ArtScroll Mishnah Series®

A rabbinic commentary to the Six Orders of the Mishnah

Rabbi Nosson Scherman / Rabbi Meir Zlotowitz
General Editors

A PROJECT OF THE

Mesorah Heritage Foundation

ששה סדרי **משנה**

THE COMMENTARY HAS BEEN NAMED **YAD AVRAHAM**
AS AN EVERLASTING MEMORIAL AND SOURCE OF MERIT
FOR THE *NESHAMAH* OF
אברהם יוסף ע"ה בן הר"ר אליעזר הכהן גליק נ"י
AVRAHAM YOSEF GLICK ע"ה
WHOSE LIFE WAS CUT SHORT ON 3 TEVES, 5735

Published by
Mesorah Publications, ltd

the mishnah

ARTSCROLL MISHNAH SERIES / A NEW
TRANSLATION WITH A COMMENTARY **YAD
AVRAHAM** ANTHOLOGIZED FROM TALMU-
DIC SOURCES AND CLASSIC COMMENTATORS.

INCLUDES THE COMPLETE HEBREW TEXT OF THE COMMENTARY
OF **RAV OVADIAH BERTINORO**

FIRST EDITION
Four Impressions ... February 1985 — December 2000
REVISED EDITION
Three Impressions ... December 2005 — November 2010
Fourth Impression ... March 2016

Published and Distributed by
MESORAH PUBLICATIONS, Ltd.
4401 Second Avenue
Brooklyn, New York 11232

Distributed in Europe by
LEHMANNS
Unit E, Viking Business Park
Rolling Mill Road
Jarrow, Tyne & Wear NE32 3DP
England

Distributed in Australia & New Zealand by
GOLDS WORLD OF JUDAICA
3-13 William Street
Balaclava, Melbourne 3183
Victoria Australia

Distributed in Israel by
SIFRIATI / A. GITLER — BOOKS
Moshav Magshimim
Israel

Distributed in South Africa by
KOLLEL BOOKSHOP
Northfield Centre, 17 Northfield Avenue
Glenhazel 2192, Johannesburg, South Africa

THE ARTSCROLL MISHNAH SERIES®
SEDER NASHIM Vol. II(a): NEDARIM
© *Copyright 2003*
by MESORAH PUBLICATIONS, Ltd.
4401 Second Avenue / Brooklyn, N.Y. 11232 / (718) 921-9000 / www.artscroll.com

ISBN 10: 0-89906-279-2
ISBN 13: 978-0-89906-279-2

Typography by CompuScribe at ArtScroll Studios, Ltd.
4401 Second Avenue / Brooklyn, N.Y. 11232 / (718) 921-9000

Printed in the United States of America
Bound by Sefercraft, Quality Bookbinders, Ltd. Brooklyn, N.Y.

⤳ Seder Nashim Vol. II(a):

מסכת נדרים
Tractate Nedarim

Translation and anthologized commentary by
Rabbi Mordechai Rabinovitch

Edited by:
Rabbi Tzvi Zev Arem

The Publishers are grateful to

YAD AVRAHAM INSTITUTE

and the

MESORAH HERITAGE FOUNDATION

for their efforts in the publication of the

ARTSCROLL MISHNAH SERIES

נְדָרַי לַה׳ אֲשַׁלֵּם נֶגְדָה נָּא לְכָל עַמּוֹ
My vows to HASHEM I will pay, in the presence, now,
of His entire people (Psalms 116:14)

מסכת זו מוקדש ע״י

משפחת קנאלל שיחי׳

מארץ ישראל ומוונצואלה

לזכר עולם לנשמות הוריהם ז״ל

ר׳ צבי הירש בן ר׳ שרגא פייוול ע״ה

ומרת פעסיא דבורה בת ר׳ יעקב דוד ע״ה

שהדריכו בנים ובנות בדרכי התורה והמצוות

This tractate is dedicated by the
Knoll Family שיחי׳
of Israel and Venezuela
in loving memory of their parents ז״ל
who raised and educated their sons and daughters
in the righteous ways of the Torah

תנצב״ה

PATRONS OF THE MISHNAH

With generosity, vision, and devotion to the perpetuation of Torah study,
the following patrons have dedicated individual volumes of the Mishnah.

SEDER ZERAIM

BERACHOS:
> In memory of
> **ר' אברהם יוסף ז"ל ב"ר אליעזר הכהן ודבורה נ"י**
> **Avraham Yosef Glick ז"ל**

PEAH:
> In memory of
> **הגאון הרב ר' אהרן ב"ר מאיר יעקב זצ"ל**
> **Rabbi Aron Zlotowitz זצ"ל**
> **והרבנית פרומא בת ר' חיים צבי ע"ה**
> **Rebbetzin Fruma Zlotowitz ע"ה**

DEMAI:
> ### Chesky and Sheindy Paneth and family
> In memory of their parents
> **ר' אברהם מרדכי בן ר' שרגא פייוועל ז"ל** – Avrohom Mordechai Mendlowitz **ז"ל**
> **ר' יעקב חיים בן ר' יחזקאל ז"ל** – Yaakov Chaim Paneth **ז"ל**
> and in memory of his brother
> **ר' משולם בן ר' יעקב חיים ז"ל** – Meshulam Paneth **ז"ל**

> ### Moshe and Esther Beinhorn and family
> In memory of their grandparents
> **ר' ישראל מרדכי ב"ר חיים צבי הי"ד וזוג' פעסיל ב"ר משה הי"ד**
> **ר' משה ב"ר שלום יוסף הי"ד וזוג' איידיל ב"ר יהודה אריה ע"ה**
> **ר' יחיאל מיכל ב"ר אברהם זאב הי"ד וזוג' שיינדל ב"ר יוסף הי"ד**
> **ר' יצחק ב"ר משה הי"ד וזוג' לאה גיטל ב"ר חיים עזרא הי"ד**

KILAYIM:
> ### Mr. and Mrs. Louis Glick
> In memory of
> **ז"ל** – Jerome Schottenstein **יעקב מאיר חיים בן אפרים אליעזר הכהן ז"ל**

SHEVIIS:
> In memory of
> **ר' אריה לייב בן שמואל יוסף ז"ל**
> **Aryeh Leib Pluchenik ז"ל**

TERUMOS:
> ### Benzi and Esther Dunner
> In memory of their grandparents
> **ר' אורי יהודה ב"ר אברהם אריה ז"ל וזוג' מרת רבקה בת שרה ע"ה**

MAASROS, MAASER SHENI:
Barry and Sipora Buls and Family
In memory of our parents

חיה שיינדל בת חיים צבי ע"ה   אברהם בן מרדכי ז"ל

Abraham and Jeanette Buls ע"ה

אלטר חיים משולם בן יעקב ז"ל   אסתר בת ראובן ע"ה

Meshulam and Esther Kluger ע"ה

and in memory of our grandparents

מרדכי בן אברהם יצחק ז"ל וזוג' רבקה בת אברהם ע"ה – בולס

חיים צבי בן דוד ז"ל וזוג' פיגא בת יצחק ע"ה – מאשקאוויטש

יעקב ז"ל הי"ד וזוג' טאבא ע"ה הי"ד – קלוגר

ראובן ז"ל הי"ד וזוג' פיגא בת יחזקאל נתן ע"ה הי"ד – שעכטר-בירנבוים

CHALLAH, ORLAH, BIKKURIM:
Yossi and Linda Segel   Danny and Shani Segel   and families
In memory of their father

ר' ברוך בן ר' יוסף הלוי ז"ל – Baruch Segel ז"ל

❧

Chesky and Sheindy Paneth and family
In memory of their parents

ר' אברהם מרדכי בן ר' שרגא פייוועל ז"ל – Avrohom Mordechai Mendlowitz ז"ל

ר' יעקב חיים בן ר' יחזקאל ז"ל – Yaakov Chaim Paneth ז"ל

and in memory of his brother

ר' משולם בן ר' יעקב חיים ז"ל – Meshulam Paneth ז"ל

❧

Moshe and Esther Beinhorn and family
In memory of their uncle

ר' אברהם זאב בן ר' יחיאל מיכל ז"ל – Avrohom Beinhorn ז"ל

SEDER MOED

SHABBOS:
Mr. and Mrs. Philip Amin
Mr. and Mrs. Lee R. Furman
In memory of their son and brother

קלמן בן ר' פסח ז"ל – Kalman Amin ז"ל

ERUVIN:
Mr. and Mrs. Lawrence M. Rosenberg
In honor of their parents

ר' גרשון בן ר' יהודה ומרת שרה שיינא בת דוב בערל עמו"ש

Judge and Mrs. Gustave Rosenberg עמו"ש

and in memory of their brother and sister

אברהם דוד ודבורה חאשא חוה בני ר' גרשון

BEITZAH:
Mr. and Mrs. Herman Wouk
In memory of their בכור and שעשועים ילד
אברהם יצחק ע״ה בן חיים אביעזר זעליג נ״י

PESACHIM:
Mr. and Mrs. Leonard A. Kestenbaum
In memory of their father זצ״ל David Kestenbaum — ר׳ דוד ב״ר אליהו זצ״ל

SHEKALIM:
In memory of **ר׳ יוסף דוד ב״ר משה גאלדוואארם זללה״ה**

ROSH HASHANAH, YOMA, SUCCAH:
ע״ה 1st Lt. Joseph Simon Bravin — ר׳ יוסף שמעון בן חיים ע״ה

TAANIS, MEGILLAH, MOED KATAN, CHAGIGAH:
In memory of
**מו״ר הרה״ג ר׳ גדליה הלוי שארר זצ״ל
HaGaon HaRav Gedalia Halevi Schorr זצ״ל**

SEDER NASHIM

YEVAMOS:
David and Rochelle Hirsch
In memory of their father Mr. Henry Hirsch ז״ל

KESUBOS:
In memory of
ע״ה Mrs. Bertha Steinmetz — מרת בילא בת ר׳ צבי מאיר ע״ה

NEDARIM:
The Knoll Family (Israel and Venezuela)
In memory of their parents
ר׳ צבי הירש בן ר׳ שרגא פייוול ע״ה
ומרת פעסיא דבורה בת ר׳ יעקב דוד ע״ה

NAZIR:
In memory of
ע״ה Yitty Leibel — יוטא ע״ה בת ר׳ יקותיאל יהודה לאי״ט

SOTAH:
In honor of the
Fifth Avenue Synagogue

GITTIN, KIDDUSHIN:
Bruce and Ruth Rappaport
In memory of his parents
ר׳ יששכר ב״ר יעקב ז״ל
ומרת בלומא שושנה בת ר׳ ברוך ע״ה

SEDER NEZIKIN

BAVA KAMMA:

In memory of

הרב שמעון ב"ר נחמיה הלוי ז"ל
Rabbi Shimon Zweig ז"ל

BAVA METZIA:

The Steinmetz family

In memory of their parents

ר' שמעון ב"ר שאול יהודה ז"ל
וזוגתו בילא בת ר' צבי מאיר ע"ה

BAVA BASRA:

In memory of

ז"ל ר' יצחק מאיר ב"ר משה ז"ל – **Mr. Irving Bunim**

SANHEDRIN:

The Zweig and Steinmetz families

In memory of

ע"ה סימא בת ר' שמעון ע"ה – **Sima Rabinowitz**

MAKKOS, SHEVUOS:

In memory of

יהושע יצחק ז"ל בן אברהם מאיר נ"י – **Joshua Waitman** ז"ל

EDUYOS:

**Mr. and Mrs. Woli and
Chaja Stern** (Saō Paulo, Brazil)

In honor of their children

Jacques and Ariane Stern   Jaime and Ariela Landau
Michael and Annete Kierszenbaum

AVODAH ZARAH, HORAYOS:

In memory of our Rebbe

מור"ר שרגא פייבל בן ר' משה זצ"ל
Reb Shraga Feivel Mendlowitz זצ"ל

AVOS:

Mr. Louis Glick   Mr. and Mrs. Sidney Glick
Mr. and Mrs. Mortimer Sklarin

In memory of their beloved mother

מרת רבקה בת ר' משה גליק ע"ה – Mrs. Regina Glick ע"ה

Mr. Louis Glick   Shimon and Mina Glick and family
Shimon and Esti Pluchenik and family

In memory of their beloved wife, mother and grandmother

מרת דבורה בת ר' שמעון גליק ע"ה – Mrs. Doris Glick ע"ה

PATRONS OF THE MISHNAH

SEDER KODASHIM

ZEVACHIM:

Mr. and Mrs. Richard Hirsch

In memory of their son

ז"ל Lawrence A. Hirsch — הילד אליעזר ז"ל בן יהודה זליג שיחי'

MENACHOS:

In memory of

ז"ל Simon Amos — שמעון בן משה עמוס ז"ל

CHULLIN:

The Steinmetz and Barouch families

In memory of

ע"ה Ruth Barouch — רבקה עטיה בת ר' שמעון ע"ה

BECHOROS:

Yad Avraham Institute

In honor of

Bruce and Ruth Rappaport

ARACHIN:

In memory of

גילה מסעודה ע"ה בת ר' יעקב נ"י
Gillah Amoch ע"ה
דפנה ע"ה בת ר' יעקב נ"י
Amy Amoch ע"ה

KEREISOS:

In memory of

ז"ל David Litman — ר' דוד ז"ל בן ר' שמעון נ"י

TEMURAH, MEILAH:

Baruch and Susie Singer and Yitzchak Ahron
Rabbi Eli Hersh and Rivky Singer
Rabbi Nussie and Ruchy Singer
Yossie and Surie Singer
Sruly Singer and Leah

In honor of

Rebbetzin Bluma Singer שתחי'

In memory of

הרה"ג ר' יצחק אהרן בן הרה"ג ר' אליהו זינגער זצ"ל
נפ' י"ג טבת תשס"א

הרה"ג ר' אליהו בן הרה"ג ר' שמעון זינגער זצ"ל
וזוגתו הרבנית רייזל בת הרה"ח ר' יששכר דוב ע"ה

הרה"צ ר' ישראל אריה ליב האלפערן בן הרה"צ ר' ברוך מסאקאליוווקא זצ"ל
וזוגתו הרבנית שבע בת הרה"ג ר' אריה ליבוש ע"ה

TAMID, MIDDOS, KINNIM:
Hashi and Miriam Herzka   Moishe and Channie Stern
Avi and Freidi Waldman   Benzi and Esti Dunner
Dovid and Didi Stern   Avrumi and Esti Stern
In honor of our dear parents
William and Shoshana Stern שיחי׳
London, England

SEDER TOHOROS

KEILIM I-II:
Leslie and Shira Westreich
Adam and Dayna — Joshua   Rayna and Dina
In memory of
ז״ל – **Larry Westreich** – אריה לייב ב״ר יהושע ז״ל
and in memory of our parents and grandparents
הרב יהושע בן מו״ר הרב הגאון יוסף יאסקא ז״ל
גיטל בת זאב וואלף ע״ה

OHOLOS:
In memory of
הרב יהושע בן מו״ר הרב הגאון יוסף יאסקא ז״ל
Rabbi Yehoshua Westreich ז״ל
and
ע״ה בת זאב וואלף ע״ה – **Gerda Westreich** ע״ה

NEGAIM:
Moshe and Esther Beinhorn and family
In memory of
יוסף דוד ז״ל בן יצחק אייזיק
Yosef Dovid Beinhorn ז״ל

PARAH:
Moshe and Esther Beinhorn and family
In memory of their uncles and aunts
אברהם צבי, חוה, רחל, חיים עזרא, אריה לייביש,
ישראל ברוך, שמואל דוד, ומשה הי״ד, והילד שלמה ע״ה
children of
יצחק בן משה שטיינבערגער ז״ל וזוג׳ לאה גיטל בת חיים עזרא ע״ה הי״ד

❧

Chesky and Sheindy Paneth and family
In memory of their grandparents
הרב יחזקאל ב״ר יעקב חיים פאנעטה ז״ל הי״ד רחל לאה בת ר׳ אשר לעמל ע״ה
הרב חיים יהודה ב״ר משולם וייס ז״ל וזוג׳ שרה רחל בת ר׳ נתן קארפל ע״ה
הרב שרגא פייוועל ב״ר משה מענדלאוויטץ זצ״ל וזוג׳ בלומא רחל בת ר׳ שמעון הלוי ע״ה
ר׳ יששכר בעריש ב״ר אברהם הלוי לאמפערט ז״ל וזוג׳ גיטל פערל בת ר׳ בצלאל ע״ה

PATRONS OF THE MISHNAH

MIKVAOS:

Mr. and Mrs. Louis Glick

In memory of his father

ר' אברהם יוסף בן ר' יהושע העשיל הכהן ז"ל

Abraham Joseph Glick ז"ל

NIDDAH:

Moshe and Esther Beinhorn and family

In memory of his beloved mother

טילא בת ר' יצחק ע"ה

Mrs. Tilli Beinhorn ע"ה

נפ' כ"ו טבת תשס"ח

MACHSHIRIN, ZAVIM:

David and Joan Tepper and family

In memory of their parents

ר' מנחם מענדל ב"ר יעקב ז"ל ומרת מינדל בת ר' אריה ליב ע"ה

Milton and Minnie Tepper ז"ל

ר' ראובן ב"ר נחמיה ז"ל ומרת עטיל בת ר' ישראל נתן נטע ע"ה

Rubin and Etta Gralla ז"ל

TEVUL YOM, YADAYIM, UKTZIN:

Barry and Tova Kohn and family

In memory of their beloved brother

הרב מנחם מנדל בן ר' יוסף יצחק אייזיק זצ"ל

HaRav Menachem Kohn זצ"ל

נפ' כ"ז מנחם אב תשס"ו

And in memory of their fathers, and grandfathers

ז"ל Josef Kohn — ר' יוסף יצחק אייזיק ב"ר בן ציון ז"ל, נפ' י' שבט תשנ"ח

ז"ל Benjamin Wiederman — ר' בנימין אלכסנדר ב"ר דוד ז"ל, נפ' ל' שבט תשס"א

and יבל"ח in honor of their mothers and grandmothers שתחי' לאוי"ט

Helene Kohn   Sylvia Wiederman

הדרן עלך ששה סדרי משנה

אָמַר ר׳ יוֹחָנָן: לֹא כָרַת הקב״ה בְּרִית עִם יִשְׂרָאֵל אֶלָּא עַל־תּוֹרָה
שֶׁבְּעַל פֶּה שֶׁנֶּאֱמַר: ,,כִּי עַל־פִּי הַדְּבָרִים הָאֵלֶּה כָּרַתִּי אִתְּךָ בְּרִית . . .״.
R' Yochanan said: The Holy One, Blessed is He, sealed a
covenant with Israel only because of the Oral Torah, as it is
said [Exodus 34:27]: For according to these words have I
sealed a covenant with you . . . (Gittin 60b).

With gratitude to *Hashem Yisbarach*, we present the Jewish public
with *Maseches Nedarim*, the third tractate of *Seder Nashim* to have
appeared in relatively quick succession. Work continues by various authors
not only on the remainder of *Nashim*, but on *Nezikin* and *Taharos* as well.
Thanks to the vision and commitment of MR. AND MRS. LOUIS GLICK, the
future of the ArtScroll Mishnah Series is assured בעזהי״ת. In their quiet,
self-effacing way, the Glicks have been a major force for the propagation of
Torah knowledge and the enhancement of Jewish life for a generation.

By dedicating the ArtScroll Mishnah Series, they have added a new dimen-
sion to their tradition of service. The many study groups in synagogues and
congregations throughout the English-speaking world are the most eloquent
testimony to the fact that thousands of people thirst for Torah learning that
is presented in a challenging, comprehensive, yet comprehensible manner.

The commentary bears the name YAD AVRAHAM, in memory of their son
AVRAHAM YOSEF GLICK ע״ה. An appreciation of the *niftar* will appear in
Tractate *Berachos*. May this dissemination of the Mishnah in his memory be
a source of merit for his soul. תנצב״ה.

We are proud and grateful that such venerable luminaries as MARAN
HAGAON HARAV YAAKOV KAMENECKI שליט״א and MARAN HAGAON
HARAV MORDECHAI GIFTER שליט״א have declared that this series should be
translated into Hebrew. *Baruch Hashem*, it has stimulated readers to echo the
words of King David: גַּל עֵינַי וְאַבִּיטָה נִפְלָאוֹת מִתּוֹרָתֶךָ, *Uncover my eyes that I
may see wonders of Your Torah* (Psalms 119:18).

May we inject two words of caution:

First, although the Mishnah, by definition, is a compendium of laws, the
final *halachah* does not necessarily follow the Mishnah. The development of
halachah proceeds through the Gemara, commentators, codifiers, responsa,
and the acknowledged *poskim*. Even when our commentary cites the
Shulchan Aruch, the intention is to sharpen the readers' understanding of the
Mishnah, but not to be a basis for actual practice. In short, this work is meant
as a first step in the study of our recorded Oral Law — no more.

Second, as we have stressed in our other books, the ArtScroll commentary is not meant as a substitute for the study of the sources. While this commentary, like others in the various series, will be immensely useful even to accomplished scholars and will often bring to light ideas and sources they may have overlooked, we strongly urge those who are able to study the classic *sefarim* in the original to do so. It has been said that every droplet of ink coming from *Rashi's* pen is worthy of seven days' contemplation. Despite the exceptional caliber of our authors, none of us pretends to take the place of the study of the greatest minds in Jewish history.

Tractate *Nedarim* discusses the different formulae that may be used in making vows and oaths; the rules governing vows that are apparently not sincere and are therefore invalid; interpretation of various unclear phraseology that may be used in vows; the parameters of someone's power to prohibit others from enjoying his possessions; the nullification of vows by a sage; and the circumstances under which they can be declared void by a husband or father.

With this volume we have the honor of introducing a new author in the Mishnah Series: RABBI MORDECHAI RABINOVITCH, currently residing in Mevasseret Zion, Israel, combines outstanding scholarship with an unusual ability to present complex ideas in a readily accessible manner. We look forward to his continued participation in the Series. This volume was edited by RABBI TZVI ZEV AREM, who continues the standard he set with his work on Tractate *Kesubos*.

We are grateful to REB DANIEL FLEISCHMANN for his very fine graphics production of this volume. He carries on the tradition established by our colleague, REB SHEAH BRANDER, who remains a leader in bringing beauty of presentation to Torah literature.

We are also grateful to the staff of Mesorah Publications: RABBI HERSH GOLDWURM, whose encyclopedic knowledge was always available; RABBI YEHEZKEL DANZIGER, RABBI AVIE GOLD, STEPHEN BLITZ, YOSAIF TIMINSKY, LEAH FREIER, CHANEE FREIER, MRS. ESTHER FEIERSTEIN, SIMIE GLUCK, MALKY GLATZER, MRS. FAIGIE WEINBAUM, MRS. JUDI DICK and MRS. SHONNIE FRIEDMAN.

Finally, our gratitude goes to RABBI DAVID FEINSTEIN שליט״א and RABBI DAVID COHEN שליט״א, whose concern, interest, and guidance have been essential to the success of the ArtScroll series since its inception.

Rabbis Nosson Scherman / Meir Zlotowitz

כ״ז שבט תשמ״ה / February 18, 1985

� Note to revised edition

We would like to acknowledge the contribution of the following individuals who worked on this revised edition, each in their own area of expertise: Rabbi Moshe Rosenblum, Rabbi Avraham Yitzchak Deutsch, Mrs. Faigie Weinbaum, Mrs. Mindy Stern, Mrs. Chumie Lipschitz, Miss Sara Rivka Spira, and Miss Sury Reinhold.

מסכת נדרים

Tractate Nedarim

General Introduction to Nedarim

◆§ *The Tractate*

Although this tractate is devoted to the laws of vows, it is included in *Seder Nashim* (the Order of Women) because a husband, under certain conditions, can revoke certain of his wife's *nedarim*. Indeed, the Torah (*Numbers* 30) devotes almost all of its treatment of the subject of *nedarim* to those made by women (ibid. v. 4ff.). The reason *Nedarim* follows *Kesubos* in the Mishnah is that a husband's right to revoke his wife's *nedarim* on his own comes only when they are fully married (see preface to Chapter 10), at which time he gives her the *kesubah* [marriage contract] (*Rambam, Introduction* to his *Mishnah Commentary*). Alternatively, since the subject of vows is discussed in *Kesubos* (Chapter 7), it was logical to follow *Kesubos* with *Nedarim* (*Shitah Mekubetzes* from *Sotah* 2a).

◆§ *Types of Nedarim*

The term נֶדֶר, *neder* [pl. *nedarim*], is used in Scripture to describe two types of vows: נִדְרֵי הֶקְדֵּשׁ, *vows of dedication to the Temple*, and נִדְרֵי אִיסּוּר, *prohibitive vows*. The former category, mentioned in *Leviticus* 22:18, *Numbers* 29:39, *Deuteronomy* 23:22ff., et al., is discussed at length in *Seder Kodashim*, the fifth order of the Mishnah. Because the English term *vow* includes any solemn promise or pledge and does not accurately convey the peculiarities of *nedarim* that will be explained below, we have usually left the term *neder* untranslated. Our tractate deals exclusively with prohibitive *nedarim* and is based on the verse (*Num.* 30:3), *When a man makes a* neder *to God, or swears an oath to bind himself with a prohibition, he shall not break his word; he shall do according to all that issues from his mouth.*

A prohibitive *neder* is one with which a person prohibits a permissible item of his own to himself or to others, or someone else's item to himself. By no means can he forbid another person's property to its owner or to anyone else other than himself (*Ran* 2a).

◆§ *Nedarim and Shevuos (Oaths)*

Prohibitive *nedarim* belong to the larger class of declarations which create halachic consequences. Of these, the most closely related to the *neder* is the *shevuah* (oath; pl. *shevuos*), which is mentioned together with the *neder* in *Numbers* 30:3. The chief distinction between them is that a *neder* interdicts an object, while a *shevuah* constrains the swearer. As the *Gemara* (2b) states: "A *neder* makes an object forbidden to the person, while a prohibitive oath forbids the person to utilize the object." Several halachic consequences result from this distinction (see 2:1ff. and commentary to 1:1).

Besides *nedarim* and oaths, the Mishnah also mentions other types of declarations which are Biblically binding (see 1:1).

✎§ The Formulae

If, for example, a person wishes to forbid a certain fruit to himself, he might declare: "The benefit of this fruit is forbidden me like an offering." The term *offering* in this statement refers to an animal that has been designated to be sacrificed in the Temple. The animal is thereby consecrated and may not be used for any other purpose. So, too, benefiting from fruit which has been designated by a *neder* to be forbidden like an offering would be prohibited. However, while use of an offering is forbidden to everyone, a *neder* may specify that the item should be forbidden to a particular person only; all others would then be permitted to use the item (*Ran* 2a).

If a person wants to deprive himself of the use of another person's fruit, he might declare, "The benefit of your fruit is forbidden me like an offering," and he would thereby be prohibited to consume or otherwise benefit from the fruit. If he wishes to forbid his fruit to someone else, he might say, "The benefit of my fruit is forbidden you like an offering," and the person whom he addressed would not be allowed to benefit from the fruit (see *Ran* 15a, s.v. הלכה). However, the declarations, "The benefit of *your* fruit is forbidden *you* like an offering," or "The benefit of *your* fruit is forbidden *him* like an offering," do not effect any prohibitions, since — as mentioned above — one cannot interdict someone else's property to anyone but himself (*Gem.* 47a, *Ran* 2a).

✎§ יָד, Yad

According to some authorities, the reference to something already prohibited — such as an offering — is an essential component of the basic *neder*. To declare, "The benefit of this fruit is forbidden me," without adding "like an offering," would be — according to this view — an incomplete *neder*; nevertheless, as long as the intent of the declaration is understood, it will be binding (*Ran to Shevuos* 20b). A *neder* such as this is known as a יָד, *yad* (handle; pl. יָדוֹת, *yados*). For, just as to hold a vessel, one need merely grasp its handle, similarly, a *neder* can be effected even if it is only partially verbalized and the entire formula is not articulated. As long as the complete formula for a *neder* can be inferred from what has been stated, the declaration is binding (*Rav* 1:1; *Rosh* 2a).

Others maintain that the reference to a forbidden item is not necessary for the basic *neder* formula; a declaration which includes no such comparison is considered a complete *neder*. Rather, the classification of *yad* would apply to a statement such as: "This fruit is to me," which omits the word *forbidden*, yet is a binding declaration provided that it was evident from the circumstances that his intention was to interdict the fruit through a *neder*. Although he did not explicitly state this intention, the fruit becomes prohibited (*Ran* 2a).

✎§ References Used in Nedarim

While a reference may not be essential to the *neder*, if it is used it must nevertheless satisfy certain criteria. In particular, only something which was previously permitted and became forbidden through a man-made stricture can be used as a reference (ibid.). An offering is a suitable reference, since the animal is consecrated — and thus made forbidden — by a person. However, something which is Biblically prohibited, such as pork, is not a valid reference (see preface to 2:1). Hence, the declaration, "This fruit is to me like pork," will not prohibit the fruit to him. On the other hand, if the statement is more detailed, the

comparison to pork will not necessarily disqualify the *neder*. For example, if a person vowed, "This fruit is forbidden for me to eat just like pork," the validity of this *neder* will depend on the two opinions concerning the basic *neder*. If the reference to a prohibited item, such as an offering, is *not* considered essential to the basic formula for a *neder*, then the above declaration can be broken into a complete basic *neder* — "This fruit is forbidden for me to eat" — with a reference appended to it — "just like pork." Since the basic *neder* is effective on its own, the reference to pork is superfluous and does not detract from it; the declaration will therefore be binding. However, according to those who hold that the basic *neder* must contain a reference to an interdicted item, the unacceptable reference to pork will invalidate the *neder*. This is because these authorities, as stated above, maintain that the statement, "This fruit is forbidden for me to eat" — which contains no reference — is only a *yad*, and is not effective unless a valid *neder* is intended. By completing the *neder* with an unacceptable reference to pork, it is evident that the intended *neder* was not a valid one (*Mishneh LeMelech, Hil. Nedarim* 1:7; *Machaneh Ephraim, Hil. Nedarim* 11).

⋑§ כִּנּוּיִים, Kinnuyim/Equivalent Terms

There are things other than offerings which are acceptable references for *nedarim*. Nevertheless, the standard reference for a *neder* originally was an offering — קָרְבָּן, *korban*, in Hebrew (*Rosh* 10a). This term later became corrupted, leading to expressions such as *konam* (קוֹנָם) and *konach* (קוֹנָח), which are also acceptable, provided that the word used in the *neder* is construed to be synonymous with *offering*. Such equivalent terms are called כִּנּוּיִים, *kinnuyim* [sing. כִּנּוּי, *kinnuy*] (*Ran* 2a).

From the examples given in the Mishnah, it seems that the term *konam* was by far the most frequently used as the reference in the formulae of *nedarim*.

⋑§ Cancellation of Nedarim

In general, a sage or a panel of three knowledgeable laymen is authorized to annul a *neder* once they ascertain that there exists a sufficient basis for annulment (*Ran* 23a; *Bechoros* 36b). The details of what constitutes a sufficient basis for annulment are discussed in Chapter 9. See also commentary to 2:1, s.v. *Grounds for Annulling a Neder*. The regulations governing the release from a *neder*, in general, are described by the Mishnah (*Chagigah* 1:8) as "hovering in the air without firm Scriptural support"; that is, they are known mainly from the Oral Law. However, when a woman makes a *neder*, there is a different method of cancellation available, since her husband or father are authorized to revoke her vows. This type of cancellation receives a lengthy Scriptural treatment (*Num.* 30:3ff.) and is discussed in the last two chapters of this tractate.

⋑§ The Biblical Commandments

A person who makes a *neder* or an oath is charged by the Torah with a positive precept to fulfill his word (*Num.* 30:3; *Deut.* 23:24); if he does not, he also violates a negative precept (ibid.; *Rambam*, Preface to *Hil. Nedarim*, and *Sefer HaMitzvos, Essin* §94 and *Lavin* §157; see *Hasagos HaRamban* ad loc.). If one intentionally contravenes a *neder* after having been duly warned, he is liable to a penalty of מַלְקוּת, lashes (*Rambam, Hil. Sanhedrin* 16:2 and *Hil. Nedarim* 1:5).

If a person (e.g., Reuven) prohibits another (Shimon) to derive some benefit from him, and Shimon violates the *neder* by enjoying the forbidden benefit, there is a controversy regarding who is penalized. *Rambam* (Hil. *Nedarim* 5:1) rules that Shimon is not liable to lashes because he had not made the *neder*. From a later ruling (ibid. 10:12), it appears that *Rambam* opines that if Reuven provided Shimon with the prohibited benefit, the former is liable (see *Lechem Mishneh* to 5:1). *Ran* (15a s.v. הלכה), however, rules that it is Shimon who is subject to lashes, for — although Reuven had declared the prohibition — it was Shimon who was thereby restricted and hence, punishable, upon its transgression (see commentary to 5:4, s.v. הֲרֵי).

⋞§ The Impropriety of Vowing

In general, the making of *nedarim* was deprecated and discouraged by the Rabbis. The *Gemara* (22a) writes that to vow is akin to building an altar outside the Temple — which is illegal — and to avoid annulling a *neder* that has already been made is like offering a sacrifice on such an altar. The simile is based on a common denominator shared by one who builds altars outside of the Temple and by one who makes prohibitive vows. Both are apt to think that what they are doing is religiously elevating, and hence, admirable; after all, they are simulating the Torah's precepts: the altar builder is imitating the sacrificial service in the Temple, and the vower is adding to the corpus of Biblical prohibitions. They fail to realize, however, that to follow precisely what the Torah commands is the true avenue to spiritual enrichment. In the words of the *Yerushalmi* (9:1): "Is what the Torah prohibits not enough for you, that you seek to interdict new things for yourself?" (*Ran* 22a). In keeping with their general disapproval of making *nedarim*, the Rabbis stated further that if a prohibitory *neder* is made, it is a *mitzvah* to seek its annulment (*Gem.* 59a). Thus, an item interdicted through a *neder* was considered to be only temporarily prohibited, on the assumption that the *neder* would eventually be annulled (ibid.; see commentary to 6:6). Accordingly, one who neglected to seek annulment for his *neder* was likened to someone who not only built illegal altars, but offered sacrifices on them as well (*Gem.* 22a).

❦   ❦   ❦

Notes Regarding the Commentary

As in the previous volumes of the Mishnah Series, every entry in the commentary has been carefully documented. Where the author has inserted a comment of his own, it is surrounded by brackets.

Certain facts concerning the classic commentators are unique to *Nedarim*. Some believe that the commentary to this tractate ascribed to *Rashi* was not written by him (*Chida* in *Shem HaGedolim*). Nevertheless, we have followed the practice of most commentators who do refer to this commentary *as Rashi*.

Also, we have two works of *Rosh* written on *Nedarim*. One is a commentary, printed on the pages of the Talmud in the standard editions; the other is the *Pesakim*, a halachic compendium usually printed at the end of the tractate. Where we quote *Rosh* without specification, we refer to his commentary.

Untranslated Hebrew terms found in the commentary are defined in the glossary at the end of the tractate (p. 230).

Acknowledgments

It is my pleasant duty to express my appreciation to the entire staff and editorial board of Mesorah Publications and Yad Avraham Institute for their assistance and encouragement throughout. Special thanks to Mr. Maxwell Rosenblum — formerly of Hartford, Connecticut — for his invaluable suggestions, and last — but not least — to my dear wife, Chana, for her selfless devotion (see *Berachos* 17a), without which this work would not have been possible.

Mordechai Rabinovitch
Mevasseret Zion, Israel
13 Shevat 5745

פרק ראשון ⁐

Chapter One

<hr>

⁐ Neder, Yad, Kinnui

Although the basic terms and concepts necessary for the understanding of this chapter have been explained at length in the General Introduction, we will review them briefly here. If a person wishes to deprive himself of the benefit of a particular item, he can make it Biblically forbidden to himself by means of a נֶדֶר, *neder* (loosely, *vow*; pl. *nedarim*). This is a type of declaration, recognized by the Torah as a binding vow, which imparts a prohibited status to an object. If, for example, a person says: "The benefit of this bread is forbidden me like an offering," it would be prohibited for him to eat or otherwise benefit from the bread. The item that the vower interdicts may belong to himself or to others. He can also prohibit his property to others, but not someone else's item to anyone but himself.

Even a *yad* — a declaration that does not contain the complete formula of a *neder* — may be effective in prohibiting an item if the speaker's intention to make a *neder* is clear, and the basic formula can be inferred. Exactly what constitutes a valid *yad* is a subject of controversy among the authorities.

According to some authorities, the reference to something already prohibited — such as an offering — is an essential component of the basic *neder*. To declare, "The benefit of this fruit is forbidden me," without adding "like an offering," would be — according to this view — a *yad*.

When referring to an offspring — קָרְבָּן, *korban*, in Hebrew — one may substitute colloquial expressions, known as כִּנּוּיִים, *kinnuyim* (equivalent terms). The most popular of these substitutes seems to have been the term *konam*.

In addition to *nedarim*, the first mishnah of this chapter also touches upon other Biblically binding declarations, such as oaths.

[א] **כָּל** כִּנּוּיֵי נְדָרִים כִּנְדָרִים, וַחֲרָמִים כַּחֲרָמִים, וּשְׁבוּעוֹת כִּשְׁבוּעוֹת, וּנְזִירוּת כִּנְזִירוּת.

ר' עובדיה מברטנורא

פרק ראשון – כל כנויי. (א) כל כנויי נדרים כנדרים. בגמרא (ג, ג) מוקמינן דרישא דמתניתין חסורי מחסרא, והכי קתני, כל ידות נדרים כנדרים כל כנויי נדרים כנדרים, אלו הן ידות נדרים האומר לחבירו מודר אני ממך מופרש אני ממך וכו', אלו הן כנויי נדרים קונם קונח קונס וכו'. ידות נדרים כמו בית יד של כלי שאוחזין אותו בו כך ידות נדרים שבהם הנדרים נאחזים, כנויי נדרים כמו המכנה שם לחבירו (בבא מציעא נח, ג) שאינו עיקרו של שם:

יד אברהם

1.

כָּל כִּנּוּיֵי נְדָרִים כִּנְדָרִים, — *All equivalent terms [used in] nedarim are like nedarim;*

As explained in the preface, if one wishes to prohibit an item to himself by means of a *neder*, he says, "This item is prohibited to me." Some authorities maintain that, to this basic formula, he must append a comparison to the kind of item that attains its forbidden status through a person's volition, such as *korban* (an offering). Accordingly, the wording of the *neder* would be: "This item is prohibited to me like a *korban*" (*Bach* to *Tur Yoreh Deah* 204, from *Tos.* 2a; *Ran* to *Shevuos* 20b; *Ritva*).

[The mishnah tells us here that if, instead of using the term *korban*, he substituted one of the equivalent terms enumerated in mishnah 2, the *neder* is valid nevertheless.]

וַחֲרָמִים כַּחֲרָמִים, — *and [those used in] charamim are like charamim,*

A חֵרֶם, *cherem* (pl. חֲרָמִים, *charamim*), is a declaration used to dedicate something as property of the *Kohanim* (priests; sing. *Kohen*). For example, if a person states: "This calf is *cherem*," the animal becomes the property of the *Kohanim* serving in the Temple at that time. Before it is given to a *Kohen*, the

designated item (in this case, the calf) is considered holy, and is forbidden for general use (*Rambam, Hil. Arachin* 6:1ff.).

There are two types of *cherem*. One designates something to become property of the *Kohen*; the other designates it as property of the Temple. When something donated to the *Kohen* through a *cherem* reaches the *Kohen's* hands, it is no longer considered holy, and there are no restrictions on its use. However, something given to the Temple by means of a *cherem* remains holy even after it is delivered, until it is redeemed (ibid.).

There is a dispute in the Mishnah (*Arachin* 8:6) regarding the declaration of a *cherem* that does not specify whether the item is intended as a contribution to the *Kohanim* or the Temple. R' Yehudah ben Beseira holds that, unless otherwise specified, the item belongs to the Temple treasury. The Sages contend conversely that such property goes to the *Kohanim*. *Rambam* (*Hil. Arachin* 6:1) rules in accordance with the latter view.

Charamim are similar to *nedarim* in that they both assign a status to an object. A *neder* designates an item as forbidden; a *cherem* designates it as

1

1. All equivalent terms [used in] *nedarim* are like *nedarim* and [those used in] *charamim* are like *charamim*, and [in] oaths are like oaths; and [in] the Naziritic declaration are like the Naziritic declaration.

YAD AVRAHAM

sacred, to be delivered either to the Temple or to the *Kohanim*, as explained above. Because of this similarity, the mishnah lists *nedarim* and *charamim* consecutively, followed by the laws for other types of declarations that are not directed at objects (*Gem.* 2b).

[Here, too, the mishnah teaches us that the equivalent expressions listed in the next mishnah may be substituted for the word *cherem* in these formulas.]

וּשְׁבוּעוֹת כִּשְׁבוּעוֹת, — *and [in] oaths are like oaths,*

[שְׁבוּעָה, *shevuah*, is an oath with which a person obligates himself to do or refrain from a specific action. An example is "*Shevuah* (i.e., I swear), that I shall not talk." A *shevuah* can create obligations as well. For example, if a person were to swear: "*Shevuah*, that I shall walk around the block," he would be bound to do so.]

The *Gemara* (2b) contrasts *nedarim* with *shevuos*: A *neder* forbids an object to a person, while a prohibitive *shevuah* interdicts the person from utilizing the object. Among the consequences of this distinction is the fact that, under Biblical law, a *neder* can affect only tangible things, whereas a *shevuah* can prohibit even intangibles, such as actions (Gem. 13b; *Ran* ad loc.).

Thus, a *shevuah* may forbid walking or talking, as such, while a *neder* intended to do the same must be made in a form prohibiting one's feet from walking or his mouth from talking (see mishnah 4 and 2:1). Or, if a person wished to prohibit himself via a *neder* to

consume a particular loaf of bread, he would say: "This loaf is forbidden like an offering, with respect to my eating it." But, if he wished to do so via a *shevuah*, he would say: "*Shevuah*, that I shall not eat this loaf" (*Ran, Tos.* 2b).

[The Hebrew term *shevuah* spawned several equivalents which may be used in lieu of it. These, too, are enumerated in the following mishnah.]

וּנְזִירוּת כִּנְזִירוּת — *and [in] the Naziritic declaration are like the Naziritic declaration.*

A *Nazir* (Nazirite) is a person who is forbidden to drink wine, cut his hair, or come into contact with the dead for thirty days because he declared, "I am a *Nazir*" (see *Num.* 6:1ff.).

[Any terms synonymous with *Nazir* will suffice to make this declaration effective; examples of these are provided in the following mishnah.]

Instead of proceeding to list the equivalent terms discussed above, the mishnah now gives examples of *yados*, incomplete *nedarim*. The *Gemara* explains that this is the result of an omission in the mishnah, and amends the text to read as follows: כָּל כִּנּוּיֵי נְדָרִים כִּנְדָרִים, וְיָדוֹת נְדָרִים כִּנְדָרִים. — *All equivalent terms [used in] nedarim are like nedarim, and all yados of nedarim are like nedarim.*

Talmudic emendations to the text of a mishnah are not rare, though it is not always clear whether an actual textual correction is being suggested, or just an interpretation.

הָאוֹמֵר לַחֲבֵרוֹ: ,,מֻדְּרַנִי מִמָּךְ'', ,,מֻפְרָשַׁנִי מִמָּךְ'', ,,מְרֻחֲקַנִי מִמָּךְ'' — ,,שֶׁאֵינִי אוֹכֵל לָךְ'',

---

ר' עובדיה מברטנורא

מודר אני ממך. אם אמר אחד מלשונות הללו, מודר אני ממך שאיני אוכל לך ושאיני טועם לך, או מופרש אני ממך שאיני אוכל לך ושאיני טועם לך, או מרוחק אני ממך שאיני אוכל לך ושאיני טועם לך, הוֹא ידות נדרים ואסור לאכול ולטעום עמו, אבל אם אמר לו מודר אני ממך בלבד, אין במשמעות דבריו אלא שלא ידבר עמו, ומופרש אני ממך בלבד משמע שלא ישא ויתן עמו, ומרוחק אני ממך בלבד משמע שלא ישב בארבע אמותיו, ואינו אסור לאכול עמו אלא אם כן פירש ואמר עם כל אחד מלשונות הללו שאיני אוכל לך ושאיני טועם לך:

יד אברהם

R' Yosef Karo, in his commentary to *Halichos Olam*, explains that the Mishnah incorporates earlier halachic statements that had been orally transmitted from generation to generation. This ancient method of study based solely on memory inevitably caused occasional variations and deletions. When composing the Mishnah, R' Yehudah Ha-Nasi retained the formulations of this oral tradition. Any omissions or corrections were subsequently recorded by the *Gemara* (see *Ittur Sofrim* to *Sefer Kerisus* 5:2:12).

For different approaches to Talmudic corrections of the Mishnah's text, see *Tiferes Yisrael (Boaz)* to *Arachin* 4:1, and ArtScroll comm. to *Beitzah* 1:2, footnote on p.16.

הָאוֹמֵר לַחֲבֵרוֹ: ,,מֻדְּרַנִי מִמָּךְ'', ,,מֻפְרָשַׁנִי מִמָּךְ'', ,,מְרֻחֲקַנִי מִמָּךְ''— *One who says to another: "I am restricted from you by a neder," "I am separated from you," [or] "I am removed from you" —*

These three phrases are to be read together with the endings *"that I shall not eat what belongs to you"* and *"that I shall not taste what belongs to you,"* which follow in the mishnah.

Thus, the declarations under discussion are: *"I am restricted from you by a neder, in that I shall not eat* (or *"taste"*) *of yours," "I am separated from you, in that I shall not eat* (or *'taste') of yours,"* etc. (*Gem.* 4b). These pronouncements are considered *yados*, since they omit explicit mention of the word אָסוּר,

prohibited, and do not make any reference to something forbidden, such as an offering. Nevertheless, they are binding. If the person who made this statement were to eat the food of the one he had spoken to, he would be violating the *neder*, and would be liable to the penalty of lashes (*Ran* 4b).

On the other hand, if a person were to declare just the first half of one of these statements, such as, *"I am restricted from you by a* neder," without the ending, *"in that I shall not eat of yours,"* it is a controversy among the authorities whether he becomes obligated thereby.

Many earlier authorities hold that, by themselves, the first halves to these statements are ambiguous. Although all of them can refer to a restriction on eating, each of them also has another implication. *I am restricted* can refer to a stricture on conversation; *I am separated* might mean a ban on business dealings; *I am removed* may indicate a prohibition against staying within another's immediate vicinity. Since a *yad* is only valid when it provides sufficient information with which to deduce the intended prohibition — and, in our case, if he declares only the first half of one of these statements, the determination of the precise intention of the *neder* is not possible —

1

1

One who says to another: "I am restricted from you by a *neder*," "I am separated from you," [or] "I am removed from you" — "in that I shall not eat,"

YAD AVRAHAM

therefore, the declaration is considered inconclusive, and hence, void (*Rosh, Ran 5a*).

Rav, however, appears to follow *Rambam* (*Hil. Nedarim* 1:23), who maintains that the first halves of these statements alone are not vague. *I am restricted* certainly implies a restriction on conversation. Similarly, *I am separated* refers to business dealings, and *I am removed*, to staying away from another"s immediate vicinity. It is only if a ban on eating another"s food is intended, that a specific clarification, *in that I shall not eat of yours*, must be added.

It is stated below (comm. to 1:4, 2:1) that a *neder* prohibiting intangibles, such as the actions of walking or talking, is only Rabbinically binding. For a *neder* to be Biblically valid, it must prohibit a tangible object. In light of this, it is possible that the declarations discussed above, such as, *I am restricted*, without the ending, *in that I shall not eat yours* — which, according to *Rambam*, prohibit intangibles like conversation and business dealings — are binding only Rabbinically. This, in fact, is the view of *R' Avraham min Hahar*. *Meiri*, however, considers even these declarations to be directed at a tangible object: the body of the person. As a precedent for this, he cites mishnah 4 which states that the *neder*, "*Konam* (an equivalent expression of *Korban*), my mouth is prohibited from speaking," is Biblically valid because the physical mouth is the tangible object of the *neder*. Under the terms of the *neder*, the mouth becomes

prohibited for speech. In a similar manner, these *yados* produce a prohibition on the physical body: "I am restricted" means "My body is restricted," and consequently, the body becomes prohibited with respect to the activities indicated: conversation, business, etc. These *yados* are therefore Biblically binding.

„שֶׁאֵינִי אוֹכֵל לָךְ" — "*in that I shall not eat,*"

This wording, used in the standard texts of the mishnah, indicates a restriction on the act of eating, rather than a prohibition on the food to be eaten. For this reason, many earlier authorities reject this reading (*Rosh* 4b; *Meiri*). The essence of a *neder* is that it assigns a prohibition status to an item. If a person wanted to forbid himself the eating of some food through a *neder*, he should declare: "This food is prohibited," rather than "I shall not eat this food." The latter declaration is the formula for an oath, which is designed to restrict a person's actions, as explained above (*Meiri; Ritva*). Although a *neder* banning an action such as eating is Rabbinically valid (*Gem.* 15b), it is assumed that the *nedarim* given here are binding even Biblically (*Tos. Yom Tov* following *Tos.* 2a). Therefore, the correct text should be „שֶׁאֲנִי אוֹכֵל לָךְ" — without a *yud* following the *aleph*. This is the same as saying „מַה שֶׁאֲנִי אוֹכֵל לָךְ" — "*that which I eat of yours.*" Thus, the full *yad* is: "I am restricted from you by a *neder*, with respect to that which I eat of yours." This declaration is clearly directed at an object — the

„שֶׁאֵינִי טוֹעֵם לָךְ" — אָסוּר. „מְנֻדֶּה אֲנִי לָךְ"
— רַבִּי עֲקִיבָא הָיָה חוֹכֵךְ בָּזֶה לְהַחְמִיר.

─────── ר' עובדיה מברטנורא ───────

רבי עקיבא היה חוכך וכו'. כלומר מתוך שפתיו זו בזו ולא רצה לאסור בפירוש, אבל היה

יד אברהם

food — and is binding under Biblical law (*Rosh* 4b; *Meiri*).

Although *Tosafos* (*Yevamos* 71a, s.v.שאני), too, agree that such a *neder* must use the term שֶׁאֵנִי, they add that the text of the mishnah reading שֶׁאֵינִי need not be changed, since the *Tanna* often does not bother to use the precise terminology necessary for that particular case. [As long as his basic intent is clear, he relies on the intelligence of the readers to understand the fine details of the law themselves.]

Rambam (and — according to the *Yachin UBoaz* edition — *Rav*, too) seems to have accepted the standard version, שֶׁאֵינִי, while maintaining that these declarations are Biblically valid (*Kesef Mishneh, Hil. Nedarim* 1:23; *Beur HaGra, Yoreh Deah* 206:20). As noted, this is problematic, since a *neder* directed at an intangible (such as eating) without mentioning a physical object (such as food) ought to be only Rabbinically binding.

This difficulty may be resolved if we assume that, as long as it is evident that the person wishes to prohibit an object — rather than an action — the precise formula used will not affect the Biblical status of the declaration (*Machaneh Ephraim*, cited below, documents this assumption; cf. *Ran* 2b). According to *Rambam*, the first halves of the declarations discussed in the mishnah, such as "I am removed," connote the specific intent to make a *neder*-type prohibition; i.e., to interdict an object. Although

by using the expression *that I shall not eat*, the person has formulated his declaration in a manner more appropriate for an oath, his intention to forbid an object by a *neder* is clear from the first half of his statement.

Therefore, the declaration, "*I am restricted from you by a neder in that I shall not eat your food*," is effective like a *neder*, and is equivalent to declaring: "*I am restricted from your food via a neder, with respect to eating it*" (*Machaneh Ephraim, Hil. Nedarim* 9).

Literally, the word לָךְ used here means *to you*. In this tractate, however, it is generally equivalent to מִשֶּׁלָּךְ and means *of yours* or *from what belongs to you*. Such a usage of this word is found in *Judges* 17:2 (*Gilyon HaShas* to 5a).

„שֶׁאֵינִי טוֹעֵם לָךְ"– — [or]*"in that I shall not taste"* —

The *Gemara* (*Shevuos* 22a) explains that *tasting* concerns even minute quantities, whereas *eating* deals with amounts that are the size of an olive or larger. A *neder* which makes no mention of eating or tasting, but is designed to forbid general benefit from a food, applies even to minute quantities (*Rambam, Hil Shevuos* 4:1 and *Hil. Nedarim* 1:5; cf. *Tos. R' Akiva* 6:7).

אָסוּר. — *is bound.*

[One who makes these declarations is obliged to fulfill them.[1]]

„מְנֻדֶּה אֲנִי לָךְ" — — "*I am excommunicated from you*" —

1. [Although the familiar translation of אָסוּר is *prohibited*, and that of מוּתָּר is *permitted*, these are based on the Biblical terms meaning *bound* and *unbound*, respectively, as in the phrase מַתִּיר אֲסוּרִים, *releases the bound* (*Psalms* 146:7). (A person is *bound* by a *prohibition*

[or] in that I shall not taste" is bound. "I am excommunicated from you" — R' Akiva hesitated with this, indicating stringency.

YAD AVRAHAM

If the purpose of this dedication is to forbid the food of the one being spoken to, it must be completed with the suffix *that I shall not eat your food*, as in the mishnah's previous set of cases. By itself, the first half of this statement indicates only a ban on staying within the other person's immediate vicinity, and not one on eating his food (*Rambam, Hil. Nedarim* 1:23).

Tosafos (7a), however, maintain that *excommunicated from you* alone, without additional clarification, already indicates a prohibition on eating the other's food. If his intention were simply to prevent being nearby that person, he would have stated so explicitly, rather than labeling himself *excommunicated*. Thus, according to *Tosafos*, the declaration under consideration here is simply: "*I am excommunicated from you*," without any further elaboration (*Tos. Yom Tov*).

Another approach is that of *Ravad* (*Hil. Nedarim* 1:24), who interprets the declaration „מְנֻדֶּה אֲנִי לָךְ, שֶׁאֵינִי אוֹכֵל לָךְ", as "*I am excommunicated from you, that I shall not eat with you.*" That is, the person may not eat any food — even his own — within the other's immediate vicinity, but he may eat even the other's food away from him.

‎רַבִּי עֲקִיבָא הָיָה חוֹכֵךְ בָּזֶה לְהַחְמִיר. — *R' Akiva hesitated with this, indicating stringency* (lit., *to be stringent*).

Literally, חוֹכֵךְ means *rubs*. That is,

R' Akiva rubbed his lips together, or rubbed his brow, unwilling to voice a decision (*Rav*). His hesitancy to rule explicitly one way or the other indicated to his followers that, in practice, they should treat the declaration מְנֻדֶּה אֲנִי לָךְ stringently and validate it (*Rosh* 7a).

R' Akiva's dilemma was whether the word מְנֻדֶּה should be interpreted as *excommunicated* or as *at a distance*. Its root, נד, is used in both senses, although the form מְנֻדֶּה generally means *excommunicated*. However, if a person said that he was imposing excommunication upon himself, it could be assumed that he was not serious and was just exaggerating; no *neder* was really intended, just an adamant refusal of his friend"s invitation (*Tos.* 7a). Therefore, if מְנֻדֶּה is interpreted as *excommunication*, R' Akiva felt that the declaration should not be binding. On the other hand, if interpreted as *at a distance*, the term should be no worse than מְרֻחֲקַנִי, *I am removed*, which is listed earlier as a legitimate way of introducing a *neder* (*Ran* 7a). [In that case, the *neder* should be valid. Unable to reach a decision on the matter, R' Akiva hesitated.]

[Since the mishnah attributes the tendency to strictly regard this declaration only to R' Akiva, it is implied that the other Sages were not at all concerned with R' Akiva's doubts. They assumed as a matter of course

from doing some act.) Therefore, where the terms *bind* and *not binding* seem more appropriate for the translation of the mishnah, we have used those terms.]

„כְּנִדְרֵי רְשָׁעִים" — נָדַר בְּנָזִיר וּבְקָרְבָּן וּבִשְׁבוּעָה. „כְּנִדְרֵי כְשֵׁרִים" — לֹא אָמַר כְּלוּם. „כְּנִדְבוֹתָם" — נָדַר בְּנָזִיר וּבְקָרְבָּן.

ר' עובדיה מברטנורא

נראה מדעתו שהיה חוסר: **כנדרי רשעים נדר בנזיר ובקרבן ובשבועה.** אם אמר הרי עלי כנדרי רשעים שנדריהס נזיר וקרבן אם אוכל ככר זו, ועבר ואכלה, חייב להיות נזיר שלשים יום ולהביא קרבן עולה וחייב מלקות כעובר על שבועת ביטוי, שהרי הזכיר בנדרו נזיר וקרבן ושבועה. ומה שאמר כנדרי רשעים, לפי שהרשעים הס שנודרים ונשבעים, לא הכשרים, שהכשרים יראים שלא לעבור על בל תאחר ונזהרים שלא להוליא שבועה מפיהם, ולפיכך כנדרי כשרים לא אמר כלום: **ובנדבותם נדר בנזיר ובקרבן.** אם אמר כנדבות כשרים הריני נזיר והרי זה קרבן אם אוכל ככר זו, ואכלה, חייב בנזיר ובקרבן, שהכשרים פעמים נודרים בנזיר לאפרושי מאיסור, ומתנדבים בקרבן ומביאים קרבנס לפתח העזרה ומקדישין אותו שם כדי שלא יבואו בה לידי מכשול. ונדבה היא כשיאמר הרי זו ונדר הרי עלי, לפיכך הכשרים מתנדבים אבל אינם נודרים כי היכי דלא ליתו לידי תקלה:

יד אברהם

that מְנֻדֶּה meant *excommunicated*, and therefore, that no serious intent to produce a *neder* existed.]

Shulchan Aruch (*Yoreh Deah* 206:3), in fact, rules that the declaration, "מְנֻדֶּה אֲנִי לָךְ, שֶׁאֵינִי אוֹכַל לָךְ — *I am excommunicated from you, in that I will not eat of yours*" is not binding (see *Beur HaGra* ibid.).

[In the following part of the mishnah, the root נדר is used in a broad sense to encompass different types of declarations, and is not limited to the description of prohibitive *nedarim*.]

„כְּנִדְרֵי רְשָׁעִים" – נָדַר בְּנָזִיר וּבְקָרְבָּן וּבִשְׁבוּעָה; — [*If one says:*] *"Like the vows of the wicked"* — *he has vowed concerning a Nazirite, an offering, and an oath.*

If a person declares: "I adopt upon myself the vows of the wicked — which are the declaration of the Nazirite, a pledge to bring an offering, and an oath — if I eat this loaf," he is not allowed to eat the loaf. If he does so, he becomes a Nazirite for the standard thirty-day period, he must offer a sacrifice at the Temple, and he is considered to have violated an oath

against eating the loaf — a transgression that is liable to the penalty of lashes (*Rav; Rambam*).

The description of the declaration of the Nazirite, the pledge to bring an offering, and the oath as "vows of the wicked" is appropriate, since careless people — unconcerned about the consequences of their words — often adopted various oaths and vows in moments of anger or the like. This laxity with respect to vow-making was considered "wicked," since the Torah treats the matter of vows and oaths with considerable gravity. However, more scrupulous people were careful to avoid swearing or vowing (*Rav; Ran; Ritva*).

„כְּנִדְרֵי כְשֵׁרִים", — לֹא אָמַר כְּלוּם; — *"Like the vows of the scrupulous"* — *he has not said anything.*

If a person declares: "I adopt upon myself the vows of the scrupulous people — which are the declaration of a Nazirite, a pledge to bring an offering, and an oath — if I eat this loaf," his statement is considered meaning-

1
1   [If one says:] "Like the vows of the wicked" — he has
vowed concerning a Nazirite, an offering, and an
oath. "Like the vows of the scrupulous" — he has not
said anything. "Like their devotional vows" — he
has vowed concerning a Nazirite and an offering.

YAD AVRAHAM

less. Scrupulous people simply did not engage in making vows; hence, to adopt *the vows of the scrupulous* amounts to adopting nothing. The person may eat the loaf without suffering any consequences (*Rav; Rambam*).

בְּנִדְבוֹתָם"., — *"Like their devotional vows" — he has vowed concerning a Nazirite and an offering.*

Although devout and scrupulous people were generally careful not to make vows and oaths, they would sometimes declare vows out of religious motivation. For example, a scrupulous person might vow to become a Nazirite in order to attain a spiritual height of devotion (*Gem.* 9b; *Ran* 9a). This is much different from the person who announces that he will become a Nazirite if he eats a certain piece of cake. That sort of declaration is flippant, and shows no sincerity on his part toward being a Nazirite (*Rambam, Hil. Nezirus* 10:14).

Similarly, if a person actually designates an animal as sacred, to be offered in the Temple, he has displayed more resolve to offer an animal than one who simply pledges to bring an offering, but fails to designate it. Devout people, upon deciding to offer a sacrifice, would bring the animal to the Temple before sanctifying it. Only there, when they were sure that their resolution could be carried out, would they designate the animal as sacred. Any chance of violating the

sanctity of the animal or neglecting to sacrifice it was thus eliminated. This practice displayed both the resolve to bring the sacrifice, as well as the concern about violating a pledge to bring an offering (*Gem.* 9b; *Ran* 9a *Rosh; Rashi; Tos.* 9b).

A declaration motivated by sincerity and resolve is called נְדָבָה, *nedavah* (pl.נְדָבוֹת,*nedavos*). A declaration lacking these elements is called *neder* (*Ran* 9a). Thus, although scrupulous people never made declarations that could be described as *nedarim*, they occasionally made sincere declarations to become a Nazirite or to sanctify an animal for an offering. These declarations are what is meant by the term בְּנִדְבוֹתָם, *like their devotional vows*, in the mishnah. For a person to adopt *the devotional vows of the scrupulous* is thus a meaningful statement, unlike *the vows of the scrupulous*, which is not. Consequently, if a person adopts *the devotional vows of the scrupulous*, he is obligated to become a Nazirite and to sanctify an animal to be offered as a sacrifice.

However, the expression *devotional vows of the scrupulous* does not include an oath. While — under appropriate circumstances — becoming a Nazirite is depicted in Scripture as admirable (see *Rambam, Hil. Nezirus* 10:14), and while offering sacrifices was a form of worship, making oaths and restrictions was not considered a way to enhance one"s

[ב] **הָאוֹמֵר** לַחֲבֵרוֹ: ,,קוֹנָם׳׳, ,,קוֹנָח׳׳, ,,קוֹנָס׳׳, הֲרֵי אֵלוּ כִּנּוּיִין לְקָרְבָּן.

—————————— ר׳ עובדיה מברטנורא ——————————

(ב) **קונם קונח קונס אלו הרי כנויין לקרבן.** לשונות של גויס הס, ויש מהס מי שקורא לקרבן כך ויש מי שקורא כך, ובכל לשון שיאמר מאלו הוא מתפיס בקרבן:

—————— **יד אברהם** ——————

spirituality. Consequently, scrupulous, devout people studiously avoided making oaths (*Ran; Meiri*).

The explanation given for this section of the mishnah follows *Rav* and *Rambam*. However, many commentators construe the phrase ,,בְּנִדְרֵי רְשָׁעִים׳׳ – נָדַר בְּנָזִיר, as referring to the case of a person who — upon noticing a Nazirite passing by — declared: "I am like the vows of the wicked." According to this view, the term וּבְקָרְבָּן describes another case in which a person, in the presence of a suitable animal, declares: "I pledge the vows of the wicked." The expression וּבִשְׁבוּעָה refers to one who, in front of some food, declares: ,,הֵימֶנּוּ כְּנִדְרֵי רְשָׁעִים׳׳ — "[away] *from it like the vows of the wicked*" (*Ran; Rosh; Rashba; Meiri*).

In each of these cases, the presence of the Nazirite, the animal, or the food reveals the intent of the phrase *like the vows of the wicked*. The respective declarations are valid and obligate the person to be a Nazirite, to bring an offering, or to abstain from the food under the force of an oath (*Ran 9a*).

If, in the identical situations, the person referred to *vows of the scrupulous* rather than *the vows of the wicked*, the declarations would be meaningless. This is because the former expression is a contradiction in terms, since scrupulous people do not usually make vows and oaths. Therefore, as explained above, the declarations of the scrupulous cannot be described as *nedarim*.

However, if — in the above cases — reference was made to *devotional vows of the scrupulous*, the law would be as follows: In the case of a passing Nazirite, if one declared: "I adopt the devotional vows of the scrupulous," he would become a Nazirite. If, in the presence of a suitable animal, he declared: "I pledge the devotional vows of the scrupulous," he would be required to bring an offering to the Temple. But, to declare in front of some food: "[Away] from it like the devotional vows of the scrupulous" would be meaningless, since this is an oath, and the scrupulous did not make oaths (ibid.).

Although the declarations in this section of the mishnah are valid, they are nevertheless not the standard form of declarations for the particular obligations being undertaken (i.e., Nazirite, sacrifice, oath), and are therefore considered *yados* (*Ritva; Ran*).

2.

The Mishnah now returns to the subject of *kinnuyim* (equivalent terms), and proceeds to present illustrations of this category.

The *Gemara* (10a) gives two accounts of the origin of these terms. R' Shimon ben Lakish maintains that these terms were invented by the Sages to be used in vows in place of the words *korban, cherem, nazir,* and *shevuah.* All of these words occur in the Torah in phrases containing God's Name. It was feared that, if the Scriptural terminology were used, force of habit would lead the speaker to finish the familiar Biblical verse. This, in turn, might cause a person to omit the primary word (*korban, che-*

1
2
2. **O**ne who says to another: *"Konam," "konach,"* [or] *"konas"* — these are equivalents for *korban.*

YAD AVRAHAM

rem, etc.) and mention only God's Name. For example, the word *korban* occurs in the phrase, קָרְבָּן לַה' — *an offering to Hashem (Lev.* 1:2). If the word *korban* was used in vows, people would get into the habit of using the familiar phrase קָרְבָּן לַה'. Apprehensive that this would lead to uttering God's Name in vain, the Sages forbade use of the Torah's terms and invented substitutes (*Ran* 10a).

R' Yochanan, however, contends that *kinnuyim* are foreign-language equivalents for the terms *shevuah, nazir, cherem,* and *korban.* Accordingly, the use of the Torah's terminology is permitted. The halachah follows this view (*Yoreh Deah* 207:1).

הָאוֹמֵר לַחֲבֵרוֹ: "קוֹנָם","קוֹנָח","קוֹנָס"– *One who says to another: "Konam," "konach," [or] "konas"* —

[He used any of these terms in place of the word *korban* in *a neder.* For example, he declared: "This food is forbidden for me like *konam."*]

The term *korban* can be used in a declaration designating an animal to be an offering. This mishnah, however, is discussing the use of the word in the context of a prohibitive *neder.* To emphasize this, the mishnah presents the case of a person who addresses another. Clearly, he is prohibiting the other's belongings to himself or vice versa, and is not sanctifying an animal (*Chiddushei R' Eliyahu Guttmacher;* see *Tos. R' Akiva*).

Meiri explains that קוֹנָם is a contraction of the words קֹדֶשׁ נָאַם — He said, "sacred." It came to be used instead of *korban,* since an animal that is to be sacrificed must be declared holy.

הֲרֵי אֵלּוּ כִּנּוּיִין לְקָרְבָּן. — *these are equivalents for korban.*

[They may be used as substitutes for the word *korban,* and their use in the formula of the *neder* is valid.]

According to the prevailing opinion that the *kinnuyim* are foreign-language equivalents, *Ran* (2a) asks why the mishnah saw the need to give examples. Why would it not have sufficed to simply state that *one may declare a neder in any language?*

Quoting *R' Yehudah ibn Chasdai*, he explains that the examples selected by the mishnah are corruptions of the Hebrew words that were incorporated into the foreign language to be used as equivalents for the original terms. Since they are not native to the foreign language, one might have thought that these words are not considered part of that language and do not qualify as legitimate terminology for vows. Therefore, the mishnah gives specific examples of such words. They are valid, since they are used and understood by speakers of the foreign language. Certainly, it follows that words which originate in the foreign language and whose meaning is synonymous with the Hebrew are valid.

Tosafos (2a) suggest a different explanation as to why the mishnah did not merely state that *one may declare a neder in any language.* For the foreign-language equivalents to be valid in a *neder,* they must be understood by the speaker. A Frenchman who did not know English could not make a *neder* using the word *sacrifice.* However, the equivalents listed in the mishnah (*konam,* etc.) may be used, and are valid even if the

„חֶרֶק", „חֶרֶךְ", „חֶרֶף" — הֲרֵי אֵלּוּ כִּנּוּיִין
לְחֵרֶם. „נָזִיק", „נָזִיחַ", „פָּזִיחַ" — הֲרֵי אֵלּוּ
כִּנּוּיִין לִנְזִירוּת. „שְׁבוּתָה", „שְׁקוּקָה", נָדַר
בְּ„מוֹתָא" — הֲרֵי אֵלּוּ כִּנּוּיִין לִשְׁבוּעָה.

[ג] הָאוֹמֵר: „לֹא חֻלִּין, לֹא אֹכַל לָךְ",

―――――― **ר' עובדיה מברטנורא** ――――――

נדר במותא. כלומר נשבע במותא, והוא כינוי של מומתא שהיא שבועה בלשון תרגום: **(ג) לחולין שאוכל לך.** הלמ"ד נקודה פתח, ומשמע לא חולין יהיה מה שאוכל לך אלא לך קדש:

יד אברהם

speaker did not understand them. [*Tosafos* apparently hold that, if a person who did not speak Hebrew used the Hebrew terms *korban, cherem, neder,* or *shevuah* in a *neder,* it would be acceptable. The equivalents in the mishnah, having developed from the original Hebrew (see *Ran,* quoted above), are also treated like Hebrew, and are acceptable for use, even if not understood.] The point of the mishnah, then, is that the equivalents listed are valid even if not understood, while foreign terms must be understood by the speaker. This differentiation would not be realized if the mishnah had simply stated that one may declare a *neder* in any language.

Ritva (*Bava Basra* 164b, s.v. ת"ר), however, disagrees and requires that the equivalents be understood in order for their use to be valid.

„חֶרֶק", „חֶרֶךְ", „חֶרֶף" – הֲרֵי אֵלּוּ כִּנּוּיִין לְחֵרֶם. — *"Cherek," "cherech," [or] "cheref" — these are equivalents for cherem.*

[They may be legitimately used as synonyms for the word *cherem.* See Mishnah 1.]

„נָזִיק", „נָזִיחַ", „פָּזִיחַ" – הֲרֵי אֵלּוּ כִּנּוּיִין לִנְזִירוּת. — *"Nazik," "naziach," [or] "paziach" — these are equivalents for*

nazir.

[Therefore, the declaration, "I am a *paziach*," for example, will obligate the person to be a full-fledged Nazirite. See mishnah 1.]

Aruch (quoted by *Meleches Shlomo;* cf. *Rashi* to *Nazir* 2a, s.v. כל) suggests that the equivalent for *cherem* and for *nazir* developed because of the similarity in the forms of the Hebrew characters. Thus, the letters ק, ף, and ךְ became confused with ם, resulting in חֶרֶךְ, חֶרֶק, חֶרֶף for חֵרֶם. (If a ם was erased, or had not been written clearly, one can easily see how it might be mistaken for the letters ק, ף or ךְ.) Similarly, ח and ק were confused with ר, and פ was confused with ר, and פ was confused with נ, leading to נָזִיק, נָזִיחַ, and פָּזִיחַ.

„שְׁבוּתָה", „שְׁקוּקָה", נָדַר בְּ„מוֹתָא" – הֲרֵי אֵלּוּ כִּנּוּיִין לִשְׁבוּעָה. — *"Shevusah," "shekukah," or [one who] swore using [the term] mosa — these are equivalents for shevuah.*

[They can be used instead of the standard term *shevuah* in the formula of an oath.]

The first two words, *shevusah* and *shekukah,* developed from *shevuah.* The third term, *mosa,* comes from the Aramaic *momasa,* which corresponds to the Hebrew *shevuah* (*Rav*). To

"Cherek," "cherech," [or] *"cheref"* — these are equivalents for *cherem;* *"nazik," "naziach,"* [or] *"paziach"* — these are equivalents for *nazir.* *"Shevusah," "shekukah,"* or [one who] swore using [the term] *mosa* — these are equivalents for *shevuah.*

3. **O**ne who says: "Not *chullin,* I shall not eat from

YAD AVRAHAM

indicate the difference in origin, the mishnah separates the first two terms from the third with the word נָדַר, [one who] swore (Tos. Yom Tov from Rosh).

The phrase "נָדַר בְּ,,מוֹתָא means *he made an oath using the term mosa.* In Rabbinic Hebrew, oaths were also called *nedarim* (Rav to 11:1; Tos. Yom Tov to 1:1); therefore, the mishnah uses the noun and verb forms of *neder* with reference to oaths as well as vows.

Instead of "נָדַר בְּ,,מוֹתָא, the version of some commentators reads: נָדַר בְּ,,מוֹהִי", *Mohi* is a corruption of מֹשֶׁה *Moshe* (Moses), and is clearly not related etymologically to the word *shevuah.* Rather, the mishnah means that someone swore by "the oath of Moshe" alluding to *Exodus* 2:21. If, instead of saying "the oath of Moshe," he said: "the oath of Mohi," the oath will be valid, since *Mohi* is equivalent to *Moshe* (Ran from Yerushalmi; Tos. Yom Tov).

3.

הָאוֹמֵר: ,,לֹא חוּלִּין, לֹא אֹכַל לָךְ" — *One who says: "Not chullin, I shall not eat from you,"*

This is to be understood as two statements: "Not *chullin* shall your food be for me; therefore, I shall not eat of it" (Radvaz, Hil. Nedarim 1:19).

Chullin means *ordinary* and *non-sacred; chullin* food is therefore permissible, But by designating another's food as "not-*chullin*," the above declaration implies that it *is* to be considered sacred, and thus forbidden (Rambam Comm.).

Rav's version of this mishnah reads somewhat differently: הָאוֹמֵר: ,,לַחוּלִּין; לַחוּלִּין (שֶׁאֹכַל לָךְ) instead of לֹא חוּלִּין and שֶׁאֹכַל לָךְ instead of לֹא אֹכַל לָךְ).

The word לַחוּלִּין is treated like a contraction of the words לֹא חוּלִּין, not-*chullin* (Gem. 11a).[1] Thus, the declaration — ,,לַחוּלִּין שֶׁאֹכַל לָךְ" — means: "Not-*chullin* [shall be] that which I eat of yours." The food is thus designated as "not-*chullin*" (i.e., sacred) and is thus forbidden to the person making the *neder* (Rav).

Had the person declared ,,לְחוּלִּין שֶׁאֹכַל לָךְ", rather than ,,לַחוּלִּין", no prohibition would result, and the food would remain permitted. This declaration — ,,לְחוּלִּין שֶׁאֹכַל לָךְ" — means "That which I eat of yours shall be *chullin.*" Since *chullin* is permissible, the food is permissible as well (Rambam; Ritva; Tur Yoreh Deah 204).

1. For this reason, when *Maharam of Rothenburg* recited the special insertion beginning with זָכְרֵנוּ in the *Shemoneh Esrei* prayer from Rosh Hashanah to Yom Kippur, he would be careful to say זָכְרֵנוּ לְחַיִּים, *Remember us for life,* rather than לַחַיִּים — which, according to this *Gemara* — would be a contraction of לֹא חַיִּים, *not life* (Tur, Orach Chaim 582; cf. Perisha ad loc. 5).

—————— ר' עובדיה מברטנורא ——————

לא כשר. יהיה אלא פסול, [והיינו] קדשים דשייך בהו כשרות ופסלות: **לא דכי.** לא מותר, כמו
איל קמלא דכן, בעבודה זרה [דף לז, א], ואף על גב דלשון מותר ואסור שייך נמי גבי
נבלה וטרפה ואנן קיימא לן (גמרא יד, א) שאין מתפיסין אלא בדבר הנידר והנדב, הואיל ויש
במשמעותו מותר גם בקדשים, הא תנן (פרק ב, ד) סתם נדרים להחמיר, דכיון דדעתו להתפיסו
בנדר אמרינן על דבר הנידר נתכוין: **טהור.** אם אמר לא טהור מה שאוכל לך: **טמא נותר**

יד אברהם

"לֹא כָשֵׁר", — *"unfit"*

He declares: "Your food shall be
unfit for me." The expression "לֹא
כָשֵׁר" is used with reference to
sacrifices, and is equivalent to the
term פָּסוּל — *unfit, disqualified* (Rav).

[A sacrificial animal may be classified as fit (כָשֵׁר) or unfit (לֹא כָשֵׁר;
פָּסוּל). For example, if a sacrificial
animal develops a disqualifying blem-
ish, it is unfit for offering on the altar
(Rambam, Hil. Isurei HaMizbei'ach
1:5ff.).

By designating another's food as לֹא
כָשֵׁר he has compared it to a
disqualified sacrificial animal. The
declaration is a valid *neder*, and the
other person's food is forbidden for
him to eat (Ritva).

The designation לֹא כָשֵׁר, *unfit*, is a
valid component in the formula of a
neder because this expression is interpreted as referring to a disqualified
sacrificial animal. This is a legitimate
reference, since the sanctity of the
animal originates from a person's
declaration (see preface to this chapter). On the other hand, if the person
were to explain that he was referring
to kosher and nonkosher food, and
not to sacrificial animals, the *neder*
would be void. This is because the
classification of food as kosher or
nonkosher is determined by the Torah — not by human designation —
and is thus not an acceptable reference
in a *neder* (see 2:1). However, in the

ab-sence of any explanation by the
person pronouncing the *neder*, the
declaration is interpreted in such a
way that it will be binding. Therefore,
לֹא כָשֵׁר is taken as a reference to a
disqualified sacrifice and not to nonkosher food.

The right to assume the more stringent
and binding interpretation when assessing
a declaration derives from the principle,
stated in 2:4, that a declaration is assumed to
be a binding one unless otherwise specified.
It is presumed that, usually, when a person
makes a declaration, he intends it to be
binding (Rosh ibid.). Thus, when food is
designated as לֹא כָשֵׁר, we interpret this as
meaning *disqualified sacrifices*, which will
validate the *neder*, rather than interpreting
the reference as meaning *nonkosher food*,
which would make the declaration unacceptable and not binding (Meiri).

וְ,"לֹא דְכֵי", — *or "not permissible,"*

[He declares: "Your food shall be
not permissible to me."]

The phrase *not permissible* might
conceivably mean *not kosher*. However, a *neder* which attempts to assign
to something the status of nonkosher
food is not valid (2:1). Therefore,
following the general assumption that
a person making a *neder* intends it to
be binding (2:4), the phrase לֹא דְכֵי, *not
permissible*, is taken to refer to a
disqualified sacrifice. This is a valid
reference for a *neder*, and the vow
"Your food is not permissible to me" is
binding (Rav).

YAD AVRAHAM

"טָהוֹר,, — "*ritually pure*"

["Your food is to me ritually pure."]

To designate something as *ritually pure* should not create any prohibitions, since this expression obviously refers to a permissible status. Therefore, *Rav* explains that the actual declaration under consideration is: "Your food is to me *not* ritually pure." The mishnah does not bother to state *not ritually pure* explicitly, since the terms דְכֵי, *permissible*, and טָהוֹר, *ritually pure*, are related (דְכֵי is Aramaic for the Hebrew זַךְ, which means *pure*), and just as in the previous phrase in the mishnah, the *neder* being discussed designated the food as לֹא דְכֵי — so too, in this phrase, the *neder* under discussion is one involving לֹא טָהוֹר (*Ran*). Indeed, in some editions of the mishnah the text reads לֹא טָהוֹר (cf. *Rif*).

Although these terms also apply to *terumah*, which is *not* a valid reference in a *neder* (as stated in 2:1), it is assumed that the person making the *neder* wishes it to be binding (*Rosh*).

"וְטָמֵא,, — or "*ritually contaminated*,"

He declares: "Ritually contaminated is your food to me" (*Rav*).

According to *Rav*, the previous case of the mishnah was a declaration designating the food as לֹא טָהוֹר, *not ritually pure*. Since this is equivalent to *tamei* (ritually contaminated; unclean) the case of *tamei* would appear to be superfluous. However, *Tosafos* (to 10b) explain that the term *tahor* in the phrase לֹא טָהוֹר is readily associated with sacrificial animals, whose ritual purity must be maintained. Hence, לֹא טָהוֹר is easily interpreted as referring to sacrifices,

albeit disqualified ones. However, the term *tamei* might have been understood as referring to something which is generally in a state of ritual contamination — namely, *chullin*, (nonsacred food). Obviously, if the *neder* designated something as *chullin*, which is completely permissible, no prohibition would ensue. Therefore, the mishnah stresses that the term *tamei* must also be understood as referring to a ritually contaminated sacrifice — and not to the commonly contaminated *chullin* — and the *neder* is binding (*Tos. Yom Tov*).

"נוֹתָר,, — "*leftover sacrificial meat*"

[He declares: "Your food is to me leftover sacrificial meat."

When an animal has been designated as a sacrifice, it becomes forbidden for general use. Upon its offering, in general, certain parts of the animal become permitted for consumption by the owner or by the *Kohen*. However, there are laws which limit the time span during which the permitted cuts may be eaten. Some offerings must be consumed within a day and a night. Others are allowed to be eaten for two days and one night. In any event, meat left over beyond the permissible time becomes forbidden, and eating it may incur the penalty of *kares* (spiritual excision and premature death). Such leftovers are called נוֹתָר, *nosar* (*Rambam, Hil. Pesulei HaMukdashim* 18:9-10).

Prior to being offered on the altar, the sacrificial animal is prohibited by human designation and, as such, is a suitable reference in a *neder*. Once offered, certain cuts of meat are

ו,,פָּגוּל" — אָסוּר. ,,כְּאִמְרָא", ,,כַּדִּירִים", ,,כָּעֵצִים",
,,כָּאִשִּׁים", ,,כַּמִּזְבֵּחַ", ,,כַּהֵיכָל", ,,כִּירוּשָׁלַיִם"; נָדַר

ר' עובדיה מברטנורא

פגול. אם אמר טמא מה שאוכל לך, וכן כולם, אסור, שכל אלו דברים הנוהגים בקדשים הם: **כאימרא.** כשה של קרבן: **בדירים.** כלשכת הטלאים או כלשכת הטלאים: **בעצים.** כגזרי עצים של מערכה: **כאישים.** כקרבנות שעל האש: **כמזבח.** כקרבנות שעל גבי המזבח: **בהיכל.** כקרבנות שבהיכל: **בירושלם.** כקרבנות שבירושלם. פירוש אחר, [כחומות ירושלים, דקסבר] שחומות ירושלים משירי הלשכה קא אתו:

יד אברהם

released from the prohibition, and become permissible. Should they be left uneaten long enough to become *nosar*, they become forbidden again; but this new prohibition is dictated by Biblical law and is *not* created by human designation. That being the case, a reference to the interdicted status of *nosar* ought not to be an acceptable reference in a *neder*, since it is not the consequence of human designation (see prefaces to 1:1, 1:4; 2:1). Yet, our mishnah appears to validate a *neder* which assigns the state of *nosar*.

To resolve this, the *Gemara* (12a) explains that a person who declares through a *neder* that something should be like *nosar* really means that it is to be like that which is subject to the laws of *nosar*. In other words, the declaration "Your food is to me *nosar*" is equivalent to saying: "Your food is to me like that which is subject to the laws of *nosar*" and refers to the sacrificial animal, whose sanctity derives from a human declaration. The reference is therefore valid, and the declaration is binding (*Tos. Yom Tov*).

ו,,פָּגוּל" — *or "pigul"* —
["Your food is to me *pigul*."]

If a sacrificial animal is slaughtered with the intention to perform one of its rites after its permitted time — viz., sprinkling its blood on the altar after sunset, offering it upon the altar after sunrise of the next day, or eating the allowed parts past one day and one night or two days and one night, the animal is considered to have been slaughtered outside the proper time. To slaughter or perform the other major sacrificial rituals with these intentions is called *pigul* (*Rambam, Hil. Pesulei HaMukdashim* 13:1). The sacrifice becomes disqualified, and one who eats willfully of the parts which normally are permitted is subject to *kares* (ibid.18:6).

Because the sacrifice is disqualified at the slaughtering, the original prohibitions that began when the animal was designated as sacrificial are never lifted. Thus, meat that is *pigul* is considered to be meat prohibited by the original human designation which — due to a disqualification — never becomes permitted. *Pigul* is therefore a valid reference for a *neder*, and the declaration designating food to be *pigul* is binding (*Ran* to 12a; *Tos.* ibid.).

אָסוּר — *[these declarations are]* binding.

The mishnah continues to list other references which are valid. However, the list is interrupted here by the word אָסוּר, *binding*. This is because the terms to follow differ from those mentioned till now. All the examples which follow in the next part of the mishnah

or "pigul" — [these declarations are] binding. "Like a lamb," "like the enclosures," "like the logs," "like the fires," "like the altar," "like the sanctuary," "like Jerusalem"; [or if] he vowed

YAD AVRAHAM

are prefaced with the comparative 'כ: כְּאִמְרָא, כַּדִּירִין etc., rather than אִמְרָא, דִּירִין, etc. In the first part of the mishnah, the terms listed do not need this preface. Hence, פִּגּוּל, טָמֵא, rather than כְּפִגּוּל, כְּטָמֵא. (The reason for this distinction is explained in the commentary to mishnah 4, s.v. רַבִּי יְהוּדָה מַתִּיר).

כְּאִמְרָא,, — "Like a lamb,"

"That is like a sacrificial lamb" (Rav; Ran). One opinion in Yerushalmi maintains that the reference here is specifically to the קָרְבַּן תָּמִיד, the twice-daily offering of a lamb in the Temple (Tos. to 10b: Ritva).

כַּדִּירִים,, — "like the enclosures,"

This could refer either to the enclosure of the Temple, in which wood for the fire on the altar was kept, or to the enclosure in which sacrificial lambs were held (Rav; Rosh).

Some explain that the reference is to the actual structure of the enclosure which was sacred. Others maintain that it refers to lambs or to the wood contained within the enclosure (see Tos. Yom Tov, s.v. כמזבח).

In any event, the structure as part of the Temple, and its contents, being reserved for the altar, were sacred by human designation and hence, valid references for a neder (ibid.).

The plural form כַּדִּירִים, rather than the singular כַּדִּיר, alludes to the two enclosures — one for wood and one for lambs (Tos. 10b; Tos. Yom Tov).

כָּעֵצִים,, — "like the logs,"

This refers to the logs of the fire on the altar. Rosh explains that a donation of wood for the altar entailed a minimum of two logs (Shekalim 6:6). Tos. Yom Tov remarks that this is why the plural form logs is used here.

כָּאִשִּׁים,, — "like the fires,"

That is, like the sacrifices which are consumed by the fires on the altar (Rav). Tosafos notes that the Torah refers to those parts of the sacrifice which are burnt on the altar as אִשִּׁים (see e.g., Lev. 1:9, 2:3). Alternatively, Yerushalmi explains that the reference here is to the actual fires burning on the altar. Tos. Tom Tov suggests that to allude to these two explanations, the mishnah uses the plural form fires.

כַּמִּזְבֵּחַ,, ,,כַּהֵיכָל,, ,,כִּירוּשָׁלַיִם;, — "like the altar," "like the sanctuary," "like Jerusalem";

These refer to offerings. Like the altar could mean any animal sacrifice, since at least part of the animal must be placed on the altar. Like the sanctuary refers to specific offerings whose blood is sprinkled inside the sanctuary of the Temple. Like Jerusalem alludes to those sacrifices which — after their offering — could be eaten anywhere within the confines of Jerusalem, even outside the Temple Mount (Rav; Tif. Yis.).

Another interpretation is that the reference here is to the actual structures of the altar, the sanctuary, and the walls of Jerusalem — all of which were sacred (Rav).

However, there is a dispute whether the walls of Jerusalem were in fact sacred or not (cf. Kiddusin 54a, and see comm. below, s.v. רַבִּי יְהוּדָה).

בְּאֶחָד מִכָּל מְשַׁמְּשֵׁי הַמִּזְבֵּחַ, אַף עַל פִּי שֶׁלֹּא הִזְכִּיר קָרְבָּן — הֲרֵי זֶה נָדַר בְּקָרְבָּן. רַבִּי יְהוּדָה אוֹמֵר: הָאוֹמֵר ,,יְרוּשָׁלַיִם" — לֹא אָמַר כְּלוּם.

ר' עובדיה מברטנורא

באחד מכל משמשי המזבח. כגון מזלגות מזרקות ומחתות, אם אמר כמזלגות שאוכל לך או כמזרקות שאוכל לך, וכן כולם, אף על פי שלא הזכיר קרבן הרי זה כנודר בקרבן: **רבי יהודה אומר האומר ירושלם.** בלא כ"ף לא אמר כלום. ותנא קמא פליג עליה. ואין הלכה כרבי יהודה:

יד אברהם

נָדַר בְּאֶחָד מִכָּל מְשַׁמְּשֵׁי הַמִּזְבֵּחַ, — *[or if] he vowed [and made reference to] one of the accessories of the altar,*

The accessories of the altar were the various tools such as forks, pitchers, and scoops used in the sacrificial service or in the cleaning of the altar (Rav; Rosh).

Thus, if he declared: "Your food is to me like forks," it is understood that he means to refer to sacrifices, and the declaration is a binding *neder* (ibid.).

[Presumably, those who explain the expression *like the enclosures, like the sanctuary,* etc. to refer to the actual structures will explain that here, too, the intention is to the accessories themselves, rather than the sacrifices.]

אַף עַל פִּי שֶׁלֹּא הִזְכִּיר ,,קָרְבָּן" – הֲרֵי זֶה נָדַר בְּקָרְבָּן. — *even though he did not mention korban — he has vowed with [reference to] an offering.*

[Following the approach that all the examples in the preceding list are, in fact, references to sacrifices, the meaning of this statement is this: Even though the word *korban* was not mentioned, his declaration is understood as referring to a sacrifice.

If we interpret some of the cases listed as comparisons to the mentioned items themselves (e.g., *like the sanctuary* refers to the structure itself), and not to sacrifices, this phrase of the mishnah will apparently be read as follows: *Even though korban*

was not mentioned or even alluded to, the declaration is as valid as one which explicitly refers to a sacrifice. This is, to refer to these sacred structures in a *neder* is as effective as referring to a sacrifice.]

רַבִּי יְהוּדָה אוֹמֵר: הָאוֹמֵר ,,יְרוּשָׁלַיִם" – לֹא אָמַר כְּלוּם. — *R' Yehudah says: One who states "Jerusalem" has not said anything.*

As a reference to a *neder*, one said "Jerusalem" and not like "Jerusalem"; therefore, the *neder* is not binding (Rav). According to this interpretation, the foregoing part of the mishnah — which prefaces the references with the comparative כ, *like*, in order that they be valid — follows R' Yehudah's opinion. The mishnah is, in effect, telling us that the comparative preposition is necessary in all those cases based on R' Yehudah's statement that saying *Jerusalem* alone — without prefacing it with *like* — is not a legitimate form of reference for a *neder*. Since this position is attributed to R' Yehudah, it may be inferred that other *Tannaim* do not require the כ, even for the cases listed above in the mishnah (Rav; Tos. Yom Tov).

Others explain that R' Yehudah does not validate a *neder* with a reference to Jerusalem, even if it has the comparative prefix, because he construes the reference to be to the walls of Jerusalem and not to sac-

[and made reference to] one of the accessories of the altar, even though he did not mention *korban* — he has vowed with [reference to] an offering. R' Yehudah says: One who states "Jerusalem" has not said anything.

YAD AVRAHAM

rifices, and he does not consider the walls of Jerusalem to be sacred. Thus, a *neder* referring to the walls of Jerusalem cannot produce a prohibition. Accordingly, the preceding part of the mishnah represents another view that validates a reference to Jerusalem either because we interpret it as referring to sacrifices eaten in Jerusalem, or because the walls of Jerusalem are considered sacred. In the latter case, even if the expression *like Jerusalem* alludes to the city"s walls,

the *neder* will be valid (*Meiri; Shitah Mekubetzes;* cf. *Yerushalmi*).

[From the next mishnah it is clear that the *Tanna* who insists on the use of the comparative preposition is R' Yehudah (*Meiri* to 1:4). Hence, the list of examples (*Meiri* to 1:4). Hence, the list of examples (*like a lamb*, etc.) follows R' Yehudah's view with respect to the use of the preposition *like*, but disputes him concerning the eligibility of *like Jerusalem* as a reference for a *neder*.]

4.

The following preface is intended to help clarify *Rav's* interpretation of this mishnah. Other approaches to some of the concepts presented here will be discussed in the following chapter.

◆§ דְּבַר הַנָּדוּר — Davar Hanadur

The Torah writes: *A man who vows a vow* (*Num.* 30:3). The seemingly redundant expression *who vows a vow*, rather than the simpler *who vows*, teaches us that a *neder* can assign to an item only the sort of prohibition which is itself the result of a declaration (*Gem.* 13a,14a; *Shevuos* 20b). A sacrificial animal, for example, is designated as such by a human declaration. Its forbidden state may therefore be assigned to something else via a *neder*. Prohibited items such as this which are created by human designation are called *davar hanadur* (*Ran* 2a).

However, when something is prohibited by the Torah, it is not a valid reference in a *neder*. For example, a *neder* stating: "Your food is to me like pork" will not be effective, since pork is forbidden by the Torah, and not by a person's designation. Prohibitions such as this, which originate in the Torah, and are not the product of human designation, are called דְּבַר הָאָסוּר, *davar haasur*. They are not valid references in a *neder* (2:1; *Gem.* 14a).

Rav (2:1), following *Rambam* (*Hil. Nedarim* 1:9ff.), adds an important detail to the definition of a *davar hanadur*. The fact that a prohibited state is created by a declaration is not enough to include it in this category. It must also be possible to produce that state voluntarily, just as a *neder* creates an interdiction purely due to a person's volition. This qualification eliminates items such as *terumah*.

Terumah is the portion of the agricultural produce which must be separated and given to the *Kohen*. It is designated as sacred and must be protected, for

[ד] **הָאוֹמֵר:** „קָרְבָּן", „עוֹלָה", „מִנְחָה",
„חַטָּאת", „תּוֹדָה", „שְׁלָמִים
שֶׁאֲנִי אוֹכֵל לָךְ" — אָסוּר. רַבִּי יְהוּדָה מַתִּיר.

──────── ר' עובדיה מברטנורא ────────

(ד) **האומר קרבן עולה מנחה חטאת תודה ושלמים.** כל הני קרבנות חובה הס, ותודה
נמי דמיא לחובה דארבעה דברים לריכין להודות, וסלקא דעתך אמינא דאין זה נודר בדבר הנדור: **ורבי
יהודה מתיר.** משום דאמרן בלא כ"ף דמי לנשבע בחיי הקרבן ובחיי העולה ואין כאן לא נדר

יד אברהם

example, from ritual contamination. Although the person has the freedom to
select and designate any part of the produce as *terumah*, he may do so only
from food subject to the obligation of *terumah*. Thus, from a fresh harvest of
grapes, for example, there is an obligation to set aside *terumah*, and all of the
grapes are suitable to fulfill this requirement. Once the selection and designation of the *terumah* is completed, however, the obligation has already been
carried out, and should one subsequently declare any of the remaining grapes
to be *terumah*, the statement will be meaningless, since *terumah* can be created
only where the obligation exists. Consequently, although the prohibited state
of *terumah* is created by human designation, it is not considered a *davar
hanadur*, and cannot be a valid reference in a *neder*, because it is not something that can be produced at will.

The coming mishnah teaches us that certain sacrifices — although they are
generally obligatory — can be caused as references in a *neder*. This is because
they can sometimes be offered voluntarily, and therefore satisfy both of *Rav's*
criteria for a *davar hanadur*: (1) Their prohibited state derives from a human
designation. (2) It is possible to produce their forbidden status at will.

הָאוֹמֵר: „קָרְבָּן", — *One who says:
"Offering,"*

[I.e., "An offering that which I eat
of yours."]

The point of the mishnah's example
is that this declaration is binding,
despite the failure to preface the word
offering with the comparative preposition *like*. This *Tanna* holds that the
intent of the person to prohibit the
other"s food through a *neder* is
obvious, even without the additional
prefix (*Ran*).

„עוֹלָה", — *"burnt-offering,"*

["A burnt-offering that which I eat
of yours."]

Although some burnt-offerings —
such as the daily *tamid*-offering or the

additional *musaf*-offerings for the
festivals — are obligatory, this term
is nevertheless a valid reference in a
neder. This is because a burnt-offering
can be offered voluntarily and is thus
a *davar hanadur* (see preface; *Tif. Yis.*).

„מִנְחָה", — *"meal-offering,"*

[There are various obligatory meal-
offerings (see *Rambam, Hil. Maasei
HaKorbanos*, Chap. 22). However, a
meal-offering can be voluntarily donated at any time (ibid. 12:4) and is
therefore in the category of a *davar
hanadur*.]

„חַטָּאת", — *"sin-offering,"*

In general, anyone who uninten-
tionally transgresses a negative pre-

4. One who says: "Offering," "burnt-offering," "meal-offering," "sin-offering," "thanksgiving-offering," [or] "peace-offering, that [which] I eat of yours" — [it is] binding. R' Yehudah permits [it].

YAD AVRAHAM

cept — which , if done deliberately, is liable to the penalty of *kares* — is obligated to bring a sin-offering as an atonement (*Rambam, Hil. Shegagos* 1:1). This type of sin-offering does not satisfy the criterion for a *davar hanadur* that it be producible voluntarily. However, there is a sin-offering which is considered voluntary — the one brought by the Nazirite at the end of his Naziritic period. Although it is incumbent upon him to bring this sacrifice, since his declaration to become a Nazirite was a voluntary act, the consequences of that declaration are also considered voluntary. Indeed, the *Gemara* (10a) tells us that there were devout people who, because they had never sinned, were never obligated to bring sin-offerings. But, out of fear that perhaps they were in need of atonement, they declared themselves Nazirites, so at the end of their Nazirite period, they would have to bring sin-offerings (*Rashi* ad loc.; cf. *Rosh*). Thus, the obligation which necessitated the bringing of the sin-offering was adopted voluntarily, and hence, the bringing of the sacrifice itself is also considered voluntary.

Because of this, a sin-offering is considered a *davar hanadur*, and is therefore a valid reference in a *neder* (*Rav* to 2:1; *Rambam, Hil. Nedarim* 1:10).

תּוֹדָה,, — *"thanksgiving-offering,"*

One could donate a thanksgiving-

offering at any time (*Rambam, Hil. Maasei HaKorbanos* 9:15). Yet, since the *Gemara* (*Berachos* 54b) lists four persons who are required to express their thanks for not being harmed,[1] the mishnah lists it here to prevent the misconception that the offering is obligatory (*Rav*).

שְׁלָמִים,, — [or] *"peace-offering,*

The Torah requires a communal peace-offering to be brought on the festival of Shavuos. Although that offering was obligatory, a person could volunteer a peace-offering of his own at any time. It is thus a *davar hanadur*, and is a valid reference for a *neder* (*Tif. Yis.*).

שֶׁאֲנִי אוֹכֵל לָךְ"- — *that [which] I eat of yours"* —

This is the conclusion of all the statements listed heretofore in the mishnah. "An offering (burnt-offering, or meal-offering, etc.) that which I eat of yours" (*Rashi*).

אָסוּר. — [it is] *binding.*

[As mentioned above, in all these cases, the reference is not prefaced by the comparative prefix, because this *Tanna* maintains that the intention of the person making the declaration is clear even without it.]

רַבִּי יְהוּדָה מַתִּיר. — *R' Yehudah permits [it].*

He maintains that there is no binding *neder* in these cases, and the

1. They are: one who journeyed at sea, who traveled through a desert, who recovered from an illness, and who was released from imprisonment (ibid.).

„הַקָּרְבָּן״, „כְּקָרְבָּן״, „קָרְבָּן שֶׁאֹכַל לָךְ״ —
אָסוּר. „לְקָרְבָּן, לֹא אֹכַל לָךְ״ — רַבִּי מֵאִיר אוֹסֵר.
הָאוֹמֵר לַחֲבֵרוֹ: „קוֹנָם פִּי הַמְדַבֵּר עִמָּךְ״, „יָדִי
עוֹשָׂה עִמָּךְ״, „רַגְלַי מְהַלְּכוֹת עִמָּךְ״ — אָסוּר.

ר׳ עובדיה מברטנורא

ולא שבועה. ורישא אשמועינן דפליג תנא קמא עליה דרבי יהודה בירושלים אם הזכירה
בלא כ״ף ואמרי דהוי נדר, וסיפא אשמועינן דפליג רבי יהודה עליה דתנא קמא אפילו בקרבן
עולה ומנחה וכו׳ כשהזכירן בלא כ״ף דלא הוי נדר: **קרבן הקרבן בקרבן שאוכל לך אסור.**
אף על גב דכל הני שמעינן להו כבר, הקרבן איצטריכא ליה, דסלקא דעתך אמינא בחיי הקרבן
קאמר. והא דתנן לקמן בפרק שני (משנה ג) הקרבן שאוכל לך מותר, התם הא קרבן קאמר,
דמשמע חיי קרבן: לקרבן לא אובל לך רבי מאיר אוסר. דנעשה כאומר לקרבן יהא לפיכך
לא אוכל לך. ואין הלכה כרבי מאיר. **קונם פי מדבר עמך.** ואף על גב דאין נדרים חלים על
דבר שאין בו ממש ודבור אין בו ממש, מכל מקום כשאמר קונם פי מדבר עמך אסר הפה מלדבר,
והפה דבר שיש בו ממש הוא, וכן יאסרו ידי למעשיהם ורגלי להלוכן, וכל כיוצא בזה:

יד אברהם

food may therefore be eaten (*Rav*).

R' Yehudah holds that when stated without the comparative preposition, the references do not indicate an intent to create a prohibited status. For example, if one declares "A burnt-offering that which I eat of yours" and not "like a burnt-offering," he might mean that the rites which make up the sacrificial service of the offering should be performed on this person''s food, and he is not referring to the prohibited state of an animal designated as a burnt-offering. Only if he added the comparative prefix, and declared the other''s food to be "like a burnt-offering" does R' Yehudah consider his intention to be to assign the forbidden state of the offering (*Ran* 11a).

An additional reason for R' Yehudah's insistence on the comparative preposition might be that without it, these declarations resemble an oath. "A burnt-offering that which I eat of yours," for example, is as though he were swearing by an offering that he will eat the other's food. By adding the

comparative preposition, however, the statement "Like a burnt-offering that which I eat of yours," is unmistakably a formula for a *neder*, and the intention to produce a *neder*-type prohibition is thus clarified (*Rav; Ran* loc. cit.; *Rambam Commentary*).

In mishnah 3, the references listed in the first part of the mishnah as creating prohibitions (*ritually unclean*, etc.) do not have the comparative prefix. *Ran* asserts that even R' Yehudah agrees that for those cases it is unnecessary, because the terms given there describe forbidden states, and their use is sufficient indication of an intent to produce a *neder*-type prohibition. On the other hand, the expressions *like a lamb, like the enclosures*, etc., enumerated in the second part of the mishnah, do not inherently represent a prohibited status, because a lamb or an enclosure is not necessarily forbidden. They therefore require the comparative prepositions in order to be valid references for a *neder*.

„הַקָּרְבָּן״, „כְּקָרְבָּן״, „קָרְבָּן שֶׁאוֹכַל לָךְ״ —

"Hakorban," "kekorban," [or] *"korban, that which I eat of yours"* — [it is] binding. *"Lekorban, I shall not eat of yours"* — R' Meir prohibits [it].

One who says to another: *"Konam* my mouth [from] talking with you," "my hand from working with you," [or] "my feet from walking with you" — [it is] binding.

YAD AVRAHAM

אָסוּר. — *"Hakorban," "kekorban,"* [or] *"korban, that which I eat of yours"* — [it is] binding.

The fact that a reference using the term *korban* (following the *Tanna* who does not require a comparative prefix) or the form *kekorban* ["like an offering"] (even according to R' Yehudah) is acceptable is not a novelty, and it would be unnecessary for the mishnah to tell us this. It is the הַקָּרְבָּן, *hakorban*, which the mishnah wishes to introduce. Although the very similar-sounding form הָא קָרְבָּן as two distinct words is not a valid reference for a *neder* (see 2:2), the expression הַקָּרְבָּן, as one word, is (*Rav*).

As two words — הָא קָרְבָּן — the meaning is *by the life of a korban*, which is the formula for an oath, and not a *neder*. As one word, הַקָּרְבָּן, the meaning is simply *the korban*. The declaration הַקָּרְבָּן שֶׁאֹכַל לָךְ is the same as saying "Your food is to me [like] the *korban*," in which the article *the* ("*the korban*") indicates some known sacrifice. This form is acceptable, and the *neder* is valid (*Rav*).

לְקָרְבָּן, לֹא אֹכַל לָךְ" – רַבִּי מֵאִיר אוֹסֵר., — *"Lekorban, I shall not eat of yours"* — R' Meir prohibits [it].

If the term לְקָרְבָּן was explained as לֹא קָרְבָּן, *not a korban* (cf. comm. to mishnah 3, s.v. הָאוֹמֵר:, לֹא חֻלִּין"), this declaration could be read as: "Not a *korban*, what I shall not eat of yours."

This double negative would imply that "What I shall eat *shall* be a *korban*, and thus, prohibited." However, the author of this ruling is R' Meir, and the *Gemara* (11a) proves that R' Meir does not accept an implied prohibition as a legitimate reference. Rather, he requires that the prohibition be stated directly. Yet surprisingly, R' Meir validates the double-negative declaration under consideration here.

The *Gemara* (13b) explains that the term לְקָרְבָּן should be understood as לְקָרְבָּן יְהֵא, *it should be an offering*. The declaration should be taken as two statements: [Your food] shall be an offering; therefore, I shall not eat it. The first statement is the *neder*, and it is binding, since the prohibition is stated directly (it should be an offering), and is not merely implied.

Under Biblical law, a *neder* directed at something intangible, such as activities like walking or talking, is not valid. Under Rabbinic law, however, even such a *neder* may be binding (2:1).

The mishnah now illustrates a formula for a *neder* which is binding even under Biblical law, although its major consequence is to ban some intangible activity.

הָאוֹמֵר לַחֲבֵרוֹ: ,,קוֹנָם פִּי הַמְדַבֵּר עִמָּךְ", ,,יָדִי עוֹשָׂה עִמָּךְ", ,,רַגְלַי מְהַלְּכוֹת עִמָּךְ" – אָסוּר. — *One who says to another: "Konam my mouth [from] talking* (lit., *that talks*) *with you," "my hand from working*

with you," [or] "my feet from walking with you" — [it is] binding.

[He may not talk, work, or walk with that person.]

The Gemara (13b) explains that the mouth, hands, or feet serve as the tangible object on which the neder is binding even under Biblical law (Rav; Rosh; cf. Ran.)

Were a person to declare simply: "Konam, my talking (working, or walking) to you" without specifying the mouth (hands, or feet) as the object of the neder, it would not be binding under Biblical law (Meiri).

There is a question discussed by the earlier authorities as to the party being deprived by these declarations. Rashi holds that the person making the declaration is prohibiting himself from enjoying the pleasure of conversation or other activity with the other person. Rashba, however, considers the neder to be directed at the other person. That is, the declaration is prohibiting the other person from enjoying the words that emanate from the mouth of the one who made the neder. Accordingly, Rashba maintains that if the speaker failed to specify some tangible object for this neder, it would not be binding at all — not even Rabbinically. The Rabbinic validation of a neder with no tangible object was enacted only for a prohibition upon oneself. But, in our mishnah, the prohibition is on the other person, and intends to forbid him from enjoying the speaker''s words. Thus, a declaration "Konam, my speech to you" that does not specify the mouth as a material object of the neder will not be valid at all — even Rabbinically (Rashba to 13b; Meiri).

פרק שני ❧

Chapter Two

As explained above (preface to 1:4), a *neder* is only capable of assigning a prohibited state which is in itself the consequence of human designation, known as *davar hanadur*. A typical example of items in this category would be a *korban* (offering), the status of which is created by a person's volition.

A forbidden status which is defined by the Torah and not created by human designation is called *davar haasur*. A typical example would be non-kosher foods, which are specified in *Leviticus* 11 and *Deuteronomy* 14. Such prohibitions cannot be assigned through a *neder*. Thus, the declaration "This fruit is forbidden to me like pork" will not be binding. Pork is Biblically interdicted, and therefore is not an acceptable reference in a *neder*.

The law that a *neder* can assign only a man-made prohibition may be understood in several ways. The simplest would seem to be the following. When a person bans something through a *neder*, he is imposing a stricture on something previously permitted. It is logical, therefore, that prohibitions which are within his jurisdiction to create be assignable through a *neder* as well. However, Divine prohibitions, which are beyond his ability to create, should similarly not be assignable via a *neder* (*Ran* 14a; cf. *Rambam, Hil. Nedarim* 1:9). A different approach is advanced by *Ritva* (to 13b and *Kiddushin* 54a; see *Avnei Nezer* 1:37). A *neder* changes the status of an object. It bestows upon it a status of forbiddance — a kind of sacredness.Thus, fruit prohibited by a *neder* is considered sacred in a sense. To transgress the *neder* and eat such fruit is to violate the sanctity of the food. On the other hand, Biblically interdicted items do not possess any special character. Rather, the objection to their use or consumption stems from the sanctity of the person. Things banned by the Torah are like pollutants for the Jew, and to partake of them is to defile oneself. Thus, the Torah forbids certain foods so that *You shall not contaminate your souls* (*Lev.* 11:44). The consumption of these foods is an abuse — not of the food, but of the person who consumes it. Following this line of thought, *Ritva* argues that it is ludicrous to attempt to assign through a *neder* the status of pork, for example, to a fruit. The substance of pork possesses no extraordinary status at all! The status of an offering, however, is indeed assignable through a *neder* because it is special. The restrictions on the general use of a sacrifice derive from its holy status which must be protected from abuse. To vow by a *neder* that some fruit is forbidden like an offering, therefore, makes sense. The *neder* would impart to the fruit a special status that must not be violated, similar to that of the sacrifice.

The mishnah now presents a list of references which are not acceptable in a *neder*, since they are items that are Biblically prohibited.

[א] וְאֵלּוּ מֻתָּרִין: „חֻלִּין שֶׁאֹכַל לָךְ״, „כִּבְשַׂר חֲזִיר״, „כַּעֲבוֹדָה זָרָה״, „כְּעוֹרוֹת לְבוּבִין״, „כִּנְבֵלוֹת״, „כִּטְרֵפוֹת״, „כִּשְׁקָצִים״,

------ ר' עובדיה מברטנורא ------

פרק שני – ואלו מותרין. (א) ואלו מותרין. חולין שאוכל לך. לסימן בעלמא נקטיה, כשם שחולין שאוכל לך אין צריך שאלה לחכם כך כל הני דאמרינן במתניתין ברישא אין צריכין שאלת חכם: **כעורות לבובין.** היו נוקבים הבהמה מחיים כנגד הלב ומוציאין הלב ומקריבין אותו לעבודה זרה, ותקרובת עבודה זרה אסור בהנאה:

------ **יד אברהם** ------

1.

וְאֵלּוּ מֻתָּרִין: — *The following are not binding:*

I.e., a declaration attempting to assign any of the following states will not be binding (*Tif.Yis.*).

חֻלִּין שֶׁאֹכַל לָךְ,, — *"[May] that which I eat of yours be chullin";*

Chullin is permitted food (see comm. to 1:3, s.v. הָאוֹמֵר: ,,לֹא חֻלִּין) and, of course, to declare someone's food to be *chullin* does not produce any prohibitions. The point of mentioning this declaration is to emphasize that the examples which follow are no more binding than if one were to declare food to be *chullin*. This teaches that a *neder* referring to Divinely interdicted items is totally ineffective — not just according to Biblical law, but under Rabbinic law as well (*Rav; Tos.* 14a, s.v. א"ה).

However, as will be seen, *Rambam* rules that if an ignorant person makes a declaration referring to a Biblically prohibited item, it is binding under Rabbinic law. Evidently, *Rambam* follows an alternate opinion in the *Gemara* which deems the case of the reference to *chullin* to be superfluous (*Tos. Yom Tov*).

כִּבְשַׂר חֲזִיר,, — *"like pork,"*

["May that which I eat of yours be like pork."

Pigs' meat, in this context, is representative of nonkosher foods. It is specifically prohibited by the Torah

(*Lev.* 11:17), and is perhaps chosen by the mishnah — rather than the meat of other Biblically interdicted animals — due to its commonness.]

כַּעֲבוֹדָה זָרָה,, — *"like an idol,"*

The Torah writes: *You shall not bring an abomination into your house* (*Deut.* 7:26) and *None of the accursed thing shall stay in your hand* (ibid., 13:18). From these verses we learn that it is forbidden to use or benefit from an idol, from any of its accessories, of from anything offered as a sacrifice to it (*Rambam, Hil. Avodah Zarah* 7:2).

[Although a statue or some other object does not become an idol unless it is designated as such by a human act or declaration — once it is so designated, its prohibition does not derive in any way from the human designation. On the contrary, the person who designates an idol intends to benefit from it and to use it. It is the Torah which creates the ban on its use. The forbidden status of an idol is therefore Biblical, and cannot be transmitted through a *neder*.]

כְּעוֹרוֹת לְבוּבִין,, — *"like perforated skins,"*

Among certain pagan cults, the hearts of animals to be offered in sacrifice to the idols were extracted through a special hole that was cut in

1. **T**he following are not binding: "[May] that which I eat of yours be *chullin*," "like pork," "like an idol," "like perforated skins," "like carcasses," "like *tereifos*," "like reptiles,"

YAD AVRAHAM

the animal's skin. As mentioned above, the use of an animal that is offered in sacrifice to an idol is Biblically forbidden. This prohibition includes even its bones, horns, and skin (*Rambam, Hil. Avodah Zarah* 7:3). Consequently, skins with the characteristic perforation would be unusable by Jews inasmuch as they were certainly taken from a Biblically forbidden animal (*Rav*).

,"כִּנְבֵלוֹת,, — "*like carcasses*,"

A kosher animal that died without *shechitah* (proper ritual slaughter) may not be eaten. This is derived from the verse (*Deut.* 14:21), *You shall not eat of anything that dies of itself.*

,"כִּטְרֵפוֹת,, — "*like tereifos*,"

An animal with a terminal disease or wound may not be eaten, even if it is ritually slaughtered. Such an animal is called a *tereifah* (pl. *tereifos*). This prohibition is based on *Ex.* 22:30 (*Rambam, Hil. Maachalos Asuros* 4:6ff.).

,"כִּרְמָשִׂים,, ,"כִּשְׁקָצִים,, — "*like reptiles*," "*like crawling creatures*,"

These are prohibited by the verse (*Lev.* 11:44), *You shall not defile yourselves with any matter of swarming thing that crawls upon the earth.*

Tos. Yom Tov, following *Ran,* notes that each example mentioned by the mishnah has unique features. Pork may not be eaten but its use for other purposes is permitted. Idols, however, may not be utilized at all. Nevertheless, if a gentile renounces his own idol, it becomes permitted. Something sacrificed to an idol, on the other hand, is permanently forbidden. So, unlike an idol which can sometimes become permitted, the prohibition of the perforated skins can never be annulled (*Rambam, Hil. Avodah Zarah* 8:9). Carcasses of unslaughtered animals are not only forbidden to eat, but are also ritually unclean under Biblical law. [A *tereifah* that has been slaughtered ritually remains forbidden for eating, but is not ritually contaminated (ibid., *Hil. Avos HaTumos* 2:6). Unlike carcasses which communicate ritual contamination only through pieces that are the size of an olive or larger, those reptiles which are ritually unclean when they are dead transmit this contamination even through pieces as small as a lentil.

⊷§ Challah and Terumah

When a dough is made, a portion of it, known as *challah*, must be separated and given to the *Kohen* (see *Num.* 15:20). Prior to its separation, the dough is forbidden for consumption by anyone. Once *challah* has been taken, the portion of *challah* itself is permitted only to a *Kohen*, but the remaining dough is permitted to all.

Similarly, *terumah* is the portion of the agricultural produce which must be given to the *Kohen*. Until *terumah* is separated, the food is forbidden for consumption by anyone. Upon separation of *terumah*, the remaining food becomes permitted. The *terumah* itself is permitted to *Kohanim* only.

Both *challah* and *terumah* are sacred, and must be treated accordingly (*Rambam, Hil. Maachalos Asuros* 10:19ff., *Hil. Bikkurim* 5:1ff., *Hil. Terumos* 6:1ff.).

ר' עובדיה מברטנורא

כחלת אהרן. שֶׁהָיָה רִאשׁוֹן לַכֹּהֲנִים. וְלֹא הֲוֵי דְּבַר הַנִּדוֹר, שֶׁאֵין חַלָּה וּתְרוּמָה בָּאִין בַּנֶּדֶר וְנִדְבָה:
הֲרֵי זֶה מוּתָּר. דְּאָמַר קְרָא (במדבר ל, ג) אִישׁ כִּי יִדּוֹר נֶדֶר, עַד שֶׁיִּדּוֹר בַּדְּבַר הַנִּדוֹר, וְתִמְצָא
שָׁאֲנִי אוֹכֵל לָךְ דְּאָמְרִינַן בְּפֶרֶק קַמָּא (משנה ד) דְּאָסוּר וְאַף עַל פִּי שֶׁאֵינוֹ דְּבַר הַנִּדוֹר, הֲוֵי טַעְמָא
דְּאֶפְשָׁר שֶׁיָּבִיא חֲטָאת חַטָּאת עַל יְדֵי נֶדֶר, כְּגוֹן שֶׁנִּדַּר בְּנָזִיר וּמִתְחַיֵּיב לְהָבִיא חֲטָאת:

יד אברהם

„בְּחַלַּת אַהֲרֹן" וְ,,כִתְרוּמָתוֹ"- — *"like the challah of Aaron"; or "like Aaron's (lit. his) terumah";*

[The separation of *challah* and *terumah* from the dough or food, and their designation as such, is a human act. Nevertheless, the mishnah classifies them as Biblically prohibited, so that a reference to them in a *neder* will not be acceptable. There are several explanations advanced by the earlier authorities as to why *terumah* and *challah* are not considered manmade prohibitions.]

As explained in the preface to 1:4, *Rav* and *Rambam* stipulate that a manmade prohibition, aside from being the consequence of a human designation, must also be producible voluntarily. Although *terumah* and *challah* satisfy the first criterion (they are produced by a human designation), they do not meet the second. The obligations to separate *terumah* and *challah* apply only to certain foods. Where no such requirements exist, they cannot be produced. One cannot take some food which is *not* subject to these obligations and declare some of it to be *challah* or *terumah*. Thus, these classifications cannot be produced voluntarily, and hence, are not considered man-made prohibitions (*Rav; Rambam*).

Other authorities do not require a man-made prohibition to be producible voluntarily. The fact that an interdict can be created by human designation is enough to classify it as

manmade (*Rosh* 12a, *Ran* ibid., *Ravad, Hil. Nedarim* 1:11). [According to this view, a different explanation must be offered as to why the states of *challah* and *terumah* may not be assigned to something else via a *neder*.]

Rosh (to 12a), quoted by *Tos. Yom Tov*, contends that the status of *challah* and *terumah* as forbidden to a non-*Kohen* is not at all the consequences of a human act. Prior to the separation of *terumah* or *challah*, the food from which it is to be taken is Biblically forbidden to all — even to *Kohanim* — and is therefore certainly not assignable via a *neder*. The subsequent prohibition of *terumah* or *challah* to a non-*Kohen* is only a remnant of the original stricture that prohibited the food to everyone. When the *terumah* and *challah* is separated, the remaining food is released from the original interdict, and becomes permissible. But the *terumah* and *challah* portions themselves become permitted only to a *Kohen*. Consequently, the declaration of something to be like these items does not create any prohibition whatsoever. On the contrary, the act of separating *challah* or *terumah* serves to release and rescind the prohibition on the rest of the food.

This being the case, the status of *terumah* or *challah* as forbidden to a non-*Kohen* is a Biblical prohibition, and is thus not the product of a human designation. Therefore, the prohibited

YAD AVRAHAM

status of *terumah* and *challah* are not considered to be manmade, and consequently — as indicated in the mishnah — are not assignable through a *neder*.

The mishnah refers to *challah* as "*the challah of Aaron.*" *Rav* suggests that this is because Aaron was the first *Kohen*. (However, Aaron himself never received *challah*. The obligation to separate *challah* took effect only after the conquest of *Eretz Yisrael*, long after Aaron's demise.)

מֻתָּר. — *[this] is not binding.*
This is the version found in the *Yachin U'Boaz* and Vilna Talmud editions. Another reading, הֲרֵי זֶה מוּתָּר, *this is not binding*, is quoted by *Rav*.

The insertion of this ruling here would appear to be unnecessary, since the mishnah opened with the phrase *The following are not binding.* It is included in order to distinguish between the cases listed by the mishnah thus far, and the following case. A declaration referring to any of the things mentioned so far is not binding in any way (see above, s.v. חֻלִּין שֶׁאֹכַל לָךְ). The coming case in the mishnah is treated more strictly, and — when

made by an ignorant person — is binding under Rabbinic law (*Tos. Yom Tov* from *Ran*).

Rambam (*Hil. Nedarim* 2:13), on the other hand, maintains that *all* the examples of the mishnah are binding under Rabbinic law when the declarations are uttered by an ignorant person.

[Accordingly, the repetition of this ruling in the mishnah could not serve to separate the examples into two groups of different severity.

However, according to *Rambam*, the examples of Biblical prohibitions are of two types. Those which are of Divine origin, such as pork, and those — such as *challah* — which although human designated, are not producible arbitrarily. Thus, the mishnah may be read as two distinct statements; 1) *The following are not binding:* ... "*like pork,*" "*like an idol,*" etc. These are all unacceptable, since they are of Biblical origin. 2) "*like ... challah ...*" or "*like ... terumah*"; *this is not binding.* This is because they can be produced voluntarily.

If the mishnah is read in this manner, the sentence "*like the challah of Aaron or ... terumah*" — *this is not binding* is an independent statement introducing a new concept, and so, the latter half is not a mere redundancy of the opening phrase in the mishnah.]

◆§ Grounds for annulling a neder

Under Biblical law, it is possible to have a *neder* annulled (*Chagigah* 10a). A request for annulment must be addressed to an outside party — either a single scholar or a panel of three laymen (*Bechoros* 36b) — who establish a basis for canceling the vow, and declare it to be null and void (*Gem.* 77b). In general, an annulment will be based on one of the following two arguments.

The first is called חֲרָטָה, *regret*. In this instance, the person argues that at the time of his declaration, he had acted impulsively and without deliberation. He now expresses sincere remorse for ever having adopted the *neder*. A typical case would be someone who made a *neder* in a fit of rage; upon regaining his equanimity, he regrets the entire incident. Thus, the *neder* was made under circumstances which are now regretted, and so, the *neder* is known as פֶּתַח (lit.,

הָאוֹמֵר לְאִשְׁתּוֹ: „הֲרֵי אַתְּ עָלַי כְּאִמָּא" —
פּוֹתְחִין לוֹ פֶּתַח מִמָּקוֹם אַחֵר, שֶׁלֹּא יָקֵל רֹאשׁוֹ
לְכָךְ.

ר' עובדיה מברטנורא

הרי את עלי כאמא. אִם עַל גַּב דְּלָאו דְּבַר הַגָּדוֹר הוּא, חִמּוּר מִכֹּל הֲנֵי דִּלְעֵיל דְּצָרִיךְ הֶתֵּירָא מִדְּרַבָּנָן אִם הוּא עִם הָאָרֶץ, וּפוֹתְחִין לוֹ פֶּתַח מִמָּקוֹם אַחֵר, כְּלוֹמַר מְבַקְּשִׁים לוֹ פֶּתַח וְטַעַם לַחֲרָטָתוֹ, וְלֹא סַגִּי בִּכְדֵי תִּהְיֶה אוֹ לְבַד עָלֶיךָ, וְכֹל זֶה שֶׁלֹּא יָקֵל רֹאשׁוֹ וְלֹא יִרְגִּיל לֶאֱסוֹר אִשְׁתּוֹ עָלָיו:

יד אברהם

opening). In this case, the panel or sage attempts to show that the declaration had been made under false pretenses (*Ran* 21b, 75b). A consequence of the *neder* — which was not realized at the time of his vow, and is undesirable — is suggested. If the person maintains that had he realized initially that his *neder* would lead to undesirable consequences, he would not have vowed, it is considered a sufficient "opening."

For example, a person made a *neder* which prohibited him to eat cake. Subsequently, all his friends — wanting him to participate at their parties — incessantly urge him to renege. A Rabbi or an annulment panel might say to him: "Had you known at the time of your vow that as a result of it, your friends would badger you, would you have made it nevertheless?" If he responds negatively, the panel may declare the *neder* null and void (*Yoreh Deah* 228:11). The reaction of his friends to the vow would thus be the necessary undesirable consequence, or the grounds on which to base the annulment.

It goes without saying that a person's contention — that had he considered the consequences, he would not have made the *neder* — must be an honest one. If he is lying, and — in reality — was prepared to suffer the unpleasant consequence, then no matter how often the *neder* is pronounced null and void, it actually remains binding. Because of this, certain "openings" are disqualified from being used as a basis for annulment, since it is assumed that, in those cases, people would be too embarrassed to state the truth. For example, it may be argued that an undesirable consequence of a *neder* might be that it would bring insults and shame to the parents of the one who made it. People would say to them, "See what a child you have raised!" or "His habits were learned at home." A panel or Rabbi could conceivably argue that had the person anticipated the anguish that his parents would have as a result of his *neder*, he would not have vowed. However, it was assumed that no one would admit that he had intended to make a *neder*, knowing that it would lead to his parents' chagrin. Thus, the claim — that had he realized the consequence of his *neder*, he would have refrained from making it — is suspect. Even if he did not care at all about his parents and had vowed with complete indifference to any harm it might bring them, it is assumed that he would not admit it. Therefore, to annul a *neder* on the basis of parental dignity was not allowed (*Yoreh Deah* 228:11 from mishnah 9:1).

הָאוֹמֵר לְאִשְׁתּוֹ: „הֲרֵי אַתְּ עָלַי כְּאִמָּא"—
One who says to his wife: "You are to me like Mother"—

It is Biblically forbidden to have sexual relations with one's mother (*Lev.* 18:7). [This prohibition is there-

2
1

One who says to his wife: "You are to me like Mother" — we find grounds to annul the *neder* from elsewhere, so that he not be lightheaded regarding such [matters].

YAD AVRAHAM

fore not assignable through a *neder*.]

However, the Rabbis, in the interest of family harmony, wished to discourage husbands from vowing against their wives (*Rosh* 14a, s.v. הא בע"ה). They therefore insisted that — although the *neder* referred to a Divine prohibition and was not binding — an ignorant person, being more prone to making *nedarim*, should be required to seek nullification if he wished to continue living with his wife. Since she is entitled to her conjugal rights, he must divorce her if he is prohibited from having relations with her (see comm. to ArtScroll *Kesubos* 5:6). Regarding a scholarly person, however, it was considered unlikely that he would make a habit of pronouncing *nedarim*, and so, in his case, the *neder* against his wife is governed by the Biblical regulations. If, as in the mishnah, he vowed against his wife, but referred to a Divine interdict — thus disqualifying the *neder* — no annulment is needed (*Rav; Rashi* 14a).

Some authorities maintain that today — with respect to this law — even scholars are treated like average citizens. Accordingly, anyone who makes a *neder* against his wife, even if he referred to a Biblical prohibition such as "Mother," would require annulment of the *neder* (*Rama, Yoreh Deah* 205:1).

פּוֹתְחִין לוֹ פֶּתַח מִמָּקוֹם אַחֵר, — *we find grounds to annul the neder* (lit., *open for him an opening*) *from elsewhere,*

That is, a declaration of regret regarding the circumstances under which the *neder* was taken is not

enough. Rather, an "opening" must be devised to serve as a basis for the annulment of the *neder* (*Rav; Rosh*).

The phrase *from elsewhere* qualifies the type of opening which may be used. In particular, it teaches that although the declaration, *You are to me like Mother*, is an abuse of his mother, the argument that this was not realized when making the declaration is not an acceptable basis for annulment. Some other "opening" *from elsewhere* — i.e., not obvious from the declaration — must be proposed. In fact, an "opening" based on parental disrespect is generally unacceptable (see preface and 9:1). This point is stressed here to emphasize that even though the *neder* of the mishnah requires annulment only under Rabbinic law (see above), the basis for annulment must satisfy the requirements to annul a Biblically recognized *neder* (*Tos. Yom Tov* from *Ran*).

A *neder* forbidding relations with one's wife by reference to *any* Biblical prohibition — not just one's mother — will be treated identically. Thus, if an ignorant person were to direct a *neder* at his wife such as "You are to me like *orlah* [fruit produced within the first three years of the planting of the tree, which is forbidden to use or benefit from (*Lev.* 19:23)]," it would require annulment under Rabbinic law. The mishnah selected the example of a reference to "Mother" merely to teach that parental disrespect cannot be used as grounds for annulment (loc. cit.).

שֶׁלֹּא יָקֵל רֹאשׁוֹ לְכָךְ. — *so that he not be lightheaded regarding such [matters].*

The Rabbis sought to discourage a

„קוֹנָם שֶׁאֵינִי יָשֵׁן", „שֶׁאֵינִי מְדַבֵּר", שֶׁאֵינִי
מְהַלֵּךְ"; הָאוֹמֵר לְאִשְׁתּוֹ: „קוֹנָם שֶׁאֵינִי מְשַׁמְּשֵׁךְ"
— הֲרֵי זֶה בְּ„לֹא יַחֵל דְּבָרוֹ".

—————— ר' עובדיה מברטנורא ——————

קונם שאיני ישן כו'. הרי זה בבל יחל מדרבנן, אבל מן התורה אין הנדר חל, דנדרים אין חלים
אלא על דבר שיש בו ממש: **קונם שאיני משמשך.** בגמרא (טו, ג) מקשה והא משועבד לה,
והיאך יכול להפקיע שעבודה בנדרו, והא הוי כאוסר פירות חבירו על חבירו, ומשני כגון דאמר
הנאת תשמישך עלי קונם, שאסר ההנאה עליו, ואין מאכילין לו לאדם דבר האסור לו:

יד אברהם

husband from freely disrupting his
family life. Aside from their concern
for the maintenance of domestic
harmony, the Rabbis also recognized
that the potential for tension — and
hence, *nedarim* — was greater in the
family than among strangers (*Rashba*
to 14a). Therefore, in order that such
matters not be taken lightly, *nedarim*
between husband and wife were
treated with great stringency. Even
when such a *neder* referred to a
Biblical prohibition, the Rabbis insisted that if it was an ignorant person
who had made the *neder*, an annulment be sought (*Rav*).

However, the declarations listed
earlier in the mishnah which are all
directed at food are not dealt with so
stringently. Those *nedarim* are not
binding at all, even under Rabbinic
law (ibid.; *Ran* 13b).

Rambam, as mentioned earlier, requires
an ignorant person to seek annulment of
any type of vow which refers to a Biblical
prohibition, even when it does not relate to
family matters. Evidently, he construes the
phrase *"We open for him an opening from
elsewhere, so that he not take such matters
lightly"* as modifying the entire mishnah,
and not just the last case of one addressing
his wife (*Tos. Yom Tov*, s.v. חולין).

Having completed a discussion of
nedarim that refer to a Biblical prohibition which can be binding only

under Rabbinic law, the mishnah now
turns to a different type of *neder*
which also is binding only under
Rabbinic law.

„קוֹנָם שֶׁאֵינִי יָשֵׁן", „שֶׁאֵינִי מְדַבֵּר",
„שֶׁאֵינִי מְהַלֵּךְ"; — *[One who says:]"Konam
on my sleeping"* (lit., *"that I sleep"), "on
my talking," [or]"on my walking";*

See comm. to 1:1, s.v. שֶׁאֵינִי. To be
binding under Rabbinic law, a *neder*
must be directed at someone tangible
(*Gem.* 3b). The acts of sleeping, talking, or walking are, of course, *not* in
this category, and can therefore not
serve as an object for a *neder* (*Rav*
from *Gem.* 15a). In 1:4, however,
nedarim are listed which do prohibit
such intangible acts. Yet, a quick
comparison will show that the formulation of those *nedarim* is much
different than the formulation of the
nedarim in this mishnah. Thus, for
example, in the case of talking, the
declaration in 1:4 reads *"Konam on my
mouth from speaking with you."* The
neder specifies a tangible object (the
mouth) at which it is directed. It is thus
effective even under Biblical law. In
our mishnah, on the other hand, the
declaration is of the form *"Konam on
my speaking."* This does *not* include
any tangible object of the *neder*.
Therefore, this type of *neder* cannot
be Biblically binding. However, the

2
1

[One who declares:] "*Konam* on my sleeping," "on my talking," [or] "on my walking"; [or] one who says to his wife: "*Konam* on my cohabitation with you" — this is governed by *He shall not violate his word* (Numbers 30:3).

YAD AVRAHAM

Rabbis saw fit to institute that even such declarations — which do not have any tangible objects — should be considered binding under Rabbinic law (*Gem.* 13b, 15a, cf. comm. to 1:4, s.v. הָאוֹמֵר).

הָאוֹמֵר לְאִשְׁתּוֹ: ,,קוֹנָם שֶׁאֵינִי מְשַׁמְּשֵׁךְ"— [or] one who says to his wife: "Konam on my cohabitation with you"—
The *Gemara* (15b) notes that the *neder* under consideration cannot be the one stated in the mishnah. The Torah requires a husband to engage in marital relations with his wife, and so she has a legal claim on him to fulfill his obligations. Now, for a husband to ban relations with his wife would amount to depriving her of her legal rights, which are tantamount to her property. But, as explained in preface to 1:1, a person cannot, through a *neder*, forbid the property of someone else to the latter. Similarly, a husband cannot — via a *neder* — deprive his wife of what is rightfully hers.

Because of this, the *Gemara* explains that the *neder* actually being discussed by the mishnah is a different one. Rather than being directed at the physical act of cohabitation, the *neder* under consideration is intended to forbid the pleasure and enjoyment that is derived from intimate relations. The actual declaration is : "*Konam*, the pleasure from my cohabitation with you" (*Rav*).

To be sure, the Torah obligates the husband to perform the physical act

of cohabitation, and the wife can legally demand that he fulfill his obligation, However, the Torah does not demand that the husband derive any pleasure from the act; that is his own prerogative. Therefore, it is within his jurisdiction to forbid this pleasure to himself through a *neder*. Thus, the prohibition of pleasure and enjoyment by a *neder* does not directly conflict with the wife's legal claims (*Rav* from *Gem.* 15b).

Because pleasure is not something tangible, it cannot be banned by a *neder* under Biblical law. This vow, therefore, which is directed at the pleasure the husband derives from marital relations, is effective only under the Rabbinic law which validates *nedarim* even when they are directed at intangibles (*Ran* to 15b).

The Rabbinic validation of this *neder*, prohibiting pleasure from cohabitation, will — in effect — forbid the couple to have relations. Although, by Biblical law, a woman is entitled to her conjugal rights (*Ex.* 21:10), *Ran* explains that the Rabbis are empowered by the Torah to prevent the active fulfillment of a positive commandment. Thus, by validating the *neder* restricting enjoyment of marital relations, the Rabbis are preventing the husband from fulfilling the positive commandment to cohabit with his wife (*Ran* 15b; see *Hagahos Maaseh Choshev* to *Shaar HaMelech*, *Hil. Shofar* 170).

Tosafos (15a, s.v. רבינא), however, understands this *neder* to be binding even under Biblical law. *Tos. Yom Tov* explains that this approach assumes that the *neder* has a tangible object.

This would be the physical body of the wife, and the *neder* would ban the wife's body with respect to the derivation of pleasure by the husband (cf. the examples in 1:4).

Although, according to *Tosafos*, it turns out that the mishnah groups the *nedarim* prohibiting walking, sleeping, and talking — which are binding only Rabbinically — together with the *neder* concerning marital relations, which *Tosafos* maintain is effective even under Biblical law, R' David ibn Zimra (*Responsa*, Vol. 3 870) explains that this grouping is intended to teach us that even the Rabbinic *neder*, if violated, carries with it a corporal punishment just as the Biblically recognized *neder* does. The punishment would be Rabbinically authorized lashes.

There is a Talmudic principle that the performance of a commandment is — in the halachic sense — not considered a benefit to the person (*Rosh Hashanah* 28a; *Eruvin* 31a). If some object is forbidden for general use or benefit, its use in the performance of a *mitzvah* would nevertheless not constitute a violation of the prohibition, because it is *not* regarded as using or deriving pleasure or benefit from the object.

For example, if a person were to prohibit a shofar from general use via a *neder*, it would still be permitted for him to blow that shofar on Rosh Hashanah in performance of the *mitzvah*. The *neder* banned deriving benefit from the shofar; but fulfilling a commandment is not considered to be deriving benefit from it.

In light of the above, the case of a *neder* prohibiting the derivation of pleasure from intimacy with one's wife would seem problematic. Since to have relations with her is a *mitzvah*, the pleasure one had therefrom should not be considered pleasure at all in the halachic sense.

To resolve this, *Ran* suggests that the Talmudic principle cited above does not apply to physical pleasures, even if experienced in the course of fulfilling a commandment. Thus, although the act of cohabitation is a *mitzvah*, the accompanying sensations of enjoyment are regarded as pleasure, and are thus prohibited by the *neder*. On the other hand, listening to the shofar does not give one physical pleasure. Therefore, a shofar forbidden by a *neder* would still be usable for the *mitzvah* of shofar-blowing. The act of shofar-blowing is a precept, and therefore does not constitute benefiting from the shofar; and listening to blasts is not considered benefiting from the shofar, since it is not a physical pleasure. A nonphysical sensation experienced while performing a *mitzvah* is included in the principle which considers the performance of commandments as not pleasurable.

Ran finds support for his premise in *Rosh Hashanah* 28a. The *Gemara* there forbids even ritual immersion in a *mikveh* (ritual pool) which has been banned by a *neder*. The immersion itself could not be subject to the ban of the *neder*, since it is a *mitzvah*, and would thus not be considered benefiting from the *mikveh*. The reason for prohibiting immersion, contends *Ran*, must be because of the physical sensation of refreshment that the person enjoys while immersing himself. Evidently, this pleasure — although experienced during the performance of a *mitzvah* (ritual immersion) — is considered to be deriving pleasure from the *mikveh*. Obviously, then — although performing a *mitzvah* is not considered to be pleasurable — physical pleasure derived during the performance of a *mitzvah* is considered pleasure.

Rashba adopts a different approach to the whole issue. He maintains that any pleasures — even physical ones, like cooling off in a pool, or those experienced during cohabitation — if derived during the performance of a *mitzvah*, are *not* considered pleasure. To explain why enjoyment of cohabitation is subject to a prohibition of a *neder* despite its occurring during the performance of a precept, *Rashba* suggests the following. The primary obligation imposed by the Torah upon the husband is to have children; to satisfy that requirement, he could marry another woman. Thus, to cohabit with this particular wife

is not necessary. Therefore, the exception stated above regarding pleasure gained while performing a *mitzvah* applies only to necessary obligations, and not to those such as the husband's relations with a specific wife. The pleasure and enjoyment he has will be considered pleasure and thus forbidden by the *neder*. (For a fuller treatment of this subject, and a reconciliation of *Rashba's* approach with the *Gemara* in *Rosh Hashanah*, see *Shaar HaMelech, Hil. Shofar* 1:3 and *Avnei Milluim* 28:60.)

הֲרֵי זֶה בְּ,,לֹא יַחֵל דְּבָרוֹ'. — *this is [governed] by "He shall not violate his word"* (*Numbers* 30:3).

This is by Rabbinic enactment only, since — as explained — for a *neder* to be binding under Biblical law, it must be directed at something tangible (*Rav*, s.v. קונם from *Gem.* 15a). The Rabbinic validation of a *neder* directed at an intangible is more strict than that of a *neder* referring to a Biblical prohibition (listed in the first part of the mishnah). In the latter case, the *neder* requires annulment only when it is made by an ignorant person. However, for a *neder* directed at an intangible, even a scholar must seek annulment of his vow (*Yoreh Deah* 213:1; *Shach* ibid.; cf. *Kesef Mishneh* and *Lechem Mishneh, Hil. Nedarim* 3:12).

The *Gemara* (15a) cites a parallel for the usage of the Biblical verse *He shall not violate his word* as the basis for a Rabbinic interdict. This is in connection with the Rabbinic law that, in a place where it is customary to prohibit something which is generally permitted, one should not violate the custom. To do so would contravene the passage quoted above.

Just as this verse is used as the basis for this Rabbinic enactment, so too, the meaning of our mishnah is that a *neder* directed at something intangible is binding only Rabbinically. Were the intention that these *nedarim*

be Biblically valid, the mishnah would have stated אָסוּר, *he is forbidden to do so*, rather than *this is governed by "He shall not violate his word"* (*Ran* 15a, s.v. רבינא).

The reason the Rabbis saw fit to recognize a *neder* directed at something intangible is explained by *Ritva*. The form of these *nedarim* — "Konam on my sleeping" or "on my talking" — is not recognizably distinct from the *neder* "Konam" or "Korban on what I eat" (1:4). Yet, the latter declaration is interpreted as being directed at the food, which is tangible, and not at the act of eating, which is not; the *neder* is therefore Biblically binding (see ibid.). If the *nedarim* of our mishnah were treated as not binding, someone might mistakenly consider the similar-sounding "Konam on what I eat" to be the same. To avoid such confusion, the Rabbis enacted that even the former type of a *neder* be considered binding and in need of annulment.

According to another approach, the basis for the Rabbinic recognition of a *neder* directed at an intangible is the aforementioned law regarding the upholding of restrictive customs. The *Gemara* cites this halachah not just to demonstrate the usage of *He shall not violate his word* in a Rabbinic context, but also to explain the rationale behind the Rabbinic enactment. A *neder* banning some intangible activity was treated like the adoption of a new custom and was thus governed by the Rabbinic decree in regard to customs. That is, just as a custom must be upheld, so ,too, should these *nedarim* be observed (*Tos. Yom Tov* from *Tos.* and *Rambam Comm.*; cf. *Yerushalmi*).

It appears that *Tosafos* considered the resolution to adopt a restriction via a *neder* as equivalent to adopting a custom. *Rambam* explains that, in general, it was a

„שְׁבוּעָה, שֶׁאֵינִי יָשֵׁן", „שֶׁאֵינִי מְדַבֵּר",
„שֶׁאֵינִי מְהַלֵּךְ" – אָסוּר.

[ב] „קָרְבָּן, לֹא אֹכַל לָךְ", „קָרְבָּן, שֶׁאֹכַל
לָךְ", „לֹא קָרְבָּן, לֹא אֹכַל
לָךְ" – מֻתָּר.

―――――――――― ר' עובדיה מברטנורא ――――――――――

שבועה שאיני ישן וכו'. אסור מן התורה, דשבועות חלין בין על דבר שיש בו ממש בין על דבר
שאין בו ממש, ואם נשבע שלא יישן שלשה ימים רלופין לילה ויום לוקה ויישן מיד, מפני שנשבע על
דבר שאי אפשר לקיימו: **(ב) קרבן לא אוכל לך כו'.** מותר, דהוי כנשבע בקרבן ונעשה כאומר
בחיי הקרבן אם אוכל לך שום דבר:

―――――――― יד אברהם ――――――――

popular custom to abide by the terms of a *neder*, even if it was directed at something intangible, and was thus technically not binding. To ignore such a *neder* would be to violate the popular custom — a course of action specifically prohibited by the Rabbinic legislation with regard to customs.

Rashash observes that the root דבר which occurs in the verse לֹא יַחֵל דְּבָרוֹ, *He shall not violate his word,* is used elsewhere in the sense of *custom* (cf. פּוֹק חֲזֵי מַאי עַמָּא דְּבַר, *Go out and see how the people conduct themselves; Eruvin* 14b). With this in mind, the verse means: *He shall not violate his custom,* and is thus very appropriate as a source for upholding customs.

„שְׁבוּעָה, שֶׁאֵינִי יָשֵׁן", „שֶׁאֵינִי מְדַבֵּר",
„שֶׁאֵינִי מְהַלֵּךְ" – אָסוּר. — *[One who swears:]* "Shevuah, that I shall not sleep," "that I shall not speak," [or] "that I shall not walk" – [is] forbidden [to do so].

An oath concerns the person making it, and his activities. Unlike a *neder* which — strictly speaking — must have a tangible object to which it imparts a prohibited status, an oath obligates the person alone, and does not affect the object or act concerning which he swears. If, for example, someone swore not to eat fruit, the status of the fruit would not be affected. The person would be prevented from eating it — not because to do so would violate some prohibited status of the fruit, but because he has restricted his person from doing so (*Gem.* 2b; *Rosh* 14b). Because of this nature of an oath, it will be Biblically binding even when directed at some intangible activity. Thus, the oath *"Shevuah, that I shall not sleep"* is valid under Biblical law (*Rav*).

The next mishnah teaches us that an oath cannot supersede any prior obligation to which the person is already bound. For example, since a Jew is commanded to eat matzah on Pesach, an oath prohibiting him from doing so will be invalid. (Contrarily, a *neder* would make the matzah forbidden to him and would thereby prevent him from meeting his obligation; see mishnah 2.) Similarly, an oath to restrict marital relations will *not* be effective, since the person is already obligated by the Biblical requirements of marriage. Thus, in this section of the mishnah, which deals with valid oaths, the case of a declaration to prevent marital relations (which is used to illustrate a *neder* directed at something intangible) is omitted (*Tos. R' Akiva*).

In connection with the oath outlawing sleep, *Rav* notes that an oath, whose terms are impossible to abide by, is not binding, and the person is guilty of having taken an oath in vain. Thus, if a person makes an oath

[One who swears:] *"Shevuah*, that I shall not sleep," "that I shall not speak," [or] "that I shall not walk" — [is] forbidden [to do so].

2. [**T** he declarations:] *"Korban*, I shall not eat of yours," *"Korban*, [if] I shall eat of yours," [and] "Not a *korban*, [what] I shall not eat of yours" — [are] not binding.

YAD AVRAHAM

to go without sleep for seventy-two consecutive hours, he is permitted to sleep even immediately, It is impossible to avoid sleeping that long, and so, the oath is not effective. However, the person is punished for having uttered a false oath.

2.

The mishnah continues the comparison of *nedarim* to oaths.

In 1:4, a *neder* which prevents a person from eating and is Biblically binding is discussed. This is *"Korban that I shall eat of yours."* The words *that I shall eat of yours* are interpreted as *that which I shall eat of yours*, and hence, that *neder* has a tangible object — the food — and is effective even Biblically. The food will be prohibited, and the person making the declaration will be forbidden to eat it.

This mishnah presents declarations which are similar sounding to the above *neder*, but which are not binding at all — not even Rabbinically. As will be seen, their formulation is inconsistent with the laws of both *nedarim* and oaths, and are therefore meaningless.

קָרְבָּן, לֹא אֹכַל לָךְ״, — *[The declarations:] "Korban, I shall not eat of yours,"*

This declaration amounts to swearing "By the life of a *korban*, I shall not eat your food." In an oath, to invoke the "life of a *korban*" is meaningless, and so the declaration has no effect (*Rav*).

If a *neder* were intended, the meaning of the words would be that the food which shall not be eaten should be like an offering. Obviously, to ban what shall not be eaten does not affect what shall be eaten, so that, as a *neder*, this declaration would have no practical consequences (*Tos. Yom Tov* from *Ran*).

הַקָּרְבָּן, שֶׁאֹכַל לָךְ״, — *"Korban, [if] I shall eat of yours,"*

The versions which read קָרְבָּן cannot be correct, since that formula is deemed binding in 1:4. The proper reading is הַקָּרְבָּן or קָרְבָּן הָא (*Tif. Yis.*). *Rav* (1:4) quotes our mishnah as reading הַקָּרְבָּן which he explains as two words — הָא קָרְבָּן, *by the life of a korban*. This, too, is a meaningless expression.

לֹא קָרְבָּן, לֹא אֹכַל לָךְ״ - מֻתָּר. — *[and] "Not a korban, [what] I shall not eat of yours" — [are] not binding.*

The designation of that which will *not* be eaten as "not a *korban*" — i.e., therefore permissible — implies that the food which *will* be eaten should be prohibited like a *korban*. Nevertheless, the mishnah deems this *neder* as meaningless in accordance with the

נדרים
ב/ב

„שְׁבוּעָה, לֹא אֹכַל לָךְ", „שְׁבוּעָה שֶׁאוֹכַל לָךְ", „לֹא שְׁבוּעָה, לֹא אֹכַל לָךְ" — אָסוּר. זֶה חֹמֶר בַּשְּׁבוּעוֹת מִבַּנְּדָרִים. וְחֹמֶר בַּנְּדָרִים מִבַּשְּׁבוּעוֹת כֵּיצַד? אָמַר: „קוֹנָם

—————— ר' עובדיה מברטנורא ——————

שבועה שלא אוכל. ולא אמרינן בחיי שבועה קאמר כדאמרינן בקרבן, דשבועה לית בה ממשא ולא שייך לומר בה בחיי שבועה: **שבועה שאוכל לך.** זמנין דשבועה שאוכל לך דלא אכילנא משמע, כגון שהיה חבירו מסרב בו לאכול ואמר ולא אכול לא אכילנא, ושוב אמר שבועה שאוכל לך, דלא אכילנא משמע, והכי קאמר בשבועה יהא עלי אי אכילנא לך: **זה חומר בשבועות.** לא מצינן לאוקמה אשבועה שֶׁ[ולא] אוכל לך וכו', דמדקתני זה חומר משמע דנדר הוי אלא דאינו חמור כשבועה, וגבי קרבן לא אוכל לך תנן דלא הוי מותר דלא נדר כלל, משום הכי צריך לאוקמה אדלעיל (משנה א) דתנינא קונס שאיני ישן שאיני מדבר הרי זה בבל יחל, ואוקימנא מדרבנן, דמדאורייתא אין הנדר חל אלא על דבר שיש בו ממש, וזה חומר בשבועות מבנדרים שהשבועה חלה אפילו על

—————— יד אברהם ——————

opinion of R' Meir, who maintains that an inferred *neder* is not valid (*Tif. Yis.*; see comm. to 1:4, s.v. לֹא „לְקָרְבָּן, אֹכַל לָךְ").

— „שְׁבוּעָה, לֹא אֹכַל לָךְ", *"Shevuah, I shall not eat of yours,"*

This is a straightforward oath not to eat another's food and is Biblically binding. According to *Rambam* (Hil. Shevuos 2:4), an oath which makes no mention of God's name is binding, but does not result in any punishment if transgressed. An oath which does mention God's name, however, is subject to the penalty of lashes, if intentionally violated, and necessitates the bringing of an offering for an accidental violation. To be punishable, according to *Rambam*, the oath here would have to be of the form *"Shevuah* to God, I shall not eat your food." *Ravad* (ibid.) maintains that an oath that omits mention of God requires the transgressor to offer a sacrifice for an accidental violation, but does not carry a penalty of lashes for intentionally transgressing the oath. *Ramban*, however, considers even an oath which makes not mention of God to be fully binding and punishable (*Tur Yoreh Deah* 237).

— „שְׁבוּעָה שֶׁאֹכַל לָךְ", *"Shevuah [if] I shall eat of yours,"*

The *Gemara* (16a) explains this declaration to be made by a person after he has already turned down an invitation to eat. When the host persists with his invitations, the exasperated guest — reinforcing his refusal — declares: *"Shevuah,* I shall eat your food," clearly intending to say "An oath upon me if I eat your food" (*Rav*).

Had the person initially responded affirmatively to the invitation, his subsequent declaration would then be constructed as a confirmation of his acceptance. In that case, the same words would mean "I take an oath obligating me to eat your food" (*Gem. ibid.*).

— „לֹא שְׁבוּעָה, לֹא אֹכַל לָךְ" - אָסוּר. *[and] "No shevuah, [for what] I do not eat"* — *[are] binding.*

This declaration — *"No shevuah* for what is not eaten" — implies that a *shevuah* be imposed with respect to

"Shevuah, I shall not eat of yours," *"Shevuah* [if] I shall eat of yours," [and] "No *shevuah,* [for what] I do not eat" — [are] binding. This is [an instance in which] oaths are more stringent than *nedarim.*

What is an instance in which *nedarim* are more stringent than oaths? [If] he said: *"Konam,*

YAD AVRAHAM

what is to be eaten, and is equivalent to having taken an oath against eating the other's food. Although this is only an inferred oath and is not stated directly, the *Gemara* (16a) attributes the ruling that is binding to R' Meir. *Ran* (based on *Shevuos* 36a) explains that despite the fact that R' Meir does not validate an inferred *neder* (see comm. to 1:4, s.v. לְקָרְבָּן), he does accept an implied oath as valid. R' Meir's source in the Torah for requiring explicit statements (and rejecting implied ones) deals with a situation where property considerations are at stake (*Kiddushin* 3:4). He generalizes this to cover cases such as *nedarim* which are similar to this in that they deal with items, rather than people. Oaths, however, affect the person, and not his possessions (cf. comm. to 1:1. s.v. וּשְׁבוּעוֹת), and they are therefore not governed by the law that legitimizes only explicit statements. Because they do not deal with property or other items, even R' Meir validates implied statements. Thus, the case of our mishnah — which implies an oath against eating another's food — is binding even according to R' Meir (*Tos. Yom Tov; Tif. Yis.*).

זֶה חֹמֶר בַּשְּׁבוּעוֹת מִבַּנְּדָרִים. — *This is [an instance in which] oaths are more stringent than nedarim.*

The designation of some oath as "more stringent" than a comparable *neder* is taken to mean that the latter,

too, is strict — but just not as strict as the oath (*Ran* from *Gem.* 16b).

Since the declarations of the first part of the mishnah (such as *"Korban,* I shall not eat your food") are not binding at all, they can certainly not qualify as "strict" *nedarim.* The *Gemara* therefore explains the comment of the mishnah *This is an instance* etc. as referring to the *nedarim* and oaths of the previous mishnah. A *neder* such as *"Konam* on my sleeping," which prohibits an intangible action, is binding under Rabbinic law. Therefore, it is considered a "strict" *neder.* But an oath to ban the same action such as *"Shevuah,* that I shall not sleep" is binding even under Biblical law. This, then, is an instance of a binding ("strict") oath that is more stringent than a comparable *neder.* The *neder* is only Rabbinically valid, whereas the oath is binding even Biblically (*Rav*).

וְחֹמֶר בַּנְּדָרִים מִבַּשְּׁבוּעוֹת כֵּיצַד? — *What* (lit., *how*) *is an instance in which nedarim are more stringent than oaths?*

Here, too, the mishnah is seeking a *neder* that is more stringent than an oath which is itself "strict" in some way. An oath, even when it is *not* binding, is still considered strict, because to utter an oath in vain is a punishable sin. Thus, even an invalid oath has halachic consequences (*Ran* 16b). A vain *neder* is, however, not a punishable offense (ibid. 14b).

[The mishnah is therefore seeking

סֻכָּה שֶׁאֲנִי עוֹשֶׂה", "לוּלָב שֶׁאֲנִי נוֹטֵל", "תְּפִלִּין שֶׁאֲנִי מַנִּיחַ" — בַּנְּדָרִים אָסוּר; בַּשְּׁבוּעוֹת מֻתָּר, שֶׁאֵין נִשְׁבָּעִין לַעֲבוֹר עַל הַמִּצְוֹת.

[ג] **יֵשׁ** נֶדֶר בְּתוֹךְ נֶדֶר, וְאֵין שְׁבוּעָה בְּתוֹךְ

ר' עובדיה מברטנורא

דבר שאין בו ממש: **תפילין שאיני מניח.** משום דאסר חפלא עליה, וחינו נרחה כנודר לבטל את המלוה, שהרי לא קבל על עלמו אלא אסר החפן עליו, ואם יקיים המלוה הויא מלוה הבחה בעבירה, ודמי למי שחייב לחכול מלה בליל הפסח ולא מלא אלא מלה של טבל או של הקדש שאסור לחכלה, אבל כל לשון שבועה הוא חוסר את עלמו מלעשות הדבר, וכיון שהוא מחוייב לעשות המלוה לאו כל כמיניה להפקיע עלמו מחיוב המלוה, ואם אמר הרי עלי קרבן אם אניח תפילין, חל הנדר וחייב להביח קרבן אם הניח תפילין

יד אברהם
---

to contrast a binding *neder* with an invalid oath, taken in vain.]

אָמַר: "קוֹנָם סֻכָּה שֶׁאֲנִי עוֹשֶׂה", "לוּלָב שֶׁאֲנִי נוֹטֵל", "תְּפִלִּין שֶׁאֲנִי מַנִּיחַ" – בַּנְּדָרִים אָסוּר; — [If] he said: "Konam, [the] succah that I am constructing"; "[the] lulav that I am taking"; "[the] tefillin that I am wearing" — as nedarim, [these declarations] are binding;

The commandments to dwell in a *succah*, take a *lulav*, and wear *tefillin* are positive obligations of the person. But, in the absence of these items, the obligations cannot be satisfied. Since a *neder* assigns a prohibition to a thing, the declaration of the mishnah designates the *succah*, *lulav*, or *tefillin* as forbidden for use.

The *neder* cannot suspend the obligation incumbent upon the person. But it can create a situation wherein it is not possible for the person to carry out his obligation. By prohibiting the object needed for fulfillment of the *mitzvah*, the *neder* precludes the possibility of its observance. Even if the person were to violate the *neder* and take the forbidden *lulav* or wear the forbidden *tefillin*, he will not have discharged his

obligation. This is because a *mitzvah* accomplished through committing a sin (in this case, the violation of a *neder*) is not acceptable (*Rav*).

In this instance, the positive precepts of *succah*, *lulav*, and *tefillin* do not override the restrictions imposed by the *neder*. Although there is a general rule that a positive precept supersedes a negative one, the violation of a *neder* is an offense against both a negative commandment — *He shall not violate his word* (Num. 30:3) — as well as a positive one — *He shall do according to all that comes from his mouth* (ibid.). In such cases, the rule that a positive precept prevails is *not* operative (*Rashba*; cf. *Tos. R' Akiva*).

From the above, it is evident that to take a *lulav* which has been forbidden by a *neder* would constitute a violation of the *neder*. However, this would seem to conflict with the general rule that the performance of a *mitzvah* is not considered a benefit to the person (see comm. to 2:1, s.v. הָאוֹמֵר לְאִשְׁתּוֹ). That rule would dictate that one cannot prohibit the use of an item for the fulfillment of a precept. *Tosafos* suggest that even a use not ordinarily regarded as a benefit can be prohibited if one specifically stimulated that he wishes to do so. Thus, the *neder* under

[the] *succah* that I am constructing," "[the] *lulav* that I am taking," "[the *tefillin* that I am wearing" — as *nedarim*, [these declarations] are binding; as oaths, they are not binding, for one may not swear to transgress the commandments.

3. **T**here is a *neder* within a *neder*, but there is not

YAD AVRAHAM

discussion does not just forbid a *lulav* from use; rather, it specifies "*lulav* which I take, and *tefillin* which I wear," indicating that the intention is to prohibit the use of the *lulav* or *tefillin*, even for the performance of the *mitzvah*. The *neder* is therefore binding even in that instance (*Ran* to 16b).

בִּשְׁבוּעוֹת מֻתָּר, — *as oaths, they are not binding,*

If an oath is made with the intention of compelling oneself to neglect the performance of a commandment, it cannot have any force. This obligation on the person to observe the Torah is already binding from Sinai, and cannot be superseded by a subsequent oath (*Rav*).

שֶׁאֵין נִשְׁבָּעִין לַעֲבוֹר עַל הַמִּצְוֹת. — *for one may not swear to transgress the commandments.*

Since oaths interdicting the performance of the precepts do not take effect, they are considered having been made in vain, and are liable to punishment of lashes if made inten-

tionally (*Rambam, Hil. Shevuos* 1:7). The mishnah thus teaches us that not only are such oaths not binding, but one is not permitted to make them (*Tif. Yis.*).

The phrase *the commandments* in the mishnah refers back to the three cases listed; viz., *succah, lulav,* and *tefillin.* It appears, then, that all these cases are fulfillment of precepts. *Shalmei Nedarim* observes — with puzzlement — that this would indicate that construction of a *succah* (as in "*Konam, [the] succah that I am constructing*") is a commandment independent of the obligation to sit in the *succah* (see *Shevuos* 29a; *Kesubos* 86a; *Rashi* to *Makkos* 8a, s.v. השתא). *Haamek She'eilah* (*Deut.* 169) points out that the *Gemara* certainly construes the mishnah as referring to sitting in the *succah.* He suggests that when a preparation for a *mitzvah* (such as constructing a *succah*) is mentioned explicitly in the Torah, it is more of a religious duty than the preparation for another precept (such as binding the species of the *lulav* or cutting a shofar) which is not specified in the Torah.

3.

יֵשׁ נֶדֶר בְּתוֹךְ נֶדֶר, — *There is a neder within a neder,*

[If a person makes a binding *neder*, and then repeats the identical declaration, intending the new *neder* to be effective in addition to the existing *neder*, the second *neder* will also be binding.]

The simplest case of a *neder* within a *neder* would seem to be the follow-

ing. A person forbids some fruit by declaring: "This fruit is forbidden to me like a sacrifice." Eating such fruit would now incur for him the penalty of *malkus* (lashes). Later, the person repeats the identical *neder*. If this second declaration were effective on top of the existing *neder*, the fruit would now be forbidden by two *nedarim*, and consequently, eating it

נדרים
ב/ד

שְׁבוּעָה. כֵּיצַד? אָמַר: "הֲרֵינִי נָזִיר אִם אֹכַל, הֲרֵינִי נָזִיר אִם אֹכַל", וְאָכַל – חַיָּב עַל כָּל אַחַת וְאֶחָת. "שְׁבוּעָה שֶׁלֹּא אֹכַל, שְׁבוּעָה שֶׁלֹּא אֹכַל", וְאָכַל – אֵינוֹ חַיָּב אֶלָּא אֶחָת.

[ד] **סְתָם** נְדָרִים – לְהַחְמִיר, וּפֵרוּשָׁם – לְהָקֵל.

ר' עובדיה מברטנורא

(ג) **חייב על כל אחת ואחת.** ויהיה נזיר שלשים יום אם אמר הריני נזיר סתם, ויביא קרבן נזיר, ויחזור להיות נזיר כמספר הפעמים שאמר שיהיה נזיר. ובשבועה אינו חייב אלא אחת, שאינו לוקה אלא מלקות אחת, אבל אם נשאל על השבועה הראשונה חלה השבועה שנייה, וכן אם נשאל על השנייה חלה השלישית, ואסור לאכול עד שיותרו כולם, מדלא תנן הרי זו שבועה אחת, אלא אינו חייב אלא אחת: (ד) **ופירושן להקל.** אף על גב דכשמפרש דבריו אזלינן בתר פירושו, כי סתם ולא פירש להחמיר אזלינן דסתם נודר דעתו לאסור:

יד אברהם

would be a violation of two *nedarim*, and would result in a punishment of two sets of lashes.

In fact, however, the second *neder* in such a case is *not* effective. This is because of the principle that אֵין אִסּוּר חָל עַל אִסּוּר, *a prohibition is not effective on something already prohibited* (*Kiddushin* 77b). Thus, for example, to declare pork to be forbidden by a *neder* will be meaningless. Pork is already forbidden, and the added prohibition intended by the *neder* does not take hold. Similarly, fruit that has been forbidden via a *neder* will not become any more prohibited by repeating the identical *neder*. The mishnah cannot then be referring to this sort of *neder* when it writes that "there is a *neder* within a *neder*" (*Tos.* 17a, s.v. יש; *Tos. Yom Tov*).

As stated below, the case of a "*neder* within a *neder*" intended here deals with the declaration of a Nazirite. *Tosafos* explain that the declaration of a Nazirite is referred to in the Torah as a *neder*.

וְאֵין שְׁבוּעָה בְּתוֹךְ שְׁבוּעָה. — *but there is*

not an oath within an oath.

[If a person makes a binding oath and then repeats the identical declaration, intending the second one to be effective on top of the first, the second oath will not be binding.]

כֵּיצַד? אָמַר: "הֲרֵינִי נָזִיר אִם אֹכַל, הֲרֵינִי נָזִיר אִם אֹכַל", וְאָכַל – חַיָּב עַל כָּל אַחַת וְאֶחָת. — *How? If he said: "I am a Nazirite if I eat, I am a Nazirite if I eat," and he eats – he is bound by each [declaration].*

[This is the mishnah's example of a *neder* within a *neder*.]

This means that for each time he repeats his declaration, he must observe a separate thirty-day Naziritic period. In the case of the mishnah — in which the declaration was said two times — he must first observe a thirty-day period, at the end of which he offers the appropriate sacrifices, followed by a second period for the second declaration (*Rav*).

Ran, quoted by *Tos. Yom Tov*, points out that hinging the adoption of the Naziritic state upon his eating ("if I eat") is not essential for the declarations to be effective. Had he simply

משניות / נדרים – פרק ב: ואלו מותרין [50]

an oath within an oath. How? If he said: "I am a Nazirite if I eat, I am a Nazirite if I eat," and he eats — he is bound by each [declaration]. "*Shevuah, that I shall not eat, shevuah, that I shall not eat,*" and he ate — he is liable only for one.

4. **I**ndeterminate *nedarim* [are treated] stringently, and their interpretation, leniently.

YAD AVRAHAM

stated, "I am a Nazirite; I am a Nazirite," without adding "if I eat," he would still be obligated to observe two thirty-day terms as a Nazirite — one for each declaration. The *Tanna* only uses a case in which the adoption of the Naziritic state is tied to an act of eating in order to make this part of the mishnah symmetrical with the next part, which discusses an oath that deals with eating.

שְׁבוּעָה שֶׁלֹּא אֹכַל, שְׁבוּעָה שֶׁלֹּא אֹכַל,״ — ״Shevuah, ״וְאָכַל - אֵינוֹ חַיָּב אֶלָּא אֶחָת. that I shall not eat; shevuah, that I shall not eat," and he ate — he is liable only for one.

[This is an illustration of an oath within an oath.]

Once a person is bound by an oath, repeating it will not obligate him any more than the original oath. If he

violates the oath by eating, he is punished for having transgressed one oath only (*Rav*).

However, the *Gemara* (18a) notes that the mishnah uses the expression *he is liable only for one* rather than saying *only one oath is effective.* This choice of words indicates that — although only the first oath is punishable — nevertheless, the subsequent declarations are not completely void. Rather, should the person have the first oath annulled (the laws regarding annulment of *nedarim* discussed in 2:1 apply equally to oaths), the second one would then automatically become binding and punishable in its wake. The only way to release the person from all the oaths would be to have them all nullified (*Rav*).

4.

סְתָם נְדָרִים - לְהַחֲמִיר, וּפֵרוּשָׁם - לְהָקֵל. *Indeterminate nedarim [are treated] stringently and their interpretation, leniently.*

[Although indeterminate *nedarim* are treated stringently, if they are interpreted as having a lenient meaning, the clarification will be accepted.]

Sometimes both a Biblical and a man-made prohibition share the same name. For example, the term x was used to describe both of these. An

indeterminate *neder* would then be of the same form "This fruit is forbidden to me like x," where x might mean either of the two prohibitions (*Meiri*).

The validity of a *neder* containing such equivocal reference will depend on the intention of the person making the *neder*. If he says that his intention was the Biblical prohibition that goes by that name, he is believed, and the declaration will not be binding; if he explains his reference to have been to

כֵּיצַד? אָמַר ,,הֲרֵי עָלַי כִּבְשַׂר מָלִיחַ", ,,כְּיֵין
נֶסֶךְ", אִם שֶׁל שָׁמַיִם נָדַר — אָסוּר; אִם שֶׁל
עֲבוֹדָה זָרָה נָדַר — מֻתָּר. וְאִם סְתָם — אָסוּר.
,,הֲרֵי עָלַי כַּחֵרֶם", אִם כְּחֵרֶם שֶׁל שָׁמַיִם
— אָסוּר; וְאִם כְּחֵרֶם שֶׁל כֹּהֲנִים — מֻתָּר;

—————— ר' עובדיה מברטנורא ——————

כבשר מליח. היינו קרבן דכתיב (ויקרא ב, יג) על כל קרבנך תקריב מלח: **בחרם של כהנים
מותר.** אף על גב דחרמי כהנים מועלים בהס עד שיבואו לידי כהנים והוי דבר הנדור, מכל
מקום סתם חרמי כהנים משמע שכבר באו ליד כהן:

the man-made interdict, the *neder* will be binding (*Tos.* 18b).

If he does not explain the intention of his reference, or if he says that he intended the interpretation of his words to be held up to the Rabbis (*Rosh, Pesakim* 2:10), the reference is stringently assumed to be to a man-made prohibition and the declaration is considered binding. The same is true if the person who made the *neder* is not available to clarify his statement. This is relevant in the case of a *neder* which is directed at another person, such as "My fruit is forbidden you like x," where x is a term used to describe both a Biblical and a man-made prohibition. If the person who made the declaration is available, he can clarify his meaning. If he is not, the declaration is treated stringently and is validated on the assumption that the man-made interdict had been intended. Thus, the person to whom the *neder* was addressed will not be permitted to eat the fruit (*Meiri*).

Rosh explains that, in the absence of a clarification to the contrary, we assume that the person intended to make a binding *neder*. For if not, why would he bother to make a declaration? Therefore, the rule is that an indeterminate *neder* is interpreted to

be binding. Nevertheless, if the person later explains that he meant something which will make the *neder* invalid, he is believed, and no prohibition will result from his declaration.

The mishnah now presents several illustrations of indeterminate *nedarim*.

כֵּיצַד? אָמַר ,,הֲרֵי עָלַי כִּבְשַׂר מָלִיחַ", ,,כְּיֵין נֶסֶךְ" — *How? He said: "[It is] to me like salted meat," [or] "wine libations"* —

Sacrificial meats were always salted before they were placed on the altar, in keeping with the verse (*Lev.* 1:3), *On all your offerings you shall put salt* (*Rav*). But, it was customary among pagans, as well, to make idolatrous offerings from salted meats (*Meiri*). Therefore, the term *salted meat* could mean sacrificial meat, which is interdicted by a man-made prohibition, or it could mean idolatrous offerings, which are Divinely forbidden [see comm. to mishnah 1, s.v. כַּעֲבוֹדָה זָרָה] (*Ran*).

Similarly, *libations* could refer to those used in the Jewish sacrificial service, which are designated as sacred and are man-made prohibitions. But, it could also mean the wine used in idol worship, which is Biblically interdicted to us (*Meiri*).

2
4

How? He said: "[It is] to me like salted meat" [or] "wine libations" — if [he vowed] of heaven, it is binding; if [he vowed] of idols, it is not binding; if it is indeterminate, it is binding. "It is to me like *cherem*" — if [he meant] a *cherem* to the Temple, it is binding; but if [he meant] a *cherem* of *Kohanim*, it is not binding;

YAD AVRAHAM

These declarations are thus indeterminate, and the law for them is as follows.

אִם שֶׁל שָׁמַיִם נָדַר – אָסוּר; — *if [he vowed] of heaven, it is binding;*

If he explained that he had been referring to meat or wine used in the Jewish sacrificial service, then his *neder* is binding (ibid.).

אִם שֶׁל עֲבוֹדָה זָרָה נָדַר – מֻתָּר; — *if [he vowed] of idols, it is not binding;*

If he explains that his reference was to meat or libations offered to idols, the declaration will not be binding, since these are Divinely interdicted (ibid.).

Tosafos and *Rosh* add that the person's explanation is accepted completely, and even under Rabbinic law, no nullification of the declaration is required (*Tos. Yom Tov*).

וְאִם סְתָם – אָסוּר. — *if it is indeterminate, it is binding.*

If he does not explain his intentions, or if he says that he intended the words to be whatever the Rabbis understood them to mean, the *neder* is interpreted stringently. The salted meat and libations referred to are assumed to be from the Jewish service. These are man-made strictures, and their *neder* is therefore binding (*Meiri; Rosh, Pesakim; Tos.*).

"הֲרֵי עָלַי כַּחֵרֶם", — *"It is to me like cherem"* —

[There are two types of declarations of *cherem*. One assigns something to the *Kohanim;* the other designates something as Temple property. Both types of property are initially sacred. However, when something donated to a *Kohen* via a *cherem* is delivered to the *Kohen,* it is no longer considered holy, and there are no restrictions on its use. Something assigned to the Temple through a *cherem,* however, remains holy even after delivery (see commentary to 1:1. s.v. וַחֲרָמִים).]

אִם כְּחֵרֶם שֶׁל שָׁמַיִם – אָסוּר; — *if [he meant] a cherem to the Temple* (lit., a *cherem of heaven*), *it is binding;*

If the person explains his reference to *cherem* to mean a *cherem* to the Temple, his declaration is binding, because the sanctity of something assigned to the Temple through a *cherem* is imposed by human designation (*Meiri*).

וְאִם כְּחֵרֶם שֶׁל כֹּהֲנִים – מֻתָּר; — *but if [he meant] a cherem of Kohanim, it is not binding;*

If he explains that by *cherem,* he intended property assigned to *Kohanim* with a *cherem* and which has already reached the *Kohen's* hands, no prohibition will result. As already mentioned, when something is assigned to a *Kohen* via a *cherem,* it loses its sanctity upon delivery to the *Kohen.* Thus, the declaration "It is to me like *cherem*," if referring to property already delivered to the *Kohen,* refers to something permissible, and no restrictions will be created (*Rav*).

וְאִם סְתָם – אָסוּר.
„הֲרֵי עָלַי כַּמַּעֲשֵׂר״, אִם כְּמַעְשַׂר בְּהֵמָה
נָדַר – אָסוּר. וְאִם שֶׁל גֹּרֶן – מֻתָּר; וְאִם
סְתָם – אָסוּר. „הֲרֵי עָלַי כַּתְּרוּמָה״, אִם
כִּתְרוּמַת הַלִּשְׁכָּה נָדַר – אָסוּר; וְאִם שֶׁל גֹּרֶן

━━━━━━━━━━━━━━━ ר׳ עובדיה מברטנורא ━━━━━━━━━━━━━━━

אם כמעשר בהמה אסור. דהוי דבר הנדור, שצריך להקדישו, ואין מעשר בהמה חוסר הדיר
כמו שמעשר דגן חוסר הגורן:

━━━

יד אברהם

Prior to delivery to the *Kohen*, the property is sacred by virtue of a human designation. Hence, had the person explained his reference to mean property assigned to a *Kohen* by a *cherem* which has *not* yet been delivered to the *Kohen*, the *neder* would be binding. However, the expression *"cherem* of *Kohanim"* is understood to mean *cherem*-property already delivered to the *Kohanim*, which is permissible for all uses. Thus, when the person explains his reference to *cherem* as meaning that it has ben assigned to *Kohanim*, the *neder* is not binding (*Rav*).

וְאִם סְתָם – אָסוּר. — *if it is indeterminate — it is binding.*

In the absence of any clarification to the contrary, the reference to *cherem* is understood to mean property that is sacred by dint of human designation. The declaration will thus be binding (*Meiri*).

„הֲרֵי עָלַי כַּמַּעֲשֵׂר״, — *[If one said:]"It is to me like a tithe"* —

The Torah obligates the separation of tithes annually from the agricultural harvest, as well as from the new flock of sheep and cattle (*Lev.* 27:30 — 33).

[There are several agricultural tithes: the first tithe, the second tithe, and the tithe for the poor. However, only the first tithe is ever referred to as simply *tithe*.]

The first tithe is given to the *Leviim*, and is *not* considered holy by most *Tannaim* (*Ritva; Meiri*). [R' Meir, quoted in *Yevamos* 86a, does regard the first tithe to be sacred.]

The tithe of animals is assigned by having the new flock pass through a gate in single file. Every tenth animal is marked and set aside to be offered as a sacrifice in the Temple. It is thus sacred (*Bechoros* 9:7).

The reference to *tithe* in the example of the mishnah may mean either the first agricultural tithe — which is not sacred — or the animal tithe, which is designated as sacred by man (*Meiri*).

אִם כְּמַעְשַׂר בְּהֵמָה נָדַר – אָסוּר; — *if he vowed like the animal tithe, it is binding;*

If he explained that by mentioning *tithe*, he intended the animal tithe, his declaration is binding.

Since a *neder* which refers to animal tithes is binding, it is clear that the prohibition of the latter is considered man-made. This is because the selection and designation of the animal as the tithe is a human act (*Tos.* 18b). Upon designation as the tithe, the

2

4

if it is indeterminate, it is binding.

[If one said:] "It is to me like a tithe" — if he vowed like the animal tithe, it is binding; if [he vowed] of the granary, it is not binding; if it is indeterminate, it is binding. "It is to me like *terumah*" — if he vowed concerning the withdrawal from the chamber, it is binding; if [he vowed] concerning the granary, it is

YAD AVRAHAM

animal is consecrated as an offering and is prohibited for general use. A reference to an animal tithe will thus create a prohibition (*Rav; Rosh*).

As discussed above (see 1:5, 2:1), *Rambam* requires a man-made prohibition to be producible voluntarily in order to be classified as a *davar hanadur*. This would seem to be inconsistent with the classification of animal tithes under this category, since it is obligatory to separate the animal tithe (*Rashash*).

However, in his *Commentary to Zevachim* 5:8, *Rambam* explains that, despite having certain unique features, the tithed animal is classified as *shelamim* (peace-offering). Since, in general, the status of a peace-offering is producible voluntarily, the prohibition of the tithe is considered manmade. (Cf. *Rambam's* treatment of sin-offerings in his *Commentary* to 1:5, see also *Rambam, Hil. Nedarim* 1:13, 2:9.)

וְאִם שֶׁל גֹּרֶן – מֻתָּר; — *if [he vowed] of the granary, it is not binding;*

[I.e., if he explained his vow to refer to the first agricultural tithe.]

According to the predominant opinion that the first tithe is permitted for all uses and is not sacred, a *neder* referring to it will not be binding. According to R' Meir, however, who maintains that the first tithe is sacred, it is treated just like *terumah* which — as explained in mishnah 1 — is not considered a man-made prohibition. Thus, the law stated here — that if a person explained his reference to be to

the first agricultural tithe, his *neder* is void — is agreed to by all (*Meiri; Ritva*).

וְאִם סְתָם – אָסוּר. — *if it is indeterminate, it is binding.*

Where no clarification is provided, the term *tithe* is interpreted such that the declaration will be binding. Thus, *tithe* is taken to refer to the animal tithe (*Meiri*).

"הֲרֵי עָלַי כַּתְּרוּמָה„, — *"It is to me like terumah"* —

Terumah literally means something that is lifted or separated. Thus, the *Kohen's* portion of the agricultural produce which is separated (lifted) from the rest is called *terumah*. Similarly, when withdrawals were made from the Temple treasury containing the revenue from the annual tax of a half shekel, the coins thus withdrawn (or separated) were called *terumah* (see *Shekalim* 3:1).

As explained in mishnah 1, *terumah* from agricultural produce is not a valid reference in a *neder*. However, the half-shekel coins were sacred and designated for use in the purchase of communal sacrifices. They were thus forbidden by a man-made prohibition, and a *neder* referring to these coins is binding.

אִם כִּתְרוּמַת הַלִּשְׁכָּה נָדַר – אָסוּר; — *if he vowed concerning the withdrawal from the chamber, it is binding;*

The *chamber* was a room in the

— מֻתָּר; וְאִם סְתָם — אָסוּר; דִּבְרֵי רַבִּי מֵאִיר.
רַבִּי יְהוּדָה אוֹמֵר: סְתָם תְּרוּמָה, בִּיהוּדָה —
אֲסוּרָה; בַּגָּלִיל — מֻתֶּרֶת, שֶׁאֵין אַנְשֵׁי גָלִיל
מַכִּירִין אֶת תְּרוּמַת הַלִּשְׁכָּה.
סְתָם חֲרָמִים, בִּיהוּדָה — מֻתָּרִין; וּבַגָּלִיל —
אֲסוּרִין, שֶׁאֵין אַנְשֵׁי גָלִיל מַכִּירִין אֶת חֶרְמֵי
הַכֹּהֲנִים.

―――――― ר' עובדיה מברטנורא ――――――

שאין אנשי גליל מכירין תרומת הלשכה. לפי שהיו רחוקים מירושלים: **שאין אנשי גליל**
מכירין חרמי כהנים. וכל מה שהיו מחרימין היו מפרישין לבדק הבית. והלכה כרבי יהודה:

――――――――― יד אברהם ―――――――――

Temple in which the coffers containing the half-shekel coins were located (*Shekalim* 3:1; *Rambam Comm.* ibid.).

The mishnah asserts that if the person explained that, with the word *terumah* he was referring to the coins withdrawn from the chamber, then his declaration will be binding (*Meiri*).

וְאִם שֶׁל גֹּרֶן – מֻתָּר; — *if [he vowed] concerning the granary, it is not binding;*

If he explained that by the word *terumah* he was referring to the *Kohen's* portion of the agricultural produce, the declaration will not be binding (ibid.).

וְאִם סְתָם – אָסוּר; דִּבְרֵי רַבִּי מֵאִיר. — *if it is indeterminate, [the neder] is binding; [these are] the words of R' Meir.*

In the absence of any other explanation by the person who made the *neder*, we assume *terumah* to mean the half-shekel coins; consequently, the *neder* is binding (ibid.).

רַבִּי יְהוּדָה אוֹמֵר: סְתָם תְּרוּמָה, בִּיהוּדָה-
אֲסוּרָה; בַּגָּלִיל - מֻתֶּרֶת, שֶׁאֵין אַנְשֵׁי גָלִיל
מַכִּירִין אֶת תְּרוּמַת הַלִּשְׁכָּה. — *R' Yehudah says: Indeterminate terumah — in Judea, it is forbidden; in Galilee, it*

is permitted, because people in Galilee are not familiar with the withdrawals from the chamber.

R' Yehudah agrees with R' Meir that an indeterminate reference should be interpreted strictly, so that the *neder* will be binding. However, where the stricter usage is not common, the term is not considered ambiguous, and is explained in accordance with the common usage (*Ran*).

Accordingly, R' Yehudah distinguishes between Judea and Galilee. In Judea, which was close to the Temple in Jerusalem, the people were familiar with both agricultural *terumah*, as well as the withdrawal of coins from the chamber. Because of this, the term *terumah* was commonly used to refer to food, as well as coins. Thus, in Judea, where the stricter usage of the word — for coins — was common, the indeterminate use of *terumah* was interpreted as referring to the coins, and the *neder* was binding. However, in Galilee, which was far from the Temple, people were generally not acquainted with the withdrawal from the chamber (*Rav*). The only *terumah* ordinarily encountered was of the

not binding; if it is indeterminate, [the *neder*] is binding; [these are] the words of R' Meir. R' Yehudah says: Indeterminate *terumah* — in Judea, it is forbidden; in Galilee, it is permitted, because people in Galilee are not familiar with the withdrawals from the chamber.

Indeterminate *charamim* — in Judea, [they] are permissible; but in Galilee, [they] are binding, because the people of Galilee are not familiar with *charamim* of *Kohanim*.

YAD AVRAHAM

agricultural variety. Thus, R' Yehudah maintains that, in Galilee, the term *terumah* is always assumed to mean agricultural *terumah*. In that case, a *neder* in Galilee which included an indeterminate reference to *terumah* should be explained according to the only common usage — agricultural *terumah*. Thus, the *neder* would not be binding (*Meiri*).

The next part of the mishnah follows the opinion of R' Elazar ben Tzadok cited in the *Gemara*. He disputes the rule stated at the beginning of the mishnah that indeterminate *nedarim* be treated stringently. Rather, he is of the opinion that an indeterminate reference will not be binding unless it is explained to be so by the person who made the *neder* (*Ran*).

סְתָם חֲרָמִים, בִּיהוּדָה – מֻתָּרִין; — *Indeterminate charamim — in Judea, they are permissible;*

Although in Judea the term *cherem* (pl. *charamim*) was used for a man-made prohibition — the Temple *cherem* — as well as for property in the hands of the *Kohen*, a lenient interpretation is adopted. Thus, R' Elazar ben Tzadok explains *charamim* to mean permissible property in the

hands of the *Kohen*, and consequently, the *neder* is not binding (*Ran* 19b, s.v. אמר אביי).

וּבַגָּלִיל – אֲסוּרִין, שֶׁאֵין אַנְשֵׁי גָלִיל מַכִּירִין אֶת חֶרְמֵי הַכֹּהֲנִים. — *but in Galilee, they are binding, because the people of Galilee are not familiar with charamim of Kohanim.*

In Galilee, it was not common to donate things to *Kohanim* with a *cherem*. Therefore *cherem* invariably meant a *cherem* to the Temple. Thus, a *neder* in Galilee which referred to *charamim*, without specifying the sort of *cherem*, could only mean a Temple *cherem*. Since the latter is man-made, the *neder* was binding.

Because the reason given for the stringent treatment of the reference in Galilee is that the people of Galilee are not familiar with *charamim* of *Kohanim*, it is clear that where there exists familiarity with this type of *cherem*, the *neder* will not be treated stringently. Rather, in a place such as Judea, where both uses were common, an indeterminate reference was interpreted leniently to mean property already delivered to the *Kohen*. That property is permissible, and therefore, the *neder* is not binding.

נְדָרִים [ה] **נָדַר** בַּחֵרֶם, וְאָמַר: ,,לֹא נָדַרְתִּי אֶלָּא
בְּחֶרְמוֹ שֶׁל יָם״; בַּקָּרְבָּן, וְאָמַר: ,,לֹא
נָדַרְתִּי אֶלָּא בְקָרְבָּנוֹת שֶׁל מְלָכִים״; ,,הֲרֵי עַצְמִי
קָרְבָּן״, וְאָמַר: ,,לֹא נָדַרְתִּי אֶלָּא בְעֶצֶם שֶׁהִנַּחְתִּי
לִי לִהְיוֹת נוֹדֵר בּוֹ״; ,,קוֹנָם אִשְׁתִּי נֶהֱנֵית לִי״, וְאָמַר:
,,לֹא נָדַרְתִּי אֶלָּא בְאִשְׁתִּי הָרִאשׁוֹנָה שֶׁגֵּרַשְׁתִּי״ —

━━━━━━━━━━━ ר' עובדיה מברטנורא ━━━━━━━━━━━

(ה) בחרמו של ים. לשון מצודה כמו אשר היא מצודים וחרמים (קהלת ז, כו): **הרי עצמי
קרבן.** אסר עצמו ככרבן על חבירו:

━━━━━━━━━━━━━━━━━━━━━━━━━━━━━━━━━━━━

יד אברהם

As already noted, this is the opinion of R' Elazar ben Tzadok. The first, anonymous *Tanna* of the mishnah, however, rules that stringency must be applied when interpreting an equivocal reference. Thus, in Judea, a reference to *cherem* will be assumed to mean a *cherem* to the Temple, and the *neder* will be binding. In Galilee, since the predominant use of *cherem* is with reference to Temple *charamim*, the *neder* will certainly be binding (*Gem.* 19b; *Ran ad loc.*; *Tos. Yom Tov*).

The position of R' Elazar ben Tzadok could have been illustrated by the mishnah in the case of a reference to *terumah*. In Judea, where *terumah* was an ambiguous term, R' Elazar would explain it to mean

agricultural *terumah*, so that the *neder* would not be binding. This example would have more clearly emphasized that a new view was being presented, since the lenient ruling would have contrasted with the previous ruling of R' Yehudah. The reason R' Elazar ben Tzadok's opinion is cited regarding a case of *charamim* is due to the tendency of the mishnah to retain the original formulation of a law. Apparently, he had initially expressed his view that ambiguous reference be treated leniently in a discussion of the case of *charamim*. Although, for the symmetry of the mishnah, it might have been better to teach this opinion with regard to a case of *terumah*, the original teaching was given priority (*Ran*, quoted by *Tos. Yom Tov*).

5.

The subject of the next mishnah is a person who offers a far-fetched and lenient explanation of his *neder*. Under Biblical law, his explanation is accepted, and the *neder* is not effective. But the Rabbis saw fit to treat such cases strictly.

נָדַר בַּחֵרֶם, וְאָמַר: ,,לֹא נָדַרְתִּי אֶלָּא בְּחֶרְמוֹ שֶׁל יָם״; — *[If]* one vowed referring to cherem, and said: "I vowed with reference to a fisherman's net" (lit., a net of the sea);

A person made a declaration of the form "This is forbidden to me like *cherem.*" As explained in the previous mishnah, the term *cherem* is an ambiguous reference. Explaining his intention, the person claims that by *cherem*, he meant a fisherman's net, which is the way the word is used in Scripture [cf. *Koheles* 7:26, *Habakkuk* 1:15] (*Rav*). [A fisherman's net bears no prohibitions, so the person is arguing that his *neder*, which referred to *cherem*, is meaningless.]

5. **[**I**f]** one vowed referring to *cherem*, and said: "I vowed with reference to a fisherman's net"; [or he vowed] referring to *korban*, and said: "I vowed with reference to gifts for kings"; [or if he declared:] "My self is [to you like a] *korban*," and he said: "I vowed with reference to a bone that I have set aside for myself to use for *nedarim*;" [or] "*Konam*, [that which] my wife benefits from me," and he said: "My declaration was directed at my first wife, whom I divorced" —

YAD AVRAHAM

בַּקָּרְבָּן, וְאָמַר: ,,לֹא נָדַרְתִּי אֶלָּא בְּקָרְבָּנוֹת שֶׁל מְלָכִים"; — *[or he vowed] referring to korban, and said: "I vowed with reference to gifts for kings";*

The term *korban* is sometimes used in the sense of *gifts for royalty*; see *Targum Onkelos* to *Genesis* 33:11 (*Meiri*). [These gifts were not sacred in any way, and to refer to them in a *neder* would not assign a prohibition.]

,,הֲרֵי עַצְמִי קָרְבָּן", וְאָמַר: ,,לֹא נָדַרְתִּי אֶלָּא בְּעֶצֶם שֶׁהֻנַּחְתִּי לִי לִהְיוֹת נוֹדֵר בּוֹ"; — *[or if he declared:] "My self is [to you like a] korban," and he said: "I vowed with reference to a bone that I have set aside for myself to use for nedarim"* (lit., *to vow with it*);

The word עַצְמִי in Hebrew means *my self*. Thus, the above declaration would ordinarily mean that he was forbidding himself to the other person (*Rav*). *However,* עַצְמִי could also mean *my bone* (as in *Gen.* 22:14), and this declaration would then mean "My bone is like a *korban*." The person argued that he specifically set aside a bone for the purpose of directing his *nedarim* at it. Thus, his *neder* was not at all intended to restrict his person from others; rather, it referred to this bone (*Tos. Yom Tov*).

,,קוֹנָם אִשְׁתִּי נֶהֱנֵית לִי", וְאָמַר: ,,לֹא נָדַרְתִּי אֶלָּא בְּאִשְׁתִּי הָרִאשׁוֹנָה שֶׁגֵּרַשְׁתִּי"– — *[or]* "Konam, my wife from benefiting from me," and he said: "My declaration was directed at my first wife whom I divorced" —

This declaration would ordinarily have been understood to be directed at his present wife. By explaining it to have been referring to his former wife, he indicates that he had no intentions whatsoever of restricting his present wife (*Meiri*).

In all these cases, the explanations offered by the person for his declaration show that his reference was no more than a play on words. The listener would be certain he had heard a binding *neder*, but in fact, the person making the declaration had intended only a meaningless statement. In the examples of עַצְמִי, קָרְבָּן, and אִשְׁתִּי, the obvious meanings (*offering, self, current wife*) would have been assumed by a listener. The case of *cherem*, notes *Meiri*, takes place in an area where *cherem* generally meant a Temple *cherem* (see mishnah 4). There, too, the average listener would assume he had heard a binding *neder*. But the far-fetched explanations offered, which

עַל כֻּלָּן אֵין נִשְׁאָלִין לָהֶן. וְאִם נִשְׁאֲלוּ — עוֹנְשִׁין אוֹתָן, וּמַחְמִירִין עֲלֵיהֶן; דִּבְרֵי רַבִּי מֵאִיר. וַחֲכָמִים אוֹמְרִים: פּוֹתְחִין לָהֶם פֶּתַח מִמָּקוֹם אַחֵר, וּמְלַמְּדִים אוֹתָן, כְּדֵי שֶׁלֹּא יִנְהֲגוּ קַלּוּת רֹאשׁ בִּנְדָרִים.

ר' עובדיה מברטנורא

אין נשאלים עליהם. אין צריכין שאלת חכם, שאמן חליס: **ואם נשאלין.** ואס עס האלך הוא זה שנדר כהאי גוונא ובא לישאל על נדרו, אין פותחין לו פתח לחרטה ואין מתירין לו, ואס עבר על נדרו זה מנדין אותו: **פותחין לו פתח ממקום אחר.** מראים לו שהנדר קיים ופותחין לו פתח מטעם אחר ומתירין לו נדרו, אבל לא טונשין ולא מחמירין. וכן הלכה:

---

involve uncommon uses of the term, show that the person intended to make a statement which appears to be a *neder*, but is, in fact, meaningless (*Tos.* 18b, s.v. סתם; *Tos. Yom Tov*).

This is considerably different from the cases of the previous mishnah. There, although a nonbinding declaration may have been intended, there was no attempt to fool people. For example, the person who declared something "to be like tithes," and intended agricultural tithes, has not made a binding *neder*. However, since the term *tithes* was widely used in the sense of agricultural tithes, he had no reason to assume that he would be misunderstood. He could not be accused of trying to trick people into thinking he had made a binding *neder*.

The examples of this mishnah employ clever puns clearly designed to fool people into thinking a binding *neder* has been made. To discourage this light-headed attitude toward *nedarim*, the Rabbis treated such cases with great severity, as discussed below (*Rambam, Hil. Nedarim* 2:12; *Tos. Yom Tov*).

עַל כֻּלָּן אֵין נִשְׁאָלִים לָהֶן. — *for all of these, they need not* (lit., *do not*) *request*

cancellation,

The *Gemara* (20a) qualifies this ruling as applying only if the above declarations were made by a scholar. His explanations — no matter how farfetched — are accepted, and the declarations are therefore not binding. He need not seek cancellation of the vows even under Rabbinic law. If, however, the declarations were made by an ignorant person, the law is different, as will be seen.

Some explain that a scholar is not likely to develop a habit of making *nedarim*. He is therefore let off lightly. An ignorant person, however, was considered more prone to developing such a habit and had to be discouraged from making a *neder*; consequently, his declarations are treated stringently (*Riva, Rashi* to 20a).

Others understand that the different treatment of the scholar and the ignorant person is due to a difference in their credibility. The explanation of a scholar — even when farfetched — is to be believed, because we do not question his veracity. On the other hand, an ignorant person who gives explanations of his statements, such as those of our mishnah, is not to be

for all of these, they need not request cancellation, and if they requested cancellation, we penalize them, and we are strict with them; [these are] the words of R' Meir.

The Sages, however, say: We find grounds to annul the *neder* from elsewhere, and we teach them, so that they not conduct themselves with levity [when dealing] with *nedarim*.

YAD AVRAHAM

believed, because we fear he is lying (*Ran* 18b).

וְאִם נִשְׁאֲלוּ- — *and if they requested cancellation,*

[They sought a Rabbi or a panel to cancel their *neder*.]

The *Gemara* (20a) construes this phrase in the mishnah to refer to an ignorant person. Some understand this expression to mean *When they request cancellation*. In other words, the ignorant person is *obligated* to seek the cancellation of his declaration (*Ran* loc. cit.). Others interpret it as *If they sought* ..., and do not obligate the ignorant person to seek cancellation. The mishnah, however, tells us the halachah of the case in which he did so (*Rav; Tos.* 20a).

The question of whether the ignorant person is obligated to seek an annulment is related to the difference, discussed above, between a scholar and an ignorant person. If the ignorant person's far-fetched explanation is not believed, then the declaration must be assumed to be binding, and a cancellation would be necessary. If his explanation is believed, then — strictly speaking — his declaration is not binding, and annulment is not obligatory. But, if the ignorant person consulted the Rabbis concerning his declaration, they required that the *neder* be annulled in order to discourage him from making *nedarim* in the future (*Shoshanim LeDavid*).

עוֹנְשִׁין אוֹתָן, — *we penalize them,*

Rav, following *Rambam*, explains this to mean that if the ignorant person violated his *neder*, he is placed under a ban. This entails being excluded from a quorum (he cannot be counted as one of the ten men needed for the prayer service), and being forbidden to bathe or cut his hair. The ban was not permanent, and was lifted upon request, once the Rabbis deemed it appropriate to do so (see *Rambam, Hil. Talmud Torah* 7:4ff).

Ran explains the penalty differently. If the ignorant person broke his vow, he is obligated to observe it for the same number of days that he broke it, before a cancellation will be granted.

[An example would be if an ignorant person vowed: "Apples are to me like *cherem*," and later explained his reference to refer to fishermen's nets. Either because we do not accept his explanation, or because we wish to discourage him from the practice of making *nedarim* in the future, the *neder* is treated strictly. If the ignorant person ate apples for ten days after making his declaration, *Ran* would hold that an annulment of his vow will be granted only if he first deprives himself of apples for a corresponding

ten days. According to *Rav* and *Rambam*, he is placed under a ban.]

וּמַחְמִירִין עֲלֵיהֶן; דִּבְרֵי רַבִּי מֵאִיר. — *and we are strict with them; [these are] the words of R' Meir.*

The *Gemara* (20a) explains this to mean that חֲרָטָה, *regret*, will not suffice to serve as a basis for annulment of the vow. A full "opening" must be sought (see mishnah 1, s.v. *Grounds for Annulling a Neder.*

וַחֲכָמִים אוֹמְרִים: פּוֹתְחִין לָהֶם פֶּתַח מִמָּקוֹם אַחֵר, — *The Sages, however, say: We find grounds to annul the neder* (lit., *open for them an opening) from elsewhere,*

Rambam understands the Sages to dispute R' Meir only with regard to the imposition of a punishment for a violation of the *neder*. Thus, the Sages maintain that no ban is imposed, even on an ignorant person. By insisting that *we find grounds to annul the neder from elsewhere*, the Sages simply mean to eliminate regret as a basis for annulment, a view identical with that of R' Meir (cf. mishnah 1, where a similar phrase is used to eliminate an annulment based on regret alone).

Another explanation is that the Sages permit an annulment to be based even on an expression of remorse. They are thus arguing with R' Meir on this point, as well as on the question of punishing for a violation. By insisting on an "opening" *from elsewhere*, they mean to say that the explanation

initially offered by the ignorant person cannot be used as the basis for an annulment. Hence, in the case of *cherem*, the Rabbis cannot annul the *neder* by suggesting that the reference was to fishermen's nets. They must base the annulment *elsewhere*; i.e., not on something used in the original explanation of the declaration. For this, however, even an expression of remorse will suffice (*Tos.* 20a).

Rav (2:1) seems to follow *Rambam* in understanding *grounds ... from elsewhere* to eliminate annulment based on regret alone. Yet, in our mishnah, he comments that the Sages hold that we do not penalize them, nor are we strict with them, suggesting — like *Tosafos* — that there are two points of contention between R' Meir and the Sages.

וּמְלַמְּדִים אוֹתָן, — *and we teach them,*
I.e., we reprove them (*Rashi*).

כְּדֵי שֶׁלֹּא יִנְהֲגוּ קַלּוּת רֹאשׁ בִּנְדָרִים. — *so that they not conduct themselves with levity [when dealing] with nedarim.*

The use of *neder*-type declarations to fool people into thinking a binding *neder* had been made was considered reprehensible. This levity was berated with harsh reproach to prevent its recurrence (*Rashi; Tos. Yom Tov*). *Rambam* (*Hil. Nedarim* 2:12) maintains that even a scholar who, as explained above, did not need a formal cancellation in the cases of the mishnah, was subjected to this rebuke.

פרק שלישי 🔊

Chapter Three

[א] **אַרְבָּעָה** נְדָרִים הִתִּירוּ חֲכָמִים: נִדְרֵי זֵרוּזִין, וְנִדְרֵי הֲבַאי, וְנִדְרֵי שְׁגָגוֹת, וְנִדְרֵי אֳנָסִים.

נִדְרֵי זֵרוּזִין כֵּיצַד? הָיָה מוֹכֵר חֵפֶץ, וְאָמַר: "קוֹנָם שֶׁאֵינִי פוֹחֵת לְךָ מִן הַסֶּלַע", וְהַלָּה אוֹמֵר: "קוֹנָם שֶׁאֵינִי מוֹסִיף לְךָ עַל הַשֶּׁקֶל" — שְׁנֵיהֶן רוֹצִין בִּשְׁלֹשָׁה דִינָרִין. רַבִּי אֱלִיעֶזֶר

—————————— ר' עובדיה מברטנורא ——————————

פרק שלישי - ארבעה נדרים. (א) ארבעה נדרים. כולהו מפרש להו ואזיל: **קונם שאני פוחת לך מן הסלע.** קונם ככר זה עלי אם אני פוחת לך מן הסלע, והסלע הוא ארבעה דינרים: **על השקל.** הוא חלי סלע: **שניהם רוצים בשלשה דינרים.** ולא היה בלבם לשם נדר, אלא המוכר נדר לזרז הלוקח שיוסיף דמים, וכן הלוקח כדי שיפחות המוכר בדמי המקח, הילכך לא הוי נדר. ואף על גב דדברים שבלב אינם דברים, היכא דמוכחא מלתא כי הכא, שכן דרך כל מוכרין ולוקחין לעשות כן חזלינן בתר דברים שבלב:

—————————— יד אברהם ——————————

1.

אַרְבָּעָה נְדָרִים הִתִּירוּ חֲכָמִים: — *The Sages permitted four nedarim:*

The *Gemara* (21b) explains this to mean that these declarations are not effective at all and do not need any cancellation. Although compatible with the guidelines for the formula of a *neder*, they are all motivated by other considerations, and are not made in order to create prohibitions.

The lack of intent to effect a prohibition is so obvious, adds *Ritva*, that even an ignorant person would not confuse these declarations with others that are actually binding. Thus, even an ignorant person who made any of these four types of declarations does not need to seek cancellation.

נִדְרֵי זֵרוּזִין, וְנִדְרֵי הֲבַאי, וְנִדְרֵי שְׁגָגוֹת, וְנִדְרֵי אֳנָסִים. — *bargaining* (lit., *urging*) *nedarim, hyperbolic* (lit., *foolish*) *nedarim, unwitting nedarim, and nedarim on conditions unavoidably unfulfilled.*

[The mishnah proceeds to give examples of each of these expressions.]

נִדְרֵי זֵרוּזִין כֵּיצַד? — *What are* (lit., *how*) *bargaining nedarim?*

Literally, זֵרוּזִין means *urging*. In the course of bargaining, a person tends to adopt a tougher position than that which he is really willing to settle for. He hopes in this way to urge the other party to moderate his position and compromise (*Rav; Rosh; Ran*).

הָיָה מוֹכֵר חֵפֶץ, וְאָמַר: "קוֹנָם שֶׁאֵינִי פוֹחֵת לְךָ מִן הַסֶּלַע", — *One was selling an item, and said: "Konam, if I sell to you for less than a sela,"*

[A *sela* is equivalent to four dinars.]

The seller, attempting to force a higher bid, insists that he cannot drop the price any lower than a *sela*. He demonstrates his adamance by declaring something to be forbidden to himself if he sells for less that four dinars.

His actual statement is something

1. **T**he Sages permitted four *nedarim:* bargaining *nedarim*, hyperbolic *nedarim*, unwitting *nedarim*, and *nedarim* on conditions unavoidably unfulfilled.

What are bargaining *nedarim*? One was selling an item, and said: *"Konam*, if I sell to you for less than a *sela,"* and the other says: *"Konam*, if I pay you more than a shekel" — both [persons] are willing at three dinars. R' Eliezer

YAD AVRAHAM

such as: *"Konam* this loaf to me if I sell to you for less than a *sela"* (*Rav; Rosh*).

וְהַלָּה אוֹמֵר: ,,קוֹנָם, שֶׁאֵינִי מוֹסִיף לְךָ עַל הַשֶּׁקֶל,, — *and the other says: "Konam, if I pay you more than a shekel" —*

[A shekel is equal to two dinars.[1]]

The buyer insists that his highest bid will be two dinars, and he displays his firmness by declaring something to become forbidden to him should he pay more than his limit. For example, his statement might be: *"Konam* this fruit to me if I pay you more than a shekel" (*Tif. Yis.*).

[The buyer and the seller have thus taken up negotiating positions designed to induce the other to moderate his demands.]

שְׁנֵיהֶן רוֹצִין בִּשְׁלשָׁה דִינָרִין. — *both [persons] are willing at three dinars.*

That is, although they appeared inflexible with the price, they both actually had a different price in mind — three dinars (*Ran*).

If the sale is indeed concluded at three dinars, the seller has apparently activated his *neder* by selling for less

than four. Similarly, the buyer has also activated his *neder* by paying more than two. In fact, however, neither one is bound by any prohibitions. The declarations are understood to have been made for bargaining purposes only and not with an intention to create a prohibition. Even while claiming to have a price limit of two or four dinars, they both were really willing to settle at three; hence, the *neder* is not binding (*Tos.* 21a, s.v. רבא).

Some authorities maintain that, although a compromise price of three dinars or so was always acceptable, the seller was never willing to sell for two, nor was the buyer ever willing to buy for four. Thus, if in the end the item is sold, for example, at two or less, the *neder* of the seller does become effective (*Ran*).

Others argue that even if a *neder* was intended for a sale at two dinars or less, it was never stated. The statement specified less than four. Since that statement was just a bargaining tactic, and not a binding *neder*, no statement has been made to effect a prohibition in the event of a sale price of two or less. Hence, even if the sale is transacted at such a price, no prohibition will result (ibid.).

1. This refers to the Mishnaic shekel, not to be confused with the Biblical shekel, which is equivalent to a *sela* (see Appendix 1 to ArtScroll *Shekalim*).

בֶּן יַעֲקֹב אוֹמֵר: אַף הָרוֹצֶה לְהַדִּיר אֶת חֲבֵרוֹ
שֶׁיֹּאכַל אֶצְלוֹ.
אוֹמֵר: ,,כָּל נֶדֶר שֶׁאֲנִי עָתִיד לִדּוֹר הוּא בָטֵל",
וּבִלְבַד שֶׁיְּהֵא זָכוּר בִּשְׁעַת הַנֶּדֶר.

ר' עובדיה מברטנורא

רבי אליעזר בן יעקב אומר אף הרוצה להדיר את חבירו כו'. מפרש בגמרא (כג, ב)
דחסורי מחסרא והכי קתני, הרוצה שיאכל חבירו אצלו ומסרב בו ומדירו, נדרי זרוזין הוא.
והרוצה שלא יתקיימו נדריו כל השנה, יעמוד בראש השנה ויאמר, כל נדר שאני עתיד לידור יהא
בטל, ויעמוד בראש השנה לאו דוקא אלא הוא הדין בכל עת שירצה ולכל זמן שיקבע: **ובלבד**
שיהיה זכור. מן התנאי בשעת הנדר ודעתו על התנאי שיהיה קיים אז הנדר בטל, אבל אם לא
נזכר מן התנאי בשעת הנדר ולא בתוך כדי דבור משעה שנדר, הנדר קיים. ואין צריך לומר אם
נזכר מן התנאי בשעת הנדר ודעתו שיהיה התנאי שיהיה בטל והנדר קיים, דפשיטא שהנדר קיים.
ומשפטי השבועות והנדרים שוין לדין זה. והלכה כרבי אליעזר בן יעקב:

יד אברהם

רַבִּי אֱלִיעֶזֶר בֶּן יַעֲקֹב אוֹמֵר: אַף הָרוֹצֶה
לְהַדִּיר אֶת חֲבֵרוֹ שֶׁיֹּאכַל אֶצְלוֹ. — R'
*Eliezer ben Yaakov says: So, too, one
who wants to direct a neder at another
so that the other person should eat with
him.*

The *Gemara* (23b) explains that the
text here is deficient (see above, comm.
to 1:1, s.v. *Talmudic Emendations of
the Mishnah*), and should be completed as follows: הָרוֹצֶה שֶׁיֹּאכַל אֶצְלוֹ
חֲבֵרוֹ וּמְסָרֵב בּוֹ וּמַדִּירוֹ נִדְרֵי זֵרוּזִין הוּא —
*One who wants his friend to eat with
him and urges him [to accept his
invitation] and directs a neder at him
— it is [in the category of] bargaining
nedarim.*

The case is that someone (e.g.,
Reuven) wants another person (Shimon) to dine with him. Shimon,
however, is reluctant to accept the
invitation. In the course of urging
Shimon to change his mind, Reuven
declares that unless Shimon accepts
the invitation, he will issue a *neder* to
ban Shimon from benefiting from any
of his (Reuven's) property. R' Eliezer

ben Yaakov maintains that this *neder*
is just a bargaining *neder,* and that
Reuven never intended to create a
prohibition. He simply wanted to
prevail upon Shimon to accept the
invitation. Thus, no interdict will take
effect even if Shimon does not accept
the invitation (*Ran 23b*, s.v. הכי).

אוֹמֵר: ,,כָּל נֶדֶר שֶׁאֲנִי עָתִיד לִדּוֹר הוּא בָטֵל".
— *He says: "Any neder that I will
make in the future is void."*

The *Gemara* (ibid.) explains that
this statement of the mishnah is
independent of the previous one,
and that it, too, is deficient. It should
read: וְהָרוֹצֶה שֶׁלֹּא יִתְקַיְּמוּ נְדָרָיו כָּל
הַשָּׁנָה, יַעֲמוֹד בְּרֹאשׁ הַשָּׁנָה וְיֹאמַר: ,,כָּל
נֶדֶר שֶׁאֲנִי עָתִיד לִדּוֹר יְהֵא בָטֵל" — *And
one who wishes that his nedarim of the
whole year not be binding, should say
(lit., rise ... and say) on Rosh Hashanah: "Any neder that I will make shall
be void."*

This refers to someone who wants
to invalidate any vows he might make
in the future. He thus declares that
any *neder* he will pronounce shall be

3
1

ben Yaakov says: So, too, one who wants to direct
a *neder* at another so that the other person should
eat with him.

He says: "Any *neder* that I will make in the
future is void." [This is effective] provided that he
remembers at the time of the *neder*.

YAD AVRAHAM

canceled. By this statement he has
made it clear that no matter what
declarations he should subsequently
make, he has no intention to produce
prohibitions through them. A *neder*
made without intent to produce a
prohibition is not binding (*Tos.* 23b,
s.v. רבא).

The requirement that a *neder* must be
made with the intent to produce a prohibition in order to be valid is also the reason
that a bargaining *neder* is not binding.
This similarity is presumably the reason
for the inclusion of this law here (*R' Zvi
Kalischer*).

Rosh Hashanah as the proper time for
this declaration is merely given as an
example. The statement would be equally
effective if made at any time, and is valid
for any time span specified (*Rav*).

The *Kol Nidrei* prayer recited at the start
of the Yom Kippur service is based on this
mishnah. The practice of reciting it on Yom
Kippur, rather than on Rosh Hashanah, the
day mentioned by the *Gemara*, is due to the
larger attendance in the synagogue on Yom
Kippur (*Tos.* 23b, s.v. ואת). Indeed, many do
have the custom to annul their *nedarim* on
the day before Rosh Hashanah (*Matteh
Ephraim* 581:49).

וּבִלְבַד שֶׁיְּהֵא זָכוּר בִּשְׁעַת הַנֶּדֶר. — [This is
effective] provided that he remembers
at the time of the neder.

That is, his future *nedarim* will be
voided only if, at the time he vows, he
recalls his earlier voidance and wants
it to apply. If, however, at the time of
his *neder* (or immediately thereafter),

he does not remember having invalidated future *nedarim*, the earlier
cancellation is not applicable, and
the *neder* will be binding. Similarly,
if, when vowing, he recalls his repudiation of all subsequent *nedarim*, but
specifically intends this prohibition, it
will be binding (*Rav; Rambam Commentary*).

Shulchan Aruch (*Yoreh Deah* 211:2)
contrarily rules that if, at the time of
vowing, the person remembered his voidance, the *neder* is binding. Only if the
repudiation was not recalled at the time of
the *neder* will the latter be canceled automatically. This is the complete antithesis of
Rav's view and is based on a version cited in
the *Gemara* (23b), in which the mishnah
reads: וּבִלְבַד שֶׁלֹּא יְהֵא זָכוּר בִּשְׁעַת הַנֶּדֶר,
*provided that he does not remember at the
time of the neder.* If the repudiation is
recalled when making the *neder*, we assume
that it is being withdrawn so that the *neder*
can be valid. Only a *neder* made when he
does *not* recall the voidance will be canceled,
since it is presumed to still be in force (*Be'er
Hagolah, Beur HaGra* ibid.).

Others (*Yoreh Deah* ibid.; *Rambam, Hil.
Nedarim* 2:4) consider the cancellation to be
effective only if, immediately after the
neder, he remembers it and relies on it.
The view in the *Gemara* which validates the
repudiation only if it is forgotten when
making the *neder* would require the same.
The text of the mishnah, which states
provided that he remembers, will thus refer
to the moment immediately after the *neder*
is made (*Bach* to *Tur* 211; see *Ohr Gadol*).

[ב] **נִדְרֵי** הַבַאי — אָמַר: ,,קוֹנָם אִם לֹא
רָאִיתִי בַּדֶרֶךְ הַזֶּה כְּיוֹצְאֵי מִצְרַיִם",
,,אִם לֹא רָאִיתִי נָחָשׁ כְּקוֹרַת בֵּית הַבַּד".
נִדְרֵי שְׁגָגוֹת — ,,אִם אָכַלְתִּי", וְ,,אִם
שָׁתִיתִי", וְנִזְכַּר שֶׁאָכַל וְשָׁתָה; ,,שֶׁאֲנִי אוֹכֵל",
וְ,,שֶׁאֲנִי שׁוֹתֶה", וְשָׁכַח וְאָכַל וְשָׁתָה; אָמַר:

ר' עובדיה מברטנורא

(ב) **נדרי הבאי.** גוזמא וספת יתר, והוא בטלמו יודע שלא היה כך: **קונם אם לא ראיתי.**
קונס עלי ככר זו אם לא ראיתי וכו': **נדרי שגגות אמר קונם.** עלי ככר זו: **אם אכלתי אם
שתיתי ונזכר שאכל ושתה.** ובשעת הנדר היה סבור שלא אכל ולא שתה, לא הוי נדר: **קונם
שאיני אוכל לך ואיני שותה, ושכח ואכל ושתה.** דבשעה שהנדר חל שהוא בשעת האכילה
והשתייה שכח את הנדר, מותר, דילפינן משבועות דכתיב (ויקרא ה, ד) האדם בשבועה דבטינן
שיהיה אדם בשעה שהשבועה חלה עליו, כלומר שיהיה זכור מן השבועה, והוא הדין בנדר:

יד אברהם

2.

נִדְרֵי הַבַאי - אָמַר: ,,קוֹנָם אִם לֹא רָאִיתִי
בַּדֶרֶךְ הַזֶּה כְּיוֹצְאֵי מִצְרַיִם", — [What are]
*hyperbolic nedarim? [A person] said:
"Konam, unless I have seen on this
road like those departing from Egypt,"*

For example, he said: "Konam this
food to me unless I have seen on this
road a group of people the size of the
Jewish nation when they departed
from Egypt" (*Rav*).

The Torah (*Ex.* 12:37) relates that the
Jewish population during the Exodus
included 600,00 men. Thus, from the
person's *neder*, it would seem that
unless he had seen a group of 600,000
the food will become forbidden to him.

However, the mishnah teaches us
that, although it is impossible for a
multitude of that size to be within a
person's range of view (see *Yerushalmi*), and although it is highly
improbable that such a massive group
passed by, the food is permitted. The
phrase *like those departing from Egypt*
is taken to be an exaggeration; it was
not intended to be understood literally. Rather, the person wished to

convey that he had seen a large group
of people. Thus, assuming that he did
in fact see a large group of people, the
food will be permitted (*Ran*).

Ran (*Shevuos* 29a) maintains that if the
person saw only a small group, one that
would not merit the hyperbolic description
like those departing from Egypt, the *neder*
will take effect, and the food will be
prohibited. *Beis Yosef* (*Yoreh Deah* 232),
however, argues that what constitutes a
"large" group is a subjective matter. Some
people consider one hundred people to be a
horde. Thus, in all cases — no matter how
many people were actually seen by the
person — his assertion that they were like
the people leaving Egypt is taken as a
legitimate exaggeration (*Tos. Yom Tov*).

,,אִם לֹא רָאִיתִי נָחָשׁ כְּקוֹרַת בֵּית הַבַּד". —
[or] *"unless I have seen a snake like a
beam of the olive press."*

He declares some food to be forbidden to him, unless he has seen a
snake resembling the beam used to
squeeze olives for their oil (*Rav*).

There are various opinions regarding the *Gemara's* description of the

2. [**W**hat are] hyperbolic *nedarim*? [A person] said: "*Konam*, unless I have seen on this road like those departing from Egypt," [or] "unless I have seen a snake like a beam of the olive press."

[What are] unwitting *nedarim*? [A person said:] "If I ate," or "If I drank," and he remembers that he ate or drank; "If I eat," or "If I drink," and he forgot, and ate or drank; [or a person said:]

YAD AVRAHAM

uniqueness of this beam: (1) It is disfigured by irregular spots (*Tos.* 25a); (2) it is full of incisions (*Rav* ibid.); (3) it is smooth (*Rosh*); (4) it is triangular (*Rambam Comm.*). In any case, the *Gemara* asserts that no snake has this feature the way the beam does.

Because the condition qualifying the *neder* (viz., *unless I have seen a snake like a beam* etc.) is clearly a fabrication, the *neder* is not binding. Had the person intended to produce a prohibition, he would not have added this condition, but would simply have stated, "*Konam*, this food is forbidden me." The addition of the impossible condition indicates that he wished only to make a hyperbolic statement regarding some bizarre snake that he had seen and did not wish to produce a prohibition; therefore, it is not binding (*Ran*).

נִדְרֵי שְׁגָגוֹת – ,,אִם אָכַלְתִּי", וְ,,אִם שָׁתִיתִי", וְנִזְכַּר שֶׁאָכַל וְשָׁתָה; — [What are] unwitting nedarim? [A person said:] "If I ate," or "If I drank," and he remembers that he ate or drank;

This refers to someone who declared that something should be forbidden to him if he ate or drank during a certain time period (*Tif. Yis.*). At the time of making the declaration, he mistakenly thought that he had not eaten or drunk, so that his *neder* would not create any prohibitions.

Only because he was certain that it would be ineffective did he make the declaration. As explained previously, in the absence of intent to create and interdict, a *neder* is not binding. Thus although he subsequently remembers that the *did* eat or drink, no prohibition results (*Rosh*).

,,שֶׁאֲנִי אוֹכֵל", וְ,,שֶׁאֲנִי שׁוֹתֶה", וְשָׁכַח וְאָכַל וְשָׁתָה; — "If I eat," or "If I drink," and he forgot, and ate or drank;

This deals with someone who declared something to become prohibited if he should eat or drink during that day. Later, he forgot his declaration and ate or drank (*Tif. Yis.*).

The eating or drinking was to have activated his *neder*. However, the mishnah tells us that since he was eating or drinking, it does not take effect. A prohibition must be created consciously, and not unwittingly, as in this case. This is derived from the verse (*Lev.* 5:4), *for all which a man utters in an oath*, in which the term *a man* is superfluous (since the verse begins with *Or a person*). The *Gemara* (*Shevuos* 26a) explains that this teaches us that an oath is valid only when the person is aware that he is effecting an oath. If, however, he activates the oath unwittingly, it does not take effect. The term *a man* is presumed to describe a person who is aware of the

„קוֹנָם אִשְׁתִּי נֶהֱנֵית לִי שֶׁגָּנְבָה אֶת כִּיסִי״, וְ,,שֶׁהִכְּתָה אֶת בְּנִי״, וְנוֹדַע שֶׁלֹּא הִכַּתּוּ וְנוֹדַע שֶׁלֹּא גְנָבַתּוּ.

רָאָה אוֹתָן אוֹכְלִים תְּאֵנִים, וְאָמַר: „הֲרֵי עֲלֵיכֶם קָרְבָּן״, וְנִמְצְאוּ אָבִיו וְאֶחָיו, [וְ]הָיוּ עִמָּהֶן אֲחֵרִים — בֵּית שַׁמַּאי אוֹמְרִים: הֵן מֻתָּרִין וּמַה שֶּׁעִמָּהֶן אֲסוּרִין; וּבֵית הִלֵּל אוֹמְרִים: אֵלוּ וָאֵלוּ מֻתָּרִין.

[ג] **נִדְרֵי** אֲנָסִים — הִדִּירוֹ חֲבֵרוֹ שֶׁיֹּאכַל אֶצְלוֹ, וְחָלָה הוּא, אוֹ שֶׁחָלָה בְנוֹ, אוֹ שֶׁעִכְּבוֹ נָהָר — הֲרֵי אֵלוּ נִדְרֵי אֲנָסִין.

ר' עובדיה מברטנורא

קונם אשתי נהנית לי שגנבה את כיסי. היינו נדרי שגגות, דכיון שנודע שלא גנבה לו נמצא שלא היה נדר: **אלו ואלו מותרין.** דנדר שהותר מקצתו הותר כולו דאינו רוצה שיחול נדרו אלא כשין שנדר אותו, וכיון שמקלתו היה שוגג נתבטל כולו: (ג) **נדרי אונסין.** דמעיקרא לא היה בדעתו שיחול הנדר אם יעכבנו אונס, וכהאי גוונא מוכיחין שהדברים שבלב הוו דברים:

יד אברהם

ramifications of his acts. Since — in our case — when he ate or drank, he forgot that these actions would effect a *neder*, no prohibition ensues. The law for a *neder* is derived from the law for an oath; consequently, the maker of a *neder*, too, must fit the description, *a man*, as described above. The *neder* of the mishnah is therefore not binding (*Rav; Rosh*).

אָמַר: „קוֹנָם אִשְׁתִּי נֶהֱנֵית לִי שֶׁגָּנְבָה אֶת כִּיסִי״, וְ,,שֶׁהִכְּתָה אֶת בְּנִי״, וְנוֹדַע שֶׁלֹּא הִכַּתּוּ וְנוֹדַע שֶׁלֹּא גְנָבַתּוּ. — [or a person] said: "Konam my wife benefiting from me, because she stole my purse," or "she beat my son," and it was discovered that she had not beaten him, and it was discovered that she had not robbed him.

Here, the person forbids his wife to benefit from him, because he accuses

her of having stolen his wallet or having beaten his son. When these accusations prove to be false, it becomes clear that the *neder* was unwitting and is not binding (*Rav; Rosh*).

Ran (25b) maintains that in order for the *neder* to be void, the reason for vowing (*because she stole*, etc.) must be clearly stated at the time of the *neder*, since it indicates that only if the premise is proven to be true will the *neder* be valid. If no reason was offered (i.e., he said: "Konam my wife benefiting from me," with no further explanation) — although he made the *neder* only because of his suspicions, it would be binding even if it turns out that the wife was not guilty (cf. *Pischei Teshuvah to Yoreh Deah* 232:2).

רָאָה אוֹתָן אוֹכְלִים תְּאֵנִים, וְאָמַר: „הֲרֵי עֲלֵיכֶם קָרְבָּן״, וְנִמְצְאוּ אָבִיו וְאֶחָיו, וְהָיוּ עִמָּהֶן אֲחֵרִים — בֵּית שַׁמַּאי אוֹמְרִים: הֵן מֻתָּרִין, וּמַה שֶּׁעִמָּהֶן אֲסוּרִין; וּבֵית הִלֵּל אוֹמְרִים: אֵלוּ וָאֵלוּ מֻתָּרִין.

3
3

"*Konam* my wife benefiting from me, because she stole my purse," or "she beat my son," and it was discovered that she had not beaten him, and it was discovered that she had not robbed him.

A person saw people eating figs, and he said: "[They are] *korban* to you," and it turned out to be his father and his brothers, and there were others with them — Beis Shammai say: They are permitted, but those with them are forbidden; Beis Hillel, however, say: Both are permitted.

3. [**W**hat are] *nedarim* with conditions unavoidably unfulfilled? His friend vowed in order that he eat with him, but he took ill, or his son took ill, or he was held back by a river — these are *nedarim* with conditions unavoidably unfulfilled.

YAD AVRAHAM

— A person saw people (lit., them) eating figs, and he said: "[They are] korban to you," and it turned out to be his father and his brothers, and there were others with them — Beis Shammai say: They are permitted, but those with them are forbidden; Beis Hillel, however, say: Both (lit., These and those) are permitted.

In this case, the owner of a fig tree saw from a distance that some people were eating his figs. Assuming them to be strangers, he declared that the figs be forbidden to them like *korban*. It turns out, however, that among the people eating figs were his father and brothers. He certainly had never intended to forbid the figs to them (*Ran*).

Beis Shammai hold that, therefore, the father and brother are exempt from the prohibition, and the figs are permitted to them. However, the *neder* does forbid the other people in the group to eat the figs. Beis Hillel, on the other hand, rule that the *neder* is completely void. Since it was made in error with respect to his relatives and is not binding on them, it is also not effective with regard to anyone else. They maintain that a *neder* cannot be binding only in part. Since the declaration referred to the whole group, it will be valid only if it can affect the whole group. However, because it is void with respect to the relatives, it is completely invalidated (*Rav*).

3.

נִדְרֵי אֳנָסִים - הִדִּירוֹ חֲבֵרוֹ שֶׁיֹּאכַל אֶצְלוֹ, וְחָלָה הוּא, אוֹ שֶׁחָלָה בְנוֹ, אוֹ שֶׁעִכְּבוֹ נָהָר - הֲרֵי אֵלּוּ נִדְרֵי אֳנָסִין. — *[What are] nedarim with conditions unavoidably unfulfilled? His friend vowed in order*

that he eat with him, but he took ill, or his son took ill, or he was held back by a river — these are nedarim with conditions unavoidably unfulfilled.

The case of the mishnah is as

נדרים [ד] נוֹדְרִין לְהָרָגִין, וְלַחֲרָמִין, וְלַמּוֹכְסִין שֶׁהִיא תְרוּמָה, אַף עַל פִּי שֶׁאֵינָה תְרוּמָה; שֶׁהֵן שֶׁל בֵּית הַמֶּלֶךְ, אַף עַל פִּי שֶׁאֵינָן שֶׁל בֵּית הַמֶּלֶךְ. בֵּית שַׁמַּאי אוֹמְרִים: בַּכֹּל נוֹדְרִין, חוּץ מִבִּשְׁבוּעָה; וּבֵית הִלֵּל אוֹמְרִים: אַף בִּשְׁבוּעָה.

ר' עובדיה מברטנורא

(ד) **להרגין.** לסטים שהורגין האדם ונוטלין את ממונו: **ולחרמין.** גזלנים שאינם הורגים, ולא זו אף זו קתני: **ולמוכסין.** במוכס העומד מאליו, אבל מוכס שהעמידו המלך בין מלך ישראל בין מלך גוי ולוקח דבר קצוב בחוק המלכות, דינא דמלכותא דינא ואסור לברוח מן המכס, וכל שכן שאסור לדור ולשבע לו לשקר: **שהן של תרומה.** אף על פי שהורגין וגוזלין אין אוכלין דבר האסור, אי נמי תרומה לא תשיבה להו, מתוך שאינה נאכלת אלא לכהנים טהורים נמכרת בזול הרבה:

יד אברהם

follows: Someone (e.g., Shimon) wishes to be the guest of another (Reuven) for a meal. But Shimon has another invitation, which he wishes to decline. He therefore asks Reuven to impose a *neder* which would make it mandatory for him to accept Reuven's invitation. Reuven obliges, and vows that unless Shimon partakes of Reuven's meal, Shimon will be barred by force of a *neder* from benefiting in any way from Reuven's property. Shimon is now able to refuse the other, conflicting invitation by pointing to the loss he will incur if he fails to attend Reuven's meal (*Gem.* 24a).

Reuven's *neder* — insisting that Shimon accept his invitation — is not comparable to a bargaining *neder* (see comm. to mishnah 1, s.v. רַבִּי אֱלִיעֶזֶר), because Shimon needs no urging to accept Reuven's invitation. On the contrary, he wants to attend, and he was the one who initiated Reuven's *neder*. Therefore, the *neder* should be

binding, and if Shimon fails to attend the meal, Reuven's property should become interdicted to him (*Ran* 24a).

However, in the mishnah's example, something occurred which prevented Shimon's attendance. For example, Shimon himself became ill, or his son took sick and needed attention, or melting snows flooded the river and prevented him from having access to Reuven's home. As a consequence, the *neder* obligating Shimon's attendance at Reuven's meal is *unavoidably unfulfilled*.

It is assumed that the *neder* was never intended to become effective under such circumstances. Although it was not explicitly stated that the *neder* should be activated only if Shimon is capable of attending and does not do so, this is assumed to be the case. Hence, when Shimon fails to attend through no fault of his own, the *neder* is not binding (*Rav*).

4.

The coming mishnah deals with extenuating circumstances under which a person is permitted to make a false *neder*. In order to prevent a robbery, for

4. **O**ne may make a *neder* for murderers, robbers, or illegal tax collectors that it is *terumah*, even though it is not *terumah*; that they belong to the royal house, even though they do not belong to the royal house.

Beis Shammai say: One may make any *neder*, but not an oath; Beis Hillel, however, say: Even an oath.

YAD AVRAHAM

example, a person makes a false claim about the status of his property. He adds credibility to his claim by reinforcing it with a *neder*. Thus, he declares: "*Konam,* this be forbidden me if my claim is not true."

When making this declaration, the person must have a time limit in mind although he does not vocalize it. (To do so would be self-defeating, since a promise to abstain from the item for only a short period does not prove his claim.) The full *neder* is really something like: "*Konam,* let this be prohibited to me for a day, if my claim is not true." Since, in fact, his claim is false, the prohibition will take effect, but only for one day. Any potential thieves, on the other hand — unaware of the time limit — assume that if the person's claim is false, this item will be forbidden him forever. They therefore accept the claim and forgo the theft.

נוֹדְרִין לְהָרָגִין, וְלַחֲרָמִין, וְלַמּוֹכְסִין שֶׁהִיא תְרוּמָה, אַף עַל פִּי שֶׁאֵינָה תְרוּמָה; שֶׁהֵן שֶׁל בֵּית הַמֶּלֶךְ, אַף עַל פִּי שֶׁאֵינָן שֶׁל בֵּית הַמֶּלֶךְ. — *One may make a neder for murderers, robbers, or illegal tax collectors that it is terumah, even though it is not terumah; that they belong to the royal house, even though they do not belong to the royal house.*

The mishnah is providing guidance on deterring a theft by murderers, robbers, or illegal tax collectors. If these criminals can be convinced that the goods which they are after are not to their liking, they will abandon their plans (*Tos.* 27b).

Apparently, thieves were not interested in *terumah* or in royal property. Although they disregarded the Torah's proscriptions against theft (or, in the case of murderers, against murder!), they were not prepared to tamper with sacred items such as *terumah*

(ibid.; *Rav; Rosh*). It was also not worth the risk to handle royal property. Thus, in order to prevent a murder and theft, a person was permitted to declare, "Let this be forbidden me if this is not *terumah* (or royal property)." As explained in the preface, he would have some time limit in mind for the prohibition (*Gem.* 28a).

The illegal tax collector mentioned here is either self-appointed, or an appointed one who collects taxes arbitrarily.

If the tax laws and the collector are legal and fair, it is forbidden to evade the taxes following the principle that the law of the kingdom (or government) is binding (*Gem.* 28a). This applies regardless of whether the ruler is a gentile or a Jew (*Rav; Choshen Mishpat* 369:6).

בֵּית שַׁמַּאי אוֹמְרִים: בַּכּל נוֹדְרִין, חוּץ מִבִּשְׁבוּעָה; וּבֵית הֵלֵּל אוֹמְרִים: אַף בִּשְׁבוּעָה. — *Beis Shammai say: One may make any neder, but not an oath;*

בֵּית שַׁמַּאי אוֹמְרִים: לֹא יִפְתַּח לוֹ בְנֶדֶר; וּבֵית
הַלֵּל אוֹמְרִים: אַף יִפְתַּח לוֹ. בֵּית שַׁמַּאי אוֹמְרִים:
בַּמֶּה שֶׁהוּא מַדִּירוֹ; וּבֵית הַלֵּל אוֹמְרִים: אַף בַּמֶּה
שֶׁאֵינוֹ מַדִּירוֹ. כֵּיצַד? אָמְרוּ לוֹ: „אֱמוֹר: ׳קוֹנָם
אִשְׁתִּי נֶהֱנֵית לִי׳ ״, וְאָמַר: „קוֹנָם אִשְׁתִּי וּבָנַי נֶהֱנִין
לִי״ — בֵּית שַׁמַּאי אוֹמְרִים, אִשְׁתּוֹ מֻתֶּרֶת, וּבָנָיו
אֲסוּרִין; וּבֵית הַלֵּל אוֹמְרִים: אֵלּוּ וָאֵלּוּ מֻתָּרִין.

───────── ר' עובדיה מברטנורא ─────────

לא יפתח לו בנדר. אם לא שאל ממנו האנס שידור לא יתחיל הוא בנדר: **במה שהוא
מדירו.** אם שאל ממנו האנס לידור לא ידור לו אלא במה שאל בלבד ולא ידור לו בדבר
אחר. וכל הני ארבעה נדרים דתנא במתניתין דין הנדרים והשבועות שוים, ומה שמותר
בנדר מותר בשבועה ואין לריכים התרה, חוץ מנדרי זרוזין בלבד שלריכים התרה מדברי
סופרים לפיכך השבועה אסורה בהם:

───────── יד אברהם ─────────

As in the case of the *neder*, the person — when making the oath — must have in mind something that will disqualify it. Thus, for a declaration of the form "Let this be forbidden to me by an oath if this is not *terumah*," he could have in mind an unsaid time limit. For an oath such as "I swear that this is *terumah*," he could have intended a play on words. Thus, *terumah*, which generally means the *Kohen's* portion of the produce, can also mean *something lifted* since the root of *terumah* (תְּרוּמָה), הרם, means *to lift*. Assuming that at one time or another, the person had lifted the produce which the thieves are after, he can safely swear that it is "*terumah*." They will assume that he means that it is sacred *terumah*, but he will actually have meant nothing more than that he at one time lifted it (*Tis. Yis.*). Similarly, if he were to swear that the goods are royal property, he could actually intend that in his household, he is "king." Therefore, the goods are "royal property" (*Meiri*).

Beis Hillel, however, say: Even an oath.

In general, an oath is considered more stringent than a *neder*. This is because in connection with an oath, the Torah writes (*Ex.* 20:7): "*For Hashem will not acquit one who utters His Name in vain*" (*Gem.* 18a).

Because of this, Beis Shammai maintain that, even in a situation such as that of the mishnah — in which a person may make a false vow in order to prevent the theft of his property — he should only use the formula of a *neder* and not of an oath (*Ran*).

Beis Hillel, on the other hand, permit the person to take even a false *oath* in order to mislead the thieves. It could be worded like a *neder*, such as this: "Let this be forbidden to me by an oath if this is not *terumah*." Or, the oath can be more direct: "I swear that this is *terumah*." Even though this is a more typical oathlike formula, Beis Hillel are not concerned that permitting it in extenuating circumstances will lead to a habit of false oaths (*Tos. Yom Tov*).

Beis Shammai say: He should not volunteer to make a *neder*; Beis Hillel, however, say: He may even volunteer. Beis Shammai say: Only what he is forced to vow; Beis Hillel, however, say: Even what he is not forced to vow. How [is this]? They told him: "Say: '*Konam*, my wife benefiting from me,'" and he said: "*Konam* my wife and my children benefiting from me" — Beis Shammai say: His wife is permitted, but his children are forbidden. Beis Hillel, however, say: Both are permitted.

YAD AVRAHAM

בֵּית שַׁמַּאי אוֹמְרִים: לֹא יִפְתַּח לוֹ בְנֶדֶר; וּבֵית הַלֵּל אוֹמְרִים: אַף יִפְתַּח לוֹ. — *Beis Shammai say: He should not volunteer to make a neder; Beis Hillel, however, say: He may even volunteer.*

According to Beis Shammai, if the robbers do not insist that the person establish his claims (that the items are *terumah* or royal property) with a *neder*, he may not do so. Although the person may make such a statement under pressure, he may not do so of his own volition. Beis Hillel, on the other hand, permits even this (*Rashi; Tif. Yis.*).

בֵּית שַׁמַּאי אוֹמְרִים: בַּמֶּה שֶׁהוּא מַדִּירוֹ; וּבֵית הַלֵּל אוֹמְרִים: אַף בַּמֶּה שֶׁאֵינוֹ מַדִּירוֹ. — *Beis Shammai say: Only what he is forced to vow; Beis Hillel, however, say: Even what he is not forced to vow.*

Although Beis Shammai agree that when the thieves insist that the victim confirm his claims with a *neder*, he may do so — nevertheless, he may not make it more extensive than the robbers call for. If he does, any addition will be binding in the regular manner (*Rav*).

[Beis Hillel, however, allow the person to extend the *neder* beyond what is being demanded, yet they still treat it as a *neder* made under extenuating circumstances. An example follows.]

כֵּיצַד? אָמְרוּ לוֹ: "אֱמֹר: 'קוֹנָם אִשְׁתִּי נֶהֱנֵית לִי'", וְאָמַר: "קוֹנָם אִשְׁתִּי וּבָנַי נֶהֱנִין לִי"- *How [is this]? They told him: "Say: 'Konam my wife benefiting from me,'" and he said: "Konam my wife and my children benefiting from me" —*

[The robbers demanded that he make a *neder* forbidding his wife to benefit from him if the goods are not *terumah* or royal property as he claims. The robbers mentioned only his wife — but when making the *neder*, he adds "*and my children.*"]

בֵּית שַׁמַּאי אוֹמְרִים: אִשְׁתּוֹ מֻתֶּרֶת, וּבָנָיו אֲסוּרִין; וּבֵית הַלֵּל אוֹמְרִים: אֵלּוּ וָאֵלּוּ מֻתָּרִין. — *Beis Shammai say: His wife is permitted, but his children are forbidden. Beis Hillel, however, say: Both are permitted.*

Beis Shammai maintain that the part of the *neder* demanded by the

---

1. Although unspoken qualifications are ordinarily disregarded in accordance with the principle that דְּבָרִים שֶׁבַּלֵּב, *words existing only in the heart*, are inefficacious (*Kiddushin* 49b-50a), under extenuating circumstances — such as those of our mishnah in which it is impossible to vocalize the qualification — even an unspoken condition is acceptable (*Gem.* 28a).

[ה] ,,הֲרֵי" נְטִיעוֹת הָאֵלּוּ קָרְבָּן אִם אֵינָן נִקְצָצוֹת", ,,טַלִּית זוֹ קָרְבָּן אִם אֵינָהּ נִשְׂרֶפֶת" — יֵשׁ לָהֶן פִּדְיוֹן; ,,הֲרֵי נְטִיעוֹת הָאֵלּוּ קָרְבָּן עַד שֶׁיִּקָּצְצוּ", ,,טַלִּית זוֹ קָרְבָּן עַד שֶׁתִּשָּׂרֵף" — אֵין לָהֶם פִּדְיוֹן.

―――――― ר' עובדיה מברטנורא ――――――

(ה) הרי נטיעות האלו קרבן אם אינן נקצצות. ראה רוח סערה באה וירא שמא יקלעו נטיעותיו ואמר הרי אלו קרבן אם אינן נקצצות, או שראה דליקה נפלה בעיר וירא על טליתו שמא תשרף ואמר הרי זו קרבן אם לא תשרף: יש להן פדיון. כשאר הקדשות, ויפדו ויקנה בדמיהן קרבן, דכיון דלא אמר הרי הן עלי כקרבן, לאו למסרינהו עליה כקרבן מיכוון אלא שיהו לקנות בדמיהן קרבן: אין להם פדיון. אלא המעות נתפסין בקדושה והנטיעות חוזרות להיות קדושות, דכיון דאמר עד שיקלעו, הכי קאמר לכשאפדה יחזרו ויקדשו עד שיקלעו:

――――――――――――――――――

יד אברהם

robbers (namely, with respect to his wife) will be modified by the unspoken qualification (e.g., that the prohibition last for only one day).[1] But the part the person added on his own (*"my children"*) will be binding as stated, with no limit, since the emergency did not require this addition.

(See mishnah 2 for another example of Beis Shammai splitting a *neder*.)

Beis Hillel, on the other hand, treat the whole *neder* identically, and permit both the wife and children to benefit from him as soon as the time limit passes (*Meiri; Yoreh Deah* 232:14).

5.

The declaration, "This is sacred for Temple maintenance," may be used to donate something for the upkeep of the Temple. Such an item would then be sacred and forbidden for general use; it may, however, be redeemed. The money used for the redemption then becomes sacred, but the item is no longer holy and may be used for any purpose (*Rambam, Hil. Arachin* 6;1,4).

It is also possible to endow all types of items, including those that are not fit for the altar, with "sacrificial sanctity." This means that the monetary equivalent of the item should be used toward the purchase of a sacrifice to be offered on the altar. Thus, for example, if a person were to sanctify a tree with "sacrificial sanctity," the tree would be considered sacred, and hence, forbid-

den for general use. It could be redeemed (and thus lose its sanctity), and the money would go toward the purchase of an offering (*Meilah* 12b).

It is commonly assumed that undoing a prohibition through the mechanism of redemption is not applicable to *nedarim*, and that the only way to nullify such an interdiction is by annulment of the *neder* (see 2:1).

Nevertheless, the *Gemara* (35a) quotes R' Meir, who maintains that when something has been prohibited "like a *korban*," and the prohibition is universal (i.e., the item has been forbidden to everyone including its owner), it is considered sacred and can be redeemed. The money will then be sacred and will go to the Temple, and the prohibition of the item will be rescinded.

3
5

5. [**I**f a person said:] "Let these saplings be an offering if they are not felled," "[Let] this cloak be an offering if it is not burnt" — they can be redeemed; "These saplings are an offering until they are felled," "This cloak is an offering until it is burnt" — they cannot be redeemed.

YAD AVRAHAM

The following mishnah deals with declarations of sanctification directed at things which are not fit to be offered as sacrifices and with their redemption. Most authorities explain that the sanctification under discussion is one of the first two types described above (i.e., Temple maintenance or sacrificial sanctity). *Ran* (28b) cites a view which attributes the mishnah to R' Meir and assumes that the "sanctity" derives from a prohibition as explained.

„הֲרֵי נְטִיעוֹת הָאֵלוּ קָרְבָּן אִם אֵינָן נִקְצָצוֹת,"
„טַלִּית זוֹ קָרְבָּן אִם אֵינָהּ נִשְׂרֶפֶת"– — *[If a person said:] "Let these saplings be an offering if they are not felled," "[Let] this cloak be an offering if it is not burnt"* —

The *Gemara* (28b) provides the following setting for these declarations. A person sees a tornado approaching and fears that it will destroy his newly planted trees. He declares that if the trees survive the storm, they should become sacred. Similarly, in the case of the cloak, a fire has broken out which the person fears will consume his cloak. He therefore declares that if his cloak survives the fire, it should be sacred (*Rav*).

The mishnah rules that the declarations are considered sincere, and the saplings or cloak will be forbidden should they survive. It might have been argued that the declarations were made out of hopelessness in the assumption

that the trees or cloak would certainly be lost, and that the declarations were really insincere. In that case, they would be ineffective (*Gem.* 28b; *Rashi*).

However, circumstantially, there is no reason to doubt the person's sincerity. It is quite appropriate for a person to promise to do a good deed if he is spared a major loss. Therefore, unlike some of the cases encountered in mishnayos 1 — 4, the declarations here are accepted at face value (ibid.; *Tif. Yis.*).

The contrast with the declarations of the previous mishnayos is the reason for the inclusion of this mish-nah here (*Tos. Yom Tov* from *Tos., Rosh*).

יֵשׁ לָהֶן פִּדְיוֹן; — *they can be redeemed;*

The mishnah could rather have said *they are sacred*. The phrase *they can by redeemed* is chosen because it makes this part of the mishnah symmetrical with the next part, in which the phrase *they cannot be redeemed* appears (*Gem.* 28b; *Tos. Yom Tov*).

„הֲרֵי נְטִיעוֹת הָאֵלוּ קָרְבָּן עַד שֶׁיִּקָּצְצוּ",
„טַלִּית זוֹ קָרְבָּן עַד שֶׁתִּשָּׂרֵף" – אֵין לָהֶם
פִּדְיוֹן. — *"These saplings are an offering until they are felled," "This cloak is an offering until it is burnt"* — *they cannot be redeemed.*

In these cases, the person sanctifies something for a limited time (i.e., *until they are felled; until it is burnt*). The stipulation is understood to mean that the sanctity should endure until the time limit is reached. This means that even if the items are redeemed before

[ו] הַנּוֹדֵר מִ„יּוֹרְדֵי הַיָּם" — מֻתָּר בְּיוֹשְׁבֵי
הַיַּבָּשָׁה; מִ„יּוֹשְׁבֵי הַיַּבָּשָׁה" —
אָסוּר בְּיוֹרְדֵי הַיָּם, שֶׁיּוֹרְדֵי הַיָּם בִּכְלַל „יוֹשְׁבֵי
הַיַּבָּשָׁה" — לֹא כְאֵלוּ שֶׁהוֹלְכִין מֵעַכּוֹ לְיָפוֹ,
אֶלָּא בְמִי שֶׁדַּרְכּוֹ לְפָרֵשׁ.

─────────── ר' עובדיה מברטנורא ───────────

(ו) מותר ביושבי יבשה. שֶׁאֵין דַּרְכָּם לָרֶדֶת לַיָּם: בכלל יושבי יבשה. שֶׁסּוֹפָם לָרֶדֶת וְלֵישֵׁב
בַּיַּבָּשָׁה: לא כאלו ההולכים מעכו ליפו. אִית דִּמְפָרְשֵׁי לָהּ הָכִי, הָא דְּתָנָן בְּרֵישָׁא דְּמַתְנִיתִין
הַנּוֹדֵר מִיּוֹרְדֵי הַיָּם מוּתָּר בְּיוֹשְׁבֵי יַבָּשָׁה דְּמַשְׁמַע הָא בְּיוֹרְדֵי הַיָּם אָסוּר, לֹא כְאֵלוּ שֶׁהוֹלְכִים מֵעַכּוֹ
לְיָפוֹ, שֶׁהַנּוֹדֵר מִיּוֹרְדֵי הַיָּם אֵינוֹ אָסוּר בָּהֶם, דְּמִשּׁוּם דֶּרֶךְ מוּעָט כָּזֶה לֹא מִיקְּרוּ יוֹרְדֵי הַיָּם. וְאִית
דִּמְפָרְשֵׁי, לֹא כְאֵלוּ הַהוֹלְכִים מֵעַכּוֹ לְיָפוֹ בִּלְבַד דְּבִכְלַל יוֹרְדֵי הַיָּם הֵם לֵיאָסֵר וְגַם יוֹשְׁבֵי יַבָּשָׁה
מִיקְּרוּ, אֶלָּא אַף בְּמִי שֶׁדַּרְכּוֹ לְפָרֵשׁ לְפִי שֶׁסּוֹפוֹ לֵירֵד לַיַּבָּשָׁה:

─────────── יד אברהם ───────────

that time, they will be automatically sanctified once again. Thus, in this case, even redemption will not succeed in rescinding the sanctity of the objects; rather, that sanctity will be automatically renewed. This is what the mishnah means by *they cannot be redeemed* (*Rav* from *Gem.* 28b).

Once the time limit has passed (e.g., the trees are felled) the automatic renewal clause will no longer be operative. If the objects are still considered sacred, they can then be redeemed. However, some maintain that when an object is sanctified only temporarily, its sanctity expires on its own at the end of the specified time. According to this view, once the trees are felled, the wood loses its sanctity and becomes fully permissible for general use (*Tos. Yom Tov* from *Rambam Comm.* and *Hil. Me'ilah* 4:11).

An interesting argument is advanced by R' Moshe of Cordova, quoted by *Ran* (28b). The assumption

that the time limit indicates an automatic renewal of sanctity persists even past the time limit until redemption. Since the sanctity persists, the only purpose in specifying a time limit would be to indicate automatic renewal of the sanctity. However, if the sanctity expires on its own once the time limit is reached, the specification of a time limit should not be viewed as a statement of automatic renewal. Rather, the time limit was specified in order to indicate the termination of the sanctity in the absence of redemption. Accordingly, if redemption is made prior to the time limit, it will be effective in permanently removing the sanctity from the object. The mishnah, which seems to say that the object cannot be redeemed, must be understood as discussing the law *after* the time limit has passed. Since, at that point, there is no more sanctity (it has expired on its own), the objects *cannot be redeemed* (*Tos. R' Akiva*).

6.

In the following mishnayos, three principles in the laws of *nedarim* are illustrated: (1) If the one who makes the *neder* does not actually intend that it should take effect, it is void (*Yoreh Deah* 232:1, *Turei Zahav* ad loc. 2). (2) The

6. One who makes a *neder* prohibiting "seafarers" is permitted to [benefit from] land dwellers; [if] "land dwellers" — he is forbidden to [benefit from] seafarers, because seafarers are included in "land dwellers" — not like those who go from Acre to Jaffa, but from someone whose custom is to voyage.

YAD AVRAHAM

vower must explicitly state what he wishes to prohibit (*Yoreh Deah* 210:1). (3) Words used in *nedarim* are interpreted according to their popular meanings (*Gem.* 30b).

הַנּוֹדֵר מִ,,יוֹרְדֵי הַיָּם'' – מֻתָּר בְּיוֹשְׁבֵי הַיַּבָּשָׁה; — *One who makes a neder prohibiting "seafarers" is permitted to [benefit from] land dwellers;*

[A person vowed with a *neder* that he be prohibited to benefit from seafarers.]

The early authorities (*Ran, Rosh, Tos.* to 30a) add that the *land dwellers* excluded from the *neder* are only those who do not regularly journey to sea. Those who do are describable as *seafarers*, even though they are currently not at sea and will be included in this *neder*.

If someone regularly rides boats, but only for short trips (*Rav*) and only on routes that hug the coast (*Rambam*), there is a question in the *Gemara* (30a) as to whether he is considered a seafarer or not. There are grounds to argue that only someone who goes out to sea on a long journey far from land is called a seafarer (see comm. below, s.v. לֹא כְאֵלּוּ). If that were the case, then only such people would be included in the *neder*. However, *Shulchan Aruch* (*Yoreh Deah* 217:33) rules that someone who prohibited "seafarers" is forbidden to benefit even from people whose trips do not involve journeys far from land.

מִ,,יוֹשְׁבֵי הַיַּבָּשָׁה'' – אָסוּר בְּיוֹרְדֵי הַיָּם, שֶׁיּוֹרְדֵי הַיָּם בִּכְלַל ,,יוֹשְׁבֵי הַיַּבָּשָׁה'' – [if] "land dwellers" — he is forbidden to [benefit from] seafarers, because seafarers are included in "land dwellers" —

Although the term *seafarers* does not include land dwellers, the term *land dwellers* includes all people, even seafarers. This is because seafarers — even those who are on long voyages — will eventually land and disembark (*Rav*). Thus, all people, including those currently at sea (*Ran*), may be referred to as *land dwellers*. Consequently, a person who declared a *neder* prohibiting himself to benefit from land dwellers is forbidden to do so from all people — land dwellers and seafarers alike (*Shulchan Aruch* loc. cit. 34).

לֹא כְאֵלּוּ שֶׁהוֹלְכִין מֵעַכּוֹ לְיָפוֹ, אֶלָּא בְמִי שֶׁדַּרְכּוֹ לְפָרֵשׁ. — *not like those who go from Acre to Jaffa, but from someone whose custom is to voyage.*

Voyage here refers to someone who goes out to sea in a large vessel for great distances from any land (*Rambam*). The route from Acre to Jaffa hugged the coast and was thus always close to land. It was not considered a *voyage*.

The mishnah's comment here modifies the previous statement that sea-

[ז] **הַנּוֹדֵר** מֵ,,רוֹאֵי הַחַמָּה'' — אָסוּר אַף
בַּסּוּמִין, שֶׁלֹּא נִתְכַּוֵּן זֶה אֶלָּא
לְמִי שֶׁהַחַמָּה רוֹאָה אוֹתוֹ.

[ח] **הַנּוֹדֵר** מֵ,,שְׁחוֹרֵי הָרֹאשׁ'' — אָסוּר
בַּקֵּרְחִין וּבְבַעֲלֵי שֵׂיבוֹת,

ר' עובדיה מברטנורא

(ז) מי שהחמה רואה אותו. מדלא [קאמר] מן הרואים: **(ח) אסור בקרחים ובבעלי
השיבות.** מדלא קאמר בבעלי השער:

יד אברהם

farers are also referred to as *land dwellers*. Lest we think that only seafarers whose route keeps them always close to land can be called *land dwellers*, the mishnah states that even people who journey far out into the ocean on a "voyage" are also referred to as land dwellers.

The word of the mishnah, *not like those who go from Acre to Jaffa, but from someone whose custom is to voyage*, must be understood in the following sense: Not *only* those who go from Acre to Jaffa are describable as land dwellers, but even someone whose custom is to voyage far out to sea is considered a land dweller (*Rav; Rambam, Hil. Nedarim 2:19; Shulchan Aruch*, loc. cit.).

Rav mentions a variant opinion in the *Gemara* which contends that people whose boat route is similar to the Acre-Jaffa route (i.e., short; near the coast) are *not* considered *seafarers*. Accordingly, in the first case of the mishnah (*one who makes a neder prohibiting seafarers*), only people who voyage out to sea will be forbidden to the person, since only they are referred to as *seafarers*. But people who go from Acre to Jaffa by boat are not *seafarers*, and will not be prohibited by the *neder*. The closing line of the mishnah refers — according to this opinion — to the first case of the mishnah and describes the seafarers who are prohibited: *Not like those who go from Acre to Jaffa, but from someone whose custom is to voyage.*

As mentioned earlier (s.v. הַנּוֹדֵר), *Shulchan Aruch* rejects this opinion, maintaining that someone who makes a *neder* prohibiting seafarers is forbidden to benefit even from people whose route is only from Acre to Jaffa. However, *Meiri* appears to prefer this view.

7.

הַנּוֹדֵר מֵ,,רוֹאֵי הַחַמָּה'' - אָסוּר אַף בַּסּוּמִין,
שֶׁלֹּא נִתְכַּוֵּן זֶה אֶלָּא לְמִי שֶׁהַחַמָּה רוֹאָה
אוֹתוֹ. — *One who makes a neder prohibiting "those who see the sun" is forbidden [to benefit] even from the blind, for he* (lit., *this one*) *referred only to those visible to the sun.*

Someone makes a *neder* prohibiting to himself any benefit from ,,רוֹאֵי הַחַמָּה'' — a phrase generally understood to mean *those who see* the sun. One would have thought that this would exclude blind people who, of course, are unable to see the sun.

Nevertheless, blind people *are* included in the term רוֹאֵי הַחַמָּה, and the person is forbidden to benefit from them. This is because the term is taken to mean *those visible to the sun*, and this includes even the blind (*Gem.* 30b; *Ran* 30a).

The reason that this expression is

7. **O**ne who makes a *neder* prohibiting "those who see the sun" is forbidden [to benefit] even from the blind, for he referred only to those visible to the sun.

8. **O**ne who makes a *neder* prohibiting "dark-headed people" is forbidden [to benefit] from bald people and hoary-haired people,

YAD AVRAHAM

construed to mean *those visible to the sun*, rather than *those who see the sun*, is explained by the *Gemara* (30b). Had the person's intention been to prohibit benefit only from people with sight and to exclude blind people, he would have merely used the term רוֹאִים, *those who see*. The apparently superfluous addition of the word חַמָּה, *sun*, indicates that this expression should be understood differently than *people who see* (*Ran* ibid.).

If רוֹאֵי הַחַמָּה is interpreted as *those visible to the sun*, the addition of the term חַמָּה assumes meaning. While the blind cannot be described as *those who see the sun*, they can be included under *those visible to the sun*. Hence, the addition of the word חַמָּה is taken to indicate that the prohibition includes even the blind, and the phrase רוֹאֵי הַחַמָּה should be understood *as those visible to the sun* (ibid.; *Turei Zahav, Yoreh Deah* 217:30).

The *Gemara* adds that a *neder* directed at *those visible to the sun* does not extend to fish or fetuses. Because the former are covered by water, and the latter by the womb, they are not considered *visible to the sun*.

From the *Gemara's* reasoning, it is evident that if רוֹאֵי הַחַמָּה were interpreted as *those who see the sun*, no legal difference could be found between that expression and simply saying רוֹאִים, *those who see*, without adding *the sun*. *Tosafos* note that this is true with respect to fish, since just as fish can see, they can see the sun. *Turei Zahav* (loc. cit.), based on *Niddah* 30b, contends that the same is true of a fetus. Not only can it see, but it can see the sun while in its mother's womb! *Rashash*, however, disputes this, and maintains that fetuses cannot see at all. They are thus not included in *those who see*, nor in *those who see the sun*.

Tosafos point out that although inanimate objects are *visible to the sun*, they are not included in the *neder*. Even when explained as *those visible to the sun*, the phrase רוֹאֵי הַחַמָּה refers only to things to which vision is relevant. Thus, animals (other than fish) will be prohibited, but inanimate objects will be permitted.

8.

הַנּוֹדֵר מִ,,שְׁחוֹרֵי הָראשׁ" – אָסוּר בַּקֵּרְחִין וּבְבַעֲלֵי שֵׂיבוֹת, — *One who makes a neder prohibiting "dark-headed people" is forbidden [to benefit] from bald people and hoary-haired people,*

The phrase שְׁחוֹרֵי הָראשׁ, *dark-headed people*, might have been construed as referring to people with dark hair on their heads.[1] Obviously, this would exclude people who are bald or

1. [The expression, *dark hair*, is mean to contrast with hair whose color has faded and become gray with age; it is not meant to exclude blond or red hair.]

וּמֻתָּר בַּנָּשִׁים וּבַקְּטַנִּים, שֶׁאֵין נִקְרָאִין שְׂחוֹרֵי
הָרֹאשׁ אֶלָּא אֲנָשִׁים.

[ט] **הַנּוֹדֵר** מִן „הַיִּלוֹדִים" — מֻתָּר בַּנּוֹלָדִים;
מִן „הַנּוֹלָדִים" — אָסוּר בַּיִּלוֹדִים.

─────────── ר׳ עובדיה מברטנורא ───────────

שאין נקראים שחורי הראש אלא אנשים. לפי שהאנשים פעמים מכסים ראשם ופעמים
מגלים ומשחרות ראשם ניכר שהם אנשים, אבל נשים לעולם הולכות וראשם מכוסה, והקטנים בין
זכרים בין נקיבות הולכין בגלוי הראש ואינם ניכרים בין זכר לנקבה, ומשום הכי לא ניקרו שחורי
הראש אלא האנשים הגדולים: (ט) **מן הילודים.** משמע שנולדו כבר: **מן הנולדים.** משמע העתידין

יד אברהם

hoary haired. However, the *Gemara* (30b) explains that had it been the intention of the person to exclude bald and hoary-haired people, he would have used a different expression. Rather than saying שְׂחוֹרֵי הָרֹאשׁ, *dark-headed people*, he would have said בַּעֲלֵי שֵׂעָר שָׁחוֹר, *people with dark hair on their head* (see *Tiferes Yerushalayim*). By selecting the former phrase, the person indicates that he is referring to people who *once* had dark hair (and not to people who currently have dark hair). Understood in this manner, the phrase שְׂחוֹרֵי הָרֹאשׁ, *people who once had dark hair*, includes both bald-headed and hoary-haired people, since both once had dark hair. Therefore, the mishnah states that one who vows not to benefit from שְׂחוֹרֵי הָרֹאשׁ is forbidden to benefit not only from people who currently have dark hair, but from bald-headed and hoary-haired people as well (*Turei Zahav* to *Yoreh Deah* 217:32).

וּמֻתָּר בַּנָּשִׁים וּבַקְּטַנִּים, שֶׁאֵין נִקְרָאִין שְׂחוֹרֵי הָרֹאשׁ אֶלָּא אֲנָשִׁים. — *but he is permitted to [benefit from] women and children, since only [adult] men are called "dark headed."*

Women always covered their heads

and were known as מְכוּסֵי הָרֹאשׁ, *those with covered heads.* Children always went about with their heads uncovered, and were consequently called מְגוּלֵי הָרֹאשׁ, *those with exposed heads.* However, adult men sometimes covered their heads, and sometimes covered their heads, and sometimes did not. They could therefore not be referred to as either *people with covered heads* or *people with exposed heads* and were rather called *dark-headed people* (*Ran* 30b).

[It is unclear what type of head-covering is being discussed here. *Tosafos* (30b, s.v. אנשים) appear to construe it as one that is required by halachah. But, since the *Gemara* describes all adult women as keeping their hair covered, this would not correspond with the contemporary practice of requiring only married women to cover their hair (see *Sheyarei Korban* to *Kesubos* 7:6; *Magen Avraham* to *Orach Chaim* 75:1; *Even HaEzer* 21:2; *Beis Shmuel* ad loc.).

Tiferes Yisrael, however, comments that gentile women, too, covered their hair. Evidently, he understood this to be a matter of custom, rather than one of halachah. Regarding men and boys, covering the head for religious reasons was not a widespread practice in Talmudic times (see *Magen Avraham* loc. cit. 2:6, *Turei Zahav* ibid., 8:3).]

In the case of our mishnah, women

3
9

but he is permitted to [benefit from] women and children, since only [adult] men are called "dark headed."

9. **O**ne who makes a *neder* prohibiting "the *yillodim*" is permitted to [benefit from] those to be born; [if] "the *noladim*" — he is forbidden to [benefit from] those already born.

YAD AVRAHAM

and children are excluded from the *neder*, since the term שְׁחוֹרֵי הָרֹאשׁ (whether in the sense of people whose

hair is currently dark, or those whose hair used to be dark) was used exclusively to refer to adult men (*Rav*).

9.

One of the examples considered in the next mishnah involves a person who forbids himself to enjoy benefits from people not yet born. A *neder* to that effect is binding despite the general rule that a person cannot sanctify something which does not yet exist. While one cannot interdict something not yet in existence to others, he may do so to himself (*Meiri; Yoreh Deah* 204:4, *Beur HaGra* ad loc.).

הַנּוֹדֵר מִן ,,הַיְלוֹדִים'' מְתָּר – בַּנּוֹלָדִים; *One who makes a neder prohibiting "the yillodim" is permitted to [benefit from] those to be born;*

The term *yillod* (pl. *yillodim*) is used in Scripture in two ways. In *Joshua* 5:5, it occurs in the sense of *those already born in the past*. In *Exodus* 1:22, however, it means *those to be born in the future*.

In the case of the mishnah, if one makes a *neder* banning benefit from *yillodim*, he is permitted to enjoy benefit from those to be born in the future. Evidently, only those already born are meant by *yillodim* and, hence, included in the *neder* (*Rav*).

Ran explains that although, in Biblical usage, the term *yillodim* is found with reference to both the past and the future, in popular use, it was confined to describing the past. Thus, when the person made a *neder* to deny himself the benefit of *yillodim*, he was

using the word as it was used by people — namely, to mean *those already born*. He is therefore permitted to benefit from those to be born in the future (*Tos. Yom Tov*).

Some commentators read this word in the mishnah as (יְלוּדִים) "*yeludim.*" This form, even in Biblical usage, occurs only in reference to those already born (see, e.g., *Job* 14:1; *I Chronicles* 14:4). If this reading is adopted, it is no longer necessary to assume that the popular usage of the word differed from its Biblical usage (see *Meiri, Ritva, Nimukei Yosef;* cf. *Chidushei HaGra*).

מִן ,,הַנּוֹלָדִים'' – אָסוּר בַּיְלוֹדִים. *[if] "the noladim" — he is forbidden to [benefit from] those already born.*

[I.e., one who makes a *neder* banning to himself the enjoyment of benefit from ,,נוֹלָדִים'' *(noladim)* is forbidden to benefit from those al-

רַבִּי מֵאִיר מַתִּיר אַף בַּיְלוֹדִים; וַחֲכָמִים אוֹמְרִים:
לֹא נִתְכַּוֵּן זֶה אֶלָּא בְּמִי שֶׁדַּרְכּוֹ לְהוֹלִיד.

―――――――― ר' עובדיה מברטנורא ――――――――

להוליד: מן הנולדים רבי מאיר מתיר אף בילודים. בגמרא (ל, ג) מפרש דחסורי מחסרא
והכי קתני, מן הנולדים אסור בילודים, רבי מאיר אומר אף הנודר מן הנולדים מותר בילודים כי
היכי דהנודר מן הילודים מותר בנולדים: **אלא ממי שדרבו להוליד.** כגון אדם ובהמה,
לאפוקי עופות ודגים שאין מולידים אלא מטילים ביצים:

―――――――――――― **יד אברהם** ――――――――――――

ready born.]

The *Gemara* (30b) notes that the
term נוֹלָד (*nolad*) and its plural form
noladim are found in Scripture referring to those to be born in the future (as
in *I Kings* 13:2), as well as to those
already born in the past (as in *Gen.*
48:5). However, the predominant
meaning apparently is *those to be born
in the future*, and this was true even in
conversational language. The statement of the mishnah that *noladim*
refers to those already born must be
understood as saying that it *also*
includes those already born. In other
words, a *neder* forswearing benefit
from *noladim* will restrict the person
not only from those to be born in the
future, but also those already born in
the past. As will be seen, this is not a
unanimous ruling (*Ran; Tos. Yom Tov*).

רַבִּי מֵאִיר מַתִּיר אַף בַּיְלוֹדִים; — *R' Meir
permits [benefit] even from those
already born;*

The wording of R' Meir's statement
seems to indicate that he permits the
person to benefit from everyone —
not just from those to be born, but
even from those already born. But, if
this is so, then *noladim*, a perfectly
legitimate term, would not include
anyone. It is impossible that this is
what R' Meir means.

Because of this difficulty, the *Gemara* (30b) emends R' Meir's ruling to
read: *Even [one who vows not to have

benefit from noladim] is permitted to
have benefit from those already born.*
In this form, the statement means that
not only does *yillodim* imply a particular tense (viz., past), but so does
noladim (viz., future). R' Meir maintains that in popular usage, the term
noladim was used exclusively to refer
to those to be born in the future.
Hence, the person who made a *neder*
prohibiting benefit from *noladim* is
forbidden to benefit from those to be
born in the future, but permitted to
benefit from those already born (*Ran*).

וַחֲכָמִים אוֹמְרִים: לֹא נִתְכַּוֵּן זֶה אֶלָּא בְּמִי
שֶׁדַּרְכּוֹ לְהוֹלִיד. — *the Sages, however,
say: This [person] referred only to that
which bears offspring.*

The Sages are explaining the previously stated ruling that a *neder*
forswearing benefit from *noladim* applies equally to those to be born and to
those already born. They regard *noladim* to mean species which give birth to
live babies, as opposed to many birds
and fish which lay eggs. People and
most mammals — whether already
born or only to be born in the future
— are all members of such species, and
so, by prohibiting to himself *noladim*,
the person is forbidding benefit from
them (*Rav from Gem. ibid.; Rambam
Commentary*).

According to the standard interpretations, the differing views expressed in the
mishnah are reflections of different assess-

3
9

R' Meir permits [benefit] even from those already born; the Sages, however, say: This [person] referred only to that which bears offspring.

YAD AVRAHAM

ments of how these terms were used in conversation. Thus, R' Meir explains *noladim* to mean *those who will be born in the future*, whereas the Sages explain it to refer to all people (*Ran; Rashi; Tos. Yom Tov*).

Nimukei Yosef finds this approach unsatisfactory. He asserts that if there is a disagreement about the way a word is used, a study should be made to determine the popular usage of the word!

Quoting *Ritva*, he therefore suggests a novel explanation of the dispute between R' Meir and the Sages concerning the connotation of *noladim*. Both agree that, in popular usage, *noladim* is used whether the intention is to those to be born in the future or to those already born in the past. However, its most common meaning is the former.

The mishnah is discussing a case of someone who used the term *noladim* in his *neder*, and subsequently forgot what he had in mind at the time of his *neder*. R' Meir rules that the less common usage may be disregarded, and we can safely assume that the person used *noladim* the way it is most often used — namely, to indicate those to be born in the future. The Sages, however, maintain, that in this case, the less common usage cannot be ignored, because it occurs in the Torah (*Gen.* 48:5). The person therefore becomes prohibited from those already born, following the less-frequent usage of *noladim*. Thus, the Sages forbid the person from all people — those to be born in the future, as well as those already born.

[This interpretation attributes to R' Meir the view that the minority usage may be disregarded, notwithstanding that, in general, R' Meir's position is that the minority must be taken into account (see *Niddah* 31b).]

10.

⋙ The Cutheans (Samaritans)

The Cutheans (or Cuthites) were a nation which was resettled in Samaria by Sennacherib to replace the Jews he had exiled therefrom. Scripture (*II Kings* 17:33) describes them as fearing God, yet worshiping idols at the same time. In an attempt to escape attacks by lions, they converted en masse to Judaism (ibid. 25ff.). Later, however, they may have adopted Judaism for no ulterior motive (*Kiddushin* 75b). Their religious observance was often flawed, because they did not take the oral law into account and concentrated on literal interpretations of the Torah. Nevertheless, those religious rituals which they did observe were followed with attention to even minute details (*Berachos* 47a et al.).

Because of questions about the sincerity of their conversion to Judaism, their halachic status was, for a time, a matter of controversy. Subsequently, the Rabbis discovered that the Cutheans continued to preach pagan beliefs and even maintained an idolatrous house of worship on Mt. Gerizim. It was then unanimously decided that they should be treated in all respects as non-Jews (*Chullin* 6a).

The following mishnah, which appears to treat the Cutheans like Jews, was formulated during the period in which their status was questionable, and follows the opinion that held them to be sincere proselytes (*Meiri; Ritva*).

[י] **הַנּוֹדֵר** מִ„שׁוֹבְתֵי שַׁבָּת" — אָסוּר בְּיִשְׂרָאֵל
וְאָסוּר בַּכּוּתִים; מֵ„אוֹכְלֵי שׁוּם" —
אָסוּר בְּיִשְׂרָאֵל וְאָסוּר בַּכּוּתִים; מֵ„עוֹלֵי יְרוּשָׁלַיִם"
אָסוּר בְּיִשְׂרָאֵל, וּמֻתָּר בַּכּוּתִים.

[יא] **„קוֹנָם** שֶׁאֵינִי נֶהֱנֶה לִבְנֵי נֹחַ" — מֻתָּר
בְּיִשְׂרָאֵל, וְאָסוּר בְּאֻמּוֹת הָעוֹלָם;

ר' עובדיה מברטנורא

(י) מאוכלי שום. אחד מעשר תקנות שתיקן עזרא שיהיו אוכלים שום לילי שבת מפני שמרבים הזרע, וליל שבת הוא זמן עונה של תלמידי חכמים: **ומותר בכותים.** שאינן עולים לרגל, ואף על גב דמדאורייתא הוא, מפני שהם שונאים ירושלים ובחרו להם הר גריזים: **(יא) מותר בישראל.** שילאו מכלל בני נח: **ואסור באומות העולם.** ואפילו באותם שהם מזרע אברהם:

יד אברהם

**הַנּוֹדֵר מִ„שׁוֹבְתֵי שַׁבָּת" — אָסוּר בְּיִשְׂרָאֵל
וְאָסוּר בַּכּוּתִים;** — *One who makes a neder prohibiting "those who rest on the Sabbath" is forbidden to [benefit from] Jews and forbidden to [benefit from] Cutheans;*

The *Gemara* (31a) notes that *those who rest on the Sabbath* refers to people commanded by the Torah to do so. Thus, a gentile — even if he were to rest on the Sabbath — would not be included, since he is not obligated to do so. However, Cutheans are treated by this mishnah like full proselytes (see preface) and are thus commanded to observe the Sabbath. They, along with all other Jews, are thus the subjects of this *neder* (*Tos. Yom Tov*).

מֵ„אוֹכְלֵי שׁוּם"– — *[if] "those who eat garlic"* —

This refers to the regulation introduced by Ezra that married men should eat garlic on Friday evening (*Bava Kamma* 82a; see 8:6). The *Gemara* designates Friday night as the time for a Torah scholar to fulfill his conjugal duties (*Kesubos* 62b). Since garlic was regarded as enhanc-

ing a man's potency, Ezra enacted that it be eaten Friday evenings (*Rav* from *Bava Kamma* ibid.). *Meiri* adds that Torah scholars, weakened by their constant exertion, were in need of something to strengthen them.

Tos. Yom Tov notes with puzzlement that *Rambam* omits this case of the mishnah from *Mishneh Torah*. In fact, he fails to record even Ezra's basic law that garlic be eaten Friday night. Evidently, *Rambam* regarded Ezra's enactment as applying only to his own generation, and not subsequently (*Rashash*; see *Rambam Commentary* 8:4).

אָסוּר בְּיִשְׂרָאֵל וְאָסוּר בַּכּוּתִים; — *he is forbidden to [benefit from] Jews and forbidden to [benefit from] Cutheans;*

This reading implies that the Cutheans, too, adhered to Ezra's enactment. Although, in general, they were only careful in the observance of Biblical law, they evidently found his regulation to their liking (*Tos. Yom Tov*).

Beis Yosef (*Yoreh Deah* 217) mentions a variant text which reads וּמֻתָּר בַּכּוּתִים, *he is permitted to [benefit from] Cutheans*. This version assumes that the latter did not follow Ezra's enact-

10. One who makes a *neder* prohibiting "those who rest on the Sabbath" is forbidden to [benefit from] Jews and forbidden to [benefit from] Cutheans; [if] "those who eat garlic" — he is forbidden to [benefit from] Jews and forbidden to [benefit from] Cutheans; [if] "the pilgrims to Jerusalem" — he is forbidden to [benefit from] Jews, but permitted to [benefit from] Cutheans.

11. [If one says:] "*Konam* what I benefit from the descendants of Noah" — he is permitted to [benefit from] Jews, but is forbidden to [benefit from] gentiles; "[*Konam*]

YAD AVRAHAM

ment. *Tiferes Yisrael* quotes *Karmei Shomron*, who relates that the Cutheans did not engage in marital relations on the Sabbath, as they considered this to be a violation of *You shall not kindle a fire ... on the Sabbath* (*Ex.* 35:3). Obviously, if they refrained from cohabitation on the Sabbath, they did not follow Ezra's rule.

מֵ,,עוֹלֵי יְרוּשָׁלַיִם" – אָסוּר בְּיִשְׂרָאֵל, וּמֻתָּר בַּכּוּתִים. — *[if] the "pilgrims to Jerusalem" — he is forbidden to [benefit from] Jews, but permitted to [benefit from] Cutheans.*

The Torah obligates Jews to appear at the Temple in Jerusalem on the three festivals: Pesach, Shavuos, and Succos. The Cutheans, however, did not revere the Temple in Jerusalem. Rather, they had a private sanctuary (later discovered to be idolatrous) on Mt. Gerizim. Since they did not participate in the triannual pilgrimage to Jerusalem, they were not included in the designation *pilgrims to Jerusalem* (*Rav; Rambam; Rosh*).

11.

,,קוֹנָם, שֶׁאֵינִי נֶהֱנֶה לִבְנֵי נֹחַ" – מֻתָּר בְּיִשְׂרָאֵל, וְאָסוּר בְּאֻמּוֹת הָעוֹלָם; — *[If one says:] "Konam what I benefit from the descendants* (lit., *children*) *of Noah" — he is permitted to [benefit from] Jews, but is forbidden to [benefit from] gentiles* (lit., *the nations of the world*);

[Regarding the term שֶׁאֲנִי (which is the version of the mishnah in the Talmud), see comm. to 1:1.]

Because Noah and his family were the only humans spared in the Great Flood (*Gen.* 7:23), all mankind is descended from Noah.

However, Abraham was singled out by God from the rest of humanity and endowed with a special sanctity, which was eventually transferred to the entire Jewish nation. The unique relationship between God and the Jewish people is thus directly trace-

„שֶׁאֵינִי נֶהֱנֶה לְזֶרַע אַבְרָהָם" — אָסוּר בְּיִשְׂרָאֵל,
וּמֻתָּר בְּאֻמּוֹת הָעוֹלָם. „שֶׁאֵינִי נֶהֱנֶה לְיִשְׂרָאֵל" —
לוֹקֵחַ בְּיוֹתֵר וּמוֹכֵר בְּפָחוֹת; „שֶׁיִּשְׂרָאֵל נֶהֱנִין לִי"
— לוֹקֵחַ בְּפָחוֹת וּמוֹכֵר בְּיוֹתֵר, אִם שׁוֹמְעִין לוֹ;

ר' עובדיה מברטנורא

אסור בישראל. וגרים נמי בכלל זרע אברהם נינהו דכתיב (בראשית יז, ה) כי אב המון גוים
נתתיך: **ומותר באומות העולם.** ואפילו באומות שהם מזרע אברהם, דלא אקרו זרע אברהם
אלא בני יעקב בלבד דכתיב (שם כא, יב) כי ביצחק יקרא לך זרע ביצחק ולא כל יצחק: **שאיני
נהנה לישראל.** משל ישראל: שאין ישראל נהנים לי. משלי: **ומוכר ביתר.** משל: אם שומעין לו
גרסינן. כלומר ימכור הדבר ביותר מכדי שויו אם ירצה חבירו לשמוע לו ולקנות ממנו החפץ
ביותר ממה שוה:

יד אברהם

able to Abraham. Hence, the Jews are
considered to descend from Abraham
(and not Noah), inasmuch as the
spiritual uniqueness of the Jews began
with Abraham. The term *descendants
of Noah*, therefore, refers solely to the
gentiles (*Ran* from *Gem.* 31a).

All non-Jews, even those who are biolog-
ical descendants of Abraham, such as
Ishmael and Esau, are described as *descendants of Noah* (*Rav*). This is because the
spiritual character with which Abraham
was endowed was conferred only upon
Isaac, not Ishmael; and upon Jacob, not
Esau [see below] (*Gem.* ibid.).

„שֶׁאֵינִי נֶהֱנֶה לְזֶרַע אַבְרָהָם" — אָסוּר
בְּיִשְׂרָאֵל, וּמֻתָּר בְּאֻמּוֹת הָעוֹלָם.
*"[Konam] what I benefit from the
progeny of Abraham"* — he is forbidden to [benefit from] Jews, but is
permitted to [benefit from] gentiles.

The *progeny of Abraham* refers to
Jews only. This is evident from the
fact that Abraham was informed by
God that his progeny would be slaves
(*Gen.* 15:13). Since it was only the
children of Jacob who were slaves in
Egypt, only they are the *progeny of
Abraham* (*Rambam Comm.*). The *Ge-
mara* (31b) notes further that God said

to Abraham, *for from Isaac shall be
your progeny* (ibid. 21:12). This indicates that only Isaac — not Ishmael
— merits the title *progeny of Abraham*. The extra word in the phrase *for
from Isaac* implies that not all of
Isaac's children will receive this title.
Thus, only Jacob and his family, and
not Esau, are the *progeny of Abraham*.

By forbidding himself benefit from
the *progeny of Abraham*, the person is
thus restricting himself from Jews
only and not gentiles.

Converts to Judaism, though not
biologically descended from Jacob,
would still be considered *progeny of
Abraham*. This is derived from the
verse (ibid. 17:5) *I have made you a
father to masses of nations*, which is
construed to refer to those who
abandoned the culture of their particular people and embraced the mono-
theism preached by Abraham; i.e.,
Judaism (see *Yerushalmi Bikkurim
1:4, Rambam Comm.* ibid.). Thus,
Abraham is the spiritual father of all
converts to Judaism and so, even a
proselyte is considered *progeny of
Abraham* (*Rav*).

what I benefit from the progeny of Abraham" —
he is forbidden to [benefit from] Jews, but is
permitted to [benefit from] gentiles. "[Konam]
what I benefit from Jews" — he must buy for
more, and sell for less; "[Konam] what Jews
benefit from me" — he must buy for less and
sell for more, if they listen to him; "[Konam]

YAD AVRAHAM

◆§ Who benefits from a transaction

The *Gemara* (31) classifies merchandise into three types, depending on the demand for the item. These are: (a) things very much in demand; (b) things for which the demand is average; and (c) things for which demand is poor.

When an item of average marketability is sold for a fair price, both the seller and the buyer are said to have enjoyed a benefit from each other through the purchase. When something is sold at a higher price than what is considered fair, the seller is said to have derived benefit from the purchaser, but not vice versa. Similarly, in a sale of an item at a reduced price, the buyer has benefited the seller, but not vice versa (*Ran* 31b).

If an article for which the demand is high is sold at a fair price, it is considered to be a benefit enjoyed by the buyer. Similarly, if an item for which there is little demand is sold for a fair price, it is regarded as a benefit derived by the seller from the buyer (ibid.).

The case of the mishnah deals with an item for which the demand is average (*Gem.* 31b).

שָׁאֵינִי נֶהֱנֶה לְיִשְׂרָאֵל" – לוֹקֵחַ בְּיוֹתֵר
וּמוֹכֵר בְּפָחוֹת; — "[Konam] what I
benefit from Jews" — he must buy
for more, and sell for less;

Someone makes a *neder* prohibiting himself from deriving benefit from *all* Jews. If he should then wish to purchase from a Jew an item of average marketability, he will have to pay more than the market price, so that only the seller will benefit. Were he to pay a fair price or a reduced price, he would be deriving benefit from another Jew, which is prohibited by his *neder*.

If he should want to sell to a Jew an item of average demand, he must sell it for a reduced price; otherwise, he will be violating his *neder* by deriving

benefit from another Jew (*Ran*; *Tos. Yom Tov*).

He would, however, be permitted to buy a poorly marketable item from — or sell a highly marketable item to — another Jew for the fair market price since, in neither case, will he be gaining a benefit from the other person (ibid.; *Yoreh Deah* 227:1).

[For further elucidation of this subject, see commentary to 4:6, s.v. וְלֹא יִמְכֹּר לוֹ.]

שֶׁיִּשְׂרָאֵל נֶהֱנִין לִי" – לוֹקֵחַ בְּפָחוֹת וּמוֹכֵר
בְּיוֹתֵר, אִם שׁוֹמְעִין לוֹ; — "[Konam] what
Jews benefit from me" — he must buy
for less and sell for more, if they listen
to him;

In this case, his *neder* made it

„שֶׁאֵינִי נֶהֱנֶה לָהֶן, וְהֵן לִי״ — יֵהָנֶה לַנָּכְרִים.
„קוֹנָם שֶׁאֵינִי נֶהֱנֶה לָעֲרֵלִים״ מֻתָּר
בְּעַרְלֵי יִשְׂרָאֵל, וְאָסוּר בְּמוּלֵי הָאֻמּוֹת;
„קוֹנָם שֶׁאֵינִי נֶהֱנֶה לַמּוּלִים״ — אָסוּר
בְּעַרְלֵי יִשְׂרָאֵל, וּמֻתָּר בְּמוּלֵי הָאֻמּוֹת, שֶׁאֵין
הָעָרְלָה קְרוּיָה אֶלָּא לְשֵׁם הַגּוֹיִם, שֶׁנֶּאֱמַר „כִּי
כָל הַגּוֹיִם עֲרֵלִים וְכָל בֵּית יִשְׂרָאֵל עַרְלֵי לֵב״,

ר' עובדיה מברטנורא

לערלים. דעתו על מי שאינו מאמין בברית מילה: **למולים.** המאמינים בברית מילה: **מותר בערלי ישראל.** כגון מי שמתו אחיו מחמת מילה: **ואסור במולי אומות.** כגון ערבי מהול וגבעוני מהול:

יד אברהם

forbidden for any Jew to derive benefit from him. Therefore, any sales or purchase he transacts with Jews must be such that *they* do not derive benefit from him. With respect to merchandise for which the demand is average, this means that if he buys something from a Jew, he must pay *less* than the fair market price. If he sells such an item to a Jew, he must sell it for *more* than the fair price (ibid.).

Obviously, nobody will want to do business with someone who overcharges and underpays, and so, this person will be unable to buy or sell to Jews, unless he finds someone willing to accept his terms. Hence, the mishnah adds — *if they listen to him* (Rav).

שֶׁאֵינִי נֶהֱנֶה לָהֶן, וְהֵן לִי״ – יֵהָנֶה לַנָּכְרִים. — *"[Konam] what I benefit from them, and they from me"* — *he may benefit gentiles.*

This refers to a *neder* which prevents him from benefiting from all other Jews, and vice versa.

Such a *neder* precludes the possibility of selling to a Jew any type of merchandise at any price, or buying it from him. In all transactions, either the buyer or seller benefits, and by the terms of the *neder*, this would be prohibited. The only ones with whom he could do business are non-Jews (*Rav*).

Ran (31a) quotes *Ra'ah*, who points out that a *neder* which is impossible to observe is not binding (see commentary to 2:1, s.v. שְׁבוּעָה, שֶׁאֵינִי יָשֵׁן — *Shevuah, that I shall not sleep*). Nevertheless, a *neder* which makes it impossible to deal with Jews is *not* considered impossible to keep, since the person can deal with non-Jews (*Tos. Yom Tov*).

Tiferes Yisrael reflects on the seemingly odd wording of the mishnah יֵהָנֶה לַנָּכְרִים, *he may benefit gentiles*, rather than לוֹקֵחַ וּמוֹכֵר לַנָּכְרִים, *he can buy and sell to gentiles.* He sees this as alluding to a situation in which the Jews, whether buying or selling, will *always* be benefiting the non-Jew. In other words, he will be overcharged by the non-Jew for what he buys, and underpaid for what he sells.

קוֹנָם, שֶׁאֵינִי נֶהֱנֶה לָעֲרֵלִים״ – מֻתָּר בְּעַרְלֵי יִשְׂרָאֵל, וְאָסוּר בְּמוּלֵי הָאֻמּוֹת; *[If one says:]"Konam what I benefit from 'the uncircumcised' "* — *he is per-*

what I benefit from them, and they from me" —
he may benefit gentiles.

[If one says:] "*Konam* what I benefit from 'the
uncircumcised' " — he is permitted to [benefit
from] uncircumcised Jews, but forbidden to
[benefit from] circumcised gentiles; "*Konam* what
I benefit from 'the circumcised' " — he is
forbidden [to benefit] from uncircumcised Jews,
but is permitted to [benefit from] circumcised
gentiles, for the term *orlah* is used only as a general
name for gentiles, as it says: *For all the nations
are uncircumcised, and the whole house of Israel
are uncircumcised in the heart (Jeremiah 9:25),*

YAD AVRAHAM

*mitted to [benefit from] uncircumcised
Jews, but forbidden to [benefit from]
circumcised gentiles;*

The term עֲרֵלִים, *areilim* (lit., *uncircumcised persons;* sing. עָרֵל, *areil*), is
used to refer to non-Jews, regardless of
whether or not they happen to be
circumcised. On the other hand, a Jew
— even if not circumcised — is not
referred to as an *areil.* [Some maintain
that this is true only if the Jew is
uncircumcised through no fault of his
own. But one who willfully neglects
his circumcision is indeed describable
as an *areil;* see *Meiri.*]

In the case of the mishnah, a *neder*
banning benefit from *areilim* amounts
to banning benefit from non-Jews
(*Avodah Zarah* 27a).

קוֹנָם שֶׁאֵינִי נֶהֱנֶה לְ׳מוּלִים׳ ״ – אָסוּר
בְּעַרְלֵי יִשְׂרָאֵל, וּמֻתָּר בְּמוּלֵי הָאֻמּוֹת,
*"Konam what I benefit from 'the
circumcised' " — he is forbidden to
[benefit from] uncircumcised Jews, but
is permitted to [benefit from] circumcised gentiles,*

The term מוּלִים, *mulim* (circumcised

persons), is used only to connote Jews,
and even an uncircumcised Jew is
referred to with this term. By making
a *neder* prohibiting benefit from
mulim, the person has restricted himself from Jews only, for non-Jews are
never referred to as *mulim,* even if
they are circumcised (ibid.).

שֶׁאֵין הָעָרְלָה קְרוּיָה אֶלָּא לְשֵׁם הַגּוֹיִם, —
*for the term orlah is used only as a
general name for gentiles,*

[The mishnah proceeds to establish
from Scripture that, indeed, the term
areil is used only to describe non-Jews.]

Regarding *nedarim,* the meaning of
a word in a popular usage is the
decisive one, not its Biblical meaning.
Nevertheless, where the popular
meaning can be supported from Scripture, the mishnah does not hesitate to
do so (*Tos.* to *Yevamos* 71a, s.v. והני).

שֶׁנֶּאֱמַר ״כִּי כָל הַגּוֹיִם עֲרֵלִים, וְכָל בֵּית
יִשְׂרָאֵל עַרְלֵי לֵב״, — *as it says: For all
the nations are uncircumcised, and the
whole house of Israel are uncircumcised in the heart (Jeremiah 9:25),*

In this verse, the gentile nations are

וְאוֹמֵר: ,,וְהָיָה הַפְּלִשְׁתִּי הֶעָרֵל הַזֶּה ...״, וְאוֹמֵר:
,,פֶּן תִּשְׂמַחְנָה בְּנוֹת פְּלִשְׁתִּים, פֶּן תַּעֲלֹזְנָה בְּנוֹת
הָעֲרֵלִים״.

רַבִּי אֶלְעָזָר בֶּן עֲזַרְיָה אוֹמֵר, מְאוּסָה הָעָרְלָה,
שֶׁנִּתְגַּנּוּ בָהּ הָרְשָׁעִים, שֶׁנֶּאֱמַר, ,,כִּי כָל הַגּוֹיִם
עֲרֵלִים״.

רַבִּי יִשְׁמָעֵאל אוֹמֵר: גְּדוֹלָה מִילָה, שֶׁנִּכְרְתוּ
עָלֶיהָ שָׁלֹשׁ עֶשְׂרֵה בְּרִיתוֹת.

רַבִּי יוֹסֵי אוֹמֵר: גְּדוֹלָה מִילָה, שֶׁדּוֹחָה אֶת
הַשַּׁבָּת הַחֲמוּרָה.

───────── ר׳ עובדיה מברטנורא ─────────

שלש עשרה בריתות. נאמרו בפרשת מילה שנאמרה לאברהם: **שהיא דוחה את השבת.**
דכתיב (ויקרא יב, ג) וביום השמיני ימול בשר ערלתו ואפילו בשבת:

יד אברהם

described as *areilim* (uncircumcised).
Yet, the above statement that this term
applies only to non-Jews might be
refuted by the end of the verse in
which the Jews are called *arlei lev* —
those with *uncircumcised* (i.e., stuffed-
up [*Metzudas Tzion* ad loc.]) *hearts*, in
not obeying God's will (*Metzudas
David* ad loc.). This might lead us to
believe that the term *areilim*, used in
the verse with respect to gentiles, also
means *arlei lev*. If that were so, we
would not be able to infer anything
about the term *areilim* by itself.

To prevent this confusion, the
mishnah adduces a proof from another verse in which the term *areil*
cannot be interpreted as *areil lev*, but
has the regular meaning of *an uncircumcised person* (*Tos. Yom Tov*
from *Rav*).

וְאוֹמֵר: ,,וְהָיָה הַפְּלִשְׁתִּי הֶעָרֵל הַזֶּה...״, —
*and it says: "And this uncircumcised
Philstine shall be ..."* (I Samuel 17:36),

In this verse, King David refers to
the Philistine, Goliath, as an *areil*, an
uncircumcised person. He does so
although Goliath could conceivably
have been born without a foreskin
and would then — strictly speaking
— be circumcised. Evidently, a non-
Jew can be referred to as an *areil*,
regardless of his physical condition.

One might counter that David
called him thus only because it was
highly unlikely that Goliath appeared
to be born without a foreskin. Consequently, this does not prove that a
gentile known to be circumcised is
nevertheless called an *areil* (ibid.).

For this reason, the mishnah cites
yet another verse:

וְאוֹמֵר: ,,פֶּן תִּשְׂמַחְנָה בְּנוֹת פְּלִשְׁתִּים, פֶּן
תַּעֲלֹזְנָה בְּנוֹת הָעֲרֵלִים״. — *and it says:
"Lest the daughters of the Philistines
rejoice, lest the daughters of the
uncircumcised be jubilant"* (II Samuel
1:20).

and it says: *And this uncircumcised Philistine shall be ... (I Samuel* 17:36), and it says: *Lest the daughters of the Philistines rejoice, lest the daughters of the uncircumcised be jubilant (II Samuel* 1:20).

R' Elazar ben Azariah says: Detestable is the foreskin, for with it the wicked are disparaged, as it says: *For all the nations are uncircumcised (Jeremiah* 9:25).

R' Yishmael says: Great is circumcision, for concerning it thirteen covenants were made.

R' Yose says: Great is circumcision which overrides the strict Sabbath.

YAD AVRAHAM

Here, the entire Philistine nation is described as *areilim* (uncircumcised). Surely, an entire nation very likely includes some who are circumcised, yet Scripture calls all of them *areilim*. Clearly, *areil* is a term used to refer to all non-Jews (ibid.).

רַבִּי אֶלְעָזָר בֶּן עֲזַרְיָה אוֹמֵר: מְאוּסָה הָעָרְלָה, שֶׁנִּתְגַּנּוּ בָהּ הָרְשָׁעִים, שֶׁנֶּאֱמַר: ,,כִּי כָל הַגּוֹיִם עֲרֵלִים.'' — *R' Elazar ben Azariah says: Detestable is the foreskin, for with it the wicked are disparaged, as it says: "For all the nations are uncircumcised" (Jeremiah* 9:25).

[The fact that the term *areil* (uncircumcised person) is reserved for reference to non-Jews shows how uncharacteristic it is for a Jew to be uncircumcised. In that vein, the chapter closes with a series of sayings praising the precept of circumcision.]

רַבִּי יִשְׁמָעֵאל אוֹמֵר: גְּדוֹלָה מִילָה, שֶׁנִּכְרְתוּ עָלֶיהָ שָׁלֹשׁ עֶשְׂרֵה בְּרִיתוֹת. — *R' Yishmael says: Great is circumcision, for concerning it thirteen covenants were made.*

This refers to the thirteen times that the word בְּרִית, *bris*, recurs in the Biblical section containing the commandment of circumcision. *Rambam*

counts the thirteen times from *Genesis* 17:1-22. However, from *Yerushalmi* it appears that the count should begin from 15:18. Evidently, *Yerushalmi* does not include one of the thirteen occurrences of the word *bris* in Chapter 17. *Meiri* omits בְּרִית עוֹלָם, *eternal covenant*, which occurs in 17:19, although it is not clear why it should be eliminated (see *Sheyarei Korban* to *Yerushalmi*).

Tos. Yom Tov suggests that the thirteen covenants correspond to the thirteen attributes of God listed in *Exodus* 34:6ff. We are taught that a prayer which incorporates these attributes cannot be ineffective; similarly, performing the commandment of circumcision must have a positive effect.

רַבִּי יוֹסֵי אוֹמֵר: גְּדוֹלָה מִילָה, שֶׁדּוֹחָה אֶת הַשַּׁבָּת הַחֲמוּרָה. — *R' Yose says: Great is circumcision which overrides the strict Sabbath.*

If the day a baby boy is to be circumcised — the eighth day of his life — falls on the Sabbath, the circumcision is performed then. This is derived from the verse, *On the eighth day his foreskin shall be cir-*

רַבִּי יְהוֹשֻׁעַ בֶּן קָרְחָה אוֹמֵר: גְּדוֹלָה מִילָה, שֶׁלֹּא נִתְלָה לוֹ לְמֹשֶׁה הַצַּדִּיק עָלֶיהָ מְלֹא שָׁעָה. רַבִּי נְחֶמְיָה אוֹמֵר: גְּדוֹלָה מִילָה, שֶׁדּוֹחָה אֶת הַנְּגָעִים.

רַבִּי אוֹמֵר: גְּדוֹלָה מִילָה, שֶׁכָּל הַמִּצְוֹת שֶׁעָשָׂה אַבְרָהָם אָבִינוּ — לֹא נִקְרָא „שָׁלֵם", עַד שֶׁמָּל, שֶׁנֶּאֱמַר: „הִתְהַלֵּךְ לְפָנַי וֶהְיֵה תָמִים". דָּבָר אַחֵר, גְּדוֹלָה מִילָה, שֶׁאִלְמָלֵא הִיא — לֹא בָרָא הַקָּדוֹשׁ בָּרוּךְ הוּא אֶת עוֹלָמוֹ, שֶׁנֶּאֱמַר: „כֹּה אָמַר יְיָ: אִם לֹא בְרִיתִי יוֹמָם וָלָיְלָה, חֻקּוֹת שָׁמַיִם וָאָרֶץ לֹא שָׂמְתִּי".

ר' עובדיה מברטנורא

שהיא דוחה את הנגעים. דדרשינן (שבת קלב, ב) ימול ואפילו במקום בהרת, ואין כאן משום קוץ בהרתו שהוא בלאו דהשמר בנגע הצרעת (דברים כד, ח):

יד אברהם

cumcised (*Lev.* 12:3), which is exegetically interpreted to mean *on the eighth day* — even if it is the Sabbath (*Rav* from *Shabbos* 131b). (However, if — for some reason — the circumcision was postponed past the eighth day, it may not be done on the Sabbath (*Rambam, Hil. Milah* 1:9; *Yoreh Deah* 266:2).

רַבִּי יְהוֹשֻׁעַ בֶּן קָרְחָה אוֹמֵר: גְּדוֹלָה מִילָה, שֶׁלֹּא נִתְלָה לוֹ לְמֹשֶׁה הַצַּדִּיק עָלֶיהָ מְלֹא שָׁעָה. — R' Yehoshua ben Korchah *says: Great is circumcision, for concerning it even Moses, the righteous one, was not spared for one hour.*

Moses, en route to Egypt, was accosted by an angel for not having attended to the circumcision of his sons (see *Exodus* 4:24ff.). The *Gemara* (32a) explains that when he arrived at the camping site, he first set up his quarters when he should have first circumcised his sons. It was for this

short delay that he was punished. From this incident, we learn the great importance of circumcision, for even someone as righteous as Moses was punished because of a slight delay in fulfilling it.

רַבִּי נְחֶמְיָה אוֹמֵר: גְּדוֹלָה מִילָה, שֶׁדּוֹחָה אֶת הַנְּגָעִים. — R' Nechemiah *says: Great is circumcision which overrides* negaim.

Negaim (sing. *nega*) are assorted growths, described in *Leviticus* 13ff., which cause a person to be in a state of ritual uncleanness. Ordinarily, it is forbidden to remove these growths. But, if a child or adult who is to be circumcised should develop one on the foreskin, the commandment of circumcision prevails over the prohibition against removing the *nega*. This applies even when the circumcision is not performed on the eighth day. Thus, R' Nechemiah adds that even

R' Yehoshua ben Korchah says: Great is circumcision, for concerning it even Moses, the righteous one, was not spared for one hour.

R' Nechemiah says: Great is circumcision which overrides *negaim*.

Rabbi says: Great is circumcision, for [despite] all the precepts which our forefathers Abraham fulfilled, he was not called "complete" until he circumcised [himself], as it says: *"Walk before Me and be perfect"* (Genesis 17:1).

Another thing: Great is circumcision, for if not for it the Holy One — Blessed is He — would not have created His world, as it says: *"So says Hashem: If not for My covenant day and night, the laws of heaven and earth I would not have put [in place]"* (Jeremiah 33:25).

YAD AVRAHAM

a circumcision which is not performed on time is great (*Maharsha*).

רַבִּי אוֹמֵר: גְּדוֹלָה מִילָה, שֶׁכָּל הַמִּצְוֹת שֶׁעָשָׂה אַבְרָהָם אָבִינוּ – לֹא נִקְרָא ,,שָׁלֵם" עַד שֶׁמָּל, שֶׁנֶּאֱמַר: ,,הִתְהַלֵּךְ לְפָנַי וֶהְיֵה תָמִים". — *Rabbi says: Great is circumcision, for [despite] all the precepts which our forefather Abraham fulfilled, he was not called "complete" until he circumcised [himself], as it says: "Walk before Me and be perfect"* (Genesis 17:1).

The verse following this one is *I will set my covenant between Me and you,* which refers to circumcision. Thus, to *walk before Me* refers to circumcision, and, by fulfilling this commandment, Abraham was *perfect* (*Gem.* 32a). *Tos. Yom Tov*, who offers a different explanation, apparently overlooked this *Gemara* (*Rashash*).

דָּבָר אַחֵר: גְּדוֹלָה מִילָה, שֶׁאִלְמָלֵא הִיא – לֹא

בָּרָא הַקָּדוֹשׁ בָּרוּךְ הוּא אֶת עוֹלָמוֹ, שֶׁנֶּאֱמַר: ,,כֹּה אָמַר ה': ,,אִם לֹא בְרִיתִי יוֹמָם וָלָיְלָה, חֻקּוֹת שָׁמַיִם וָאָרֶץ לֹא שָׂמְתִּי". — *Another thing: Great is circumcision, for if not for it the Holy One — Blessed is He — would not have created His world, as it says: "So says HASHEM: If not for My covenant day and night, the laws of heaven and earth I would not have put [in place]"* (Jeremiah 33:25).

In context, this verse refers to the laws of nature. God states that just as the natural laws, such as the cycles of day and night, do not cease, so too His affection for the Jewish people will not cease. He will restore them to the Land of Israel and to their former glory (*Rashi ad loc.*).

The *Tanna* exegetically interprets the verse to indicate that, if not for the covenant of circumcision, the world would not have been created (ibid.).

פרק רביעי &

Chapter Four

[א] אֵין בֵּין הַמֻּדָּר הֲנָאָה מֵחֲבֵרוֹ לַמֻּדָּר הֵימֶנּוּ מַאֲכָל, אֶלָּא דְרִיסַת הָרֶגֶל

—————— ר' עובדיה מברטנורא ——————

פרק רביעי – אין בין המודר. (א) אין בין מודר. אלא דריסת הרגל. לעבור דרך ארצו או להשאיל כלים שאין עושין בהם אוכל נפש, שמותרין במודר הימנו מאכל ואסורין במודר הימנו הנאה:

יד אברהם

1.

The following mishnah contrasts the restrictions that apply to someone who is prohibited by a *neder* from enjoying general benefits from another with the restrictions which affect someone prohibited only from food-related benefits.

אֵין בֵּין הַמֻּדָּר הֲנָאָה מֵחֲבֵרוֹ — *There are no [differences] between someone prohibited by a neder to benefit from another* Shulchan Aruch (*Yoreh Deah* 221:1) explains this to mean that a person (e.g., Reuven) forbade the benefit of his property to another (Shimon) by declaring: "*Konam*, benefit from my property to you." Thus, Shimon is forbidden to derive benefit from Reuven's property, but is apparently not forbidden to benefit from Reuven himself.

Shalmei Nedarim adds that this mishnah cannot be discussing declarations forbidding benefit from a person — as opposed to his property — since, in that case, the mishnah would be making a serious omission. For example, someone forbidden to benefit in general from a person is prohibited to sleep with him in the same bed or bathe with him in the same bed or bathe with him in a pool (see mishnah 4). But someone restricted only from deriving food-related benefits from a person would be allowed to share a bed or bath with him. Why, then, does our mishnah — which lists the differences between a general prohibition and one limited to food-related benefits — not list this example? If we assume, however, that our mishnah is dealing only with declarations prohibiting benefit

from someone's property, this difficulty is solved. The benefit enjoyed when sharing a bath or a bed is not from the other person's property, but from the person himself. If they are bathing in a small pool, when one of them moves, he causes water to flow over the other one, thereby benefiting him; if they sleep in one bed during the winter each makes it warmer for the other (see commentary ibid.). Consequently, it has no relevance to our mishnah, which is concerned with a *neder* banning the derivation of benefit from property.

It is interesting to note that *R' Akiva Eiger* does not seem to interpret the mishnah this way. The *Gemara* (32b) attributes our mishnah to *R' Eliezer*, who maintains that a person who makes a *neder* forbidding himself to benefit from another may not even enjoy benefits which are ordinarily regarded to be worthless (an example of which is give below, s.v. אֶלָּא). In his *Tos. R' Akiva* to 5:1, *R' Akiva Eiger* establishes that those who dispute *R' Eliezer* and consider negligible benefits to be permitted disagree only about a *neder* which forbids having benefit from the person. But, with respect to a *neder* which outlaws benefiting from a *thing*, everyone agrees that even "worthless" benefits are forbidden. Since, as men-tioned, the *Gemara* attributes our mishnah to *R' Eliezer* alone, it follows that the mishnah must be dealing with a *neder* forbidding benefit from

1. **T**here are no [differences] between someone prohibited by a *neder* to benefit from another and someone prohibited by a *neder* to derive food-related benefits from him, except for treading by foot

YAD AVRAHAM

the person, not from his property. Furthermore, as *Shalmei Nedarim* notes, *Pnei Yehoshua* to *Megillah* 8a clearly interprets our mishnah as referring to such a *neder*.

[In the course of the chapter, the distinction between a *neder* banning enjoyment of benefit from the person and a *neder* banning derivation of benefit from his property will become clearer. At this point, however, suffice it to say that if Shimon is forbidden to benefit from Reuven, the person, he may not use Reuven's property. Although the *neder* does not imbue Reuven's property with a forbidden status vis-a-vis Shimon, use of the property amounts to a benefit from Reuven who owns it. On the other hand, if only Reuven's *property* is forbidden by the *neder*, then benefit from Reuven himself (such as sharing a bath, as mentioned above) is permitted. See, however, *Turei Zahav* to *Yoreh Deah* 221:16, who attempts to equate these two types of *nedarim* (cf. *Chidushei R' Akiva Eiger* ibid.).]

לַמֻּדָּר הֵימֶנּוּ מַאֲכָל, — *and someone prohibited by a neder to derive food-related benefits from him,*

A food-related benefit in the context of this mishnah is any benefit which can lead to food. Thus, for example, it would be forbidden for Shimon to receive money from Reuven, since money can be used to purchase food (*Meiri; Ritva*). Similarly, anything used to assist in the preparation of food is considered to lead to eating. Consequently, as will be seen, all sorts of utensils used in food preparation will be prohibited for Shimon's use (*Ritva*).

The precise *neder* under consideration here is explained by the *Gemara* (33a) to be: "Any benefit from you which leads to food

shall be *konam* to me." An alternative formula, "The benefit from your food is *konam* to me," is rejected by the *Gemara*, since that declaration would not forbid pots and pans, for example, and the *neder* of the mishnah clearly does.

The expression, *benefit from food*, which presumably encompasses more than just eating, would forbid benefits that are attainable without eating. For example, to take chewed grain and place it on a wound as a salve is a benefit from grain itself that does not involve eating (*Ran*).

At first, *Rav* explains the *neder* being discussed in the mishnah to be the one rejected by the *Gemara*. Although he subsequently seems to correct this, citing the accepted version, it is strange that he should mention the wrong version altogether (*Tos. Yom Tov*). [In addition, *Rambam*, in his *Commentary*, mentions only the *neder* rejected by the *Gemara*. Obviously, the matter requires further study.]

אֶלָּא דְּרִיסַת הָרֶגֶל — *except for treading by foot*

The difference between one forbidden by a *neder* to benefit from another and one forbidden to desire food-related benefits from him is that, in the former case, Shimon, who is prohibited to benefit from Reuven, may not walk across Reuven's property. This prohibition is binding even with regard to property which Reuven generally leaves open, and which he allows people to walk across (*Ran; Tos.*). Although traversing such property might be considered a "worthless" benefit, since it is available to all at no cost, the mishnah follows the opinion of R' Eliezer, who maintains that even benefits to which

וְכֵלִים שֶׁאֵין עוֹשִׂין בָּהֶן אֹכֶל נֶפֶשׁ.
הַמֻּדָּר מַאֲכָל מֵחֲבֵרוֹ — לֹא יַשְׁאִילֶנּוּ נָפָה
וּכְבָרָה וְרֵחַיִם וְתַנּוּר; אֲבָל מַשְׁאִיל לוֹ חָלוּק
וְטַבַּעַת וְטַלִּית וּנְזָמִים, וְכָל דָּבָר שֶׁאֵין עוֹשִׂין בּוֹ
אֹכֶל נֶפֶשׁ. מְקוֹם שֶׁמַּשְׂכִּירִין כַּיּוֹצֵא בָהֶן — אָסוּר.

--- ר' עובדיה מברטנורא ---

נפה וכברה רחים ותנור. שמתקנים בהס אוכל נפש, וכל שכן קדרה ושפוד שהאוכל טומד
בתוכו. ומודר מאכל דתנן במתניתין הוא שיאמר לו הנאת מאכלך עלי קונס: **מקום שמשכירין**
כיוצא בהם. דכיון דדרך להשכיר כיוצא בזה והוא מוחל לו השכירות, באותם הדמים יכול לקנות
אוכל נפש, והוא הדירו מהנאה המביאה לידי מאכל:

יד אברהם

people do not attach any value are
forbidden by a *neder* (*Gem.* 32b).

If Shimon were restricted only from
food-related benefits, he would be
allowed to walk on Reuven's property, since this is not food related
(*Ritva*).

The *Gemara* poses the question that, in a
case in which Shimon is forbidden from
food-related benefits only, if he crossed
Reuven's property as a shortcut on the way
to a meal, has he violated his *neder*? The
question is raised by the *Gemara* (33a), and
left unresolved.

וְכֵלִים שֶׁאֵין עוֹשִׂין בָּהֶן אֹכֶל נֶפֶשׁ. — *and*
utensils not used for food.

Benefit from such utensils does not
lead to eating; therefore, it would be
permitted to someone forbidden only
from food-related benefits; unless he
received a benefit that saved him
money. Someone forbidden to enjoy
general benefits from another would,
of course, be prohibited from using
any of the latter's utensils, including
those not used for food (*Ritva*).

הַמֻּדָּר מַאֲכָל מֵחֲבֵרוֹ - לֹא יַשְׁאִילֶנּוּ —
Someone prohibited by a neder *from*
deriving food [related benefits] from
another should not lend him

I.e., if Shimon, for example, is

forbidden by a *neder* from deriving
food-related benefits from Reuven,
the latter should not lend Shimon the
following items (*Meleches Shlomo*).

נָפָה וּכְבָרָה וְרֵחַיִם — *a flour-sieve, a*
grain-sieve, a mill,

The translation follows *Rambam*
(*Comm.* to *Sheviis* 5:9). Elsewhere
(*Keilim* 15:4), *Rambam* notes that the
grating of a flour-sieve is finer than
that of a grain-sieve.

It is not clear, however, why the
flour-sieve should be mentioned before the grain-sieve. The order of
preparing flour was to sift the grain
in a grain-sieve to remove chaff and
other waste, then to grind the grain
into flour, and then to sift the flour
into a flour-sieve. One would have
expected the listing in the mishnah to
read: *a grain-sieve, a mill, a flour-sieve.*

Because of this difficulty, *Tiferes*
Yisrael suggests that the term נָפָה here
is a fan used in the winnowing. If that
is so, then the items are indeed listed in
the order of their use. First, the wheat
is processed by winnowing which
involves a fan; later, the grain is sifted
with the grain-sieve, and, finally, the
grain is ground into flour with a mill.
(Support for *Tiferes Yisrael's* theory

4
1
and utensils not used for food.

Someone prohibited by a *neder* from deriving food-[related benefits] from another should not lend him a flour-sieve, a grain-sieve, a mill, or an oven; but he may lend him a shirt, a ring, a cloak, earrings, and anything not used for food. [In] a place where things like these are rented, it is prohibited.

YAD AVRAHAM

may be found in *Rashi* to *Tannis* 3b, s.v. אפשר בנפוותא, who cites the Mishnaic phrase נָפָה וּכְבָרָה to explain נִפְוָותָא as a fan used in winnowing.)

וְתַנּוּר; — *or an oven;*

Tos. Yom Tov suggests that the oven mentioned here is not the one used to bake bread. The baking procedure in those times involved sticking the dough directly on the wall of the oven where it baked. This meant that the oven was in contact with the finished edible product, viz., the bread. But the other food-related utensils listed (sieves and mill) are all used in preliminary procedures, and do not come into contact with the finished product. Accordingly, *Tos. Yom Tov* proposes that the oven mentioned here is similar to the modern one, into which pots and pans containing food are placed. The oven itself never comes into contact with food, and is therefore similar to the other utensils listed.

The reason the mishnah's examples are all of utensils not directly in contact with edible food is to stress that benefit from these utensils is also forbidden as being food related, and not just the benefit from those which produce a ready-to-eat product (*Ran*; *Rosh*).

אֲבָל מַשְׁאִיל לוֹ חָלוּק וְטַבַּעַת וְטַלִּית וּנְזָמִים, וְכָל דָּבָר שֶׁאֵין עוֹשִׂין בּוֹ אֹכֶל נֶפֶשׁ. — *but he may lend him a shirt, a ring, a cloak,*

earrings, and anything not used for food.

Some text read: *a shirt, a cloak, a ring, or earrings.* The items are thus organized into two groups — garments [shirt, cloak] and jewelry [ring, earrings] (*Rashash*).

The use of these things are not food related, and are permitted even to someone forbidden only from any benefit which leads to food (*Ritva*). [On the other hand, for someone forbidden to derive general benefit from another, use of these items would be prohibited.]

It is conceivable that someone might borrow clothes or jewelry in order to gain entrance to some fancy dinner. Whether or not such a use would make borrowing the clothes a food-related benefit is left undecided by the *Gemara* (33a).

וְכָל דָּבָר שֶׁאֵין עוֹשִׂין בּוֹ אֹכֶל נֶפֶשׁ. — *and anything not used for food.*

It is unclear whether this is the end of the previous statement — *he may lend him a shirt ... and anything not used for food,* or the beginning of the following one — *Anything not used for food in a place where things like these are rented is prohibited* (*Rashash*).

מְקוֹם שֶׁמַּשְׂכִּירִין כַּיּוֹצֵא בָהֶן – אָסוּר. — *[In] a place where things like these are rented, it is prohibited.*

Where items such as these, which

[ב] הַמֻּדָּר הֲנָאָה מֵחֲבֵרוֹ — שׁוֹקֵל [לוֹ] אֶת שִׁקְלוֹ, וּפוֹרֵעַ אֶת חוֹבוֹ,

(ב) שׁוֹקֵל לוֹ שִׁקְלוֹ. מַחֲצִית הַשֶּׁקֶל שֶׁחַיָּיב כָּל אֶחָד מִיִּשְׂרָאֵל בְּכָל שָׁנָה לְצוֹרֶךְ קָרְבְּנוֹת צִבּוּר, וְהַמֻּדָּר יָכוֹל לִשְׁקֹל לוֹ בִּשְׁבִילוֹ דְּמִצְוָה בְּעָלְמָא קָעָבִיד: **וּפוֹרֵעַ לוֹ חוֹבוֹ.** אִית דְּמוֹקְמֵי לָהּ דַּוְקָא בְּחוֹב שֶׁהִתְנָה לוֹהּ עִם הַמַּלְוֶה שֶׁלֹּא יִפְרָעֶנּוּ אֶלָּא לִכְשֶׁיִּרְצֶה וְלֹא יוּכַל הַמַּלְוֶה לְכָפְלוֹ, וְהַשְׁתָּא לֹא אַהֲנֵי לֵיהּ מִידֵי בַּמֶּה שֶׁפָּרַע חוֹבוֹ. וְאִית דְּמוֹקְמֵי לָהּ בְּכָל חוֹב שֶׁבָּעוֹלָם, שֶׁאֵינוֹ אֶלָּא מוֹנֵעַ אֶת בַּעַל חוֹבוֹ שֶׁלֹּא יִתְבָּעֶנּוּ, וּמְנִיעַת תְּבִיעָה אֵינָהּ בַּכְּלָל הֲנָאָה:

יד אברהם

are not food related, are ordinarily rented, it is prohibited to borrow them, even if the *neder* only specifies food-related benefits. For example, if Reuven, from whom Shimon is forbidden to derive any food-related benefit, lends a suit to the latter in a place in which suits are rented, rather than borrowed, he has thereby enabled Shimon to save the cost of rental, and money is considered a food-related benefit, since it can be used to acquire food. Thus, Shimon has received a food-related benefit from Reuven which is forbidden by the *neder*. Consequently, *in a place where things like these are rented*, it is prohibited (*Rav; Rosh; Ran*).

2.

As stated above, if Reuven saves Shimon the expense of renting something, it is considered a financial benefit received by the latter from the former. Evidently, money that Shimon saves because of Reuven is as forbidden a benefit as if, for example, Reuven were to give Shimon a gift. However, it can be argued that this conclusion is valid only where Reuven deals with Shimon directly. (See *Rashash* to 35b; cf. *Chidushei R' Akiva* to *Yoreh Deah* 221:2.)

What if Shimon is in debt to a third party (e.g., Levi)? Obviously, if Levi releases his claim on Shimon, the latter will save money. What if Reuven (from whom Shimon may not benefit) gives Levi the money owed to him by Shimon, thus removing Levi's claim on Shimon? Is the money thus saved by Shimon considered to be a benefit received from Reuven? Or, perhaps, since Reuven has not given anything directly to Shimon, but has simply prevented a creditor from pursuing him, the money Shimon saves is not a benefit received from Reuven.

The question here is not whether Shimon has received a benefit. Certainly, it is a great benefit to Shimon to have his debt paid for him. However, this benefit did not come to him directly from Reuven, since the latter dealt solely with Levi, and benefited Shimon only indirectly.

Rather, the question is whether an indirect benefit is included in the *neder* (*Rashba; Meiri*).

The *Gemara* (33a) demonstrates that this question is the subject of a debate in *Kesubos* 13:2, in which Chanan maintains that to eliminate a claim is *not* the same as directly giving a positive benefit to someone. In the succeeding mishnayos, this issue is central. Although the halachah follows Chanan (see *Even HaEzer* 70:8;

2. **S**omeone prohibited by a *neder* to benefit from another — [the latter] may contribute his half shekel [for him], pay his debt,

YAD AVRAHAM

Choshen Mishpat 128:1), *Rav* and *Tos. Yom Tov* consider the following mishnayos from both points of view. [Their approach will be adopted in the commentary.]

הַמֻּדָּר הֲנָאָה מֵחֲבֵרוֹ– — *Someone prohibited by a neder to benefit from another —*

[For example, Shimon is prohibited from deriving general benefit from Reuven.]

שׁוֹקֵל [לוֹ] אֶת שִׁקְלוֹ, — *[the latter] may contribute his half shekel [for him],*

As long as the Temple stood, it was obligatory for every Jewish man to contribute an annual tax of a half shekel to the Temple (*Rambam, Hil. Shekalim* 1:1ff). If a person had not given it by a certain time, he was coerced into doing so (ibid. 7).

The mishnah states that, although Shimon is prohibited from benefiting from Reuven, it is permitted for Reuven to contribute the half shekel to the Temple on behalf of Shimon, and this will not be considered a benefit to the latter. Reuven has simply eliminated the Temple's claim from Shimon (*Ran*).

Those who disagree with Chanan, and consider the removal of a claim to be equal to directly benefiting a person, explain the mishnah in the following manner:

Under certain circumstances (see *Rambam, Hil. Shekalim* 3:9), half shekels that were sent via an agent to Jerusalem, but were stolen before they were delivered, do not have to be replaced by the senders. Although it was customary for the senders to replace them, it was not obligatory to do so.

Accordingly, the mishnah can be interpreted as referring to a case in which Shimon had already sent in his half shekel, but it was stolen before it reached the Temple, and consequently, he was not obligated to replace it. Reuven then went ahead and donated a half shekel on Shimon's behalf. Here, Reuven's donation has not even removed a claim from Shimon, since Shimon was no longer obligated to pay. Even though the custom was that someone in Shimon's position did replace the half shekel, he could not be forced to do so. Consequently, all agree that Shimon has received no benefit from Reuven, and so, the latter was permitted to donate the money in the former's behalf (*Tos. Yom Tov* from *Ran*).

וּפוֹרֵעַ אֶת חוֹבוֹ, — *pay his debt,*

[Reuven may pay to Levi the money owed to him by Shimon, and it is not considered to be a benefit received by Shimon from Reuven.]

Here, too, the payment to Levi accomplished nothing more than the elimination of a claim on Shimon, and it is not considered that the latter gained any direct benefit from Reuven (*Rav*).

Those who treat prevention of a loss as equivalent to a benefit explain the mishnah to be dealing with the following case. When Levi initially gave Shimon the money, he made it clear that he would not demand repayment; Shimon would pay it back only if he wanted to. Thus, when Reuven went on his own initiative to pay Levi for Shimon, he was not removing any claim from Shimon, because there was no real claim on him. Consequently, Shimon has not derived any benefits from Reuven;

נְדָרִים
ד/ב
וּמַחֲזִיר לוֹ אֶת אֲבֵדָתוֹ. מָקוֹם שֶׁנּוֹטְלִין עָלֶיהָ
שָׂכָר — תִּפּוֹל הֲנָאָה לַהֶקְדֵּשׁ.

ר' עובדיה מברטנורא

וּמַחֲזִיר לוֹ אֲבֵדָתוֹ. בֵּין שֶׁהָיוּ נִכְסֵי מַחֲזִיר אֲסוּרִים עַל בַּעַל אֲבֵדָה בֵּין שֶׁהָיוּ נִכְסֵי בַּעַל אֲבֵדָה אֲסוּרִים עַל הַמַּחֲזִיר מִשּׁוּם דִּמְצֵי קָעָבֵיד: **וּבְמָקוֹם שֶׁנּוֹטְלִין עָלֶיהָ שָׂכָר תִּפּוֹל הֲנָאָה לַהֶקְדֵּשׁ.** כְּשֶׁנִּיהֶם מוֹדְרִים הֲנָאָה זֶה מִזֶּה, אִם הוּא נוֹטֵל שָׂכָר נִמְצָא שָׂכָר נֶהֱנָה וְאִם אֵינוֹ נוֹטֵל שָׂכָר נִמְצָא מֵהֲנָה, לְפִיכָךְ תִּפּוֹל הֲנָאָה לַהֶקְדֵּשׁ, וְלֹא אָמְרִינַן יוֹלִיךְ הֲנָאָה לְיַם הַמֶּלַח, לְפִי שֶׁאֵסֶר עָלָיו הַנָּאָתוֹ כַּהֶקְדֵּשׁ, הִילְכָךְ כָּל הֲנָאָה הַבָּאָה לְיָדוֹ מִמֶּנּוּ הֶקְדֵּשׁ הִיא:

יד אברהם

and hence, it was permitted for Reuven to pay Levi (Rav).

וּמַחֲזִיר לוֹ אֶת אֲבֵדָתוֹ. — and return his lost article to him.

There are two possible cases to which the mishnah may be referring, and the law is the same in both. The first possibility is that Shimon (who is forbidden to benefit from Reuven) has lost something, and Reuven has found it. When Reuven returns it to Shimon, Shimon is not actually benefiting from Reuven, since the article he is receiving has been his all along. Furthermore, any efforts Reuven puts into returning the article are not done as a favor to Shimon — so that it may be said that the latter had a service performed for him by Reuven. Rather, since it is a Biblical obligation to return a lost article (Deut. 22:1ff), any efforts invested by Reuven are done in fulfillment of the precept, and not to benefit Shimon (Ritva; Shalmei Nedarim to 33b, s.v. בפי' הראש).

The second possibility is that Reuven has lost something, and Shimon has found it. On the surface, there is no obvious reason for Shimon not to return the article to Reuven. It is, after all, permitted for Reuven to benefit from Shimon! However, there is a subtle point involved. Because return-

ing lost articles is a Biblical imperative, the principle that one's involvement with a mitzvah exempts him from other mitzvos applies (Berachos 11a et al.). Thus, if a poor person were to approach Shimon while the latter is returning the lost article to Reuven, Shimon would be exempt from giving him charity. His involvement with the commandment to return a lost article exempts him from the obligation to give charity at that time (Bava Kamma 56b).

But, in that case, Shimon has saved money (that would otherwise have been given to the poor person) as a consequence of returning Reuven's property. In other words, Shimon has used Reuven's property to save himself money, and has thus benefited from Reuven (Tos. 33b, s.v. דמהני).

However, the Gemara (33b) says that the coincidence of a poor person arriving just when Shimon is involved with returning Reuven's property is a highly unlikely occurrence. Therefore, when Shimon forbids himself to benefit from Reuven, it is assumed that he did not intend to include a rare benefit such as this in the prohibition; consequently, he may return the lost article (Ran 33b, s.v. פרוטה).

and return his lost article to him. [In] a place
where [people] take a reward for this, the benefit
should go to the Temple.

YAD AVRAHAM

מְקוֹם שֶׁנּוֹטְלִין עָלֶיהָ שָׂכָר – תִּפֹּל הֲנָאָה
לַהֶקְדֵּשׁ. — *[In] a place where [people]
take a reward for this, the benefit
should go* (lit., *fall*) *to the Temple.*

The case under consideration here
concerns a place in which it was
customary for the loser of an item to
reward the finder for its return
(*Rambam Comm.*), and where both
the loser and the finder were prohibited to benefit from each other (*Rav*).
For example, Reuven has prohibited
Shimon to benefit from him, and vice
versa.

If Shimon finds an item which
Reuven lost, it will be problematic
for Shimon to return the item to
Reuven. For if Shimon takes the
customary reward from Reuven, he
will be benefiting from Reuven, something disallowed by the *neder*. But if
he forgoes the reward, he is benefiting
Reuven by saving him the reward
money, which is also forbidden. To
overcome this problem, the mishnah
rules that *the benefit* — i.e., the reward
— should go to the Temple, so that
Shimon will not receive it, and will not
derive a benefit from Reuven. Con-
comitantly, Reuven will not have
saved the reward money, since he
gives it to the Temple.

The reward money might have
been disposed of in other ways by
which neither Reuven nor Shimon
would benefit therefrom. For example,
the mishnah could have advised that
it be thrown into the sea. However,
because — as a result of the *neder* —
the benefit becomes forbidden like an

offering, it is considered to assume a
degree of sanctity. Thus, the reward
money — which, in this case, is the
benefit — is considered sacred, and is
therefore donated to the Temple (*Rav*
from *Rosh* 33a, s.v. תפול).

Tos. Yom Tov challenges the above
explanation, which is based on the
premise that, in the case of the
mishnah, rewards were given for the
return of lost articles. Returning a lost
article is obligated by the Torah, and it
is not permitted to take payment for
fulfilling a commandment (*Bechoros*
29a). Both *Tur* and *Shulchan Aruch*
(*Choshen Mishpat* 265:1) explicitly
state, based on Talmudic passages,
that we are commanded to return lost
articles without receiving compensation.

Because of this difficulty, *Tos. Yom
Tov* prefers *Ran's* interpretation. In
Bava Metzia 2:9, we are taught that if
a person takes time off from work in
order to retrieve and return a lost item to
someone, he is partially compensated
by the loser of the item for the loss of
income he sustains. The *reward* referred to by the mishnah is the compensation for the loss incurred by the
finder, and not a reward for returning
the item.

Accordingly, *Ran* translates the
phrase מְקוֹם שֶׁנּוֹטְלִין עָלֶיהָ שָׂכָר to
mean *a case in which [the finder] is
entitled to compensation*, while *Rambam* and *Rav* render it *a place where
[people] take a reward*; i.e., a city in
which it was customary to reward
people who returned lost articles.

[ג] **וְתוֹרֵם** אֶת תְּרוּמָתוֹ וּמַעְשְׂרוֹתָיו לְדַעְתּוֹ, וּמַקְרִיב עָלָיו קִנֵּי זָבִין, קִנֵּי זָבוֹת, קִנֵּי יוֹלְדוֹת, חַטָּאוֹת וַאֲשָׁמוֹת. וּמְלַמְּדוֹ מִדְרָשׁ, הֲלָכוֹת, וְאַגָּדוֹת, אֲבָל

―――――――― ר' עובדיה מברטנורא ――――――――

(ג) ותורם תרומתו ומעשרותיו לדעתו. כגון שאמר כל הרוצה לתרום יבא ויתרום, אבל לא יאמר לו לתרום שהרי עושהו שליח והנאה היא לו שנעשה שליחותו: **ומקריב לו קיני זבין וזבות.** כהן שהדיר את ישראל הנאה ממנו יכול להקריב קרבנותיו שמביא על זב וזבה ויולדת: **ומלמדו מדרש.** ספרא וספרי שהוא מדרש הפסוקים: **הלכות.** הלכה למשה מסיני: **אגדות.** דברי חכמים [שהסמיכום] על הפסוקים ללמדו דברי כל הני, שאין אדם רשאי ליקח שכר

יד אברהם

3.

וְתוֹרֵם אֶת תְּרוּמָתוֹ וּמַעְשְׂרוֹתָיו לְדַעְתּוֹ, — *He may separate his terumah and tithes with his knowledge,*

Even if Shimon is forbidden to derive benefit from Reuven, the latter is nevertheless permitted to separate the *terumah* and tithes which it is incumbent upon the former to set aside. This is true only if the food being designated a *terumah* is Shimon's, in which case he derives no material gain from Reuven (*Tos. Yom Tov;* cf. *Meiri, Tos. R' Akiva Eiger*).

The law is that, when taking off *terumah* and tithes from someone else's produce, the *terumah* will be sacred, and the remaining food will become permitted only if the portions were set aside with the permission of the owner (see *Rambam, Hil. Terumos* 4:2). Thus, for Reuven's designation of *terumah* to be effective, he must have Shimon's consent. On the other hand, Shimon may not ask Reuven outright to do so, since, if Reuven acts by appointment of Shimon, then Shimon is said to have benefited, because someone followed his instructions (*Gem.* 36b). To circumvent this problem, therefore, Shimon — instead of specifically appointing Reuven — announces that anyone

who wishes to separate his *terumah* and tithes may do so. Such a proclamation is considered sufficient consent so that anyone may separate the *terumah* and tithes, but it does not classify whoever should do so as an agent of Shimon. This is what the mishnah means by *with his* knowledge. That is, Shimon must have granted permission for anyone to separate his *terumah* and tithe for him, but must not have appointed whoever should do so to be his representative. Under these conditions, when Reuven acts, he does so on his own, so that Shimon does not have the benefit and satisfaction of someone fulfilling his instructions (*Rav*).

וּמַקְרִיב עָלָיו — *and he may sacrifice for him*

If Reuven is a *Kohen*, he is permitted to sacrifice an offering brought by Shimon, who is forbidden to benefit from him (*Rav*). This is because the *Kohanim*, when conducting the sacrificial service, are not acting in the agency of the person offering the sacrifice; rather, they are acting in the service of God (*Rambam, Hil. Nedarim* 6:5, cited by *Tos. Yom Tov*). That being the case, Reuven's

3. **H**e may separate his *terumah* and tithes with his knowledge, and he may sacrifice for him [the bird-offerings of *zavin, zavos*, and postpartum women, [and the] sin-offerings and guilt-offerings [of *metzoraim*].

He may teach him *Midrash, Halachos*, and *Agga-*

YAD AVRAHAM

participation in Shimon's offering is not in the capacity of Shimon's representative. Thus, Shimon is not considered to be benefiting from Reuven when the latter carries out the various steps in the sacrificial ritual (*Ran* 35b, s.v. הא).

קְנֵי זָבִין, קְנֵי זָבוֹת, קְנֵי יוֹלְדוֹת, חַטָּאוֹת, וַאֲשָׁמוֹת. — *[the] bird-offerings (lit. nests) of zavin, zavos, and postpartum women, [and the] sin-offerings and guilt-offerings [of metzoraim].*

In the case described above, Reuven, the *Kohen*, may sacrifice *any* offering brought by Shimon. The mishnah specifies these offerings because they commonly share the fact that they permit their owner to partake of the sacrificial meat (*Tos. Yom Tov* from *Rav*). *Zavim, zavos,* postpartum women, and *metzoraim* are people in various states of ritual uncleanness, whose laws are described at length in *Leviticus* 12-15. Even after their process of purification is well under way (i.e., they have been immersed in a ritual bath following the preliminaries necessary for their state of uncleanness), they remain forbidden to consume meat or any foods until they bring a specific sacrifice (*Rambam, Hil. Mechuserei Kapparah* 1:1ff.) In the case of the *zav, zavah,* and postpartum woman, the sacrifice is a bird-offering; in the case of a *metzora*, it is an animal-offering which includes a sin-offering

and a guilt-offering. As long as these sacrifices are not brought, these people are said to be lacking atonement (ibid.). Although the offering of these sacrifices restores to their owners the right to eat sacrificial food, this physical pleasure is not considered to be a benefit derived directly from the *Kohen* (*Meiri; Ran* 35b, s.v. הא). [Rather, Shimon — upon having his sacrifice offered — becomes permitted to eat sacrificial meat by virtue of a privilege granted to him by the Torah, and not because of the *Kohen*.] The mishnah selects the example of offerings for people "lacking in atonement" to stress that, even in these cases, when the owner of the offering gains a physical pleasure — the eating of sacrificial foods — this is not a benefit derived from the *Kohen*. This is certainly true regarding the standard sacrifice, which involves no such granting of a right — the function of the *Kohen* is considered independent of the person offering the sacrifice. The *Kohen* acts on behalf of God, and not on behalf of the person whose sacrifice he is attending to (*Meiri; Ran* ibid., s.v. אלא; *Tos. Yom Tov*).

The term קְנֵי literally means *nests of ...* It is used because the offering of *zavim*, etc., are birds (*Ran*).

וּמְלַמְּדוֹ מִדְרָשׁ, הֲלָכוֹת, וְאַגָּדוֹת, — *He may teach him Midrash, Halachos, and Aggados,*

Strictly speaking, it is forbidden for

לֹא יְלַמְּדֶנּוּ מִקְרָא; אֲבָל מְלַמֵּד הוּא אֶת בָּנָיו וְאֶת בְּנוֹתָיו מִקְרָא. וְזָן אֶת אִשְׁתּוֹ וְאֶת בָּנָיו, אַף עַל פִּי שֶׁהוּא חַיָּב בִּמְזוֹנוֹתֵיהֶם.

─────────── ר' עובדיה מברטנורא ───────────

כדי ללמד את חבירו את כל אלה, ואין כאן הנאה דמלוה קעביד: **אבל לא ילמדנו מקרא.** שמותר ליטול שכר על למוד המקרא שאינו נוטל אלא שכר פסוק טעמים לנגן המקראות כהלכתן, ולאו דאורייתא הוא ושרי ליטול שכר עליו, ואם אינו נוטל שכר מהנה ואם נוטל נמלא נהנה, ודוקא במקום שנהגו ליטול שכר על המקרא, אבל במקום שאין נוטלין שכר על המקרא אף המקרא שרי ללמדו: **אבל מלמד הוא את בנו.** ואף על גב דמלוה על האב ללמד את בנו וזה מוליאו מידי חובתו, לא מקרי הנאה דמלות לאו ליהנות נתנו, וגם אפשר שהיה מולא אחר שהיה מלמדו חנם:

─────────── **יד אברהם** ───────────

a teacher of Torah to receive remuneration for his service. This is derived by the *Gemara* (37a) from the verse (*Deut.* 4:5), *See, I have taught you laws and ordinances just as I have been instructed by God*, which is exegetically interpreted to mean that just as Moses received instruction in Torah from God gratis, so too did he teach the Torah to the Jewish people for no charge, and similarly, they should continue to receive instruction in Torah without having to pay for it (*Rambam, Hil. Talmud Torah* 1:7; cf. *Ran* 37a).

Accordingly, only such Torah as was received by Moses from God is included in this prohibition. As will be seen, the traditional chanting of the verse is not of Biblical origin, and is therefore not included in the interdiction. Consequently, the teaching of Scripture — if it includes lessons in chanting the verses — can be done for remuneration (*Gem.* 37a; *Ran*). The entire Oral Law, on the other hand, is included in the prohibition against taking payment for teaching Torah (*Meiri*) [because it, too, was received

by Moses from God].

Thus the mishnah states that if Shimon is forbidden to benefit from Reuven, it is still permitted for Reuven to teach him the Oral Law at no charge. Since teaching of the Oral Law was always without compensation, Reuven's free lessons have not saved Shimon any money. The knowledge which Shimon acquires in the course of his studies is also not considered a benefit derived from Reuven. This is because the study of Torah is the fulfillment of a Biblical commandment, and benefit derived from the performance of a commandment is not considered a benefit [see 2:1] (*Meiri*).

As illustrations of disciplines of the Oral Law which are taught without remuneration, the mishnah lists *Midrash*, *Halachos*, and *Aggados*. *Rav*, following *Rosh* (36b), defines these as follows: *Midrash* comprises the legal commentaries written by the *Tannaim* on the Torah such as *Sifra* and *Sifrei*; *Halachos* are laws received orally by Moses at Sinai (הֲלָכָה לְמשֶׁה מִסִּינַי); and *Aggados* refer to Rabbinic teachings

dos, but he may not teach him Scripture; however, he may teach his sons and his daughters Scripture. He may feed his wife and children, even though he is obligated in their sustenance.

YAD AVRAHAM

[presumably the allegorical and homiletic ones] based on Biblical verses.

אֲבָל לֹא יְלַמְּדֶנּוּ מִקְרָא; — *but he may not teach him Scripture;*

Lessons in reading Scripture included instruction in chanting the Biblical verse with the appropriate melody. The tune used when reading the Torah was not taught to Moses by God (see *Rosh* 37a), and is thus not included in the prohibition against teaching Torah for money. That is why — even in ancient times — Torah teachers were paid. Consequently, Reuven's free lessons save Shimon the cost of a teacher. It is thus forbidden for Reuven to do this, since he thereby benefits Shimon (*Rav*).

Note that in this case, the money saved by Shimon is a benefit, although elimination of a claim which also saves one money is not. The reason for this, as explained in the preface to mishnah 2, is that where Reuven deals directly with Shimon, even saving the latter money is treated as a benefit. Only the elimination of the claim of a third party is not a benefit. Thus, in our case — in which Reuven teaches Shimon Scripture, and forgoes payment owed him by Shimon — he is benefiting Shimon, which is forbidden (*Rashash*).

The widespread modern practice of compensating teachers of Torah is based on the argument that the person is being paid not for his teaching, but for his time (*Yoreh Deah* 246:5). Since it is accepted today that a teacher of any discipline of Torah is entitled to compensation, he may

not teach for free to someone forbidden by a *neder* to benefit from him. Even if one teaches only the Oral Law, he is saving his student money, which is forbidden by the *neder* (ibid. 221:2).

אֲבָל מְלַמֵּד הוּא אֶת בָּנָיו וְאֶת בְּנוֹתָיו מִקְרָא. — *however, he may teach his sons and his daughters Scripture.*

Although it is forbidden for Reuven to teach Torah to Shimon, it is permissible for him to teach Shimon's children without demanding remuneration. Shimon can argue that he has not been saved any money by Reuven's act, since he could always have found some other teacher who would also have given his children instruction free of charge (*Rav*).

Many versions of this Mishnah omit the words *and his daughters*, presumably reflecting the question of whether it is permissible to teach one's daughter Torah; see *Sotah* 3:4 (*Tos. Yom Tov*).

Chidushei HaGra (*Yoreh Deah* 246:6), however, cites this mishnah as the source for the *Rambam's* ruling (*Hil. Talmud Torah* 1:13) which permits teaching the Written Law (i.e., Scripture) to girls.

וְזָן אֶת אִשְׁתּוֹ וְאֶת בָּנָיו, אַף עַל פִּי שֶׁהוּא חַיָּב בִּמְזוֹנוֹתֵיהֶם. — *He may feed his wife and children, even though he is obligated in their sustenance.*

I.e., Reuven may feed the wife of Shimon (who is forbidden to benefit from Reuven), even though by doing so, he is discharging Shimon's obligation to provide for his wife and

וְלֹא יָזוּן אֶת בְּהֶמְתּוֹ, בֵּין טְמֵאָה בֵּין טְהוֹרָה.
רַבִּי אֱלִיעֶזֶר אוֹמֵר: זָן אֶת הַטְּמֵאָה, וְאֵינוֹ זָן אֶת
הַטְּהוֹרָה. אָמְרוּ לוֹ: מַה בֵּין טְמֵאָה לִטְהוֹרָה?
אָמַר לָהֶן: שֶׁהַטְּהוֹרָה — נַפְשָׁהּ לַשָּׁמַיִם וְגוּפָהּ
שֶׁלּוֹ, וּטְמֵאָה — נַפְשָׁהּ וְגוּפָהּ לַשָּׁמַיִם. אָמְרוּ
לוֹ: אַף הַטְּמֵאָה נַפְשָׁהּ לַשָּׁמַיִם וְגוּפָהּ שֶׁלּוֹ,
שֶׁאִם יִרְצֶה — הֲרֵי הוּא מוֹכְרָהּ לַגּוֹיִם אוֹ
מַאֲכִילָהּ לַכְּלָבִים.

─────────── ר' עובדיה מברטנורא ───────────

ולא יזון את בהמתו. דניחא ליה בפטומה וקא מהני ליה: **טמאה נפשה וגופה לשמים**
דלמלאכה קיימא ואינו חושש על פטומה: **שאם ירצה מוכרה לעובדי כוכבים.** לאכילה ונוטל
דמים יתירים בשביל פטומה:

יד אברהם

children (*Meiri*; cf. *Rosh*).

This is yet another example of eliminating a claim from Shimon (viz., the claim of his wife and children), which it is permitted for Reuven to do (*Tos. 38a*).

Those who regard the saving of money brought about by the elimination of a claim to be a benefit received explain that the food provided to Shimon's wife and children is extra food, above and beyond what Shimon was obligated to give. This surplus food is simply a gift of Reuven to Shimon's wife and children. It saves Shimon no money, and is thus not a benefit received by Shimon from Reuven (*Tos. Yom Tov*; cf. *Ran*).

וְלֹא יָזוּן אֶת בְּהֶמְתּוֹ, בֵּין טְמֵאָה בֵּין טְהוֹרָה.
רַבִּי אֱלִיעֶזֶר אוֹמֵר: זָן אֶת הַטְּמֵאָה, וְאֵינוֹ זָן
אֶת הַטְּהוֹרָה. — *However, he may not feed his animal, whether [it be] nonkosher or kosher. R' Eliezer says: He may feed the nonkosher one, but not the kosher one.*

Nonkosher animals were, of course, not maintained for eating. They were used for work (*Rav*).

The first, anonymous *Tanna* argues

that feeding Shimon's animals enhances their worth, and so, for Reuven to provide food for Shimon's animal is to give Shimon a real benefit. R' Eliezer, however, counters that only animals intended for eating are enhanced by feeding; work animals, however — and hence, as far as Jews are concerned, all nonkosher animals — are not improved by feeding.

Ran, quoted by *Tos. Yom Tov*, observes that R' Eliezer's distinction applies only to extra, non-essential food which could serve only to fatten the animals. Fattening animals intended for eating is desirable; but fattening work animals makes them sluggish and unproductive, and so, it is undesirable. Thus, even R' Eliezer agrees that Reuven cannot feed work animals their daily food requirements, because to do so would directly benefit Shimon. He takes exception with the first *Tanna* only with regard to unnecessary extras, because he contends that Shimon does not benefit by

However, he may not feed his animal, whether [it be] nonkosher or kosher. R' Eliezer says: He may feed the nonkosher one, but not the kosher one.

They said to him: What is the difference between a kosher and a nonkosher [animal]? He said to them: For the kosher one's soul belongs to heaven, but its body belongs to him; whereas the nonkosher one — [both] its soul and body belong to heaven. They said to him: Even the nonkosher one — its soul belongs to heaven, but its body belongs to him, for, if he wants, he can sell it to a non-Jew or feed it to dogs.

YAD AVRAHAM

having his work animals fattened.

The mishnah now continues with the dialogue between the first *Tanna* and R' Eliezer.

אָמְרוּ לוֹ: מַה בֵּין טְמֵאָה לִטְהוֹרָה? אָמַר לָהֶן: שֶׁהַטְּהוֹרָה – נַפְשָׁהּ לַשָּׁמַיִם וְגוּפָהּ שֶׁלּוֹ, וּטְמֵאָה – נַפְשָׁהּ וְגוּפָהּ לַשָּׁמַיִם. — *They said to him: What is the difference between a kosher and a nonkosher [animal]? He said to them: For the kosher one's soul belongs to heaven, but its body belongs to him; whereas the nonkosher one — [both] its soul and body belong to heaven.*

When the kosher animal's soul goes to heaven — that is, when the animal is slaughtered — its body goes to the owner; i.e., he eats it. Therefore, the owner is interested in the fattening of the animal (*Tos.* 38).

However, when the nonkosher animal dies, the owner cannot eat it. Therefore, since he has no enjoyment from the body, he has no interest in it being fattened (*Tif. Yis.*).

אָמְרוּ לוֹ: אַף הַטְּמֵאָה נַפְשָׁהּ לַשָּׁמַיִם וְגוּפָהּ שֶׁלּוֹ, שֶׁאִם יִרְצֶה – הֲרֵי הוּא מוֹכְרָהּ לַגּוֹיִם אוֹ מַאֲכִילָהּ לַכְּלָבִים. — *They said to him:*

Even the nonkosher one — its soul belongs to heaven, but its body belongs to him, for, if he wants, he can sell it to a non-Jew or feed it to dogs.

A person can utilize the flesh of the nonkosher animal as well, for he can sell it to non-Jews, or for dog food.

If the animal is fattened, it can fetch a higher price, and so the fattening of even nonkosher work animals is also a benefit for their owner (*Rav*).

Tiferes Yisrael suggests that R' Eliezer did not accept this argument, since — at present — the purpose of retaining the nonkosher animal was not in order to sell it, but in order to use it for work, and — for work — fattening is not a benefit. The fact that, under certain circumstances, fattening could be a benefit for nonkosher animals (i.e., if they died) did not concern him. On the other hand, the first *Tanna* held that the possibility of realizing a benefit from the fattening of the animal was enough to make if forbidden for Reuven to feed Shimon's animal.

[ד] **הַמֻּדָּר** הֲנָאָה מֵחֲבֵרוֹ, וְנִכְנַס לְבַקְּרוֹ —
עוֹמֵד, אֲבָל לֹא יוֹשֵׁב.
וּמְרַפְּאֵהוּ רְפוּאַת נֶפֶשׁ, אֲבָל לֹא רְפוּאַת מָמוֹן.

— **ר' עובדיה מברטנורא** —

(ד) עומד אבל לא יושב. מתניתין איירי כשנכסי המבקר אסורים על החולה, ובמקום שנוטלין
שכר על הישיבה עם החולה, שאם יושב עמו ואינו נוטל שכר הנהוג הרי מהנהו, אבל עמידה זמן
מועט הוא ואין רגילין ליטול עליה שכר: **רפואת הנפש.** רפואת גופו: **רפואת ממון.** רפואת
בהמתו. לפי שחייב אדם לרפאות את חבירו כשחלה שנאמר (דברים כב, ב) והשבותו לו לרבות אבדת
גופו, ומלוה קעביד, לפיכך אף על פי שהדירו הנאה ממנו מרפאו בידיו כשחלה בגופו, ואם חלתה
בהמתו אינו יכול לרפאה בידים מפני שמהנהו, אבל אומר לו סם פלוני יפה לה סם פלוני רע לה:

יד אברהם

4.

הַמֻּדָּר הֲנָאָה מֵחֲבֵרוֹ, וְנִכְנַס לְבַקְּרוֹ – עוֹמֵד,
אֲבָל לֹא יוֹשֵׁב. — *[If] someone was
prohibited by a neder to benefit from
another, and [the latter] entered to visit
him, he may stand, but not sit.*

The case here involves someone
(e.g., Shimon), who is sick in bed, and
another person (e.g., Reuven), from
whom he may not benefit. Reuven
now visits Shimon in a locale where it
is customary to pay someone who
spends time with a sick person (*Rav*).

Were Reuven to sit with Shimon,
he would be entitled to remuneration;
to forgo it would be to benefit Shimon.
Thus, the mishnah rules that Reuven
may stand — i.e., visit him briefly —
but *may not sit* — i.e., make an
extended visit — with him without
compensation, since that would be
benefiting Shimon (*Rav; Rambam*).

If, during his visit, Reuven remained
standing, no payment would be forth-
coming. Payment was advanced for
long visits which involved sitting, but
not for "standing" visits which were
brief. Therefore, Reuven may visit
Shimon even for free, as long as he
(Reuven) remains standing (*Rav*).

From the above, it is clear that where
Reuven excuses Shimon from paying

him, he is considered to have given a
direct benefit to Shimon (cf. preface to
mishnah 2). But a "standing" visit by
Reuven, which does not create monetary indebtedness, is not considered a
benefit derived by Shimon from Reuven. Apparently, any improvement
in ailing Shimon's frame of mind
resulting from Reuven's visit is not
considered to be a benefit derived by
Shimon from Reuven! Rather, since we
are commanded to visit the sick,
Reuven's visit is his personal fulfillment of a commandment. He is serving
God — not Shimon — with his visit.
The fact that Shimon might enjoy the
visit and have his mood improved is
only considered a by-product of Reuven's action, and not something that
Reuven "gives" to Shimon. Hence,
Shimon's enjoyment of the visit is not
considered a benefit derived from
Reuven, and is permitted (*Ran* 39b;
see *Meiri*, who maintains that an
improved mood is not a "real" benefit).

If, conversely, Reuven were prohibited
from benefiting from Shimon, the *Gemara*
(39a) rules that Reuven would still be
permitted to visit Shimon, even though to
do so would mean walking on the latter's
property, which should be forbidden as in
mishnah 1. The *Gemara*, however, explains

4

4. [If] someone was prohibited by a *neder* to benefit from another, and [the latter] entered to visit him, he may stand, but not sit. He may afford him a healing of [his] person, but not a healing of [his] property.

YAD AVRAHAM

that, when prohibiting someone to have benefit from him, a person does intend to exclude the banned party from benefits that are of crucial importance to himself (the person issuing the ban). Thus, when Shimon forbade Reuven to enjoy any benefit from him, he never interdicted him to enter his property for the purpose of visiting him, if he should take sick.

וּמְרַפְּאֵהוּ רְפוּאַת נֶפֶשׁ, — *He may afford him a healing of [his] person* (lit., *heal him a healing of the soul*),

If Reuven is a doctor, he may treat Shimon although the latter is not allowed to benefit from him. The *Gemara* (*Sanhedrin* 73a) classifies medical care as an instance of returning a lost item. To heal a patient is to return his health to him. Consequently, a doctor may treat even a patient who is prohibited from deriving benefit from him. Just as in mishnah 2, a person may return a lost article to its loser even if the latter is prohibited from deriving benefit from the finder — so too, in this case, the doctor is simply returning a "lost item," and the patient is receiving only that which was his to begin with — his health. As for the doctor's personal efforts on behalf of the patient, these are expended in fulfillment of the commandment to save lives. Thus, the doctor is acting in the service of God — not the patient — and any benefit to the patient is incidental to that (*Rav*; *Ran* 41b).

Ran points out, however, that any

medicines used may not be supplied by the doctor. To do so would be to directly give the patient an extra benefit. *Rosh* adds that Reuven, the doctor in the mishnah's case, provided his services gratis (*Tos. Yom Tov*). [Since Shimon is not considered to have benefited, it is clear that he did not save money. Evidently, doctors did not take remuneration for their services, which they viewed as the performance of a *mitzvah*, and not a livelihood.]

אֲבָל לֹא רְפוּאַת מָמוֹן. — *but not a healing of [his] property.*

[I.e., his animals.]

This refers to a case in which other, equally competent animal doctors are available. In that case, the treatment of the animal by this doctor would not be categorized as "returning a lost article" since the animal is not "lost"; any of the available veterinarians can treat it. In the previous case of a sick person, on the other hand, even the availability of alternative medical care does not change the fact that this particular doctor "found" his health. This is because people do not necessarily respond to any doctor. Even if several doctors of equal ability treat a patient, he might respond and be cured by only one of them (*Tos. Yom Tov* from *Ran*).

In the mishnah's case — in which other animal doctors are at hand — Reuven may not personally treat Shimon's animal, but he may offer advice on what medicines should be administered. In general, offering

וְרוֹחֵץ עִמּוֹ בְּאַמְבָּטִי גְדוֹלָה, אֲבָל לֹא בִּקְטַנָּה. וְיָשֵׁן עִמּוֹ בַּמִּטָּה. רַבִּי יְהוּדָה אוֹמֵר: בִּימוֹת הַחַמָּה, אֲבָל לֹא בִּימוֹת הַגְּשָׁמִים, מִפְּנֵי שֶׁהוּא מְהַנֵּהוּ. וּמֵסֵב עִמּוֹ עַל הַמִּטָּה.

וְאוֹכֵל עִמּוֹ עַל הַשֻּׁלְחָן, אֲבָל לֹא מִן הַתַּמְחוּי; אֲבָל אוֹכֵל הוּא עִמּוֹ מִן הַתַּמְחוּי הַחוֹזֵר.

ר' עובדיה מברטנורא

אבל לא בקטנה. מפני שמהנהו כשמגביה עליו את המים: **אבל לא בימות הגשמים.** מפני שמחממו. והלכה כרבי יהודה: **אבל לא מן התמחוי.** לא יאכל עמו בכלי אחד, שמא יניח מלאכול מנה יפה שבו כדי שיאכל זה שמודר הנאה ממנו, או שמא יקרב לפניו חתיכה שיאכל ונמצא מהנהו: **אבל אוכל הוא מן התמחוי החוזר.** לבעל הבית, ראובן אוכל בקערה שיודע שכשיחזירנה לבעל הבית יחזור בעל הבית וישלחנה לשמעון שמודר הנאה ממנו, ולא חיישינן שמא ישייר בקערה כדי שיאכל ממנה שמעון ונמלא מהנהו:

יד אברהם

advice was not considered to be providing Shimon with a real benefit (*Rav; Tos. Yom Tov*). *Beis Yosef* (*Yoreh Deah* 221) adds, however, that if there are consultation fees for medical advice, then Reuven may not advise Shimon for free, since to exempt Shimon from the fees is to benefit him.

וְרוֹחֵץ עִמּוֹ בְּאַמְבָּטִי גְדוֹלָה, אֲבָל לֹא בִּקְטַנָּה. — *He may bathe with him in a large pool, but not in a small one.*

In a small pool, if a person moves, he causes water to flow over anyone else in it. Thus, Reuven may not bathe in a small pool together with Shimon, who is forbidden to benefit from him, since — if Reuven moves — he will be causing water to go over Shimon, and thereby benefiting him. In a large pool, however, there is no problem for the two to bathe simultaneously (*Rav*).

וְיָשֵׁן עִמּוֹ בַּמִּטָּה. רַבִּי יְהוּדָה אוֹמֵר: בִּימוֹת הַחַמָּה, אֲבָל לֹא בִּימוֹת הַגְּשָׁמִים, מִפְּנֵי שֶׁהוּא מְהַנֵּהוּ. — *He may sleep with him on the [same] bed. R' Yehudah says: In the summer, but not in the*

winter, for [then] he benefits him.

R' Yehudah disagrees with the first anonymous opinion and maintains that Reuven may share a bed with Shimon only during the summer, since the latter has no benefit from this. But, in the winter, Reuven's presence on the bed makes it warmer — a benefit for Shimon. The halachah is in accordance with R' Yehudah (*Rav*; see comm. to mishnah 1, s.v. אֵין בֵּין).

The *Gemara* (41b) cites the opinion of R' Meir, who disputes the last two rulings of the mishnah, and disallows Reuven from bathing with Shimon even in a large pool, and similarly prohibits sharing a bed with him even in the summer. His reaction is that if we were to permit these instances, when no benefit is involved, people would come to bathe in small pools or share beds in winter, which does involve forbidden benefits.

וּמֵסֵב עִמּוֹ עַל הַמִּטָּה. — *But he may recline with him on the bed.*

Even in the winter. Sitting on the same bed is permitted; we do not fear that Reuven will fall asleep, thus warming it up for Shimon (*Tos. Yom Tov from Rosh*).

He may bathe with him in a large pool, but not in a small one.

He may sleep with him on the [same] bed. R' Yehudah says: In the summer, but not in the winter, for [then] he benefits him. But he may recline with him on the bed.

He may eat with him on the [same] table, but not from the [same] plate; however, he may eat with him from a plate which goes back [to the host].

YAD AVRAHAM

וְאוֹכֵל עִמּוֹ עַל הַשֻּׁלְחָן, — *He may eat with him on the [same] table,*

Here, Reuven and Shimon are each eating their own food, but sitting at the same table. The mishnah states that to prohibit this for fear that Reuven might share his food with Shimon, and thus benefit him, is not warranted (*Meiri*).

Rashbah (41b) asks why this case is different from the case of two people, one of whom is eating milk products, and the other, meat. There, it is prohibited for them to sit at the same table, lest they share their food, which would mean they would be combining milk and meat, a prohibited combination (*Yoreh Deah* 88). Here, too, since it is forbidden under the *neder* for them to share their food, we should forbid them from eating at the same table!

Rashba answers that perhaps the fear of violating a *neder* weighs more heavily on people than other prohibitions. Thus, extra precautionary measures might be necessary to prevent consumption of a milk and meat combination, but they are not necessary to prevent violation of a *neder*.

Rosh, quoted by *Tos. Yom Tov*, resolves *Rashba's* question differ-

ently. If Reuven had forbidden Shimon to benefit from him, it may be assumed that they are not on the best of terms with each other. In that case, they will certainly not share any food. But two people who are friendly — and one eats meat and the other milk — might very well share their food. Therefore, the Rabbis restricted them from eating at the same table.

אֲבָל לֹא מִן הַתַּמְחוּי; — *but not from the [same] plate;*

The problem with them eating from the same plate is that Reuven might leave over some portion for Shimon, or might even push it to Shimon's side of the plate. This will be giving Shimon a benefit, which is forbidden (*Rav*).

— אֲבָל אוֹכֵל הוּא עִמּוֹ מִן הַתַּמְחוּי הַחוֹזֵר. *however, he may eat with him from a plate which goes back [to the host].*

Some versions do not include the word עִמּוֹ, *with him*. Thus, the case here is of Reuven eating alone from the plate. He knows that, when he finishes, the host will take back the plate, refill it , and give it to Shimon. The mishnah rules that it is permitted for Reuven to eat from such a plate. And we do not fear that Reuven might leave over some portion on the

לֹא יֹאכַל עִמּוֹ מִן הָאֵבוּס שֶׁלִּפְנֵי הַפּוֹעֲלִים.
וְלֹא יַעֲשֶׂה עִמּוֹ בָאֻמָּן; דִּבְרֵי רַבִּי מֵאִיר.
וַחֲכָמִים אוֹמְרִים: עוֹשֶׂה הוּא בְרָחוֹק מִמֶּנּוּ.

—————————— ר׳ עובדיה מברטנורא ——————————

הָאֵבוּס שֶׁלִּפְנֵי הַפּוֹעֲלִים. כלי גדול שממלאים אותו ואוכלים בו כל הפועלים ביחד: **לֹא יַעֲשֶׂה עִמּוֹ בָאֻמָּן.** לא יקצור עמו באותה שורה שהוא קוצר, שגורם לו שממהר לעשות מלאכתו כשמולא המקום פנוי ונמלא מהגנו. ואין הלכה כרבי מאיר:

יד אברהם

plate for the host to serve to Shimon, which would be providing the latter with a forbidden benefit (*Rav; Rambam*).

Those readings which include *with him* in the text explain that the case here involves a plate from which Reuven and Shimon eat simultaneously, and which is constantly refilled by the host. Although, in the previous case, it was forbidden for Reuven and Shimon to eat from the same plate, this was because of the possibility that Reuven might save a portion to give Shimon. However, in this instance — in which the plate is constantly being refilled by the host — there is no reason for Reuven to look out for Shimon. Shimon will certainly get as much food as he wants without Reuven's help. Therefore, Reuven may eat *with him* from the plate which is constantly being refilled (*Rashba; Rosh*).

לֹא יֹאכַל עִמּוֹ מִן הָאֵבוּס שֶׁלִּפְנֵי הַפּוֹעֲלִים — *He may not eat with him from the workers' food bowl* (lit., *the feedbox that is before the workers*).

This bowl was a large receptacle which was filled with food, and from

which the workers all ate together. It was not constantly refilled. Therefore, it resembles the case above of two people eating together from the same plate, which is forbidden. Despite the enormous size of this bowl, it is feared that Reuven might save a piece for Shimon, or push one to him (*Rav; Tif. Yis.*)

וְלֹא יַעֲשֶׂה עִמּוֹ בָאֻמָּן; דִּבְרֵי רַבִּי מֵאִיר. וַחֲכָמִים אוֹמְרִים: עוֹשֶׂה הוּא בְרָחוֹק מִמֶּנּוּ. — *He may not work with him on the same row; [these are] the words of R' Meir. The Sages, however, say: He may work far from him.*

If Reuven and Shimon were working in a field in close proximity to each other, they would benefit from each other's presence. For example, if they were harvesting grain near each other, any clearing opened by Reuven enables Shimon to work with greater ease. Thus, to work on the same row near each other is certainly forbidden (*Rav*). The disagreement between R' Meir and the Sages concerns working far apart. R' Meir forbids even this as a precaution, lest they come to work near each other; the Sages are not concerned with this possibility (*Tos. Yom Tov* from *Gem. 41b*).

5.

◆§ Shemittah — the Sabbatical Year

Every seventh year of a cycle dating back to Biblical times, known as *Shemittah*, the Sabbatical year, it is forbidden to farm the land of *Eretz Yisrael*.

He may not eat with him from the workers' food bowl.

He may not work with him on the same row; [these are] the words of R' Meir. The Sages, however, say: He may work far from him.

YAD AVRAHAM

Furthermore, anything which grows then is considered ownerless and may be taken and eaten by anyone (see *Ex.* 23:11; *Rambam, Hil. Sheviis*). Although it is only the produce of the seventh year which is ownerless, and not the land upon which it grows, it is permitted on the seventh year to enter anybody's field for the purpose of taking agricultural produce. It is as though the Torah has made even the field ownerless with respect to using it in order to gain access to what is grown there. However, all other uses of the field remain within the sole jurisdiction of the owner, so that to enter the field for the purpose not related to taking the produce is forbidden without the owner's permission (*Gem.* 42b; *Ran* ad loc.).

The following mishnah discusses the effect of the seventh year on a *neder*. In the commentary to mishnah 1, s.v. אֵין בֵּין, it is stated that there is a difference between a *neder* which forbids Shimon to derive benefit from Reuven, and one forbidding Shimon to derive benefit from Reuven's property. *Ran* (31a, s.v. לוקה) notes that it is not within a person's power to forbid to his friend something not yet in existence. Thus, if Reuven forbids benefit from all his property to Shimon, the *neder* will affect only things already belonging to Reuven. But something he acquires subsequent to the *neder*, although it already existed at that time, is not forbidden to Shimon. (At the time of the *neder*, it is considered not to have existed in terms of being Reuven's property, because prior to his acquisition of it, he could not have prohibited it to Shimon.) On the other hand, if Shimon was forbidden to benefit from Reuven himself, then even property acquired after the *neder* would be forbidden for Shimon's use. In such a case, the forbidden item is Reuven himself who, of course, exists at the time of the *neder*. Using Reuven's property is therefore considered benefiting from him, no matter when the property was acquired.

There is also another important distinction. The *Gemara* (34b) considers the question of a loaf of bread belonging to Reuven, which he forbids to Shimon by declaring: "My loaf is forbidden to you." If Reuven should then give the loaf as a gift to Shimon, it may be argued that the loaf — no longer being Reuven's — is permitted. *Ran* (ibid., s.v. בעא) points out that had the loaf been forbidden to Shimon as a result of a declaration by Reuven that "Benefit from me is forbidden to you," this argument would not be relevant. When receiving the loaf as a gift, Shimon is benefiting from Reuven.

This mishnah, according to the *Gemara* (42 a,b), illustrates the principle that if something is forbidden by a *neder* made by its owner, it remains so even if it leaves that person's property. *Ran* (ibid., s.v. אם) asserts that the *neder* being discussed here contains no possessives, and is therefore not affected by the

[ה] הַמֻּדָּר הֲנָאָה מֵחֲבֵרוֹ לִפְנֵי שְׁבִיעִית — לֹא יֵרֵד לְתוֹךְ שָׂדֵהוּ, וְאֵינוֹ אוֹכֵל מִן הַנּוֹטוֹת. וּבַשְּׁבִיעִית — אֵינוֹ יוֹרֵד לְתוֹךְ שָׂדֵהוּ, אֲבָל אוֹכֵל הוּא מִן הַנּוֹטוֹת. נָדַר הֵימֶנּוּ מַאֲכָל לִפְנֵי שְׁבִיעִית — יוֹרֵד

ר' עובדיה מברטנורא

(ה) מן הנוטות. פירות תלויין הנוטין חוץ מן הפרדס: **ובשביעית לא ירד לתוך שדהו.** אף על גב דפירות שביעית רחמנא אפקרינהו, גוף הקרקע לא אפקר רחמנא, וחיישינן שמא בשעה שאינו אוכל מן הפירות ישהה בשדה ויתעכב שם ויהנה מגוף הקרקע שאינו הפקר:

יד אברהם

arguments mentioned earlier in connection with a *neder* of the form "My loaf, etc." Here, the *neder* is: "Benefit from *this property* is forbidden to you." The property remains interdicted even when it leaves the ownership of Reuven, who made the *neder*. Had Reuven's *neder* been "Benefiting from *me* is forbidden to you," it would be prohibited for Shimon to benefit from Reuven's property only as long as to do so would constitute a benefit from Reuven himself. If, however, Reuven were to sell his property to a third party, or, if it was otherwise removed from his ownership, Shimon would be permitted to benefit from the property which is no longer affiliated with Reuven.

In the following mishnah, where — according to the *Gemara* — it is shown that property of Reuven which he forbids to Shimon with a *neder* remains forbidden even when the seventh year makes it ownerless, it is clear that the *neder* under consideration is of the form "Benefit from this property is forbidden to you like *korban.*"

הַמֻּדָּר הֲנָאָה מֵחֲבֵרוֹ לִפְנֵי שְׁבִיעִית— — *Someone prohibited by a neder made prior to Shemittah to benefit from another*

Reuven makes a *neder* during one of the six non-*Shemittah* years, in which he bans Shimon from deriving any benefit from his property (*Tos. Yom Tov* from *Rashi*; *Ran* 42b).

לֹא יֵרֵד לְתוֹךְ שָׂדֵהוּ, — *may not enter* (lit., *descend into*) *his field,*

Shimon may not enter Reuven's field. Since the *neder* prohibited derivation of benefit in general, walking on Reuven's field would be a violation of the *neder* (see mishnah 1) (*Tos.*; *Rashi*).

וְאֵינוֹ אוֹכֵל מִן הַנּוֹטוֹת. — *and may not eat overhanging fruit.*

That is, fruit growing on branches of Reuven's tree that extended beyond the boundaries of his property (*Rav*). To reach such fruit, it is not necessary to enter Reuven's field. Nevertheless, it is prohibited for Shimon to pick fruit from such branches, since the fruit belongs to Reuven, and Shimon may not derive benefit from him (*Tos. Yom Tov* from *Rashi*; *Tos.*).

Even during *Shemittah*, when the fruit becomes ownerless, it remains forbidden for Shimon to partake of it (*Tos. Yom Tov* from *Rashi*). This illustrates the law that a person can prohibit his things through a *neder*, so

5. **S**omeone prohibited by a *neder* made prior to *Shemittah* to benefit from another may not enter his field, and may not eat overhanging fruit. However [if the *neder* was made] in *Shemittah*, he may not enter his field, but he may eat from the overhanging fruit.

[If] prior to *Shemittah*, he made a *neder* prohibiting food-related benefits, he   may enter

YAD AVRAHAM

that they remain interdicted even if they leave his ownership. Thus, although Reuven's fruit becomes ownerless during that year, it had already become forbidden to Shimon in advance of *Shemittah*, and the prohibition remains in force even though Reuven's ownership of the fruit is suspended during the Sabbatical year [see preface] (*Gem.* 42a).

וּבַשְׁבִיעִית– — *However [if the neder was made] in Shemittah,*

[If Reuven made the *neder* during the seventh year.]

אֵינוֹ יוֹרֵד לְתוֹךְ שָׂדֵהוּ, — *he may not enter his field,*

The *neder* is effective even during *Shemittah* on the land which still belongs to Reuven; therefore, Shimon may not enter the field (*Rav*).

אֲבָל אוֹכֵל הוּא מִן הַנּוֹטוֹת. — *but he may eat from the overhanging fruit.*

The fruit of *Shemittah* does not belong to Reuven, and therefore cannot be banned by him for Shimon (see preface to 1:1). Hence, Shimon may eat the fruit from the branches extending outside Reuven's land. In reality, Shimon is permitted to eat fruit from inside the field as well, since none of the fruit belongs to Reuven and, therefore, none of the fruit is subject to the *neder*.

However, in order to reach it, Shimon needs to walk on Reuven's land — and the *neder* did take effect on the land. Under Biblical law, the *neder* could not prevent Shimon from walking on the land in order to pick the fruit. In the Sabbatical year, use of the land for the purpose of reaching its fruit is removed by the Torah from the jurisdiction of the owner (*Rashi, Tos.; Ran* 42b). Therefore, the *neder* should not prevent such a use. However, the Rabbis ruled that if Shimon were permitted to enter the field for the fruit, he might come to use the land for some other purpose such as lying down and resting on the ground. Control over this use of the land was not removed by the Torah from the owner, and so, the *neder* prohibits it. To prevent such a violation of the *neder*, the Rabbis forbade Shimon to enter the field altogether, but allowed him to pick any fruit he could reach without entering the field (*Rav from Gem.* 42b).

נָדַר הֵימֶנּוּ מַאֲכָל לִפְנֵי שְׁבִיעִית– — *[If] prior to Shemittah, he made a neder prohibiting food-related benefits* (lit., *food*),

In the sixth year, for example, Reuven forbade Shimon from deriving any food-related benefits from his property (*Rashi*).

לְתוֹךְ שָׂדֵהוּ, וְאֵינוֹ אוֹכֵל מִן הַפֵּרוֹת; וּבַשְּׁבִיעִית — יוֹרֵד וְאוֹכֵל.

[ו] הַמֻּדָּר הֲנָאָה מֵחֲבֵרוֹ — לֹא יַשְׁאִילֶנּוּ, וְלֹא יִשְׁאַל מִמֶּנּוּ; לֹא יַלְוֶנּוּ, וְלֹא יִלְוֶה מִמֶּנּוּ; וְלֹא יִמְכּוֹר לוֹ, וְלֹא יִקַּח מִמֶּנּוּ.

—————————— **ר׳ עובדיה מברטנורא** ——————————

(ו) המודר הנאה מחבירו לא ישאילנו. גזירה שמא ישאל ממנו והוא אסר הנאת אותו פלוני עליו, וכן לא ילונו גזירה שמא ילוה ממנו: **ולא ימכור לו.** בפחות משויו, גזירה שמא יקח ממנו נמי בפחות משויו וכמלא כהנה:

————————————————————————

יד אברהם

— יוֹרֵד לְתוֹךְ שָׂדֵהוּ, וְאֵינוֹ אוֹכֵל מִן הַפֵּרוֹת; *he may enter the field, but may not eat the fruits;*

Shimon may enter the field, since — as explained in mishnah 1 — walking on Reuven's property is not a food-related benefit, and is not prohibited by the *neder*. Nevertheless, he may not eat the fruit, even during *Shemittah*. Although the fruit is then ownerless, it remains forbidden by force of the *neder* which took effect prior to *Shemittah* (ibid.).

וּבַשְּׁבִיעִית — יוֹרֵד וְאוֹכֵל. — *[if he made*

the neder] in Shemittah, he may enter [the field] and eat.

If, during the Sabbatical year, Reuven made a *neder* forbidding to Shimon any food-related benefits from his property, the *neder* prohibits neither walking on the field nor eating the fruit. This is because walking on the field is not a food-related benefit, and, since the fruit is ownerless during *Shemittah*, it cannot be prohibited to Shimon by Reuven's *neder*. The fruit is therefore permitted to Shimon, and he may enter the field and pick it (*Tos.*).

6.

הַמֻּדָּר הֲנָאָה מֵחֲבֵרוֹ — *Someone prohibited by a neder to benefit from another* [Shimon is forbidden to benefit from Reuven by virtue of a *neder*.]

Some commentators (*Rashash; R' Yoel Chasid*) suggest that, according to *Rav*, the case in question deals exclusively with a *neder* which Shimon imposed upon himself, and not with a *neder* directed at him by Reuven. For example, Shimon had declared: "Konam, benefit from Reuven to me." Had Shimon become forbidden as a result of Reuven declaring, "Benefit from me shall be forbidden to Shimon," then — according to these authorities — the law of the mishnah would not apply. The basis for making such a distinction will be explained below.

When money is borrowed, the money eventually repaid is almost never the actual coins or bills borrowed; rather, money of an equivalent worth is returned. When a thing is borrowed, however, the thing itself is returned to the lender, and not some equivalent replacement. The Hebrew language distinguishes between these two categories, referring to the borrowing and lending of *things* as שְׁאֵלָה, and the borrowing and lending of money as הַלְוָאָה (*Ran* 42b, s.v. ולא).

לֹא יַשְׁאִילֶנּוּ, וְלֹא יִשְׁאַל מִמֶּנּוּ; לֹא יַלְוֶנּוּ, וְלֹא יִלְוֶה מִמֶּנּוּ; — *shall not lend him, nor shall he borrow from him; he shall not lend him money, nor shall he borrow money from him;*

Shimon, who is forbidden to benefit

4
6

the field, but may not eat the fruits; [if he made the *neder*] in *Shemittah*, he may enter [the field] and eat.

6. **S**omeone prohibited by a *neder* to benefit from another shall not lend him, nor shall he borrow from him; he shall not lend him money, nor shall he borrow money from him; he shall not sell to him, nor shall he buy from him.

YAD AVRAHAM

from Reuven, may not lend money or anything else to Reuven. Even though, when Shimon lends something to Reuven, he does not enjoy any benefit from the latter, it is forbidden for him to do so. This is a Rabbinic enactment, and was instituted as a precaution lest — by lending to Reuven — Shimon would be led to also borrowing from him, which would be prohibited by the *neder* (*Rav*).

In a case in which the prohibition of Shimon was initiated by Reuven, and not self-imposed by Shimon, it may be presumed that Reuven bears some grudge against Shimon, to which he gives expression by forbidding the latter to derive any benefits from him (cf. mishnah 4, s.v. וְאוֹכֵל). If this is true, then it is plausible that Reuven would never agree to lend anything to Shimon even if Shimon lent things to him. Following this reasoning, some authorities (see above) note that, in his explanation of the mishnah, *Rav* specifies that the *neder* forbidding Shimon to benefit from Reuven was made by Shimon himself.

Tos. Yom Tov finds this qualification difficult, arguing that the law of the mishnah should apply equally to the case in which Reuven directed the *neder* at Shimon. However, we can refute *Tos. Yom Tov*'s argument if we accept the premise that, in a case that Reuven bans Shimon, he will also not agree to lend him anything, since he bears some grudge against him. If this is so, then the precaution of the mishnah prohibiting Shi-

mon from lending to Reuven lest he borrow from him is unnecessary, because Reuven will never lend him in any event. The mishnah's precautionary enactment is logical only in a case that Reuven bears no malice for Shimon, and might lend him something. That would be true only if the prohibition on Shimon was self-imposed. It is for this reason that *Rav* limits the law of the mishnah to such a case (*Rashash; R' Yoel Chasid*).

וְלֹא יִמְכֹּר לוֹ, וְלֹא יִקַּח מִמֶּנּוּ. — *he shall not sell to him, nor shall he buy from him.*

Most authorities explain that this ruling, too, is based on a Rabbinic enactment. Thus, Shimon shall not sell to Reuven even though the sale is not considered a benefit for Shimon (see below), lest he come to buy from Reuven, which would be a benefit and, hence, prohibited (*Rav; Rambam Comm.; Ran* 43a).

The assertion that Shimon's selling something to Reuven would not constitute a benefit for Shimon, and is therefore prohibited only Rabbinically, needs clarification. It has been stated above (comm. to 3:11) that, when an item of average marketability is sold at a fair price, both the seller and the buyer are considered to have derived some benefit from each other. If that were the case in our mishnah, then Shimon's selling to Reuven would be prohibited under the terms of the *neder*, and not just as a

אָמַר לוֹ: „הַשְׁאִילֵנִי פָרָתְךָ". אָמַר לוֹ: „אֵינָהּ
פְּנוּיָה". אָמַר: „קוֹנָם שָׂדִי שֶׁאֲנִי חוֹרֵשׁ בָּהּ
לְעוֹלָם". אִם הָיָה דַּרְכּוֹ לַחֲרוֹשׁ — הוּא אָסוּר,
וְכָל אָדָם מֻתָּרִין; אִם אֵין דַּרְכּוֹ לַחֲרוֹשׁ —
הוּא וְכָל אָדָם אֲסוּרִין.

ר' עובדיה מברטנורא

אם היה דרכו לחרוש הוא אסור. דלא איכוין אלא שלא יחרוש הוא עצמו כמו שהיה רגיל אבל
אחרים יחרשו: **ואם אין דרכו לחרוש.** דעתו היה שלא יחרשו בה לא הוא ולא אחרים:

יד אברהם

precautionary measure. The only case in which a seller does not benefit from the buyer is when the item is sold below cost. Therefore, that must be the case of the mishnah, and the intent is that Shimon should not sell to Reuven for less than cost, although to do so is not a benefit to the former. It is prohibited only to prevent the possibility of Shimon buying from Reuven for less than cost in violation of the *neder* (*Rav; Tos. Yom Tov*).

Just as it is Rabbinically forbidden for Shimon to sell to Reuven at less than cost, so too is it prohibited for him to buy from Reuven at more than the fair price. Although buying something at an excessive price is not considered a benefit for the buyer, it is interdicted lest he come to sell to Reuven at a high price which would be a benefit to him from Reuven and, consequently, a violation of the *neder* (*Turei Zahav* to *Yoreh Deah* 221:28). Thus, the Rabbis forbade Shimon to engage even in a transaction in which he is not considered the beneficiary, lest he partake in one in which he is (*Rav; Tos. Yom Tov*).

In the case of 3:11, although the person forbade upon himself to have benefit from all Jews, he was nonetheless permitted to conduct such transaction from which he does not derive a benefit. Thus, he was allowed to sell for less and buy for more than the fair price; no Rabbinic enactment was made to disallow such transactions. The reason for the greater stringency in the case of our mishnah is that the scope of the *neder* under consideration here is quite limited. Only Shimon's dealings with Reuven are affected; he may do business with anyone else. Therefore, imposing a precautionary restriction upon Shimon does not make the situation intolerable for him. In the case of 3:11, on the other hand, were the Rabbis to forbid Shimon from participating even in transactions which bring him no benefit, they would be creating circumstances that would be almost impossible to withstand. Although he would be allowed to deal with non-Jews, this was considered a very desperate alternative. Therefore — to afford him some possibilities of doing business with Jews — the Rabbis refrained from adding to his prohibitions (*Ran* 43, s.v. אביי).

Rosh (42b) construes the mishnah as dealing with actual violations of the *neder*, and not just a Rabbinic enactment. Unlike the previous statement, [He] *shall not lend him* and *he shall not lend him money*, which are Rabbinic prohibitions, the ruling *He shall not sell to him, nor shall he buy from him* is a result of the *neder* itself. The mishnah is discussing an item of average marketability being sold at a fair price. Whether Shimon is the buyer or the seller, he will derive some benefit from Reuven, and this is prohibited by the *neder*.

According to *Rosh*, therefore, it is

He said to him: "Lend me your vow." He responded: "It is not available." He said: "*Konam*, my field with respect to ever plowing [it] with it." If it was his practice to plow, he is forbidden, but other people are permitted; if it is not his practice to plow, he and all [other] people are forbidden.

YAD AVRAHAM

permitted even Rabbinically for Shimon to buy from Reuven at a high price, and to sell to him at a low price, since, in both cases, Shimon does not benefit from Reuven. The Rabbis saw no need for legislation here, because — if, for example, Shimon sold to Reuven for less than cost — it is assumed that he did so in order to avoid benefiting from Reuven. Obviously, then, he is cognizant that it is forbidden for him to benefit from Reuven, and there is therefore no need to fear that this will lead him to buy from Reuven for less than cost (*Cheshek Shlomo* to 3:11).

According to this interpretation, the halachah in this case involving individuals is precisely the same as that of the case in 3:11 dealing with all Jews. Indeed, in his commentary (30b), *Rosh* writes that the mishnah in 3:11 could just as well have been formulated in terms of a *neder* directed at an individual, rather than one directed at all Jews.

The next case of the mishnah is discussed here incidentally by the *Tanna*, since it involves שְׁאֵלָה, *loan of items*, which was mentioned in the preceding section of the mishnah (*Meiri*).

הַשְׁאִילֵנִי פָּרָתָךְ״. — *He said to him: "Lend me your cow."*

A person (e.g., Levi), who is not subject to any *nedarim* (*Rashi*), addresses another (e.g., Yehudah), and

asks to borrow his cow (*Tif. Yis.*).

אָמַר לוֹ: ,,אֵינָהּ פְּנוּיָה״. — *He responded* (lit. *said to him*): "It is not available."

Yehudah refuses Levi's request, explaining that the cow is being used, and is not available (*Rashi*).

אָמַר: ,,קוֹנָם, שָׂדִי שֶׁאֲנִי חוֹרֵשׁ בָּהּ לְעוֹלָם״. — *He said: "Konam, my field with respect to ever plowing [it] with it."*

Levi, angry because he did not get the cow, makes a *neder* which prohibits him to use it for plowing his field (*ibid.*; *Tur Yoreh Deah* 218). [Ordinarily, if someone other than Levi were now to plow the latter's field with this cow, Levi would be said to have enjoyed a prohibited benefit. However, in our case, the mishnah qualifies the consequences of Levi's declaration by determining his intention, as follows.]

אִם הָיָה דַרְכּוֹ לַחֲרוֹשׁ – הוּא אָסוּר, וְכָל אָדָם מֻתָּרִין; — *If it was his practice to plow, he is forbidden, but other people are permitted;*

If Levi always did his plowing by himself, we interpret his declaration as prohibiting only direct benefit from the cow. That is, only when he himself plows with the cow has he used it in a prohibited manner. But for others to plow his field for him with this cow is permitted. Even though he has benefited from the cow, he never intended this type of benefit to be forbidden (*Rav*).

אִם אֵין דַּרְכּוֹ לַחֲרוֹשׁ – הוּא וְכָל אָדָם אֲסוּרִין.

[ז] הַמֻּדָּר הֲנָאָה מֵחֲבֵרוֹ, וְאֵין לוֹ מַה יֹּאכַל – הוֹלֵךְ אֵצֶל הַחֶנְוָנִי, וְאוֹמֵר: "אִישׁ פְּלוֹנִי מֻדָּר מִמֶּנִּי הֲנָאָה, וְאֵינִי יוֹדֵעַ מָה אֶעֱשֶׂה". וְהוּא נוֹתֵן לוֹ, וּבָא וְנוֹטֵל מִזֶּה.

הָיָה בֵיתוֹ לִבְנוֹת, גְּדֵרוֹ לִגְדּוֹר, שָׂדֵהוּ לִקְצוֹר

―――――― ר' עובדיה מברטנורא ――――――

(ז) ואין לו מה יאכל. אורחא דמלתא נקט והוא הדין אפילו יש לו מה יאכל: **ובא זה ונוטל מזה.** אם ירצה ליתן לו, ואינו עובר על נדרו, אבל אינו יכול לכופו לשלם לו דהא לא אמר לו תן לו ואני אפרע, ואם אמר לו תן לו ואני אפרע אסור, דהא שליח שוייה:

יד אברהם

— if it is not his practice to plow, he and all [other] people are forbidden.

If Levi generally had hired help to plow his field, we interpret his dec-

laration as forbidding the benefit of the field being plowed with Yehudah's cow even by people other than himself (Rav).

7.

הַמֻּדָּר הֲנָאָה מֵחֲבֵרוֹ, וְאֵין לוֹ מַה יֹּאכַל― — [If] someone is prohibited by a neder to benefit from another, and he does not have what to eat,

[For example, Shimon is not permitted to benefit from Reuven, and he is short of food. The mishnah shows how Reuven can be instrumental in resolving Shimon's predicament, without Shimon violating the terms of the neder.]

The technique Reuven uses would be allowed even if Shimon was not short of food, but the mishnah selects the more common case of Shimon in need of food, and without the means to acquire it (Rav).

הוֹלֵךְ אֵצֶל הַחֶנְוָנִי, — [the other person] goes to the storekeeper,

Reuven goes to the storekeeper (Meiri).

The mishnah writes the storekeeper, rather than a storekeeper, to indicate that Reuven may even go to

his regular storekeeper, who often gives him things on credit (Ran).

וְאוֹמֵר: "אִישׁ פְּלוֹנִי מֻדָּר מִמֶּנִּי הֲנָאָה, וְאֵינִי יוֹדֵעַ מָה אֶעֱשֶׂה". — and says: "So-and so is prohibited by a neder to benefit from me, and I don't know what to do."

Reuven apprises the storekeeper of Shimon's situation. If the storekeeper now responds by providing Shimon with food, it is not considered that the storekeeper did so as an agent of Reuven. At no time did Reuven request him to supply Shimon. He simply informed him of the situation, and the storekeeper acted on his own (Rav).

וְהוּא נוֹתֵן לוֹ, — He gives him,

The storekeeper supplies Shimon if he should so desire. Shimon is permitted to accept the goods, since this does not violate the neder. Although Reuven had a role in inspiring the storekeeper to act, the latter's deed

7. [I f] someone is prohibited by a *neder* to benefit from another, and he does not have what to eat, [the other person] goes to the storekeeper, and says: "So-and-so is prohibited by a *neder* to benefit from me, and I don't know what to do." He gives him, and collects from this one.

[If] he had a house to be built, a fence to be erected, [or] a field to be harvested, [the other

YAD AVRAHAM

was independently motivated. He is not an agent of Reuven, and thus, to accept goods from him is not equivalent to benefiting from Reuven (*Rav; Rosh*).

וּבָא וְנוֹטֵל מִזֶּה. — *and collects from this one.*

[The storekeeper, after supplying Shimon, may then return to Reuven, who may pay him for whatever was given to Shimon.]

Since Reuven did not appoint him to give food to Shimon, the storekeeper has no legal claim on Reuven (ibid.); at most, he has a claim on Shimon for the food he supplied. Nevertheless, it is permissible for Reuven to pay the storekeeper, since — as explained in mishnah 2 — it is permitted for Reuven to eliminate a claim from Shimon. The mishnah thus states only that Reuven is allowed to pay the storekeeper, but is not obligated to do so (*Rambam Comm.; Tos. Yom Tov*).

Those who treat the elimination of a claim like a real benefit must explain this case somewhat differently. *Tosafos* (*Bava Kamma* 109a, s.v. ב"ח), quoted by *Tos. Yom Tov*, suggest that the storekeeper did not sell to Shimon on credit; rather, he gave Shimon an outright gift. In turn, Reuven — should he be so inclined — gives the storekeeper a gift for the same amount. Since the store-

keeper has no accounts to settle with Shimon, Reuven's gift to the storekeeper is not at all related to Shimon, and is therefore permissible.

The next case in the mishnah is another illustration of how Reuven, from whom Shimon may not benefit, can still be instrumental in having assistance reach Shimon without actually directing it to him.

According to most authorities, there is no difference halachically between the examples of the mishnah. However, *Kesef Mishneh* (Hil. *Nedarim* 7:12) suggests that *Rambam* did distinguish between them. In the first case of the mishnah in which Shimon's hunger is a vital concern, it is permitted from the outset for Reuven to hint to the storekeeper; but — in the following cases — in which the concerns are not so crucial, the ruling applies only where it is a *fait accompli*; i.e., where Reuven has already initiated the process.

הָיָה בֵיתוֹ לִבְנוֹת, גְּדֵרוֹ לִגְדּוֹר, שָׂדֵהוּ לִקְצוֹר — *[If] he had a house to be built, a fence to be erected, [or] a field to be harvested,*

[Shimon — who is forbidden to benefit from Reuven — needs any or all of these services, but cannot afford them.]

הוֹלֵךְ אֵצֶל הַפּוֹעֲלִים, וְאוֹמֵר: ,,אִישׁ פְּלוֹנִי
מֻדָּר מִמֶּנִּי הֲנָאָה, וְאֵינִי יוֹדֵעַ מָה אֶעֱשֶׂה". הֵם
עוֹשִׂין עִמּוֹ, וּבָאִין וְנוֹטְלִין שָׂכָר מִזֶּה.

[ח] **הָיוּ** מְהַלְּכִין בַּדֶּרֶךְ, וְאֵין לוֹ מַה יֹּאכַל —
נוֹתֵן לְאַחֵר לְשׁוּם מַתָּנָה, וְהַלָּה מֻתָּר
בָּהּ. אִם אֵין עִמָּהֶם אַחֵר — מַנִּיחַ עַל הַסֶּלַע אוֹ עַל
הַגָּדֵר, וְאוֹמֵר: ,,הֲרֵי הֵן מֻפְקָרִים לְכָל מִי שֶׁיַּחְפּוֹץ",
וְהַלָּה נוֹטֵל וְאוֹכֵל; וְרַבִּי יוֹסֵי אוֹסֵר.

――――――― ר' עובדיה מברטנורא ―――――――

(ח) **ורבי יוסי אוסר.** דכיון שאין שם אחר שיכול לזכות אלא הוא הוי כמתנה. ואין הלכה כרבי
יוסי. ודוקא באין לו מה יאכל הוא דשרו רבנן אבל באינש אחרינא לא:

יד אברהם

הוֹלֵךְ אֵצֶל הַפּוֹעֲלִים, וְאוֹמֵר: ,,אִישׁ פְּלוֹנִי
מֻדָּר מִמֶּנִּי הֲנָאָה, וְאֵינִי יוֹדֵעַ מָה אֶעֱשֶׂה".
[the other person] goes to the workers,
and says: "So-and-so is prohibited by a
neder to benefit from me, and I don't
know what to do."

[Reuven approaches some workers
and informs them of Shimon's plight,
but does not instruct them in any
way.]

הֵם עוֹשִׂין עִמּוֹ, וּבָאִין וְנוֹטְלִין שָׂכָר מִזֶּה.
They may work for him, and collect
wages from this one.

The workers, on their own, attend

to whatever it is that Shimon needs,
but the latter does not have the funds
to cover the cost of the job. As in the
previous case, Reuven may compen-
sate the workers, since he is simply
eliminating a claim from Shimon, and
not providing him with a real benefit
(Rambam Comm.; Tos. Yom Tov).

If we hold that elimination of a claim is a
benefit, then the case here involves workers
who helped Shimon voluntarily and free of
charge. Thus, whatever Reuven gives the
workers is a gift to them, and has no bearing
on Shimon (see Tos. Yom Tov).

8.

In this mishnah, it is clear that, once Reuven's property (in particular, his
food) leaves his possession, it is no longer subject to the neder he declared
while it belonged to him. Accordingly, the mishnah is dealing either with a
neder which prohibits Shimon from benefiting from Reuven himself, or one
in which Reuven specified that he was interdicting his property. Once the
property is transferred to a third party, Shimon may benefit from it, since to
do so is no longer considered benefiting from Reuven (s.v. בעא, and 42b, s.v.
אם; Chidushei R' Akiva Eiger to Turei Zahav Yoreh Deah 221:16; see preface to
mishnah 5 Ran 34b, 42b).

הָיוּ מְהַלְּכִין בַּדֶּרֶךְ, וְאֵין לוֹ מַה יֹּאכַל— [If]
they were traveling on the road, and he
did not have what to eat,

Reuven, Shimon, and Levi were
traveling together, and Shimon, who
is forbidden to benefit from Reuven,

person] goes to the workers, and says: "So-and-so is prohibited by a *neder* to benefit from me, and I don't know what to do." They may work for him, and collect wages from this one.

8. [**I**f] they were traveling on the road, and he did not have what to eat, he gives [food] to someone else as a gift, and that one is permitted it. If there is no one else with them, he puts [it] on a rock or on a fence, and says: "These are free for whoever should want," and that one takes and eats; R' Yose, however, forbids [this].

YAD AVRAHAM

no longer has any food. Reuven happens to have some extra food, and wishes to give some of it to Shimon, but cannot do so directly because of the *neder*. To hint to Levi that he should give the food, and that Reuven would remunerate him in the manner of the previous mishnah, is not a likely solution, since Levi had probably taken only enough food for himself, and not enough to give away any (*Meiri*). [Therefore, the mishnah must devise a new method to enable Reuven to get food to Shimon without violating the *neder*.]

נוֹתֵן לְאַחֵר לְשׁוּם מַתָּנָה, וְהַלָּה מֻתָּר בָּהּ. —
he gives [food] to someone else as a gift, and that one is permitted it.

[Reuven gives some food to Levi as a gift. Levi then proceeds to offer it to Shimon, who is permitted to benefit from things belonging to Levi.]

Tos. Yom Tov follows the view of *Rosh*, who permits this method only when Shimon is without food. If Shimon has some food, however, it is not allowed, because there is always the fear that Reuven does not sincerely give the food to Levi as a gift.

After all, his true objective is that it reach Shimon, and if the gift to Levi is not meant sincerely, then it remains Reuven's property and is forbidden for Shimon to eat. Because of this concern, *Rosh* permits this manner of giving a third party a gift only in extreme circumstances such as when Shimon is completely out of food. *Tos. Yom Tov* appears to have understood *Rav* as agreeing with *Rosh*. However, *Tos. R' Akiva* maintains that *Rav* disagrees, and permits the method of this mishnah even when Shimon is not in dire need.

אִם אֵין עִמָּהֶם אַחֵר – מַנִּיחַ עַל הַסֶּלַע אוֹ עַל
הַגָּדֵר, וְאוֹמֵר: "הֲרֵי הֵן מֻפְקָרִים לְכָל מִי
שֶׁיַּחְפֹּץ", וְהַלָּה נוֹטֵל וְאוֹכֵל; — *If there is no one else with them, he puts [it] on a rock or on a fence, and says: "These are free for whoever should want," and that one takes and eats;*

If Reuven and Shimon are alone on the road, the only way for Reuven to transfer food to Shimon without violating the *neder* is to declare the food to be ownerless. The food is thus no longer owned by Reuven, and is available for repossession by

anyone who takes it. *That one* (Shimon) may now gain possession of it and eat it without transgressing the *neder* (*Ran*).

וְרַבִּי יוֹסֵי אוֹסֵר. — *R' Yose, however, forbids [this].*

R' Yose agrees in principle with the first, anonymous *Tanna* that it is permitted for Shimon to take possession of something made ownerless by Reuven. However, he is concerned that, if that is permitted, Reuven might declare something ownerless by announcing: "This is free for taking, but only by Shimon." This

would not be a valid renunciation of ownership, and Shimon would be forbidden to take it. To prevent this from occurring, R' Yose disallowed the entire method (*Ran; Tos. Yom Tov* explaining *Rav*).

Although *Tos. R' Akiva* holds that *Rav* allows transfer to a third party even when Shimon is not in great need, as in the first case of the mishnah he admits that the second method of declaring the food to be ownerless is allowed by *Rav* only if Shimon is in genuine need because the first *Tanna*, who permits the method, and whom the halachah follows, only allows it to be employed in extreme circumstances.

פרק חמישי ‌
Chapter Five

If a property is owned by a partnership of two or more persons, there are laws which govern whether one of them has the right to insist that the property be divided so that each partner gets his rightful share. Once the property would be distributed among the partners, each would be the full owner of his share, and would have no rights in any other part of the property. In the absence of such a distribution, the partners jointly use the entire property.

If the property in question is land, the crucial criterion is area; a division can be made only if each partner will receive at least four square cubits. Should the land not be large enough for this, no partner can insist that it be divided (*Bava Basra* 1:6; *Choshen Mishpat* 171:3).

Regarding *nedarim*, these considerations have numerous ramifications. A person has no authority to effect a prohibition which will restrict others from something he himself does not own (see preface to 1:1). Obviously, this does not apply to a shared property which is divided among partners; his share is his to do with as he pleases. Before the property is distributed, however — at which time all the partners are equally entitled to use the entire property — it may be argued that since no single partner can claim exclusive ownership, none of them can prohibit it to others with a *neder*.

A distinction may be drawn between the type of property which one of the partners can insist be divided, and one which he cannot. A property of the former category — since it will almost certainly be divided eventually — might be treated as consisting of individual shares, albeit unidentified at this point, even before the actual distribution is carried out. However, a property which cannot be divided without the consent of all the partners might be considered jointly shared by all of them, rather than comprising distinct and individually owned shares. In that case, perhaps it would not be within the jurisdiction of any partners to forbid his share to another (see *Ran* 45b).

[א] **הַשֻּׁתָּפִין** שֶׁנָּדְרוּ הֲנָאָה זֶה מִזֶּה —
אֲסוּרִין לִכָּנֵס לֶחָצֵר. רַבִּי
אֱלִיעֶזֶר בֶּן יַעֲקֹב אוֹמֵר: זֶה נִכְנָס לְתוֹךְ שֶׁלּוֹ,
וְזֶה נִכְנָס לְתוֹךְ שֶׁלּוֹ; וּשְׁנֵיהֶם אֲסוּרִים לְהַעֲמִיד

━━━━━━━━━━ ר' עובדיה מברטנורא ━━━━━━━━━━

פרק חמישי – השותפין. (א) השותפין. שיש לכל אחד מהם בית בחצר והחצר שלפני הבתים
שניהם שותפם בה, ובזמן שיש בחצר דין חלוקה, והוא שהיה לכל בית ובית ארבע אמות בחצר
לפני הבית ונשאר עוד מן החצר ארבע אמות לזה וארבע אמות לזה, בהא מודו כולי עלמא
דשניהם אסורים ליכנס בחצר עד שיחלוקו הואיל ויש בה דין חלוקה. ולא נפליגו רבי אליעזר
ורבנן אלא בחצר שאין בה דין חלוקה, רבנן אמרי כל אחד מהם בשל חברו הוא נכנס, ורבי
אליעזר בן יעקב סבר יש ברירה והאי בדידיה קאזיל והאי בדידיה קאזיל:

━━━━━━━━ **יד אברהם** ━━━━━━━━

1.

הַשֻּׁתָּפִין שֶׁנָּדְרוּ הֲנָאָה זֶה מִזֶּה— *Partners who have prohibited with a neder the benefit of each other*

Reuven and Shimon are joint owners of a property. Reuven has made a *neder* forbidding himself to benefit from Shimon's property, and Shimon has done the same regarding Reuven (*Rav; Tos. R' Akiva*). Alternatively, Shimon has forbidden benefit from his property to Reuven, and vice versa (*Tif. Yis.* from *Gem.* 46a).

The *Gemara* (46b) explains that, if the shared property is such that any partner can coerce the other to divide it (see preface), all agree that the *nedarim* are effective in banning both Reuven and Shimon from entering the property. We do not say, for example, that Reuven — when entering the property — is, in fact, treading on his own share of the property which would be permitted, since it was never forbidden to him by a *neder*; rather, since Reuven's personal share can and will be deci-sively identified and isolated by distributing the property, we do not permit Reuven to walk on anything that is not his with certainty, and might be Shimon's. Therefore, prior to the distribution, neither partner can enter the shared property; after the distribution, either of them can enter his own share of the property (*Rav* following *Rambam; Rashba* disagrees; see *Ran* 46b, s.v. אבל).

The mishnah, which presents a difference of opinion concerning the shared property, is discussing a property not large enough for a partner to be able to force distribution. In such a case we do not view the property as necessarily heading toward division. Instead, it is assumed that the partners will share the property in common without dividing it up. Therefore, we treat the partners as though each of them owns the entire property indi-vidually. This is accomplished by assuming that the partnership agree-ment provides for a rotation of own-ership among the partners. Thus, the initial agreement arranges that the property shall belong for a period of time to Reuven, and for another period to Shimon. The idea be-hind such an arrangement is to achieve

5
1

1. **P**artners who have prohibited with a *neder* the benefit of each other are forbidden to enter the yard. R' Eliezer ben Yaakov says: This one is entering into his own [property], and this one is entering into his own [property]; but both are forbidden to install

YAD AVRAHAM

that, when Reuven uses the property, it belongs completely to him, and when Shimon uses the property, it belongs completely to him. Clearly, the precise sequence of ownership cannot be known at the outset. On the other hand, it may be said with certainty that the original partnership agreement allows for definite ownership of the entire property by each partner at some time.

The following dispute between R' Eliezer ben Yaakov and the Sages revolves on whether this lack of specificity regarding the sequence of ownership is significant (*Ran*).

אֲסוּרִין לִכָּנֵס לֶחָצֵר. — *are forbidden to enter the yard.*

This is the opinion of the Sages who consider such property (in this case, *the yard*) to be comprised of the independent — but unidentifiable — shares of each partner. Since no distribution of these shares is in the offing, they maintain that we cannot identify the shares, and hence, cannot distinguish between Reuven's part and Shimon's. Therefore, if — for example — Reuven were to enter the yard, he might be treading on Shimon's property, which is forbidden to him by the *neder*. Hence, they are forbidden to enter the yard (ibid.).

As explained previously, the partnership agreement provided that, during Reuven's use of the property, it should belong solely to Reuven;

therefore, when Reuven enters, he should be entering his *own* property — something he is permitted to do. However, the Sages maintain that since the times that each partner will use the property are unknown at the time of the agreement, it is not an effective agreement. Therefore, rather than assuming the property to belong on a rotational basis to one partner at a time, we assume that each partner constantly owns a share of the property. Therefore, if either of them enters, he might be walking on the other partner's share — something forbidden to him by the *neder* (ibid.).

רַבִּי אֱלִיעֶזֶר בֶּן יַעֲקֹב אוֹמֵר: זֶה נִכְנָס לְתוֹךְ שֶׁלּוֹ, וְזֶה נִכְנָס לְתוֹךְ שֶׁלּוֹ; — *R' Eliezer ben Yaakov says: This one is entering into his own [property], and this one is entering into his own [property];*

R' Eliezer considers the partnership agreement to be binding. Although the sequence of ownership is not known initially, it becomes identified as the partners use the property. The crucial thing which the contract must specify is *who* owns the property. This it does by making clear that each partner will at some time own the whole property. Accordingly, when Reuven comes into the yard, he is entering a property which is totally his, and is, of course, permitted. Thus, R' Eliezer ben Yaakov rules that access to the property is not curtailed by the *neder* (*Ran*).

שָׁם רֵחַיִם וְתַנּוּר, וּלְגַדֵּל תַּרְנְגוֹלִים.
הָיָה אֶחָד מֵהֶם מֻדָּר הֲנָאָה מֵחֲבֵרוֹ, לֹא יִכָּנֵס
לֶחָצֵר. רַבִּי אֱלִיעֶזֶר בֶּן יַעֲקֹב אוֹמֵר: יָכוֹל הוּא
לוֹמַר לוֹ: ,,לְתוֹךְ שֶׁלִּי אֲנִי נִכְנָס, וְאֵינִי נִכְנָס לְתוֹךְ
שֶׁלָּךְ״. וְכוֹפִין אֶת הַנּוֹדֵר לִמְכּוֹר אֶת חֶלְקוֹ.

[ב] **הָיָה** אֶחָד מִן הַשּׁוּק מֻדָּר מֵאֶחָד מֵהֶם הֲנָאָה

ר' עובדיה מברטנורא

ושניהם אסורים להעמיד שם רחים וכו'. ומודה רבי אלעזר בן יעקב בכל הני דשותפים
מעכבים זה על זה, דלא שייך להתיר מטעם ברירה, דכיון דבידו לעכב עליו ואינו מעכב נמלא
מהנהו: **וכופין את הנודר למכור את חלקו.** דחיישינן מאחר שרואה את חברו נכנס ישכח
ויכנס גם הוא, אבל כששניהם אסורים לא חיישינן, ודוקא כשנדר מעלמו שלא יהנה בשל חברו
הוא דכופין אותו למכור חלקו, אבל אם חברו הדירו שלא יהנה ממנו, אנוס הוא ואין כופין אותו
למכור דמלי אית ליה למיעבד, ואם אמרת כן כל שותף ידיר את חברו שלא יהנה ממנו, כדי
שיכופו אותו למכור לו חלקו: **(ב) היה אחד מן השוק וכו'.** להודיעך כחו דרבי אלעזר בן
יעקב נקט לה, דאפילו אחד מן השוק שאין לו חלק בחלר שרי ליה רבי אלעזר בן יעקב ליכנס
מטעם ברירה. והלכה כרבי אלעזר בן יעקב:

יד אברהם

**וּשְׁנֵיהֶם אֲסוּרִים לְהַעֲמִיד שָׁם רֵחַיִם וְתַנּוּר,
וּלְגַדֵּל תַּרְנְגוֹלִים.** — *but both are
forbidden to install a mill or an oven
there, or to raise chickens.*

No partnership allows for one
partner to introduce into the property
things which affect the entire property and which reduce its availability
to the remaining partners (see *Meiri*).
Even R' Eliezer ben Yaakov, who
legitimizes a rotational ownership,
agrees that no partner has the right
to unilaterally introduce an oven or a
mill into the yard. To do so inevitably
affects the whole yard, as well as
reduces it in size. It is thus a form of
deriving benefit from the other partner's property which is prohibited by
the *neder* (*Meiri; Ran*).

**הָיָה אֶחָד מֵהֶם מֻדָּר הֲנָאָה מֵחֲבֵרוֹ, לֹא יִכָּנֵס
לֶחָצֵר. רַבִּי אֱלִיעֶזֶר בֶּן יַעֲקֹב אוֹמֵר: יָכוֹל הוּא
לוֹמַר לוֹ: ,,לְתוֹךְ שֶׁלִּי אֲנִי נִכְנָס, וְאֵינִי נִכְנָס
לְתוֹךְ שֶׁלָּךְ״.** — *[If] one of them was*

*prohibited by a neder from benefiting
from the other, he may not enter the
yard. R' Eliezer ben Yaakov says: He
may say to him: "I am entering my
own [property]; I am not entering
yours."*

This is identical to the previous
case, except that instead of both
partners being bound by a *neder*, only
one of them is forbidden to benefit
from the other (*Tos. 46a, s.v.* הָיָה).
Thus, for example, Reuven and Shimon are joint holders of a property,
and the latter makes a *neder* forbidding himself to benefit from Reuven
(*Rav; Rambam; Ran*). [Once again, the
issue is whether the claim that the
partner is entering his own property is
a valid one.]

וְכוֹפִין אֶת הַנּוֹדֵר לִמְכּוֹר אֶת חֶלְקוֹ. — *We
force the one who made the neder to sell
his share.*

Shimon, who imposed the prohibi-

5
2

a mill or an oven there, or to raise chickens.

[If] one of them was prohibited by a *neder* from benefiting from the other, he may not enter the yard. R' Eliezer ben Yaakov says: He may say to him: "I am entering my own [property]; I am not entering yours." We force the one who made the *neder* to sell his share.

2. [**I**f] someone from the street was prohibited by a *neder* to benefit from one of them,

YAD AVRAHAM

tion upon himself, is forced to sell his share, because — were he to retain his ownership — he would inevitably be drawn into violating the *neder*. Because — upon observing Reuven, who has no such restrictions, coming and going freely — Shimon might be led to do the same out of jealousy, thereby violating his *neder* (*Rav; Rosh* 45b).

To enforce the *neder* and prevent its violation, a partner who imposes upon himself a prohibition restricting his access to the joint property is obligated to sell his share. This punishment is applied, because the person made a *neder* which he will probably not be able to keep (*Ran*).

However, had Shimon been forbidden as a consequence of a *neder* made by Reuven, he would not be penalized. Since Shimon did not initiate the

prohibition, he should not be made to suffer by selling his share because of it. On the other hand, Reuven, who initiated the *neder*, is also not punishable, since he did not make a *neder* which *he* cannot keep; obeying the *neder* is Shimon's responsibility (*Rav*, as understood by *Tos. Yom Tov; Ran*; see commentary to mishnah 4, s.v. הֲרֵי). *Rambam* (*Hil. Nedarim* 7:5), however, rules in such a case that Reuven is forced to sell his share.

This last statement of the mishnah would appear to be the view of the first, anonymous *Tanna*, since — according to R' Eliezer ben Yaakov — it is permitted for Shimon to enter the property (*Tos.* 46a, s.v. היה; *Rashi*). *Ran* maintains, however, that, since Shimon may not assemble an oven on the property, even R' Eliezer ben Yaakov requires him to sell his share, lest he come to do so out of jealousy when he sees Reuven doing it.

2.

הָיָה אֶחָד מִן הַשׁוּק מֻדָּר מֵאֶחָד מֵהֶם הֲנָאָה — *[If] someone from the street was prohibited by a neder to benefit from one of them,*

A third party (e.g., Levi), who is not a partner in the property, is forbidden by a *neder* to benefit from Reuven, a partner of Shimon (*Rashi*).

[The mishnah addresses the question of whether Levi can enter the property held jointly by Reuven and Shimon. Will that constitute trespassing on Reuven's property — a violation of the *neder* — or can Levi claim that he is treading on Shimon's property, which is permitted?

— לֹא יִכָּנֵס לֶחָצֵר. רַבִּי אֱלִיעֶזֶר בֶּן יַעֲקֹב אוֹמֵר: יָכוֹל הוּא לוֹמַר לוֹ: ,,לְתוֹךְ שֶׁל חֲבֵרְךָ אֲנִי נִכְנָס, וְאֵינִי נִכְנָס לְתוֹךְ שֶׁלָּךְ''.

[ג] הַמֻּדָּר הֲנָאָה מֵחֲבֵרוֹ, וְיֶשׁ לוֹ מֶרְחָץ וּבֵית הַבַּד מֻשְׂכָּרִים בָּעִיר, אִם יֶשׁ לוֹ בָּהֶן תְּפִיסַת יָד — אָסוּר.

ר' עובדיה מברטנורא

(ג) **המודר הנאה מחבירו ויש לו מרחץ ובית הבד. וכו'.** ראובן שנאסר עליו ליהנות בנכסי שמעון ויש לשמעון בעיר מרחץ ובית הבד שהשכירן לאחרים ובא ראובן להשתמש בהן, רואין אם נשאר [לשמעון] מקום בזה המרחץ ובית הבד שלא השכירו כגון בור בבית המרחץ וכיוצא בזה, אסור לראובן להשתמש בהם, ואם לאו מותר:

יד אברהם

יָכוֹל הוּא לוֹמַר לוֹ: ,,לְתוֹךְ שֶׁל חֲבֵרְךָ אֲנִי נִכְנָס, וְאֵינִי נִכְנָס לְתוֹךְ שֶׁלָּךְ''. — *he may not enter the yard. R' Eliezer ben Yaakov says: He may say to him: "I am entering into your partner's property; I am not entering into yours."*

Rav notes that this case — which applies R' Eliezer ben Yaakov's ruling to a third party — is an indication of how far his opinion goes. Even though Reuven is a partner in the property, Levi's presence there is a form of Shimon's use of the property (*Rashba*), and this identifies the property at that time as being Shimon's.

The halachah follows R' Eliezer ben Yaakov (*Yoreh Deah* 226:1), and so, Levi may enter the property. However, if he enters for any reason other than for Shimon, his entry is forbidden, since then his claim that he is entering Shimon's property is meaningless (ibid.).

For example, Reuven made a *neder*, forbidding benefit from his property to Shimon (*Tur Yoreh Deah* 221).

These questions will depend on the dispute in the previous mishnah between R' Eliezer ben Yaakov and the Sages regarding the nature of the partnership. According to the former, if the entire ownership of the property fluctuates between the partners, then Levi — if he were visiting Shimon — could argue that his entry into the property is a form of Shimon's use of the property, at which time it becomes his; therefore, Levi should be allowed to enter it. If, however, we follow the Sages' approach, the two partners are considered to own the property concurrently, and their individual shares cannot be identified. Consequently, Levi may not enter there even to visit Shimon, since he might be treading on Reuven's property.]

Thus, Levi's rights of access to the shared yard will depend on the earlier dispute as follows:

לֹא יִכָּנֵס לֶחָצֵר. רַבִּי אֱלִיעֶזֶר בֶּן יַעֲקֹב אוֹמֵר:

3.

הַמֻּדָּר הֲנָאָה מֵחֲבֵרוֹ, — *Someone prohibited by a neder to benefit from another,*

he may not enter the yard. R' Eliezer ben Yaakov says: He may say to him: "I am entering into your partner's property; I am not entering into yours."

3. **S**omeone prohibited by a *neder* to benefit from another, who owns a bathhouse or an olive press which are being leased in the city — if he has an interest in them, it is forbidden;

YAD AVRAHAM

וְיֵשׁ לוֹ מֶרְחָץ וּבֵית הַבַּד מֻשְׂכָּרִים בָּעִיר, — *who owns a bathhouse or an olive press which are being leased in the city —*

[*He* refers to the one whose property is forbidden (in our example, Reuven).]

The example of a bathhouse or an olive press is purely illustrative; the considerations of the mishnah apply equally to any other type of property (*Rashba*).

The mishnah states that, when Reuven makes his *neder*, these concerns of his are being leased to a third party (*Rav*). The right of Shimon to use the press or the bathhouse will depend on whether or not it was included by Reuven in his *neder*. This, in turn, will depend on the term of the lease, as will be seen.

However, *Tos. Yom Tov*, following *Rashba*, notes that the question of whether Reuven included these enterprises in his *neder* is pertinent only if they had already been leased prior to his *neder*. If, on the other hand, the bathhouse or olive press was rented out only *after* the *neder* was made, it was certainly included in the prohibition. Furthermore, renting is not considered a change in ownership. Thus, even while under the control of the lessee, the property remains Reuven's and is forbidden to Shimon. The mishnah deals only with property already rented at the time Reuven makes his *neder*, and considers the possibility that, although it still belongs to Reuven, perhaps he did not include it in his prohibition.

Rav indicates that the lessee must be a third party, and not Shimon, at whom the *neder* is directed. Were Shimon renting Reuven's property, it certainly would be included in the prohibition.

Rashba, however, is uncertain about this, and *Ritva* asserts that the mishnah's ruling applies even to a case in which Shimon is the lessee.

[It is possible that the seemingly superfluous phrase of the mishnah *in the city* supports *Rav's* position and means: If the bathhouse or olive press is rented to someone *in the city*, i.e., other than Shimon (see *Meiri*).

אִם יֶשׁ לוֹ בָּהֶן תְּפִיסַת יָד – אָסוּר; — *if he has an interest in them, it is forbidden;*

If Reuven retained a share in the property for himself even while it was leased out, he certainly had it in mind when he declared benefit from his property to be forbidden to Shimon. Consequently, it is forbidden for the latter to benefit from it.

What it is exactly that Reuven retains is the subject of controversy. *Rav* follows *Rambam*, who explains

אֵין לוֹ בָהֶן תְּפִיסַת יָד — מֻתָּר.
הָאוֹמֵר לַחֲבֵרוֹ: ,,קוֹנָם, לְבֵיתְךָ שֶׁאֲנִי נִכְנָס'',
וְ,,שָׂדְךָ שֶׁאֲנִי לוֹקֵחַ'', מֵת אוֹ שֶׁמְּכָרוֹ לְאַחֵר —
מֻתָּר.

,,קוֹנָם, לְבַיִת זֶה שֶׁאֲנִי נִכְנָס'', ,,שָׂדֶה זוֹ שֶׁאֲנִי
לוֹקֵחַ'', מֵת אוֹ שֶׁמְּכָרוֹ לְאַחֵר — אָסוּר.

ר' עובדיה מברטנורא

ומת או שמכרם לאחר מותר. דכיון שאמר [ביתך] שדך לא נתכוון אלא בזמן שהם שלו, אבל
אם אמר בית זה או שדה זו אסרם עליו לעולם:

יד אברהם

אֵין לוֹ בָהֶן תְּפִיסַת יָד – מֻתָּר. — *if he does
not retain an interest in them, it is
permitted.*

If Reuven's involvement in the
property does not entail any of the
interests mentioned above, he certainly did not include it in his
prohibition, and it is permitted for
Shimon to use. However, if, when
making the *neder*, Reuven specified
that the prohibition should include
even such property, it becomes forbidden, since it is within the jurisdiction of the owner to forbid even
property that he rented to someone
else (*Tos.* 46a, s.v. אם; *Yoreh Deah*
221:6).

הָאוֹמֵר לַחֲבֵרוֹ: ,,קוֹנָם, לְבֵיתְךָ שֶׁאֲנִי נִכְנָס''
וְ,,שָׂדְךָ שֶׁאֲנִי לוֹקֵחַ'', — *[If] someone
says to another: "Konam, your house,
with respect to my entering it," or
"your field with respect to my buying
[it],"*

The person who makes this *neder*
(e.g., Shimon) is forbidden to enter the
other's house or buy his field. Since the
neder specifies *your house* or *your field*,
the prohibition will endure only as
long as the house or field belongs to
that individual (Reuven); if they leave

that Reuven has excluded some part of
the property from the lease. For
example, Reuven retains complete
possession of one tub in the bathouse,
and rents out the bathhouse together
with all the remaining tubs. By virtue
of the tub he keeps himself, Reuven is
said to have the entire bathhouse in
mind when he pronounces his *neder*,
and so, the entire bathhouse becomes
forbidden for Shimon to use (see
Chidushei R' Eliyahu Guttmacher).
[As mentioned earlier, property rented
from Reuven is still owned by him,
and he can prohibit it via a *neder* to
others such as Shimon, if he so pleases.]

Ran explains that Reuven's interest
is the receipt of a fixed percentage of
the annual profit realized by the
various concerns. He thus has actual
holdings in the entire business.

Rosh suggests yet another approach. The property is assumed to
have been included in Reuven's
neder only if he pays some taxes on
it. How-ever, if all taxes are paid by
the lessee, Reuven is not considered
to hold an interest in it, and the
property would not have been included in his *neder*.

5
3

if he does not retain an interest in them, it is permitted.

[If] someone says to another: "Konam, your house, with respect to my entering it," or "your field, with respect to my buying [it]," [and] he died or sold it to another person, it is permitted.

[If he said:] "Konam, this house, with respect to my entering," [or] "this field, with respect to my buying [it]," [and] he died or sold it to another, it is forbidden.

YAD AVRAHAM

Reuven's possession, they become permitted (Rav).

מֵת אוֹ שֶׁמְּכָרוֹ לְאַחֵר – מֻתָּר. — [and] he died or sold it to another person, it is permitted.

If Reuven dies or sells his property, it is no longer his, and — under the terms of the neder — becomes permitted to Shimon (Rav). The same is true if Reuven gives the property to someone as a gift (Ran). [However, if he rents out the property after Shimon has forbidden it to himself with his neder, the property remains forbidden, since such property still belongs to Reuven (see commentary above, s.v. וְיֵשׁ לוֹ).]

The early authorities note that the prohibition will not be lifted if Reuven should sell the house to Shimon. While it might be argued that, once Shimon takes possession, the house is no longer Reuven's, and should therefore be permitted, it is assumed that when Shimon forbade himself to enter Reuven's house, what he really meant was to forbid a house whose

entry was dependent on Reuven. If he buys the house from Reuven, the possibility of entering has been created through the latter by selling it to him; therefore, it remains forbidden. If Reuven sells it to a third party, however, the possibility of entry is controlled by that person, and Shimon may therefore enter the house, and — if he so desires — purchase it from the new owner (Rashba, Meiri to 46b).

„קוֹנָם, לְבַיִת זֶה שֶׁאֲנִי נִכְנָס", „שָׂדֶה זוֹ שֶׁאֲנִי לוֹקֵחַ", מֵת אוֹ שֶׁמְּכָרוֹ לְאַחֵר – אָסוּר. — [If he said:] "Konam, this house, with respect to my entering," [or] "this field, with respect to my buying [it]," [and] he died or sold it to another, it is forbidden.

Here, Shimon directs his neder not at your house or your field, but at this house and this field. The prohibition is not defined in terms of Reuven, the current owner, but is directed at the field or house, regardless of who owns them. Hence, the prohibition persists even if Reuven dies or sells the property (Rav).

4.

Under the laws of nedarim, a person is empowered to ban another person's use of his property (see General Introduction). The following mishnayos

‫[ד] ‏"הֲרֵינִי עָלֶיךָ חֵרֶם" — הַמֻּדָּר אָסוּר;‬
‫"הֲרֵי אַתְּ עָלַי חֵרֶם" — הַנּוֹדֵר‬
‫אָסוּר; "הֲרֵינִי עָלֶיךָ וְאַתְּ עָלַי" — שְׁנֵיהֶם‬
‫אֲסוּרִין. וּשְׁנֵיהֶם מֻתָּרִין בְּדָבָר שֶׁל עוֹלֵי בָבֶל,‬
‫וַאֲסוּרִין בְּדָבָר שֶׁל אוֹתָהּ הָעִיר.‬

ר' עובדיה מברטנורא

‫(ד) הריני עליך חרם. הנאתי תהיה אסורה עליך כחרס שלא תוכל להנות ממני: המודר‬
‫אסור. אף על פי שלא ענה אמן, שאדם יכול לאסור על חבירו שלא יהנה ממנו: הרי אתה עלי‬
‫חרם. שאסר על עצמו כל הנאה שתבוא לו מחבירו, הנודר אסור: בדבר של עולי בבל. כגון‬
‫בור של עולי רגלים שהיו עולים מבבל לארץ ישראל לרגל, והיה הבור באמצע הדרך, וידן‬
‫של כל ישראל שוה בו, והוי כהפקר ולא כדבר שהוא של שותפים:‬

יד אברהם

discuss whether a person who has contributed toward the development and maintenance of public property can claim to own a share in such property, and therefore, possess also the right to forbid it by a *neder* to some other person.

‫"הֲרֵינִי עָלֶיךָ חֵרֶם" – הַמֻּדָּר אָסוּר;‬ — *[If one says:]* "I am to you *cherem*," the person prohibited by the neder is forbidden;

If, for example, Reuven said to Shimon: "I am to you *cherem*," it is the same as saying: "Benefit from me shall be forbidden to you like *cherem*," and it is prohibited for Shimon to derive benefit from Reuven. Although Shimon did not issue the declaration himself, nor did he answer *amen* to it, he is nevertheless bound to obey it (*Rav*).

‫"הֲרֵי אַתְּ עָלַי חֵרֶם" – הַנּוֹדֵר אָסוּר;‬ — "You are to me cherem" — the person making the neder is forbidden;

[If Shimon declared it interdicted for himself to benefit from Reuven, the prohibition would take effect.]

In the previous case, Shimon is forbidden via a *neder* issued by Reuven. In this instance, the prohibition on Shimon is self-imposed; he is

restricted by a *neder* which he himself made. *Rambam* maintains that when someone is restricted as a consequence of a *neder* declared by another person — such as in the preceding case — he is not subject to the penalty of lashes for the violation of the *neder*. *Rambam* construes the verse (*Num.* 30:3) *He shall not break his word*, which is the basis for punishing one who violates a *neder*, as referring only to a *neder* that is describable as *his word*. That is, only when violating a *neder* that he himself had made is the offender liable to lashes. Otherwise — although he is bound to observe the terms of the *neder* — he is not punishable for its transgression (see *Hil. Nedarim* 5:1f; *Lechem Mishneh* ad loc.).

Ran (15a) rejects this distinction, and understands the verse to mean simply that one may not violate the words of the *neder*. Accordingly, he maintains that, whether or not the

4. **[**If one says:] "I am to you *cherem*," the person prohibited by the *neder* is forbidden; "You are to me *cherem*" — the person making the *neder* is forbidden; "I am to you and you are to me" — both are forbidden. Both are permitted in something of the pilgrims from Babylon, but are forbidden in something of that city.

YAD AVRAHAM

person restricted by the *neder* had issued it himself, he is subject to the penalty of lashes for its violation.

הֲרֵינִי עָלֶיךָ וְאַתְּ עָלַי'' – שְׁנֵיהֶם אֲסוּרִין,, — "I am to you and you are to me" — both are forbidden.

[If Reuven forbids to Shimon the benefit from himself like *cherem*, as well as forbidding to himself any benefit from Shimon, neither of them may derive benefit from each other.]

וּשְׁנֵיהֶם מֻתָּרִין בְּדָבָר שֶׁל עוֹלֵי בָבֶל, — *Both are permitted in something of the pilgrims from Babylon,*

During the Second Temple period, the largest group of pilgrims to the Temple came from Babylon, where most Jews lived. To assist the many people who made the journey, wells were dug along the main highways, which were designated as public property of the Jewish people. All Jews were entitled to take water from these wells, and one could not prevent another from doing so (*Rav*).

In the following mishnah, more examples of property of *the pilgrims from Babylon* are given, and it is evident that this is the general term used to describe any public property of the Jewish people.

Since no individual had the right to restrict access of any other Jew to public facilities, he could not — in the context of *nedarim* — be considered an owner of a share in these facilities. That is, he was not empowered to declare a *neder* which would forbid his share in these facilities to some other person. To do so would be attempting to forbid property which is not his to someone else — an ability beyond one's jurisdiction. Therefore, *both are permitted in something of the pilgrims from Babylon* (*Rav*; *Tos. Chadashim*).

וַאֲסוּרִין בְּדָבָר שֶׁל אוֹתָהּ הָעִיר. — *but are forbidden in something of that city.*

Examples of city property are given in the next mishnah. Essentially, these were municipal facilities built with funds collected from the residents of the city. They were open for use to the general public, including even residents of other cities. However, local citizens had a say in deciding such things as the sale of such properties, and thus exercised more control over these than the people from other locales. The municipal facilities were thus considered to be the joint property of the city residents, and not the public property of the Jewish people. It was within a resident's right to forbid the use of his share to someone else via a *neder* (*Tos. Yom Tov* from *Ran*).

[ה] **וְאֵיזֶהוּ** "דָּבָר שֶׁל עוֹלֵי בָבֶל"? כְּגוֹן הַר הַבַּיִת, וְהָעֲזָרוֹת, וְהַבּוֹר שֶׁבְּאֶמְצַע הַדֶּרֶךְ. וְאֵיזֶהוּ "דָּבָר שֶׁל אוֹתָהּ הָעִיר"? כְּגוֹן הָרְחָבָה, וְהַמֶּרְחָץ, וּבֵית הַכְּנֶסֶת, וְהַתֵּבָה, וְהַסְּפָרִים. וְהַכּוֹתֵב חֶלְקוֹ לַנָּשִׂיא. רַבִּי יְהוּדָה אוֹמֵר, אֶחָד כּוֹתֵב לַנָּשִׂיא וְאֶחָד כּוֹתֵב לַהֶדְיוֹט.

— ר' עובדיה מברטנורא —

(ה) הרחבה. השווקין שבעיר: **והתיבה.** שמניחין בה ספרים: **והספרים.** שקונאים בני העיר ללמוד בהם: **והכותב חלקו לנשיא.** מפרש בגמרא (מח, א) דהכי קתני, ומה תקנתן, יכתבו חלקן לנשיא, כלומר אלו שנדרו הנאה זה מזה ואסורים להשתמש ברחובה של עיר ובתיבה ובספרים, יכתוב כל אחד מהם חלקו שיש לו ברחבה ובתיבה ובספרים לנשיא, ואחר כך יוכל כל אחד מהם להשתמש בהם, שבממון של נשיא הם משתמשים ואין אחד מהם נהנה משל חבירו: **רבי יהודה אומר אם ירצו יכתבו חלקם להדיוט.** אלא שאם כתבו לנשיא אין צריך לזכות לו על ידי אחר, דמשום חשיבותו של נשיא קונה אף על פי שלא זיכה לו על ידי אחר, ובהדיוט לא קנה עד שיזכה לו על ידי אחר:

יד אברהם

5.

וְאֵיזֶהוּ "דָּבָר שֶׁל עוֹלֵי בָבֶל"? כְּגוֹן הַר הַבַּיִת, וְהָעֲזָרוֹת, וְהַבּוֹר שֶׁבְּאֶמְצַע הַדֶּרֶךְ. — *What is "something of the pilgrims from Babylon?" [Things] like the Temple Mount, the Temple Court, and the well in the middle of the highway.*

All these facilities were constructed and maintained with funds collected from the entire Jewish people (*Rambam, Hil. Shekalim* 4:8, see *Kesef Mishneh* ad loc.). Thus, every Jew has rights to these facilities, and cannot be denied access to them. Accordingly, even if Reuven has interdicted the benefit of his property to Shimon, the *neder* does not affect these public properties, which are beyond Reuven's domain (*Rav; Tos. Yom Tov*).

In fact, the entire Temple was considered public property, and not just the area of the Temple Mount and the courtyards. The mishnah selects only these, however, because any Jew was permitted to enter there; the more sacred areas, such as the Sanctuary or the court of the *Kohanim*, were off limits to most Jews (*Tos. Yom Tov*).

According to some opinions, Jerusalem was treated as public property of the Jewish people, and therefore, no *neder* could be made forbidding the use of the city to another person. Others, however, consider Jerusalem to be municipal property belonging to the residents of the city (*Tos. Yom Tov; Tif. Yis.*).

Baal HaMaor (to end of Tractate *Beitzah*) indicates a different reason to explain the status of the Temple compound, with respect to *nedarim*. Rather than being public property of the Jewish people, it was no one's property; as a sacred place, it belonged to Heaven, not to any mortal. Practically speaking, this approach is no different than the previous explanation

5. **W**hat is *something of the pilgrims from Babylon?* [Things] like the Temple Mount, the Temple Court, and the well in the middle of the highway. What is *something of that city?* [Things] like the public square, the bathhouse, the synagogue, the ark, and the books.

One who assigns his share to the president — R' Yehudah says: Both one who assigns to the president, and one who assigns to an ordinary person.

YAD AVRAHAM

with regard to *nedarim.* As long as the property does not belong to a person, he cannot forbid it with a *neder* to someone else. Thus, sacred property — which belongs to Heaven, and not to people — is not affected by *nedarim* that one person directs at another.

וְאֵיזֶהוּ ,,דָּבָר שֶׁל אוֹתָהּ הָעִיר"? כְּגוֹן הָרְחָבָה, וְהַמֶּרְחָץ, וּבֵית הַכְּנֶסֶת, וְהַתֵּבָה, וְהַסְּפָרִים. — *What is "something of that city?'* [Things] like the public square, the bathhouse, the synagogue, the ark, and the books.

These facilities were funded from municipal taxes or donations (*Rav*), and were considered the property of the people of that city, rather than of the Jewish people in general. As such, the city residents had a say in the control of these properties, and all residents were considered their joint owners. Their rights in these properties were sufficient to allow them to include these in their *nedarim.*

Thus, if Reuven was a resident, and made a *neder* forbidding Shimon to benefit from his property, the latter would be prohibited, for example, to use the city bathhouse (*Ran* 48a, s.v. אסורין).

וְהַכּוֹתֵב חֶלְקוֹ לַנָּשִׂיא, — *One who assigns his share to the president* —

The *Gemara* (48a) explains this to mean that if two residents of a city are prohibited via a *neder* to benefit from each other, they may still use municipal properties if each of them assigns his share in these properties to the president. In other words, they can relinquish their shares in the city property by assigning it to the president, so that if either of them should use the city property, he will not be benefiting from the *other.*

President, as used here, refers to the person responsible for the affairs of the city, such as the monarch or the governor (*Meiri*). The governing authority is considered to be the embodiment of the public. Therefore, by transferring his share to the leader, rather than a private citizen, Reuven's share is no longer standard municipal property, but assumes the status of public property (see *Tzofnas Paneiach* to *Hil. Nedarim* 7:2, *Tiferes Yaakov* 33).

רַבִּי יְהוּדָה אוֹמֵר: אֶחָד כּוֹתֵב לַנָּשִׂיא, וְאֶחָד כּוֹתֵב לַהֶדְיוֹט. — *R' Yehudah says: Both one who assigns to the president, and one who assign to an ordinary person.*

[R' Yehudah points out that the people bound by a *neder* can assign their shares to a private citizen as well. As the property of that third party and not of one of them, they are both permitted to

מַה בֵּין כּוֹתֵב לַנָּשִׂיא לְכוֹתֵב לַהֶדְיוֹט? שֶׁהַכּוֹתֵב
לַנָּשִׂיא אֵינוֹ צָרִיךְ לְזַכּוֹת. וַחֲכָמִים אוֹמְרִים: אֶחָד
זֶה וְאֶחָד זֶה צְרִיכִין לְזַכּוֹת; לֹא דִבְּרוּ בַנָּשִׂיא
אֶלָּא בַהֹוֶה. רַבִּי יְהוּדָה אוֹמֵר: אֵין אַנְשֵׁי גָלִיל
צְרִיכִין לִכְתּוֹב, שֶׁכְּבָר כָּתְבוּ אֲבוֹתֵיהֶם עַל יְדֵיהֶם.

[ו] הַמֻּדָּר הֲנָאָה מֵחֲבֵרוֹ וְאֵין לוֹ מַה יֹּאכַל
— נוֹתְנוֹ לְאַחֵר לְשׁוּם מַתָּנָה,
וְהַלָּה מֻתָּר בָּה.

ר' עובדיה מברטנורא

אנשי גליל אין צריכין לזכות. אנשי גליל קנטרנים היו ובכעסן היו נודרים הנאה זה מזה,
עמדו אבותיהן וכתבו חלקיהן לנשיא, שאם בניהם אחריהם ידרו הנאה זה מזה לא יהיו אסורים
ברחבה של עיר או בתיבה או בספרים, דממון נשיא הס:

יד אברהם
---

use the municipal properties.]

מַה בֵּין כּוֹתֵב לַנָּשִׂיא לְכוֹתֵב לַהֶדְיוֹט?
שֶׁהַכּוֹתֵב לַנָּשִׂיא אֵינוֹ צָרִיךְ לְזַכּוֹת. —
*What is the difference between one
who assigns to the president, and one
who assigns to an ordinary person?
That one who assigns to the president
need not [give it to someone] to take
possession on behalf [of the president].*

In general, when assigning a property to some person in the latter's
absence, the procedure requires that
someone represent the designated
recipient and take title on his behalf
(*Choshen Mishpat* 234:1). R' Yehudah
contends, however, that when assigning one's share to the president, this is
not necessary. The transfer to the
president is effected through the
resolve of the giver, even without
any formal procedure of acquisition
[see below] (*Rashash*, based on *Tos.* to
Bechoros 18b).

[In keeping with the approach that
assigning to the president amounts to a
designation of the property as public

property, the president himself is not really
acquiring anything; rather, the entire Jewish people is the beneficiary. Therefore, one
may understand that the ordinary protocol
for private acquisition might not apply (cf.
Tos. Yom Tov, s.v. והכותב, *Tif. Yis.*).]

וַחֲכָמִים אוֹמְרִים: אֶחָד זֶה וְאֶחָד זֶה צְרִיכִין
לְזַכּוֹת; לֹא דִבְּרוּ בַנָּשִׂיא אֶלָּא בַהֹוֶה. — *The
Sages, however, say: Both this one and
that one must [give their share to
someone] to take possession on [their
behalf]; they spoke of the president
only [to reflect] the current [practice].*

The Sages maintain that even when
designating his share to the president,
Reuven may not rely on his own
resolve alone. He must conduct formal
acquisition proceedings and hand the
deed to someone acting on behalf of
the president. Procedurally, then,
there is no difference between assigning one's share to the president or to a
private citizen. Nevertheless, it was
most common to assign one's share to
the president, since a president was
hardly likely to ban it with a *neder*.

5
6

What is the difference between one who assigns to the president, and one who assigns to an ordinary person? That one who assigns to the president need not [give it to someone] to take possession on behalf [of the president]. The Sages, however, say: Both this one and that one must [give their share to someone] to take possession on [their behalf]; they spoke of the president only [to reflect] the current [practice]. R' Yehudah says: The people of Galilee need not assign, since their fathers have already assigned for them.

6. **[I**f] someone is prohibited by a *neder* to benefit from another, and he has nothing to eat, [the other person] may give it to someone else as a gift, and he is permitted it.

YAD AVRAHAM

On the other hand, a private citizen might do to Reuven as Reuven had done to Shimon, and declare a *neder* which would deny Reuven access to the facilities (*Tos. Yom Tov* from *Ran*).

[If property assigned to the president was treated like public property of the Jewish people, it was beyond anyone's jurisdiction to forbid it. This would explain why it was prevalent to assign one's share to the president rather than to a private citizen, who would still be able to interdict it with a *neder*.]

רַבִּי יְהוּדָה אוֹמֵר: אֵין אַנְשֵׁי הַגָּלִיל צְרִיכִין — לִכְתּוֹב, שֶׁכְּבָר כָּתְבוּ אֲבוֹתֵיהֶם עַל יְדֵיהֶם.
R' Yehudah says: The people of Galilee need not assign, since their fathers have already assigned for them.

The *Gemara* (48a) explains that the

residents of Galilee were notorious for their quarrelsomeness and the constant banning of their belongings to each other. In order to permanently overcome this problem as it effected municipal property, all the citizens of Galilee assigned their holdings in the public properties to the president. Thus, no citizen of Galilee could ever forbid his share in municipal holdings, because they were presidential property, and therefore not affected even if *nedarim* were made. There was no need to assign their municipal holdings to a third party, since their forefathers had already done so on their behalf (*Rav*).

6.

הַמֻּדָּר הֲנָאָה מֵחֲבֵרוֹ, וְאֵין לוֹ מַה יֹּאכַל — נוֹתְנוֹ לְאַחֵר לְשׁוּם מַתָּנָה, וְהַלָּה מֻתָּר בָּהּ.
[If] someone is prohibited by a neder to benefit from another, and he has

nothing to eat, [the other person] may give it to someone else as a gift, and he is permitted it.

Essentially, this is the same as the

מַעֲשֶׂה בְּאֶחָד בְּבֵית חוֹרוֹן שֶׁהָיָה אָבִיו מֻדָּר הֵימֶנּוּ הֲנָאָה, וְהָיָה מַשִּׂיא אֶת בְּנוֹ. וְאָמַר לַחֲבֵרוֹ: "חָצֵר וּסְעוּדָה נְתוּנִים לְךָ בְּמַתָּנָה, וְאֵינָן לְפָנֶיךָ אֶלָּא כְּדֵי שֶׁיָּבוֹא אַבָּא וְיֹאכַל עִמָּנוּ בַּסְּעוּדָה". אָמַר לוֹ: "אִם שֶׁלִּי הֵם — הֲרֵי הֵם מֻקְדָּשִׁין לַשָּׁמָיִם"! אָמַר לוֹ: לֹא נָתַתִּי [לְךָ] אֶת שֶׁלִּי שֶׁתַּקְדִּישֵׁם לַשָּׁמָיִם". אָמַר לוֹ: "לֹא נָתַתָּ לִי אֶת שֶׁלְּךָ אֶלָּא שֶׁתְּהֵא אַתָּה וְאָבִיךָ אוֹכְלִים וְשׁוֹתִים וּמִתְרַצִּים זֶה לָזֶה, וִיהֵא עָוֹן תָּלוּי בְּרֹאשׁוֹ".

ר' עובדיה מברטנורא

(ו) **ומעשה בבית חורון. וכו'.** בגמרא (מח, א) מפרש דמתניתין חסורי מחסרא והכי קתני, ואם הוכיח סופו על תחלתו אסור, ומעשה נמי בבית חורון באחד שהוכיח סופו על תחלתו וכו': **ואינן לפניך אלא שיבא אבא ויאכל.** אלמא לא נתנס אלא כדי שיבא אביו ויאכל ואסור, אבל אם אמר הרי הן לפניך ואם רצונך יבא אבא ויאכל, מותר, ואם סעודתו מוכחת עליו שהרבה בסעודה יותר ממה שהיה צריך ונכרין הדברים שבשביל שבא אביו עשה כדי שיבא ויאכל, אסור:

יד אברהם

case already discussed in 4:8, in which Reuven — from whom Shimon may not benefit — gives food to a third party as a gift, thus enabling Shimon to partake of it.

In the present case, however, Shimon runs out of food in the city, rather than — as in 4:8 — on the road (*Rosh*). Since, in the city, there are other people who can help him, we might have thought that Reuven should not be allowed to circumvent the *neder*. Therefore, the mishnah teaches that even in the city, Reuven may donate food to a third party, thus making it permissible to Shimon (*Tif. Yis.*).

The earlier mishnah also teaches us something not evident from the present mishnah. Despite the urgency of Shimon's situation in 4:8 — in having run short of food while traveling — Reuven may not use the tactic of declaring his food ownerless (see 4:8) unless no third person is available. As long as a third person is present, the only way to escape the ban is for Reuven to present the food as a gift to the third person (*Meiri*).

The *Gemara* (48a) explains that Reuven's gift of the food must be sincere; if it is not, then the gift is not legally valid. In that case, it remains forbidden to Shimon, even if he takes it from the hands of the third party. An illustration of this follows.

מַעֲשֶׂה בְּאֶחָד בְּבֵית חוֹרוֹן שֶׁהָיָה אָבִיו מֻדָּר הֵימֶנּוּ הֲנָאָה, וְהָיָה מַשִּׂיא אֶת בְּנוֹ. וְאָמַר לַחֲבֵרוֹ: "חָצֵר וּסְעוּדָה נְתוּנִים לְךָ בְּמַתָּנָה, וְאֵינָן לְפָנֶיךָ אֶלָּא כְּדֵי שֶׁיָּבוֹא אַבָּא וְיֹאכַל עִמָּנוּ בַּסְּעוּדָה". — *It happened that a person in Beis Choron, whose father was prohibited by a neder to benefit from him, was marrying off his son. He said to another: "[The] courtyard and banquet are given to you as a gift, but are yours (lit., before you) only so that Father can come and eat with us at the banquet."*

It happened that a person in Beis Choron, whose father was prohibited by a *neder* to benefit from him, was marrying off his son. He said to another: "[The] courtyard and banquet are given to you as a gift, but are yours only so that Father can come and eat with us at the banquet." He replied: "If they are mine, then they are dedicated to Heaven." He said: "I did not give [you] what was mine in order for you to dedicate it to Heaven." He replied: "You gave me yours only so that you and your father could eat and drink and appease each other, and the sin should be on my head."

YAD AVRAHAM

This specification that *"[they] are yours only so that Father can come and eat with us at the banquet"* indicates that the gift is not sincere. The person wanted it to appear that he had given the yard and feast away, but had not really intended to do so (*Rav*).

Mention is made of both the yard and the food, since the father — being forbidden to benefit from his son — would not be able to eat his son's food nor enter his property; see 4:1 (*Kehati*).

אָמַר לוֹ: "אִם שֶׁלִּי הֵם – הֲרֵי הֵם מֻקְדָּשִׁין לַשָּׁמַיִם!" — *He replied (lit., said): "If they are mine, then they are dedicated to Heaven."*

[And are thus forbidden for general use.] The other person is trying to force him to admit that the gift was not really genuine (*Ritva*).

אָמַר לוֹ: "לֹא נָתַתִּי [לְךָ] אֶת שֶׁלִּי שֶׁתַּקְדִּישֵׁם לַשָּׁמַיִם". אָמַר לוֹ: "לֹא נָתַתָּ לִי אֶת שֶׁלְּךָ אֶלָּא שֶׁתְּהֵא אַתָּה וְאָבִיךָ אוֹכְלִים וְשׁוֹתִים וּמִתְרַצִּים זֶה לָזֶה, וִיהֵא עָוֹן תָּלוּי בְּרֹאשׁוֹ". — *He said: "I did not give [you] what was mine in order for you to dedicate it to Heaven." He replied: "You gave me*

yours only so that you and your father could eat and drink and appease each other, and the sin should be on my (lit., his) head."

[It was common not to articulate unpleasant thoughts about oneself in the first person. Rather, a third-person form was used, euphemistically making it appear as though someone else was being referred to (see *Gen.* 26:10, *Rashi* ad loc.; *Ex.* 1:10, *Rashi* ad loc., s.v. וְעָלָה).

This incident illustrates that the gift must be genuine if it is to circumvent the obstacle of the *neder*. Some interpret one reading in the *Gemara* (48a) as suggesting that, if the gift had been given without comment, and only later, the person had mentioned: "Father can be invited, if you so desire," we treat the gift as being sincere. However, had this same comment been made at the time of the gift — "The yard and food are yours as a gift; Father can be invited if you want" — this would indicate a lack of sincerity (*Rashba*; cf. *Rav*).

Others construe the *Gemara* as maintaining that no person sincerely gives

וּכְשֶׁבָּא דָבָר לִפְנֵי חֲכָמִים, אָמְרוּ: כָּל מַתָּנָה שֶׁאֵינָה, שֶׁאִם הִקְדִּישָׁהּ אֵינָה מְקֻדֶּשֶׁת — אֵינָה מַתָּנָה.

יד אברהם

away a wedding banquet. The claim that one is doing so is therefore certainly fraudulent, and such a gift is not valid under any circumstances (*Ran*).

וּכְשֶׁבָּא דָבָר לִפְנֵי חֲכָמִים, אָמְרוּ: כָּל מַתָּנָה שֶׁאֵינָה, שֶׁאִם הִקְדִּישָׁהּ אֵינָה מְקֻדֶּשֶׁת – אֵינָה מַתָּנָה. — *When the matter came before the Sages, they said: Any gift which is not [sincere] — which, if sanctified, is not sacred — is not a gift.*

[The Rabbis pointed out that if the yard and the banquet were truly being

relinquished, the recipient should have the right to do with them whatever he wishes. But, in fact, they were never really given away, and this is why the recipient's attempt to sanctify them was objected to. Thus, any gift which is not actual, as displayed by the inability of the recipient to do with it as he pleases, is not a valid gift, and does not affect a *neder*.]

It is possible to give someone a gift on the

5
6

When the matter came before the Sages, they said: Any gift which is not [sincere] — which, if sanctified, is not sacred — is not a gift.

YAD AVRAHAM

condition that he not sanctify it. Such a gift would be valid unless the person violated the condition and sanctified it (*Choshen Mishpat* 241:5). Nevertheless, this law does not conflict with the conclusion of our mishnah. The mishnah is referring to gifts which were presented without stipulating any legal conditions. Such gifts may indeed be put to any use the recipient desires. However, when a condition which is halachically valid is stipulated, the gifts will be subject to the condition. [1] In the incident related in our mishnah, no legal conditions were specified, and so, the recipient would have been within his rights to dedicate the yard and banquet, if they had been sincerely given to him (*Yerushalmi; Ran; Tos. Yom Tov*).

1. The criteria for halachically valid conditions are discussed in *Even HaEzer* 38:2*ff*.; see also *Choshen Mishpat* 241:9.

פרק ששי ‎⇜
Chapter Six

The next chapter deals with the connotation of various terms which might be used in a *neder*. As has already been discussed (3:6*ff*), the gauge used in interpreting the scope of a *neder* is the meaning of the words of the *neder* in popular usage (*Gem.* 49a). The mishnah provides numerous examples to illustrate this, but it should be kept in mind that, on a practical level, the final determination depends on the place and time in which the *neder* was made (*Yoreh Deah* 217:1). *Rav* (6:2) observes that when a term is used to describe more than one thing, the *neder* is applied to all the possible meanings. This is so even if most people use it for only one thing, and only a minority used it to mean something else. *Turei Zahav* (*Yoreh Deah* 208:1), however, qualifies this rule. If the term in question defines the item being prohibited, it is indeed given the widest interpretation, and even a minority usage is taken into account. But, where the term in question is only a reference in the *neder*, the minority usage can be ignored. For example, in a place where the term *salt meat* was generally used to describe sacrificial meat, but was used by some people to refer to ordinary meat which was salted, if someone was to declare:

"These fruits are forbidden to me like salted meat," the reference *like salted meat* would be understood on the basis of the majority usage of the term as meaning sacrificial meat. [Even if the person later claimed that he had intended only ordinary meat, he would not be believed, and the *neder* would be binding (*Yoreh Deah* 208:1).] But, if someone were to declare a *neder* prohibiting "salted meat" to himself, the prohibition would include even ordinary meat which had been salted. When considering the item being prohibited, even the minority usage is taken into account.

[א] הַנּוֹדֵר מִן „הַמְבֻשָּׁל" — מֻתָּר בַּצָּלִי וּבַשָּׁלוּק. אָמַר: „קוֹנָם תַּבְשִׁיל שֶׁאֵינִי טוֹעֵם" — אָסוּר בְּמַעֲשֵׂה קְדֵרָה רַךְ, וּמֻתָּר בְּעָבֶה. וּמֻתָּר בְּבֵיצַת טְרָמִיטָא וּבִדְלַעַת הָרְמוּצָה.

ר' עובדיה מברטנורא

פרק ששי – הנודר מן המבושל. (א) הנודר מן המבושל. שאמר קונס מבושל עלי: **מותר בצלי ובשלוק.** כל שנתבשל יותר מבשולו הראוי נקרא שלוק: **מעשה קדרה רך.** שנאכל עם הפת: **עבה.** שנאכל בלא פת: **ביצת טרמיטא.** מבושלת במים חמים ומשמרים אותה שלא תקפה: **ובדלעת הרמוצה.** דלעת שטומנים אותה ברמץ הוא אפר חם ומתמתק בכך:

יד אברהם

1.

הַנּוֹדֵר מִן „הַמְבֻשָּׁל" – מֻתָּר בַּצָּלִי — One who makes a neder prohibiting "what is cooked" is permitted what is roasted

I.e., he declares: "Konam, what is cooked to me" (Rav).

The meaning of a declaration is determined by the popular usage of the terminology employed, and not by some other usage such as, for example, Biblical parlance (Gem. 49a). Thus, although the Scriptural usage of the Hebrew term בִּישׁוּל, cooking, includes even something roasted (ibid.), in the context of nedarim, the word must be defined as it is used by people. Since, popularly, it did not refer to something roasted, the prohibition banning what is cooked did not apply to what was roasted (ibid.); hence, he is permitted that which is roasted.

וּבַשָּׁלוּק. — and what is overcooked.

The translation follows Rav and Rosh. Others maintain that שָׁלוּק should be understood as undercooked. They argue that something over-

cooked would certainly be included when people say what is cooked (Ran; Tos.).

A different approach is adopted by Tos. Rid, who understands שָׁלוּק to describe not the degree of cooking, but rather, the method. According to him, when something is cooked together with spices, it is referred to as מְבֻשָּׁל; when it is cooked by itself in plain water, it is called שָׁלוּק. [This ex-planation is also evident from Rambam, Hil. Nedarim 9:1; see, however, Terumos 10:11 and Avodah Zarah 2:6.]

אָמַר: „קוֹנָם, תַּבְשִׁיל שֶׁאֵנִי טוֹעֵם"– [If] he said: "Konam, cooked food, with respect to my tasting [it],"

This declaration prohibits tasting cooked food. Cooked food here means foods prepared in any manner which are eaten together with bread. Thus, roasted and overcooked food — although not included in the expression what is cooked — are included in the term cooked food, since it is eaten with bread (Rav, Tos. Yom Tov

1. **O**ne who makes a *neder* prohibiting "what is cooked" is permitted what is roasted and what is overcooked. [If] he said: "*Konam*, cooked food, with respect to my tasting [it]," he is forbidden [to taste] soft food made in a pot, but is permitted [to taste] solids. He is permitted [to taste] soft-boiled eggs and a gourd baked in hot ashes.

YAD AVRAHAM

from *Gem.* 49a).

From *Tur* 217 and *Rambam, Hil. Nedarim* 9:1, it appears that there is no substantial difference between the terms *what is cooked* and *cooked food*. Rather, the two examples of the mishnah are drawn based on the parlances in two different locales. In one city, the expression *cooking* did not include roasting and other forms of cooking; in the other city, it did. Thus — in the first example — roast is permitted to the person, while in this case, it is not. [The mishnah presented these apparently conflicting cases to demonstrate that the final determinant is the way the local populace uses the words.]

Regarding the term שֶׁאֵינִי, see *Tos. Yom Tov* here and commentary to 1:1, s.v. שֶׁאֵינִי אוֹכֵל. In the commentary ibid., s.v. שֶׁאֵינִי טוֹעֵם, the difference between the terms *tasting* and *eating* is also explained.

אָסוּר בְּמַעֲשֶׂה קְדֵרָה רַךְ, וּמֻתָּר בְּעָבֶה. — *he is forbidden [to taste] soft food made in a pot, but is permitted [to taste] solids.*

This refers to foods like grits and porridge (*Tos. Yom Tov*), which coagulate upon being cooked, and were eaten by people in both their liquid and solid states (*Ran*). If the edible form was basically liquid, it was eaten with bread and therefore was considered a *cooked food*. If it was eaten as a solid, it was not taken with bread and

was not considered a *cooked food* (*Rav*).

וּמֻתָּר בְּבֵיצַת טְרָמִיטָא — *He is permitted [to taste] soft-boiled eggs*

The translation of this term follows *Rav* and *Rambam*, who stress that great care was taken to ensure that the egg did not harden (see *Rambam Comm.* and *Hil. Nedarim* 9:7). The *Gemara* (50b) describes this type of preparation of an egg as follows: "A servant who makes it is worth one thousand dinar, for it is immersed one thousand times into hot water and one thousand times into cold water, until it becomes so small that it can be swallowed" [without chewing (*Ran*)].

This food is permitted, because people did not eat it with bread, and this *Tanna* maintains that such dishes are not considered *cooked food* (*Tos. Yom Tov*).

וּבִדְלַעַת הָרְמוּצָה. — *and a gourd baked in hot ashes.*

There is a certain species of gourd which is naturally bitter, but, upon being baked in hot ashes, becomes edible (*Rav; Rosh* 51; *Rambam Comm.* to 6:1 and to *Kilayim* 1:2; *Yerushalmi* ibid.). [This, too, was not included in the category of *cooked food.*]

[ב] **הַנּוֹדֵר** מִ„מַּעֲשֵׂה קְדֵרָה" — אֵינוֹ אָסוּר אֶלָּא מִמַּעֲשֵׂה רְתַחְתָּה. אָמַר: „קוֹנָם הַיּוֹרֵד לַקְּדֵרָה שֶׁאֵינִי טוֹעֵם" — אָסוּר בְּכָל הַמִּתְבַּשְּׁלִין בַּקְּדֵרָה.

[ג] **מִן** „הַכָּבוּשׁ" — אֵינוֹ אָסוּר אֶלָּא מִן הַכָּבוּשׁ שֶׁל יָרָק; „כָּבוּשׁ שֶׁאֵינִי טוֹעֵם" — אָסוּר בְּכָל הַכְּבוּשִׁים. מִן „הַשָּׁלוּק"

ר׳ עובדיה מברטנורא

(ב) ממעשה רתחתה. אוכל עשוי מקמח שהורתח בקדרה. וכללא דמלתא, בנדרים הלך אחר לשון בני אדם לפי הזמן והמקום, ואי איכא דוכתא דקרו לגלי מבושל ולמבושל גלי הנודר מן המבושל אסור בגלי, וכן כל כיוצא בזה, ואי רובא קרי ליה הכי הכי ומיעוטא קרי ליה לא אמרינן זיל בתר רובא אלא הוי ספק נדרים וכל ספק נדרים להחמיר: **(ג) אינו אסור אלא מן הכבוש של ירק.** דסתם כבוש של ירק הוא. **כבוש שאיני טועם.** משמע כל מיני כבוש, וכן שלוק גלוי מליח בלא ה"א משמע כל מינים של שלוק ושל גלוי ושל מליח:

יד אברהם

2.

הַנּוֹדֵר מִ„מַּעֲשֵׂה קְדֵרָה" - אֵינוֹ אָסוּר אֶלָּא מִמַּעֲשֵׂה רְתַחְתָּה. — *One who makes a neder prohibiting "something prepared in a pot" is forbidden only a boiled food.*

A *neder* prohibiting *something prepared in a pot*, without specifying whether the food must be soft or solid, is construed as referring to a specific dish made of flour and soft bread which was boiled in a pot. Because it was boiled, it was also known as מַעֲשֵׂה רְתַחְתָּה, which incorporates the Hebrew root רתח meaning *boil* (*Rav*; *Rambam Comm.*).

However, *Rosh* (49a) and *Tur* (Yoreh Deah 217) maintain that all foods — whose final stage of preparation is that it is boiled in a pot — are included here, but something made ready by frying in a pan would be permitted (*Tos. Yom Tov*).

אָמַר: „קוֹנָם הַיּוֹרֵד לַקְּדֵרָה שֶׁאֵינִי טוֹעֵם"— — *[If] he said: "Konam, what goes into a pot with respect to my tasting it," he is forbidden whatever is cooked in a pot.*

The term *what goes into a pot* was not used to refer to some specific dish. It was used to describe anything cooked in a pot (*Tos. Yom Tov*).

Rosh and *Tur* interpret this expression to include any food that, at some time during its preparation, was cooked in a pot. Thus, something which is first cooked and then fried will be included under *what goes into a pot* (*Tos. Yom Tov* from *Beis Yosef* 217). [Such a food would not be included in the expression *something prepared in a pot* of the preceding case, since the final stage of preparation did not involve cooking it in a pot.]

2. **O**ne who makes a *neder* prohibiting "something prepared in a pot" is forbidden only a boiled food. [If] he said: "*Konam*, what goes into a pot, with respect to my tasting it," he is forbidden whatever is cooked in a pot.

3. **[I**f he prohibited] "the preserved food," he is forbidden only preserved vegetables; "preserved food, with respect to my tasting" — he is forbidden all preserved foods. "The seethed food"

YAD AVRAHAM

3.

מִן "הַכָּבוּשׁ" – אֵינוֹ אָסוּר אֶלָּא מִן הַכָּבוּשׁ שֶׁל יָרָק; — *[If he prohibited]* "*the preserved food," he is forbidden only preserved vegetables;*

If someone made a *neder* prohibiting "the *preserved food*," the proscription extends only to preserved vegetables, and not to other preserved foods such as meats. The reason for this is that he used the definite article *the*. Thus, the *neder* is of the form: "*Konam*, the preserved food to me." Consequently, the *neder* is understood to be directed only at the most common preserved food — namely, vegetables — and not at all types of preserved food (*Rav; Rambam Comm.*).

"כָּבוּשׁ שֶׁאֵינִי טוֹעֵם" – אָסוּר בְּכָל הַכְּבוּשִׁים. — *"preserved food, with respect to my tasting" — he is forbidden all preserved foods.*

In this case, the *neder* was directed at preserved food in general, and not just at *the* preserved food. Therefore, all preserved foods — vegetables and meats alike — are included in the prohibition (*Rav*).

The difference between this case and the preceding one is the absence of the definite article. The words *with respect to my tasting*, which the mishnah seems to emphasize in the present case, should not be construed as the reason for the wider scope of this *neder*. Rather, the mishnah teaches that even when stating *with respect to my tasting* [as opposed to *with respect to my eating* (*Ravad, Hil. Nedarim* 9:2 and *Kesef Mishneh* ibid.)], the *neder* is given the widest interpretation only when the definite article is omitted. But, if the person were to direct the *neder* at *the preserved food*, even if he stated *with respect to my tasting* (e.g., "*Konam*, the preserved food, with respect to my tasting") the *neder* would be assumed to apply only to preserved vegetables (*Ran*).

The mishnah continues with several other examples of terms — which, when introduced by the definite article — refer only to the predominant form, while, if mentioned without the definite article, are all inclusive.

אֵינוֹ אָסוּר אֶלָּא מִן הַשָּׁלוּק שֶׁל בָּשָׂר; "שָׁלוּק שֶׁאֵינִי טוֹעֵם" — אָסוּר בְּכָל הַשְּׁלָקִים. מִן "הַצָּלִי" — אֵינוֹ אָסוּר אֶלָּא מִן הַצָּלִי שֶׁל בָּשָׂר; דִּבְרֵי רַבִּי יְהוּדָה; "צָלִי שֶׁאֵינִי טוֹעֵם" — אָסוּר בְּכָל הַצְּלוּיִים. מִן "הַמָּלִיחַ" — אֵינוֹ אָסוּר אֶלָּא מִן הַמָּלִיחַ שֶׁל דָּג; "מָלִיחַ שֶׁאֵינִי טוֹעֵם" — אָסוּר בְּכָל הַמְּלוּחִים.

[ד] "דָּג, דָּגִים שֶׁאֵינִי טוֹעֵם" — אָסוּר בָּהֶן, בֵּין גְּדוֹלִים בֵּין קְטַנִּים, בֵּין מְלוּחִין בֵּין טְפֵלִין, בֵּין חַיִּין בֵּין מְבֻשָּׁלִין; וּמֻתָּר בְּטָרִית טְרוּפָה וּבַצִּיר.

ר' עובדיה מברטנורא

(ד) **דג דגים שאיני טועם.** לֹא דָג וְלֹא דָגִים וְהַכֹּל בְּמַשְׁמַע: **טפלין.** מַבְלֵי מֶלַח: **בטרית טרופה.** דָג שֶׁחוֹתְכִים אוֹתוֹ חֲתִיכוֹת חֲתִיכוֹת וּמוֹכְרִים אוֹתוֹ וְיֵשׁ לוֹ שֵׁם בִּפְנֵי עַצְמוֹ וְאֵינוֹ בִּכְלַל דָּג וְדָגִים: **ציר.** מֵי הַיּוֹצְאִים מִן הַדָּגִים הַמְּלוּחִים:

יד אברהם

מִן "הַשָּׁלוּק" – אֵינוֹ אָסוּר אֶלָּא מִן הַשָּׁלוּק שֶׁל בָּשָׂר; "שָׁלוּק שֶׁאֵינִי טוֹעֵם" – אָסוּר בְּכָל הַשְּׁלָקִים. — "The seethed food" — he is forbidden only seethed meat; "seethed food, with respect to my tasting" — he is forbidden all seethed foods.

[Here, the standard seethed dish was meat, and so, a *neder* directed at *the seethed food* affected only meat.]

Some texts read: *seethed vegetables,* rather than *seethed meat (Tos. Yom Tov).* [That version presumes the predominant seethed food to be vegetables.]

מִן "הַצָּלִי" – אֵינוֹ אָסוּר אֶלָּא מִן הַצָּלִי שֶׁל בָּשָׂר; דִּבְרֵי רַבִּי יְהוּדָה; "צָלִי שֶׁאֵינִי טוֹעֵם" – אָסוּר בְּכָל הַצְּלוּיִים. מִן "הַמָּלִיחַ" – אֵינוֹ אָסוּר אֶלָּא מִן הַמָּלִיחַ שֶׁל דָּג; "מָלִיחַ שֶׁאֵינִי טוֹעֵם" – אָסוּר בְּכָל הַמְּלוּחִים. — "The

roast" — he is forbidden only roasted meat; [these are] the words of R' Yehudah; "roast, with respect to my tasting" — he is forbidden all roasted foods. "The salted food" — he is forbidden only salted fish; "salted food with respect to my tasting" — he is forbidden all salted foods.

[Here, too, the most common roasted and salted foods were meat and fish, respectively.]

Our approach here follows *Rav.* However, some authorities explain the mishnah to revolve not on the use of the definite article, but on the inclusion of the phrase *with respect to my tasting;* where this is added, the broader meaning is assumed (*Ran*).

4.

"דָּג, דָּגִים שֶׁאֵינִי טוֹעֵם" – אָסוּר בָּהֶן בֵּין גְּדוֹלִים בֵּין קְטַנִּים, בֵּין מְלוּחִין בֵּין טְפֵלִין, בֵּין חַיִּין בֵּין מְבֻשָּׁלִין; — [If one said: "Konam] fish, fishes, with respect to my tasting," he is forbidden them

whether large or small, whether salted or unsalted, whether raw or cooked;

Fish is taken to refer to large fish which are sold individually and are therefore referred to in the singular.

— he is forbidden only seethed meat; "seethed food, with respect to my tasting" — he is forbidden all seethed foods. "The roast" — he is forbidden only roasted meat; [these are] the words of R' Yehudah; "roast, with respect to my tasting" — he is forbidden all roasted foods. "The salted food" — he is forbidden only salted fish; "salted food with respect to my tasting" — he is forbidden all salted foods.

4. **[I**f one said: "*Konam*] fish, fishes, with respect to my tasting," he is forbidden them whether large or small, whether salted or unsalted, whether raw or cooked; but he is permitted hashed *taris* and brine. One who

YAD AVRAHAM

Fishes refers to smaller fish which are sold in quantity; hence, they are indicated by the plural. By specifying both the singular and the plural forms, the person is applying his prohibition to all varieties of fish — *large or small, salted or unsalted, raw or cooked* (*Ran*).

Rambam (*Comm.*) understands *fish, fishes* to be phrased in the style of such expressions as *Song of Songs, futility of futilities* (*Ecc.* 1:2), etc., in which the repeated term amplifies the meaning. Thus, the repetition of the term *song*, for example, indicates the ultimate song. Here, too, the repetition of *fish* indicates that the entire range of fish is being considered (cf. *Rashash*).

וּמֻתָּר בְּטָרִית טְרוּפָה וּבַצִּיר. — *but he is permitted hashed taris and brine.*

According to *Rav*, *taris* is a particular species of fish. It was sold as a hash which was referred to by name, and was not included in a general reference to fish. *Rosh* adds another explanation,

according to which *taris* is the term used to describe ground fish in general, whereas the expression *fish, fishes* used in the *neder* refers only to whole fish and not ground fish (*Rosh; Ran*).

Brine — despite possessing the flavor of fish — is not referred to as fish, and is not included in the prohibition. However, the *Gemara* (52b) raises the possibility that because the *neder* specifies *with respect to my tasting,* something like brine — which carries the taste of fish — should also be prohibited. If that is so, then the mishnah — which permits brine — must be referring to brine which was collected before the *neder* was made, so that the fish flavor it contains derives from permitted fish. But brine which contains the flavor of prohibited fish — extracted after the *neder* — is forbidden. The halachah follows this opinion (*Shach* to *Yoreh Deah* 217:18; *Taz* ibid. 16).

הַנּוֹדֵר מִן "הַצַּחֲנָה" — אָסוּר בְּטָרִית טְרוּפָה, וּמֻתָּר בַּצִּיר וּבַמֻּרְיָס. הַנּוֹדֵר מִטָּרִית טְרוּפָה — אָסוּר בַּצִּיר וּבַמֻּרְיָס.

[ה] **הַנּוֹדֵר** מִן "הֶחָלָב" — מֻתָּר בַּקּוֹם; וְרַבִּי יוֹסֵי אוֹסֵר. מִן "הַקּוֹם" — מֻתָּר בֶּחָלָב. אַבָּא שָׁאוּל אוֹמֵר: הַנּוֹדֵר מִן "הַגְּבִינָה" — אָסוּר בָּהּ, בֵּין מְלוּחָה בֵּין טְפֵלָה.

─────── **ר' עובדיה מברטנורא** ───────

ומוריס. שומן היוצא מדגים מלוחים: **צחנה.** תערובת מיני דגים טרופים נקראים צחנה, ודוגמתו במסכת עבודה זרה (דף מ, א) הָהִיא אַרְבָּא דְלַחֲנָתָא: **ומותר בציר ובמוריס.** הואיל ואין עיקר ממשות הדג מובלע בהם: **הנודר מטרית טרופה אסור בציר ובמורייס.** דכיון דהזכיר טרופה, מכל דבר שמטורב בו מין דג משמע: **(ה) קום.** הוא נסיובי דחלבא, מיס היוצאים מן הגבינה: **אבא שאול אומר בו' בין מלוחה בין טפלה.** דלא תימא הגבינה המיוחדת שבגבינה משמע ואין דרך לאכלה בלא מלח. והלכה כאבא שאול:

─────── **יד אברהם** ───────

הַנּוֹדֵר מִן "הַצַּחֲנָה" — אָסוּר בְּטָרִית טְרוּפָה, וּמֻתָּר בַּצִּיר וּבַמֻּרְיָס. — *One who makes a neder prohibiting "assorted hashed fish" is forbidden hashed taris, but permitted brine and fish juice.*

Hashed *taris* is included in *assorted hashed fish* since it, too, is hashed fish (*Tos. Yom Tov*). However, brine and fish juice are not included, since they do not contain actual pieces of fish (*Rav*).

הַנּוֹדֵר מִטָּרִית טְרוּפָה — אָסוּר בַּצִּיר וּבַמֻּרְיָס. — *One who makes a neder prohibiting "hashed taris" is forbidden brine and fish juice.*

Since *taris* was always hashed, the redundant reference to *hashed taris* is understood as including the by-product of the grinding process. Thus, brine and fish juice are also forbidden (*Rosh*).

The version of some authorities reads: *is permitted brine and fish juice* (*Ran*). This follows the previous case, which excludes brine and fish juice from the category of general hashed fish, because they do not contain actual pieces of fish (see *Tos. Yom Tov*).

5.

הַנּוֹדֵר מִן "הֶחָלָב" — מֻתָּר בַּקּוֹם; — *One who makes a neder prohibiting "the milk" is permitted whey;*

Whey was not called *milk*, and so, was not included in the prohibition. The translation of קום as *whey* follows *Rav* and *Rambam* (*Comm.*

and *Hil. Nedarim* 9:8). *Ravad* (ibid.), however, explains it to be curdled milk. [Although, as a form of milk, one might expect curdled milk to be included under the category of milk, according to *Ravad*, the mishnah states that it is not. Perhaps this is

6
5

makes a *neder* prohibiting "assorted hashed fish" is forbidden hashed *taris*, but permitted brine and fish juice. One who makes a *neder* prohibiting "hashed *taris*" is forbidden brine and fish juice.

5. **O**ne who makes a *neder* prohibiting "the milk" is permitted whey; R' Yose, however, forbids it. "The whey" — he is permitted milk. Abba Shaul says: One who makes a *neder* prohibiting "the cheese" is forbidden it, whether it is salted or unsalted.

YAD AVRAHAM

because, in this *neder*, milk was prefaced with the definite article *the*. In accordance with mishnah 3, this would indicate only what is most commonly referred to as milk, and not other forms such as curdled milk.]

וְרַבִּי יוֹסֵי אוֹסֵר. — *R' Yose, however, forbids it.*

The *Gemara* (52b) explains that, in R' Yose's town, whey was also called *milk* and this is the basis of the ruling. Thus, there is no fundamental dispute here. The rulings cited are simply a reflection of the language in use in different regions (*Tos. Yom Tov*).

,,הַקּוּם'' - מֻתָּר בְּחָלָב. — *"The whey" — he is permitted milk.*

[All agree that a *neder* forbidding whey does not apply to milk.]

אַבָּא שָׁאוּל אוֹמֵר: הַנּוֹדֵר מִן ,,הַגְּבִינָה'' אָסוּר בָּהּ, בֵּין מְלוּחָה בֵּין טְפֵלָה. — *Abba Shaul says: One who makes a neder prohibit-*

ing "the cheese" is forbidden it, whether it is salted or unsalted.

Rav follows *Rosh* who explains that Abba Shaul's point is that cheese — even when prefaced by the definite article — is taken to mean both salted and unsalted cheese.

Shoshannim LeDavid adds that, according to Abba Shaul, the case of *the cheese* is not an exception. Rather, Abba Shaul disputes the general contention of mishnah 3 that the use of a definite article is an indication that only something well known is being referred to. He maintains that each case must be judged on its own merit, and not in the light of some general rule.

Ran, however, construes Abba Shaul to be stressing not just that unsalted cheese is common, but that unsalted cheese is also called cheese. Thus, whether he refers to it with the definite article or not, the person is assumed to be prohibiting both salted and unsalted cheeses (*Tos. Yom Tov*).

6.

The next mishnayos deal with the status of flavors or juices extracted from foods forbidden by a *neder*.

[ו] הַנּוֹדֵר מִן ,,הַבָּשָׂר'' – מֻתָּר בָּרֹטֶב

וּבַקִּיפָה; וְרַבִּי יְהוּדָה אוֹסֵר. אָמַר רַבִּי יְהוּדָה: מַעֲשֶׂה וְאָסַר עָלַי רַבִּי טַרְפוֹן בֵּיצִים שֶׁנִּתְבַּשְּׁלוּ עִמּוֹ. אָמְרוּ לוֹ: וְכֵן הַדָּבָר! אֵימָתַי? בִּזְמַן שֶׁיֹּאמַר: ,,בָּשָׂר זֶה עָלַי'', שֶׁהַנּוֹדֵר מִן הַדָּבָר וְנִתְעָרֵב בְּאַחֵר, אִם יֵשׁ בּוֹ בְּנוֹתֵן טַעַם – אָסוּר.

ר' עובדיה מברטנורא

(ו) **מותר ברוטב ובקיפה.** רוטב הנקפא בשולי הקדירה נקרא קיפה: **רבי יהודה אוסר.** הואיל ויש בו טעם בשר. ואין הלכה כרבי יהודה: **אימתי בזמן שאמר בשר זה עלי.** דכיון דאמר בשר זה שווייה עליה חתיכה דאיסורא ואסור בטעמו, אבל אם אמר קונם בשר עלי לא אסר טעמו אלא בדבר הנקרא בשר:

יד אברהם

הַנּוֹדֵר מִן ,,הַבָּשָׂר'' – מֻתָּר בָּרֹטֶב – *One who makes a neder prohibiting ''meat'' is permitted meat juice*

Meat juice is not meat, and was therefore not intended when the prohibition specifying meat was stated.

As will be seen, there are formulae of *nedarim* which are understood to forbid juice as well. However the standard *neder*, ''Konam, meat to me,'' prohibits only what is called meat, and not meat juice (*Rav; Rosh*).

וּבַקִּיפָה; – *and jelled meat juice;*

The translation follows *Rav*. However, it is not clear why the mishnah found it necessary to rule concerning both meat juice and jelled meat juice — two items which are essentially identical (*Tos. Yom Tov*).

Rosh explains this to be a gel of meat juice and strands of meat which collected at the bottom of the pot. Although this gel contains some actual meat, it is not referred to as meat, and is therefore not included in the prohibition.

Another interpretation is *spices* (*Rambam Comm.; Rav* to *Chullin* 9:11).

וְרַבִּי יְהוּדָה אוֹסֵר. – *R' Yehudah, however, forbids [them].*

R' Yehudah assumes that anything with the flavor of meat was included in the prohibition; accordingly, meat juice is forbidden (*Rav*).

אָמַר רַבִּי יְהוּדָה: מַעֲשֶׂה וְאָסַר עָלַי רַבִּי טַרְפוֹן בֵּיצִים שֶׁנִּתְבַּשְּׁלוּ עִמּוֹ. – *Said R' Yehudah: It happened that R' Tarfon forbade me the eggs which were cooked with it.*

[In support of his position, R' Yehudah recounts a personal incident in which R' Tarfon forbade eggs that had been cooked together with meat which was forbidden by a *neder*. Clearly, this was because the eggs had absorbed the flavor of the meat. This demonstrates, then, that the prohibition includes anything which carries the flavor of the meat.]

אָמְרוּ לוֹ: וְכֵן הַדָּבָר! אֵימָתַי? בִּזְמַן שֶׁיֹּאמַר: ,,בָּשָׂר זֶה עָלַי'', שֶׁהַנּוֹדֵר מִן הַדָּבָר וְנִתְעָרֵב בְּאַחֵר, אִם יֵשׁ בּוֹ בְּנוֹתֵן טַעַם – אָסוּר. – *They said to him: It is true! When? At a*

6. **O**ne who makes a *neder* prohibiting "meat" is permitted meat juice and jelled meat juice; R' Yehudah, however, forbids [them]. Said R' Yehudah: It happened that R' Tarfon forbade me the eggs which were cooked with it. They said to him: It is true! When? At a time that he says: "This meat to me," because one who prohibits a thing with a *neder* and it mixes with another thing — if there is enough to give a flavor, it is forbidden.

YAD AVRAHAM

time that he says: "This meat to me," because one who prohibits a thing with a neder and it mixes with another thing — if there is enough to give its flavor, it is forbidden.

The Rabbis who disputed R' Yehudah answered him that, indeed, R' Tarfon's ruling was justified. But not because a prohibition against meat automatically includes things such as eggs which have absorbed the flavor of the meat. Rather, it was because the case in question involved a formula of a *neder* which was directed not at meat in general, but at a specific piece of meat. That is, the person declared concerning a specific piece of meat: "This meat is to me *konam*." In such a case, not only is the piece of meat proper forbidden, but anything which has acquired its flavor is also forbidden. This is why R' Tarfon forbade the eggs (*Rav*).

When eggs are cooked together with meat, they are said to have acquired the flavor of the meat as long as the meat constitutes one-sixtieth or more of the mixture. If the meat were present in amounts of less than one-sixtieth of the amount of eggs, the flavor of the meat would be considered annulled, and the eggs would be permitted (*Tif. Yis*).

Ran argues that the flavor of meat forbidden by a *neder* can be annulled only by a flavor of a different species; thus, the flavor of the meat could be annulled in the egg. But, if the meat forbidden by a *neder* were cooked together with other pieces of permitted meat, even if there were sixty times as much permitted meat, all the meat would be forbidden.

The reason for this, explains *Ran* (52a), is that the operative mechanism in the law of annulment of a prohibition in a mixture is the existence of a dissimilarity between the forbidden item and the rest of the mixture. When two things are dissimilar, the predominant one overwhelms the other in a mixture, causing it to lose its identity; but, when two things are similar, they act to reinforce their identity rather than destroy it.

Ordinarily, when something forbidden is mixed together with something permitted — whether of the same species or a different one — the contrast between the permissibility of one thing and the forbiddenness of the other is enough to activate the law of annulment. Thus, if a piece of unslaughtered beef were cooked in sixty times as much permitted beef, the latter would be said to have annulled the flavor issuing from the forbidden piece. Therefore, the permitted pieces will remain permitted. So too, if the nonkosher beef were cooked in sixty times as many eggs, the eggs remain permitted because they have annulled any forbidden flavor deriving from the nonkosher meat.

This is all true for a permanently prohib-

[ז] הַנּוֹדֵר מִן „הַיַּיִן" — מֻתָּר בְּתַבְשִׁיל שֶׁיֵּשׁ בּוֹ טַעַם יָיִן. אָמַר: „קוֹנָם יַיִן זֶה שֶׁאֵינִי טוֹעֵם", וְנָפַל לַתַּבְשִׁיל — אִם יֶשׁ בּוֹ בְּנוֹתֵן טַעַם הֲרֵי זֶה אָסוּר. הַנּוֹדֵר מִן „הָעֲנָבִים" — מֻתָּר בַּיַּיִן; מִן „הַזֵּיתִים" — מֻתָּר בַּשֶּׁמֶן. אָמַר: „קוֹנָם זֵיתִים וַעֲנָבִים אֵלּוּ שֶׁאֵינִי טוֹעֵם" — אָסוּר בָּהֶן וּבַיּוֹצֵא מֵהֶן.

────────── ר' עובדיה מברטנורא ──────────

(ז) **מותר בתבשיל שיש בו טעם יין.** כרבנן דרבי יהודה:

יד אברהם

ited item such as unslaughtered meat. Such meat can never become permitted, and so, its state of forbiddenness stands in sharp contrast to the permissibility of the rest of the mixture (the kosher beef, or the eggs in the case above).

But, a piece of meat prohibited by a *neder* does not possess such a clear-cut state of forbiddenness. This is because the *Gemara* (59a) states that it is incumbent upon a person to seek cancellation of any prohibitions which he creates. Therefore, since *nedarim* are supposed to be revoked, they are treated like temporary prohibitions. A piece of meat forbidden today by a *neder* will become permissible as soon as the *neder* is canceled.

For a temporary prohibition, the contrast between the permissibility of the rest of the mixture and the temporarily prohibited item is not pronounced. Therefore, only where some other contrast is present can the laws of annulment apply. Accordingly, only where the item prohibited by a *neder* is mixed with a different species will it be annulled if it is less than one-sixtieth. The contrast between the species compensates for the insufficient

contrast between the already-permitted and the soon-to-be permitted states. But, if the item prohibited by a *neder* mixes with permissible items of the identical species, the laws of annulment do not apply. In the absence of any contrasts, the character of the forbidden item is reinforced and not annulled.

Therefore, the mishnah deliberately selects a case of meat, that had been prohibited by a *neder*, and was subsequently cooked with eggs. As distinct species, the laws of annulment apply even though the meat is only temporarily prohibited. Thus, if the eggs are not sixty times as much as the meat, they are forbidden; if they are sixty times the meat, they will be permitted. On the other hand, if this meat were cooked with permitted meat, even if the permitted meat were sixty times as much, the entire mixture would be forbidden. For even something bearing only temporary prohibition — when mixed with the same species — cannot be annulled. (For a further discussion of *Ran's* theories on the laws of annulment, see *R' Akiva Eiger*, Responsa Vol. 1 189, 209; see also *Beis Meir* to *Yoreh Deah* 102.)

7.

הַנּוֹדֵר מִן „הַיַּיִן" — מֻתָּר בְּתַבְשִׁיל שֶׁיֵּשׁ בּוֹ טַעַם יָיִן. — *One who makes a neder prohibiting "wine" is permitted a cooked dish which has the taste of wine in it.*

This follows the opinion of the Sages, who dispute R' Yehudah in the previous mishnah, and maintain that, when some general species is forbidden by a *neder*, the prohibition is not

6
7

7. **O**ne who makes a *neder* prohibiting "wine" is permitted a cooked dish which has a taste of wine in it. [If] he said: "*Konam*, this wine with respect to my tasting [it]," and it fell into a cooked dish — if it is enough to give flavor, it is forbidden. One who makes a *neder* prohibiting "grapes" is permitted wine; [if he makes a *neder* prohibiting] "olives," he is permitted oil. [If] he said: "*Konam*, these olives and grapes with respect to my tasting [them]," he is forbidden them and what comes from them.

YAD AVRAHAM

intended to include more than the species itself. However, something which has merely absorbed the flavor of the forbidden species was not intended, and is permitted (*Rav*).

In the previous mishnah, this was illustrated with meat juices which remain permitted — according to the Sages — even though the meat itself has been forbidden. This is because the juice is not referred to as *meat*, and, thus — although it carries the flavor of meat — it was not included in the *neder*. In the present case, the wine itself, which has been forbidden, mixes with some dish which then acquires the flavor of wine. Although the actual wine has been absorbed — and not some extract as in the case of meat juice — the mishnah teaches us that the dish remains permitted. Only something in a form referred to as *wine* is prohibited by the *neder*. But, a cooked dish — despite having absorbed and having the flavor of wine — is not called *wine*. It is therefore permitted (*Tif. Yis*; see *Rashash*).

אָמַר: "קוֹנָם יַיִן זֶה שֶׁאֵינִי טוֹעֵם", וְנָפַל לַתַּבְשִׁיל — *[If] he said: "Konam, this*

wine with respect to my tasting [it]," and it fell into a cooked dish —

[Rather than prohibiting wine in general, the person here prohibits some specific bottle of wine — "*this wine.*" Because of this, even something which has only absorbed the flavor of the wine, although is is not called wine, is forbidden (see previous mishnah).]

אִם יֵשׁ בּוֹ בְּנוֹתֵן טַעַם הֲרֵי זֶה אָסוּר. — *if it is enough to give flavor, it is forbidden.*

[If the wine amounts to one-sixtieth or more of the cooked dish, it is considered to give flavor, and the dish is forbidden.]

הַנּוֹדֵר מִן "הָעֲנָבִים" – מֻתָּר בַּיַּיִן; מִן "הַזֵּיתִים" – מֻתָּר בַּשֶּׁמֶן. אָמַר: "קוֹנָם זֵיתִים וַעֲנָבִים אֵלּוּ שֶׁאֲנִי טוֹעֵם" – אָסוּר בָּהֶן וּבַיּוֹצֵא מֵהֶן. — *One who makes a neder prohibiting "grapes" is permitted wine; [if he makes a neder prohibiting] "olives," he is permitted oil. [If] he said: "Konam, these olives and grapes with respect to my tasting [them]," he is forbidden them and what comes from them.*

This is another illustration of a *neder* directed at a fruit. The *neder* ordinarily is not assumed to include

[ח] הַנּוֹדֵר מִן "הַתְּמָרִים" — מֻתָּר בִּדְבַשׁ תְּמָרִים. מִ"סְּתָוָנִיּוֹת" — מֻתָּר בְּחֹמֶץ סְתָוָנִיּוֹת. רַבִּי יְהוּדָה בֶּן בְּתֵירָא אוֹמֵר: כֹּל שֶׁשֵּׁם תּוֹלַדְתּוֹ קְרוּיָה עָלָיו, וְנוֹדֵר הֵימֶנּוּ — אָסוּר אַף בַּיּוֹצֵא הֵימֶנּוּ. וַחֲכָמִים מַתִּירִין.

--- ר' עובדיה מברטנורא ---

(ח) סְתָוָנִיּוֹת. ענבים רעים הנשארים בגפנים [בימות] הסתיו ואינס ראוים ליין ועושים מהם חומץ: בל ששם תולדתו קרויה עליו. ואף על פי שגשתגה נקראת על שם עיקרו, כמו דבש תמרים חומץ סתוניות: וחכמים מתירין. איכא בין תנא קמא לחכמים, דתנא קמא סבר הנודר בסתוניות מותר בחומץ מהן ואסור בסתוניות, וחכמים מתירין בסתוניות עצמן, דכיון דסתוניות לאו בני אכילה נינהו כי נדר מסתוניות דעתו על החומץ היוצא מהן לא על הסתוניות עצמן. והלכה כחכמים. פירוש אחר, וחכמים מתירין חומץ הסתוניות כמו דבש תמרים, דסבירא להו לחכמים דין בדברים הראוים לאכילה בין שאינן ראויין לאכילה האוסר דבר אחד על עצמו מותר ביוצא ממנו:

--- יד אברהם ---

"Konam, these olives and grapes," omitting "with respect to my tasting," the prohibition would still include juices extracted from the forbidden fruit. If he said: "Konam, olives and grapes with respect to my tasting — without specifying these olives and grapes — the Gemara questions whether the phrase with respect to my tasting ought to be construed as including even juices extracted from the olives and grapes. The question is left undecided by the Gemara, and — in practice — we give such a neder the broadest meaning and assume that it prohibits the wine and oil which come from the grapes and olives as well (Tos. Yom Tov).

the juices extracted from these fruits; namely, wine or oil. [Even though grapes and olives were kept primarily in order to be squeezed for their juice (Chullin 14b), the juices had distinct names (wine, oil) and were not referred to by the name of the fruit (grapes, olives).]

However, when the neder specified these olives or grapes, then anything extracted from the designated fruits was prohibited (Tif. Yis.).

The Gemara (52b) asserts that the entire formula of the mishnah, "Konam, these olives and grapes with respect to my tasting [them]," is not necessary in order to effect a prohibition on juices extracted from the forbidden fruit. Had the person said:

8.

הַנּוֹדֵר מִן "הַתְּמָרִים" — מֻתָּר בִּדְבַשׁ תְּמָרִים — מִ"סְּתָוָנִיּוֹת" — מֻתָּר בְּחֹמֶץ סְתָוָנִיּוֹת. One who makes a neder prohibiting "dates" is permitted date honey. [If he makes a neder prohibiting] "winter grapes," he is permitted vinegar of winter grapes.

[Since the neder is directed at dates or at winter grapes in general, and the formula of the neder does not indicate that their by-products are included, the honey or vinegar extracted from the dates or winter grapes are permitted.]

The honey extracted from dates

8. **O**ne who makes a *neder* prohibiting "dates" is permitted date honey. [If he makes a *neder* prohibiting] "winter grapes," he is permitted vinegar of winter grapes. R' Yehudah ben Beseira says: Whenever the derivative carries the name of its source, and he makes a *neder* prohibiting the source, he is forbidden the derivative as well. The Sages, however, permit it.

YAD AVRAHAM

and vinegar derived from winter grapes are not referred to simply as *honey* or *vinegar*. Rather, their source is always identified, and they are called *date honey* or *vinegar* of winter grapes. However, this is done in order to distinguish them from bee honey and other vinegars, and not because they retain in some way the character of dates and grapes (*Tos. Yom Tov from Ran*). Thus, they are not included when dates and winter grapes are mentioned (*Rav*).

רַבִּי יְהוּדָה בֶּן בְּתֵירָא אוֹמֵר: כָּל שֶׁשֵּׁם תּוֹלַדְתּוֹ קְרוּיָה עָלָיו, וְנוֹדֵר הֵימֶנּוּ – אָסוּר אַף בַּיוֹצֵא הֵימֶנּוּ. — *R' Yehudah ben Beseira says: Whenever the derivative carries the name of its source, and he makes a neder prohibiting the source, he is forbidden the derivative as well.*

R' Yehudah ben Beseira maintains that, in general, if a derivative is always identified by its source, it is included when reference is made to the source. Thus, someone who — via a *neder* — forbids dates or winter grapes will also be forbidden date honey and vinegar of winter grapes (*Rav*).

וַחֲכָמִים מַתִּירִין. — *The Sages, however, permit it.*

[That is, the person who prohibited dates or winter grapes is allowed date honey or vinegar of winter grapes.]

The *Gemara* (53a), according to *Ran* (ad loc.), distinguishes between the opinion attributed here to the Sages and the view stated anonymously at the beginning of the mishnah as follows. According to the Sages, when someone prohibits winter grapes, not only is the vinegar permitted — since it is not included in the category of winter grapes — the winter grapes themselves are permitted. This is because winter grapes are not edible. Consequently, we assume that the person — when stating his *neder* — was not directing it at the grapes, but at the vinegar. Since there is no intention to forbid the grapes, they remain permitted. The vinegar, on the other hand — despite the person's assumed intention to forbid it — remains permitted. It will be forbidden only if it is mentioned in the *neder*; this declaration mentions only *winter grapes*, which is not acceptable name for the vinegar. Thus, the *neder* is totally ineffective, and the person may enjoy benefit from both the winter grapes and their vinegar (*Rav; Rosh*).

Rav also mentions a different approach, according to which the first opinion of the mishnah permits derivatives only when their source is edible. But, vinegar of winter grapes, which is derived from something inedible, will be forbidden even by a *neder*

[ט] הַנּוֹדֵר מִן „הַיַּיִן" — מֻתָּר בְּיֵין תַּפּוּחִים;

מִן „הַשֶּׁמֶן" — מֻתָּר בְּשֶׁמֶן שֻׁמְשְׁמִין; מִן „הַדְּבַשׁ" — מֻתָּר בִּדְבַשׁ תְּמָרִים; מִן „הַחֹמֶץ" — מֻתָּר בְּחֹמֶץ סְתְוָנִיּוֹת; מִן „הַכְּרֵשִׁין" — מֻתָּר בַּקַּפְלוֹטוֹת; מִן „הַיָּרָק" — מֻתָּר בְּיַרְקוֹת הַשָּׂדֶה, מִפְּנֵי שֶׁהוּא שֵׁם לְוַאי.

[י] מִן „הַכְּרוּב" — אָסוּר בָּאַסְפַּרְגּוֹס; מִן „הָאַסְפַּרְגּוֹס" — מֻתָּר בַּכְּרוּב.

—————————— ר' עובדיה מברטנורא ——————————

(ט) **קפלוטות.** מין ממיני הכרתים הגדלים בארץ ישראל: **שהוא שם לווי.** הבא לומר ירקות שדה צריך לחבר שם לירק ולומר ירקות שדה, וכן כולם, אבל בשביעית, לפי שאין ירקות גינה מצויין שאין גדולין בלא עבודה ואוכלים ירקות שדה, לפיכך ירקות סתם בשביעית הוו ירקות שדה, מה שאין כן בשאר שני השבוע: (י) **אספרגוס.** מין כרוב הוא, אלא שאין כרוב נקרא בשם אספרגום. פירוש אחר, אספרגום, המים שנשלקו בהם הכרוב:

—————————— יד אברהם ——————————

which refers only to the grapes with no mention of the vinegar. However, this approach is not consistent with our texts

which read: *[If he makes a neder prohibiting] winter grapes, he is permitted vinegar of winter grapes (Rashash).*

9.

הַנּוֹדֵר מִן „הַיַּיִן" - מֻתָּר בְּיֵין תַּפּוּחִים; *One who makes a neder prohibiting "wine" is permitted apple wine;*

[The term *wine* refers to wine made from grapes. Apple wine is always referred to with the accompanying appellate *apple*, and never as *wine* alone.]

מִן „הַשֶּׁמֶן"- *[if he prohibited]"oil",*

[I.e., a person made a *neder* prohibiting oil.]

מֻתָּר בְּשֶׁמֶן שֻׁמְשְׁמִין; *— he is permitted sesame oil;*

The term *oil* alone refers to olive oil. Sesame oil is always called by its own name, and not included in a *neder* referring simply to *oil* (Tos. Yom Tov from *Rashi*).

מִן „הַדְּבַשׁ"- *[if]"honey,"*

[A person made a *neder* prohibiting

honey.]

מֻתָּר בִּדְבַשׁ תְּמָרִים; *— he is permitted date honey;*

Honey alone means bee honey (Tos. Yom Tov from Tur). [Date honey is not intended, unless explicitly mentioned.]

This is true only for popular usage, which — as far as *nedarim* are concerned — is the determining factor. However, in Biblical nomenclature, the term *honey* alone means date honey (Tif. Yis.; see, however, Mishneh LeMelech, Hil. Bikkurim 2:19).

מִן „הַחֹמֶץ" - מֻתָּר בְּחֹמֶץ סְתְוָנִיּוֹת; מִן „הַכְּרֵשִׁין" - מֻתָּר בַּקַּפְלוֹטוֹת; *[if] "vinegar," he is permitted vinegar of winter grapes; [if] "leek," he is permitted leeks with a head;*

Vinegar alone refers to wine vine-

9. **O**ne who makes a *neder* prohibiting "wine" is permitted apple wine; [if he prohibited] "oil," he is permitted sesame oil; [if] "honey," he is permitted date honey; [if] "vinegar," he is permitted vinegar of winter grapes; [if] "leek," he is permitted leeks with a head; [if] "vegetables," he is permitted wild vegetables because it is an appellative.

10. **[I**f one made a *neder* prohibiting] "cabbage," he is forbidden *ispargos*; [if] "*ispargos*," he is permitted cabbage. [If]

YAD AVRAHAM

gar (*Tif. Yis.*). *Leek* does not ordinarily include the related *leek with a head* (*porrum capitatum*) (*Aruch*, quoted by *Meleches Shlomo*).

[*if*] מִן ,,הַיָּרָק" – מֻתָּר בְּיַרְקוֹת הַשָּׂדֶה, *vegetables, he is permitted wild vegetables,*

Ordinarily, when a person refers to *vegetables*, he means *cultivated vegetables*, and not those which grow wild on their own. However, during *Shemittah* (the Sabbatical year,) when farming is forbidden, the standard vegetable is the wild one. Thus, during that year, the law would be that a *neder* prohibiting vegetables

interdicts wild ones, but not cultivated ones (*Rav*). Where cultivated vegetables were imported to the Holy Land during *Shemittah*, the term *vegetables* included both the imported, cultivated vegetables as well as the local wild ones (*Tos. Yom Tov*).

מִפְּנֵי שֶׁהוּא שֵׁם לְוַי. — *because it is an appellative.*

[That is, all the species listed in the mishnah are described by a specific epithet, and are thus ordinarily not intended when reference is made to the general class to which they belong.]

10.

מִן ,,הַכְּרוּב" – אָסוּר בָּאִסְפַּרְגוֹס; מִן ,,הָאִסְפַּרְגוֹס", – מֻתָּר בַּכְּרוּב. — [*If one made a neder prohibiting*] *"cabbage," he is forbidden ispargos; [if] "ispargos," he is permitted cabbage.*

According to one definition, *ispargos* is a species of a cabbage.[1] It is thus included when a *neder* is directed at

cabbage in general. However, a *neder* aimed at *ispargos* alone prohibits only it, and not other varieties of cabbage (*Rav*).

Another explanation is that *ispargos* is the water in which cabbage was cooked (*Rav*; *Rambam Comm.*). It was also called *cabbage*, and, therefore,

1. [Though the vegetable *asparagus* is included in the same general classification as cabbage, it does not seem that it could be considered a species of the latter. We have therefore left *ispargos* untranslated.]

„הַגְּרִיסִין" — אָסוּר (מִן הַ) [בַּ]מִקְפָּה, וְרַבִּי יוֹסֵי
מַתִּיר; מִן „הַמִּקְפָּה" — מֻתָּר בַּגְּרִיסִין. מִן
„הַמִּקְפָּה" — אָסוּר בַּשּׁוּם, וְרַבִּי יוֹסֵי מַתִּיר; מִן
„הַשּׁוּם" — מֻתָּר בַּמִּקְפָּה. מִן „הָעֲדָשִׁים" —
אָסוּר בָּאֲשִׁישִׁין, [וְרַבִּי יוֹסֵי מַתִּיר]; מִן
„הָאֲשִׁישִׁים" — מֻתָּר בָּעֲדָשִׁים. „חִטָּה, חִטִּים
שֶׁאֵינִי טוֹעֵם" — אָסוּר בָּהֶן בֵּין קֶמַח בֵּין פַּת.
„גְּרִיס, גְּרִיסִין שֶׁאֵינִי טוֹעֵם" — אָסוּר בָּהֶן בֵּין
חַיִּין בֵּין מְבֻשָּׁלִים. רַבִּי יְהוּדָה אוֹמֵר: „קוֹנָם גְּרִיס
אוֹ חִטָּה שֶׁאֵינִי טוֹעֵם" — מֻתָּר לָכוֹס חַיִּים.

מן הגריסין אסור במקפה. שאף על פי שהם נתונים לתוך המקפה עדיין שם גריסין עליהם:
ורבי יוסי מתיר. דקסבר מקפה של גריסין מיקרו גריסין גרידא לא מיקרו: מקפה. תבשיל עב
של קטנית או של ליקי קדרה: הנודר מן המקפה אסור בשום. רגילים היו לתת שום בכל
מקפה כדי שיתן טעם, והשום הוא המקפה: אסור באשישין. פסולת של עדשים. ואין הלכה
כרבי יוסי [בכלתי] בצי דמתניתין: חטה חטים שאיני טועם. חטה משמע פת אפויה, חטים
משמע לכוס:

יד אברהם

would be forbidden via a *neder*
prohibiting cabbage. However, cabbage was not referred to as *ispargos*, so
that, if *ispargos* were prohibited,
cabbage would remain permitted
(*Tos. Yom Tov*).

מִן „הַגְּרִיסִין" — אָסוּר (מִן הַ) [בַּ]מִקְפָּה, וְרַבִּי
יוֹסֵי מַתִּיר; — [If] "grits", he is forbidden
*grits pottage; R' Yose, however, per-
mits it.*

Coarsely ground beans or grain
were cooked in a soup containing grits
along with oil and garlic. The mishnah
considers the grits to retain their
character even while becoming an
ingredient of this pottage. The grits
soup is thus forbidden even by a *neder*
directed at grits. However, R' Yose
argues that once they have been
prepared as a pottage, the grits are no

longer referred to as plain grits (*Rav*).

מִן „הַמִּקְפָּה" – מֻתָּר בַּגְּרִיסִין. – [If] "grits
pottage," he is permitted grits.

[All agree that grits, in general, are
not intended when a person forbids
grits pottage, and they therefore
remain permitted.]

מִן „הַמִּקְפָּה" – אָסוּר בַּשּׁוּם, וְרַבִּי יוֹסֵי מַתִּיר;
מִן „הַשּׁוּם" – מֻתָּר בַּמִּקְפָּה. – [If] "grits
pottage," he is [also] forbidden garlic;
R' Yose, however, permits it; [if]
"garlic," he is permitted grits pottage.

[The *Tannaim* argued whether garlic — since it is an ingredient in the
pottage — was referred to as *pottage*.
But everyone agrees that pottage was
not called *garlic*.]

מִן „הָעֲדָשִׁים" – אָסוּר בָּאֲשִׁישִׁים, [וְרַבִּי יוֹסֵי
מַתִּיר]; מִן „הָאֲשִׁישִׁים" – מֻתָּר בָּעֲדָשִׁים.
[If] "lentils," he is forbidden waste of

6
10

"grits," he is forbidden grits pottage; R' Yose, however, permits it. [If] "grits pottage," he is permitted grits. [If] "grits pottage," he is [also] forbidden garlic; R' Yose, however, permits it; [if] "garlic," he is permitted grits pottage. [If] "lentils," he is forbidden waste of lentils; R' Yose, however, permits it; [if] "waste of lentils," he is permitted lentils. [If one says:] "Wheat grain, wheat grains, with respect to my tasting [them]," he is forbidden them whether [in the form of] flour or bread; "Grits, grits with respect to my tasting [them]," he is forbidden them whether raw or cooked. R' Yehudah says: [If he says:] "*Konam,* grits or wheat grain with respect to my tasting," he is permitted to chew them raw.

YAD AVRAHAM

lentils; R' Yose, however, permits it; [if] "waste of lentils," he is permitted lentils.

The translation follows *Rav,* and is based on *Rosh* (53b). *Yerushalmi* explains אֲשִׁישִׁים to be *roasted lentils, ground and kneaded with honey, and fried* — that is, a kind of cake made of lentil flour with honey. The dispute in the mishnah centers on whether this was still called *lentils,* R' Yose maintaining that it was not.

„חִטָּה, חִטִּים שֶׁאֵינִי טוֹעֵם" – אָסוּר בָּהֶן בֵּין קֶמַח בֵּין פַּת. „גְּרִיס, גְּרִיסִין שֶׁאֵינִי טוֹעֵם" – אָסוּר בָּהֶן בֵּין חַיִּין בֵּין מְבֻשָּׁלִים. — *[If one says:] "Wheat grain, wheat grains, with respect to my tasting [them]," he is forbidden them whether [in the form of] flour or bread; "Grits, grits with respect to my tasting [them]," he is forbidden them whether raw or cooked.* [גְּרִיס, גְּרִיסִין denotes the singular and plural forms of *grits.*]

Just as in mishnah 4, where the explicit mention of the singular and

the plural forms of the word *fish* is taken to indicate all the forms of fish, so too, the mention of the singular and the plural forms of *wheat* and *grits* are indicative of an intention to include different forms.

Thus, the singular form of *wheat* may be used to describe a loaf of bread which is a single, solid unit, but not flour, which is composed of many grains. On the other hand, the plural form is used to describe flour, but not bread. Nevertheless, when mentioned together, both forms are included (*Ran*).

[Similarly, the singular form *split bean* might describe a cooked dish of split beans which merge into one unit; but, a collection of raw, split beans would be described by the plural form. Together, both forms are included.]

As in mishnah 4, *Rambam* explains that the broader interpretation of the *neder* is not due to mention of both singular and plural forms, but to repetition of the root. This repetition amplifies the meaning, and gives

[167] **THE MISHNAH/NEDARIM** — Chapter Six: *HaNodeir Min HaMevushal*

it the broadest definition. The *neder*, therefore, include all the varieties of the forbidden item.

רַבִּי יְהוּדָה אוֹמֵר: ,,קוֹנָם גְּרִיס אוֹ חִטָּה שֶׁאֵינִי טוֹעֵם'' – מֻתָּר לָכֹס חַיִּים. — *R' Yehudah says:* [*If he says:*] "*Konam, grits or wheat grain with respect to my tasting,*" *he is permitted to chew them raw.*

R' Yehudah is not disputing the preceding rulings of the mishnah; rather, he is illustrating them by way of an example. If someone forbade *wheat grain* or *grits* (in the singular form), he will be permitted to chew them raw. The singular form, as explained above, can describe grits or wheat grain cooked together into a unit. But, as independent entities (i.e., when raw), only the plural form is appropriate (*Tos. Yom Tov*).

Some authorities do understand R' Yehudah as disagreeing with the previous opinion. According to them, the first view maintains that, whether the singular or plural form is used, the *neder* includes both the raw and the cooked form. They understand the mishnah as though it said "*wheat grain or wheat grains with respect to my tasting,*" and it would mean that either form of the word includes both the raw and the cooked states. R' Yehudah, however, disputes this, and maintains that the singular form describes the cooked state only (*Tos.* 53a, s.v. חטא; see *Lechem Mishneh, Hil. Nedarim* 9:9).

פרק שביעי ⋘

Chapter Seven

A number of definitions will be helpful for a clearer understanding of the next mishnayos. The enormous variety of edible vegetables can be classified into distinct categories. There are the grains: wheat, barley, and certain related species — used primarily for bread and cereals. There are legumes, such as beans and peas. Both legumes and grains are edible seeds. Some vegetables are not seeds, but rather other parts of the plant; lettuce and cabbage, for example, are from the leafy part of the plant, while radishes are from the root. Vegetables which are not seeds can be referred to as *greens*, corresponding to the Hebrew יָרָק, *yarak* (sing.), or יְרָקוֹת, *yerakos* (pl.). This is usually so with respect to vegetables which are leafy or those that are eaten raw. However, those vegetables which are not leafy, or are edible only upon cooking, might not be considered *greens*, and would be called *fruit* instead. Thus, a gourd — which was edible only after cooking — would ordinarily not be included under the category of greens, but rather that of fruits (*Tos. Rid; Meiri*).

[א] **הַנּוֹדֵר** מִן „הַיָּרָק" — מֻתָּר בַּדְּלוּעִין;
וְרַבִּי עֲקִיבָא אוֹסֵר. אָמְרוּ לוֹ
לְרַבִּי עֲקִיבָא: וַהֲלֹא אוֹמֵר אָדָם לִשְׁלוּחוֹ: „קַח לִי
יָרָק", וְהוּא אוֹמֵר: „לֹא מָצָאתִי אֶלָּא דְלוּעִין".
אָמַר לָהֶם: כֵּן הַדָּבָר; אוֹ שֶׁמָּא אוֹמֵר הוּא לוֹ:
„לֹא מָצָאתִי אֶלָּא קִטְנִית"? אֶלָּא שֶׁהַדְּלוּעִין
בִּכְלָל „יָרָק", וְקִטְנִית אֵינָן בִּכְלָל „יָרָק". וְאָסוּר
בְּפוֹל הַמִּצְרִי לַח, וּמֻתָּר בַּיָּבֵשׁ.

—————— ר' עובדיה מברטנורא ——————

פרק שביעי – הנודר מן הירק. (א) הנודר מן הירק. לא מצאתי אלא דלועין. ואם מין
ירק הוא אמאי לא זבין ליה: **כן הדבר.** וממשם אני מביא ראיה, שמא אומר לא מלאתי אלא

יד אברהם

1.

הַנּוֹדֵר מִן „הַיָּרָק" — *One who makes a neder prohibiting greens*

The *Gemara* (54a) explains the *neder* in question to be: "*Konam*, to me greens cooked in a pot." The stipulation *cooked in a pot* would seem to indicate that the person wants to prohibit even vegetables which are not edible raw, and must be cooked in a pot (*Ran*).

But a *neder* can prohibit only something included in the words of the declaration. Even if the person desires to prohibit a certain thing, if he fails to articulate the *neder* in such a way as to include that thing, it will remain permitted (see comm. to 6:8, s.v. וַחֲכָמִים מַתִּירִין). Thus, if vegetables which are only edible when cooked cannot be called *greens*, the *neder*,' "*Konam*, to me, greens cooked in a pot," will not prohibit them (*Ran*).

מֻתָּר בַּדְּלוּעִין; — *is permitted gourds;*

The gourds mentioned are inedible without cooking (*Ran*).

וְרַבִּי עֲקִיבָא אוֹסֵר. — *R' Akiva, however, forbids [them].*

R' Akiva argues with the Rabbis —

the first anonymous opinion in the mishnah — as to whether such gourds can be included in the words of the *neder*. The Rabbis maintain that these bitter gourds cannot be referred to as *greens*, since greens can always be eaten raw; R' Akiva disagrees (*Rosh; Ran*).

[In the ensuing debate, they each attempt to find support for their position from a typical example of the usage of the term *greens* in an everyday situation. As mentioned previously, definitions of the words of a *neder* are based on their popular meaning (see preface to 6:1).]

אָמְרוּ לוֹ לְרַבִּי עֲקִיבָא: — *They said to R' Akiva:*

[The Rabbis reasoned with R' Akiva.]

וַהֲלֹא אוֹמֵר אָדָם לִשְׁלוּחוֹ: „קַח לִי יָרָק", וְהוּא אוֹמֵר: „לֹא מָצָאתִי אֶלָּא דְלוּעִין". — *Doesn't a person say to his agent: "Buy me greens," and he says: "I found only gourds"?*

The Rabbis recount a typical exchange, which — they maintain — supports their contention that bitter gourds are not called *greens*. A person

7
1

1. **O**ne who makes a *neder* prohibiting greens is permitted gourds; R' Akiva, however, forbids [them]. They said to R' Akiva: Doesn't a person say to his agent: "Buy me greens," and he says: "I found only gourds"? He said to them: Indeed, it is so; but does he say to him: "I found only legumes"? [It is] only [because] bitter gourds are included under the category of greens, but legumes are not included under the category of greens. He is forbidden fresh Egyptian beans, but permitted dry [ones].

YAD AVRAHAM

sends someone to the market with instructions to purchase greens. The market, however, is out of everything except bitter gourds. The agent returns to his sender, and reports: *"I found only gourds."*

The Rabbis contend that, if *greens* included even bitter gourds — which are edible only after cooking — the agent would not have returned for further instructions. He would have purchased the gourds, and thus fulfilled his mission (*Rav*). Since, however, it is commonplace that the agent in this situation returns for further direction, it is evident that bitter gourds are not included under the category of greens (*Tos.*). [Therefore, the *neder* of the mishnah which is directed at *greens* does not prohibit bitter gourds.]

אָמַר לָהֶם: כֵּן הַדָּבָר; — *He said to them: Indeed, it is so;*

R' Akiva counters that the incident adduced by the Rabbis to support their position actually supports his (*Rav*).

אוֹ שֶׁמָּא אוֹמֵר הוּא לוֹ: ,,לֹא מָצָאתִי אֶלָּא קְטָנִית"? — *but does he say to him: "I found only legumes"?*

If the agent who has been instructed to buy greens will find legumes, will he report this to the sender? No. But he

will mention that he could find only gourds! (*Rashi; Rosh*).

אֶלָּא שֶׁהַדְּלוּעִין בִּכְלָל ,,יָרָק", וְקִטְנִית אֵינָן בִּכְלָל ,,יָרָק". — *[It is] only [because] bitter gourds are included under the category of greens, but legumes are not included under the category of greens.*

It is because legumes are certainly not intended by the words *greens*, but gourds might be. Therefore, he consults his sender to ascertain whether gourds would satisfy his need (*Rav; Rosh*).

Accordingly, when he says *greens cooked in a pot*, he may very well intend to include things that are only edible after cooking, which are also sometimes called *greens*, in particular, bitter gourds. Therefore, R' Akiva rules that he is forbidden bitter gourds (*Rav*).

Although R' Akiva prohibits bitter gourds to someone making this *neder*, he does not impose a penalty of lashes for eating gourds in violation of the *neder* (*Gem.* 54a). This is because R' Akiva is not certain that gourds are intended. However, since they might be, he stringently interprets the *neder* and forbids them out of doubt. But, something forbidden only out of doubt does not carry a corporal penalty for its violation (*Ran*).

וְאָסוּר בְּפוֹל הַמִּצְרִי לַח, וּמֻתָּר בַּיָּבֵשׁ. — *He is forbidden fresh Egyptian beans, but permitted dry [ones].*

[ב] הַנּוֹדֵר מִן „הַדָּגָן" – אָסוּר בְּפוֹל הַמִּצְרִי
יָבֵשׁ; דִּבְרֵי רַבִּי מֵאִיר. וַחֲכָמִים
אוֹמְרִים: אֵינוֹ אָסוּר אֶלָּא בַּחֲמֵשֶׁת הַמִּינִין. רַבִּי
מֵאִיר אוֹמֵר: הַנּוֹדֵר מִן „הַתְּבוּאָה" – אֵינוֹ אָסוּר
אֶלָּא בַּחֲמֵשֶׁת הַמִּינִין. אֲבָל הַנּוֹדֵר מִן „הַדָּגָן" –
אָסוּר בַּכֹּל, וּמֻתָּר בְּפֵרוֹת הָאִילָן וּבַיָּרָק.

[ג] הַנּוֹדֵר מִן „הַכְּסוּת" – מֻתָּר בַּשַּׂק, בַּיְרִיעָה,
וּבַחֲמִילָה. אָמַר: „קוֹנָם צֶמֶר
עוֹלֶה עָלַי" – מֻתָּר לְהִתְכַּסּוֹת בְּגִזֵּי צֶמֶר; „פִּשְׁתָּן
עוֹלֶה עָלַי" – מֻתָּר לְהִתְכַּסּוֹת בַּאֲנִיצֵי פִשְׁתָּן.

ר' עובדיה מברטנורא

קטנית, ומדקא אתי להמלך על הדלוטין אלמא מין ירק הוא. והלכה כחכמים: **(ב) אסור בפול**
המצרי יבש. דדגן כל מידי דמידגן משמע, כל דבר שעושין ממנו כרי, והא נמי מדגן הוא:
הנודר מן הדגן אסור בכל. מיני קטניות שעושין מהן כרי. ואין הלכה כרבי מאיר: **(ג) בשק**
ביריעה ובחמילה. מיני בגדים גסים ועבים ביותר ואין בני אדם רגילים להתכסות בהם:
מותר בגיזי צמר. שלא נתכוין אלא לבגד גמר:

יד אברהם

When the Egyptian bean is fresh, it is called a *green*. However, when dried, it is no longer called a *green* (*Ran*; see

next mishnah). [Thus, the *neder* here which bans *greens* prohibits fresh Egyptian beans, but not dry ones.]

2.

הַנּוֹדֵר מִן „הַדָּגָן" – אָסוּר בְּפוֹל הַמִּצְרִי יָבֵשׁ;
דִּבְרֵי רַבִּי מֵאִיר. וַחֲכָמִים אוֹמְרִים: אֵינוֹ אָסוּר
אֶלָּא בַּחֲמֵשֶׁת הַמִּינִין. — *One who makes a neder prohibiting dagan is forbidden dry Egyptian beans; [these are] the words of R' Meir. The Sages, however, say: He is forbidden only the five varieties.*

Dagan is a term used generally with reference to grain. The word describes the procedure of piling up the grain in a granary. This procedure was used with dry Egyptian beans as well, and so, R' Meir considers them to be also included in the term *dagan* (*Rav*). However, the Sages maintain that the word *dagan* was used exclusively

for the five principal varieties of grain; viz., wheat, barley, spelt, rye or oats. See *Challah* 1:2, *Pesachim* 2:5, *Menachos* 10:7 (*Meiri*).

רַבִּי מֵאִיר אוֹמֵר: הַנּוֹדֵר מִן „הַתְּבוּאָה" –
אֵינוֹ אָסוּר אֶלָּא בַּחֲמֵשֶׁת הַמִּינִין. אֲבָל,
הַנּוֹדֵר מִן „הַדָּגָן" – אָסוּר בַּכֹּל, — *R' Meir says: One who makes a neder prohibiting tevuah is forbidden only the five grains. However, one who makes a neder from dagan is forbidden all,*

I.e., all things which are piled up similar to grain (*Rashi*).

R' Meir comments that there is, in fact, a term reserved exclusively for the five grains. This is the word

7
2-3

2. **O**ne who makes a *neder* prohibiting *dagan* is forbidden dry Egyptian beans; [these are] the words of R' Meir. The Sages, however, say: He is forbidden only the five varieties. R' Meir says: One who makes a *neder* prohibiting *tevuah* is forbidden only the five grains. However, one who makes a *neder* from *dagan* is forbidden all, but he is permitted fruit of the tree, and greens.

3. **O**ne who makes a *neder* prohibiting clothing is permitted sackcloth, sheets of cloth, and heavy fabric. [If] he said: "*Konam*, wool [from] coming upon me," he is permitted to clothe himself with wool shearings; "Flax [from] coming upon me," he is permitted to clothe [himself] with stalks of flax.

YAD AVRAHAM

tevuah. However, according to R' Meir, *dagan* is not limited to the five grains; rather, it denotes any product which, like grain, is piled. Thus, for example, beans — which are piled — will be forbidden by a *neder* prohibiting *dagan*. In particular, the dry Egyptian bean will be prohibited, since it is piled (ibid.). [But the fresh Egyptian bean will be permitted, since in that form it is called a *green* (7:1).]

וּמֻתָּר בְּפֵרוֹת הָאִילָן וּבַיָּרָק. — *but he is permitted fruit of the tree, and greens.*

This is because fruits and greens are not piled, and are certainly not called *dagan* (*Rosh* 55a).

3.

הַנּוֹדֵר מִן ,,הַכְּסוּת" – מֻתָּר בַּשַּׂק, בַּיְרִיעָה, וּבַחֲמִילָה. — *One who makes a neder prohibiting clothing is permitted sack-cloth, sheets of cloth, and heavy fabric.*

The materials listed by the mishnah — *sackcloth, sheets of cloth, and heavy fabric* — were all very coarse and heavy, and were not commonly used in clothing (*Rav*). [Consequently, a *neder* prohibiting *clothing* does not include these cloths.]

Sackcloth was a weave of goats' hair, *sheets of cloth* refers to coarsely woven cloth which was unsewn, and *heavy fabric* was a very thick, water-

resistant material. The latter two were used for protection against rain (*Rambam; Tos. Yom Tov*).

אָמַר: ,,קוֹנָם צֶמֶר עוֹלֶה עָלַי" – מֻתָּר לְהִתְכַּסוֹת בְּגִזֵּי צֶמֶר; ,,פִּשְׁתָּן עוֹלֶה עָלַי" – מֻתָּר לְהִתְכַּסוֹת בַּאֲנִיצֵי פִשְׁתָּן. — *[If] he said: "Konam, wool [from] coming upon me," he is permitted to clothe himself with wool shearings; "Flax [from] coming upon me," he is permitted to clothe [himself] with stalks of flax.*

The prohibitions here are understood as being directed at garments of

רַבִּי יְהוּדָה אוֹמֵר: הַכֹּל לְפִי הַנּוֹדֵר. טָעַן וְהֵזִיעַ וְהָיָה רֵיחוֹ קָשֶׁה, אָמַר: „קוֹנָם צֶמֶר וּפִשְׁתִּים עוֹלִים עָלַי" — מֻתָּר לְהִתְכַּסּוֹת, וְאָסוּר לְהַפְשִׁיל לַאֲחוֹרָיו.

[ד] **הַנּוֹדֵר** מִן „הַבַּיִת" — מֻתָּר בָּעֲלִיָּה; דִּבְרֵי רַבִּי מֵאִיר. וַחֲכָמִים אוֹמְרִים: עֲלִיָּה בִּכְלָל „הַבַּיִת". הַנּוֹדֵר מִן „הָעֲלִיָּה" — מֻתָּר בַּבַּיִת.

ר׳ עוֹבַדְיָה מִבַּרְטְנוּרָא

הכל לפי הנודר. לפי שעת הנדר, כיון שניכר שמחמת כובד משאו נדר, מותר להתכסות. והלכה כרבי יהודה: **(ד) הנודר מן הבית.** שלא יכנס לבית, מותר לכנס לעלייה, דלאו בכלל בית הוא:

יד אברהם

wool or flax (*Rav*). [Thus, a wool or linen suit would be forbidden; but wool shearings or flax stalks, not being garments, would not.]

רַבִּי יְהוּדָה אוֹמֵר: הַכֹּל לְפִי הַנּוֹדֵר — *R' Yehudah says: All depends on the person making the neder.*

R' Yehudah maintains that the *neder* must be interpreted according to the context in which it was uttered (*Ran; Tos.*).

טָעַן, — *If he was carrying a load,*

[I.e., of flax or wool.]

וְהֵזִיעַ וְהָיָה רֵיחוֹ קָשֶׁה, אָמַר: „קוֹנָם צֶמֶר וּפִשְׁתִּים עוֹלִים עָלַי" - מֻתָּר לְהִתְכַּסּוֹת, וְאָסוּר לְהַפְשִׁיל לַאֲחוֹרָיו. — *and he perspired and smelled badly, [and] he said: "Konam, wool or flax [from] coming upon me," he is permitted to clothe [himself with these], but is forbidden to carry bundles [of these] on his back.*

If a person declares: "Konam, wool or flax from coming upon me," as a reaction to the discomfort he experi-

ences while carrying loads of raw wool and flax, then the *neder* is assumed to prohibit only *carrying* loads of wool or flax; wearing these materials, however, would be permitted (*Meiri*).

According to *Rambam* (*Hil. Nedarim* 8:8), if a person was uncomfortable wearing a wool suit and he declared: "*Konam*, wool from coming upon me," he would be prohibited from wearing woolen clothes, but not from carrying loads of wool. But, if there was no circumstantial evidence with which to determine the extent of the prohibition (i.e., the person was neither wearing nor carrying wool at the time of his *neder*), R' Yehudah would prohibit him both from wearing and carrying wool.

Rosh (*Pesakim* 7:3), however, maintains that — where no indications are present — the *neder*, "*Konam*, wool from coming upon me," forbids only wearing wool, but not carrying loads of wool (*Tos. Yom Tov*).

The standard method for transporting bundles of wool or flax manually was to sling the bundles

R' Yehudah says: All depends on the person making the *neder*. If he was carrying a load, and he perspired and smelled badly, [and] he said: "*Konam*, wool or flax [from] coming upon me," he is permitted to clothe [himself with these], but is forbidden to carry bundles [of these] on his back.

4. **S**omeone who makes a *neder* prohibiting a house is permitted the upper story; [these are] the words of R' Meir. The Sages, however, say: The upper story is included in the [term] *house*. One who makes a *neder* prohibiting from the upper floor is permitted the house.

YAD AVRAHAM

over one's shoulder and onto his back. It is for this reason that the mishnah mentions carrying bundles on his back. However, he would be equally forbidden to carry them in his hands in front of himself (*Tos. Yom Tov*).

4.

הַנּוֹדֵר מִן ,,הַבַּיִת״ — *Someone who makes a neder prohibiting a house*

That is, the *neder* forbids him to enter a particular house (*Rav*). To qualify as a house, a building must encompass a minimum area of 4x4 cubits (*Yerushalmi* to *Maasros* 3:3; *Meiri*).

מֻתָּר בָּעֲלִיָּה; דִּבְרֵי רַבִּי מֵאִיר. — *is permitted the upper story; [these are] the words of R' Meir.*

R' Meir maintains that, when people talk about a house, they intend only the lower floor (which was presumably the main residence) (*Rosh* 56a).

וַחֲכָמִים אוֹמְרִים: עֲלִיָּה בִּכְלָל ,,הַבַּיִת״. — *The Sages, however, say: The upper story is included in the [term] house.*

The Sages disagree, and consider an upper story also to be included in the popular usage of the term *house* (*Ran*). Accordingly, for someone who forbade a house with respect to entering it, the Sages would forbid him to enter the upper story as well. This is so even if there is no access to the upper story from inside to the ground floor (*Yad Avraham* to *Yoreh Deah* 217:28).

הַנּוֹדֵר מִן ,,הָעֲלִיָּה״ - מֻתָּר בַּבַּיִת. — *One who makes a neder prohibiting from the upper floor is permitted the house.*

Everyone agrees that the entire house is not included in the term *upper floor* (*Tos. Yom Tov* from *Rashi*). [Therefore, someone who prohibited himself from entering an upper floor would be allowed to enter the ground floor.]

[ה] **הַנּוֹדֵר** מִן ,,הַמִּטָּה" — מֻתָּר בַּדַּרְגָּשׁ;
דִּבְרֵי רַבִּי מֵאִיר. וַחֲכָמִים אוֹמְרִים:
דַּרְגָּשׁ בִּכְלַל ,,מִטָּה". הַנּוֹדֵר מִן ,,הַדַּרְגָּשׁ" — מֻתָּר
בַּמִּטָּה. הַנּוֹדֵר מִן ,,הָעִיר" — מֻתָּר לְכָנֵס לִתְחוּמָה
שֶׁל עִיר, וְאָסוּר לְכָנֵס לְעִבּוּרָהּ; אֲבָל הַנּוֹדֵר מִן
,,הַבַּיִת" — אָסוּר מִן הָאֲגַף וְלִפְנִים.

ר' עובדיה מברטנורא

(ה) דרגש. מטה קטנה שנותנין אותה לפני מטה גדולה וממנה עולין למטה הגדולה: **לתחומה**
של עיר. אלפים אמה לכל רוח סביבותיה. עבורה של עיר, הבתים היוצאים ממנה בתוך שבעים
אמה ושיריים, כאשה מעוברת שכריסה בולט לחוץ: **האגף.** [מקום] נעילת הדלת, ודוגמתו יגיפו
הדלתות בספר עזרא (נחמיה ז, ג). ואין הלכה כרבי מאיר בכולה מתניתין:

יד אברהם

5.

הַנּוֹדֵר מִן ,,הַמִּטָּה" — מֻתָּר בַּדַּרְגָּשׁ; דִּבְרֵי רַבִּי
מֵאִיר. וַחֲכָמִים אוֹמְרִים: דַּרְגָּשׁ בִּכְלַל
,,מִטָּה". — *One who makes a neder prohibiting a bed is permitted the footstool; [these are] the words of R' Meir. The Sages, however, say: A footstool is included in the [term] bed.*

The translation follows the view in the *Gemara* (56b), which renders דַּרְגָּשׁ, *dargash*, as *footstool*, a kind of small bed upon which one stepped in order to get to the larger bed (*Rav; Rambam*).

The dispute between R' Meir and the Sages concerns whether, in ordinary conversation, this *dargash* was included when reference was made to a bed (*Tos.* 56a, s.v. מותר).

הַנּוֹדֵר מִן ,,הַדַּרְגָּשׁ" — מֻתָּר בַּמִּטָּה. — *One who makes a neder prohibiting a footstool is permitted the bed.*

All, however, agree that a regular bed was never called *dargash* (*Tos. Yom* from *Rashi*). Consequently, a *neder* directed at the footstool does not affect the bed.

⋗§ Techum/The Sabbath Boundary

On the Sabbath it is prohibited to go more than two thousand cubits beyond the city limits. This boundary is known as the *techum*.

The limits from which the *techum* is measured may, in fact, extend beyond the actual city. If, for example, there is even a single residence within 70 ⅔ cubits from the edge of the city, it is incorporated into the city, and the two thousand-cubit *techum* is measured from it. The 70 ⅔-cubit extension is called עִבּוּר, *ibbur*. These concepts are discussed at length in tractate *Eruvin* (see ibid. 5:1ff. and General Introduction to ArtScroll ed.).

הַנּוֹדֵר מִן ,,הָעִיר" — מֻתָּר לְכָנֵס לִתְחוּמָה שֶׁל
עִיר, וְאָסוּר לְכָנֵס לְעִבּוּרָהּ; — *One who makes a neder prohibiting a city is permitted to enter the techum of the city, but is forbidden to enter the extension;*

When people talk about a city, they do not usually include the *techum*. However, the extension of 70 ⅔ cubits is popularly treated as part of the city (*Shach* to *Yoreh Deah* 217:35). Consequently, a *neder* directed at a city prohibits the person from entering the

5. **O**ne who makes a *neder* prohibiting a bed is permitted the footstool; [these are] the words of R' Meir. The Sages, however, say: A footstool is included in the [term] *bed*. One who makes a *neder* prohibiting a footstool is permitted the bed. One who makes a *neder* prohibiting a city is permitted to enter the *techum* of the city, but is forbidden to enter the extension; but one who makes a *neder* prohibiting a house is forbidden from the doorframe and inward.

YAD AVRAHAM

city proper, as well as the extended city limits. However, he is allowed to enter the two thousands cubits which constitute the *techum* (*Rav*).

אֲבָל הַנּוֹדֵר מִן ,,הַבַּיִת" – אָסוּר מִן הָאֲגַף וְלִפְנִים. — *but one who makes a neder prohibiting a house is forbidden from the doorframe and inward.*

From the fact that the extension to the city limits is included within the

term *city*, we might conclude that, similarly, the term *house* ought to include the house along with its threshold which extends outdoors. To avoid this misconception, the mishnah states that a *neder* directed at a house includes only whatever is enclosed by the door of the house. The threshold which extends outdoors, however, is not included (*Tos. Yom Tov*).

6.

The following mishnah considers the status of things which were generated from something forbidden by a *neder*. The first type discussed is something received in exchange for the item prohibited by a *neder*. In general, under Biblical law, if an item which is forbidden for general use is exchanged for some permitted item, the latter does not acquire any forbidden status as a result of the transaction (*Kiddushin* 58a). This is true except for items forbidden as idolatrous and for produce of *Shemittah*, the Sabbatical year. For these things, the replacement assumes the prohibition of the forbidden item. Thus, for example, if an idol or a product of the Sabbatical year is sold, the money received in exchange for it is prohibited for use in the same manner as the item which it replaces (ibid.). There is a question as to whether, under Rabbinic law, the above rules were left intact (see *Gem.* 47a). According to *Ran* (47b and *Avodah Zorah* 54b), even under Rabbinic law, a permitted item received in exchange for a forbidden item remains permitted. If someone, for instance, were to sell fruit that is *orlah*,[1] he would be permitted to use the money received in exchange for the fruit. However, *Rashi* (*Chullin* 4b and

---

1. עָרְלָה, *orlah*: Fruit produced within the first three years from the planting of a tree is forbidden for use (*Lev.* 19:23).

קוֹנָם פֵּרוֹת הָאֵלּוּ עָלַי״, „קוֹנָם הֵן עַל פִּי״,
„קוֹנָם הֵן לְפִי״ — אָסוּר בְּחִלּוּפֵיהֶן

――――――――――――――― ר׳ עובדיה מברטנורא ―――――――――――――――

(ו) **אסור בחליפיהן ובגדוליהן.** אם החליפן לכתחלה אסור המחליף בדמיהן, דרבנן גזרו על
דמי איסורי הנאה, וגדולי קונס אסורים כגדולי הקדש:

יד אברהם

Avodah Zarah 54b) states that the person who conducts a transaction with an
item forbidden for general use is Rabbinically forbidden from deriving benefit
from the revenue. According to *Rashi*, if someone were to sell *orlah* fruit, it
would be prohibited for him to use the money he received in exchange for
forbidden fruit. However, to someone other than the seller, the money would
remain permitted.

The application of these laws to items forbidden from general use by a
neder would seem to lead to the following conclusion. If we maintain — like
Rashi — that someone who exchanges a forbidden item is then forbidden to
use the replacement, we would expect this to be the case for *nedarim* as well.
Thus, if someone forbade himself an apple for general use via a *neder*, and
then sold the apple, he ought to be forbidden under Rabbinic law from using
the proceeds of the apple. If, however, there is no such Rabbinic injunction, as
Ran maintains, although it is initially forbidden for him to sell the apple (see
Ran 47a), if he went ahead and did so, its proceeds ought to be permitted for
his use, expost facto (see *Tos. R' Akiva* 7:7).

There is, however, another legal category which is relevant in the case of
items prohibited by a *neder*. Something which has been designated as sacred
(e.g., property of the Temple) is redeemable. Upon redemption, the sanctity of
the sacred item is transferred to the redeeming money, while the originally
designated item loses its sanctity (*Rashi* to *Succah* 40b). This feature of items
that are dedicated as sacred may be meaningful for *nedarim*, since the standard *neder* assigns to its object the status of a sacred item. It is conceivable,
then, that included in the person's intent is that even something received in
exchange for the item prohibited by the *neder* should itself be forbidden just
like something exchanged for a sacred item (*Ran* 57a, s.v. קונם). Of course,
unlike something sacred, an item prohibited by a *neder* is not redeemable, and
does not lose its forbidden status in exchange for something else (*Gem.* 86b; cf.
3:5 and *Gem.* 35a).

A second category discussed by the mishnah is something that grows out
of an item prohibited, by a *neder*. For example, if a person prohibits an onion
via a *neder*, and then plants the onion, what is the law concerning what now
grows from the onion? Does it have the forbidden status of the onion, or were
such products of the onion never included in the prohibition? [The status of
things which grow from prohibited items, in general, is not altogether clear.
Something which grows out of *terumah*, for example, is Biblically permitted,
but Rabbinically forbidden (*Rash* to *Terumos* 9:4). However, it would seem
from the mishnah (ibid.). that something grown from other items designated
as sacred would be permitted even Rabbinically. Yet *Rav* (to our mishnah)

6. [**I**f a person said:] "*Konam,* these fruits to me," "may they be *konam* for my mouth," [or] "may they be *konam* to my mouth," he is forbidden whatever is received in exchange for them,

YAD AVRAHAM

follows *Rosh* and *Ran* who indicate that it is forbidden (see *Rashash, Mareh HaPonim* to *Yerushalmi* 7:7; cf. *Rambam, Hil. Me'ilah* 5:6,11).] As will be seen in the following mishnah, certain formulae of *nedarim* are assumed to include even that which grows from the item prohibited by the *neder.*

קוֹנָם פֵּרוֹת הָאֵלּוּ עָלַי", קוֹנָם הֵן עַל פִּי", "קוֹנָם הֵן לְפִי"— — [If a person said:] "Konam, these fruits to me," "may they be konam for my mouth," [or] "may they be konam to my mouth,"

Notwithstanding the comments *for my mouth* or *to my mouth,* it is assumed that a *neder* intending to forbid only eating — and not general benefit — would state as much explicitly. Thus, these declarations are all construed as banning some fruit from general use (*Rosh*). Accordingly, the fruits interdicted under the *neder* are governed by the rules relevant to items forbidden from general use, and, in particular, by the laws which apply to something generated by a forbidden item (see preface). *Rosh* adds that the specification, *these fruits,* is not crucial. Even if the person were to declare, for example, "*Konam,* apples to me," directing the prohibition at all apples — rather than a particular few — the law of the mishnah would apply nevertheless.

Ran, however, understands the mishnah to be discussing only prohibitions which are directed at specific items. By isolating *these fruits* (or, in the other examples, *may they be,* in which *they* refers to specific fruits), the declaration indicates that the specific objects of the *neder* should be forbidden with stringency of

something sacred. According to *Ran,* the operative law here is the law for sacred items (see preface).

אָסוּר בְּחִלּוּפֵיהֶן — *he is forbidden whatever is received in exchange for them,*

Rav explains this to be a Rabbinic restriction and a reflection of the general Rabbinic enactment regarding items forbidden for general use. That is, not only is the item itself interdicted, but if someone exchanged it for something permitted, the person who made the transaction would be forbidden to benefit from the permitted item (see preface). In the example of the mishnah — in which the *neder* forbids fruits only for the person who made the declaration — if he himself sells the fruit, he is Rabbinically forbidden to benefit from the money acquired from the sale. If someone else sells the fruits, the person who made the *neder* would be allowed to benefit from the money received, since the Rabbinic restriction applies only to the person who exchanges the forbidden item (*Tos. Yom Tov*). *Rav*'s explanation follows that of *Rosh.*

However, *Ran* — who does not acknowledge a Rabbinic restriction against someone who exchanges a forbidden item (see preface) — maintains that the prohibition of the item

וּבְגִדּוּלֵיהֶן. ״שֶׁאֵינִי אוֹכֵל״ וְ״שֶׁאֵינִי טוֹעֵם״ —
מֻתָּר בְּחִלּוּפֵיהֶן וּבְגִדּוּלֵיהֶן, בְּדָבָר שֶׁזַּרְעוֹ כָלֶה;
אֲבָל בְּדָבָר שֶׁאֵין זַרְעוֹ כָלֶה — אֲפִלּוּ גִדּוּלֵי
גִדּוּלִין אֲסוּרִין.

— ר' עובדיה מברטנורא —

שאיני אוכל שאיני טועם. לא אסר עליו אלא אכילה וטעימה מהם בלבד: **אבל בדבר
שאין זרעו כלה.** כגון בצלים וכיוצא בהן, אפילו גדולי גדולים הוי כמו גוף האיסור כיון
שאין הזרע כלה:

יד אברהם

received in replacement of the forbidden fruit is a Biblical prohibition. *Ran* understands these *nedarim*, which are directed at specific items (see above), to intend a prohibition of equal intensity to that of a sacred item. Thus, the *neder* itself is tantamount to specifying that just as the replacement of a sacred item is sacred, so too, the replacement of this prohibited item shall itself be prohibited by the *neder*. Therefore, money received, for example, in exchange for the prohibited fruits, is itself prohibited by the *neder*. Accordingly, even if someone else sells the forbidden fruit, the money received will be forbidden to the person who made the *neder*, since the *neder* banned the fruit, as well as whatever it generates (*Tos. R' Akiva* 7:7).

וּבְגִדּוּלֵיהֶן. — *and whatever grows from them.*

[If the *neder* is directed at something which can be planted, then whatever grows from it will also be prohibited.] *Rav* follows *Rosh* and *Ran*, who relate this ruling to the law that something grown from a thing which has been dedicated as sacred is itself sacred. [However, as noted in the preface, this law is not altogether clear.]

Rashba (47a) associates this with the law that what grows from a food designated as *terumah* is itself treated

as *terumah* (*Terumos* 9:4).

שֶׁאֵינִי אוֹכֵל״ וְ״שֶׁאֵינִי טוֹעֵם״— — *"With respect to my eating," or "with respect to my tasting,"*

That is, he declared: "Konam, this fruit to me with respect to my eating/tasting." Here, the prohibition is explicitly limited to eating or tasting, and does not include other benefits from the fruit (*Rav*).

מֻתָּר בְּחִלּוּפֵיהֶן וּבְגִדּוּלֵיהֶן, — *he is permitted whatever is received in exchange for them and whatever grows from them,*

[Since benefit from the fruit is permitted, the fruit is not governed by the laws for things from which benefit is forbidden; nor is the prohibition here intended to confer upon the fruit a "sacred" status. On the contrary, it is limited solely to eating or tasting. Consequently, revenue from the sale of the forbidden item, and similarly, anything grown from it, are permitted.

As far as the permissibility of things grown from the forbidden item, there is one qualification, as follows:]

בְּדָבָר שֶׁזַּרְעוֹ כָלֶה; אֲבָל בְּדָבָר שֶׁאֵין זַרְעוֹ כָלֶה — אֲפִלּוּ גִדּוּלֵי גִדּוּלִין אֲסוּרִין. — *if it is a thing whose seed decomposes; but for a thing whose seed does not decompose,*

and whatever grows from them. "With respect to my eating," or "with respect to my tasting," he is permitted whatever is received in exchange for them and whatever grows from them, if it is a thing whose seed decomposes; but for a thing whose seed does not decompose, even what is grown from what was grown is forbidden.

YAD AVRAHAM

even what is grown from what was grown is forbidden.

Most plants grow from a seed which decomposes as part of the growth process. No remnant of the original seed would be found if one were to dig up the plant. However, certain vegetables — such as onions and garlic (*Rav; Terumos* 9:6) — if planted, will produce new plants without decomposing themselves.

The mishnah states that the previous ruling, *he is permitted ... whatever grows from them,* is true only for species whose seed decomposes. The new plant is an entity independent of the forbidden seed, and is thus permitted. However, if the item forbidden was — for example — onions, even if the prohibition were limited only to eating, any new onion plants produced by the forbidden onions would also be prohibited. Furthermore, if this new crop were replanted, and produces another new generation of onions, they, too, would be forbidden. The reason for this is that, since the originally forbidden onions remain extant, the plants they generate are treated not as independent entities, but as an amalgam including some of the forbidden onions. And — as explained in 6:6 — an item prohibited by a *neder* mixed with a like species is never nullified. Thus, the new

onions which are considered to include some of the prohibited onions are forbidden. Even if these are planted to produce a third generation, the new generation of onions still is considered to contain some fraction of the original forbidden onions, and so, they, too, will be interdicted. Hence, the mishnah states: *what is grown from what was grown [from the forbidden item] is forbidden (Tos. Yom Tov* from *Ran;* cf. *Tif. Yis.* 31).

Most authorities understand the mishnah's distinction between two types of seeds as applying to the first case of the mishnah as well. That is, when someone forbids having general benefit from fruit by declaring, "*Konam* these fruits to me," the mishnah states that *he is forbidden ... whatever grows from them.* This implies that the next generation of plants — namely, what grows from what was grown from the forbidden fruit — is permitted; only *whatever grows from them* was forbidden. The mishnah then states that this inference is correct only for plants whose seed decomposes; regarding those whose seeds do not decompose, however, all subsequent generations will be forbidden (*Tos. Yom Tov* from *Ran*).

Ritva does not apply the mishnah's distinction to the first case. He maintains that when the mishnah states: *he is for-*

[ז] הָאוֹמֵר לְאִשְׁתּוֹ: „קוֹנָם מַעֲשֵׂה יָדַיִךְ
עָלַי", „קוֹנָם הֵן עַל פִּי", „קוֹנָם
הֵן לְפִי" — אָסוּר בְּחִלּוּפֵיהֶן וּבְגִדּוּלֵיהֶן. „שֶׁאֵינִי
אוֹכֵל", „שֶׁאֵינִי טוֹעֵם" — מֻתָּר בְּחִלּוּפֵיהֶן
וּבְגִדּוּלֵיהֶן, בְּדָבָר שֶׁזַּרְעוֹ כָלֶה; אֲבָל בְּדָבָר שֶׁאֵין
זַרְעוֹ כָלֶה — אֲפִלּוּ גִדּוּלֵי גִדּוּלִין אֲסוּרִים.

ר' עובדיה מברטנורא

(ז) **קונם מעשה ידיך עלי.** אסר כל מה שהיא עושה ומכינה לו, ואם נטעה אילן גדוליו אסורין:

יד אברהם

bidden … whatever grows from them, all subsequent generations are forbidden, even those of species whose seed disintegrates. Even though the seed has vanished, the first generation is forbidden, because we construe the intention of the *neder* as including it. Similarly, argues *Ritva*, all subsequent generations may be presumed to have been included in the scope of the *neder* (see *Chidushei R' Akiva* to *Yoreh Deah* 216:1).

7.

The *Tanna* continues to illustrate the laws discussed in the preceding mishnah.

הָאוֹמֵר לְאִשְׁתּוֹ: „קוֹנָם מַעֲשֵׂה יָדַיִךְ עָלַי", — *One who says to his wife: "Konam, your handiwork to me,"*

A husband declares a *neder* banning himself benefit from anything his wife makes or prepares for him (*Rav*). The *neder* affects not only what she has already made, but even what she will make in the future, since a person restricting himself through a *neder* can forbid even things not yet existing (*Gem.* 47a). Some authorities rule that, since the raw materials belong to the husband, the *neder* forbids only the increased value resulting from the wife's input in the creation of the finished product. For example, when the wife bakes a bread from flour and water, the bread is worth more than the original flour and water. The difference in price between the finished product and the raw ingredient is what the *neder* forbids. The finished product is sold, and the value of the forbidden appreciation must be discarded (*Ritva*), or given to the wife (*Ran; Rashba*). However, the cost of the initial ingredients, having never been forbidden by the *neder*, may be used by the husband (see *Ran* 57a; *Rashba*).

קוֹנָם הֵן עַל פִּי", „קוֹנָם הֵן לְפִי" — *"they are konam for my mouth," [or] "they are konam to my mouth,"*

[As in the previous mishnah, these declarations impose a ban on derivation of general benefit, and not just eating. However, the mention of *my mouth* would seem to indicate that the prohibition is directed at edible things only, and is forbidding their benefit. This would explain why *Rosh, Tosafos,* and *Meiri* interpret the mishnah to be discussing a prohibition directed only at foods prepared by the wife, and not at other things she might make, such as clothes. However, *Ritva* specifically mentions wool spun by the wife as an article forbidden to the

7. **O**ne who says to his wife: "*Konam*, your handiwork to me," "they are *konam* for my mouth," [or] "they are *konam* to my mouth," he is forbidden whatever is received in exchange for them and whatever grows from them. "With respect to my eating," "with respect to my tasting," he is permitted whatever is received in exchange for them and whatever grows from them, if it is a thing whose seed decomposes; but for a thing whose seed does not decompose, even what is grown from what was grown is forbidden.

YAD AVRAHAM

husband in the mishnah's case. *Rav* echoes *Rosh's* statement on this issue verbatim, but deletes the mention of food, indicating that the *neder* applies to anything the wife produces, not just food. Perhaps the declaration, "*Konam, your handiwork to me*," is aimed at all the wife's work, while the declarations, "*they are konam for/to my mouth*," deal with food products only.]

אָסוּר בְּחִלּוּפֵיהֶן וּבְגִדּוּלֵיהֶן. — *he is forbidden whatever is received in exchange for them and whatever grows from them.*

According to *Rosh* (cited in commentary to previous mishnah), the restriction on whatever is received in exchange for the forbidden item is part of the wider Rabbinic enactment which governs the exchange of items that are forbidden for general use. According to *Ran* (57a), this *neder* — by detailing specific objects for prohibition — is more intense, and includes even what is generated by the forbidden item. In the previous mishnah, the specification was accomplished by clearly stating "these

fruits." In the present case, the prohibition is limited to products created by his wife. Not all cakes, for example, are being forbidden — only those baked by his wife. Thus, this *neder* is understood to be an intense one which includes whatever is received in exchange for the forbidden items, and whatever grows from them.

שֶׁאֵינִי אוֹכֵל", "שֶׁאֵינִי טוֹעֵם" – מֻתָּר בְּחִלּוּפֵיהֶן וּבְגִדּוּלֵיהֶן, — *"With respect to my eating," "with respect to my tasting," he is permitted whatever is received in exchange for them and whatever grows from them,*

As in the preceding mishnah, a *neder* restricting only eating or tasting does not extend to things generated by the forbidden item. *Ran* notes that this is repeated here to stress that the same rule applies even to a *neder* with specified objects (e.g., *these fruits*, "*your handiwork*") which might be expected to be more intense and encompassing (*Tos. Yom Tov*).

בְּדָבָר שֶׁזַּרְעוֹ כָלֶה; אֲבָל בְּדָבָר שֶׁאֵין זַרְעוֹ כָלֶה – אֲפִלּוּ גִדּוּלֵי גִדּוּלִין אֲסוּרִין. — *if it is a thing whose seed decomposes; but for a thing whose seed does not decompose,*

[ח] **„שְׁאַתְּ** עוֹשָׂה אֵינִי אוֹכֵל עַד הַפֶּסַח״,
„שְׁאַתְּ עוֹשָׂה אֵינִי מִתְכַּסֶּה
עַד הַפֶּסַח״, עָשְׂתָה לִפְנֵי הַפֶּסַח — מֻתָּר
לֶאֱכוֹל וּלְהִתְכַּסּוֹת אַחַר הַפֶּסַח. „שְׁאַתְּ עוֹשָׂה
עַד הַפֶּסַח אֵינִי אוֹכֵל״, וְ„שְׁאַתְּ עוֹשָׂה עַד
הַפֶּסַח אֵינִי מִתְכַּסֶּה״, עָשְׂתָה לִפְנֵי הַפֶּסַח —
אָסוּר לֶאֱכוֹל וּלְהִתְכַּסּוֹת אַחַר הַפֶּסַח.

ר' עובדיה מברטנורא

(ח) **שאת עושה איני אוכל עד הפסח.** הכי משמע, שאת עושה עכשיו איני אוכל עד הפסח,
אבל לאחר הפסח אני אוכל. אבל כל מה שאת עושה עד הפסח איני אוכל, משמע, כל מה שאת
עושה מהיום עד שיבא הפסח איני אוכל אותו לעולם אפילו לאחר הפסח:

יד אברהם

even what is grown from what was
grown is forbidden.

If the *neder* had been limited to
eating or tasting, and the wife planted
something whose seed decomposes,
that which is produces by the plant is
permitted. The efforts invested in the
planting are his wife's handiwork,
and the fruit or vegetable resulting is
considered something received in exchange for the wife's work which is
not forbidden. But, if she planted
something which does not decompose, the product grown is considered
to be the actual work of her hands.
Since subsequent generations of the
plant all contain some of the original
which did not decompose, they are all
considered her handiwork — and not
an exchange for her word — and are
forbidden (*Meiri*).

With regard to all the cases in this
mishnah and the one preceding it, in which
any outgrowth of the forbidden item is also
prohibited, *Ravad* (*Hasagos* to *Hil. Nedarim*
5:16) raises an intriguing question. There is
a general rule that anything brought into
existence through the combined operation
of two factors, of which one is permitted

and the other forbidden, is itself permitted
(*Avodah Zarah* 49a; *Rambam, Hil. Avodah
Zarah* 7:14; *Yoreh Deah* 142:11). Accordingly, if a seed which has been forbidden by
a *neder* is planted, anything which grows
from it is the product of both the seed which
is forbidden, as well as the earth which is
permitted; therefore, it ought to be permitted. This would contradict our mishnah,
which rules that what grows from the seed
is forbidden.

Avnei Miluim (Responsa §6), based on
Ran (*Avodeh Zarah* 49a), explains that the
rationale behind the law permitting something produced by the joint action of
forbidden and permitted factors is the law
of בִּיטוּל, *bitul* (nullification). That is, the
influence of the forbidden factor in the
creation of the product is negated by the
influence of the permitted factor. Accordingly, this principle may be applied only
where the law of *bitul* is applicable, but
not to prohibitions stemming from *nedarim*, since they are considered temporary.
(This is explained at length in the
commentary to 6:6, s.v. אָמְרוּ לוֹ.) They
are, therefore, also not affected by the law
which permits the product of permissible
and forbidden factors. Consequently, the
mishnah rules that *what is grown from
them is forbidden*.

8. **[** If a person said:] "What you make I shall not eat until *Pesach*," [or] "What you make I shall not wear until *Pesach*," [what] she makes before *Pesach* he is permitted to eat or wear after *Pesach*. "What you make until *Pesach* I shall not eat," [or] "what you make until *Pesach* I shall not wear," he is forbidden to eat or wear after *Pesach* [what] she made before *Pesach*.

YAD AVRAHAM

8.

Because the previous mishnah mentions a wife's handiwork, the next mishnah proceeds to discuss another case involving the wife's work (*Meiri*).

שֶׁאַתְּ עוֹשָׂה אֵינִי אוֹכֵל עַד הַפֶּסַח", "שֶׁאַתְּ עוֹשָׂה אֵינִי מִתְכַּסֶּה עַד הַפֶּסַח", — *[If a person said:] "What you make I shall not eat until Pesach," [or] "What you make I shall not wear until Pesach,"*

[A husband forbade himself to eat or wear any food or clothing his wife might make. The formulation of the prohibition includes a time limit (*until Pesach*), which is construed to mean that the prohibition of wearing or eating will be in effect only until *Pesach*. Hence:]

עֲשָׂתָה לִפְנֵי הַפֶּסַח – מֻתָּר לֶאֱכוֹל וּלְהִתְכַּסּוֹת אַחַר הַפֶּסַח. — *[what] she makes before Pesach he is still permitted to eat or wear after Pesach.*

After *Pesach*, the husband may eat or wear anything the wife made, even if she had made it before the festival, because the restriction ends at *Pesach* (*Rav; Tos. Yom Tov*).

"שֶׁאַתְּ עוֹשָׂה עַד הַפֶּסַח אֵינִי אוֹכֵל", וְ"שֶׁאַתְּ עוֹשָׂה עַד הַפֶּסַח אֵינִי מִתְכַּסֶּה", — *"What you make until Pesach I shall not eat," [or] "what you make until Pesach I shall not wear,"*

In this declaration, the time limit defines the object of the prohibition *what you make until Pesach*. The duration of the prohibition is, however, unlimited (*Rav*). Therefore:

עֲשָׂתָה לִפְנֵי הַפֶּסַח – אָסוּר לֶאֱכוֹל וּלְהִתְכַּסּוֹת אַחַר הַפֶּסַח. — *he is forbidden to eat or wear after Pesach [what] she made before Pesach.*

That is, he is permanently forbidden to eat or wear anything his wife made during the time between his declaration and *Pesach* (*Rav*). [Something she made after the festival is not included in the prohibition at all.]

9.

The mishnah presupposes the reader's awareness that the festival of *Succos* is celebrated in Tishrei, the first month of the Jewish calendar, and is followed by *Pesach* (Passover) in Nissan, the seventh month. It was common for *Succos* to be referred to as simply *the Festival*, and this terminology is employed by our mishnah (see *Tos. Yom Tov* to *Rosh Hashanah* 1:2).

[ט] ,,**שֶׁאַתְּ** נֶהֱנֵית לִי עַד הַפֶּסַח אִם תֵּלְכִי לְבֵית אָבִיךְ עַד הֶחָג״, הָלְכָה לִפְנֵי הַפֶּסַח — אֲסוּרָה בַּהֲנָאָתוֹ עַד הַפֶּסַח. אַחַר הַפֶּסַח, בְּלֹא יַחֵל דְּבָרוֹ. ,,שֶׁאַתְּ נֶהֱנֵית לִי עַד הֶחָג אִם תֵּלְכִי לְבֵית אָבִיךְ עַד הַפֶּסַח״, וְהָלְכָה לִפְנֵי הַפֶּסַח — אֲסוּרָה בַּהֲנָאָתוֹ עַד הֶחָג; וּמֻתֶּרֶת לֵילֵךְ אַחַר הַפֶּסַח.

───────── ר' עובדיה מברטנורא ─────────

(ט) **שאת נהנית לי עד הפסח אם הולכת את לבית אביך עד החג.** מי שהיה עומד אחר החג ואמר הנאתו עליה עד הפסח אם תלך לבית אביה עד החג: **לאחר הפסח בלא יחל דברו.** כלומר, אם הלכה לאחר הפסח, עוברת בבל יחל למפרע על מה שנהנית ממנו קודם הפסח:

───────────────────────

יד אברהם

,,שֶׁאַתְּ נֶהֱנֵית לִי עַד הַפֶּסַח אִם תֵּלְכִי לְבֵית אָבִיךְ עַד הֶחָג״, — *[If a person said:* "Konam] whatever benefit you have from me before Pesach, if you go to your father's house before the Festival" —

[I.e., "If you go to your father's house before *Succos*, any benefit you have from me before *Pesach* shall be forbidden like *konam*."]

This declaration was issued by the husband to his wife sometime following *Succos* but before *Pesach* (*Rav*). [Clearly, the condition — *if you go ... before the Festival* — is binding even after the prohibition has ended. For example, if the declaration was made in Kislev, the third month of the year, the condition would be in force for the succeeding nine months until *Succos* in the first month of the next year. But the prohibition against benefiting from her husband can last no longer than four months left between the time of the declaration and *Pesach*.

Being a conditional prohibition, it will take effect only if the condition is met. Thus, only if the wife visits her father's house before *Succos* will any prohibition ensue.

The law for this type of declaration is as follows:]

הָלְכָה לִפְנֵי הַפֶּסַח – אֲסוּרָה בַּהֲנָאָתוֹ עַד הַפֶּסַח; — *if she went before Pesach, she is forbidden to have any benefit from him until Pesach;*

By visiting her father's house, she has activated the prohibition. It includes any benefits derived from the time of the declaration through *Pesach* (*Rambam, Hil. Nedarim* 10:12). Thus, not only benefits she derives after going to her father's house are forbidden, but — retroactively — any benefit received from the time the *neder* was made will be forbidden. If the declaration had been made in the third month, and she went to her father's house in the fourth month, any benefit she may have received in the preceding month will now have become forbidden. As long as there is a possibility of fulfilling the condition which will activate the prohibition, any benefit the wife may have between the time of the *neder* and *Pesach* may possibly become forbidden retroactively. Because of this, the

9. **[I**f a person said: "*Konam*] whatever benefit you have from me before *Pesach*, if you go to your father's house before the Festival" — if she went before *Pesach*, she is forbidden to have any benefit from him until *Pesach*; [if she went] after *Pesach*, [she is liable for] "he shall not break his word." ["*Konam*] whatever benefit you have from me before the Festival, if you go to your father's house before *Pesach*" — if she went before *Pesach*, she is forbidden to benefit from him until the Festival; but she is permitted to go after *Pesach*.

YAD AVRAHAM

Gemara (15a) rules that the wife must assume that the prohibition will be activated and behave accordingly. In other words, even though the prohibition has not yet been activated, the wife must behave as though it were. From the moment the declaration is made, she must desist from deriving any benefit from her husband until *Pesach*. In this way, even if she should subsequently visit her father's house, she will not have retroactively enjoyed a forbidden benefit (*Tos. Yom Tov*).

אַחַר הַפֶּסַח – בְּ,,לֹא יַחֵל דְּבָרוֹ". — *[if she went] after Pesach, [she is liable for] "he shall not break his word."*

I.e., if she went to her father's house after *Pesach* — while the condition was still in force — the prohibition will be retroactively initiated, and any benefit she may have had prior to *Pesach* will turn out to have been forbidden. Or — in the words of the mishnah — such benefits will have contravened the *neder*, and she will have transgressed the Biblical prohibition *he shall not break his word* [*Num.* 30:3] (*Rav*). This is because if

someone — through a *neder* — forbids another to benefit from him or his property, the other person transgresses *he shall not break his word* if he benefits from that which was prohibited (*Tos. Yom Tov* from *Rosh*).

Rambam (*Hil. Nedarim* 10:12) appears to explain the mishnah to mean that, although benefit from her husband was explicitly forbidden only until *Pesach*, the husband is prevented by the *neder* from giving his wife any benefit as long as the condition is binding; namely, until *Succos*. *Ravad* (*ad loc.*) disagrees vehemently.

שֶׁאַתְּ נֶהֱנֵית לִי עַד הֶחָג, אִם תֵּלְכִי לְבֵית אָבִיךְ עַד הַפֶּסַח", — *["Konam]whatever benefit you have from me before the Festival, if you go to your father's house before Pesach"* —

[In this case, too, the declaration is made following *Succos*, but before the next *Pesach*. But, in this instance, the prohibition against benefiting from her husband is of longer duration than the condition Thus:]

וְהָלְכָה לִפְנֵי הַפֶּסַח – אֲסוּרָה בַהֲנָאָתוֹ עַד הֶחָג; — *if she went before Pesach, she is forbidden to benefit from him until the Festival;*

By going to her father's house in

advance of *Pesach*, the condition for activating the prohibition is met. Any benefit from the time of the declaration until the following *Succos* will thus be forbidden by the *neder* (*Tos. R' Akiva*).

וּמְתֶּרֶת לֵילֵךְ אַחַר הַפֶּסַח. — *but she is permitted to go after Pesach.*

Going to her father's house after Passover is not connected with the prohibition; hence, *she is permitted to go after Pesach,* and no transgressions will result. This is a rather obvious statement, but is included in order to complete the symmetry of the mishnah (*Tos.* 15b; *Tos. R' Akiva*).

פרק שמיני ‏&

Chapter Eight

[א] **קוֹנָם** יַיִן שֶׁאֲנִי טוֹעֵם הַיּוֹם" — אֵינוֹ
אָסוּר אֶלָּא עַד שֶׁתֶּחְשַׁךְ; "שַׁבָּת
זוֹ" — אָסוּר בְּכָל הַשַּׁבָּת, וְשַׁבָּת שֶׁעָבְרָה; "חֹדֶשׁ
זֶה", אָסוּר בְּכָל הַחֹדֶשׁ, וְרֹאשׁ חֹדֶשׁ לְהַבָּא;

—————————— ר' עובדיה מברטנורא ——————————

פרק שמיני – קונם יין. (א) קונם יין. עד שתחשך. שכן דרך לשון בני אדם כשאומרים היום
רוצים לומר עד השלמת היום: **שבת זו.** היה עומד באמצע השבוע ואמר שבת זו, אסור בכל
השבוע: **והשבת לשעבר.** ואסור נמי ביום השבת כי הוא בכלל השבוע שעבר: **חדש זה
אסור בכל החדש.** אם עומד באמצע החדש ואמר חדש זה, אסור עד תשלום החדש, ויום ראש
חדש להבא, ומותר ביום ראש חדש כי הוא נמנה עם החדש הבא, ואפילו היה ראש חדש ביום
שלשים לחדש שעבר. וכן שנה זו, אם עמד באמצע השנה ואמר שנה זו, אסור עד תשלום השנה,
ומותר בראש השנה שהוא נמנה עם השנה העתידה לבא:

—————————— יד אברהם ——————————

1.

"קוֹנָם יַיִן שֶׁאֲנִי טוֹעֵם הַיּוֹם" — — "Konam,
*wine, with respect to my tasting [it]
today"* —

[I.e., a person forbids wine with a
neder which is to endure for a limited
time: *today*.] The law would be identical were he to state יוֹם זֶה, *this day* (*Tif.
Yis; Shach, Yoreh Deah* 220:2).

Obviously, the mishnah's choice of
a case involving wine is only an
example; the same would be true
regarding any food or drink (*Tif. Yis*.).

אֵינוֹ אָסוּר אֶלָּא עַד שֶׁתֶּחְשַׁךְ; — *it is
forbidden [to him] only until dark;*

The term *today* (or *this day*) is not
used to indicate a twenty-four-hour
time span. Rather, it means whatever
time remains until the completion of
the day (*Rav*). A day is defined as
lasting from nightfall to nightfall
(*Chullin* 5:5). Nightfall is determined
by the appearance of three stars in the
sky (*Meiri*; cf. *Nimukei Yosef*). [If, for
example, nightfall came at 7:30 p.m.,
no matter whether the declaration
was issued at 9 p.m. the previous
night, 7 a.m. in the morning, or 7 p.m.
in the evening, the prohibition would

expire at 7:30 p.m.]

Although, with the completion of
the day at nightfall, the Scriptural
prohibition on the wine is ended, the
Rabbis required the person to seek
cancellation of his *neder* before drinking wine (*Rav*, s.v. אם). The reason for
this is explained below.

"שַׁבָּת זוֹ" — — *"this week"* —

A person, sometimes during the
course of the week, declared wine to
be forbidden for him *"this week"*
(*Rav*).

אָסוּר בְּכָל הַשַּׁבָּת, וְשַׁבָּת שֶׁעָבְרָה; — *it is
forbidden [to him] throughout the
week, and [the] Sabbath [is included
in the week] preceding [it]* (lit., *that has
passed*);

If, for example, he made the *neder*
on Tuesday, wine would be forbidden
to him from the time of the declaration
until the completion of the Sabbath.
This is because the Sabbath is included with the week that precedes it
(*Rav*), since people speak of the Sabbath as the last day of the week, and
so, *this week* ends with the end of the
Sabbath (*Ran*; *Tos*.).

8
1

1. "**K**onam, wine, with respect to my tasting [it] today" — it is forbidden to him only until dark; "this week" — it is forbidden [to him] throughout the week, and [the] Sabbath [is included in the week] preceding [it]; "this month" — it is forbidden [to him] throughout the month, and Rosh Chodesh is included in the coming [month];

YAD AVRAHAM

Even if, on Sabbath afternoon, a person were to forbid something for "*this week*," the prohibition would end just a few hours later with the end of that Sabbath (*Shach* loc. cit., 220:7; *Meiri*).

In connection with this case, as well as with all the subsequent cases of the mishnah (*this month, this year*, etc.), there is a question whether at the end of the specific time, the item is automatically permitted, or whether — as in the case of *this day* — it remains Rabbinically forbidden until cancellation of the *neder* is obtained. *Rav* (end of mishnah) equates all these cases, and requires cancellation of the *neder* even after the time has elapsed. His opinion is quoted by *Bach* (*Yoreh Deah* 220) and *Shach* (ibid. 10), who support it. However, *Rama* (ibid. 3) follows *Rabbeinu Yerucham* and others who disagree and maintain that, for a *neder* limited to *this week*, all restrictions are lifted at the conclusion of the week, and no cancellation must be sought. Only for the case of *this day* was such cancellation required for the reasons explained below.

חֹדֶשׁ זֶה,, — "*this month*" —

The Hebrew month follows the lunar cycle, and is either twenty-nine or thirty days long. The first day of every month is celebrated as a mini-holiday and is called *Rosh Chodesh*. Rosh Chodesh is celebrated for one day when it follows a month of twenty-nine days. In a thirty-day month, the thirtieth day is celebrated as Rosh Chodesh along with the following day which is the first day of the new month; thus, Rosh Chodesh is two days (*Rambam, Hil. Kiddush HaChodesh* 8:1ff.). Although, in a two-day Rosh Chodesh, the first day is actually the last day of the preceding month — in popular conversation, both days of this minifestival are treated as belonging to the new month (*Tos. Yom Tov*). Consequently...

אָסוּר בְּכָל הַחֹדֶשׁ, וְרֹאשׁ חֹדֶשׁ לְהַבָּא; — *it is forbidden [to him] throughout the month, and Rosh Chodesh is included in the coming [month];*

Since Rosh Chodesh is popularly associated with the coming month, a prohibition stemming from a *neder* specifying *this month* will expire with the advent of Rosh Chodesh at the end of the twenty-ninth day of the month even if the month has thirty days, because the thirtieth day of the month serves as the first day of Rosh Chodesh (*Rav*). Furthermore, if a person made a *neder* on the *first* day of a two-day Rosh Chodesh, he will be bound by it for thirty days until the next Rosh Chodesh. Although — legally — the first day of a two-day Rosh Chodesh is the end of the preceding month, the term *this month* is used to indicate the time from one Rosh Chodesh to the next (*Meiri; Shach* to *Yoreh Deah* 220:12).

„שָׁנָה זוֹ" — אָסוּר בְּכָל הַשָּׁנָה, וְרֹאשׁ הַשָּׁנָה
לֶעָתִיד לָבוֹא; „שָׁבוּעַ זֶה" — אָסוּר בְּכָל
הַשָּׁבוּעַ, וּשְׁבִיעִית שֶׁעָבְרָה. וְאִם אָמַר: „יוֹם
אֶחָד", „שַׁבָּת אֶחָת", „חֹדֶשׁ אֶחָד", „שָׁנָה
אֶחָת", „שָׁבוּעַ אֶחָד" — אָסוּר מִיּוֹם לְיוֹם.

[ב] „עַד הַפֶּסַח" — אָסוּר עַד שֶׁיַּגִּיעַ; „עַד

ר' עובדיה מברטנורא

שבוע זה. היה עומד באמלע השמטה ואמר שבוע זה, אסור עד תשלום השמטה, והשביעית
בכלל שמטה שעברה: אם אמר יום אחד שבת אחת חדש אחד שנה אחת שבוע אחד.
אסור מיום ליום, אם עומד באמלע היום ואומר יום אחד אסור עד למחר כעת הזאת, וכן אם
עומד בשמונה לחדש ואמר חדש אחד אסור עד שמונה לחדש הבא, וכן בשנה, וכן בשמטה, וכן אם
אמר קונם עלי יין יום, סתם, או שבת או חדש או שנה או שבוע סתם, אף על פי שלא אמר יום אחד, שבת
אחת, חדש אחד, דינו מעת לעת. והאומר קונם עלי יין היום, אף על פי שהוא מותר כשתחשך,
צריך שאלה לחכם, גזירה כשאמר היום שמא יבא להתיר כשיאמר יום סתם, דמיחלף ליה בין יום
להיום, או בין שבת זו לשבת סתם, וכן כולם: (ב) עד הפסח אסור עד שיגיע. דבלשון בני אדם
עד ולא עד בכלל:

יד אברהם

„שָׁנָה זוֹ" – אָסוּר בְּכָל הַשָּׁנָה, וְרֹאשׁ הַשָּׁנָה
לֶעָתִיד לָבוֹא; — "this year" — it is
forbidden [to him] throughout the year,
and Rosh Hashanah [is included in the
year] to come;

In Rosh Hashanah (1:1), the Mishnah describes a number of different
types of years, each one with a
different day designated as its New
Year. However, regarding nedarim,
the New Year is those two days that
are popularly known as such — the
Rosh Hashanah festival observed on
the first two days of the month of
Tishrei (Rosh Hashanah 12b; Rambam,
Hil. Nedarim 10:4). A neder that was
stipulated to last this year will expire
with the start of Rosh Hashanah.

„שָׁבוּעַ זֶה" — "this Sabbatical cycle"
—

[In Jewish law, every fiftieth year is
celebrated as Yovel (Jubilee). The
intervening forty-nine years are di-

vided into seven cycles of seven years
each (Lev. 5:8-10). The seventh year of
each such cycle is the Shemittah
(Sabbatical year), in which agricultural work is forbidden in Eretz Yisrael
(ibid. v. 2). Accordingly, the third year
after a Jubilee would belong to the first
Sabbatical cycle, while the tenth year
would belong to the second cycle, etc.]

אָסוּר בְּכָל הַשָּׁבוּעַ, וּשְׁבִיעִית שֶׁעָבְרָה. — [it
is] forbidden throughout the Sabbatical
cycle, and the Sabbatical year [is included in the cycle] preceding it.

[The period of time defined by
"this Sabbatical cycle" ends with the
conclusion of the Sabbatical year,
which is observed at the end of the
cycle.]

וְאִם אָמַר: „יוֹם אֶחָד", „שַׁבָּת אֶחָת", „חֹדֶשׁ
אֶחָד", „שָׁנָה אֶחָת", „שָׁבוּעַ אֶחָד" – אָסוּר
מִיּוֹם לְיוֹם. — But if he said: "One day,"
"one week," "one month," "one year,"
[or] "one Sabbatical cycle" — [it is]

8
2

"this year" — it is forbidden [to him] throughout the year, and Rosh Hashanah [is included in the year] to come; "this Sabbatical cycle" — [it is] forbidden throughout the Sabbatical cycle, and the Sabbatical year [is included in the cycle] preceding it. But if he said: "One day," "one week," "one month," "one year," [or] "one Sabbatical cycle" — [it is] forbidden [to him] from [that] day until [the next] day.

2. **"U**ntil *Pesach"* — it is forbidden until [*Pesach*]

YAD AVRAHAM

forbidden [to him] from [that] day until [the next] day.

[It is forbidden to him from the time he made the *neder* until the same moment on the next day, week, month, or Sabbatical cycle, depending on the *neder*.]

The specification *one day* refers to a full twenty-four-hour period; *one week* to a period of seven full twenty-four-hour days; and so on, for each of the expressions in the mishnah. Thus, if — for example — a person at 3 p.m. on Tuesday declared wine to be forbidden to him for *one day*, the prohibition would be in effect for a twenty-four-hour period until Wednesday 3 p.m. Similarly, if at 3 p.m. on Tuesday, he made such a *neder* with a time limit of *one week*, the prohibition would last until Tues-

day 3 p.m. of the following week (*Shach* loc. cit. 11; cf. *Beis Yosef* to *Yoreh Deah* 220, s.v. קונם).

The Rabbis were concerned that people might confuse a *neder* specifying *one day*, which creates a twenty-four-hour prohibition, with a *neder* specifying *today* or *this day*, in which case the prohibition lasts only until nightfall. To prevent this from happening, it was instituted that a *neder* specifying *today* should not expire automatically at nightfall; rather, the person is required to seek cancellation of the *neder* after nightfall. In this way, even if the person mistakenly thought the prohibition to be over earlier than it actually was, he would be corrected upon presenting his case to the Sage or panel for annulment (*Rashi* 60a, s.v. גזירה).

2.

עַד הַפֶּסַח,, — *"Until Pesach"* —

[That is, the person forbids something to himself via a *neder*, in which he stipulates that the prohibition shall last *"until Pesach."* The issue in question is whether *until* should be interpreted as *until, and including* or as *until, and not including.*]

אָסוּר עַד שֶׁיַּגִּיעַ; — *it is forbidden until*

[Pesach] arrives;

The mishnah rules that, in conversational usage, *until* is construed to mean *until, but not including* (*Rav*). Therefore, the prohibition ends with the arrival of *Pesach*.

Bach (*Yoreh Deah* 220, s.v. האוסר) rules that here, too, cancellation of the *neder* is needed, and the prohibition does not end automatically, because he contends that, in

שֶׁיְּהֵא" — אָסוּר עַד שֶׁיֵּצֵא; "עַד לִפְנֵי הַפֶּסַח" — רַבִּי מֵאִיר אוֹמֵר: אָסוּר עַד שֶׁיַּגִּיעַ; רַבִּי יוֹסֵי אוֹמֵר: אָסוּר עַד שֶׁיֵּצֵא.

[ג] **עַד** הַקָּצִיר", "עַד הַבָּצִיר", "עַד הַמָּסִיק" — אֵינוֹ אָסוּר אֶלָּא עַד שֶׁיַּגִּיעַ.

ר' עובדיה מברטנורא

עד שיהא אסור עד שיצא. דמשמע כל זמן שהוא הווה: **עד לפני הפסח רבי מאיר אומר אסור עד שיגיע.** דלא מעייל אינש נפשיה אספיקא, ודבר המבורר לקרות פני הפסח קאמר, והיינו עד שיגיע, ורבי יוסי סבר מעייל אינש נפשיה לאסור בכל מה שיוכל להסתפק. והלכה כרבי יוסי: **(ג) עד הקציר.** של חטים ושעורים: **עד הבציר.** של ענבים: **עד המסיק.** של זיתים: **אינו אסור אלא עד שיגיע.** הואיל ואין לקציר ולבציר זמן קבוע, כדמפרש ואזיל, לא שנא אמר עד שיהא לא שנא אמר עד שיגיע אינו אסור אלא עד שיגיע, שכל דבר שאין זמנו קבוע אין בדעת הנודר להכניס עצמו באסור זמן שאין ידוע לו, ולפיכך אמרינן דודאי עד שיגיע קאמר:

יד אברהם

this instance as well, confusion could arise between the case of *until Pesach*, which means the start of *Pesach*, and *until it is* [*Pesach*], which means the end of *Pesach* (see *Taz* ibid. 3; *Shach* ad loc. 19).

"עַד שֶׁיְּהֵא" — אָסוּר עַד שֶׁיֵּצֵא; — *"until it is* [*Pesach*]' — [it is] forbidden until [*Pesach*] ends;*

The expression, *until it is*, is understood as equivalent to *until, and as long as it is*. Thus, the prohibition remains in force until the end of *Pesach* (*Rav*)

"עַד לִפְנֵי הַפֶּסַח"— *"until before Pesach"* —

The expression *before Pesach* certainly means *prior to the beginning of Pesach*. However, even the days of the festival itself can be referred to as *before Pesach*, inasmuch as it precedes what remains of *Pesach*. The third day of the holiday is still "before *Pesach*," since tomorrow will still be *Pesach*. As long as but a moment remains of the festival, the moment preceding it can be called *before Pesach* (*Rashi* to *Kiddushin* 64b; cf. *Rosh* 61a, quoted by *Tos. Yom Tov*). [Thus, the expres-

sion *until before Pesach* is of somewhat uncertain meaning.]

רַבִּי מֵאִיר אוֹמֵר: אָסוּר עַד שֶׁיַּגִּיעַ; — *R' Meir says: It is forbidden until* [*Pesach*] *arrives;*

R' Meir contends that a person — when using an expression of questionable meaning — intends only its most certain interpretation. Since *until before Pesach* certainly describes the moment before the beginning of the holiday, R' Meir assumes this to be the person's intention. Therefore, with the arrival of *Pesach*, the prohibition ceases (*Rav*).

רַבִּי יוֹסֵי אוֹמֵר: אָסוּר עַד שֶׁיֵּצֵא. — *R' Yose says: It is forbidden until* [*Pesach*] *ends.*

R' Yose disagrees and maintains that a person expects the broadest possible interpretation to be applied to his words. Since *before Pesach* can be understood to describe even the closing moments of the festival, R' Yose rules that the prohibition remains in effect until the end of *Pesach* (*Rav*).

arrives; "until it is [*Pesach*]" — [it is] forbidden until [*Pesach*] ends; "until before *Pesach*" — R' Meir says: It is forbidden until [*Pesach*] arrives; R' Yose says: It is forbidden until [*Pesach*] ends.

3. **"U**ntil the harvest," "until the vintage," "until the olive-picking" — it is forbidden only until [these times] arrive.

YAD AVRAHAM

Rav's explanation of the dispute between R' Meir and R' Yose follows the *Gemara* here (61b). However, in *Kiddushin* (65a), the *Gemara* explains this dispute differently. Rather than revolving on a general assessment of the intention of people's expressions, the question these *Tannaim* are addressing is the meaning of the word פְּנֵי.

R' Meir construes it to mean *before*, since it derives from פָּנִים, *face*; that is, when one thing faces another it is *before* it. Thus, לִפְנֵי פֶּסַח means *before Pesach*. But R' Yose derives פְּנֵי from the verb לִפְנוֹת which means *to turn [and face]*. In this instance, the *neder* endures until the festival *turns away*; i.e., until it ends.

3.

„עַד הַקָּצִיר", „עַד הַבָּצִיר", „עַד הַמָּסִיק"– — *"Until the harvest," "until the vintage," "until the olive-picking"* —

[A person made a *neder*, stipulating its time limit as *until the harvest*, etc.] This case refers both to someone who said: "*until the harvest*," etc., as well as if he said, "until it is the harvest" (or "until it is the vintage," etc.) (*Rav; Rambam, Hil. Nedarim* 10:7; *Rosh; Ran*). [Although, in the example of one who made a *neder* "*until Pesach*" in the previous mishnah, a distinction was drawn between the phrase *until* and *until it is*, this distinction does not apply here, and the law is identical in all instances.]

אֵינוֹ אָסוּר אֶלָּא עַד שֶׁיַּגִּיעַ. — *it is forbidden only until [these times] arrive.*

That is, the prohibition ends with the start of the harvest season, not with its end. The mishnah's inclusion of the seemingly superfluous word *only* teaches us that whatever ex-

pression is used — be it just *until* or *until it is* — the prohibition lasts *only* until the designated time arrives, and not until it ends (*Rosh*, quoted by *Tos. Yom Tov*).

The reason for this is that the harvest season is not an event having a set time and is therefore unlike the *Pesach* festival, which has both a known starting date — the fifteenth of Nissan — as well as a known duration — seven days according to Biblical law. Since a person is not dealing with unknowns in the latter case, when stating "until it is Pesach" he might mean *until and as long as it is Pesach*. But when referring to the harvest season, neither the start nor the end are predictable. It is therefore assumed that a person does not intend to adopt a prohibition of uncertain duration, and even if he says, "until it is the harvest," he means only until the harvest begins (*Rav; Ran,* quoted by *Tos. Yom Tov*).

זֶה הַכְּלָל: כֹּל שֶׁזְּמַנּוֹ קָבוּעַ, וְאָמַר: "עַד שֶׁיַּגִּיעַ"
— אָסוּר עַד שֶׁיַּגִּיעַ; אָמַר: "עַד שֶׁיְּהֵא" — אָסוּר
עַד שֶׁיֵּצֵא. וְכֹל שֶׁאֵין זְמַנּוֹ קָבוּעַ, בֵּין אָמַר: "עַד
שֶׁיְּהֵא", בֵּין אָמַר: "עַד שֶׁיַּגִּיעַ" — אֵינוֹ אָסוּר
אֶלָּא עַד שֶׁיַּגִּיעַ.

[ד] "עַד הַקַּיִץ", "עַד שֶׁיְּהֵא הַקַּיִץ" — עַד
שֶׁיַּתְחִילוּ הָעָם לְהַכְנִיס בַּכַּלְכַּלּוֹת;
"עַד שֶׁיַּעֲבֹר הַקַּיִץ" — עַד שֶׁיְּקַפְּלוּ הַמַּקְצוּעוֹת;

ר' עובדיה מברטנורא

(ד) **עד הקיץ עד שיהא הקיץ.** בין אמר עד הקיץ בין אמר עד שיהא הקיץ אינו אסור אלא עד
שיתחילו העם להכנים להכניס בכלכלות, כלומר שקולעים תאנים הרבה ומכניסים אותם בסלים: **עד**
שיקפלו המקצועות. המחללאות שמיבשים עליהם התאנים, לאחר שנתיבשו מקפלין אותן
מחללאות ומניחין אותן לשנה הבאה:

יד אברהם

בֵּין אָמַר: "עַד שֶׁיַּגִּיעַ" – אֵינוֹ אָסוּר אֶלָּא עַד
שֶׁיַּגִּיעַ. — *Whatever has no set time —
whether he said: "until it is," [or]
whether he said: "until it arrives" —
it is forbidden only until it arrives
(Rav).*

This is illustrated by the case of our
mishnah which equates the law for
until it is the harvest to that for *until
the harvest*, and rules for both that *it is
forbidden only until it arrives.*

Those who include the harvest season
under events with a *set time* explain
whatever has no set time to refer to a *neder*
limited by something random, such as
"until Mr. X goes to a certain place."
Obviously, Mr. X could stay in that place
as long as he wants. Consequently, even if
the *neder* were formulated as "until Mr. X is
in that place," we would not consider the
prohibition to last as long as Mr. X is there,
because we have no way of predicting how
long he will be there. Rather, the prohibition would end as soon as he goes there
(*Tos., Meiri, Rashba* ibid.).

זֶה הַכְּלָל: כֹּל שֶׁזְּמַנּוֹ קָבוּעַ, וְאָמַר: "עַד
שֶׁיַּגִּיעַ" – אָסוּר עַד שֶׁיַּגִּיעַ; אָמַר: "עַד
שֶׁיְּהֵא", אָסוּר עַד שֶׁיֵּצֵא- — *This is the
rule: Whatever has a set time, and he
said: "until it arrives," it is forbidden
until it arrives; [if]he said: "until it is,"
it is forbidden until it ends.*

Most authorities explain *set time* to
mean an event of known duration. The
example of this would be the *nedarim*
of the previous mishnah, referring to
Pesach (*Ran; Rosh*).

Some authorities also include in this
category events which occur annually, not
withstanding that they are of unknown
duration (*Tos.* 60b; *Meiri* and *Rashba*
quoting "*some commentators*"). Accordingly, they regard the harvest season as an
event having a set time. They consequently
read the first part of our mishnah as
discussing only a case of *until the harvest.*
But if he were to say "*until it is the harvest*,"
the prohibition would last until the conclusion of the harvest. (See *Rashba* for a further
discussion *of this approach.*)

וְכָל שֶׁאֵין זְמַנּוֹ קָבוּעַ, בֵּין אָמַר: "עַד שֶׁיְּהֵא",

---

8

4

This is the rule: Whatever has a set time, and he said: "until it arrives," it is forbidden until it arrives; [if] he said: "until it is," it is forbidden until it ends. Whatever has no set time — whether he said: "until it is," or whether he said: "until it arrives" — it is forbidden only until it arrives.

4. "Until the fig-picking" [or] "until it is the fig-picking," [it is forbidden] until the people begin to bring in [the figs] in baskets; "until the fig-picking passes" [it is forbidden] until the mats are folded up;

YAD AVRAHAM

4.

"עַד הַקַּיִץ,, "עַד שֶׁיְּהֵא הַקַּיִץ,,– — *"Until the fig-picking" [or] "until it is the fig-picking"*

[A person made a *neder*, stipulating that the prohibition last *until the fig-picking*.]

The translation follows *Ran* (61b), who explains קַיִץ to derive from a root meaning *to pick by hand*. Fig-picking, which was done by hand, was therefore called קַיִץ. *Rambam* (*Comm.*) translates the word as *summer*, and explains that the time at which the figs ripened enough to be eaten was popularly called *summer* (*Tos. Yom Tov*).

עַד שֶׁיַּתְחִילוּ הָעָם לְהַכְנִיס בַּכַּלְבָּלוֹת; — *[it is forbidden] until the people begin to bring in [the figs] in baskets;*

Since the fig-picking was an event of unknown duration, and thus one without a set time, even a declaration of the form *until it is the fig-picking* is taken to mean *until the start of the fig-picking season*. That is, *until the people begin to bring the figs in baskets* (*Ran*).

As it stands, this ruling would seem to conflict with those who include any annual

event in the category of *whatever has a set time* (see commentary to previous mishnah); indeed, this is the reason most authorities reject that view (see *Tos.*, *Meiri*, *Rashba* cited ibid.).

עַד שֶׁיַּעֲבֹר הַקַּיִץ,, — *"until the fig-picking passes"*

[By stating explicitly that the prohibition should last *"until the fig-picking passes,"* the person indicates that he wants it to persist until the end of the fig-picking season.]

עַד שֶׁיְּקַפְּלוּ הַמַּקְצוּעוֹת; — *[it is forbidden] until the mats are folded up;*

The translation follows *Rav* and *Rambam*, who explain that the figs were laid out on mats to be dried. When most of these had been folded up and stored for the following year, the fig season could safely be assumed to be over (*Gem.* 61b; *Rambam*, *Hil. Nedarim* 10:9).

Ran translates הַמַּקְצוּעוֹת as *folding knives* used to fashion piles of figs into cylindrical blocks. *Shulchan Aruch* (*Yoreh Deah* 220:17) adopts this translation as well, but see *Sheyarei Korban* to *Yerushalmi* 8:4, who challenges it.

„עַד הַקָּצִיר" — עַד שֶׁיַּתְחִילוּ הָעָם לִקְצוֹר קְצִיר
חִטִּין, אֲבָל לֹא קְצִיר שְׂעוֹרִים. הַכֹּל לְפִי מְקוֹם
נִדְרוֹ, אִם הָיָה בָּהָר — בָּהָר, וְאִם הָיָה בַּבִּקְעָה
— בַּבִּקְעָה.

[ה] **עַד** „הַגְּשָׁמִים", „עַד שֶׁיִּהְיוּ הַגְּשָׁמִים" —
עַד שֶׁתֵּרֵד רְבִיעָה שְׁנִיָּה. רַבָּן שִׁמְעוֹן
בֶּן גַּמְלִיאֵל אוֹמֵר: עַד שֶׁיַּגִּיעַ זְמַנָּהּ שֶׁל רְבִיעָה.

ר' עובדיה מברטנורא

הכל לפי מקום נדרו. אם רוב תבואות המקום חטין עד קציר חטים, ואם שעורים עד קציר
שעורים, וכן אם היה בהר בשעת הנדר עד שיגיע זמן הקציר והבליר בהר, ואם בבקעה עד
שיגיע זמן הקציר והבליר של בקטה: **(ה) עד הגשמים עד שיהיו גשמים.** בחיוא לשון משתי
לשונות הללו שהוליא מפיו, מותר כיון שהתחילו הגשמים לירד ברביעה שניה, שהיא בשנה
המאוחרת בראש חדש כסליו, הילכך הנודר עד הגשמים אסור עד ראש חדש כסליו, אלא אם כן
ירדו גשמים בתחלת זמן שהוא בשנה המבכרת [בשבעה עשר] במרחשון, ובשנה הבינונית
בעשרים ושלשה בו. וכן הלכה. ולא כרבן שמעון בן גמליאל שאומר עד שיגיע זמנה של רביעה:

יד אברהם

„עַד הַקָּצִיר" — *"until the harvest"*

This *neder* was made in a place
which cultivated crops of both wheat
and barley (*Tos.* 62b), the latter
harvest beginning earlier than the
wheat harvest (*Rashi* ibid.).

עַד שֶׁיַּתְחִיל הָעָם לִקְצוֹר קְצִיר חִטִּין, אֲבָל
לֹא קְצִיר שְׂעוֹרִים. — *[it is forbidden]*
until the people begin to gather in the
wheat harvest, not the barley harvest.

Because barley is usually used for
animal food, and not for human
consumption (*Tif. Yis.* 23), the wheat
harvest was considered the major
harvest, and was referred to simply
as *the harvest* (*Tos.* 62b). Consequently, a prohibition lasting *until*
the harvest would end when people
begin to harvest the wheat.

This was not a hard-and-fast rule,
however, and was truly only in locales
where *the harvest* was popularly
construed as meaning the wheat
harvest. But if the major crop was

barley, and *the harvest* was used with
reference to the barley harvest, then
the *neder* would be interpreted accordingly (*Rav; Rosh; Ran*).

הַכֹּל לְפִי מְקוֹם נִדְרוֹ: — *Everything is*
according to the place of his neder:

[That is, the language used in the
declaration is assessed according to the
place in which it was made. If, for
example, the *neder* was made in a place
in which *the harvest* meant the wheat
harvest, it would be interpreted accordingly; if it was made in a place where
the harvest meant the barley harvest,
that interpretation would be adopted.]

אִם הָיָה בָּהָר - בָּהָר; וְאִם הָיָה בַּבִּקְעָה-
בַּבִּקְעָה. — *if he was in the mountain,*
[the neder refers to the harvest] in the
mountain; if he was in the valley, [it
refers to the harvest] in the valley.

The harvest in *Eretz Yisrael* arrives
sooner in the lowlands than in the
mountains. The meaning of *until the*

"until the harvest" [it is forbidden] until the people begin to gather in the wheat harvest, not the barley harvest. Everything is according to the place of his *neder:* if he was in the mountain, [the *neder* refers to the harvest] in the mountain; if he was in the valley, [it refers to the harvest] in the valley.

5. "Until the rains" [or] "until the rains are" [it is forbidden] until the second rain falls. R' Shimon ben Gamliel says: Until the time for [that] rain arrives. "Until the

YAD AVRAHAM

harvest would then depend on where the *neder* was made. If, for example, it was made in the mountains, even if the person subsequently went to the valley where the harvest begins earlier, he would remain prohibited until the harvest had begun in the mountains (*Rav; Gem.* 62b).

5.

עַד הַגְּשָׁמִים" „, "עַד שֶׁיִּהְיוּ הַגְּשָׁמִים"– — *"Until the rains," [or] "until the rains are"*

The rains do not have a set time, since they are of unknown duration (see mishnah 3). Consequently, whether a person bans something *until the rains* or *until the rains are,* the prohibition does not persist until the end of the rains, but expires at the beginning of the rains (*Ran; Rosh*).

[However, what precisely constitutes the start of *the rains* is subject to question. Is it the time at which the rains are expected, or is it only the actual rainfall?]

עַד שֶׁתֵּרֵד רְבִיעָה שְׁנִיָּה. — *[it is forbidden] until the second rain falls.*

The use of the plural form *rains* was construed as indicating the second rain. Furthermore, since the person said *"rains,"* rather than *"the second rain,"* his words are understood to refer to the actual rainfall, and not just

the expected date of the rain (*Bach* to *Tur Yoreh Deah* 220).

רַבָּן שִׁמְעוֹן בֶּן גַּמְלִיאֵל אוֹמֵר: עַד שֶׁיַּגִּיעַ זְמַנָּהּ שֶׁל רְבִיעָה. — *R' Shimon ben Gamliel says: Until the time for [that] rain arrives.*

R' Shimon ben Gamliel concurs with the first, anonymous opinion that the reference is to the second rain, but he does not agree that the use of the form *rains* is an indication that the person means the actual rainfall (*Ran* 63a). Rather — since the expected date for the second rain is known, while the date when the rain will actually fall is not — we assume that the person intended the prohibition to endure only until the time when the second rain is expected (*Ran* 62b).

The *Gemara* (63a) cites a variety of opinions as to the expected date for the second rain. *Shulchan Aruch* (*Yoreh Deah* 220:18) follows *Rambam* (*Hil. Nedarim* 10:11), who fixes it as the

„עַד שֶׁיִּפְסְקוּ גְּשָׁמִים" — עַד שֶׁיֵּצֵא נִיסָן כֻּלּוֹ;
דִּבְרֵי רַבִּי מֵאִיר. רַבִּי יְהוּדָה אוֹמֵר: עַד שֶׁיַּעֲבוֹר
הַפֶּסַח.

„קוֹנָם יַיִן שֶׁאֵינִי טוֹעֵם הַשָּׁנָה", נִתְעַבְּרָה
הַשָּׁנָה — אָסוּר בָּהּ וּבְעִבּוּרָהּ; „עַד ר'אשׁ אֲדָר",
עַד ר'אשׁ אֲדָר הָרִאשׁוֹן; „עַד סוֹף אֲדָר" — עַד
סוֹף אֲדָר הָרִאשׁוֹן.

ר' עובדיה מברטנורא

רבי יהודה אומר עד שיעבור הפסח. וְהִלְכָה כְּרַבִּי יְהוּדָה:

יד אברהם

twenty-third day of the month of Cheshvan for *Eretz Yisrael* and its neighboring countries.

The halachah is in accordance with the first opinion in the mishnah (see *Tos. Yom Tov, Bach* loc. cit.). Thus, *until the rains* creates a prohibition which lasts until the second rains actually fall. To qualify as *second rains*, they must come after the expected date; that is, they must fall following the twenty-third of Cheshvan. Before that, any rain which falls is not counted as part of the *second rains* (*Rambam; Yoreh Deah* ibid.; see also *Rambam Comm.* to *Peah* 8:1).

„עַד שֶׁיִּפְסְקוּ גְּשָׁמִים" – עַד שֶׁיֵּצֵא נִיסָן כֻּלּוֹ;
דִּבְרֵי רַבִּי מֵאִיר. רַבִּי יְהוּדָה אוֹמֵר: עַד
שֶׁיַּעֲבֹר הַפֶּסַח. — *"Until the rains stop" — [it is forbidden] until Nissan is over; [these are] the words of R' Meir. R' Yehudah says: Until Pesach is over.*

R' Meir and R' Yehudah disagree with respect to what constitutes the end of the rainy season. The opinions they express here are consistent with those attributed to them in *Taanis* 1:2 (see ArtScroll comm. ibid.), where R' Meir rules that we continue praying for rain [by saying וְתֵן טַל וּמָטָר, *and give dew and rain*, in the *Shemoneh Esrei*

prayer (*Korban HaEdah*)] until the end of Nissan, while R' Yehudah contends that this prayer is no longer recited once *Pesach* ends (*Yerushalmi* 8:5).

In *Taanis* (4b), the *Gemara* concludes that there are two versions of R' Yehudah's opinion: One is that the prayer for rain is to be said until the end of *Pesach*; the other, that it be said only until the first day of *Pesach*. The halachah follows the latter version of R' Yehudah's ruling — that the prayer is recited only until the first day of *Pesach* (*Rambam, Hil. Tefillah* 2:15; *Shulchan Aruch Orach Chaim* 117:1). This would seem to indicate that we consider the rainy season to be ended by the first day of *Pesach*. Yet, when stating the law of our mishnah, both *Rambam* (*Hil. Nedarim* 10:11) and *Shulchan Aruch* (*Yoreh Deah* 220:19) rule that *until the rains stop* means until the end of *Pesach*! (*Beur HaGra* ibid.).

In resolving this difficulty, *Sheyarei Korban* (to *Yerushalmi* 8:5) points out that *Yerushalmi* (*Taanis* 1:2) explains that the reason the prayer for rain is said only until the first day of *Pesach* is "in order for the holidays to conclude with dew, since dew is always a good sign." This refers to the custom of replacing the mention of rain (מוֹרִיד הַגֶּשֶׁם) in the *Shemoneh Esrei* prayer with the mention of dew (מוֹרִיד הַטָּל). It was deemed auspicious to mention *dew* rather than *rain* in the festival prayers (*Korban HaEdah* ad loc.). In other words, even if R'

rains stop" — [it is forbidden] until Nissan is over;
[these are] the words of R' Meir. R' Yehudah says:
Until *Pesach* is over.

[If one says:] *"Konam*, wine, with respect to my
tasting it this year," and the year was extended, it is
forbidden during it and during its extension; "until
the start of Adar" — [it is forbidden] until the start
of the first Adar; "until the end of Adar" — [it is
forbidden] until the end of the first Adar.

YAD AVRAHAM

Yehudah ruled that the prayer for rain be
said only until the first day of *Pesach*, this
was not because the day marked the end of
the rainy season. It was rather for the
purpose of mentioning the dew in the
prayers. It follows that the end of the rainy
season, according to both versions of R'
Yehudah's statement in *Taanis*, was at the
end of *Pesach*, as is evident from our
mishnah. Hence, *Rambam* and *Shulchan
Aruch* are justified in ruling, on the basis of
our mishnah, that the rainy season ends
with the conclusion of *Pesach*, although
they also rule that the prayer for rain
should only be said until the first day of
Pesach.

קוֹנָם יַיִן שֶׁאֵינִי טוֹעֵם הַשָּׁנָה", נִתְעַבְּרָה,,
הַשָּׁנָה — *[If one says:]"Konam*, wine,
with respect to my tasting it this year,"
and the year was extended,*

Although mishnah 1 rules that *this
year* means *until Rosh Hashanah*, one
might think that this applies only to a
regular twelve-month year, but not to
a leap year which has thirteen months,
due to the addition of a second month
of Adar (see *Rosh Hashanah* 7a;
Rambam, Hil. Kiddush HaChodesh
4:1). If a person, at the beginning of
such a year, introduces a prohibition
for *this year*, he might mean only for
the following twelve months, which
ordinarily would bring him to the
next Rosh Hashanah but which, in a

leap year, ends one month before
Rosh Hashanah (*Ran*).

To avoid this misconception, the
mishnah rules:

אָסוּר בָּהּ וּבְעִבּוּרָהּ; — *it is forbidden
during it and during its extension;*

That is, the prohibition remains in
effect until Rosh Hashanah, notwithstanding that if the *neder* had been
made at the start of the year, it will last
for thirteen months (*Ran*).

Furthermore, if — during a leap year — a
person declared that a prohibition should
last "one year," it endured for thirteen
months, since the duration of one year is
measured by the year at hand (*Rosh*, quoted
by *Tos. Yom Tov*). However, *Rambam (Hil.
Nedarim* 10:4) and *Shulchan Aruch (Yoreh
Deah* 220:7) rule that a time limit of *one year*
is always interpreted to mean *until the same
moment the following year*, as in mishnah 1.
Thus, if the *neder* was made before the
second Adar, then to reach the same
moment of the succeeding year will take
thirteen months; therefore, the prohibition
will last that long. But, if the *neder* was
made after the additional Adar, the corresponding moment of the next year will be
only twelve months away, and the prohibition will endure for that amount of time.

עַד רֹאשׁ אֲדָר" – עַד רֹאשׁ אֲדָר הָרִאשׁוֹן;,,
עַד סוֹף אֲדָר" – עַד סוֹף אֲדָר הָרִאשׁוֹן.,, —
"until the start of Adar" — [it is for-
bidden] until the start of the first Adar;

רַבִּי יְהוּדָה אוֹמֵר: ,,קוֹנָם יַיִן שֶׁאֵינִי טוֹעֵם עַד
שֶׁיְּהֵא הַפֶּסַח'' — אֵינוֹ אָסוּר אֶלָּא עַד לֵיל
הַפֶּסַח, שֶׁלֹּא נִתְכַּוֵּן זֶה אֶלָּא עַד שָׁעָה שֶׁדֶּרֶךְ
בְּנֵי אָדָם לִשְׁתּוֹת יָיִן.

[ו] **אָמַר:** ,,קוֹנָם בָּשָׂר שֶׁאֵינִי טוֹעֵם עַד
שֶׁיְּהֵא הַצּוֹם'' — אֵינוֹ אָסוּר
אֶלָּא עַד לֵילֵי הַצּוֹם, שֶׁלֹּא נִתְכַּוֵּן זֶה אֶלָּא עַד
שָׁעָה שֶׁדֶּרֶךְ בְּנֵי אָדָם לֶאֱכוֹל בָּשָׂר.

ר' עובדיה מברטנורא

(ו) **לילי הצום.** ליל צום כפור, שמצוה להרבות בסעודה בערב צום כפור:

יד אברהם

"until the end of Adar" — [it is for-bidden] until the end of the first Adar.

[The mishnah states that the start of Adar refers to the start of Adar I, and similarly, the end of Adar refers to the end of Adar I. Obviously, when people wish to refer to the second Adar, they do so explicitly.]

Some texts read: "until the end of Adar" — [it is forbidden] until the end of the second Adar. Accordingly, both Adars were viewed as one long month which started at the beginning of Adar I and ended with the conclusion of Adar II (Tos. Yom Tov from Rosh).

רַבִּי יְהוּדָה אוֹמֵר: ,,קוֹנָם יַיִן שֶׁאֵינִי טוֹעֵם עַד שֶׁיְּהֵא הַפֶּסַח''— R' Yehudah says: [If one says:] "Konam, wine, with respect to my tasting [it] until it is Pesach,"

6.

אָמַר: ,,קוֹנָם בָּשָׂר שֶׁאֵנִי טוֹעֵם עַד שֶׁיְּהֵא הַצּוֹם''— [If one] said: "Konam, meat, with respect to my tasting [it] until it is the fast,"

The mishnah continues here with another example of a neder in which one specifies a time limit beginning with until it is, which R' Yehudah

In mishnah 2, it is stated that the expression until it is Pesach means until the end of the Passover holiday. R' Yehudah argues, however, that a prohibition imposed on wine until it is Pesach should be an exception, since the person surely intends to celebrate the Seder, which includes the consumption of the four cups of wine (Rashi 63b). Thus, he rules:

אֵינוֹ אָסוּר אֶלָּא עַד לֵיל הַפֶּסַח, שֶׁלֹּא נִתְכַּוֵּן זֶה אֶלָּא עַד שָׁעָה שֶׁדֶּרֶךְ בְּנֵי אָדָם לִשְׁתּוֹת יָיִן. — it is forbidden only until the night of Pesach, since his intention was only until the time when it is customary for people to drink wine.

[That is, by until it is Pesach in this case, he meant until that time during Pesach when it is customary to drink wine — namely, the Seder.]

maintains should be an exception to the general rule of mishnah 3. The fast referred to is the fast of Yom Kippur (Rav; Rambam Ran).

Because it is considered a mitzvah to eat a large feast on the day before Yom Kippur (Rav; Rosh Hashanah 9a; Orach Chaim 604:1), which custom-

R' Yehudah says: [If one says:] "*Konam*, wine, with respect to my tasting [it] until it is *Pesach*," it is forbidden only until the night of *Pesach*, since his intention was only until the time when it is customary for people to drink wine.

6. [I]f one] said: "*Konam*, meat, with respect to my tasting [it] until it is the fast," it is forbidden only until [before] the night of the fast, since his intention was only until the time when it is customary for people to eat meat.

YAD AVRAHAM

arily consisted of fowl and fish[1] (*Tosafos* to *Chullin* 83a, s.v. וכדברי and *Kesubos* 5a, s.v. אלא), and the law is that a *neder* banning meat generally prohibits animal meat and fowl, and sometimes even fish (*Gem.* 54b; *Rambam, Hil. Nedarim* 9:6; *Yoreh Deah* 217:8), it follows that, in this case of a prohibition on meat *until it is the fast*, if we explain it to mean *until the fast ends*, the person will be prevented from partaking of the pre-Yom Kippur meal. Therefore, R' Yehudah rules:

אֵינוֹ אָסוּר אֶלָּא עַד לֵילֵי הַצּוֹם, שֶׁלֹּא נִתְכַּוֵּן זֶה אֶלָּא עַד שָׁעָה שֶׁדֶּרֶךְ בְּנֵי אָדָם לֶאֱכוֹל בָּשָׂר. — *it is forbidden only until [before] the night of the fast, since his intention was only until the time when it is customary for people to eat meat.*

In other words, the person is permitted to have meat in his pre-Yom Kippur meal, since we interpret his *neder* as imposing a prohibition lasting until — but not including — that meal (*Ran*). Thus, according to R' Yehudah, the phrase *until it is the fast* not only does not mean *until the end of*

the fast; it does not even mean *until the start of the fast*. Rather, it means *until the pre-Yom Kippur meal*, which is somewhat before the start of the fast (ibid.; see *Tif. Yis.*).

The translation follows *Ran*, who permits the person to have meat in the pre-fast meal. Consequently, לֵילֵי הַצּוֹם cannot mean *the night of the fast*, which would be its literal meaning, but must be understood as *the meal before the night of the fast*.

Rashash contends that, indeed, the mishnah may be taken literally. Instead of explaining *the fast* of the mishnah as referring to the fast of Yom Kippur which begins at sundown, he suggests (based on *Rashi*, see also *Ritva*) that the intention is to one of the four minor fasts (the Fast of Gedalyah, the Tenth of Teves, the Seventeenth of Tammuz, and the Fast of Esther), on which eating is prohibited only by day. Thus, if we assume that to prepare themselves for fasting, people ate meat the night before the fast, then by *until the fast*, the person meant only *until the night before the fast*, when people ate meat. The words of the mishnah may thus be taken literally.

(For a discussion of the mishnah's use of the plural form לֵילֵי, see *Tos. Yom Tov* to *Terumos* 8:3.)

1. In the northern part of *Eretz Yisrael* it was customary to eat animal meat for the pre-Yom Kippur meal (see *Chullin* 5:3).

רַבִּי יוֹסֵי בְּנוֹ אוֹמֵר: ,,קוֹנָם שׁוּם שֶׁאֵינִי טוֹעֵם
עַד שֶׁתְּהֵא שַׁבָּת" — אֵינוֹ אָסוּר אֶלָּא עַד לֵילֵי
שַׁבָּת, שֶׁלֹּא נִתְכַּוֵּן זֶה אֶלָּא עַד שָׁעָה שֶׁדֶּרֶךְ בְּנֵי
אָדָם לֶאֱכוֹל שׁוּם.

[ז] **הָאוֹמֵר** לַחֲבֵרוֹ: ,,קוֹנָם שֶׁאֲנִי נֶהֱנֶה לָךְ
אִם אֵין אַתָּה בָא וְנוֹטֵל לְבָנֶיךָ
כּוֹר אֶחָד שֶׁל חִטִּין וּשְׁתֵּי חָבִיּוֹת שֶׁל יַיִן" — הֲרֵי
זֶה יָכוֹל לְהָפֵר אֶת נִדְרוֹ שֶׁלֹּא עַל פִּי חָכָם, וְיֹאמַר
לוֹ: ,,כְּלוּם אָמַרְתָּ אֶלָּא מִפְּנֵי כְבוֹדִי? זֶהוּ כְבוֹדִי!"

―――――― ר' עובדיה מברטנורא ――――――

קוֹנָם שׁוּם שֶׁאֵינִי טוֹעֵם וכו'. שֶׁעֶזְרָא תִּקֵּן שֶׁיְּהוּ אוֹכְלִים שׁוּם בְּלֵילֵי שַׁבָּת מִפְּנֵי שֶׁמַּרְבֶּה הַזֶּרַע.
וְאֵין הֲלָכָה לֹא כְּרַבִּי יְהוּדָה וְלֹא כְּרַבִּי יוֹסֵי בְּנוֹ, אֶלָּא כִּדְאָמְרִינַן לְעֵיל בְּמַתְנִיתִין, כֹּל שֶׁזְּמַנּוֹ קָבוּעַ,
אָמַר עַד שֶׁיַּגִּיעַ, אָסוּר עַד שֶׁיַּגִּיעַ, עַד שֶׁיְּהֵא, אָסוּר עַד שֶׁיְּהֵא: **(ז) זֶהוּ כְבוֹדִי.** שֶׁאֲפַרְנֵס בְּנֵי מֶשֶׁל:

יד אברהם

רַבִּי יוֹסֵי בְּנוֹ אוֹמֵר: ,,קוֹנָם שׁוּם שֶׁאֵינִי טוֹעֵם
עַד שֶׁתְּהֵא שַׁבָּת" — R' Yose, his son,
says: [If one says:]"Konam, garlic with
respect to my tasting [it] until it is the
Sabbath,"

[R' Yose, the son of R' Yehudah,
who was cited in the previous mishnah, follows with another example of a
neder using the expression *until it is*,
which, according to him, ought to be
an exception to the rule of mishnah 3.]

אֵינוֹ אָסוּר אֶלָּא עַד לֵילֵי שַׁבָּת, — *it is
forbidden only until the night of the
Sabbath,*

[And not until the end of the
Sabbath, as it would be if the rule of
mishnah 3 were applied.]

שֶׁלֹּא נִתְכַּוֵּן זֶה אֶלָּא עַד שָׁעָה שֶׁדֶּרֶךְ בְּנֵי אָדָם
לֶאֱכוֹל שׁוּם. — *since his intention was
only until the time when it is customary for people to eat garlic.*

As explained in the commentary to
3:10, Ezra instituted that married men
eat garlic on Friday evening — specifi-

cally, the beginning of the night — in
order to increase their potency (*Rambam Comm,* s.v. ר"י). This night is
considered an appropriate time for
marital relations. For Torah scholars, it
is the one time during the week when
they are required to fulfill their conjugal
duty (*Kesubos* 52a; see ArtScroll commentary ibid. 5:6). In addition, on the
Sabbath, one is obligated to enjoy every
possible pleasure (*Rambam* ibid.). Accordingly, it was customary for people
to eat garlic on Friday night. [R' Yose
therefore assumes that this person who
banned for himself garlic *until it is the
Sabbath* did not mean *until the Sabbath
is over,* but *until the Sabbath comes.*]

Ran follows the view of *Rambam* (*Comm.*),
who rejects the opinions of R' Yehudah and
R' Yose, and maintains that all these cases
("wine ... until it is Pesach"; "meat ... until it
is the fast"; "garlic ... until it is the Sabbath")
are governed by the rule of mishnah 3.

However, some authorities do accept the
opinions of R' Yehudah and R' Yose (*Tos.
Yom Tov*).

R' Yose, his son, says: [If one says:] "*Konam*, garlic, with respect to my tasting [it] until it is the Sabbath," it is forbidden only until the night of the Sabbath, since his intention was only until the time when it is customary for people to eat garlic.

7. **[I**f] someone says to another: "*Konam*, whatever benefit I might derive from you, unless you come and take for your children one *kor* of wheat and two barrels of wine," such a person can annul his *neder* without recourse to a sage, if he says to him: "Did you say [that] other than for my honor? That is my honor!"

YAD AVRAHAM

7.

הָאוֹמֵר לַחֲבֵרוֹ: "קוֹנָם שֶׁאֲנִי נֶהֱנֶה לָךְ אִם אֵין אַתָּה בָּא וְנוֹטֵל לְבָנֶיךָ כּוֹר אֶחָד שֶׁל חִטִּין וּשְׁתֵּי חָבִיּוֹת שֶׁל יַיִן," — *[If] someone says to another: "Konam, whatever benefit I might have from you, unless you come and take for your children one kor of wheat and two barrels of wine,"*

Kor is a measure of volume equivalent to thirty *seah* (*Rav* to *Kilayim* 2:9). A gift of such dimensions was sizable, and would only have been inspired by a desire to share his gratitude for numerous gifts or other benefits he had received from this other person (*Rosh* 24a; *Meiri* ibid.). The person's insistence that the other take the gift for his children, rather than for his own use, was a polite way to offer a gift (*Rosh* loc. cit.).

הֲרֵי זֶה יָכוֹל לְהָפֵר אֶת נִדְרוֹ שֶׁלֹּא עַל פִּי חָכָם, — *such a person can annul his neder without recourse to a sage,*

[There is a way for the prohibition to be released without seeking annulment from a sage or panel, and without the other person's taking the gift.]

וְיֹאמַר לוֹ: — *if* (lit., *and*) *he says to him:*

"כְּלוּם אָמַרְתָּ אֶלָּא מִפְּנֵי כְבוֹדִי? זֶהוּ כְבוֹדִי!" — *"Did you say [that] other than for my honor? That is my honor!"*

The intended recipient asserts that the true intention of the person making the declaration was to honor him, and that this can be accomplished without actually taking the gift. On the contrary, he argues that he is honored simply by the offer of such a gift. People hearing that he was made such an offer will already accord him respect (*Meiri* 24a; *Ran* ibid.). Furthermore, to refuse such an offer is also an honor; he says: "My honor is to despise the taking of gifts" (*Rosh* ibid.; cf. *Proverbs* 15:27). Thus, without actually taking the wheat and wine, the person has satisfied the conditions for abolishing the prohibition (*Meiri* loc. cit.).

Yerushalmi adds that although this holds true ordinarily, if the one who made the declaration insists that his intention was not to honor the other person, but rather to honor himself

וְכֵן הָאוֹמֵר לַחֲבֵרוֹ: „קוֹנָם שֶׁאַתָּה נֶהֱנֶה לִי אִם אֵין אַתָּה בָא וְנוֹתֵן לִבְנִי כּוֹר אֶחָד שֶׁל חִטִּין וּשְׁתֵּי חָבִיּוֹת שֶׁל יַיִן" — רַבִּי מֵאִיר אוֹמֵר: אָסוּר עַד שֶׁיִּתֵּן; וַחֲכָמִים אוֹמְרִים: אַף זֶה יָכוֹל לְהָפֵר אֶת נִדְרוֹ שֶׁלֹּא עַל פִּי חָכָם, וְיֹאמַר לוֹ: „הֲרֵי אֲנִי כְּאִלּוּ הִתְקַבַּלְתִּי".

הָיוּ מְסָרְבִין בּוֹ לָשֵׂאת בַּת אֲחוֹתוֹ, וְאָמַר: „קוֹנָם שֶׁהִיא נֶהֱנֵית לִי לְעוֹלָם"; וְכֵן הַמְגָרֵשׁ אֶת אִשְׁתּוֹ, וְאָמַר: „קוֹנָם אִשְׁתִּי נֶהֱנֵית לִי לְעוֹלָם"

ר' עובדיה מברטנורא

היו מסרבין בו לשאת את בת אחותו. מפצירין בו שישא את בת אחותו מפני שהיא בת גילו ואמרינן (יבמות סג, ב) הנושא את בת אחותו הכתוב עליו אומר (ישעיה נח, ז-ט) ומבשרך לא תתעלם אז תקרא וה' יענה:

יד אברהם

with the fact that the other person accepted a gift from him, then the condition is understood literally. Unless the person actually takes the gift, or the *neder* is annulled, the prohibition will remain in force (*Ran* loc. cit.; *Shach* to *Yoreh Deah* 232:46).

וְכֵן הָאוֹמֵר לַחֲבֵרוֹ: „קוֹנָם שֶׁאַתָּה נֶהֱנֶה לִי אִם אֵין אַתָּה בָא וְנוֹתֵן לִבְנִי כּוֹר אֶחָד שֶׁל חִטִּין וּשְׁתֵּי חָבִיּוֹת שֶׁל יַיִן" — *Similarly, someone who says to another: "Konam, whatever benefit you might derive from me, unless you come and give my son one kor of wheat and two barrels of wine"* —

In this case, the person making the declaration (e.g., Reuven) demands a large gift from another (e.g. Shimon), or else the latter will be deprived of the right to benefit from him (Reuven). Presumably, Reuven has been giving Shimon a lot of benefit while not receiving much in return. To bring this situation to an end, Reuven declares that henceforth, unless Shimon deli-

vers a large gift to Reuven's son, Shimon will be banned from receiving any benefit from Reuven (*Meiri*; *Rosh* 24a;).

רַבִּי מֵאִיר אוֹמֵר: אָסוּר עַד שֶׁיִּתֵּן; — *R' Meir says: It is binding until he gives;*

R' Meir takes the stipulation literally, and maintains that, unless Shimon physically delivers the gift of wheat and wine, the prohibition will go into effect. *Ran* (24a, 63b) quotes *Yerushalmi*, which construes R' Meir's statement as disputing the first case of the mishnah as well. That is, according to R' Meir, if the person who made the stipulation *unless you come and take*, etc. does not explicitly state that his intention is only to honor the person, we take him literally, and the prohibition is effective until the person receives the gift. *Tosafos* (63b, s.v. ר"מ), however, interpret R' Meir as disagreeing only in this case (*Tos. Yom Tov*).

8
7

Similarly, someone who says to another: "*Konam*, whatever benefit you might derive from me, unless you come and give my son one *kor* of wheat and two barrels of wine" — R' Meir says: It is binding until he gives; the Sages, however, say: This person, too, can annul his *neder* without recourse to a sage, if he says: "It is as if I have received."

[If] they were urging him to marry his sister's daughter, and he said: "*Konam*, whatever benefits she derives from me forever"; likewise, [if] one was divorcing his wife, and said: "*Konam*, whatever benefit my wife derives from me forever,"

YAD AVRAHAM

וַחֲכָמִים אוֹמְרִים: אַף זֶה יָכוֹל לְהָפֵר אֶת נִדְרוֹ שֶׁלֹּא עַל פִּי חָכָם, וְיֹאמַר לוֹ: "הֲרֵי אֲנִי כְּאִלּוּ הִתְקַבַּלְתִּי". — *the Sages, however, say: This person, too, can annul his neder without recourse to a sage, if he says: "It is* (lit., *I am*) *as if I have received."*

Reuven's stipulation was that he receive something from Shimon. But even if he were to receive it, he could always return it, if he so desired.

Therefore, if he wishes to do so, there is no point in going through the motions. Reuven can forgo his demands on Shimon by declaring that he considers it as if he had actually received the gift, and returned it (*Rashba*, quoted by *Ran* 24a). The condition for preventing the prohibition has thus been satisfied, and the prohibition is released without recourse to a sage or panel for annulment.

הָיוּ מְסָרְבִין בּוֹ לָשֵׂאת בַּת אֲחוֹתוֹ, — *[If] they were urging him to marry his sister's daughter,*

It was considered virtuous to marry one's sister's daughter (*Rav* from

Yevamos 62b). *Rashbam* extends this to any niece, even one's brother's daughter. The mishnah discusses, marriage to one's sister's daughter, since that was a much more common occurrence (*Tos.* to *Yevamos* 62b, s.v. והנושא).

וְאָמַר: "קוֹנָם שֶׁהִיא נֶהֱנֵית לִי לְעוֹלָם"; — *and he said: "Konam, whatever benefit she derives from me forever";*

[Although the *neder* appears to forbid to her all benefits from him, the circumstances under which it was made — as a reaction to pressure to marry — would indicate that his purpose was to avoid the marriage, and that only the benefit of marriage was being interdicted.]

וְכֵן הַמְגָרֵשׁ אֶת אִשְׁתּוֹ, וְאָמַר: "קוֹנָם אִשְׁתִּי נֶהֱנֵית לִי לְעוֹלָם"- — *likewise [if] one was divorcing his wife, and said "Konam, whatever benefit my wife derives from me forever,"*

[Here, too, the circumstances under which the prohibition was imposed indicate that *benefits* refers only to marriage, not to all benefits.]

הֲרֵי אֵלּוּ מֻתָּרוֹת לֵהָנוֹת לוֹ, שֶׁלֹּא נִתְכַּוֵּן זֶה — אֶלָּא לְשׁוּם אִישׁוּת. הָיָה מְסָרֵב בַּחֲבֵרוֹ שֶׁיֹּאכַל אֶצְלוֹ, אָמַר: "קוֹנָם לְבֵיתְךָ שֶׁאֵינִי נִכְנָס"; "טִפַּת צוֹנֵן שֶׁאֵינִי טוֹעֵם לָךְ" — מֻתָּר לִכָּנֵס לְבֵיתוֹ וְלִשְׁתּוֹת מִמֶּנּוּ צוֹנֵן, שֶׁלֹּא נִתְכַּוֵּן זֶה אֶלָּא לְשׁוּם אֲכִילָה וּשְׁתִיָּה.

ר' עובדיה מברטנורא

שלא נתכוון זה אלא לשם אכילה ושתיה. ומיהו גס באכילה ושתיה מותר הואיל ולא הוליא מפיו אכילה ושתיה, דבנדרים בעינן שיוליא בשפתיו כדכתיב (במדבר ל, ג) ככל היולא מפיו יעשה, ולא דמי לרישא, דאישות בכלל הנאות איתיה:

יד אברהם

הֲרֵי אֵלּוּ מֻתָּרוֹת לֵהָנוֹת לוֹ, שֶׁלֹּא נִתְכַּוֵּן זֶה אֶלָּא לְשׁוּם אִישׁוּת. — *they are permitted to have benefit, since his intention was only for marriage.*

Both the wife being divorced and the niece are forbidden to marry (or remarry) the person who made the *neder*, but any other benefits from him are permitted.

Unlike the prohibition of *"wine … until it is Pesach"* (mishnah 5), *"meat … until it is the fast"* (mishnah 6), or *"garlic … until it is the Sabbath"* (ibid.), for which the person's possible intentions are disregarded by most authorities (see commentary ibid.), here all agree that the circumstantial evidence is

overwhelming, and thus serves as a sufficient basis upon which to interpret the terms of the *neder* (*Tos. Yom Tov* to mishnah 6, s.v. שלא נתכון).

הָיָה מְסָרֵב בַּחֲבֵרוֹ שֶׁיֹּאכַל אֶצְלוֹ, אָמַר: — *[If] he was urging another to eat with him, [and] he said:*

[I.e., the person who was invited replied:]

"קוֹנָם לְבֵיתְךָ שֶׁאֵינִי נִכְנָס"; "טִפַּת צוֹנֵן שֶׁאֵינִי טוֹעֵם לָךְ" — *"Konam, your house, with respect to my entering [it]'; [or] "a drop of your cold water, with respect to my tasting [it],"*

[In refusing the invitation, the

8
7

they are permitted to have benefit, since his intention was only for marriage. [If] he was urging another to eat with him, [and] he said: "*Konam*, your house, with respect to my entering [it]"; [or] "a drop of your cold water, with respect to my tasting [it]," he is permitted to enter his house and to drink his cold water, for his intention was only for eating and drinking.

YAD AVRAHAM

person bans himself from entering the inviter's home, or even from tasting a drop of his water. However, since the *neder* was made in order to refuse an invitation to eat, it is evident that he does not mean to implement such drastic restrictions upon himself.]

מֻתָּר לִכָּנֵס לְבֵיתוֹ וְלִשְׁתּוֹת מִמֶּנּוּ צוֹנֵן, שֶׁלֹּא נִתְכַּוֵּן זֶה אֶלָּא לְשׁוּם אֲכִילָה וּשְׁתִיָּה. — *he is permitted to enter his house and to drink his cold water, for his intention was only for eating and drinking.*

[The restrictions are considered to have been declared without real intent to prohibit (see 3:1ff.), and are therefore not binding.]

Rav follows the view of *Rosh* (*Commentary* to 21a and *Pesakim* 8:5), who rules that the person is permitted even to eat and drink the

host's food. Although he may have intended to forbid it, he did not articulate that prohibition, and it therefore is not effected. However, *Beis Yosef* (*Yoreh Deah* 218) point out that, in our editions of the *Tosefta* (4:8), it is explicit that a prohibition on eating or drinking the host's food is created. This is further evident from *Rambam* (*Hil. Nedarim* 8:10), who rules that, although the person may enter the host's home and take his cold water, he may not partake of the particular meal whose invitation he had rejected with his *neder*. Accordingly, *Shulchan Aruch* (loc. cit. 4) rules that, in the case of our mishnah, although the person is permitted to enter the house or taste cold water, he may not partake of the meal.

פרק תשיעי ୫§

Chapter Nine

୫§ Annulment of a Neder

In the commentary to 2:1, s.v. *Grounds for Annulling a Neder*, it was explained that if an "opening" for a *neder* can be found, the *neder* could be annulled by a panel of three laymen or by an expert sage.

In general, the sage or panel attempted to uncover a foreseeable, but objectionable, consequence of the *neder*, which was not sufficiently realized by the person at the time of his declaration. If, upon reflection, the person contends that had he taken this consequence into account at that time, he would never have made his declaration, a "way out" — which can serve as a basis for the annulment of the *neder* — has been found. The panel or sage repeats the formula, "It is permitted you," three times, and the *neder* is annulled (*Yoreh Deah* 228:3,7).

It must be emphasized that the statement of annulment has no effect unless the person honestly believes that had he realized the consequences of the *neder*, he would not have made it. If this is not so, no matter how many times a panel or sage annuls the *neder*, it remains binding (ibid. 228:10).

[א] **רַבִּי** אֱלִיעֶזֶר אוֹמֵר: פּוֹתְחִין לָאָדָם בִּכְבוֹד אָבִיו וְאִמּוֹ; וַחֲכָמִים אוֹסְרִין. אָמַר רַבִּי צָדוֹק: עַד שֶׁפּוֹתְחִין לוֹ בִּכְבוֹד אָבִיו וְאִמּוֹ, יִפְתְּחוּ לוֹ בִּכְבוֹד הַמָּקוֹם. אִם כֵּן, אֵין נְדָרִים!

ר' עובדיה מברטנורא

פרק תשיעי – רבי אליעזר. (א) רבי אליעזר אומר פותחין לאדם בכבוד אביו ואמו. כגון שיאמרו לו, אילו היית יודע שיאמרו העולם לאביך ולאמך ראו גדולים שגדלתם, כמה בנכס קל בנדרים, ונמלאת מזלזל בכבודם, כלום היית נודר, **וחכמים אוסרין.** דחיישינן שמא משקר, כי הוא בוש לומר שלא היה מניח מלידור בשביל כבודם, ונמצא שחכם מתיר נדר זה בלא חרטה. ומיירי שהוא אינו מתחרט מעיקרא מעיקרו, דקיימא לן פותחין בחרטה, ואין צריך למצוא לו פתח בשעה שהוא מתחרט מעלמו מעיקרו: **יפתחו לו בכבוד המקום.** על מלתיה דרבי אליעזר קא פריך, כי היכי דפותחין בכבוד אביו ואמו ולא חיישינן שמא ישקר, יפתחו לו נמי בכבוד המקום ויאמרו לו אילו היית יודע שתקרא רע לפני המקום כלום היית נודר, ואמרו לו חכמים דרבי אליעזר מהא ולא לא תסייען, דהא רבי אליעזר מודה בהא דודאי ישקר, דלא חליף אינש כולי האי דיאמר שלא היה מניח בשביל כבוד המקום, ולא דמי לרבן שמעון בן גמליאל דפתח לההוא גברא בוטה יש גברא כדמקרות חרב כו' (משלי יב, יח), דהתם אומר לו מן הפסוקים כהך דתנן במתניתין שעובר על לא תשנא ולא תקום ולא תטור, אבל כשמזכירין לו כבוד המקום חז ודאי משקר. והלכה כחכמים:

יד אברהם

1.

רַבִּי אֱלִיעֶזֶר אוֹמֵר: פּוֹתְחִין לָאָדָם בִּכְבוֹד אָבִיו וְאִמּוֹ; — *R' Eliezer says: They may find grounds to annul a neder for a person with the honor of his father and his mother;*

A panel or sage may invoke the honor of a person's parents to devise an "opening" for his *neder*. For example, they might ask him, "Had you known that people would chide your parents by saying: 'See the children you have raised — how lightheaded your son is with regard to making *nedarim!*' thus bringing embarrassment to them, would you have made the *neder*?" (Rav; Rosh). If the person answers: "No, I would not have made the *neder*, had I realized that this would be the outcome," R' Eliezer maintains that an "opening" has been found, and the *neder* can be annulled (Rashi).

וַחֲכָמִים אוֹסְרִין. — *the Sages, however, forbid [it].*

The Sages forbid the use of such an "opening." This is because they contend that, out of embarrassment to display before the panel or the sage his disregard for his parents' honor, the person might be untruthful when responding that he would not have made the *neder*; it is possible that he actually is not concerned about his parents' honor, and would have made the *neder* in any case (Rav).

[Obviously, R' Eliezer opines that we are not concerned with this possibility, because a person whose parents' honor is of no concern to him would also be impudent enough to admit this openly.]

אָמַר רַבִּי צָדוֹק: עַד שֶׁפּוֹתְחִין לוֹ בִּכְבוֹד אָבִיו וְאִמּוֹ, יִפְתְּחוּ לוֹ בִּכְבוֹד הַמָּקוֹם. — *Said R'*

9
1

1. **R**′ Eliezer says: They may find grounds to annul a *neder* for a person with the honor of his father and his mother; the Sages, however, forbid [it]. Said R′ Tzadok: Before they find grounds to annul the *neder* for him with the honor of his father and his mother, they should do so with the honor of God. If so, no *nedarim*!

YAD AVRAHAM

Tzadok: Before they find grounds to annul the neder for him with the honor of his father and his mother, they should do so with the honor of God.

[The term הַמָּקוֹם (lit., *the place*) is used to refer to God, the Omnipresent (see *R′ Avraham Min HaHar; Bereishis Rabbah* 68).]

R′ Tzadok reasons that, if R′ Eliezer's argument is valid, it ought to be possible to annul a *neder* on the grounds that it is an affront to the dignity of God, since He does not look favorably upon people who create such prohibitions (see *Gem.* 2a, 77b). For, if indeed, people will unabashedly acknowledge their irreverence for their parents, a person who would have made his *neder* despite being aware that it constitutes an abuse to the honor of God will also admit to it. Consequently, a person — who, upon being informed about Divine disapproval of *nedarim*, expresses regret at having made his *neder* — should be believed. Thus, *the honor of God* should be a valid argument with which to annul a *neder* (*Rav; Rosh*).

[Evidently, it was known that even R′ Eliezer did not allow the use of an "opening" based on Divine honor. Thus, by demonstrating that R′ Eliezer's position regarding parental honor leads to the conclusion that the "Divine honor" argument is valid, R′ Tzadok hoped to refute R′ Eliezer's view.]

אִם כֵּן, אֵין נְדָרִים! — *If so, no nedarim!*

Some commentators understand this statement as being addressed to R′ Tzadok, who had hoped to support the position of the Sages by rejecting R′ Eliezer's opinion. The Sages, however, explained to him that his argument was not valid, since R′ Eliezer distinguished between parental honor and Divine honor, maintaining that parental honor can be used as an "opening," while Divine honor is not. This is because even a person who is contemptuous enough to assert his readiness to embarrass his parents would not admit to a similar intention to offend the Divine honor, for no one would be brazen enough to declare his indifference to the Almighty's will. Thus, even R′ Eliezer cannot allow the *honor of God* argument to be used as an "opening," since the veracity of the person's response is in question.

Accordingly, the text of the mishnah: *If so, no nedarim!* is laconic, an abridgment of the statement: *They said to him: If so, no nedarim will be properly annulled!* That is, if the "Divine dignity" argument were to be used as an "opening," no annulments could be trusted, since the person's declared change of heart with regard to his *neder* would always be suspect (*Rav* and *Rosh*, based on *Abaye's* interpretation in the *Gemara* 64a).

[213] THE MISHNAH/NEDARIM — Chapter Nine: *R′ Eliezer*

וּמוֹדִים חֲכָמִים לְרַבִּי אֱלִיעֶזֶר בְּדָבָר שֶׁבֵּינוֹ לְבֵין אָבִיו וְאִמּוֹ, שֶׁפּוֹתְחִין לוֹ בִּכְבוֹד אָבִיו וְאִמּוֹ.

ר׳ עובדיה מברטנורא

שביעו לבין אביו ואמו. כגון שהדיר את אביו מנכסיו:

יד אברהם

Rava, however, offers a different explanation. He construes this statement of the mishnah to be an abridgment of: *If so, no nedarim will be brought to a sage or a panel for annulment!* In other words, if the *honor of God* "opening" is acceptable, people will no longer turn to a sage or a panel to seek annulment of their *nedarim*. Since it is universally applicable, they will apply it on their own, thinking that doing so suffices to annul their *neder*. But, in fact, this is not so, since only a second party (a sage or a panel) can nullify one's *neder*, as the *Gemara* (*Chagigah* 10a) deduces from the verse (*Num.* 30:2), *He shall not break his word*, from which the Rabbis interpret that others may, indeed, break his word [i.e., by nullifying it] (*Rashi, Ran* 64b). Therefore, to prevent this from happening, an "opening" as extensive as one based on Divine honor was invalidated even by R' Eliezer. The problem that the "opening" of parental honor will also lead people to nullify *nedarim* on their own was not as serious, since the argument that a *neder* is offensive and embarrassing to parents was not always relevant. Thus, people would not automatically assume it to be a sufficient "opening," and would only have their *nedarim* nullified with that argument by presenting their cases to a sage or a panel (*Ran* 64b).

Rambam (*Comm.* here and to *Nazir* 5:4) appears to explain that both the Sages and R' Eliezer accept an "opening" based on parental honor. Their dispute is whether or not this "opening" requires the regular annulment procedure (a presentation before a sage or panel). R' Eliezer holds that if the parents claim to be embarrassed by the *neder*, it is thereby annulled, while the Sages maintain that the regular procedure is needed. The phrase *if so, no nedarim!* is read as part of R' Tzadok's statement, which is that if the offensiveness of a *neder* suffices to annul it without recourse to a sage or panel, no *nedarim* will be brought for annulment to a sage or panel, since all *nedarim* are offensive to God. But this cannot be, since — as mentioned above — the Torah indicated that annulment is attained only through the involvement of a sage or panel (see *Yerushalmi* and *Keren Orah*). R' Eliezer's response to this challenge is not recorded by the mishnah.

Aside from the unlikelihood that R' Eliezer introduces the new concept that a *neder* can be annulled on its own without following the standard procedure, there are other peripheral difficulties that have been raised concerning *Rambam's* interpretation of this mishnah. For a fuller discussion see R' *Avraham Min HaHar, Meiri, Lechem Mishneh* to *Hil. Nedarim* 8:5, and *Einayim LaMishpat* to 64a.

וּמוֹדִים חֲכָמִים לְרַבִּי אֱלִיעֶזֶר בְּדָבָר שֶׁבֵּינוֹ לְבֵין אָבִיו וְאִמּוֹ, — *The Sages agree with R' Eliezer, however, that — for a matter between him and his father and mother —*

This is a prohibition which the person directs at his parents. For example, he forbids his parents from deriving benefit from his property (*Rav*), or vice versa (*Meiri*).

שֶׁפּוֹתְחִין לוֹ בִּכְבוֹד אָבִיו וְאִמּוֹ. — *they may find grounds to annul his neder*

9
1

The Sages agree with R' Eliezer, however, that — for a matter between him and his father and mother — they may find grounds to annul his *neder* with the honor of his father and mother.

YAD AVRAHAM

with the honor of his father and mother.

As stated above, the reason that the Sages did not ordinarily allow parental honor to be used as the basis for an "opening" was that they were concerned that a person would not be so brazen as to admit his irreverence and disregard for his parents. However, a person who actually directs a *neder* at his parents clearly does not disguise his impudence. It may therefore be assumed that if he, in fact, would have made his *neder* even with the knowledge that it would subsequently cause his parents anguish, he would openly admit to it before the panel or the sage. The "opening" is therefore acceptable (*Gem.* 54b; *Tos. Yom Tov*).

According to Rava's interpretation of the mishnah (*Gem.* ibid.), discussed above, an "opening" is disqualified if wide application would lead to popular neglect of the correct annulment procedure. Indeed, according to him, this is why the Sages in general were opposed to an "opening" based on parental honor (*Ran* 64b). However, it was felt that to allow this "opening" to be used only in the limited case of *a matter between him and his father and mother* would not create such a problem, and the person would not be led to annul the *neder* on his own (*Gem.* 64b). [Hence, the Sages agree that, in a matter affecting the relationship between him and his parents, an "opening" based on parental honor is acceptable.]

2.

The basic element in the technique of finding an "opening" for a declaration is the change of heart the person has with respect to the original *neder*. Had he realized the full consequence of his *neder*, he would never have made it (see *Yoreh Deah* 228:12).

This mishnah discusses a consequence of the *neder*, which — even had the vower foreseen it — would not have deterred him from making the *neder*. For example, an unusual or unlikely development takes place which makes it difficult for the person to abide by his *neder*, and brings him to seek its annulment. Even if the person would have realized this eventuality when making his *neder*, it would not have prevented him from doing so. Rather, he would have convinced himself that such an occurrence is unlikely, and should not interfere with his intentions. In such a situation, the argument, "Had I realized the full consequences of the *neder*, I would not have made it," is not relevant, since — even if he had considered this eventuality — he would have gone ahead with his *neder* nevertheless. It would seem, then, that such an unexpected turn of events ought not to constitute a satisfactory opening. However, as will be demonstrated in the coming mishnah, the matter is subject to dispute (*Rav; Rosh*).

[ב] וְעוֹד אָמַר רַבִּי אֱלִיעֶזֶר: פּוֹתְחִין בְּנוֹלָד;
וַחֲכָמִים אוֹסְרִים. כֵּיצַד? אָמַר:
"קוֹנָם שֶׁאֵינִי נֶהֱנֶה לְאִישׁ פְּלוֹנִי", וְנַעֲשָׂה
סוֹפֵר, אוֹ שֶׁהָיָה מַשִּׂיא אֶת בְּנוֹ בְּקָרוֹב,

────────── ר' עובדיה מברטנורא ──────────

(ב) ועוד אמר רבי אליעזר. קולא אחרת בנדרים: **פותחין בנולד.** בנדרים, כגון דבר שאינו מצוי ונולד ונתחדש אחר שנדר, ואילו ידע בשעת הנדר שיתחדש דבר זה לא היה נודר: **וחכמים אוסרים.** דטעמא דחרטה משום שעל ידי חרטה נעקר הנדר מעיקרו, ובדבר שאינו מצוי אינו נעשה נדר [עקור] מעיקרו, כי בשביל זה לא היה מניח מלדור כי היה סבור שלא יבא לעולם: **ונעשה סופר.** תלמיד חכם והכל צריכים לו:

────────── יד אברהם ──────────

— וְעוֹד אָמַר רַבִּי אֱלִיעֶזֶר: פּוֹתְחִין בְּנוֹלָד;
R' Eliezer also said: They can find grounds to annul a neder on the basis of an unexpected development;

R' Eliezer maintains that even an unlikely development can serve as the basis for an "opening." While it is true that, had the person considered the *possibility* of this unlikely occurrence developing, he would have discounted it, if he had known with certainty at the time of the *neder* that it would actually transpire, he would not have made the *neder* (*Rav*). Although, of course, the person had no way of knowing the future, R' Eliezer asserts — on the basis of Biblical precedent (see below) — that even unforeseeable developments, which cause the vower to have second thoughts about his *neder*, may be used as an "opening" (*Gem.* 64b).

וַחֲכָמִים אוֹסְרִין. — *the Sages, however, prohibit it.*

The Sages insist that the development which inspires a change of heart regarding the *neder* must be one that was possible to anticipate initially. Then, the fact that the person neglected to do so is attributed to an

oversight on his part and indicates that the *neder* was made without the vower realizing its ramifications. It is this element of fault with the *neder* that the sage or panel can point to and use to nullify the *neder* at its origin. Similar to an unwitting *neder* (described in 3:2), which never takes effect because it was based on a misconception, here it is demonstrated that, had certain factors been realized at the time of the *neder*, it would not have been made; consequently, it may now be annulled (see *Rambam*, quoted by *Taz, Yoreh Deah* 228:16; *Ran* 21b, 76b; cf. *Rav*).

However, if the undesirable consequence of the *neder* is unlikely to occur, then neglecting to take it into account cannot be considered a mere flaw in the *neder*, for, even if the vower had realized it, he would have gone ahead with his *neder* nevertheless, confident that the undesirable consequence would never happen (*Rav*).

Moreover, the Biblical precedent which R' Eliezer uses to establish the validity of such "openings" is rejected by the Sages. According to the Midrash (cited by *Rashi* to *Ex.* 2:21), Moses

2. **R**′ Eliezer also said: They can find grounds to annul a *neder* on the basis of an unexpected development; the Sages, however, prohibit it. How? [If] he said: "*Konam,* my having benefit from So-and-so," and he became a scribe, or was shortly to marry off his son, and he said:

YAD AVRAHAM

took an oath not to abandon Jethro and return to Egypt. Yet, when God revealed to him that his enemies, Dasan and Aviram, had died (*Ex.* 4:19), he was permitted to return to Egypt. Clearly, argues R′ Eliezer, the untimely death of Moses' enemies was considered an "opening" for his oath. Had he known when swearing that they were to die shortly, he would not have sworn.

The Sages, however, demonstrate that the Torah's reference to the "death" of Dasan and Aviram actually means that they had become poor. [Poverty is considered like death (*Gem.* 7b).] Having thus lost their influence, they were no longer a threat to Moses. Since a person's turning poor is a foreseeable and likely contingency, it thus qualifies as an acceptable "opening." Accordingly, Moses' oath was repealed by a common "opening," and is therefore not a precedent for R′ Eliezer's position (*Ran* 64b; *Tos. Yom Tov*).

[The mishnah now offers several illustrations of unlikely future developments which, according to the Sages, are not appropriate for "openings."]

כֵּיצַד? אָמַר: ,,קוֹנָם שֶׁאֵינִי נֶהֱנֶה לְאִישׁ
פְּלוֹנִי'', וְנַעֲשֶׂה סוֹפֵר, — *How? [If] he*

said: "*Konam, my having benefit from So-and-so," and he became a scribe,*

[So-and-so became a scribe.] The translation follows *Meiri* and *Tosafos,* who render סוֹפֵר as *scribe,* and this is the common interpretation. *Rav* follows *Rosh* who renders it *scholar*[1] (see *Rashi* to *Avodah Zarah* 2b, s.v. וסופריה, *Kiddushin* 30a; cf. ibid. 4:13). In either case, the idea is that the person at whom the *neder* was directed suddenly assumed a position which would make it impossible to avoid him. If he was appointed to be the town scribe, his services would be needed for preparation of documents (*Meiri*); if he became a scholar, his services would be needed in that capacity (*Rav*).

אוֹ שֶׁהָיָה מַשִּׂיא אֶת בְּנוֹ בְּקָרוֹב, — *or was shortly to marry off his son,*

When depriving himself of the privilege to benefit from this person, he did not realize that the latter would soon be celebrating a wedding which he would have to attend (*Tos.*). He would have to enter his house to hear the *sheva berachos,* the seven nuptial blessings (*Meiri*).

וְאָמַר: — *and he said:*

[The person who made the declaration said:]

---

1. See commentary to ArtScroll *Ezra* 7:6, p. 154 that the familiar expression עֶזְרָא הַסוֹפֵר, *Ezra HaSofer,* does not mean that Ezra was a scribe, but that he was a scholar.

וְאָמַר: "אִלּוּ הָיִיתִי יוֹדֵעַ שֶׁהוּא נַעֲשֶׂה סוֹפֵר, אוֹ
שֶׁהוּא מַשִּׂיא אֶת בְּנוֹ בְּקָרוֹב — לֹא הָיִיתִי נוֹדֵר!";
"קוֹנָם לְבַיִת זֶה שֶׁאֵינִי נִכְנָס", וְנַעֲשָׂה בֵּית
הַכְּנֶסֶת, וְאָמַר: "אִלּוּ הָיִיתִי יוֹדֵעַ שֶׁהוּא נַעֲשֶׂה
בֵּית הַכְּנֶסֶת — לֹא הָיִיתִי נוֹדֵר!" — רַבִּי אֱלִיעֶזֶר
מַתִּיר, וַחֲכָמִים אוֹסְרִין.

[ג] **רַבִּי** מֵאִיר אוֹמֵר, יֵשׁ דְּבָרִים שֶׁהֵן כְּנוֹלָד
וְאֵינָן כְּנוֹלָד; וְאֵין חֲכָמִים מוֹדִים לוֹ.
כֵּיצַד? אָמַר: "קוֹנָם שֶׁאֵינִי נוֹשֵׂא אֶת פְּלוֹנִית,
שֶׁאָבִיהָ רָע", אָמְרוּ לוֹ: "מֵת", אוֹ שֶׁעָשָׂה תְשׁוּבָה;

ר' עובדיה מברטנורא

או שהיה משיא את בנו בקרוב לא הייתי נודר. וכגון שנדרו לזמן ולא היה סבור שישיא את
בנו בתוך אותו זמן ויצטרך לילך לחופה בנו. והלכה כחכמים: **(ג) יש דברים שהם כנולד.**
נראין כנולד ואינם כנולד, ופותחין בהם: **אמרו לו מת וכו'.** ואף על גב דמיתה נולד הוי, הואיל
ופירש בשעת נדרו בעבור מה היה נודר, נעשה כתולה נדרו בדבר, כאילו פירש כל זמן שאביה
קיים, הלכך לא הוי נולד. אבל תנאי גמור לא הוי, הילכך צריך התרה, ובירושלמי **(ח, ג)** מוכח
שאין צריך התרה, וכן פירש רמב"ס:

יד אברהם

"אִלּוּ הָיִיתִי יוֹדֵעַ שֶׁהוּא נַעֲשֶׂה סוֹפֵר, אוֹ
שֶׁהוּא מַשִּׂיא אֶת בְּנוֹ בְּקָרוֹב - לֹא הָיִיתִי
נוֹדֵר!" — *"If I had known that he
would become a scribe, or that he was
about to marry off his son, I would not
have made the neder!";*

The mishnah is dealing with a case
in which the *neder* had a time limit
appended to it. Thus, even if the vower was aware that the object of his
neder had a marriageable son, he could
still argue that had he realized that a
wedding was to take place in the near
future — within the time limit — he
would not have made the *neder* (*Rav
following Rosh*).

"קוֹנָם לְבַיִת זֶה שֶׁאֵנִי נִכְנָס", וְנַעֲשָׂה בֵּית
הַכְּנֶסֶת, אָמַר: "אִלּוּ הָיִיתִי יוֹדֵעַ שֶׁהוּא נַעֲשֶׂה
בֵּית הַכְּנֶסֶת - לֹא הָיִיתִי נוֹדֵר!"— *[or if
one said:] "Konam, this house, with*

*respect to my entering [it]," and it was
made into a synagogue, [and] he said:
"If I had known that it would be made
into a synagogue, I would not have
made the neder"* —

[This is another illustration of an
unlikely and unexpected occurrence
which, although it prompts the person
to seek annulment of his *neder*, cannot
be used as an "opening," according to
the Sages.]

רַבִּי אֱלִיעֶזֶר מַתִּיר, וַחֲכָמִים אוֹסְרִין. — *R'
Eliezer permits it; the Sages, however,
forbid it.*

The mishnah repeats the views of
R' Eliezer and the Sages in order to
summarize the mishnah (*Ran*). The
halachah is in accordance with the
opinion of the Sages (*Rav; Yoreh Deah
228:12*).

25 — not applicable

"If I had known that he would become a scribe, or that he was about to marry off his son, I would not have made the *neder*!"; [or if one said:] "*Konam*, this house, with respect to my entering [it]," and it was made into a synagogue, [and] he said: "If I had known that it would be made into a synagogue, I would not have made the *neder*!" — R' Eliezer permits it; the Sages, however, forbid it.

3. **R'** Meir says: There are things which are like unexpected developments, and are not like unexpected developments; the Sages, however, do not agree with him. How? [If one] said: "*Konam*, my marrying So-and-so, because her father is evil," [and] they told him: "He died," or that he had repented;

YAD AVRAHAM

3.

רַבִּי מֵאִיר אוֹמֵר: יֵשׁ דְּבָרִים שֶׁהֵן כְּנוֹלָד, וְאֵינָן כְּנוֹלָד; — R' *Meir says: There are things which are like unexpected developments, and are not like unexpected developments;*

That is, there are things which might appear as though they should be treated like unexpected developments and should therefore not be acceptable for "openings"; yet, they are not treated as such, and are accepted (*Rav*).

וְאֵין חֲכָמִים מוֹדִים לוֹ. — *the Sages, however, do not agree with him.*

This is the standard version of the mishnah's text, which is followed by *Tosafos.* However, *Rambam, Ran, Meiri,* and others read: *The Sages agree. Rosh,* who discusses both readings, concludes that the preferred version is the latter — *The Sages agree with him* (*Tos. Yom Tov*).

כֵּיצַד? — *How?*

[The mishnah now presents some illustrations of R' Meir's case.]

אָמַר: „קוֹנָם שֶׁאֵינִי נוֹשֵׂא אֶת פְּלוֹנִית, שֶׁאָבִיהָ רַע", — *[If one] said: "Konam, my marrying So-and-so, because her father is evil,"*

[This *neder* forbids him to marry a certain woman, whose father is an evil man. Although he did not stipulate that the prohibition is made only on the condition that her father remain evil, it is clear that this was what prompted the *neder*.]

אָמְרוּ לוֹ: „מֵת", אוֹ שֶׁעָשָׂה תְּשׁוּבָה; — *[and] they told him: "He died," or that he had repented;*

At the time the *neder* was made, the father was alive and well, but evil. Surely, that he should die or repent would be classified as an *unexpected development* (*Gem.* 65a). Nevertheless, in the case of the mishnah, this is exactly what happens, and some time

„קוֹנָם לְבַיִת זֶה שֶׁאֵינִי נִכְנָס, שֶׁהַכֶּלֶב רַע בְּתוֹכוֹ״, אוֹ „שֶׁהַנָּחָשׁ בְּתוֹכוֹ״, אָמְרוּ לוֹ: „מֵת הַכֶּלֶב״, אוֹ שֶׁנֶּהֱרַג הַנָּחָשׁ, הֲרֵי הֵן כְּנוֹלָד וְאֵינָן כְּנוֹלָד. וְאֵין חֲכָמִים מוֹדִים לוֹ.

[ד] וְעוֹד אָמַר רַבִּי מֵאִיר: פּוֹתְחִין לוֹ מִן הַכָּתוּב שֶׁבַּתּוֹרָה, וְאוֹמְרִים לוֹ: „אִלּוּ הָיִיתָ יוֹדֵעַ שֶׁאַתָּה עוֹבֵר עַל ׳לֹא תִקֹּם׳, וְעַל ׳לֹא תִטֹּר׳, וְעַל ׳לֹא תִשְׂנָא אֶת אָחִיךָ בִּלְבָבֶךָ׳, ׳וְאָהַבְתָּ לְרֵעֲךָ כָּמוֹךָ׳,

---

יד אברהם

after the *neder* was put into effect, the person learns that the father unexpectedly died or repented. While, ordinarily, such developments would not qualify for a "way out" of the *neder*, the present case is different. For, by mentioning that he was proscribing the marriage to himself because of the evil father, it is as if he had explicitly stated that the prohibition should endure only as long as the objectionable factor — the father's evil — is present (*Rav*).

קוֹנָם לְבַיִת זֶה שֶׁאֵינִי נִכְנָס, שֶׁהַכֶּלֶב רַע בְּתוֹכוֹ״, אוֹ „שֶׁהַנָּחָשׁ בְּתוֹכוֹ״, אָמְרוּ לוֹ: „מֵת הַכֶּלֶב״, אוֹ שֶׁנֶּהֱרַג הַנָּחָשׁ, — "Konam, this house, with respect to my entering because an evil dog is in it," or "because a snake is in it," [and] they told him: "The dog died," or that the snake had been killed —

[Here, too, although the *neder* does not expressly stipulate that the prohibition shall endure only as long as the evil dog or snake inhabit the house, it gives that impression.]

הֲרֵי הֵן כְּנוֹלָד, וְאֵינָן כְּנוֹלָד. וְאֵין חֲכָמִים מוֹדִים לוֹ. — these are things which are

like unexpected developments, but are not like unexpected developments. The Sages, however, do not agree with him.

According to *Rambam* (Hil. Nedarim 8:1f.) and *Shulchan Aruch* (*Yoreh Deah* 228:19), once the person is informed that the motive for his *neder* has been eliminated, he is automatically released from the prohibition. This is because the *neder* is interpreted as though it actually stated that the prohibition should endure only as long as the father is evil, or the snake or dog is present. When and if that condition no longer exists (i.e., the father repents, the dog dies, etc.), the prohibition ceases.

[*Rav*, while citing conflicting opinions on this issue, appears to follow *Rosh* (65a) who contends that, because the *neder* did not explicitly stipulate that the prohibition hinges on the existence of some condition, annulment by a sage or panel is needed. However, *Rosh* himself in his *Pesakim* (9:3) cites *Yerushalmi* that no annulment is needed, and appears to concur with *Rambam*.]

"Konam, this house, with respect to my entering because an evil dog is in it" or "because a snake is in it," [and] they told him: "The dog died," or that the snake had been killed — these are things which are like unexpected developments, but are not like unexpected developments. The Sages, however, do not agree with him.

4. **R**' Meir also said: They can find ground to annul his *neder* from what is written in the Torah, and they say to him: "If you had known that you transgress *'You shall not take vengeance'* (*Lev.* 19:18), or *'You shall not bear a grudge'* (ibid.), or *'You shall not hate your brother in your heart'* (ibid. v. 17), or *'You shall love your fellow as yourself'* (ibid. v. 18),

YAD AVRAHAM
4.

וְעוֹד אָמַר רַבִּי מֵאִיר: פּוֹתְחִין לוֹ מִן הַכָּתוּב שֶׁבַּתּוֹרָה, — *R' Meir also said: They can find grounds to annul his neder from what is written in the Torah,*

Although, in mishnah 1, we are taught that to bring to the vower's attention that *neder*-making is an affront to the Divine honor is *not* a valid opening, this mishnah tells us that to point out to him that his *neder* may constitute a contravention of some specific commandment *written in the Torah* is a suitable opening. This is because a person will not admit to the panel or the sage his disregard for the Divine honor, but may admit to having transgressed a specific precept of the Torah. Thus, when asked if he would have made the *neder* despite knowing that it conflicts with a Biblical verse, he would not be afraid to answer affirmatively. Accordingly, if he answers "no," he is believed, and the *neder* is nullified (*Rav* 9:1; *Ran* 64a;

Rosh ibid.; cf. *Shach, Yoreh Deah* 228:17; *Meiri*).

וְאוֹמְרִים לוֹ: ,,אִלּוּ הָיִיתָ יוֹדֵעַ שֶׁאַתָּה עוֹבֵר עַל 'לֹא תִקֹּם', וְעַל 'לֹא תִטֹּר', — *and they say to him: "If you had known that you transgress 'You shall not take vengeance' (Lev. 19:18), or 'You shall not bear a grudge' (ibid.),*

An example of vengeance would be if a person refuses to lend another some tool, and the latter responds with a *neder* depriving the former of the use of his tool (*Rosh* 65b; *Tos. Yom Tov*).

וְעַל 'לֹא תִשְׂנָא אֶת אָחִיךָ בִּלְבָבֶךָ', 'וְאָהַבְתָּ לְרֵעֲךָ כָּמוֹךָ', — *or 'You shall not hate your brother in your heart' (ibid. v. 17), or 'You shall love your fellow as yourself' (ibid. v. 18).*

If, for example, he vowed not to inquire into the well-being of his fellow (*Rosh*), or, out of hate, he banned someone from deriving any benefit from him (*Rashi*).

'וְחֵי אָחִיךָ עִמָּךְ' — שֶׁמָּא יַעֲנִי וְאֵין אַתָּה יָכוֹל לְפַרְנְסוֹ". וְאָמַר: „אִלּוּ הָיִיתִי יוֹדֵעַ שֶׁהוּא כֵן — לֹא הָיִיתִי נוֹדֵר!" — הֲרֵי זֶה מֻתָּר.

[ה] פּוֹתְחִין לָאָדָם בִּכְתֻבַּת אִשְׁתּוֹ. וּמַעֲשֶׂה בְּאֶחָד שֶׁנָּדַר מֵאִשְׁתּוֹ הֲנָאָה וְהָיְתָה, כְּתֻבָּתָהּ אַרְבַּע מֵאוֹת דִּינָרִין, וּבָא לִפְנֵי רַבִּי עֲקִיבָא, וְחִיְּבוֹ לִתֵּן לָהּ כְּתֻבָּתָהּ.

───── **ר' עובדיה מברטנורא** ─────

(ד) **אילו הייתי יודע שבן הוא לא הייתי נודר הרי זה מותר.** אחר שיתירנו החכם. וכל המודר הנאה מחבירו כשמתירו לו אין מתירין אלא בפני חבירו, דכתיב (שמות ד, יט) ויאמר ה' אל משה במדין לך שוב, אמר לו הקדוש ברוך הוא למשה במדין נדרת לך והתר את נדרך, לפי שנשבע משה לחותנו שלא יזוז ממדין בלא רשותו, דכתיב (שם ב, כא) ויואל משה לשבת את האיש, והוצרכו הקדוש ברוך הוא ללכת להתיר נדרו בפניו: (ה) **פותחין לו בכתובת אשתו.** בפרטון כתובתה אם נדר לגרשה:

───── **יד אברהם** ─────

'וְחֵי אָחִיךָ עִמָּךְ' - שֶׁמָּא יַעֲנִי, וְאֵין אַתָּה יָכוֹל לְפַרְנְסוֹ." — [or] 'That your brother may live with you' (ibid. 25:36) — perhaps he will grow poor, and you will not be able to support him [would you have vowed?]."

[That is, the Torah commands us to sustain our impoverished fellow Jews. But, by forbidding another to benefit from one's belongings, he is making it impossible to assist the other person should the latter need help.]

This "opening" is valid even if the person at whom the neder is directed grows poor following the neder. As seen in the commentary to mishnah 2 (s.v. וַחֲכָמִים אוֹסְרִין), becoming poor is not considered an unexpected development.

The statement that this neder makes it impossible for the vower to support the impoverished object of the neder needs clarification. Why prevent the vower from contributing to the public charities so that the other person can turn to them for assistance? As soon as

the money is acquired by the public charities, it becomes permitted to Shimon, the person at whom the neder was directed, since it is no longer considered the vower's property (see 4:7ff).

The *Gemara* (65b) explains, however, that before a person turns to public funds he approaches those close to him (*Ran*). Moreover, according to *Rosh* (65b, s.v. אינו), the public funds need not assist someone who has not first turned to his relatives (see *Keren Orah*). If, at that time, the neder makes Reuven unable to help, he already transgresses the obligation to sustain one's brother (*Tos. Yom Tov*).

וְאָמַר: „אִלּוּ הָיִיתִי יוֹדֵעַ שֶׁהוּא כֵן - לֹא הָיִיתִי נוֹדֵר!" - הֲרֵי זֶה מֻתָּר. — *If he said: "Had I known that this was so, I would not have made the neder" – it is permitted.*

[That is, this claim is sufficient grounds to have the neder annulled by a sage or a panel of three.] *Rav* (following *Rambam Comm.*) adds that,

[or] *'That your brother may live with you'* (ibid. 25:36) — perhaps he will grow poor, and you will not be able to support him [would you have vowed?]" If he said: "Had I known that this was so, I would not have made the *neder!*" — it is permitted.

5. **T**hey can find grounds to annul a man's *neder* by [reason of] his wife's *kesubah*. It happened once that a person made a *neder* prohibiting benefit from his wife, and her *kesubah* was four hundred dinars. He came before R' Akiva, who obligated him

YAD AVRAHAM

when seeking to nullify a *neder* directed at another person, both parties must be at the annulment proceedings (see *Gem.* 65a; *Rambam, Hil. Shevuos* 6:7).

5.

פּוֹתְחִין לָאָדָם בִּכְתֻבַּת אִשְׁתּוֹ. — *They can find grounds to annul a man's neder by [reason of] his wife's kesubah.*

The *kesubah* (marriage contract) is a document given to the wife upon marriage containing, among other matters, the settlement of a stated amount due her should she be widowed or divorced (see General Introduction to ArtScroll *Kesubos*).

Payment of the *kesubah* is not considered an unexpected development, and hence, may be used to devise an "opening" for a *neder* (*Tos.* 65b; *Meiri*).

וּמַעֲשֶׂה בְּאֶחָד שֶׁנָּדַר מֵאִשְׁתּוֹ הֲנָאָה, — *It happened once that a person made a neder prohibiting benefit from his wife,*

[For example, he declared that the enjoyment he experiences on having relations with her should be forbidden him with a *neder* (see 2:1). Such a *neder*, which makes it impossible for the husband to fulfill his conjugal duty toward his wife, obligates him to

give her a divorce (see commentary to *Kesubos* 5:6; *Yoreh Deah* 235:1).]

Meiri explains the case as involving a *neder* depriving his wife from benefiting from him, which, in the cases detailed in *Kesubos* Chapter 7, also necessitate the husband to divorce her. However, the standard text of the mishnah reads: שֶׁנָּדַר מֵאִשְׁתּוֹ הֲנָאָה, *[he] made a neder, prohibiting benefit from his wife*, and not vice versa.

Rav follows *Rosh* (65b), who construes our mishnah to mean that the husband made a *neder* to divorce her. Since a *neder* can only prohibit and not obligate one to do an act (see General Introduction and *Ran* 8a, s.v. והלא), this comment needs explanation. From *Gittin* 46b, it appears that a *neder* to divorce is of the form: "Konam, fruits to me, unless I divorce my wife." Thus, the *neder* forces him to divorce her (see *Rav* to *Gittin* 4:7). *Gilyonei HaShas* notes that the expression, נָדַר לְגָרֵשׁ — *he made a neder to divorce*, occurs in *Tosefta Gittin* 3:8.

אָמַר לוֹ: ,,רַבִּי! שְׁמוֹנֶה מֵאוֹת דִּינָרִין הִנִּיחַ
אַבָּא, וְנָטַל אָחִי אַרְבַּע מֵאוֹת וַאֲנִי אַרְבַּע
מֵאוֹת, לֹא דַיָּהּ שֶׁתִּטּוֹל הִיא מָאתַיִם, וַאֲנִי
מָאתַיִם?״ אָמַר לוֹ רַבִּי עֲקִיבָא: ,,אֲפִלּוּ אַתָּה
מוֹכֵר שְׂעַר רֹאשְׁךָ, אַתָּה נוֹתֵן לָהּ כְּתֻבָּתָהּ.״
אָמַר לוֹ: ,,אִלּוּ הָיִיתִי יוֹדֵעַ שֶׁהוּא כֵּן — לֹא
הָיִיתִי נוֹדֵר!״ וְהִתִּירָהּ רַבִּי עֲקִיבָא.

[ו] **פּוֹתְחִין** בְּיָמִים טוֹבִים וּבְשַׁבָּתוֹת.

(ו) **פותחין בימים טובים ובשבתות.** אם נדר להתענות או שלא לאכול בשר לזמן קבוע,
אומרים לו אילו שמת אל לבך לשבתות וימים טובים שבתוך זמן זה כלום היית נודר, ואין זה פותח
בכבוד המקום:

וְהָיְתָה כְתֻבָּתָהּ אַרְבַּע מֵאוֹת דִּינָרִין, וּבָא
— לִפְנֵי רַבִּי עֲקִיבָא, וְחִיְּבוֹ לִתֵּן לָהּ כְּתֻבָּתָהּ.
*and her kesubah was four hundred
dinars. He came before R' Akiva, who
obligated him to pay her kesubah to
her.*

R' Akiva obligated him to divorce
her and pay the settlement of four
hundred dinars due her (*Ritva*).

אָמַר לוֹ: ,,רַבִּי! שְׁמוֹנֶה מֵאוֹת דִּינָרִין הִנִּיחַ
אַבָּא, וְנָטַל אָחִי אַרְבַּע מֵאוֹת וַאֲנִי אַרְבַּע
מֵאוֹת. לֹא דַיָּהּ שֶׁתִּטּוֹל הִיא מָאתַיִם, וַאֲנִי
מָאתַיִם?״ — *He said to him: "Rabbi!
Father left eight hundred dinars, my
brother took four hundred, and I took
four hundred. Is it not enough that she
should take two hundred and I, two
hundred?'*

Although, in modern times, the kesubah may be paid even with chattels,
such as money, this is an innovation
established in the Geonic period (*Rambam Hil. Ishus* 16:7; *Even HaEzer* 100:1).
However, in Talmudic times, the kesubah was payable only with land (see
Kesubos 8:7 and comm. ad loc.).

Accordingly, the *Gemara* (65b)
explains that the father bequeathed
eight hundred dinars worth of land.
The husband in our case, who in-
herited four hundred dinars, apparently owns no other property. He
therefore pleaded with R' Akiva that
he be allowed to retain two hundred
dinars worth of land for himself, and
pay the wife only two hundred of the
four hundred dinars that is owed her.

In general, the law for a debtor who
claims bankruptcy allows him to
retain for himself enough to cover
food for a month and clothes for a
year (*Bava Metzia* 113b). However,
the obligation in not abrogated, and
— should his financial condition
improve — he must pay what remains
of his debt (*Gem.* 66a).

אָמַר לוֹ רַבִּי עֲקִיבָא: ,,אֲפִלּוּ אַתָּה מוֹכֵר שְׂעַר
רֹאשְׁךָ, — *R'*
אַתָּה נוֹתֵן לָהּ כְּתֻבָּתָהּ.״
*Akiva said to him: "Even if you have to
sell the hair on your head, you must
pay her kesubah to her."*

"Even if you have to sell the hair on

to pay her *kesubah* to her. He said to him: "Rabbi! Father left eight hundred dinars, my brother took four hundred, and I took four hundred. Is it not enough that she should take two hundred and I, two hundred?" R' Akiva said to him: "Even if you have to sell the hair on your head, you must pay her *kesubah* to her." He said to him: "Had I known that this was so, I would not have made the *neder*." Thereupon, R' Akiva permitted her.

6. **T**hey can find grounds to annul a *neder* by [reason of] festivals or Sabbaths.

YAD AVRAHAM

your head to provide sustenance for yourself, *you must pay her kesubah to her* from the land" (*Gem.* 65b). The Gemara must interpret the mishnah this way, because shorn human hair, being movable, is not suitable for payment of a *kesubah* (see *Tif. Yis.* 18). He did not mean, however, that the husband must hand over the four hundred dinars of land immediately. For, if to do so would leave the husband bankrupt, he is entitled to retain a certain amount for his basic needs, as mentioned above (see *Ara-chin* 6:3). He meant, rather, that the obligation remains in force until it is fully paid with land (*Tos. Yom Tov*).

אָמַר לוֹ: ,,אִלּוּ הָיִיתִי יוֹדֵעַ שֶׁהוּא כֵן – לֹא הָיִיתִי נוֹדֵר". וְהִתִּירָהּ רַבִּי עֲקִיבָא. — *He said to him:"Had I known that this was so, I would not have made the neder." Thereupon, R' Akiva permitted her.*

[The translation *permitted her* follows the standard texts. It must be explained to mean that R' Akiva annulled the husband's *neder* using the payment of the *kesubah* as the "opening"; hence, she was again permitted to her husband.

Another reading is וְהִתִּירוֹ (*Shinuyei Nuschaos*), which would translate either as *he permitted it* — referring to the *neder* — or *he permitted him*, referring to the husband.]

6.

פּוֹתְחִין בְּיָמִים טוֹבִים וּבַשַׁבָּתוֹת. — *They can find grounds to annul a neder by [reason of] festivals or Sabbaths.*

If someone made a *neder* to fast or to abstain from meat for a fixed period of time, the occurrence within that period of a festival or a Sabbath may be used to devise an "opening" (*Rav*).

If, for example, he adopted a thirty-day ban on meat, not realizing that a

festival — during which one must eat meat (see *Rambam Comm.*). — falls within that period, the sage or panel might then ask him if he would have made the *neder* had he realized this. If he answers negatively, the *neder* can be annulled (*Rav; Rosh*).

Similarly, if he was aware that his period of abstention included Sabbath or a festival, but he was not aware that

בָּרִאשׁוֹנָה הָיוּ אוֹמְרִים: אוֹתָן הַיָּמִים — מֻתָּרִין, וּשְׁאָר כָּל הַיָּמִים — אֲסוּרִין; עַד שֶׁבָּא רַבִּי עֲקִיבָא וְלִמֵּד, שֶׁהַנֶּדֶר שֶׁהֻתַּר מִקְצָתוֹ — הֻתַּר כֻּלּוֹ.

[ז] כֵּיצַד? אָמַר: „קוֹנָם שֶׁאֵינִי נֶהֱנֶה לְכֻלְּכֶם", הֻתַּר אֶחָד מֵהֶן — הֻתְּרוּ כֻלָּן. „שֶׁאֵינִי נֶהֱנֶה לָזֶה וְלָזֶה", הֻתַּר הָרִאשׁוֹן —

אוֹתָן הַיָּמִים. שׁמֻלּא להֶס פֶתח להתחרט, מוּתּרים, שֶׁהֻחכּס מתירין: **וּשְׁאָר הַיָּמִים.** שֶׁאֵין עליהֶס חרטה, נֶשׁארין בּאיסורֶן: **שֶׁנֶּדֶר שֶׁהֻתַּר מִקְצָתוֹ הוּתַּר כֻּלּוֹ.** אַף עַל פּי שֶׁלּא מֻלּא פֶתח עַל כוּלּוֹ, דּלא נֶדר מֵטיקרמֵ אֶלּא עַל דּעת שֶׁיֻתקיֵיס כוּלּוֹ, נמֻלּא התֶרֶת מקֶצתוֹ פֶתח לכוּלּוֹ: **(ז) לָזֶה וְלָזֶה.** כּגוֹן שֶׁאֶסֶר הֶראשׁוֹן עֶליו בּקוֹנס, ואֶמֶר עֶל הֶשֶׁני הֶרי זֶה כֶראשׁוֹן וֶעֶל הֶשׁלישׁי הֶרי זֶה כֶשׁני, וכֵן כּוּלּס, הוּתַּר הֶראשׁוֹן הוּתּרוּ כוּלּס, שֶׁכּוּלּס תּלוּיֵין בּוֹ:

on these days one must eat meat, and he claims that, had he realized this, he would not have made a *neder*, then it may be annulled (*Meiri*).

בָּרִאשׁוֹנָה הָיוּ אוֹמְרִים: אוֹתָן הַיָּמִים — מֻתָּרִין, וּשְׁאָר כָּל הַיָּמִים — אֲסוּרִין; — *At first they used to say: Those days are permitted, but all the other days are forbidden —*

[Originally, it was the practice in such a case to rule that the prohibition remain in force except on the Sabbath or festivals, for which days it is annulled. The obligation to eat on those special days does not conflict with a desire to abstain from food on ordinary days. Thus, only with respect to the Sabbath and the festival was the *neder* based on a lack of information; for ordinary days, however, the prohibition could remain intact.]

עַד שֶׁבָּא רַבִּי עֲקִיבָא וְלִמֵּד, שֶׁהַנֶּדֶר שֶׁהֻתַּר מִקְצָתוֹ - הֻתַּר כֻּלּוֹ. — *until R' Akiva*

7.

כֵּיצַד? — *How?*

[Following R' Akiva's ruling in the

came and taught that a *neder* which has been nullified in part is nullified in its entirety.

Even though no "opening" was found with respect to ordinary weekdays, R' Akiva maintains that, when declaring a prohibition, the person wants it to be effective as declared, or not at all. Hence, as long as an "opening" for just part of the *neder* can be found, the entire *neder* will be annulled (*Rav; Rosh*). *Ran* cites *Yerushalmi*, according to which R' Akiva finds support for this argument in the verse (*Num.* 30:3), *Like all that issues from his mouth he shall do*, which he interprets to mean that a *neder* is binding only when *all* of it is binding. Thus, R' Akiva taught on the basis of this verse that *a neder which has been nullified in part is nullified in its entirety* (*Tos. Yom Tov*).

previous mishnah that a *neder* is either effective in its entirety or not at all, the

At first they used to say: Those days are permitted, but all the other days are forbidden — until R' Akiva came and taught that a *neder* which has been nullified in part is nullified in its entirety.

7. **H**ow? [In a case where someone] said: "*Konam*, what benefit I derive from any of you," if one of them is permitted — they are all permitted. "What I benefit from this one and from this one," if the first one is permitted —

YAD AVRAHAM

mishnah now provides guidelines with which to assess a declaration that produces more than one forbidden entity. The determining factor will be whether the declaration entails more than one prohibition, each one banning a specific item, or whether all the forbidden items are generated by a single prohibition.

In the latter case, in which a single *neder* prohibits several independent entities, R' Akiva's rule that *a neder nullified in part is nullified in its entirety* applies. But, if each interdicted item is the consequence of an independent prohibition, the annulment of one prohibition has no bearing on the remaining items which remain forbidden.]

אָמַר: "קוֹנָם שֶׁאֵינִי נֶהֱנֶה לְכֻלְכֶם", — [In a case where someone] said: "Konam, what benefit I derive from any (lit., all) of you,"

[He addresses a group of several persons and declares the benefit he might derive from any of them to be forbidden to himself.]

הֻתַּר אֶחָד מֵהֶן - הֻתְּרוּ כֻלָּן. — if one of them is permitted — they are all permitted.

That is, if the prohibition is abrogated with regard to even one member

of the group by a sage or panel, the *neder* is completely voided (*Shach, Yoreh Deah* 229:4; see also mishnah 8). [A declaration directed at "*any of you*" is considered one *neder*. Therefore, R' Akiva's rule applies, and a nullification of part of the *neder* nullifies all of it.]

"שֶׁאֵינִי נֶהֱנֶה לָזֶה וְלָזֶה", — "What I benefit from this one and from this one" —

[And so on, specifying each member of the group he wishes to prohibit to himself.]

The *Gemara* (26b) explains that the case under consideration involves a declaration in which he made a series of prohibitions, each one based on the one preceding it. For example, he declares: "*Konam*, benefit from Reuven to me." He then adds that Shimon should be like Reuven, and Levi like Shimon, etc.

From *Rav* (following *Rosh* 66a) it appears that the text of the mishnah (*from this one and from this one*) is not the text of the actual declarations, and that the *Gemara* is amending the mishnah (*Shoshannim LeDavid; Tos. Yom Tov*). If, on the other hand, someone were to use the formula which appears in the mishnah — *from*

הַתְּרוּ כֻלָּן; הֻתַּר הָאַחֲרוֹן — הָאַחֲרוֹן מֻתָּר, וְכֻלָּן אֲסוּרִין; הֻתַּר הָאֶמְצָעִי — הֵימֶנּוּ וּלְמַטָּה מֻתָּר, הֵימֶנּוּ וּלְמַעְלָה אָסוּר. שֶׁאֵינִי נֶהֱנֶה לָזֶה קָרְבָּן, וְלָזֶה קָרְבָּן — צְרִיכִין פֶּתַח לְכָל אֶחָד וְאֶחָד.

[ח] **,,קוֹנָם** יַיִן שֶׁאֵינִי טוֹעֵם, שֶׁהַיַּיִן רַע לַמֵּעַיִם'',

---

ר' עובדיה מברטנורא

לזה קרבן ולזה קרבן. הא מתניתין רבי שמעון היא דאמר גבי שבועת הפקדון (שבועות לח, א) אם היו חמשה תובעים אותו וכפר ונשבע והודה שאינו חייב לזה קרבן ולזה קרבן על כל אחד עד שיאמר שבועה לכל אחד ואחד, והכא נמי צריך שיאמר לזה קרבן ולזה קרבן, אבל חכמים אומרים אם אמר שבועה שאיני לך ולא לך ולא לך על כל אחד ואחד, חייב על כל לזה ולזה ולא זה ולא לזה, אף על פי שלא הזכיר קרבן על כל אחד הוי כל אחד נדר בפני עצמו. וכן הלכה:

יד אברהם

this one and from this one — the law will be different, as explained below.

However, *Rambam* (Hil. Nedarim 4:11) seems to construe the *Gemara* as interpreting the mishnah's formula, and not as making a textual correction. In other words, if someone declared, *"Konam, what I benefit from this one and from this one,"* it is tantamount to forbidding the first person with a *neder*, and making the second person like the first (*Tos. Yom Tov*). *Lechem Mishneh* (Hil. Nedarim 4:11) and *Beur HaGra* (Yoreh Deah 229:4) both note that these differing approaches to the mishnah appear to depend on two variant texts of the *Gemara*.

הֻתַּר הָרִאשׁוֹן – הַתְּרוּ כֻלָּן; הֻתַּר הָאַחֲרוֹן – הָאַחֲרוֹן מֻתָּר, וְכֻלָּן אֲסוּרִין; הֻתַּר הָאֶמְצָעִי — הֵימֶנּוּ וּלְמַטָּה מֻתָּר, הֵימֶנּוּ וּלְמַעְלָה אָסוּר. *if the first one is permitted — they are all permitted; if the last one is permitted — the last one is permitted, but all the others are forbidden; if one in between* (lit., *the middle one*) *is permitted — from him and down are permitted, from him and up are forbidden.*

Since, as explained, the prohibition

of each subsequent person is based on the preceding prohibition, the mishnah rules that those prohibited later remain prohibited only as long as the earlier prohibitions remain. Thus, if — for example — ten people are forbidden by this *neder*, all are dependent on the first person's being forbidden. Should a sage or panel find reason to annul the *neder* with regard to the first person, the remaining nine persons are automatically also permitted, since the basis for their prohibition has been removed.

If, however, the prohibition of the last one is nullified, benefit from him will be permitted, but benefit from the first nine persons will remain interdicted. Since each person was specified by the vower saying (according to *Rav*:) "this one shall be like this one," or (according to *Rambam*:) "from this one and from this one," each prohibition is considered to derive from a distinct *neder* and R' Akiva's rule does not apply (*Rosh* 26b, s.v. וסיפא).

Similarly, if one of the intermediate persons is released from the *neder*, all the persons whose prohibition fol-

they are all permitted; if the last one is permitted —
the last one is permitted, but all the others are
forbidden; if one in between is permitted — from him
and down are permitted, from him and up are
forbidden. "What I benefit from this one is *korban*,
and from this one, *korban*" — grounds to annul each
neder are needed.

8. **[** If one said:] "*Konam*, wine, with respect to my
tasting [it] because wine is bad for the bowels,"

YAD AVRAHAM

lowed his — and therefore, depended
on his — are released. But all those that
preceded his remain forbidden (ibid.).

שֶׁאֵינִי נֶהֱנֶה לָזֶה קָרְבָּן, וְלָזֶה קָרְבָּן" —
צְרִיכִין פֶּתַח לְכָל אֶחָד וְאֶחָד. — "*What I
benefit from this one is korban, and
from this one, korban*" — *grounds to
annul each neder are needed.*

Here, each person is forbidden by
distinct declaration of prohibition;
hence, R' Akiva's rule does not apply
(*Rav*).

The specific mention of the word
korban in connection with each person from whom benefit is being
forbidden is what separates one prohibition from the other. The *Gemara*
(66a) attributes this view to R' Shimon, who follows a similar approach
in *Shevuos* 5:3. The Sages (ibid.),
however, would consider the prohibitions to be unrelated, even without
repeated mention of the word *korban*.
According to *Rav*, the Sages maintain

that a declaration of the form, "*Konam, what I benefit from this one and
from this one, etc.,*" creates unrelated
prohibitions. Although the mishnah
above appears to classify such a
declaration as creating interdependent prohibitions, *Rav*, as noted
above, construes that section of the
mishnah to have been changed by the
Gemara (see above).

According to *Rambam*, the formula
from this one and from this one creates
interdependent prohibitions. However, if a person were to declare,
"*Konam, what I benefit from this
one, from this one, from this one,
etc.,*" without the conjunction *and*, the
Sages would treat this as creating
unrelated prohibitions, to which R'
Akiva's rule does not apply (*Rambam,
Hil. Nedarim* 4:11).

Rav rules in accordance with the Sages.
Shulchan Aruch (*Yoreh Deah* 229:1), however, seems undecided.

8.

The Mishnah continues to illustrate the principle stated above (mishnah 6),
that a *neder* which has been canceled in part is canceled completely.

„קוֹנָם יַיִן שֶׁאֵינִי טוֹעֵם שֶׁהַיַּיִן רַע לַמֵּעַיִם", —
*[If one said:] "Konam, wine, with
respect to my tasting [it] because wine*

is bad for the bowels,"
[A person forbids himself all wine
on the assumption that it is injurious.]

אָמְרוּ לוֹ: ,,וַהֲלֹא הַמְיֻשָּׁן יָפֶה לַמֵּעַיִם?" — הֻתַּר
בַּמְיֻשָּׁן; וְלֹא בַמְיֻשָּׁן בִּלְבַד הֻתַּר, אֶלָּא בְּכָל הַיַּיִן.
,,קוֹנָם בָּצָל שֶׁאֵינִי טוֹעֵם, שֶׁהַבָּצָל רַע לַלֵּב", אָמְרוּ
לוֹ: ,,הֲלֹא הַכֻּפְרִי יָפֶה לַלֵּב?" — הֻתַּר בַּכֻּפְרִי; וְלֹא
בַכֻּפְרִי בִּלְבַד הֻתַּר, אֶלָּא בְּכָל הַבְּצָלִים. מַעֲשֶׂה
הָיָה, וְהִתִּירוּ רַבִּי מֵאִיר בְּכָל הַבְּצָלִים.

─────────── ר' עובדיה מברטנורא ───────────

(ח) ולא במיושן בלבד הותר אלא בכל היין. ודוקא שאמר אילו ידעתי כן לא הייתי נודר
כלל או הייתי אומר יושן ישן מותר וחדש אסור, אבל אמר אילו הייתי יודע הייתי אומר כל יין אסור
עלי חוץ מן הישן, הרי זה אין מותר לו אלא הישן בלבד, וכל שאר יין אסור:

─────────── יד אברהם ───────────

אָמְרוּ לוֹ: ,,וַהֲלֹא הַמְיֻשָּׁן יָפֶה לַמֵּעַיִם?" —
הֻתַּר בַּמְיֻשָּׁן; — [and] they said to him:
"But isn't old wine good for the
bowels?" — he is permitted aged wine;

In *Bava Basra* (6:3), the mishnah explains that aged wine is at least three
years old. Since such wine is good for the
bowels, the *neder* was based on incorrect
information. Therefore, he is permitted
aged wine without having the *neder*
annulled, since — with regard to aged
wine — there was no intent to prohibit
(*Ran* 66a; *Meiri*; see *Rashash*).

וְלֹא בַמְיֻשָּׁן בִּלְבַד הֻתַּר, אֶלָּא בְּכָל הַיַּיִן. —
and not only is he permitted aged wine
but all wine.

[Since the *neder* is canceled with
respect to aged wine, it is completely
canceled, following R' Akiva's rule
(mishnah 6).]

However, this case differs somewhat from those discussed above. In
those instances, the release from part of
the *neder* was accomplished through
annulment based on an "opening."
Here, the part of the *neder* which is
canceled is based on misinformation.
There was never an intention to forbid
wine that is not detrimental to one's
health, and so, the *neder* which intended to restrict all wine was in error.

Therefore, *Darkei Moshe* (*Yoreh
Deah* 232:5) and *Shach* (ibid. 229:4)
contend that this difference leads to the
following distinction based on the
Gemara (26b). Whereas, in the cases of
mishnayos 6 and 7, once part of the *neder* is nullified, the rest also falls away, in
this case — in which the cancellation of
part was due to its being in error — the
cancellation of the rest of the *neder* will
depend on the person's reaction upon
discovering his mistake. If, on learning
that aged wine is not damaging to the
health, he states that, had he known
this, he would not have made the *neder*
at all, or he would have used a different
formulation altogether, the *neder* is
canceled in its entirety in accordance
with R' Akiva's rule. If, however, he
reacts by saying that he would have
made the *neder* using the same formula,
with an addition of a clause excluding
aged wine, then the remaining *neder* is
not canceled. He will indeed be permitted aged wine, but he will be
forbidden other wines.

An example of a new formulation
of the *neder* would be the declaration:
"Used wine is permitted; new wine is
forbidden like *konam*." This bears no
resemblance to the original declara-

[and] they said to him: "But isn't old wine good for the bowels?" — he is permitted aged wine; and not only is he permitted aged wine but all wine. "*Konam*, onions, with respect to my tasting [them] because onions are bad for the heart," [and] they said to him: "But isn't village onion good for the heart?" — he is permitted the village onion; and not only is he permitted the village onion, but also all onions. It once happened, and R' Meir permitted him all onions.

YAD AVRAHAM

tion: "*Konam*, wine, with respect to my tasting, etc." The entire original declaration is therefore canceled (*Rav*).

An example of the original declaration with a clause appended to it would be: "*Konam*, wine, with respect to my tasting it, except for aged wine." If the person indicates that he would have amended his original declaration in this fashion, we say that his original declaration is not completely annulled. Rather, we interpret it as though it never included aged wine. Thus, while he is permitted aged wine, he is forbidden all other wines (*Rav*).

Tos. Yom Tov to mishnah 6 quotes *Rosh*, who interprets mishnah 7 as relating also to the case of a *neder*, part of which was canceled due to error. In light of the above, however, it is clear that, in such a case, the person's reaction must be analyzed before R' Akiva's rule can be applied. [Accordingly, in the commentary to mishnayos 6 and 7, we have explained the cancellation of part of the *neder* to be due to an "opening" only. If, on the other hand, the cancellation had its origin in a *neder* based on misinformation, then the extent to which the person rejects his initial formulation must be taken into account.]

,,קוֹנָם בָּצָל שֶׁאֵינִי טוֹעֵם, שֶׁהַבָּצָל רַע לַלֵב'',
— אָמְרוּ לוֹ: ,,הֲלֹא הַכֻּפְרִי יָפֶה לַלֵב?'' —
"*Konam*, onions (lit., an onion), with

respect to my tasting [them] because onions are bad for the heart," [and] they said to him: "But isn't the village onion good for the heart?'"

The translation follows *Rav* (*Terumos* 2:5) and *Aruch* (s.v. כפר). *Tosafos* (26b, s.v. כופר) explains כֻּפְרִי to be the name of a place [Cyprus (?)]. *Rosh* (26b) renders it *a large, fully ripened onion* (cf. *Rashi* to *Bava Kamma* 80a, s.v. כלבים, and to *Yevamos* 59a, s.v. כופרי).

הֻתַּר בַּכֻּפְרִי; וְלֹא בַּכֻּפְרִי בִּלְבַד הֻתַּר, אֶלָּא בְּכָל הַבְּצָלִים. — *he is permitted the village onion; and not only is he permitted the village onion, but also all onions.*

Again, R' Akiva's rule that the *neder* will be entirely canceled if a part of it is canceled will apply only if the person — upon learning of his error — totally rejects his original formulation.

If, however, he reacts by saying that he would have declared: "All onions ... except village onions," although he is permitted village onions, he is forbidden all others (*Rav; Yoreh Deah* 232:9).

מַעֲשֶׂה הָיָה, וְהִתִּירוּ רַבִּי מֵאִיר בְּכָל הַבְּצָלִים. — *It once happened, and R' Meir permitted him all onions.*

[In contrast with the earlier practice

[ט] **פּוֹתְחִין** לָאָדָם בִּכְבוֹד עַצְמוֹ וּבִכְבוֹד
בָּנָיו. אוֹמְרִים לוֹ: ,,אִלּוּ הָיִיתָ
יוֹדֵעַ שֶׁלְּמָחָר אוֹמְרִין עָלֶיךָ: 'כָּךְ הִיא וֶסְתּוֹ שֶׁל
פְּלוֹנִי, מְגָרֵשׁ אֶת נָשָׁיו', וְעַל בְּנוֹתֶיךָ יִהְיוּ
אוֹמְרִין: 'בְּנוֹת גְּרוּשׁוֹת הֵן; מָה רָאֲתָה אִמָּן שֶׁל
אֵלּוּ לְהִתְגָּרֵשׁ?' ". וְאָמַר: אִלּוּ הָיִיתִי יוֹדֵעַ שֶׁכֵּן
– לֹא הָיִיתִי נוֹדֵר!" – הֲרֵי זֶה מֻתָּר.

ר' עובדיה מברטנורא

(ט) פותחין לאדם בכבוד עצמו ובכבוד בניו. אם נדר לגרש את אשתו: מה ראתה אמן
להתגרש. אם לא שנמצא בה ערות דבר, ונמצא פוגם את בניו, ולא חיישינן שמא ישקר שהוא
אינו מתחרט אלא שהוא בוש לומר שאינו חושש לכבוד בניו:

יד אברהם

(mentioned in mishnah 6) before R'
Akiva's teaching became widespread,
R' Meir implemented R' Akiva's
ruling in an actual case. The mishnah

mentions this, presumably to establish R' Akiva's ruling as prevalent,
and indeed, the halachah follows it
(see *Yoreh Deah* 229:1, 232:7).]

9.

פוֹתְחִין לָאָדָם בִּכְבוֹד עַצְמוֹ וּבִכְבוֹד בָּנָיו —
*They can find grounds to annul a
person's neder by [reason of] his own
honor or the honor of his children.*

If a person made a *neder* which
forces him to divorce his wife (see
mishnah 5), the ensuing damage to his
reputation, or that of his children,
may be used as an argument for an
"opening" with which to annul his
neder (*Rav*).

אוֹמְרִים לוֹ: ,,אִלּוּ הָיִיתָ יוֹדֵעַ שֶׁלְּמָחָר אוֹמְרִין
עָלֶיךָ: 'כָּךְ הִיא וֶסְתּוֹ שֶׁל פְּלוֹנִי, מְגָרֵשׁ
אֶת נָשָׁיו', — *They say to him: "If you
would have known that tomorrow
they would say about you: 'Such
is the habit of So-and-so — he
divorces his wives,'*

[People talking about him in this
fashion will affect his respectability.
This may be used as an "opening" if
the person concedes that, had he

realized this undesirable consequence,
he would not have made the *neder*.]

Although a person who makes a
neder depriving himself of something
seems to be prepared to endure
physical suffering, he is not prepared
to see his reputation ruined. Thus, one
who, for example, forbade fruit for
himself unless he divorces his wife
(see commentary to mishnah 5) is
believed if he claims that he would
not have made the *neder* had he
realized that it would hurt his reputation (*Tif. Yis.* 30).

וְעַל בְּנוֹתֶיךָ יִהְיוּ אוֹמְרִין: — *and about
your daughters they will say:*

The knowledge that people will
gossip about his wife and daughters
serves as a deterrent for the *neder*. For
if his wife's reputation is damaged, it
will affect their daughters' chances of
marriage, since people assume that the

9. **T**hey can find grounds to annul a person's *neder* by [reason of] his own honor or the honor of his children. They say to him: "If you would have known that tomorrow they would say about you: 'Such is the habit of So-and-so — he divorces his wives,' and about your daughters they will say: 'They are daughters of a divorced woman; what did their mother see to bring about her divorce?' [would you have vowed?]." If he said: "Had I known that this would be so, I would not have vowed!" — it is permitted.

daughters emulate their mothers (*Tos. Yom Tov*).

'בְּנוֹת גְּרוּשׁוֹת הֵן, מָה רָאֲתָה אִמָּן שֶׁל אֵלּוּ לְהִתְגָּרֵשׁ?." — *They are daughters of a divorced woman; what did their mothers see to bring about her divorce? [would you have vowed?]"*

That is, "What did she find so appealing to involve herself in, knowing that it would lead to her divorce?" In other words, people would suspect the mother of adultery (*Tos. Yom Tov*).

Some texts have: "*What did he see in their mother that caused him to divorce her?*" (*Rishon LeTzion*).

וְאָמַר: ,,אִלּוּ הָיִיתִי יוֹדֵעַ שֶׁכֵּן - לֹא הָיִיתִי נוֹדֵר!" — *If he said: "Had I known*

that this would be so, I would not have vowed!" —

The person's claim that consideration for his honor or that of his children would have made him refrain from making the *neder* is believed. We do not suspect that a person would be too embarrassed to admit that he would have made the *neder* in spite of his children's honor; if it were so, he would admit it. Thus, when he contends that it is not the case, he is believed (*Rav*).

הֲרֵי זֶה מֻתָּר. — *it is permitted.*

That is, the sage or panel declare the *neder* to be permitted on the basis of this "opening" (*Rambam*).

10.

In the case of one who forbids marriage of some woman "because her father is evil" (mishnah 3), the declaration is interpreted as though it read "as long as her father is evil.' The mention of the factor — the father's wickedness — which prompted the *neder* enables us to classify the declaration as one which hinges on the existence of that factor. Once that circumstance ceases to exist, even if it is because of an unexpected development, the prohibition is lifted (see commentary ibid.).

In this mishnah, a *neder* that seems to mention the factor which prompted it is nevertheless not treated like a conditional *neder*. The reasons for this will be discussed below.

[י] ,,**קוֹנָם** שֶׁאֵינִי נוֹשֵׂא אֶת פְּלוֹנִית
כְּעוּרָה'', וַהֲרֵי הִיא נָאָה;
,,שְׁחוֹרָה'', וַהֲרֵי הִיא לְבָנָה; ,,קְצָרָה'', וְהֲרֵי
הִיא אֲרֻכָּה — מֻתָּר בָּהּ. לֹא מִפְּנֵי שֶׁהִיא
כְּעוּרָה וְנַעֲשֵׂית נָאָה, שְׁחוֹרָה וְנַעֲשֵׂית לְבָנָה,
קְצָרָה וְנַעֲשֵׂית אֲרֻכָּה, אֶלָּא שֶׁהַנֶּדֶר טָעוּת.
וּמַעֲשֶׂה בְּאֶחָד שֶׁנָּדַר מִבַּת אֲחוֹתוֹ הֲנָיָה,
וְהִכְנִיסוּהָ לְבֵית רַבִּי יִשְׁמָעֵאל וְיִפּוּהָ. אָמַר לוֹ
רַבִּי יִשְׁמָעֵאל: ,,בְּנִי! לָזוֹ נָדַרְתָּ?'' אָמַר לוֹ:

ר' עובדיה מברטנורא

(י) אלא שהנדר טעות. מעיקרו, שבשעת הנדר היתה לבנה, ואינו צריך שאלה לחכם: **מעשה באחד שנדר וכו'.** בגמרא (סו, א) מפרש דחסורי מחסרא, והכי קתני, רבי ישמעאל קומר אפילו כעורה ונעשית יפה שחורה ונעשית לבנה, ומעשה נמי וכו', דתנא קמא לא שרי אלא בזמן שהיה הנדר טעות מעיקרו כגון שהיתה יפה בשעת הנדר, ורבי ישמעאל סבר שאף על פי שלא נעשית יפה אלא לאחר הנדר הנדר מותר, דכין שיכולין ליפותה לא היתה כעורה מעיקרא. ואין הלכה כרבי ישמעאל:

יד אברהם

,,**קוֹנָם שֶׁאֵינִי נוֹשֵׂא אֶת פְּלוֹנִית כְּעוּרָה'', וַהֲרֵי
הִיא נָאָה**; ,,**שְׁחוֹרָה'', וַהֲרֵי הִיא לְבָנָה**;
,,**קְצָרָה'', וַהֲרֵי הִיא אֲרֻכָּה**– — [If one
says:] "Konam, my marrying So-and-
so the ugly," and, in fact, she is good
looking; "dark," and she is fair;
"short," and she is tall —

The person mentions what
prompted his neder — the woman's
supposed ugliness, darkness, or shortness. However, the neder is not treated
as depending on the continuation of
these states. One explanation for this is
that, instead of saying:, "Konam … So-
and-so because she is ugly," the person
says, "Konam … So-and-so, the ugly."
The mention of her ugliness comes,
then, not to describe the motivation for
the neder, but to identify the object of
the prohibition (the ugly woman).
Therefore, there is no justification for
interpreting the declaration to mean

"as long as she is ugly" (Ran 65b, s.v.
תנא; Tos. Yom Tov).

A different explanation is advanced
by Rashba, who maintains that the
wording is not crucial. Even if the
factor which prompts the neder is
mentioned only as an identifying detail, the neder is assumed to be conditional on that factor. Thus, in the case
of mishnah 3, even if the person were to
declare, for example, "Konam, my
marrying the daughter of So-and-so
the evil" (rather than "Konam … So-
and-so because her father is evil"), the
prohibition would be in force only as
long as the father remained evil (Meiri
65a). However, in our case, even if he
said, "because she is ugly," the neder
would not be treated as a conditional
one. This is because ugliness (as well as
darkness and shortness) is usually not a
temporary condition, and conse-

10. **[I**f one says:] "*Konam*, my marrying So-and-so the ugly," and, in fact, she is good looking; "dark," and she is fair; "short," and she is tall — he is permitted her. [This is] not because she was ugly and became good looking, or dark and became fair, or short and became tall, but because the *neder* was an error.

It happened once that someone made a *neder* prohibiting benefit from his sister's daughter, and they brought her to R' Yishmael's house, and made her beautiful. R' Yishmael said to him: "My son, regarding this woman did you vow?" He said to him:

YAD AVRAHAM

quently, it is not plausible to interpret the declaration to mean "as long as she is ugly." However, it is sensible to say, *as long as her father is evil*, since — although it is unlikely — it is not unheard of for someone to repent or die unexpectedly. Therefore, in the examples of mishnah 3, the *neder* is treated as a conditional one (*Ran 65b; Tos. Yom Tov*).

מֻתָּר בָּהּ. — *he is permitted her.*
[He is allowed to marry her. Even though the *neder* is not dependent on her ugliness (or shortness, etc.) as explained above, when it is discovered that she is ugly, dark, or short, the *neder* is annulled.]

לֹא מִפְּנֵי שֶׁהִיא כְעוּרָה וְנַעֲשֵׂית נָאָה, שְׁחוֹרָה וְנַעֲשֵׂית לְבָנָה, קְצָרָה וְנַעֲשֵׂית אֲרֻכָּה, — [This is] *not because she was ugly and became good looking, or dark and became fair, or short and became tall,*
[That is, if, at the time of the *neder*, she was indeed ugly, dark, or short, and later, she somehow became beautiful, fair, or tall, the prohibition would remain in force. The ruling *he is permitted her* applies only to the

case in which it was discovered that, even at the time of the *neder*, she was beautiful, fair, or tall. Thus, the *neder* was originally based on false premises and is not binding.]

אֶלָּא שֶׁהַנֶּדֶר טָעוּת. — *but because the neder was an error.*
And is therefore null and void even without recourse to a sage or panel (*Rav*).

וּמַעֲשֶׂה בְּאֶחָד שֶׁנָּדַר מִבַּת אֲחוֹתוֹ הֲנָיָה, — *It happened once that someone made a neder prohibiting benefit from his sister's daughter,*
[Compare 8:7.]

וְהִכְנִיסוּהָ לְבֵית רַבִּי יִשְׁמָעֵאל, וְיִפּוּהָ. — *and they brought her to R' Yishmael's house, and made her beautiful.*
The *Gemara* (66b) explains that she had uncomely false teeth, and R' Yishmael replaced them with golden ones. This considerably improved her appearance.

אָמַר לוֹ רַבִּי יִשְׁמָעֵאל: — *R' Yishmael said to him:*
[I.e., to the person who made the *neder*.]

„לָאו". וְהִתִּירוֹ רַבִּי יִשְׁמָעֵאל. בְּאוֹתָהּ שָׁעָה
בָּכָה רַבִּי יִשְׁמָעֵאל וְאָמַר: בְּנוֹת יִשְׂרָאֵל נָאוֹת
הֵן, אֶלָּא שֶׁהָעֲנִיּוּת מְנַוַּלְתָּן". וּכְשֶׁמֵּת רַבִּי
יִשְׁמָעֵאל הָיוּ בְּנוֹת יִשְׂרָאֵל נוֹשְׂאוֹת קִינָה
וְאוֹמְרוֹת: „בְּנוֹת יִשְׂרָאֵל אֶל רַבִּי יִשְׁמָעֵאל
בְּכֶינָה".

וְכֵן הוּא אוֹמֵר בְּשָׁאוּל: „בְּנוֹת יִשְׂרָאֵל אֶל
שָׁאוּל בְּכֶינָה".

יד אברהם

„בְּנִי! לָזוֹ נָדַרְתָּ?" אָמַר לוֹ: „לָאו". וְהִתִּירוֹ
רַבִּי יִשְׁמָעֵאל. — ''My son, regarding this
woman did you vow?'' He said to him:
''No.'' Thereupon R' Yishmael permitted [her].

The change in appearance that the
woman underwent transpired after
the *neder* was made. Thus, at the time
of the *neder*, she was indeed uncomely, and the declaration ought
not be considered one based on misinformation. Nevertheless, R' Yishmael nullified the *neder* when her
appearance changed. Some explain
that he reasoned that, since it was
possible to beautify her, she was never
really ugly, and, the *neder* is indeed

considered one based on false information (*Rav; Rosh* 66a). Others suggest that R' Yishmael, like R' Eliezer in
mishnah 2, was of the opinion that an
''opening'' may be based on an
unexpected development (*Ran* 66a;
cf. *Rambam Comm.*). Thus, when she
unexpectedly was made beautiful, the
prohibition could be annulled by a
sage or panel who would use the new
circumstance as an ''opening.'' Whatever R' Yishmael's reason, the halachah does not follow his view (*Ran;
Yoreh Deah* 232:6).

בְּאוֹתָהּ שָׁעָה — *At that time*
[Upon witnessing the metamor-
phosis the girl underwent.]

"No." Thereupon, R' Yishmael permitted [her].

At that time R' Yishmael wept and said: "The daughters of Israel are beautiful, but poverty makes them ugly."

When R' Yishmael died, the daughters of Israel raised a lament, saying: "Daughters of Israel, weep over R' Yishmael." And so, too, it says about Saul (*II Samuel* 1:24): *Daughters of Israel, weep over Saul.*

YAD AVRAHAM

בָּכָה רַבִּי יִשְׁמָעֵאל וְאָמַר: ,,בְּנוֹת יִשְׂרָאֵל נָאוֹת הֵן, אֶלָּא שֶׁהָעֲנִיּוּת מְנַוַּלְתָּן''. — *R' Yishmael wept and said: "The daughters of Israel are beautiful, but poverty makes them ugly."*

[Compare *Negaim* 2:1.]

וּכְשֶׁמֵּת רַבִּי יִשְׁמָעֵאל הָיוּ בְנוֹת יִשְׂרָאֵל נוֹשְׂאוֹת קִינָה וְאוֹמְרוֹת: ,,בְּנוֹת יִשְׂרָאֵל אֶל רַבִּי יִשְׁמָעֵאל בְּכֶינָה''. — *When R' Yishmael died, the daughters of Israel raised a lament, saying: "Daughters of Israel, weep over R' Yishmael."*

[R' Yishmael's sensitivity for the plight of the Jewish women did not go unnoticed, and on his passing, they deeply mourned his loss.]

וְכֵן הוּא אוֹמֵר בְּשָׁאוּל: ,,בְּנוֹת יִשְׂרָאֵל אֶל שָׁאוּל בְּכֶינָה''. — *And so, too, it says about Saul (II Samuel 1:24): Daughters of Israel, weep over Saul.*

[As the verse there continues: *who clothed you in scarlet delicately, who put ornaments of gold upon your apparel.*]

The *Gemara* (66b) relates how, upon R' Yishmael's death, a eulogist paraphrased the above verse: "Daughters of Israel, weep over R' Yishmael, who clothed you in scarlet delicately, who put ornaments of gold upon your apparel" (*Meiri*).

פרק עשירי ◄

Chapter Ten

✑§ Introduction

✑§ הֲפָרָה — Revocation by the Father and / or Husband

The remainder of the tractate deals with the special laws governing the revocation and confirmation of a woman's *nedarim* by her father and/or her husband, known as הֲפָרָה.

✑§ Difference Between הֲפָרָה/Revocation and הַתָּרָה/Annulment

This type of revocation (see *Num.* Chap. 30) differs fundamentally from the cancellation of a *neder* by a sage or panel, dealt with by the Mishnah in previous chapters. When a sage finds grounds to annul the *neder* and pronounces it permitted, the *neder* is retroactively canceled and is considered to have never existed (*Kesubos* 74b). Thus, if a person violated his *neder* and then had it canceled by a sage, he incurs no penalty for the violation. Since the *neder* has been retroactively annulled, he has committed no infraction (*Rosh, Pesakim* 10:11). But revocation by a husband or father is capable only of discontinuing the prohibition effected by the *neder*. From the moment they revoke it, it is canceled; until then, however, it has been binding (*Nazir* 21b; *Yoreh Deah* 234:51). Consequently, if the wife violated her *neder* before her husband revoked it, she is punishable (*Rambam, Hil. Nedarim* 12:19; *Rosh* loc. cit.).

This difference between the two procedures reflects itself in the formulae used to cancel the *neder*. A sage in such a case declares: "מוּתָּר,, — literally, "*permitted*," while a husband or father declares "מוּפָר,, — literally, "*breached*," or "*discontinued*." Should one employ the formula of the other, the cancellation will be ineffective (*Gem.* 77b).

Ramban (*Responsa* 262, quoted by *Beis Yosef* to *Yoreh Deah* 228 and *Turei Zahav* ibid. 4) suggests that this is analogous to someone who finds a rope tied in a knot. If he unties the knot, he restores the rope to its original state; however, if he cuts the rope, the knot remains, but it is no longer binding. The Hebrew word מוּתָּר, *permitted*, literally means *untied*; it is therefore an appropriate term for a sage's annulment, which completely undoes the *neder* as if it never existed. The word מוּפָר, *revoked*, however, connotes that an obstacle exists, but has been overcome; it is thus appropriate to describe the revocation by a husband or father (ibid.; see also *Ran* 77b, s.v. אמר).

[Note: To avoid confusion, we have consistently translated הֲפָרָה as *revocation*, and הַתָּרָה as *annulment* or *nullification*, although these English terms are synonymous.]

✑§ A Girl's Stages of Maturity

A girl from birth until her twelfth birthday is considered a minor. After that time, if she has already developed two pubic hairs — as is usually the case — she is no longer a minor, and enters an intermediate stage, during which she is called a

נַעֲרָה, *naarah*. Six months later, she is known as a בּוֹגֶרֶת, *bogeres*[1] (*Rav; Ramban, Hil. Ishus* 2:1ff. from *Niddah* 47a).

∝§ The Father's Authority over Nedarim

Once a girl has become a *bogeres*, her *nedarim* are no longer within her father's jurisdiction (mishnah 2). Thus, the last stage during which the father has authority over her *nedarim* is when she is a *naarah*. The *Tanna's* purpose in discussing the *naarah* here is to emphasize this. However, prior to her becoming a *naarah* — that is, when she is still a minor — the father does exercise control over her *nedarim* (*Ran*).

During most of her years as a minor, any *nedarim* she makes are not effective at all, and need no revocation whatsoever. However, during her last year as a minor, this is not the case. From her eleventh birthday until her twelfth, if — upon examination — she displays an understanding of *nedarim*, they will be binding (*Rav*). After that time, even if she has not grown two pubic hairs, her *nedarim* are binding although she does not comprehend them (*Niddah* 45b; *Rambam, Hil. Nedarim* 11:1ff.; *Yoreh Deah* 233:1f.; *Shach* ad loc. 2).

Thus, prior to becoming a *naarah*, there are two situations in which her *nedarim* would be effective: 1) the year between her eleventh and twelfth birthdays, provided she understands *nedarim*; 2) from her twelfth birthday until she grows two pubic hairs and becomes a *naarah*. In both cases, her *nedarim* are effective, but are subject to revocation by her father (*Ran; Rambam* loc. cit. 11:6; *Shulchan Aruch* loc. cit. 234:1).

∝§ Erusin and Nisuin

According to Biblical law, there are two stages to marriage. The first is known as אֵרוּסִין, *erusin*, or קִדּוּשִׁין, *kiddushin*. We have translated the former as *betrothal* only for lack of a better English equivalent. The truth is, however, that *erusin* is very different from a mere engagement in that, during this stage — in most respects — the couple is legally married (see General Introduction to ArtScroll *Kesubos*, p. 6).

The second stage of marriage is called נִשּׂוּאִין, *full marriage*. This is effected by a procedure called *chupah*, and it completes the marriage process (see ibid., p. 7). In earlier times, the period of *erusin* lasted a long time — usually a year (see *Kesubos* 5:2). Following the *erusin* ceremony, the bride returned to her father's home and remained there until the *nisuin*. Later, it became customary to perform both stages of the marriage at the wedding.

After *nisuin*, a woman is no longer under her father's jurisdiction; hence only her husband may revoke her *nedarim* (ibid. 4:4). During the *erusin*, however, she is subject to the joint authority of both her father and her husband. How this affects her *nedarim* is the subject of the following mishnayos.

---

1. If a girl grows two pubic hairs later than usual, *Rav* (*Kesubos* 3:8) holds that, as long as she has already grown them by the time she is twelve and half years old, she is deemed a *bogeres* at that age. If they grow anytime thereafter, she becomes a *bogeres* immediately. According to *Rambam* (ibid.), however, whenever she grows the hairs — provided that she is over twelve years old — six months are counted and only then is she considered a *bogeres*.

[א] נַעֲרָה הַמְאֹרָסָה, אָבִיהָ וּבַעְלָהּ מְפִירִין נְדָרֶיהָ. הֵפֵר הָאָב וְלֹא הֵפֵר הַבַּעַל, הֵפֵר הַבַּעַל וְלֹא הֵפֵר הָאָב — אֵינוֹ מוּפָר, וְאֵין צָרִיךְ לוֹמַר שֶׁקִּיֵּם אֶחָד מֵהֶן.

ר' עובדיה מברטנורא

פרק עשירי – נערה המאורסה. (א) נערה המאורסה. בת שתים עשרה שנה ויום אחד והביאה שתי שערות קרויה נערה, עד שנה חדשים. ובת אחת עשרה שנה ויום אחד נדריה נבדקים, אם ידעה לשם מי נדרה ולשם מי הקדישה נדרה נדר, ואף היא אביה ובעלה מפירין נדריה: **הפר האב ולא הפר הבעל.** משום דהוה אפשר למטעי ולפרש אביה ובעלה מפירין נדריה, או אביה או בעלה, תנא הפר האב ולא הפר הבעל וכו', לאשמועינן דתרווייהו צריכין להפר: **ואין צריך לומר שקיים אחד מהם.** שאם קיים אחד מהם אין השני יכול להפר, והא קמשמע לן שאף על פי שנשאל האחד מהם שקיים, על הקמתו, על הקמתו, כדקיימא לן נשאלים על הקימם (גמרא כד, א), אין זה שנשאל על הקימם יכול להפר יותר, הואיל ולא היו כולים להפר שניהם להפר בבת אחת:

יד אברהם

1.

נַעֲרָה הַמְאֹרָסָה, — *A naarah who is betrothed —*

[See preface.]

אָבִיהָ וּבַעְלָהּ מְפִירִין נְדָרֶיהָ. — *her father and her husband revoke her nedarim.*

That is, in order for the *neder* to be canceled, both the father and the husband must revoke it. This is derived from the phrase (*Num.* 30:17) *between a man and his wife, between a father and his daughter* being a naarah in her father's house.

The expression, *a naarah in her father's house*, is understood to mean that she is a *naarah* who is nevertheless still in her father's house. In other words, she is still partially under his authority. This refers to a *naarah* who is betrothed; although she is to some extent already subject to her husband's jurisdiction, she is still *in her father's house*. The juxtaposition in this verse of the phrases, *man and his wife* and *father and his daughters*, teaches us that the *nedarim* of a betrothed girl can be canceled only if both the husband and the father

revoke them (*Gem.* 68a, according to *Ran* ibid, and *Malbim* to *Num.* loc. cit; *Tos. Yom Tov*).

הֵפֵר הָאָב וְלֹא הֵפֵר הַבַּעַל, הֵפֵר הַבַּעַל וְלֹא הֵפֵר הָאָב — אֵינוֹ מוּפָר; — *[If] the father revoked [a neder], but the husband did not revoke [it, or if] the husband revoked [it], but the father did not revoke [it], it is not revoked;*

To prevent one from misinterpreting the previous statement as meaning that her father *or* her husband revokes her *nedarim*, the mishnah states very clearly that the revocation of one party without the other is ineffective, and the *neder* will not be revoked (*Rav* from *Gem.* 67a).

Rosh (ibid.) notes that any misunderstanding could have been avoided had the mishnah simply stated: "Her father and her husband revoke her *nedarim* together." He remarks, however, that such an expression does not conform to the Mishnaic style.

As stated below (mishnah 8), if a certain amount of time passes from when the husband or father first learns of the *neder*, he forfeits his right of revocation, and the *neder* is automatically confirmed. Thus, the

10
1

1. **A** *naarah* who is betrothed — her father and her husband revoke her *nedarim*. [If] the father revoked [a *neder*], but the husband did not revoke [it, or if] the husband revoked [it], but the father did not revoke [it], it is revoked; certainly [this is so] if one of them confirmed [the *neder*].

YAD AVRAHAM

mishnah, when stating here: *If the father revoked, but the husband did not*, means that he did not revoke the *neder* within the allotted time (*Tos. Yom Tov*; cf. *Rashash*).

וְאֵין צָרִיךְ לוֹמַר שֶׁקִּיֵּם אֶחָד מֵהֶן. — *certainly [this is so] if one of them confirmed [the neder].*

[I.e., if either the husband or the father actually confirmed the *neder*, it goes without saying that the necessary revocation by the two of them is lacking, and the *neder* is not revoked.]

Since this statement is an obvious extension of the previous one, it seems superfluous. The *Gemara* (67a) therefore explains that the mishnah is adding something new here. The law is that the revocation of a *neder* is final, and cannot be retracted; confirmation of a *neder*, on the other hand, may be repealed (*Gem.* 69a, 79a). The procedure for repealing the confirmation of a *neder* is the same as that used to annul a *neder* — by appealing to a sage or a panel (*Rashi* ibid.).

Suppose that the husband confirmed his bride's *neder*. This would make the *neder* irrevocable, since the necessary condition for cancellation — the revocation by both the husband and the father — will not have been met. But, what if, subsequently, the husband seeks — and gains — repeal of his confirmation of the *neder*? It is precisely this case that the mishnah is referring to when it tells us that once

either the husband or father has confirmed the *neder* — even if the confirmation is subsequently repealed — the *neder* still stands.

There is considerable controversy concerning the meaning of the *Gemara's* statement. *Rav* follows *Rambam* (*Hil. Nedarim* 13:21) and *Rosh* (67a), who construe it to mean that the one who confirmed the *neder* cannot subsequently revoke it, even if the confirmation was repealed. This is because, in the case of a betrothed *naarah*, whose *nedarim* require joint revocation by the father and husband in order to cancel it, it must be possible for them to revoke the *neder* together at all times from when it was made until the revocation. This requisite is not met if the husband confirms the *neder*, after which he cannot revoke it — even if they had been fully married — until his confirmation is repealed. Thus, revocation in this case is no longer possible — even if the confirmation is subsequently repealed — because of this period of time that the husband was unable to revoke the *neder* (see *Rosh* ibid.; *Keren Orah* ibid.; *Beur HaGra, Yoreh Deah* 234:16). Accordingly, the *neder* will stand. *Shulchan Aruch* (*Yoreh Deah* 234:6) rules in accordance with this view.

Rambam, however, interprets the *Gemara* differently. He contends that the case under consideration is that, for example, the father revokes the

נדרים]ב[**מֵת** הָאָב — לֹא נִתְרוֹקְנָה רְשׁוּת לַבַּעַל. מֵת הַבַּעַל — נִתְרוֹקְנָה רְשׁוּת לָאָב. בָּזֶה

─────────── **ר׳ עובדיה מברטנורא** ───────────

)ב(מת האב לא נתרוקנה רשות לבעל. שֶׁאֵין הַבַּעַל מֵפִיר נִדְרֵי אִשְׁתּוֹ עַד שֶׁתִּכָּנֵס: **מת הבעל נתרוקנה רשות לאב.** וּמֵפֵר כָּל יְמֵי נַעֲרוּתָהּ דִּכְתִיב)במדבר ל, יז(בִּנְעוּרֶיהָ בֵּית אָבִיהָ:

─────────────── **יד אברהם** ───────────────

neder, but the husband confirms it. The point of the *Gemara* is that the husband's confirmation of the *neder* renders the father's revocation ineffective. Thus, even if the confirmation is subsequently repealed and the husband revokes the *neder*, it will be necessary for the father to revoke it once again; if he chooses not to, the *neder* is still binding. However, if he does, the *neder* is revoked (*Hil. Ramban* 10:1; *Ran* 67a).

Meiri (to 67a) goes even further and maintains that confirmation by the husband does not cancel the effectiveness of the father's revocation of the *neder*. To be sure, the *neder* is not revoked as long as the husband's confirmation is in force. But, as soon as the confirmation is repealed, the original revocation of the *neder* by the father is reactivated. To revoke the *neder* now, it is only necessary for the husband to add his revocation. The *Gemara's* point is that repeal of a confirmation does not, in itself, amount to revocation. If the *neder* is to be revoked, the husband must add his revocation to that of the father; otherwise, the *neder* will remain in force.

Rashba (67a) questions the *Gemara's* reasoning in the case of a confirmation which has been repealed by a sage. Since repeal by a sage is retroactive (see preface), the confirmation should be viewed as never having existed. How, then, could a repealed confirmation affect subsequent revocation of a *neder*?

He answers that it does so only in a case in which it was the husband who had revoked the *neder*, and the father who had confirmed it. He holds that, although revocation of the *neder* by both the husband and the father is needed, they are not equal partners. Rather, the father's role is more crucial than the husband's. Thus, if the husband revoked the *neder*, his revocation is considered "weak." If it is then followed with a confirmation by the father — even one which is later repealed — the revocation is totally ineffective, and must be repeated once again along with the father's revocation in order to revoke the *neder*. However, if it was the father who first revoked the *neder*, and the husband who confirmed it, then — when the husband repeals his confirmation — the father does *not* need to repeat his revocation. Rather, the husband's revocation — following the repeal of his confirmation — combines with the father's initial revocation. This is because the father's revocation, which is considered "strong," is not affected by a confirmation on the part of the husband which is later repealed.

Ran (loc. cit.) offers another explanation, which does not differ between the father and the husband. However, since it is necessary for both of them to revoke the *neder*, revocation by only one of them is considered "weak," and thus, is affected even by a confirmation which is subsequently repealed.

[According to *Meiri*, on the other hand, neither the husband's nor the father's revocation is so weak as to be voided by a subsequently repealed confirmation. The entire issue is only whether the repeal of the confirmation is itself a revocation, or whether explicit revocation is needed.]

2. **I**f the father dies, the [sole] right does not fall to the husband. If the husband dies, the [sole] right falls to the father. In this matter,

YAD AVRAHAM

2.

Having stated in the previous mishnah that revocation by both the father and husband is needed to revoke a betrothed girl's *nedarim*, the *Tanna* now examines the law when one of the two loses his jurisdiction over her *nedarim*.

מֵת הָאָב - לֹא נִתְרוֹקְנָה רְשׁוּת לַבַּעַל. — *If the father dies, the [sole] right does not fall to the husband.*

A husband is unable to revoke his wife's *nedarim* on his own until she is fully married [see preface to mishnah 1] (*Rav*). Thus, the betrothed *naarah* whose father has died cannot have her *nedarim* revoked by her husband. Even after the marriage is consummated — at which time her husband enjoys the right to revoke her *nedarim* on his own — this right extends only to *nedarim* made following the final stage of the marriage. But he cannot revoke *nedarim* his wife had made during her *erusin* period (*Gem.* 67a).

This law — that the death of the father does not invest the betrothed husband with the right to revoke *nedarim* on his own — is derived by the *Gemara* (70a) from the phrase (*Num.* 30:17) בִּנְעֻרֶיהָ בֵּית אָבִיהָ, *being a naarah in her father's house.* This verse, which is understood as dealing with a betrothed *naarah*, teaches us that, as long as she is a *naarah*, she is considered as still remaining, in some way, *in her father's house*. Thus, even when the father has died, the *naarah* has not fully left his domain. Her betrothed husband, therefore, cannot exercise sole rights over her *nedarim*, since she remains attached to *her father's house* (*Rashi; Tos. Yom Tov*). Needless to say, if a sage finds an

"opening" for her *neder*, he can permit it on that basis (*Meiri*).

מֵת הַבַּעַל - נִתְרוֹקְנָה רְשׁוּת לָאָב. — *If the husband dies, the [sole] right falls to the father.*

[During his lifetime, the betrothed husband held rights to revoke his bride's *nedarim* together with her father. Upon the husband's death — if the girl has not yet become a *bogeres* — she reverts to the full control of her father, who one again may revoke her *nedarim* on his own.]

The *Gemara* (70b) distinguishes between *nedarim* of which her betrothed husband was aware before his death, and those of which he was not, and finds Scriptural support in each case for the return of the sole right of revoking her *nedarim* to the father (see *Tos. Yom Tov*).

However, if the husband, prior to his death, had confirmed her *neder*, the father would not be able to revoke it now (*Gem.* 68b, 72a; *Yoreh Deah* 234:11).

Rambam (*Hil. Nedarim* 11:19) holds that, if the husband revoked a *neder* before his death, and the father first learned of the *neder* after the husband's death, the father cannot revoke it now on his own. *Turei Zahav* (ibid. 23), however, disputes this interpretation of *Rambam's* opinion (see also *Beur HaGra* ibid. 30).

The terminology used by the mishnah to denote the transference of this

יָפֶה כֹּחַ הָאָב מִכֹּחַ הַבַּעַל.
בְּדָבָר אַחֵר יָפֶה כֹּחַ הַבַּעַל מִכֹּחַ הָאָב,
שֶׁהַבַּעַל מֵפֵר בְּבֶגֶר, וְהָאָב אֵינוֹ מֵפֵר בְּבֶגֶר.

—— ר׳ עובדיה מברטנורא ——

והאב אינו מפר בבגר. כדכתיב (שם ל, ז) בבית אביה חביה בנעוריה:

יד אברהם

שֶׁהַבַּעַל מֵפֵר בְּבֶגֶר, וְהָאָב אֵינוֹ מֵפֵר בְּבֶגֶר. — *for a husband can revoke [his wife's nedarim] even after she has been a bogeres, while the father cannot revoke her nedarim once she becomes a bogeres.*

That the father loses control over his daughter's *nedarim* once she becomes a *bogeres* is derived from the phrase (*Num.* 30:4), *in the house of her father, being a naarah*, which implies that he has authority over her only while she is a *naarah*; once she becomes a *bogeres*, however, she is independent of her father's house (*Rav; Rosh*).

However, the statement that *a husband can revoke even after she has become a bogeres* is problematic. The *husband* referred to is clearly the betrothed husband, since the whole point of the mishnah is to compare the rights of the betrothed husband with the father. The previous mishnah states that, during the *erusin* period, he can revoke *nedarim* only together with the father. This is because, until the completion of the marriage, his bride is not yet regarded as being completely in his domain (*Kesubos* 4:5). Although becoming a *bogeres* may suffice to release her from her father's control, it does not place her completely into her husband's domain (*Gem.* 70b). How, then, can the betrothed husband revoke her *nedarim* alone before they are fully married?

The *Gemara* (70b) explains that the mishnah follows the opinion of R' Eliezer (mishnah 5; see ibid.), who

---

right is נִתְרוֹקְנָה which, literally, means *emptied* (from the root רק, *empty*). The *Tanna* analogizes this case with one who empties the contents of a bag into someone else's hands; he is left empty handed, while the other person now holds the complete contents of the bag. So too — in this case — when the husband dies, his entire share of the rights is ''emptied'' into the father's hands. The latter now exercises complete control over his daughter's *nedarim*, despite the period of her *erusin* when she was subject to her husband's authority as well (*Rosh* 68a).

בָּזֶה יָפֶה כֹּחַ הָאָב מִכֹּחַ הַבַּעַל. — *In this matter, the power of the father surpasses that of the husband.*

[That is, in the preceding case, the power of the father surpasses that of the betrothed husband. For the father — even after his daughter's *erusin* — can again acquire sole rights to revoke her *nedarim* in the event that the husband dies before completing the marriage, and she is not yet a *bogeres* (see preface to mishnah 1). The betrothed husband, however, can only revoke her *nedarim* together with the father.]

בְּדָבָר אַחֵר יָפֶה כֹּחַ הַבַּעַל מִכֹּחַ הָאָב, — *In another matter, the power of the husband surpasses that of the father,*

[In another matter — namely, in the case to follow — a situation is devised in which the betrothed husband has the sole right to revoke his wife's *nedarim*.]

the power of the father surpasses that of the husband.

In another matter, the power of the husband surpasses that of the father, for a husband can revoke [his wife's *nedarim*] even after she has been a *bogeres*, while the father cannot revoke her *nedarim* once she becomes a *bogeres*.

YAD AVRAHAM

contends that the husband acquires the complete rights to revoke his wife's *nedarim* on his own as soon as he becomes obligated to support her, even if this obligation should begin before they are fully married. Thus, if a man should betroth a *bogeres*, he will acquire the right to revoke her *nedarim* as soon as he becomes responsible for her support, even if the marriage has not yet been completed. (For the circumstances under which a husband becomes obligated to support his wife even before they are fully married, see mishnah 5 and *Kesubos* 5:2.) It is to such a case that the mishnah refers (*Gem.* 70b; *Ran; Tos. Yom Tov*).

The halachah rejects R' Eliezer's opinion and follows the view of the Sages (mishnah 5), who rule that only the actual completion of the marriage

gives the husband the right to revoke his wife's *nedarim* on his own. The anonymous inclusion of R' Eliezer's position in our mishnah — usually an indication of general agreement — was done in order to symmetrize the mishnah and not to assert R' Eliezer's view as the prevalent opinion (*Tos. Yom Tov* and *Rashash*).

Yerushalmi explains our mishnah as being unrelated to mishnah 5. It quotes the opinion of R' Lazer (not to be confused with R' Eliezer — *Keren Orah* 68a, 70b) that a *bogeres* who is betrothed becomes immediately subject to her husband's authority with regard to *nedarim*. Our mishnah follows this view of R' Lazer.

Interestingly, *Tos. Rid* (7) attempts to interpret our *Gemara* in a similar fashion (see commentary to mishnah 5).

3.

The Torah writes that if a father or a husband wishes to revoke a *neder* he must do so on the day he hears of it (*Num.* 30:6,9,13). Even if he learns of the *neder* many years after it had been made, he may revoke it, provided he does so on that day (see mishnah 8).

In the case of a betrothed girl whose *nedarim* are under the joint authority of her father and her husband, *Rambam* (*Hil. Nedarim* 12:17) maintains that not only is their right of revocation limited to the day on which they first learn of the *neder*, but it is also applicable only if they both learn of the *neder* on the same day. Thus, if the father became aware of the *neder* on Monday and revoked it, while the husband first learned of it on Tuesday — even if the husband revokes it immediately — the revocation will remain ineffective. Only if they both become aware of and revoke the *neder* on the same day can it be revoked.

[ג] **נָדְרָה** וְהִיא אֲרוּסָה, נִתְגָּרְשָׁה בּוֹ בַיּוֹם, נִתְאָרְסָה בּוֹ בַיּוֹם, אֲפִלּוּ לְמֵאָה — אָבִיהָ וּבַעְלָהּ הָאַחֲרוֹן מְפִירִין נְדָרֶיהָ. זֶה הַכְּלָל: כָּל שֶׁלֹּא יָצְאָת לִרְשׁוּת עַצְמָהּ שָׁעָה אַחַת — אָבִיהָ וּבַעְלָהּ הָאַחֲרוֹן מְפִירִין נְדָרֶיהָ.

ר' עובדיה מברטנורא

(ג) **נתגרשה בו ביום.** שֶׁמֵּט הָאָב, שֶׁאִם עִבֵּר הַיּוֹם שׁוּב אֵינוֹ יָכוֹל לְהָפֵר: **ונתארסה.** לְאַחַר, בּוֹ בַיּוֹם: **אביה ובעלה האחרון מפירין נדריה.** שֶׁנָּדְרָה בִּפְנֵי הָאַרוּס הָרִאשׁוֹן, שֶׁהָאַחֲרוֹן מֵפֵר בְּקוּדְמִין: **כל זמן שלא יצאה לרשות עצמה.** לֹא מֵחֲמַת בֶּגֶר וְלֹא מֵחֲמַת נִשּׂוּאִין:

יד אברהם

Hilchos Ramban (10:1), however, argues that there is no requirement that the father and the husband must hear of the *neder* and revoke it on the same day. As long as each one revoked the *neder* on the day which he first learned of it, the revocation is efficacious, even if these days are far apart.

This dispute is based upon the interpretation of the verse (*Num.* 30:8), *And her husband heard ... on the day of his hearing,* which is explained by *Rambam* (loc. cit.) to mean that *her [betrothed] husband heard [of the neder] on the same day of his* (the father's) *hearing.* He thus concludes that they both must learn of the *neder* on the same day. *Ramban* disagrees. (See *Bach* to *Yoreh Deah* 234, *Turei Zahav* ibid. 6; cf. *Haamek Davar* to *Num.* 30:8.)

If neither the husband or the father revokes the *neder* by the end of that day, it is tantamount to confirmation of the *neder* (*Gem.* 79a). [Thus, if a betrothed *naarah* made a *neder*, and, for example, the husband did not revoke it by the end of the day on which he learned of it, it is no longer possible for the *neder* to be revoked. For, although the father might yet revoke it when he learns of it — according to *Ramban's* view cited above, that they need not revoke on the same day — his revocation will be ineffective, since the husband is considered to have already confirmed the *neder*.]

In a similar vein, the *Gemara* (71bf.) questions whether their divorce after the husband's learning of the *neder* should be considered a confirmation or not. One might argue that — since the husband knows that, upon the divorce, he loses his right to revoke her *nedarim* — his failure to exercise this right is equivalent to confirmation. Most authorities consider the question to have been left undecided (*Ramban, Hil. Nedarim* 11:17; *Yoreh Deah* 234:20).

נָדְרָה וְהִיא אֲרוּסָה, נִתְגָּרְשָׁה — *If she vowed while she was betrothed, [and] was divorced*

And her father heard about the *neder*, but her husband did not (*Rav,* according to *Tos. Yom Tov; Ramban, Hil. Nedarim* 11:11; *Yoreh Deah* 234:18; *Shach* ad loc. 34).

It is necessary to stipulate that the betrothed husband did not know of the *neder*, because, if he did, his subsequent divorce might be considered a confirmation of the *neder*, thus precluding its revocation (see *Tos. Yom Tov; Kesef Mishneh, Hil. Nedarim* 11:11).

בּוֹ בַיּוֹם, — *on the same day,*

3. **I**f she vowed while she was betrothed, [and] was divorced on the same day [and] betrothed [again] that same day, even to a hundred [men] — her father and her current husband revoke her *nedarim*.

This is the general rule: As long as she had never entered into a state of independence for even one hour, her father and her current husband revoke her *nedarim*.

YAD AVRAHAM

That is, she was divorced on the same day in which her father learned of her *neder*. This is an essential factor in this case because once the father learns of her *neder*, he has the right to revoke it only until the end of the day (mishnah 8). Since the mishnah wishes to construct a case in which the father plays a part in revoking the *neder*, the events must take place on the same day (*Ran*).

נִתְאָרְסָה בּוֹ בַּיּוֹם, אֲפִלּוּ לְמֵאָה– — *[and] betrothed [again] that same day, even to a hundred [men] —*

[I.e., even if she was betrothed and divorced that day to many different men.

A girl who is not yet a *bogeres*, upon being divorced before she is fully married, returns to her father's jurisdiction (mishnah 2). If she becomes betrothed once again, the authority over her *nedarim* is shared by her new husband and her father.]

אָבִיהָ וּבַעֲלָהּ הָאַחֲרוֹן מְפִירִין נְדָרֶיהָ. — *her father and her current* (lit., *last*) *husband revoke her nedarim.*

The point the mishnah wishes to convey is that the new husband, together with the father, can revoke *nedarim* that had been made prior to the *erusin*, including even those that

were made while she was betrothed to a previous husband (*Rav*). The *Gemara* (71a) derives this from the verse (*Num.* 30:6), *if she will be [betrothed] to a man, and have nedarim upon her,* which is construed as referring to *nedarim* that were made even prior to the *erusin* (*Tos. Yom Tov*).

This rule — which allows a betrothed husband, together with the father, to revoke *nedarim* made even before the *erusin* — does not apply to a fully married husband. The latter has jurisdiction only over *nedarim* made following the completion of the marriage (see next mishnah).

זֶה הַכְּלָל: כָּל שֶׁלֹּא יָצָאת לִרְשׁוּת עַצְמָהּ שָׁעָה אַחַת, אָבִיהָ וּבַעֲלָהּ הָאַחֲרוֹן מְפִירִין נְדָרֶיהָ. — *This is the general rule: As long as she had never entered into a state of independence for even one hour, her father and her current husband revoke her nedarim.*

This means that, if — following her divorce — a girl does not attain a state of independence, and is still subject to her father's jurisdiction, when she becomes betrothed once again, control of her *nedarim* is shared by her father and her new husband. A state of independence is achieved only if she is divorced after a completed marriage, or if she becomes a *bogeres*. To be independent *for even one hour* means,

דֶּרֶךְ [ד] תַּלְמִידֵי חֲכָמִים, עַד שֶׁלֹּא הָיְתָה בִתּוֹ יוֹצְאָה מֵאֶצְלוֹ אוֹמֵר לָהּ: "כָּל נְדָרִים שֶׁנָּדַרְתְּ בְּתוֹךְ בֵּיתִי — הֲרֵי הֵן מוּפָרִין". וְכֵן הַבַּעַל, עַד שֶׁלֹּא תִכָּנֵס לִרְשׁוּתוֹ אוֹמֵר לָהּ: "כָּל נְדָרִים שֶׁנָּדַרְתְּ עַד שֶׁלֹּא תִכָּנְסִי לִרְשׁוּתִי — הֲרֵי הֵן מוּפָרִין",

---
ר' עובדיה מברטנורא

(ד) **עד שלא היתה בתו יוצאה מאצלו.** קודם שתצא לרשות הבעל, וכן האחרום אומר לה כן עד שלא תכנס לרשותו, שמשנכנסה לרשותו אינו יכול להפר, שאין הבעל מפר בקודמין. ושמעינן ממתניתין שהבעל יכול להפר נדרי אשתו אפילו בלא שמיעה, מדקתני וכן הבעל עד שלא תכנס לרשותו אומר וכו':

יד אברהם
---

for example, that she is divorced from a completed marriage and is betrothed an hour later. Since she was divorced from a completed marriage, she is no longer subject to her father's jurisdiction, and he cannot revoke her *nedarim*. A betrothed husband can never revoke *nedarim* on his own (mishnah 1). Consequently, any *nedarim* binding on this woman or those that she makes prior to being fully married can never be revoked (*Rav; Meiri*). [Of course, they can still be annulled by a sage or panel.]

The *Gemara* (89a) remarks that the principle here — *This is the general rule* — alludes to a case in which the husband's agents have come to take the betrothed girl to the *chupah*, the completion of the marriage ceremony. Once she leaves her father's home in the company of these agents, the completion of the marriage process is under way, and her father can no longer revoke her *nedarim*. [Whether at that point she is considered sufficiently under the husband's authority for him to revoke her *nedarim* on his own is a subject of controversy (see commentary to mishnah 5, s.v. עַד).] However, if the father himself or his agents join the husband's agents, she is not yet considered independent of her father's authority. Thus, at that point, her father may still revoke her *nedarim* together with her husband [cf. *Kesubos* 4:5 and ArtScroll comm. there] (*Tos. Yom Tov*).

4.

דֶּרֶךְ תַּלְמִידֵי חֲכָמִים, — *It was the custom of scholars [that]*

The mishnah cites this practice of scholars as an example for all others to follow. It is not a recommendation merely for educated people (*Gilyonei HaShas*).

עַד שֶׁלֹּא הָיְתָה בִתּוֹ יוֹצְאָה מֵאֶצְלוֹ — *as long as one's daughter had not left him,*

I.e., before she is fully married, and

her *nedarim* would be completely out of his control because she will have come under her husband's authority, and only he will be able to revoke her *nedarim*. However, the husband's control extends only to the *nedarim* she makes following the *chupah*. Those made during the *erusin*, on the other hand, cannot be revoked by the husband after the *chupah*; they must

4. **I**t was the custom of scholars [that] as long as one's daughter had not left him, he would say to her: "All *nedarim* which you have made in my house are revoked." And so, too, the husband — before she would come under his authority — would say to her: "All *nedarim* which you have made prior to coming under my authority are revoked,"

YAD AVRAHAM

be revoked by the father and the husband together before the completion of the marriage (*Ran*).

אוֹמֵר לָהּ: ,,כָּל נְדָרִים שֶׁנָּדַרְתְּ בְּתוֹךְ בֵּיתִי – הֲרֵי הֵן מוּפָרִין.'' — *he would say to her: "All nedarim which you have made in my house are revoked."*

The mishnah stresses that the formula used was a general one directed at all her *nedarim*, and not some specific ones of which the father was aware. Evidently, it is not necessary for the father to be aware of his daughter's *neder* in order to revoke it. Although the Torah (*Num.* 30:5) writes: *her father hears her neder*, this is to teach us that, in order to revoke his daughter's *nedarim*, a person must have the ability to hear; a deaf person, therefore, is not eligible. However, a person who can hear need not actually hear about a particular *neder* in order to revoke it (*Ran* 72b, s.v. אמר; *Tos. Yom Tov*; see comments of *Meiri* cited below).

[A father may make such a declaration only with regard to *nedarim* his daughter has already made. He cannot, however, revoke the *nedarim* she will make in the future (see mishnah 7).]

וְכֵן הַבַּעַל, עַד שֶׁלֹּא תִכָּנֵס לִרְשׁוּתוֹ, — *And so, too, the husband — before she would come under his authority —*

That is, before the bride would come under his complete jurisdiction by virtue of the *chupah* [see following

mishnah] (*Tos. Yom Tov*).

Meiri notes that even those who require that both the husband and father revoke the *nedarim* of a betrothed girl on the same day (see *Rambam, Hil. Nedarim* 12:17; preface to mishnah 3) insist on this only when the *neder* is being revoked after the father and husband had heard of it. But, in the case under consideration — in which the *nedarim* are being revoked without knowing whether or not any had been made — this does not apply. Accordingly, in this case, the father need not revoke the *neder* on the same day as the husband.

אוֹמֵר לָהּ: ,,כָּל נְדָרִים שֶׁנָּדַרְתְּ עַד שֶׁלֹּא תִכָּנְסִי לִרְשׁוּתִי – הֲרֵי הֵן מוּפָרִין,'' — *would say to her: "All nedarim which you have made prior to coming under my authority are revoked,"*

The mishnah teaches us that a husband need not be aware of a particular *neder* in order to revoke it (*Rav; Rambam Comm.*).

[Though *Rav* and *Rambam* do not indicate that the same is true of the father, they do not mean to exclude the latter. They merely chose the husband as an example (see *Ran* 72b; *Lechem Mishneh, Hil. Nedarim* 12:13).]

Thus, in all cases of revocation of a woman's *nedarim* by her father and/or husband, the revocation is effective even without knowing if a *neder* had

נדרים שֶׁמִּשֶּׁתִּכָּנֵס לִרְשׁוּתוֹ אֵינוֹ יָכוֹל לְהָפֵר.

[ה] **בּוֹגֶרֶת** שֶׁשָּׁהֲתָה שְׁנֵים עָשָׂר חֹדֶשׁ, וְאַלְמָנָה שְׁלֹשִׁים יוֹם, רַבִּי אֱלִיעֶזֶר אוֹמֵר:

—————— ר' עובדיה מברטנורא ——————

(ה) **בוגרת ששהתה שנים עשר חדש.** בוגרת שאין אביה מפר נדריה ותבטוה ליגסא, ושהתה שנים עשר חדש שמכאן ואילך בעלה חייב במזונותיה: **ואלמנה.** שֶׁשָּׁהֲתָה שלשים יום משתבטוה ליגסא שהיא אוכלת משל בעלה: **רבי אליעזר אומר הואיל**

יד אברהם

indeed been made (*Yoreh Deah* 234:25; *Ran* 73a, s.v. משום).

Rosh, however, disputes this ruling and insists that revocation requires prior knowledge of the *neder*. The general formula mentioned by the mishnah was stated by the father or the husband only to provoke the girl to inform him of any *nedarim* she had made. But the actual revocation was declared only after they learned of the *neder* (see *Gem.* 72b). This opinion is recorded by *Rama*, loc. cit.

שֶׁמִּשֶּׁתִּכָּנֵס לִרְשׁוּתוֹ אֵינוֹ יָכוֹל לְהָפֵר. — *for once she comes under his authority, he cannot revoke [them].*

[I.e., once they are fully married, he can no longer revoke the *nedarim* she made prior to that time.]

This is derived from the verse (*Num.* 30:11), *If in her husband's house she vowed*, which implies that the fully married husband has authority only over *nedarim* uttered in his "house" (*Rosh* 67a, s.v. שאין).

5.

A betrothed girl — whose husband informed her that he wishes to complete the marriage — is given twelve months to prepare her jewelry, clothes, and whatever else she needs. This rule applies to a girl who was betrothed before she became a *bogeres*. If she had reached that stage prior to the *erusin*, she is given twelve months from the day she became a *bogeres*. If she is betrothed more than twelve months after becoming a *bogeres*, she is given thirty days from the time she is notified by the husband that he wishes to complete the marriage. The shorter time allotted to a *bogeres* is due to the consideration that she is more concerned with marriage and has already made some preparations. Similarly, a widow who became betrothed is given thirty days after her new husband's notification. Having been married before, she already has the necessary jewelry, etc., and thus requires less time to prepare (*Kesubos* 5:2 and 57b, according to *Rashi* ad loc.; *Even HaEzer* 56:1).

If the time allotted for preparation passes, and thus the husband fails to complete the marriage, he becomes obligated to support her (*Kesubos* 5:2; *Shulchan Aruch* loc. cit. 3). This mishnah discusses whether this has any bearing on the husband's right to revoke his wife's *nedarim*.

בּוֹגֶרֶת — *A bogeres*

As explained in the commentary to mishnah 2, once a girl reaches this stage, her father no longer exercises control over her *nedarim* (*Rav*).

for once she comes under his authority, he cannot
revoke [them].

5. **A** *bogeres* who had waited twelve months —
or a widow, thirty days — R' Eliezer says:

שֶׁשָּׁהֲתָה שְׁנֵים עָשָׂר חֹדֶשׁ, — *who had
waited twelve months —*
[The time for her preparation has
passed without her betrothed husband completing the marriage. Thus,
he is now obligated to support her.]
Rav appears to hold that this
twelve-month period begins on the
day she receives notification from the
husband of his desire to complete the
marriage.

Tos. Yom Tov argues that, if this is
so, we must make the unlikely assumption that the notification was
received on the very day she became a
bogeres. For, if it was received any time
after that, the twelve months would
begin from the day she became a
bogeres and not from the day of notification, as stated in *Even HaEzer* 56:1;
hence, it would be less than twelve
months from the time of her notification until the expiration of her pre-
paratory time. Indeed, the *Gemara*
(70b) appears to raise this very issue
and, because of it, explains the mishnah differently (see below).

It is noteworthy that *Tosafos* (*Kesubos*
57b, s.v. בגורה and s.v. תיובתא) maintain —
unlike *Shulchan Aruch* — that, if the *erusin*
took place before she became a *bogeres*, and
the husband notified her that he wishes to
complete the marriage sometime after she
became a *bogeres*, she is given twelve
months from the time of notification.
[Perhaps *Rav* here follows *Tosafos'* view.]

There are, in fact, several different
approaches to our mishnah, which
depend on a variety of versions and
interpretations of the *Gemara.*

Rosh (70b), quoted by *Tos. Yom Tov,*
understands the mishnah as dealing
with a girl who had already been a
bogeres for twelve months and was
then betrothed. The law in her case is
that she has thirty days from the time
of notification to prepare for her
marriage, as stated later in the mishnah. The phrase, *A bogeres who had
waited twelve months,* means that
twelve months have passed since she
became a *bogeres.*

Ran (70b) interprets the *Gemara*
(ibid.) to mean that the mishnah
should read: *A bogeres and one who
has waited twelve months.* That is,
two cases are being discussed: that of a
bogeres whose preparation time varies
according to the time elapsed since she
became a *bogeres,* and the case of a girl
who is not yet a *bogeres,* whose
preparation time is twelve months.

However one reads the mishnah,
the relevant point is that the girl in
question has completed the time
allotted in order for her to prepare
for marriage, and it is thus obligatory
upon her betrothed husband to provide for her sustenance (*Rav*).

וְאַלְמָנָה שְׁלֹשִׁים יוֹם, — *or a widow,
thirty days —*
That is, the thirty-day preparation
period allotted to a widow from the
time she is notified by her betrothed
husband has passed (*Rav;* see preface).

According to *Rosh,* cited above, the
thirty days specified here is the preparation period for the two preceding
cases — a *bogeres* who has been in that

הוֹאִיל וּבַעְלָהּ חַיָּב בִּמְזוֹנוֹתֶיהָ — יָפֵר; וַחֲכָמִים אוֹמְרִים: אֵין הַבַּעַל מֵפֵר עַד שֶׁתִּכָּנֵס לִרְשׁוּתוֹ.

ר' עובדיה מברטנורא

וּבַעְלָהּ חַיָּב בִּמְזוֹנוֹתֶיהָ. הוּא מֵיפֵר אֶת נְדָרֶיהָ. וְאֵין הֲלָכָה כְּרַבִּי אֱלִיעֶזֶר:

יד אברהם

stage for at least twelve months, and a widow.

רַבִּי אֱלִיעֶזֶר אוֹמֵר: הוֹאִיל וּבַעְלָהּ חַיָּב בִּמְזוֹנוֹתֶיהָ – יָפֵר; — *R' Eliezer says: Since her husband is responsible for her sustenance, he can revoke [her nedarim];*

I.e., by himself. R' Eliezer reasons that, because the girl is dependent on her husband for sustenance, she makes *nedarim* contingent upon his approval. Therefore, although — strictly speaking — she is not under his authority until they are fully married, he may already revoke her *nedarim* by himself (*Gem.* 73b; *Ran*).

וַחֲכָמִים אוֹמְרִים: — *the Sages, however, say:*

Ran (73b) identifies *the Sages* as R' Yehoshua who was the usual disputant of R' Eliezer (cf. *Ran* 74b, s.v. הכא; *Gilyonei HaShas* 73b).

אֵין הַבַּעַל מֵפֵר — *A husband cannot revoke [her nedarim]*

They disagree with R' Eliezer's assertion that dependence on a betrothed husband for sustenance causes the woman to vow subject to her husband's approval. Therefore, although he is obligated to support her, he cannot yet revoke her *nedarim* by himself (*Ran* 73b; see mishnah 2).

R' Eliezer's argument that a woman vows conditional to her husband's approval is attributed to R' Pinchas. R' Eliezer applied the argument to this case of a woman dependent on her husband's support, but, actually, R' Pinchas' statement had been made in much wider context — namely, in

order to explain the rationale behind the law that gives every husband the right to revoke his wife's *nedarim*. The commentators point out that R' Pinchas' theory is not an isolated opinion, but is unanimously agreed to (see *Ran* 73b; *Ritva* to 66b; *Tos.* to *Niddah* 46b).

Accordingly, a question presents itself: If the reason a husband has the right to revoke his wife's *nedarim* is that she makes them conditional to his approval, why is it necessary for the Torah to tell us that a husband has the power to revoke his wife's *nedarim*?

Among the solutions suggested are these:

R' Pinchas' reasoning is just the opposite: *Because* a woman knows that the Torah gave a husband the right to revoke his wife's *nedarim*, she vows subject to his approval even in cases [such as ours] in which the husband would not be empowered by the Torah to revoke it (*Tos.* to *Niddah* 46b).

Because most women make their *nedarim* conditional to the approval of their husbands, the Torah legislated that the *nedarim* of all married women may be revoked by the husbands, even if a particular woman claims to have made her *neder* regardless of whether or not her husband would approve (*Rashba, Responsa* Vol. 4 310; *Tos. HaRosh* to *Niddah* 46b).

Ordinarily, an unspoken condition is legally ineffective. Therefore, had the Torah not granted the husband the power of revocation, even if a woman intended that her *neder* be subject to her husband's approval, the condition would not take effect if she did not verbalize it (*Ritva* to 66b).

For further discussion of this issue, see *Shalmei Nedarim* to 66b and *Gilyonei HaShas* to 73b.

עַד שֶׁתִּכָּנֵס לִרְשׁוּתוֹ. — *until she has entered his authority.*

I.e, until the marriage is completed (*Tif. Yis.*).

10
5
Since her husband is responsible for her sustenance, he can revoke [her *nedarim*]; the Sages,
however, say: A husband cannot revoke [her
nedarim] until she has entered his authority.

The *Gemara* (89a) indicates that, once the girl has been given over to agents of the husband who will take her to the *chupah*, she is considered to have left her father's jurisdiction. The father is thus no longer capable of revoking her *nedarim*, even together with the betrothed husband.

Whether — at that point — the husband acquires the right to revoke her *nedarim* on his own is questionable. Some treat the girl's leaving her father's home to go to the husband's home as the beginning of the *chupah*, and assume that, even at that time, the husband is able to revoke her *nedarim* on his own (*Yoreh Deah* 234:8). Others contend that, although she has left her father's home, she has not yet entered her husband's home. Thus, neither of them can revoke her *nedarim* (*Tur* 234; *Shulchan Aruch* loc. cit.). A third opinion maintains that the husband may not revoke her *nedarim* until the marriage is completed, but that once it has been, he may revoke on his own even those made between the time she left her father's house in order to come to his, and the time she became fully married (*Turei Zahav* to *Yoreh Deah* 234:9; *Ritva* to 89a).

The halachah follows the view of the Sages (*Rav; Shulchan Aruch* 5).

It is generally assumed that the dispute of R' Eliezer and the Sages applies to all the cases listed at the start of the mishnah. *Tos. Rid* (7), however — like *Ran* (cited above) — reads the mishnah as meaning that three cases are being discussed: (1) a *bogeres*; (2) a girl who is not yet a *bogeres*, and has had twelve months of preparation; and (3) a widow. He contends that there is no argument regarding the first case. Rather, since — upon becoming a *bogeres* — she leaves her father's authority, if she subsequently is betrothed, she immediately comes under her husband's jurisdiction with regard to *nedarim*. The mishnah thus gives instances in which a betrothed husband can revoke *nedarim* on his own even before they are fully married. The first case is a betrothed *bogeres*; all agree that the husband can revoke her *nedarim* on his own during the *erusin*. The other cases are subject to the dispute of R' Eliezer and the Sages (see commentary to mishnah 2).

6.

When a man dies without children, the Torah (*Deut.* 25:5ff.) commands that one of his brothers (referred to as the *yavam*, pl., *yevamin*) marry his widow (the *yevamah*). This marriage is called *yibum* and takes place when the brother and the widow engage in a conjugal act. The usual *chupah* is neither required nor effective in the case of *yibum*. According to Biblical law, there is also no need to perform *erusin* first. The Torah also provides a mechanism, known as *chalitzah* ("taking off the shoe"), by which the widow can be released from her attachment to the brothers (*Rambam, Hil. Yibum* 1:1ff.; *Even HaEzer* 156; see General Introduction to ArtScroll *Yevamos*, pts.4).

The status of a woman awaiting *yibum* is questionable. Does her impending

[ו] שׁוֹמֶרֶת יָבָם, בֵּין לְיָבָם אֶחָד בֵּין לִשְׁנֵי יְבָמִין – רַבִּי אֱלִיעֶזֶר אוֹמֵר: יָפֵר. רַבִּי יְהוֹשֻׁעַ אוֹמֵר: לְאֶחָד, אֲבָל לֹא לִשְׁנַיִם. רַבִּי עֲקִיבָא אוֹמֵר: לֹא לְאֶחָד וְלֹא לִשְׁנַיִם.

ר' עובדיה מברטנורא

(ו) **שומרת יבם וכו' רבי אליעזר אומר יפר.** כשעשה בה יבמה מאמר מיירי, דסבירא ליה לרבי אליעזר מאמר קונה ביבמה קנין גמור מן התורה, ואם היא נערה ויש לה אב, אביה ויבמה שעשה בה מאמר מפירין נדריה: **רבי יהושע אומר לאחד ולא לשנים.** דלא סבירא ליה לרבי יהושע מאמר קונה קנין גמור, מיהו סבירא ליה דים זיקה, וזיקה ככנוסה, וכשאין שם אלא יבם אחד מיפר, אבל כשיש שני יבמין אין שום אחד מהם מיפר שאין ברירה: **רבי עקיבא אומר לא לאחד ולא לשנים.** דסבר זיקה אינה ככנוסה, ומאמר אינו קונה קנין גמור מן התורה:

יד אברהם

marriage to her brother-in-law create any bond between them, so that she may be considered betrothed to him? Or, perhaps — since they do not need *chupah* to be married — her status is that of a fully married woman? It is also possible that no bond whatsoever exists, and although she is not free to marry anyone else, neither is she considered betrothed to her brother-in-law. These questions become more perplexing in a case in which she has more than one brother-in-law. For, even if she could be considered as betrothed or married to one of them, she cannot be betrothed or married to two men at once!

Another question that presents itself is this: In view of the fact that *erusin* is not necessary before *yibum*, if — in such a case — the brother-in-law does perform the usual *erusin* ceremony with the widow, does it have any legal effect?

All these questions are particularly relevant with regard to *nedarim*, for the answer to them will decide whether the brother-in-law in such a case has any jurisdiction over the widow's *nedarim*. If they are betrothed, he should share the authority with her father; if they are fully married, he should have the sole jurisdiction; if they are considered totally unmarried, he should have no rights until the marriage is consummated. In this mishnah, the *Tannaim* debate the above questions.

שׁוֹמֶרֶת יָבָם, בֵּין לְיָבָם אֶחָד בֵּין לִשְׁנֵי יְבָמִין – — *A woman awaiting a yavam — whether one yavam or two yevamin —*

The *Gemara* (74a) suggests two interpretations of the mishnah's case. The first is that one of the brothers-in-law betrothed their deceased brother's widow. The question is whether *erusin* by a *yavam* has any effect.

The second approach is that no *erusin* took place (*Rosh* 74a; cf. *Meiri*),

but one of the brothers was obligated by the court to provide for the widow's sustenance. The dispute of the preceding mishnah regarding a connection between the obligation to provide sustenance and the right to revoke *nedarim* is thus continued in this mishnah.

רַבִּי אֱלִיעֶזֶר אוֹמֵר: יָפֵר. — *R' Eliezer says: He may revoke [her nedarim].*

R' Eliezer maintains that *erusin* by

6. **A** woman awaiting a *yavam* — whether one *yavam* or two *yevamin* — R' Eliezer says: He may revoke [her *nedarim*]. R' Yehoshua says: [When she awaits] one, but not two. R' Akiva say: Neither [when she awaits] one, nor two.

YAD AVRAHAM

the brother-in-law is effective and grants him the right to revoke her *nedarim* (*Rav*).

Alternatively, R' Eliezer is consistent with his position, stated in the previous mishnah, that the obligation to provide sustenance brings with it the right to revoke *nedarim* (*Ran* 74b).

Rav writes that R' Eliezer regards the *erusin* in this case as enabling the brother-in-law to jointly revoke *nedarim* with her father. Thus, the *erusin* here creates a state similar to ordinary *erusin*. However, the *Gemara* (74b) is uncertain of this, since it is possible that *erusin* by a *yavam* produces a bond between him and the *yevamah* equivalent to that existing between a fully married husband and wife. Accordingly, the *yavam* would be entitled to revoke her *nedarim* on his own (*Ran* 74a, s.v. ורי׳ יהושע; see *Tos. Yom Tov*).

רַבִּי יְהוֹשֻׁעַ אוֹמֵר: לְאֶחָד, אֲבָל לֹא לִשְׁנַיִם. — *R' Yehoshua says:* [When she awaits] one, but not two.

R' Yehoshua holds that the *erusin* of a *yavam* to a *yevamah* has no effect (*Rav*). He also disagrees with R' Eliezer's view that a man's obligation to support a woman entitles him to revoke her *nedarim* (*Ran* 74b; *Rashba*; see comm. to previous mishnah s.v. וחכמים אומרים).

Rather, R' Yehoshua maintains that, as soon as the childless brother dies, a bond exists between his widow and his brother who eventually marries her. Therefore, if the deceased had only one brother, he may revoke her

nedarim (*Rav*). However, if he had more than one brother, the identity of the one with this right is unknown in advance of the actual *yibum*; thus, none can revoke her *nedarim* (*Ran* 74a; cf. *Rosh*; *Rashi* to *Yevamos* 29b).

Furthermore, the Torah states (*Num.* 30:14): *her husband can confirm it, and her husband can revoke it,* implying that, for the revocation of a *neder* to be effective, the husband must be identifiable as such (*Tos. R' Akiva* from *Ran*).

Rav appears to attribute to R' Yehoshua the view that the automatic bond between the *yavam* and the *yavamah* is equivalent to a full marriage in that he may revoke her *nedarim* on his own. Perhaps *Rav* preferred this approach rather than explaining the bond as being equivalent to *erusin*, since the latter probability is not expressly propounded anywhere in the Talmud, while the former is (*Tos. Yom Tov*).

רַבִּי עֲקִיבָא אוֹמֵר: לֹא לְאֶחָד וְלֹא לִשְׁנַיִם. — *R' Akiva says: Neither [when she awaits] one, nor two.*

R' Akiva disputes all the arguments advanced by his colleagues, contending that a brother-in-law — whether he be the only candidate for *yibum* or one of several brothers — has no control over the widow's *nedarim*. Thus, according to R' Akiva, *erusin* here has no effect, nor is there any special bond uniting the widow to her brother-in-law (*Rav*).

אָמַר רַבִּי אֱלִיעֶזֶר: מָה אִם אִשָּׁה שֶׁקָּנָה הוּא לְעַצְמוֹ הֲרֵי הוּא מֵפֵר נְדָרֶיהָ, אִשָּׁה שֶׁהִקְנוּ לוֹ מִן הַשָּׁמַיִם אֵינוֹ דִין שֶׁיָּפֵר נְדָרֶיהָ! אָמַר לוֹ רַבִּי עֲקִיבָא: לֹא, אִם אָמַרְתָּ בְּאִשָּׁה שֶׁקָּנָה הוּא לְעַצְמוֹ, שֶׁאֵין לַאֲחֵרִים בָּהּ רְשׁוּת, תֹּאמַר בְּאִשָּׁה שֶׁהִקְנוּ לוֹ מִן הַשָּׁמַיִם, שֶׁיֵּשׁ לַאֲחֵרִים בָּהּ רְשׁוּת? אָמַר לוֹ רַבִּי יְהוֹשֻׁעַ: עֲקִיבָא, דְּבָרֶיךָ בִּשְׁנֵי יְבָמִין; מָה אַתָּה מֵשִׁיב עַל יָבָם אֶחָד? אָמַר לוֹ: אֵין הַיְבָמָה גְמוּרָה לַיָּבָם כְּשֵׁם שֶׁהָאֲרוּסָה גְמוּרָה לְאִישָׁהּ.

ר' עובדיה מברטנורא

אשה שקנה הוא לעצמו. היינו ארוסתו: **הרי הוא מיפר נדריה.** בשותפות עם אביה: **אשה שהקנו לו מן השמים.** דהיינו יבמתו: **אינו דין שיפר נדריה.** בשותפות עם אביה: **שיש לאחרים רשות בה.** שגם היא זקוקה לשאר אחיו: **מה אתה משיב על יבם אחד.** כלומר תשובתך טובה על דברי רבי אליעזר שאומר שמפר אפילו כשיש שני יבמין, מה תשיבני על דברי שאני אומר לאחד ולא לשנים: **אין היבמה גמורה ליבם.** להתחייב מיתה הבא עליה כשם שהארוסה גמורה לאישה לענין חיוב מיתה. והלכה כרבי עקיבא:

יד אברהם

אָמַר רַבִּי אֱלִיעֶזֶר: מָה אִם אִשָּׁה שֶׁקָּנָה הוּא לְעַצְמוֹ הֲרֵי הוּא מֵפֵר נְדָרֶיהָ, — *Said R' Eliezer: If he can revoke the nedarim of a wife whom he acquired on his own,*

That is, if he betroths a girl of his own choice, he is granted the right by the Torah to revoke her vows in conjunction with her father (Rav).

אִשָּׁה שֶׁהִקְנוּ לוֹ מִן הַשָּׁמַיִם אֵינוֹ דִין שֶׁיָּפֵר נְדָרֶיהָ! — *surely he can revoke the nedarim of a wife acquired for him by Heaven!*

His brother's widow is put before him for marriage by an act of Heaven. Thus, R' Eliezer argues that, if betrothing a woman of his choice endows him with certain rights, betrothing a woman whom God himself instructs him to marry should certainly obtain for him those rights. Therefore, a *yavam* who betroths his brother's widow ought to be able to revoke her *nedarim* (Rav).

אָמַר לוֹ רַבִּי עֲקִיבָא: לֹא, אִם אָמַרְתָּ בְּאִשָּׁה שֶׁקָּנָה הוּא לְעַצְמוֹ, שֶׁאֵין לַאֲחֵרִים בָּהּ רְשׁוּת; — *Said R' Akiva to him: No; if you said this for a woman he acquired on his own, [it is because] others have no rights to her;*

R' Akiva demonstrates that even if *erusin* by a *yavam* is regarded as significant, it is not comparable with ordinary *erusin*. When someone betroths a woman as the first stage of marriage, she can no longer be betrothed by any other man. Thus, if Reuven betroths Leah, and then Shimon does the same, the latter's act is totally meaningless. This feature of *erusin*, which uniquely associates the betrothed woman to her husband, is what constitutes the authority over her, manifesting itself in the right to revoke her *nedarim* (Tif. Yis.).

Said R' Eliezer: If he can revoke the *nedarim* of a wife whom he acquired on his own, surely he can revoke the *nedarim* of a wife acquired for him by Heaven! Said R' Akiva to him: No; if you said this for a woman he acquired on his own, [it is because] others have no rights to her; shall you say this for a woman acquired for him by Heaven, to whom others do have rights? Said R' Yehoshua to him: Akiva, your words [apply] when there are two *yevamin*; what do you answer when there is one *yavam*? He said to him: The *yevamah* is not as complete [a wife] to the *yavam*, as a betrothed woman is a complete [wife] to her husband.

YAD AVRAHAM

תֹּאמַר בְּאִשָּׁה שֶׁהִקְנוּ לוֹ מִן הַשָּׁמַיִם, שֶׁיֵּשׁ לַאֲחֵרִים בָּהּ רְשׁוּת? — *shall you say this for a woman acquired for him by Heaven, to whom others do have rights?*

The woman awaiting *yibum* must marry one of her deceased husband's brothers; each of the brothers is equally eligible to marry her. Accordingly, if Reuven betroths her, and then his brother Shimon also betroths her , the *erusin* of the latter is also effective and, consequently, she requires a divorce from both of them (*Rashi*, from *Yevamos* 50a; see Art-Scroll commentary ibid. 5:1, p. 136). Or, if after Reuven's *erusin*, Shimon hands her a bill of divorce, it becomes forbidden even for Reuven to marry her, and she must be released through *chalitzah* (*Ran* 74b; *Yevamos* 50a, 53a).

The lack of exclusivity inherent in the *erusin* by a *yavam* indicates a lack of control. Hence, says R' Akiva: Shall you say that *erusin* of a wife given to him by Heaven, in whom the other brothers also have rights, shall invest him with rights of

revocation of her *nedarim*? (*Tif. Yis.*).

אָמַר לוֹ רַבִּי יְהוֹשֻׁעַ: עֲקִיבָא, דְּבָרֶיךָ בִּשְׁנֵי יְבָמִין; מָה אַתָּה מֵשִׁיב עַל יָבָם אֶחָד? — *Said R' Yehoshua to him: Akiva, your words [apply] when there are two yevamin; what do you answer when there is one yavam?*

R' Yehoshua counters that R' Akiva's response suffices to refute R' Eliezer's view — that the brother-in-law who betrothed or was obligated in sustenance can revoke *nedarim* — on the grounds that the equal claim of the other brothers weakens the rights of this brother. But, argues R' Yehoshua, how do you refute my opinion that, if there is only one brother-in-law, he may revoke the widow's *nedarim* on the basis of a special bond between them? (*Rav*).

אָמַר לוֹ: אֵין הַיְבָמָה גְּמוּרָה לַיָּבָם כְּשֵׁם שֶׁהָאֲרוּסָה גְּמוּרָה לְאִישָׁה. — *He said to him: The yevamah is not as complete [a wife] to the yavam, as a betrothed woman is a complete [wife] to her husband.*

R' Akiva rejects the argument that a "special bond" creates a status equi-

[ז] הָאוֹמֵר לְאִשְׁתּוֹ: ,,כָּל הַנְּדָרִים שֶׁתִּדְּרִי מִכָּאן עַד שֶׁאָבוֹא מִמָּקוֹם פְּלוֹנִי
הֲרֵי הֵן קַיָּמִין'' – לֹא אָמַר כְּלוּם. ,,הֲרֵי הֵן מוּפָרִין'' – רַבִּי אֱלִיעֶזֶר אוֹמֵר: מוּפָר. וַחֲכָמִים אוֹמְרִים: אֵינוֹ מוּפָר. אָמַר רַבִּי אֱלִיעֶזֶר: אִם הֵפֵר נְדָרִים שֶׁבָּאוּ לִכְלַל אִסּוּר, לֹא יָפֵר נְדָרִים שֶׁלֹּא בָאוּ לִכְלַל אִסּוּר? אָמְרוּ לוֹ: הֲרֵי הוּא אוֹמֵר: ,,אִישָׁהּ יְקִימֶנּוּ וְאִישָׁהּ יְפֵרֶנּוּ''.

─────── ר' עובדיה מברטנורא ───────

(ז) הרי הן קיימין לא אמר כלום. דהוה ליה קיום בטעות, לפי שיש נדרים שלא יחפוץ בקיומן: הרי הן מופרין רבי אליעזר אומר מופר. דמסתמא אין אדם רוצה בנדרי אשתו: נדרים שבאו לכלל איסור. לאחר שנדרה אסורה בהם אם לא יפר לה הבעל:

יד אברהם

valent to *erusin* and thereby entitles the *yavam* to revoke her *nedarim*. He demonstrates this by noting that, although both a woman who is betrothed and one awaiting *yibum* are prohibited to cohabit with others, nevertheless, the penalty for one who commits adultery with the former is death by stoning, while for adultery with the latter, it is only lashes. This shows that the two states are not comparable, and that the *yevamah* is not as united to her brother-in-law as a betrothed woman is to her husband. Therefore, R' Akiva maintains that, whether the deceased has one or more brothers, none of them may revoke the widow's *nedarim*, until they actually marry her (*Rav; Rambam; Tos. Yom Tov*).

7.

הָאוֹמֵר לְאִשְׁתּוֹ:—*One who says to his wife:*

The same is true if a father said this to his daughter (*Rambam, Hil. Nedarim 13:9; Rama to Yoreh Deah 234:28*). *Ohr Sameach* (to Rambam loc. cit.), however, develops a theory that R' Eliezer's argument stated below applies only to a husband and wife, and not a father and daughter.

,,כָּל הַנְּדָרִים שֶׁתִּדְּרִי מִכָּאן עַד שֶׁאָבֹא מִמָּקוֹם פְּלוֹנִי הֲרֵי הֵן קַיָּמִין''—*All the nedarim which you shall make, from now until I return from such and such a place are confirmed,''*

[That is, he issues in advance a confirmation of *nedarim* to be made during a certain time period.]

לֹא אָמַר כְּלוּם. — *has said nothing.*

His confirmation in advance could not possibly have been sincere, for he did not know what *nedarim* would become confirmed as a consequence of it. Perhaps his wife will make *nedarim* that are embarrassing or painful to him! Therefore — despite his declaration — we assume that he did not mean it sincerely, and his confirmation is not effective (*Rav; Rosh* to 72b and to *Nazir* 12b).

Gilyon Maharsha (Yoreh Deah 234:28) notes that — according to this approach —

7. **O**ne who says to his wife: "All the *nedarim* which you shall make, from now until I return from such and such a place are confirmed," he said nothing. [But if he says:] "they shall be revoked" — R' Eliezer says: [They are] revoked. The Sages, however, say: [They are] not revoked. Said R' Eliezer: If he can revoke *nedarim* which are already binding, should he not be able to revoke *nedarim* which are not yet binding? They said to him: It says (*Numbers* 30:14): *Her husband can confirm it, and her husband can revoke it* —

YAD AVRAHAM

if the husband specified a particular *neder* in his advance confirmation, the confirmation would be effective. Since he knows exactly what he is confirming, his sincerity is not suspect (cf. *Tif. Yis.* 34, *Chidushei R' Nechemiah Yerushalimski;* see also *Rashash* to 75a).

Others point out that nowhere do we find a basis for confirmation of *nedarim* not yet made, and, in the absence of Scriptural proof to that effect, we assume that it does not exist, even if he specified a particular *neder* (*Gilyon Maharsha* loc. cit. explaining *Ran* 75a; *R' Eliezer of Metz,* quoted by *Rosh* 75a; see *Tos. R' Akiva,* whose question was anticipated by *Rosh*).

Rashash (75a) adds that an early source construes the phrase (*Num.* 30:3), *to bind a prohibition upon himself,* as explicitly excluding advance confirmation, for it implies that one can create prohibitions upon himself, but he cannot prohibit for others (i.e., confirm their prohibitions) before they themselves have made them (*Sifrei* ibid., according to *Yalkut Shimoni* 785; see also *Malbim,* and *Rabbeinu Hillel* to *Sifrei*).

"הֲרֵי הֵן מוּפָּרִין,,– — *[But if he says:] "they shall be revoked"* —

[That is, he issued an advance revocation of her *nedarim*.]

רַבִּי אֱלִיעֶזֶר אוֹמֵר: מוּפָר. — *R' Eliezer says: [They are] revoked.*

The earnestness of revocation is not in doubt, since a husband generally is against his wife making *nedarim* (*Rav; Rosh* 72b).

וַחֲכָמִים אוֹמְרִים: אֵינוֹ מוּפָר. — *The Sages, however, say: [They are] not revoked.*

[They maintain that advance revocation is not acceptable. The basis of the dispute between R' Eliezer and the Sages follows.]

אָמַר רַבִּי אֱלִיעֶזֶר: אִם הֵפֵר נְדָרִים שֶׁבָּאוּ לִכְלָל אִסּוּר, לֹא יָפֵר נְדָרִים שֶׁלֹּא בָּאוּ לִכְלָל אִסּוּר? — *Said R' Eliezer: If he can revoke nedarim which are already binding, should he not be able to revoke nedarim which are not yet binding?*

The logic of this argument is that a *neder* which has already effected a prohibition ought to be more difficult to revoke than one which has not even been declared, and is, at most, potential. Since the Torah legislates that a husband (or father) has the rights to revoke actual *nedarim,* it follows that they should be able to revoke potential ones as well (*Ran* 75a).

אָמְרוּ לוֹ: הֲרֵי הוּא אוֹמֵר: ,,אִישָׁהּ יְקִימֶנּוּ וְאִישָׁהּ יְפֵרֶנּוּ,, — *They said to him: It says (Numbers 30:14): "Her husband*

אֶת שֶׁבָּא לִכְלָל הָקֵם – בָּא לִכְלָל הָפֵר; לֹא בָא לִכְלָל הָקֵם – לֹא בָא לִכְלָל הָפֵר.

[ח] **הֲפָרַת** נְדָרִים – כָּל הַיּוֹם. יֵשׁ בַּדָּבָר לְהָקֵל וּלְהַחְמִיר. כֵּיצַד? נָדְרָה בְּלֵילֵי שַׁבָּת

ר' עובדיה מברטנורא

שבאו לכלל הקם. נדרים שחלו כבר: **(ח) הפרת נדרים.** שאמרה תורה (במדבר ל, טו) ואם ביום שמוע אישה יניא אותה: **כל היום.** עד שתחשך שנאמר ביום שמעו, והא דכתיב (שם ל, טו) מיום אל יום, נריכא, דלא תימא ביממא אין בליליא לא, קמשמע לן דזימנין שיש לו זמן להפר מעת לעת, כגון אם נדרה בתחלת הלילה: **ויש בדבר להקל ולהחמיר.** כלומר פעמים שיש להפרה זמן מועט ופעמים זמן מרובה: **נדרה בלילי שבת.** האי דנקט בלילי שבת לאשמועינן שמפירין נדרים בשבת ואפילו שלא לצורך השבת, והכא איהו מתיר בשבת אלא נדרים שהן לצורך השבת, ואף על פי שהיה לו פנאי מבעוד יום יכול להתיר לצורך השבת: **שאם לא**

יד אברהם

can confirm it, and her husband can revoke it" —

[The Sages agree with R' Eliezer that, in general, to revoke something actual is harder than to revoke something potential. However, if Scripture indicates otherwise, it obviously must be followed (*Gem. 76a, Ran ad loc.*). Accordingly, the Sages adduced Scriptural support for their position.]

אֶת שֶׁבָּא לִכְלָל הָקֵם – בָּא לִכְלָל הָפֵר; לֹא בָא לִכְלָל הָקֵם – לֹא בָא לִכְלָל הָפֵר. — *that which can be confirmed can be revoked; that which cannot be confirmed cannot be revoked.*

The above verse was traditionally understood to equate the type of *neder* which one can revoke to that which he can confirm (*Tif. Yis.*; cf. *Ran*). Just as confirmation is effective only for actual *nedarim* (see above, s.v. לֹא אָמַר כְּלוּם) — so, too, is revocation of *nedarim* by the husband or father valid only for actual *nedarim*.

The concern of the mishnah is with *nedarim* that have not yet been made. However, a *neder* that has already been declared but will not take effect until later is different. Thus, if she made a *neder* that wine be prohibited to her if she goes to a certain place, her declaration will become binding only when she goes to the forbidden place. Nevertheless, once her declaration has been made — even before it becomes binding — the father and/or husband may revoke it (*Gem. 90a; Yoreh Deah* 228:17, 234:69; see commentary to 11:1, s.v. אִם אֲרָחַן).

8.

הֲפָרַת נְדָרִים – כָּל הַיּוֹם. — *Revocation of nedarim [is valid] the entire day.*

When the *neder* of a woman becomes known to her husband or father, and he wishes to revoke it, there is a time limit set by the Torah by when he must do so. This deadline is the nightfall of the day on which he became aware of the *neder*, as it says (*Num.* 30:9): *If, on the day her husband hears of it, he revokes it* (*Rav; Rosh*) and (v. 6) *If her father revokes it on the day he hears of it* (*Rambam*).

If that day passes, and nightfall sets in, they can no longer revoke the *neder* (*Rav*). Failure to revoke the *neder*

that which can be confirmed can be revoked; that which cannot be confirmed cannot be revoked.

8. **R**evocation of *nedarim* [is valid] the entire day. This fact can be lenient or stringent. How? If she made a *neder* on the night of Sabbath,

YAD AVRAHAM

within the allotted time is tantamount to confirmation, as stated in v. 15: *If her husband remains silent from one day to the next, he has confirmed her nedarim ... he has confirmed them, because he was silent during the day he heard them.*

The *Gemara* (76b) explains that the phrase, *from one day to the next,* teaches us that the entire time from the moment the *neder* becomes known until the deadline is reached is valid for its revocation. Thus, if the *neder* became known during the night it could be revoked already then (*Rav*), and not just during daylight, as one might have thought from the phrase *on the day he hears of it* (*Rashi* 76b). Accordingly, for a *neder* which became known at the beginning of the night, the period of revocation would be the twenty-four hours, until the following nightfall (*Rav*).

יֵשׁ בַּדָּבָר לְהָקֵל וּלְהַחֲמִיר. — *This fact can be lenient or stringent.*

This means that, because there is a fixed deadline, the actual time during which revocation is possible varies according to how early or late in the course of the day the *neder* became known. When this period for revoking is longer, the law is considered "lenient"; when the period is shorter, the law is considered "stringent" (*Rav*). If, instead, there has been a fixed time limit for revocation — for example, twenty-four hours from whenever

the *neder* became known — the law would be considered neither stringent nor lenient, since the person would always have the same amount of time to revoke it, regardless of when it became known (*Ran* 76b).

The *Gemara* (76b) quotes a view that disputes the law of our mishnah, maintaining that, in fact, the time for revoking *nedarim* is constant; namely, twenty-four hours from when the *neder* became known. After some discussion, the *Gemara* concludes that the halachah does not follow that opinion. Consequently, most authorities rule in accordance with our mishnah (*Rabbeinu Chananel* to *Shabbos* 157a; *Tos.* (ibid.), s.v. והלכתא; *Rambam, Hil. Nedarim* 12:15; *Yoreh Deah* 234:21). However, some authorities had a variant reading in the *Gemara* that the halachah does follow that view (*Rosh* 76b).

כֵּיצַד? נָדְרָה בְּלֵילֵי שַׁבָּת- — *How? If she made a neder on the night of Sabbath,*

In Jewish law the day begins and ends with nightfall (see *Gen.* 1:5). Hence, *the night of Sabbath* means the night following Friday and preceding Saturday, which is the start of the Sabbath (*Tos. Yom Tov*).

The mishnah illustrates a long period of revocation with the example of a woman whose *neder* became known on the night of the Sabbath. The same would be true regarding any other day of the week, but, by using this example, the mishnah is incidentally teaching us that *nedarim* may be revoked on the Sabbath, even if they did not prohibit anything that

יָפֵר בְּלֵילֵי שַׁבָּת, וּבְיוֹם הַשַּׁבָּת עַד שֶׁתֶּחְשַׁךְ. נָדְרָה עִם חֲשֵׁכָה — מֵפֵר עַד שֶׁלֹּא תֶחְשַׁךְ, שֶׁאִם חָשְׁכָה וְלֹא הֵפֵר — אֵינוֹ יָכוֹל לְהָפֵר.

ר' עובדיה מברטנורא

הפר וחשכה אינו יכול להפר. שאין הפרת נדרים מעת לעת אלא אם כן נדרה מתחלת הלילה. ולענין הפרה אינו מועיל עד שיאמר מופר לך כלישנא דקרא, דהפרת הבעל הוא מכאן ולהבא בלא טעם, כמו את בריתי הפר (בראשית יז, יד), וחכם הוא שאומר מותר לך אין כאן נדר ואין כאן שבועה שהוא עוקר הנדר מעיקרו, ואם אמר החכם בלשון הפרה והבעל בלשון התרה, אינו מותר ואינו מופר. ואם אמר אם לא נדרת מדירך אני, דבריו קיימים, ואין צריך שיאמר קיים ליכי, הואיל ואפילו שתק כל אותו היום הנדר קיים, בדבור כל דהו נמי הוי קיום. ובשבת יאמר עלי אכלי טלי שתי, ולא יפר כדרך שיאמר בחול, והנדר בטל מאליו, ואם אינו יכול להכריחה מבטל בלבו ואין צריך להוציא בשפתיו, ודוקא בטול כגון טלי אכלי שהוא טלי מכריחה לעבור על נדרה הוא שמועיל אם חשב בלבו אף על פי שלא הוציא בשפתיו, אבל הפרה שאינו מכריחה לעבור על הנדר צריך להוציא בשפתיו ולא סגי אם הפר אם הפר בלבו:

יד אברהם

would affect her enjoyment of the day (*Rav; Ran*).

Thus, not only a prohibition imposed on clothes or food — which are needed on the Sabbath — may be revoked, but even one forbidding use from a car, for example — which she is prohibited to use on the Sabbath in any case — may be revoked.

This law is recorded in *Shabbos* 24:5 (see ArtScroll commentary ibid.), where the Mishnah adds that the law for the annulment of a *neder* by a sage or panel is different. Using that method, only *nedarim* that affect things necessary for the Sabbath may be annulled on the Sabbath (*Rav* from *Gem.* 77a).

יָפֵר בְּלֵילֵי שַׁבָּת, וּבְיוֹם הַשַּׁבָּת עַד שֶׁתֶּחְשַׁךְ. — *he can revoke it during the night of the Sabbath, or on the Sabbath day before nightfall.*

[He has until nightfall at the conclusion of the Sabbath to revoke her *nedarim*. If she made the *neder* early on the night of Sabbath, the husband has a full twenty-four hours to exercise his right. This is the mishnah's example of a long period for revoking.]

נָדְרָה עִם חֲשֵׁכָה– — *If she vowed just before dark,*

As the Sabbath was nearing its conclusion (*Ran; Tif. Yis.*).

מֵפֵר עַד שֶׁלֹּא תֶחְשַׁךְ, — *he must revoke it before nightfall,*

In this case, only a short time is available for the husband to revoke her *neder*, illustrating a stringent aspect of the law, which sets the deadline for revoking as the end of the day (*Ran*).

It is unlikely that a *neder* made shortly before the end of the Sabbath will have any bearing on the needs of the Sabbath. The Sabbath meals have already been eaten, and such things as jewelry are no longer needed (*Rashi* 77a; *Tos. Yom Tov*). The fact that this *neder* may be revoked on the Sabbath demonstrates again that even *nedarim* not affecting the Sabbath may be revoked on the Sabbath (*Gem.* 77a).

he can revoke it during the night of the Sabbath, or on the Sabbath day before nightfall. If she vowed just before dark, he must revoke it before nightfall, for if it became dark, and he had not revoked it, he can no longer revoke [it].

YAD AVRAHAM

שֶׁאָם חָשְׁכָה וְלֹא הֵפֵר – אֵינוֹ יָכוֹל לְהָפֵר. — *for if it became dark, and he had not revoked it, he can no longer revoke [it].*

Even though the sanctity of the Sabbath may be extended past darkness, the right to revoke the *neder* in this case expires with darkness (*Yad Shaul*, quoted by *Shalmei Nedarim*).

With regard to revoking *nedarim* on the Sabbath, the *Gemara* (77b) states that the procedure should be differentiated from that used during the week. The man should not say to his wife on the Sabbath, "It is revoked for you," in the manner which he would do during the week, but he should say to her: "Take this (which your *neder* prohibited) and eat it," or "take this and drink it," and the *neder* becomes automatically void.

The *Gemara* continues: *R' Yochanan says: And he must revoke it in his heart.* *Ran* (ibid.) interprets R' Yochanan's statement to mean that he must think in his heart the standard formula for revoking, "the *neder* is revoked." At first glance, this would appear to conflict with a subsequent statement of the *Gemara* (79a) that to revoke a *neder* in one's heart without verbalizing it is ineffective. *Ran* (77b), however, explains that an unspoken revocation is unacceptable only when it is not accompanied by an oral indication of the husband's or father's intention. But, in our case, the unspoken revocation is accompanied by oral instructions to his wife to contravene the terms of her *neder*. The combination of this oral indication of objection to the *neder* and his thinking that it should be revoked suffices to revoke the *neder*. *Ran's* approach is followed by *Tur*

(*Yoreh Deah* 234) and *Shulchan Aruch* (ibid. 38).

Others explain that, when R' Yochanan said that he must revoke it in his heart, he did not mean that the revocation formula should be recited mentally. Rather, he meant that it should be whispered. But, if he failed to do even this and did not verbalize the formula at all, the revocation will not be effective, as stated in the *Gemara* 79a (*Ritva; R' Eliezer of Metz*, quoted by *Rosh* 77b).

Rambam (*Commentary* and *Hil. Nedarim* 13:14ff.) adopts a different approach, according to which a husband may cancel his wife's *nedarim* by either of two methods: a) revocation (הֲפָרָה), b) negation (בִּטוּל). Negating the *neder* means to force his wife to actively violate her prohibition. Thus, if she had made a *neder* not to eat a certain food, and he forced her to eat it, the *neder* is automatically canceled even without an accompanying oral statement that he rejects the *neder*. This is different than revocation, for which only an explicit statement declaring the *neder* to be void is required.

Thus, *Rambam* (ibid.) explains that, on the Sabbath, the husband should cancel his wife's *nedarim* via the method of negation, since this requires no oral statement of revocation. [Indeed, R' Yochanan, in his directive regarding the cancellation of *nedarim* on the Sabbath (,,צָרִיךְ שֶׁיְבַטֵּל בְּלִבּוֹ''), uses the term בִּטוּל, negation (*Rambam Commentary*).] Once the husband does this, even if the wife disobeys him and refuses to contravene her prohibition, it is canceled simply because the husband pressured her to do so. However, in this case, the husband must also mentally cancel the *neder* (*Beur HaGra* to *Yoreh Deah* 234:93; *Lechem*

Mishneh to *Hil. Nedarim* 13:7; cf. *Tos. Yom Tov*). *Malbim* (*Num.* 30:6) finds support for *Rambam's* view in the fact that the Torah uses two different verbs when discussing cancellation of the *neder* by a husband —

הֵנִיא, *disallow*, and הֵפֵר, *revoke* (v. 9). Basing himself on *Sifrei* (ibid.), he explains that הֵנִיא corresponds to *Rambam's* concept of negation, while הֵפֵר refers to revocation (see also *Haamek Davar* ad loc.).

פרק אחד עשר ﷺ
Chapter Eleven

The previous chapter taught us that the husband/and or father of a woman —
depending on her age and marital status — are empowered by the Torah to revoke
her *nedarim*. The mishnah now discusses the type of *nedarim* they can revoke. The
Gemara (82a) states a general rule: A husband may revoke all his wife's *nedarim*,
except for those which prohibit someone else from deriving benefit from her. The
nedarim that he can revoke fall into two categories — those which involve self-denial
and those that affect their mutual relationship.

The Torah writes (*Num.* 30:14): *Every neder and every binding oath involving self-
denial, her husband can confirm it, and her husband can revoke it.* This teaches that a
husband has authority over his wife's *nedarim* if they involve self-denial — that is,
they cause her some deprivation (*Meiri* here and to 82a). Another phrase (ibid. v. 17), בֵּין
אִישׁ לְאִשְׁתּוֹ, *between a man and his wife*, was understood by the Rabbis to mean that
any *neder* which affects their mutual relationship [by anguishing the husband (*Shitah
Mekubetzes* 79b; cf. *Meiri* to mishnah 2)] is also within his jurisdiction (*Gem.* 79b).

Many authorities maintain that a father's right to revoke his daughter's *nedarim* is
also limited to these two types — namely, those that involve self-denial, and those that
disrupt the relationship between him and his daughter because they distress him (*Ran*
68a, s.v. לומר; *Rosh* 79a; *Yoreh Deah* 234:58, *Shach* ad loc. 72). However, *Rambam* (*Hil.
Nedarim* 12:1) is of the opinion that a father has the right to revoke any of his daughter's
nedarim (see *Lechem Mishneh* ad loc., *Turei Zahav* loc. cit. 48, *Beur HaGra* ibid. 111).

The *Gemara* (79b) differentiates between the revocations of the two kinds of *nedarim*
that are subject to the husband's authority. If he revokes a *neder* which affects their
mutual relationship but does not involve self-denial, the revocation will endure only as
long as they are married, or — if they divorce — only as long as she does not marry
another man. If she does — even should she subsequently be divorced or widowed —
since she may no longer remarry her first husband (*Deut.* 23:4; *Rambam, Hil. Gerushin*
11:12f.), the *neder* becomes reactivated (*Ran, Rosh, Tos.* 79b; *Yoreh Deah* 234:58; cf. *Meiri,
Keren Orah* to 79b). The husband's revocation of *nedarim* which involve self-denial,
however, is binding even if they divorce, and she marries another man (ibid.).

There is another distinction between the husband's revocation of these two types
of *nedarim*. A *neder* that affects their mutual relationship can be revoked by the
husband only to the extent that if affects him; if it has consequences for others as
well, he has no authority over those aspects of the *neder*. Thus, if — for example —
she prohibits cohabitation with all Jews — including her husband — his revocation
will permit her to cohabit with him, but will not release the prohibition for others
(see mishnah 12). Contrastingly, if he revokes a *neder* which involves self-denial, the
entire *neder* is canceled — not only what relates to him, but what affects others as
well (*Ran* 82b, s.v. ורב אסי).

In this chapter, the mishnah delineates the types of *nedarim* a husband may revoke.

[א] וְאֵלּוּ נְדָרִים שֶׁהוּא מֵפֵר, דְּבָרִים שֶׁיֵּשׁ בָּהֶם עִנּוּי נֶפֶשׁ: ,,אִם אֶרְחַץ", וְ,,אִם לֹא אֶרְחַץ"; ,,אִם אֶתְקַשֵּׁט", וְ,,אִם לֹא אֶתְקַשֵּׁט".

————————— ר' עובדיה מברטנורא —————————

פרק אחד עשר – ואלו נדרים. (א) אלו נדרים. בגמרא (פ, ג) מפרש דנדרים ושבועות קתני, דבלשון חכמים שבועות בכלל נדרים הס: אם ארחץ ואם לא ארחץ. הכי קאמר, הנאת רחילה אסורה עלי לעולם אם ארחן היוס, הרי נדר. אם לא ארחן, שבועה שלא ארחן, הרי שבועה. וכן אם אתקשט, הנאת קשוט אסורה לעולם אם אתקשט אס אתקשט היוס. אם לא אתקשט, שבועה שלא אתקשט:

יד אברהם

1.

וְאֵלּוּ נְדָרִים — *These are nedarim*

The mishnah here is speaking of oaths as well as *nedarim*. In Talmudic parlance, the term *nedarim* also includes oaths (*Rav* from *Gem*. 80b). This is evident from a previous mishnah (1:1; see commentary ad loc.): [*If one says:*] *"Like the nedarim of the wicked,"* he has vowed concerning ... *an oath* (*Rambam Commentary* quoting *Gem*. loc. cit.).

The *Gemara* (ibid.) also cites another version of the mishnah, which specifically mentions oaths: *These are nedarim and oaths,* etc.

That the following laws apply equally to *nedarim* and oaths is clear from the verse (*Num*. 30:14) upon which they are based: *Every neder and every binding oath,* etc. (*Meiri*).

שֶׁהוּא מֵפֵר, — *that he can revoke* —

This refers to the husband and/or father of a woman who made such a *neder* or oath, depending on who has jurisdiction over her at the time [see preface to Chapter 10] (*Rav; Ran; Tos.; Rosh*).

This view stems from *Sifrei*, which hermeneutically derives a comparison of the husband and the father from the verse (*Num*. 30:17) *between a man and his wife, between a father and his daughter* (*Tos. Yom Tov*).

Some authorities, however, main-

tain that, as long as a woman is under her father's authority, he can revoke *all* her *nedarim* and oaths — not only those which involve self-denial or affect their mutual relationship. They base this opinion on the phrase כָּל נְדָרֶיהָ, *all her nedarim* (*Num*. 30:6), which deals with the father's authority in this area (*Rambam, Hil. Nedarim* 12:1; see *Meiri, Yoreh Deah* 234:58).

Radbaz (*Hil. Nedarim* 12:1) notes that the mishnah's use of the singular form, *he can revoke,* supports *Rambam's* view that only the husband has limitations with regard to the *nedarim* he may revoke. If the father was also subject to such restrictions, the mishnah should have said: "These are *nedarim* which they may revoke," referring to both the husband and the father.

דְּבָרִים שֶׁיֵּשׁ בָּהֶם עִנּוּי נֶפֶשׁ: — *those that involve self-denial:*

[The husband and/or the father of the vower may revoke those *nedarim* which impose affliction or abstinence on her.] This is derived from verse 14: *Every neder and every binding oath involving self-denial — her husband can confirm it, and her husband can revoke it* (*Rashi*).

It is exegetically derived from verse 17, בֵּין אִישׁ לְאִשְׁתּוֹ, *between a man and his wife,* that a husband is authorized to revoke not only *nedarim* involving self-denial, but also those that affect

1. **T**hese are *nedarim* that he can revoke — those that involve self-denial: "If I bathe," or "If I do not bathe"; "If I adorn myself," or "If I do not adorn

YAD AVRAHAM

their mutual relationship by either engendering strife between them or by distressing the husband (see preface). However, the mishnah singles out *those that involve self-denial* because they can be revoked permanently; i.e., the revocation is in force even if he dies or divorces her, and she marries another man. *Nedarim* that affect their relationship, on the other hand, can be revoked by the husband only for as long as she does not marry another man; once she remarries, however, the *neder* is reactivated. Thus, the intent of the mishnah is : *These are nedarim that he can revoke permanently* (*Rav* to mishnah 2, *Tos. Yom Tov*, from *Gem*. 79b).

אָם אֶרְחַץ,, — *"If I bathe,"*

This is the condition upon which the *neder* hinges. That is, she makes the following declaration: "The pleasure of bathing shall be prohibited to me forever *if I bathe* today" (*Rav* from *Gem*. 80b).

Although the woman making this *neder* could simply avoid bathing that day, and the prohibition would then not be activated, the husband may nevertheless annul the *neder*. This is because refraining from bathing for even one day is considered self-denial (*Gemara* 80a).

The mishnah teaches us incidentally that, although the prohibition does not go into effect until she violates the condition, the husband may nevertheless revoke the *neder* as soon as it has been declared (*Ran* 80b, s.v. אלא; see commentary to 10:7, s.v. אֶת שֶׁבָּא).

וְאָם לֹא אֶרְחַץ,, — *or "If I do not bathe"*;

She swears that she will not bathe (*Rav* from *Gem*. 80b). [As mentioned above, in Talmudic terminology the term *nedarim* includes oaths as well.]

Some authorities maintain that if a woman's *neder* or oath imposes self-denial (such as refraining from bathing) upon herself for even a very short period of time (e.g., an hour), it is sufficient grounds for revocation by the husband and/or father (*Rav* to mishnah 2; *Meiri*; *Rambam, Hil. Nedarim* 12:4; see *Mishneh LaMelech* ad loc.).

אָם אֶתְקַשֵּׁט,, — *"If I adorn myself,"*

Here, too, the mishnah means that she made the following *neder*: "The pleasure of adornment be prohibited to me forever if I adorn myself today" (*Rav* from *Gem*. 80b).

Adornment in this instance refers to beautification of the face, such as applying make-up to the eyes or face. Refraining from these — even for one day (or one hour, according to *Rav*, *Meiri*, et al., cited above) — is considered self-denial, in the opinion of this anonymous *Tanna* (*Ran*, quoted by *Tos. Yom Tov*).

Meiri adds that *adornment* also includes beautifying oneself with clothes and jewelry.

The mishnah is teaching us that abstaining not only from a necessity such as bathing is considered self-denial, but even from adornment, which is not that vital for one's health and cleanliness (*Tif. Yis.*).

וְאָם לֹא אֶתְקַשֵּׁט.,, — *or "If I do not adorn myself."*

She swears that she will not adorn herself (*Rav* from *Gem*. 80b).

אָמַר רַבִּי יוֹסֵי: אֵין אֵלּוּ נִדְרֵי עִנּוּי נָפֶשׁ.

[ב] **וְאֵלּוּ** הֵם נִדְרֵי עִנּוּי נָפֶשׁ: אָמְרָה: ״קוֹנָם
פֵּרוֹת הָעוֹלָם עָלַי״ — הֲרֵי זֶה יָכוֹל
לְהָפֵר; ״פֵּרוֹת מְדִינָה עָלַי״ — יָבִיא לָהּ מִמְּדִינָה
אַחֶרֶת. ״פֵּרוֹת חֶנְוָנִי זֶה עָלַי״ — אֵינוֹ יָכוֹל לְהָפֵר;

— ר' עובדיה מברטנורא —

אמר רבי יוסי אין אלו נדרי ענוי נפש. אגדר בלבד פליג רבי יוסי על תנא קמא, ואמר, דהנאת
רחיצה אסורה עלי לעולם אם תרחץ היום אין זה נדר של ענוי נפש, שהרי אפשר לה שלא תרחץ היום
ולא תהיה הנאת רחיצה אסורה עליה לעולם, ומגיעת יום אחד מרחיצה אינו ענוי נפש, דניוול של
יום אחד לא הוי ניוול. ואין הלכה כרבי יוסי. ובין האב ובין הבעל הבטל נדרי טיווי נפש [הוא ד]מפירים,
דכתיב (במדבר ל, יז) בין איש לאשתו בין אב לבתו מקים אב לבטל, מה בעל אינו מפר אלא נדרי
ענוי נפש אף אב אינו מפר אלא נדרי ענוי נפש. ורמב״ס (הלכות נדרים יב, א) פסק שהאב מפר כל
נדרים ושבועות אפילו אותן שאין של ענוי נפש שנאמר (במדבר ל, ה) כל נדריה ואסריה:

— יד אברהם —

R' — אָמַר רַבִּי יוֹסֵי: אֵין אֵלּוּ נִדְרֵי עִנּוּי נָפֶשׁ.
Yose said: These are not nedarim of self-denial.

According to *Rav*, if the woman swore that she would not bathe or adorn herself indefinitely, even R' Yose would concur that this is considered self-denial, and hence, the husband and/or father may revoke the oath (*Tos. Yom Tov* to mishnah 2).

Rav seems to contradict himself by writing, in his commentary to mishnah 2, that a woman's oath not to adorn herself indefinitely is classified as one that affects their mutual relationship, but not one of self-denial (ibid.).

Other commentaries construe R' Yose's view to be that abstaining from bathing or adornment, even indefinitely, is not considered self-denial. Accordingly, even if she were to fulfill the condition by bathing that day, and thereby become forbidden to bathe again forever, the husband and/or father would nevertheless be unable to revoke the *neder* as being one of self-denial. They would also not be

empowered to revoke an oath forbidding bathing or adornment, regardless of whether or not the woman had spe-cified a time limit (*Ran* 80b, s.v. אלא, and 81a, s.v. איבעיא; *Rosh*; *Meiri*).

There is a dispute in the *Gemara* (81a) whether R' Yose agrees that in fact, the husband may revoke such ne-darim, because the physical repulsiveness of a wife not bathing or adorning herself for even one day is regarded as a matter affecting their mutual relationship, in which case the husband may revoke the *neder*, albeit not necessarily on a permanent basis. (As explained in the preface, the husband's revocation of *nedarim* which affect their mutual relationship is effective only as long as — in the event that they divorce — she does not marry another man.) The *Gemara* concludes that he may indeed annul them for this reason (*Tos. Yom Tov*).

myself." R' Yose said: These are not *nedarim* of self-denial.

2. **T**hese are *nedarim* of self-denial: [If] she said: "*Konam*, the fruits of the world to me," he may revoke it; "[*Konam*] the fruits of [this] country" — he can bring her [fruit] from another country. "[*Konam*] the fruits of this storekeeper to me" — he cannot revoke it;

YAD AVRAHAM

2.

וְאֵלוּ הֵם נִדְרֵי עִנּוּי נֶפֶשׁ: — *These are nedarim of self-denial:*

This is the continuation of R' Yose's statement in mishnah 1 (*Ran; Tos. Yom Tov*).

אָמְרָה: ,,קוֹנָם פֵּרוֹת הָעוֹלָם עָלַי'' - הֲרֵי זֶה יָכוֹל לְהָפֵר; — *[If] she said: "Konam, the fruits of the world to me," he may revoke it;*

To deprive herself of some food, whether it be fruits — as in the example of the mishnah — or any other food, is regarded even by R' Yose as self-denial (*Meiri*).

[However, if the prohibition is such that it does not completely proscribe the food to her, it is not deemed self-denial by R' Yose, as follows:]

,,פֵּרוֹת מְדִינָה עָלַי'' - יָבִיא לָהּ מִמְּדִינָה אַחֶרֶת. — *"[Konam] the fruits of [this] county" — he can bring her [fruit] from another country.*

The translation follows *Rav* and *Meiri*, who explain that, even if the prohibition forbids fruit of her own country to her, it is not considered self-denial by R' Yose, because she can easily get the same fruit from another country, either by her husband's going to get them, or by having them

delivered (*Meiri*). On the other hand, those who dispute R' Yose in mishnah 1 (henceforth to be referred to as *the Rabbis*) argue that such a *neder* is deemed self-denial, since fruit from other countries may sometimes not be available (*Meiri*).

Ran, however, contends that R' Yose concurs that a *neder* interdicting the fruit of her own country is regarded as self-denial. He disagrees only with the Rabbis' opinion that a *neder* prohibiting fruit from some other country is considered self-denial (see *Tos. Yom Tov*).

Although R' Yose does not consider this a *neder* of self-denial, he agrees that it should be classified as one that affects their mutual relationship (*Gem.* 82b; see *Rosh* and *Meiri*), since it imposes the added burden on him to get fruit from elsewhere, which he resents doing (*Meiri*). [As explained in the preface to this chapter, the classification of the *neder* would determine whether or not the revocation would be a permanent one (see ibid.).]

,,פֵּרוֹת חֶנְוָנִי זֶה עָלַי'' - אֵינוֹ יָכוֹל לְהָפֵר; — *"[Konam] the fruits of this storekeeper to me" — he cannot revoke it;*

R' Yose does not consider this prohibition self-denying since she can eat the fruits of other storekeepers. As in the case above, this does not

וְאִם לֹא הָיְתָה פַּרְנָסָתוֹ אֶלָּא מִמֶּנּוּ — הֲרֵי זֶה יָפֵר. דִּבְרֵי רַבִּי יוֹסֵי.

[ג] **קוֹנָם** שֶׁאֵינִי נֶהֱנֶה לַבְּרִיּוֹת — אֵינוֹ יָכוֹל לְהָפֵר, וִיכוֹלָה הִיא לֵהָנוֹת

ר' עובדיה מברטנורא

(ב) אם לא היתה פרנסתו אלא ממנו. שהוא מאמינו עד שירויח ויפרע לו: **הרי זה יפר דברי רבי יוסי.** רבי יוסי לטעמיה דסבירא ליה שאין הבעל מפר כל נדר שיש בו ענוי נפש, שהוא מחלק בין ענוי מרובה לענוי מועט, ובין ענוי של זמן מרובה לזמן מועט. וכל מתניתין דהאי פירקא מזלא כותיה ואינה הלכה. אלא הבעל מפר כל נדר שיש בו ענוי נפש, בין של יום אחד ואפילו שעה אחת, בין של זמן מרובה, בין ענוי גדול בין ענוי קטן. וכן מפר נדרים ושבועות בדבר שבינו לבינה אף על פי שאין בהם ענוי נפש, כגון אם נשבעה או נדרה שלא תכחול או שלא תתקשט. וכן אם נדרה שלא תאכל מפירות מדינה זו, הבעל מפר, שטורח הוא לו להביא לה פירות ממדינה אחרת, והוי דברים שבינו לבינה. ומה בין נדרים ושבועות שבינו לבינה לנדרים ושבועות שיש בהם ענוי נפש, נדרים ושבועות שיש בהם ענוי נפש מפר לעצמו ולאחרים, כגון אם נדרה שלא תאכל בשר ולא תשתה יין, מפר לה והיא מותרת לאכול ולשתות ואפילו לאחר שתתאלמן או תתגרש ותנשא לאחר. ונדרים ושבועות שבינו לבינה, כגון אם אסרה עליה תשמיש של כל אדם לעולם או שלא תכחול ותתקשט לעולם, מפר חלקו ותהא משמשתו וכוחלת ומתקשטת כל זמן שהיא תחתיו, וכשתתאלמן או תתגרש, תהיה אסורה בתשמיש כל אדם ולכחול ולהתקשט, וכן כל כיוצא בזה: **(ג) קונם שאיני נהנית לבריות אינו יכול להפר.** שאין זה מנדרי עינוי נפש, שהרי יכולה להתפרנס משל בעל, דבעל לאו בכלל בריות הוא. והא מתניתין נמי רבי יוסי היא, ואין כן הלכה כדפרישנא לעיל. ולא מיבעיא אי אמרה קונם שאני נהנית לבריות שאסרה הנאת כל הבריות עליה, שהוא מיפר משום נדרי ענוי נפש אליבא דחכמים, אלא אפילו אמרה קונם שאני נהנית לפלוני שלא אסרה עליה אלא הנאת אותו פלוני בלבד, הבעל מיפר משום דברים שבינו לבינה, שטורח הוא לו כשלא תהנה מאותו פלוני, והתורה אמרה בין איש לאשתו, כל דבר שבין איש לאשתו הבעל מיפר:

יד אברהם

mean that the husband cannot revoke the *neder* at all. Rather, *he cannot revoke it* as a self-denying *neder* [i.e., on a permanent basis], but he may revoke it as a *neder* affecting their relationship. The Rabbis, however, disagree, since it might be that fruit would be unavailable from any other storekeeper (*Meiri*).

וְאִם לֹא הָיְתָה פַּרְנָסָתוֹ אֶלָּא מִמֶּנּוּ – הֲרֵי זֶה יָפֵר. — *but, if he was his only source for provisions, he can revoke it.*

That is, the particular storekeeper whose fruits the wife banned is the only one who allows the husband to purchase on credit (*Rav*). Therefore, when he is short of cash, he will be unable to purchase fruit from any other storekeeper. If fruit from this storekeeper is forbidden to his wife, she will be unable to eat any fruit. Hence, even R' Yose agrees that it is considered a *neder* of self-denial [and may be revoked permanently] (*Ran*).

דִּבְרֵי רַבִּי יוֹסֵי. — [These are] the words of R' Yose.

The *Gemara* (82a) notes that this attribution is superfluous, since this entire mishnah is obviously a continuation of R' Yose's statement in

but, if he was his only source for provisions, he can revoke it. [These are] the words of R' Yose.

3. **[I**f one's wife said:] *"Konam, what I benefit from people,"* he cannot revoke it, and she can benefit

YAD AVRAHAM

the previous mishnah. Nevertheless, it is mentioned here to point out that the remaining mishnayos of the chapter also follow R' Yose's view (*Tos. Yom Tov*).

This is important for us to know, since we might otherwise assume that the following mishnayos, which are stated anonymously, represent a majority opinion, and thus should be favored by the halachah. However, since they are attributed to R' Yose alone, they do not have the weight of majority opinion, and may be rejected in favor of the Rabbis' view (*Ran 82b; Tos. Yom Tov*).

Indeed, some authorities do rule in ac-

cordance with R' Yose's opinion (see *Ran* 81a, 82b; *Lechem Mishneh* to *Hil. Nedarim* 12:1, s.v. שלא תבחול, and 12:5).

Rav, both here and in the preceding mishnah, states that the halachah does not follow R' Yose; however, when summing up the final law, he appears inconsistent (see *Tos. Yom Tov*).

Rambam (*Commentary*) also rejects R' Yose's opinion. However, in his *Mishneh Torah*, there are apparent inconsistencies which lead some authorities to assume that he retracted from his position in the *Commentary* and ruled in accordance with R' Yose's view (see *Tos. Yom Tov, Rabbeinu Avraham min HaHar* to 82a, *Lechem Mishneh, Hi. Nedarim* 12:1, *Tzofnas Paneach* ibid.).

3.

קוֹנָם, שֶׁאֵינִי נֶהֱנֵה לַבְּרִיּוֹת״- — *[If one's wife said:] "Konam, what I benefit from people,"*

This declaration would make it forbidden for her to acquire anything beneficial (e.g., food) from any person directly. However, it is assumed that the term *people* does not include her husband, so that if he acquires food from someone, it is permitted for her to receive it from him (*Rav*). This is not tantamount to deriving benefit from those included in her ban, since the prohibition was not directed at "the property of any people" — in which case the property (e.g., food) would be prohibited even if it reached her through her husband. Rather, the *neder* forbids her to benefit from the

people themselves, and therefore, when she gets it from her husband, she benefits from him, which is permitted, and not from them (*Ran 83b; Rosh*; see also preface to Chapter 4 and *Ran* 31a, s.v. ומוכר).

אֵינוֹ יָכוֹל לְהָפֵר, — *he cannot revoke it,*

Since this *neder* allows for the possibility of her receiving sustenance via her husband, R' Yose [whose view this mishnah follows (*Rav*)] maintains that the husband cannot revoke it as a *neder* involving self-denial. He does concede, however, that it may be revoked because it affects their mutual relationship (*Rosh 83b*). *Rav* notes that the Rabbis, who argue with R' Yose, classify this *neder*, which

בַּלֶּקֶט וּבַשִּׁכְחָה וּבַפֵּאָה. ,,קוֹנָם כֹּהֲנִים וּלְוִיִם נֶהֱנִים לִי" — יִטְּלוּ עַל כָּרְחוֹ. ,,כֹּהֲנִים אֵלּוּ וּלְוִיִם אֵלּוּ נֶהֱנִים לִי" — יִטְּלוּ אֲחֵרִים.

ר' עובדיה מברטנורא

וִיכוֹלָה לֵיהָנוֹת בלקט שכחה ופיאה. הכי קאמר, ועוד טעמא אחרינא שקונס שאני נהנית לבריות אין הבעל מיפר, שהרי יכולה ליהנות מלקט שכחה ופיאה, שאינה נהנית מן הבריות, דמתנות עניים נינהו, ונמצא שאין כאן עינוי נפש: **קוֹנָם כהנים ולוים נהנים לי.** כי היכי דקונס שאני נהנית לבריות מותרת במתנות עניים, הכי נמי המדיר כהנים ולוים מנכסיו מותרים במתנות כהונה ולויה:

יד אברהם

prohibits her from deriving benefit from anyone (other than her husband), as one involving self-denial. He adds further, that even a *neder* preventing her only from benefiting from a single individual affects their mutual relationship, and is therefore revocable. This is because if the wife must avoid a particular person it can impose inconveniences on her husband.

Rambam (*Commentary*) appears to construe R' Yose's ruling here as meaning that *he cannot revoke it* as absolute; i.e., the *neder* is regarded neither as one of self-denial nor as one that affects their mutual relationship. The Rabbis, he maintains, treat the *neder* of this mishnah as one that affects their mutual relationship (see *Keren Orah*).

וִיכוֹלָה הִיא לֵהָנוֹת בַּלֶּקֶט וּבַשִּׁכְחָה וּבַפֵּאָה. — *and she can benefit from the gleanings, the forgotten sheaf and the corner of the field.*

לֶקֶט, *gleanings,* refers to what falls from the harvester as he gathers his bundles (*Lev.* 19:9; *Peah* 4:10; *Rambam, Hil. Matnos Aniyim* 1:4ff.). שִׁכְחָה, *forgotten sheaf,* includes what he overlooked when collecting the bundles into a heap, or when cutting the standing grain (*Deut.* 24:19; ibid.). פֵּאָה, *corner of the field,* is what one is obligated to leave standing (usually at the corner of the

field) in a field being harvested. All these are reserved exclusively for the poor, who may partake of them even against the will of the owner of the field (*Rambam* ibid.).

The mishnah is telling us that another way for the woman to sustain herself without someone else giving food to her husband, yet without violating her *neder* banning benefit from people, is to take these gifts reserved for the poor. Since the owner of the field has no authority over who may take these portions, they are considered ownerless (*Tif. Yis.*). Therefore, taking them is not regarded as benefiting from the owner (*Rosh; Tos. Yom Tov*), and it is not a violation of the *neder* (*Rav*). Needless to say, she has no right to partake of these gifts unless her husband is poor and unable to support her (*Tif. Yis.*).

The underlying concept of this case — that, if one partakes of property which is considered ownerless, it is not deemed as benefiting from any person — is also illustrated with the following example, but not in the context of a *neder* declared by one's wife (*Rav; Rambam Commentary*).

,,קוֹנָם כֹּהֲנִים וּלְוִיִם נֶהֱנִים לִי" — *[If one said:] "Konam, Kohanim or Leviim benefiting from me"* —

from the gleanings, the forgotten sheaf, and the corner of the field.

[If one said:] "*Konam*, *Kohanim* or *Leviim* benefiting from me" — they may take [it] against his will. "[*Konam*], these *Kohanim* or these *Leviim* benefiting from me" — others may take [it].

YAD AVRAHAM

[This is a new case, and applies to any person making such a *neder*.]

The Torah (*Num.* 18:21ff.) obligates certain portions to be separated from agricultural produce and given to *Kohanim* and *Leviim*. The owner of the produce may choose which *Kohanim* or *Leviim* should receive his dues. In the *Gemara* (84b-85a) there is a controversy as to whether this privilege [טובַת הַנָאָה] is considered to be of monetary value (see *Tos. Yom Tov*). Even if this right does have such value, and he is thus considered the owner of these dues until they are given to the *Kohen* or *Levi*, if he declares benefit from him to be forbidden to *Kohanim* and *Leviim*, he loses the privilege of choosing to which of them to give the gifts, and hence, any ownership in them. This is because these dues are of no use to him, being permitted only to *Kohanim* and *Leviim*, and therefore, it is obvious that the intent of his declaration is to renounce even this privilege in the gifts (*Gem.* ibid.; *Ran* ad loc.). Accordingly:

יִטְּלוּ עַל כָּרְחוֹ. — *they may take [it] against his will.*

Since the owner has forfeited any rights he may have had in this produce, the *Kohanim* and *Leviim* may partake of it, and it is not regarded as benefiting from him (*Rav*; *Tos. Yom Tov*).

On the basis of the above, *Rashba*, quoted by *Ran* (85a), concludes that if a person forbids himself to benefit from his own property effectively forfeiting any rights he has in it, this declaration is tantamount to a renunciation of ownership, entitling any outsider to take possession of his belongings (see *Ran* ibid.; *Meiri*; *Machaneh Ephraim Hil. Zechiyah* 4; *Nesivos HaMishpat* 275:1).

„כֹּהֲנִים אֵלוּ וּלְוִיִּם אֵלוּ נֶהֱנִים לִי" — *"[Konam] these Kohanim or these Leviim benefiting from me"* —

Here, rather than including all *Kohanim* or *Leviim* in his ban, he limits the prohibition to specific persons. Since there remain *Kohanim* whom he permits to benefit from him, he has not renounced his right to distribute the dues to whom he sees fit; he has merely limited it somewhat. Accordingly, he retains these rights, and if one of the specified *Kohanim* partakes of the dues, he is violating the terms of the *neder* by deriving benefit from the owner (*Tos. Yom Tov*). Thus:

יִטְּלוּ אֲחֵרִים. — *others may take [it].*

[Those *Kohanim* or *Leviim* not specified in the ban may take the gifts.]

Even according to those who maintain that the privilege of choosing the recipient *Kohen* or *Levi* is not regarded as being of monetary value, it nevertheless gives the owner of the produce sufficient authority to proscribe certain *Kohanim* or *Leviim* from taking the dues without his permission. This is because a *neder* that prohibits benefiting from a certain item in-

[ד] **,,קוֹנָם** שֶׁאֵינִי עוֹשָׂה עַל פִּי אַבָּא" וְ,,עַל פִּי אָבִיךְ" וְ,,עַל פִּי אָחִי" וְ,,עַל פִּי אָחִיךְ" — אֵינוֹ יָכוֹל לְהָפֵר. ,,שֶׁאֵינִי עוֹשָׂה עַל פִּיךְ" — אֵינוֹ צָרִיךְ לְהָפֵר. רַבִּי עֲקִיבָא אוֹמֵר: יָפֵר, שֶׁמָּא תַעְדִּיף עָלָיו יוֹתֵר מִן הָרָאוּי לוֹ. רַבִּי יוֹחָנָן בֶּן נוּרִי אוֹמֵר: יָפֵר, שֶׁמָּא יְגָרְשֶׁנָּה וּתְהֵי אֲסוּרָה עָלָיו.

===== ר' עובדיה מברטנורא =====

(ד) קוֹנָם שֶׁאֵינִי עוֹשָׂה עַל פִּי אבא. הקדש יהא כל מה שאני טושה מלבוש טל פי אבא, כלומר, שלא יוכל אבא ליהנות ממטשה ידי, אינו יכול להפר, שאין זה דברים שבינו לבינה. ובהא מודו כולי טלמא שאוסרת הנאתה טל פלוני אין הבטל מיפר. וכן הלכה: **על פיך אינו צריך להפר.** משום דמשעבדא ליה, ואף על גב דהקדש מוליא מידי שעבוד, אלמוה רבנן לשעבודא דבעל דבטל שאין הקונס מפקיע שעבודו: **יפר שמא תעדיף עליו יותר מן הראוי לו.** והקדש חל טל החלק הטודף שאינו תחת שעבודו, לפיכך לריך להפר, והספרה מוטלת בו משום דהו דברים שבינו לבינה, שאי אפשר שלא יתערב אותו הטודף בשל בטלה: **רבי יוחנן בן נורי אומר יפר שמא יגרשנה.** וטיקר מטשה ידיה לריך הפרה שמא יגרשנה ויפקט שעבודיה דבטל, ואז יחול הנדר ותהא אסורה לחזור לו. והלכה כרבי יוחנן בן נורי. ובאומרת יקדשו ידי לטושיהם, דידים איתנהו בטולם, וחל טליהם הקדש:

===== יד אברהם =====

cludes also benefits from it that are ordinarily considered worthless [see 4:1] (*Meiri; Kesef Mishneh* to *Hil. Nedarim* 7:11 quoting *R' Meir HaMeili; see Tos. Yom Tov; Keren Orah* to 84b).

4.

,,קוֹנָם שֶׁאֵינִי עוֹשָׂה עַל פִּי אַבָּא" וְ,,עַל פִּי אָבִיךְ" וְ,,עַל פִּי אָחִי" וְ,,עַל פִּי אָחִיךְ"- — *[If one's wife said:] "Konam, my handiwork to Father" or "to your father" or "to my brother" or "to your brother,"*

That is, she declares it to be forbidden for any one of these people to benefit from her work (*Rav*).

אֵינוֹ יָכוֹל לְהָפֵר. — *he is unable to revoke it.*

As explained in the preface to mishnah 1, a *neder* which prohibits someone other then a woman's husband to benefit from her is considered neither one of self-denial [since it restricts others, not herself (*Meiri*), nor one that affects their mutual relationship [since he remains permitted to benefit from her work (*Rosh*)]. Therefore, all agree that the *neder* of the mishnah cannot be revoked by the husband (*Rav; Rambam Commentary*).

Generally, one cannot prohibit to someone else the benefit of something that does not yet exist. For example, if one says: "*Konam*, the fruits of my tree to So-and-So" before any fruits had yet grown, the *neder* is inefficacious (*Gem.* 47a). Nonetheless, in this case, the handiwork that the woman will produce after she made the *neder* will be forbidden to her father, because the ban interdicts her hands, with respect to what they produce, rather than the produce itself. Since, of course, her hands exist now, the

4. **[I**f one's wife said:] *"Konam,* my handiwork to Father" or "to your father" or "to my brother" or "to your brother," he is unable to revoke it; [*"Konam,*] my work to you" — he need not revoke it. R' Akiva says: He should revoke it lest she produce more than his due. R' Yochanan ben Nuri says: He should revoke it lest he divorce her, and she will then be forbidden to him.

YAD AVRAHAM

prohibition is effective for benefits derived from her handiwork in the future (*Gem.* 85b; *Meiri*; see *Ran* 16b s.v. אמר; *Tos. Yom Tov,* s.v. שמא).

שֶׁאֵינִי עוֹשָׂה עַל פִּיךְ״, — [*"Konam]* my work to you" —

In this case, the wife addresses her husband, and declares the benefit from her handiwork to be forbidden to him (*Meiri*). According to the *kesubah* (marriage contract), a husband must provide sustenance for his wife in exchange for which he is granted the rights to her handiwork (*Kesubos* 58b; see ArtScroll commentary ibid. 4:4, p.80).

אֵינוֹ צָרִיךְ לְהָפֵר. — *he need not revoke it.*

[Such a *neder* is not effective, and it is therefore unnecessary for the husband to revoke it.]

Ordinarily, if a person were to interdict via a *neder* an item upon which someone else has a lien, the prohibition would take effect. Nevertheless, the Rabbis instituted that, with regard to the items which a wife is obligated to give her husband, such as her handiwork (and vice versa, see *Ran* 15b, s.v. והא), his claim to such things is tantamount to ownership, so that she cannot forbid it to him (*Rav; Kesubos* 59b). To do so would be to prohibit her husband to benefit from his own property, which is beyond the

scope of a *neder* (see preface to 1:1; *Rambam, Hil. Nedarim* 12:9f.).

רַבִּי עֲקִיבָא אוֹמֵר: יָפֵר, שֶׁמָּא תַעְדִּיף עָלָיו יוֹתֵר מִן הָרָאוּי לוֹ. — *R' Akiva says: He should revoke it lest she produce more than his due.*

R' Akiva maintains that, if the wife produces handiwork beyond her normal output, she may retain it for herself; the husband has no claim to it, and it is within her jurisdiction to prohibit it to him. Thus, the *neder* in our mishnah would forbid this surplus to him. The husband is empowered to revoke this *neder,* because — since, in practice, it is impossible to precisely separate her extra output from her ordinary work — tension is bound to arise between husband and wife, classifying this *neder* as one which affects their mutual relationship (*Rav*).

The first *Tanna,* however, contends that even her surplus work belongs to the husband, so that there is no produce of the wife's upon which the prohibition could take effect (*Tos. Yom Tov*).

רַבִּי יוֹחָנָן בֶּן נוּרִי אוֹמֵר: יָפֵר, שֶׁמָּא יְגָרְשֶׁנָה וּתְהֵי אֲסוּרָה עָלָיו. — *R' Yochanan ben Nuri says: He should revoke it lest he divorce her, and she will then be forbidden to him.*

R' Yochanan ben Nuri argues that, although the Rabbis enacted that the

[ה] **נָדְרָה** אִשְׁתּוֹ, וְסָבוּר שֶׁנָּדְרָה בִתּוֹ; נָדְרָה
בִתּוֹ, וְסָבוּר שֶׁנָּדְרָה אִשְׁתּוֹ; נָדְרָה
בְנָזִיר, וְסָבוּר שֶׁנָּדְרָה בְקָרְבָּן; נָדְרָה בְקָרְבָּן,
וְסָבוּר שֶׁנָּדְרָה בְנָזִיר; נָדְרָה מִן הַתְּאֵנִים, וְסָבוּר
שֶׁנָּדְרָה מִן הָעֲנָבִים; נָדְרָה מִן הָעֲנָבִים, וְסָבוּר
שֶׁנָּדְרָה מִן הַתְּאֵנִים — הֲרֵי זֶה יַחֲזוֹר וְיָפֵר.

────────── ר׳ עובדיה מברטנורא ──────────

(ה) **הרי זה יחזור ויפר.** דהפרה בטעות לא הויא הפרה עד שיכוין לאשה שנדרה, דכתיב
(במדבר ל, יג) לא הניא אותה, עד שתהיה ההפרה לעלמה של הנודרת. וגם שיכוין לנדר שנדרה,
דכתיב (שם פסוק ה) ושמע אביה את נדרה, עד שידע איזה נדר נדרה:

────────── יד אברהם ──────────

husband's rights to his wife's handiwork prevent her *neder* from taking
hold, this is so only as long as he has
these rights. Should they divorce,
however, in which case his rights to
her produce would be terminated, her
produce would become forbidden to
him by virtue of that *neder* (*Rav; Tos.
Yom Tov* from *Ran; Rosh* 86b).

If the prohibition becomes effective, anything his ex-wife produces
henceforth will be forbidden to him.
In that case, it will be impossible for
them ever to remarry — since, in
marriage, he could not possibly avoid
benefiting from her handiwork. Consequently, the prohibition of her work
to him, although it will be effective
only if they divorce, may eventually
interfere with a subsequent desire to
remarry. Thus, according to R' Yochanan ben Nuri, it is a *neder* which
affects their mutual relationship (*Rosh*
79b, s.v. שמיא).

The disagreement of the other *Tannaim* in
the mishnah with R' Yochanan ben Nuri
may be about the possibility of the declaration becoming effective once the husband
loses his right through divorce. R' Yochanan
ben Nuri holds that the Rabbinic enactment
discussed above, which gives the husband's
claim to his wife's handiwork the status of
ownership, merely suspends the *neder* during the marriage; therefore, should they
divorce, the *neder* would be activated. The
other *Tannaim*, however, maintain that the
enactment dissolves the *neder* completely,
because a *neder* that does not take effect as
declared is automatically void (*Ran* 85b; see
Shaar HaMelech, cited in commentary to
mishnah 12, s.v. וּתְהֵא).

5.

נָדְרָה אִשְׁתּוֹ, וְסָבוּר שֶׁנָּדְרָה בִתּוֹ; — [If] his
*wife vowed, and he thought it was his
daughter who had vowed;*

A man, having been informed that
his daughter made a *neder*, revoked it
(*Rama, Yoreh Deah* 234:31). According to some authorities, the mishnah
refers even to a case in which he knew
whether it was his daughter or wife
who had made the *neder*, but he assumed it to be his daughter and made
the revocation on that assumption
(*Bach* to *Yoreh Deah* 234; see *Shach*
ibid. 47 and *Turei Zahav* ibid. 31). [He
later discovered that it had actually
been his wife who had vowed.]

נָדְרָה בִתּוֹ, וְסָבוּר שֶׁנָּדְרָה אִשְׁתּוֹ; — [or if]
his daughter vowed, and he thought it

11
5

5. **[**If] his wife vowed, and he thought it was his daughter who had vowed; [or if] his daughter vowed and he thought it was his wife who had vowed; [or if] she vowed [to become] a Nazirite, and he thought that she had vowed concerning an offering; [or if] she vowed concerning an offering, and he thought that she had vowed [to become] a Nazirite; [or if] she made a *neder* prohibiting figs, and he thought that she had made a *neder* prohibiting grapes; [or if] she made a *neder* prohibiting grapes; and he thought that she had made a *neder* prohibiting figs — he must revoke the *neder* again.

YAD AVRAHAM

was his wife who had vowed;

[This is the reverse of the previous example. Here, he revoked a *neder* which he assumed had been made by his wife, and, in fact, had been made by his daughter.]

נָדְרָה בְנָזִיר, וְסָבוּר שֶׁנָּדְרָה בְקָרְבָּן; נָדְרָה בְקָרְבָּן, וְסָבוּר שֶׁנָּדְרָה בְנָזִיר; — *[or if] she vowed [to become] a Nazirite, and he thought that she had vowed concerning an offering; [or if] she vowed concerning an offering, and he thought that she had vowed [to become] a Nazirite;*

In this case, there was no misinformation as to who had made the *neder*, but as to what it had been about. For example, a woman declared herself a Nazirite, but her husband was informed that she had made a *neder* that some item should be prohibited to her like an offering (*Tos.* 86b). [He then revoked the *neder* on the basis of this false information.]

נָדְרָה מִן הַתְּאֵנִים, וְסָבוּר שֶׁנָּדְרָה מִן הָעֲנָבִים; נָדְרָה מִן הָעֲנָבִים, וְסָבוּר שֶׁנָּדְרָה מִן

הַתְּאֵנִים— *[or if] she made a neder prohibiting figs, and he thought that she had made a neder prohibiting grapes; [or if] she make a neder prohibiting grapes, and he thought that she had made a neder prohibiting figs —*

[In these cases, he had been misinformed as to the item she had interdicted.]

הֲרֵי זֶה יַחֲזֹר וְיָפֵר. — *he must revoke the neder again.*

[This applies to all the cases in this mishnah.]

His original revocation, having been made while misinformed, is not valid. This is derived from the phrase (*Num.* 30:6), *But if her father disallows her*, which teaches us that he must know exactly who pronounced the *neder*, and the phrase (ibid. v. 5), *and her father hears her neder*, which implies that he must know precisely the nature and object of the *neder* when revoking it (*Rambam, Commentary and Hil. Nedarim* 12:21; cf. *Rav, Tos. Yom Tov*).

Because the information he initially

[ו] אָמְרָה: ,,קוֹנָם תְּאֵנִים וַעֲנָבִים אֵלּוּ שֶׁאֵינִי טוֹעֶמֶת״, קַיָּם לַתְּאֵנִים — כֻּלּוֹ קַיָּם; הֵפֵר לַתְּאֵנִים — אֵינוֹ מוּפָר עַד שֶׁיָּפֵר אַף לָעֲנָבִים. אָמְרָה: ,,קוֹנָם תְּאֵנִים שֶׁאֵינִי טוֹעֶמֶת וַעֲנָבִים שֶׁאֵינִי טוֹעֶמֶת״ — הֲרֵי אֵלּוּ שְׁנֵי נְדָרִים.

─────────── ר׳ עובדיה מברטנורא ───────────

(ו) קיים לתאנים כולו קיים כו'. וטעמא, דכתיב (במדבר ל, יד) אישה יקימנו, יקים ממנו, כשקיים מקלתו קייס כולו. אבל יפירנו דליכא למדרש הכי, אינו מופר עד שיפר כולו. ואלו דברי יחיד וחינה הלכה, אלא הלכה כחכמים שאומרים מקיש הקמה להפרה, מה הפרה מה שהפר הפר ומה שלא הפר לא הפר, דהא ליכא למדרש הפרה במקלת, אף הקמה מה שקיים קיים ומה שלא קיים לא קיים, דמיקימנו נמי לא דרשינן הקמה במקלת, אלא אחריה דקרא למכתב הכי, ואף על גב דבהתרת חכם אמרינן נדר שהותר מקלתו הותר כולו, בהפרת הבעל והאב אינו כן:

יד אברהם

received was incorrect, *the day that he hears it* (ibid. v. 6) in this case would be the day in which he receives accurate information (*Rashba; Meiri*). When he hears that it was actually his wife who had vowed, or that the *neder* had, in fact, been directed at grapes, he has until the end of that day to revoke the *neder* (*Rambam, Hil. Nedarim* 12:21; *Yoreh Deah* 234:32).

Even if the husband — upon hearing the original, wrong information — had confirmed the *neder*, it does not take effect, and later, upon receiving the correct facts, he can revoke it (*Tosefta* 7:6, quoted by *Ran*; see *Keren Orah*).

6.

אָמְרָה: ,,קוֹנָם תְּאֵנִים וַעֲנָבִים אֵלּוּ שֶׁאֵינִי טוֹעֶמֶת״, — [If] she said: "Konam, these figs and grapes, with respect to my tasting [them],"

The law of the mishnah applies whether she proscribed specific figs and grapes, or figs and grapes in general (*Meiri; see Tos. Yom Tov*).

קַיָּם לַתְּאֵנִים — כֻּלּוֹ קַיָּם; — [and] he confirmed [the neder with regard] to figs, it becomes confirmed in its entirety;

This is because, in connection with confirming a *neder*, the Torah (*Num.* 30:14) writes: אִישָׁהּ יְקִימֶנּוּ, *her husband can confirm it*, and the word יְקִימֶנּוּ can also be understood as a contraction of יָקִים מִמֶּנּוּ, *can confirm [part] of it.* Thus, even if he confirms only part of the *neder* (e.g., with regard to figs), the

entire *neder* is confirmed, and both figs and grapes are prohibited (*Rav*).

הֵפֵר לַתְּאֵנִים — אֵינוֹ מוּפָר עַד שֶׁיָּפֵר אַף לָעֲנָבִים. — *if he revoked the neder with regard to figs, it is not revoked until he revokes it with regard to grapes as well.*

The reason that partial revocation is not as effective as partial confirmation is that regarding revoking *nedarim*, the Torah (loc. cit.) writes יְפֵרֶנּוּ, *he can revoke it*, which cannot be interpreted to mean *he shall revoke [part of] it*. Thus, unlike partial confirmation, which validates the entire *neder*, partial revocation is not effective (*Rav*).

Some explain that revoking part of the *neder* — in this instance, with regard to figs — does succeed in permitting figs alone. The mishnah, however,

6. **[**I**f] she said: "*Konam,* these figs and grapes, with respect to my tasting [them]," [and] he confirmed [the *neder* with regard] to figs, it becomes confirmed in its entirety; if he revoked the *neder* with regard to figs, it is not revoked until he revokes it with regard to grapes as well. [If] she said: "*Konam,* figs with respect to my tasting [them], and grapes with respect to my tasting [them]," these are two *nedarim.***

YAD AVRAHAM

means that this partial revocation does not rescind the remainder of the prohibition (regarding grapes), until he revokes that part of the *neder* as well (*Tos. Yom Tov* from *Ran*).

Others maintain that, if the husband revokes only part of the *neder,* nothing has been accomplished, and the entire *neder* remains in force; if he wishes to revoke the *neder,* he must revoke it completely (*Ramban; Ran* 82b, s.v. ורב, and 87b, s.v. אבל prefers this approach).

Rav follows *Rambam* (*Commentary* and *Hil. Nedarim* 13:10), who rejects the ruling in our mishnah, and follows the opinion of the Sages mentioned by the *Gemara* (87b), which equates confirming a *neder* to revoking one, and maintains that partial confirmation, too, does not confirm the entire *neder. Rosh,* however, rules in accordance with the anonymous *Tanna* of our mishnah (see *Beis Yosef, Yoreh Deah* 234, and *Rama* ibid. 36).

Although annulment by a sage or panel of even part of a *neder* suffices to cancel the entire *neder* (9:6ff.; see 3:2,4), revocation by a husband is different (*Rav; Rambam Comm.*). This is because of the fundamental difference between these two methods of rescinding a *neder,* discussed in the preface to 10:1. A sage or panel retroactively annuls the *neder* by finding an "opening." Since the person intended the entire *neder* to be binding, and his initial declaration is shown to have been based on a misunderstanding, the whole *neder* is canceled. Revocation by a husband, on the other hand, does not take into account the thoughts of his wife when she made the *neder.* Rather, it discontinues the prohibition she imposed from the moment of revocation and onward. There is therefore no reason why partial revocation should cancel the entire prohibition (*Rosh* 82b, s.v. באחת, quoted by *Tos. Yom Tov*).

Ran (27a) cites *Ramban,* who distinguishes between annulment by a sage or panel on the basis of an "opening," in which case partial annulment cancels the entire *neder,* and annulment based on an expression of regret (see 2:1), in which case partial annulment does not rescind the entire *neder.* See also *Maharit,* Vol. 1 19.

אָמְרָה: ,,קוֹנָם תְּאֵנִים שֶׁאֵינִי טוֹעֶמֶת וַעֲנָבִים שֶׁאֵינִי טוֹעֶמֶת'' – הֲרֵי אֵלּוּ שְׁנֵי נְדָרִים. — [*If*] she said: "*Konam,* figs with respect to my tasting [them], and grapes with respect to my tasting [them]," these are two nedarim.

[The husband's confirmation with regard to one of the prohibited items has no effect on the other.]

[ז] ,,**יוֹדֵעַ** אֲנִי שֶׁיֵּשׁ נְדָרִים, אֲבָל אֵינִי יוֹדֵעַ
שֶׁיֵּשׁ מְפִירִין" — יָפֵר. ,,יוֹדֵעַ אֲנִי
שֶׁיֵּשׁ מְפִירִין, אֲבָל אֵינִי יוֹדֵעַ שֶׁזֶּה נֶדֶר" — רַבִּי
מֵאִיר אוֹמֵר: לֹא יָפֵר; וַחֲכָמִים אוֹמְרִים: יָפֵר.

───────── ר' עובדיה מברטנורא ─────────

(ז) **איני יודע שיש מפירין.** שיש לו רשות להפר. ביום שנודע לו שיש לו רשות להפר, שהוא
עליו כיום שמעו: **איני יודע שזה נדר.** וצריך הפרה: **רבי מאיר אומר לא יפר.** דכיון שיודע
שיש בידו להפר, אף על פי שלא ידע שהוא נדר מכל מקום נדר היה לו להפר. ואין הלכה כרבי מאיר:

יד אברהם

According to *Tosafos* (87b, s.v.
ורבי), the declaration here is: "*Konam*, figs, with respect to my tasting
them, and *konam*, grapes with respect
to my tasting them." It is the repetition
of *konam* which makes this declaration like two separate *nedarim*. It
appears that in some versions, such
as that of *Rosh*, the term *konam* is
repeated in the very text of the
mishnah. *Ran* (87b, s.v. אמר) considers the repetition of *with respect to
my tasting* to be the reason we regard
this statement as two *nedarim* [and the
actual text of the declaration is thus
exactly as recorded in the mishnah]

(*Tos. Yom Tov*).

The *Gemara* (86b) identifies R'
Shimon as the author of this ruling,
in accordance with a similar approach
he adopts in *Shevuos* 5:3 [see 9:7] (*Tos.
Yom Tov*).

The consequence of the fact that
this statement is considered two separate *nedarim* is that if the husband
revoked (or confirmed) one part of the
neder (e.g., regarding figs), he can still
confirm (or revoke) the other part
(regarding grapes), since the two
halves are treated as two distinct,
complete *nedarim*, and not as parts
of one long *neder* (*Rav; Meiri*).

7.

,,יוֹדֵעַ אֲנִי שֶׁיֵּשׁ נְדָרִים, אֲבָל אֵינִי יוֹדֵעַ שֶׁיֵּשׁ
מְפִירִין" — *[If a man said:]* "*I know
that there are nedarim, but I did not
know that they could be revoked* (lit.,
there are revokers),"

A woman made a *neder*, and her
husband (or her father, as the case may
be) failed to revoke it during the day he
learnt of it (*Rambam Comm.*). Ordinarily, this would constitute a confirmation of the *neder*, and it would no
longer be revocable (*Num.* 30:15; *Rambam, Hil. Nedarim* 12:15,18). However,
in the case of our mishnah, on the day
the husband first learnt of the *neder*, he
was unaware that he possessed the right

to revoke it (*Ran*).

יָפֵר. — *he can revoke [the neder].*

The day he learns of his right to
revoke her *nedarim* is considered *the
day he hears of it* (*Rav*), and he has
until the end of that day to revoke it
(*Rambam, Hil. Nedarim* 12:20; *Yoreh
Deah* 234:21).

The earlier day, on which he first
found out about his wife's declaration,
is not regarded as *the day he hears of it*,
since "hearing of it" means to become
aware of the *neder* while knowing of
the right to revoke it. But, here, on
hearing of the *neder*, he did not know

7. **[I**f a man said:] "I know that there are *nedarim*, but I did not know that they could be revoked," he can revoke [the *neder*]. [But if he said:] "I know that *nedarim* could be revoked, but I did not know that this was a *neder*" — R' Meir says: He cannot revoke [it]; the Sages, however, say: He can revoke [it].

YAD AVRAHAM

his rights; consequently, that day is not considered *the day he hears of it* (*Tos.* 87b, s.v. יודע).

‎,,יוֹדֵעַ אֲנִי שֶׁיֵּשׁ מְפִירִין, אֲבָל אֵינִי יוֹדֵעַ שֶׁזֶּה נֶדֶר"– — *[But if he said:] "I know that nedarim could be revoked, but I did not know that this was a neder"* —

In this case, he claims that, although he knew all along that there were certain *nedarim* which a husband could revoke (those involving self-denial and those which affect their mutual relationship), he did not know that her declaration was a valid *neder*, and it therefore needed revocation (*Rav; Rosh* 78b). *Ran* explains his claim to be that he did not know that this *neder* was of the category he was empowered to revoke.

‎רַבִּי מֵאִיר אוֹמֵר: לֹא יָפֵר; — *R' Meir says: He cannot revoke [it];*

R' Meir argues that, since when he first heard of his wife's *neder*, he already knew that he was empowered to revoke her *nedarim*, he should have done so just to be safe, even though he did not know that her *neder* was valid (*Rav; Meiri*). His failure to revoke it is therefore considered a confirmation of the *neder* (*Rosh* 78b).

Some explain that, even if he had revoked it upon first hearing of it, the *neder* would not be canceled. Since he did not know that the *neder* could be revoked or that it needed revocation, his knowledge of

it is incomplete and so, he is not considered to have "heard of the *neder*" sufficiently to be able to revoke it. On the other hand, his knowledge on that day is considered complete enough, relative to what he discovered subsequently (that it can be or needs to be revoked), so that the first day does count as *the day he hears of it*. Thus, according to R' Meir, he cannot revoke the *neder* in such a case at all — not on the day he initially learns of it, nor on a later day when he discovers that it needed to be or could have been revoked (*Ran* 87b).

‎וַחֲכָמִים אוֹמְרִים: יָפֵר. — *the Sages, however, say: He can revoke [it].*

They do not regard the day he first learnt of the *neder* as *the day he hears of it*, since his knowledge of the status of the *neder* was incomplete (*Tos.* 87b, s.v. יודע). When he discovers that the *neder* needs to be revoked, and that this can be done by him, he has until the end of that day to do so (*Yoreh Deah* 234:21; see *Radbaz, Hil. Nedarim* 12:20).

Those who explain R' Meir as holding that revocation of the *neder* on either day is invalid construe the Sages as maintaining that the *neder* may be revoked on the earlier day. That is, if on the day he first learnt of it, he revoked it — although he did not yet know that it needed to be or could be revoked — the *neder* is canceled. But, on the later date, when he becomes aware of the status of the *neder*, even the Sages do not permit revocation (*Ran*).

[ח] **הַמֻּדָּר** הֲנָאָה מֵחֲתָנוֹ, וְהוּא רוֹצֶה לָתֵת
לְבִתּוֹ מָעוֹת — אוֹמֵר לָהּ: ,,הֲרֵי
הַמָּעוֹת הָאֵלּוּ נְתוּנִין לָךְ בְּמַתָּנָה, וּבִלְבַד שֶׁלֹּא
יְהֵא לְבַעֲלִיךְ רְשׁוּת בָּהֶן, אֶלָּא מַה שֶׁאַתְּ נוֹשֵׂאת
וְנוֹתֶנֶת בְּפִיךְ".

[ט] **וְנֶדֶר** אַלְמָנָה וּגְרוּשָׁה ... יָקוּם עָלֶיהָ".

─────────────── **ר' עובדיה מברטנורא** ───────────────

(ח) ובלבד שלא יהא לבעליך רשות בהם. ותגאו קיים ולא קנה הבעל, ואף על גב
דבמתנה זו מלילו מן הטורח, שהרי אשתו ניזונת מן המעות הללו ומזונותיה היו עליו, אלולי
מעותא אינה חשובה הנאה: **(ט) ונדר אלמנה וגרושה כו'.** לגופיה לא צריך קרא, דכיון דאין
לה בעל, מי יפר. אלא כשנדרה כשהיא אלמנה, לזמן, ולא הגיע זמן הנדר עד שנשאת:

─────────────────────────────────

יד אברהם

8.

One of the provisions of the *kesubah* (marriage contract) assigns to the
husband the usufruct of gifts that the wife receives during the course of their
marriage. (*Rambam, Hil. Ishus* 12:4, 16:2; *Even HaEzer* 85; see General Introduction to ArtScroll *Kesubos*, p. 6). This does not apply to gifts of food,
however, since the husband is obligated in any case to provide food for his
wife (*Ran*). Thus, if someone from whom the husband was forbidden to
benefit was to give the wife food, the husband is not entitled to it in any way,
and the prohibition has not been violated (ibid.; 4:3). However, if the same
person were to give the wife some gift other than food, he would thereby also
be giving the husband the usufruct of that gift, which would constitute a
violation of the *neder* (*Turei Zahav, Yoreh Deah* 22:3).

In this mishnah, a method is described by which one can present a woman
with a gift in such a manner that the husband — who is forbidden to benefit
from him — does not gain from it, thereby circumventing the prohibition.

הַמֻּדָּר הֲנָאָה מֵחֲתָנוֹ, — *One who is
prohibited by a neder to benefit from
his father-in-law,*

The translation follows *Tos. Yom
Tov* who vowelizes חתנו (which
would ordinarily be read as חֲתָנוֹ,
son-in-law) as חָתְנוֹ, *father-in-law.*

Some texts have: הַמֻּדָּר חֲתָנוֹ הֲנָאָה
מִמֶּנּוּ; *One whose son-in-law is
prohibited by a neder to benefit from
him* (*Shinuyei Nuschaos* from a re-
sponsum of *Rambam*). [Whatever the

version, the case remains the same:
someone is forbidden to derive benefit
from his father-in-law.]

וְהוּא רוֹצֶה לָתֵת לְבִתּוֹ מָעוֹת– — *and he
wants to give money to his daughter —*

[I.e., the father-in-law wants to give
money to his daughter.]

Money is used here in contrast with
food, which — as explained in the
preface — is not problematic. But a
gift of money to his daughter would
ordinarily mean a simultaneous gain

8. **O**ne who is prohibited by a *neder* to benefit from his father-in-law, and he wants to give money to his daughter — he says to her: "This money is given to you as a gift, provided that your husband has no rights in it, but that you put it in your mouth."

9. **B**ut the neder *of a widow or of a divorcee ... shall stand against her* (Numbers 30:10). How?

YAD AVRAHAM

for the son-in-law and would constitute a breech of the *neder* (Tos. Yom Tov, from Ran; Shach, Yoreh Deah 222:1; Turei Zahav ibid.). [The mishnah therefore constructs a case in which the father can give money to his daughter in such a way that her husband does not gain any benefit from his gift.]

אוֹמֵר לָהּ: ,,הֲרֵי הַמָּעוֹת הָאֵלוּ נְתוּנִים לָךְ בְּמַתָּנָה, וּבִלְבַד שֶׁלֹא יְהֵא לְבַעֲלִיךְ רְשׁוּת בָּהֶן, אֶלָּא מַה שֶׁאַתְּ נוֹשֵׂאת וְנוֹתֶנֶת בְּפִיךְ.'' — *he says to her: "This money is given to you as a gift, provided that her husband has no rights in it, but that you put it in your mouth."*

He stipulates that she use the money solely to acquire food for eating. He might equally have specified that it be reserved for some other use, such as clothes (Yoreh Deah ibid.).

The father's statement includes two parts: (1) a condition that the husband may not use the gift, and (2) a specification of how his daughter should use it. Were the father only to state the first part — that the husband not have any rights to the money — it

would not be sufficient. Since he did not also specify how she should use the money, the husband would gain the unsufructuary rights to the gift, and the *neder* would thus be violated (ibid.). If, on the other hand, he stated only what the gift should be used for, there is disagreement among the later authorities. Tos. Yom Tov considers such a statement effective in restricting the husband from benefiting from the gift. Shach (Yoreh Deah 222:2) and Turei Zahav (ibid. 2), however, disagree (see Pischei Teshuvah ibid. 1).

The conditions attached to the gift accomplish that the son-in-law does not gain any rights to the gift, so that the *neder* is not violated thereby. Ran explains that this is because the daughter is not being given an absolute gift. It is given her only for a particular use, and is hers only if she uses it that way. Although a husband generally gains automatic rights in his wife's acquisition, this is not a usual type of acquisition, and so, is not included in the general rule (Ran, quoted by Tos. Yom Tov).

9.

,,וְנֵדֶר אַלְמָנָה וּגְרוּשָׁה ... יָקוּם עָלֶיהָ.'' כֵּיצַד? — *"But the neder of a widow or of a divorcee ... shall stand against her"* (Numbers 30:10). How?

This verse refers to a woman who has become widowed or divorced from a full marriage [and not just from *erusin*, the first stage of marriage] (Rashi

כֵּיצַד? אָמְרָה: "הֲרֵינִי נְזִירָה לְאַחַר שְׁלֹשִׁים יוֹם", אַף עַל פִּי שֶׁנִּשֵּׂאת בְּתוֹךְ שְׁלֹשִׁים יוֹם — אֵינוֹ יָכוֹל לְהָפֵר.

נָדְרָה וְהִיא בִּרְשׁוּת הַבַּעַל — מֵפֵר לָהּ. כֵּיצַד? אָמְרָה: "הֲרֵינִי נְזִירָה לְאַחַר שְׁלֹשִׁים", אַף עַל פִּי שֶׁנִּתְאַלְמְנָה אוֹ נִתְגָּרְשָׁה בְּתוֹךְ שְׁלֹשִׁים — הֲרֵי זֶה מוּפָר. נָדְרָה בּוֹ בַיּוֹם, נִתְגָּרְשָׁה בּוֹ בַיּוֹם, הֶחֱזִירָהּ בּוֹ בַיּוֹם — אֵינוֹ יָכוֹל לְהָפֵר.

—————————— ר' עובדיה מברטנורא ——————————

אינו יכול להפר. אַף עַל פִּי שֶׁהַנֶּדֶר חָל כְּשֶׁהִיא תַחְתָּיו, דִּבְתַר שָׁעַת הַנֶּדֶר אָזְלִינָן: **נדרה בו ביום, גרשה בו ביום, והחזירה בו ביום.** וְאַחַר כָּךְ שָׁמַע אֶת נִדְרָהּ: **אינו יכול להפר.** כֵּיוָן שֶׁיָּצְאָת בִּרְשׁוּת עַצְמָהּ בֵּין נֶדֶר לַהֲפָרָה, דְּאֵין הַבַּעַל מֵפֵר בְּקוֹדְמִין:

ad loc.; see *Malbim* ibid.). In that case, however, this verse — which indicates that the *neder* of a widow or a divorcee stands and cannot be revoked — would seem superfluous. For, in her current state, she has no husband [nor does her father have any more rights (see 10:3)]; how could her *nedarim* possibly be revoked? (*Rav*). [This is the mishnah's question: *How?*]

אָמְרָה: "הֲרֵינִי נְזִירָה לְאַחַר שְׁלֹשִׁים יוֹם", — אַף עַל פִּי שֶׁנִּשֵּׂאת בְּתוֹךְ שְׁלֹשִׁים יוֹם— *[If] she said: "I will be a Nazirite after thirty days" — even if she marries within the thirty days,*

The mishnah asserts that the verse is needed for a case in which she declares a *neder* — e.g., to become a Nazirite — which will take effect only after thirty days. In the interim, she remarries, so that when the *neder* is scheduled to take effect, she will have a husband (*Rav*).

אֵינוֹ יָכוֹל לְהָפֵר. — *he cannot revoke it.*
The verse teaches us that, although the *neder* takes effect while she is under her new husband's jurisdiction,

he cannot revoke it, since it had been declared while she was independent (*Rav; Meiri*).

[Having established that it is her status at the time the *neder* is made which is decisive, the mishnah proceeds to illustrate a situation in which — because of this law — the husband's revocation is effective.]

נָדְרָה וְהִיא בִּרְשׁוּת הַבַּעַל – מֵפֵר לָהּ. — *[If] she vowed while under her husband's authority, he may revoke it.*

[That is, if she made the *neder* while they were married, even if she is independent at the time it actually takes effect, his revocation is valid nevertheless.]

כֵּיצַד? אָמְרָה: "הֲרֵינִי נְזִירָה לְאַחַר שְׁלֹשִׁים", אַף עַל פִּי שֶׁנִּתְאַלְמְנָה אוֹ נִתְגָּרְשָׁה בְּתוֹךְ שְׁלֹשִׁים— *How? If she said: "I will be a Nazirite after thirty [days]" — even if she is widowed or divorced within the thirty [days],*

Sometime after making this declaration she is divorced or widowed, so that when her *neder* is to take effect, she is independent. Neverthe-

[If] she said: "I will be a Nazirite after thirty days" — even if she marries within the thirty days, he cannot revoke it.

[If] she vowed while under her husband's authority, he may revoke it. How? If she said: "I will be a Nazirite after thirty [days]" — even if she is widowed or divorced within the thirty [days], it is revoked. [If] she vowed on the same day, [and] was divorced on the same day, [and] he took her back on the same day, he cannot revoke it.

YAD AVRAHAM

less, the revocation is efficacious, since she was under her husband's domain when she made the *neder* (*Meiri*; see commentary to 10:7, s.v. אֶת שֶׁבָּא).

הֲרֵי זֶה מוּפָר. — *it is revoked.*

If, upon learning of this *neder*, the husband revoked it (*Ritva*).

[To conclude the discussion of women who became divorced or widowed after a complete marriage, the mishnah goes on to delineate to what extent becoming independent removes her from anyone else's authority.]

נָדְרָה בּוֹ בַיּוֹם, — *[If] she vowed on the same day,*

I.e., on the day she was married (*Ran* 89a).

נִתְגָּרְשָׁה בּוֹ בַיּוֹם, — *[and] was divorced on the same day,*

The sequence of events is that she marries, makes a *neder*, and is divorced — all on the same day. The reason the mishnah chooses a case in which the *neder* was made on the day of the marriage is to emphasize that the woman's father no longer has any authority over her. Although, earlier on this very day, if she had not yet become a *bogeres*, he did have such privileges [either alone or in conjunction with the betrothed husband (see

10:1)], once she is married, he loses these rights altogether (*Ran*). [After the divorce, she is independent, having left the domain of both her father and her husband. But ...]

הֶחֱזִירָהּ בּוֹ בַיּוֹם- — *[and] he took her back on the same day,*

[Her ex-husband remarries her.] *Rav* follows *Rosh*, who explains that, although the *neder* was made during the first marriage, the husband only learnt of it later in the day, when they were married for the second time. Had the husband become aware of the *neder* during the first marriage and not revoked it prior to their divorce, the act of divorce would preclude subsequent revocation (*Yoreh Deah* 234:14,20; *Turei Zahav* ibid. 16; *Shach* 27). [The mishnah therefore deals with the case in which the husband learns of the *neder* after the divorce.]

אֵינוֹ יָכוֹל לְהָפֵר. — *he cannot revoke it.*

[Even though the husband becomes aware of the *neder* once they are married again, at which time he does have the authority to revoke the *nedarim* his wife will make from now on, he does not have rights to revoke those she had made prior to their second marriage, notwithstand-

זֶה הַכְּלָל: כָּל שֶׁיָּצְאָת לִרְשׁוּת עַצְמָהּ שָׁעָה אַחַת — אֵינוֹ יָכוֹל לְהָפֵר.

[י] **תֵּשַׁע** נְעָרוֹת נִדְרֵיהֶן קַיָּמִין: (א) בּוֹגֶרֶת, וְהִיא "יְתוֹמָה"; (ב) נַעֲרָה וּבָגְרָה,

───────── ר׳ עובדיה מברטנורא ─────────

(י) תשע נערות נדריהן קימים. נערות לאו דוקא: **בוגרת והיא יתומה.** שנשאת ומת בעלה כשהיא נערה, והיא יתומה בחיי האב, שאחר שנשאת אין לאביה רשות בה, ובגרה אחר כך ונדרה, נדרה קיים, שאין האב יכול להפר שהרי היא בוגרת, ועוד שהיא יתומה בחיי האב:

───────── יד אברהם ─────────

ing that it had been made during a marriage to him on the very same day.] As explained in the commentary to 10:4, this is derived from the verse (Num. 30;11), *If in her husband's house she vowed*, which means that the husband can revoke only *nedarim* made in his current "house," i.e., his current marriage (*Tos. Yom Tov*).

זֶה הַכְּלָל: כָּל שֶׁיָּצְאָת לִרְשׁוּת עַצְמָהּ שָׁעָה אַחַת – אֵינוֹ יָכוֹל לְהָפֵר. — *This is the general rule: If any woman had entered into her own authority for even one hour, he cannot revoke her neder.*

The *Gemara* (89a) explains that this

generalization comes to include the case in which the father or his agents give over his betrothed daughter to agents of her husband to be taken to the *chupah*, the completion of the marriage. This already constitutes her independence from the father's domain, and he no longer has any jurisdiction over her *nedarim*. Similarly, at this stage, the husband cannot revoke any *nedarim* made prior to the time his father-in-law gives his wife over to his agents, since they were made prior to the full marriage, and are beyond his jurisdiction (*Tos. Yom Tov; see 10:3*).

10.

There are three developments which bring to an end a father's jurisdiction over his daughter's *nedarim*. These are: becoming a *bogeres*, complete marriage, and the father's death.

As explained in the commentary to 10:1, most authorities maintain that a woman becomes a *bogeres* six months after she becomes a *naarah*. A *naarah* is a girl over the age of twelve, who has grown two pubic hairs (see ibid.).

According to *Tos. Rid*, however, it is possible for a girl to become a *bogeres* even before the passage of these six months if she displays certain physical changes (see *Niddah* 47a), such as the developments of breasts. See *Ravad, Maggid Mishneh,* and *Lechem Mishneh* to *Rambam, Hil. Ishus* 2:8.

If a betrothed girl becomes a *bogeres*, her *nedarim* cannot be revoked, since — during her betrothed status — the combined revocation of both her husband and father is needed, and, since she is a *bogeres*, her father is no longer able to revoke her *nedarim* (see 10:2).

The *chupah*, which effects a full marriage, transfers a woman into her husband's domain (10:2; *Kesubos* 4:4f.). The termination of such a marriage,

This is the general rule: If any woman had entered into her own authority for even one hour, he cannot revoke her *neder*.

10. **T**here are nine *naaros* whose *nedarim* stand: [1] a *bogeres* who is an "orphan"; [2] a *naarah* who became a *bogeres*, and is an

YAD AVRAHAM

whether by death of the husband or by divorce, leaves her independent, as explained in the previous mishnah.[1] If, at that time, the girl is not yet a *bogeres*, she is known as "an orphan in her father's lifetime" (*Rambam Commentary; Yevamos* 13:6). This means that — although a father ordinarily has authority over his daughter while she is a minor — in this case, since she has already been fully married, she is considered independent even though she is not yet mature. Thus, she is like an orphan, who — having no father — is not subject to his jurisdiction (*Rashi* to *Yevamos* 109a, s.v. קטנה). The status of such a girl with regard to the father's rights over her *nedarim* is discussed in the coming mishnah.

תֵּשַׁע נְעָרוֹת נִדְרֵיהֶן קַיָּמִין: — *There are nine naaros whose nedarim stand:*

Rav follows *Rosh*, who remarks that the term נְעָרוֹת, which usually refers to girls who have not yet reached the state of *bogeres*, is used loosely here, since the mishnah goes on to list cases that involve a *bogeres* (*Tos. Yom Tov*).

However, *Rambam* (*Commentary*) explains that, indeed, the term is used in its strict sense, since — in all the following cases — the girl was a *naarah* when she was betrothed. This interpretation is followed by *Meiri*

and *R' Avraham min Hahar.*

The point of the mishnah's opening statement is that, in all the nine examples which follow, the *nedarim* are irrevocable. As will be seen, the nine examples can be reduced to three basic principles, but, in order to sharpen our minds, the mishnah developed all the different possibilities from those three principle (*Ran* from *Yerushalmi; Tos. Yom Tov*).

בּוֹגֶרֶת וְהִיא ,,יְתוֹמָה"; — *[1] a bogeres who is an "orphan";*

[I.e., she becomes — so to speak —

1. Upon the termination of an *erusin* (the first stage of marriage), however, she is once again subject to her father's jurisdiction, if she has not yet become a *bogeres* (10:2).

When a girl's father dies, his heirs do not inherit the authority to revoke her *nedarim* (*Tos. Rid* 11:24). Therefore, the *nedarim* of any orphan girl who is not fully married are irrevocable. Even if she is betrothed, her husband is unable to revoke her *nedarim* alone (10:2).

A girl who is not yet a *bogeres* and becomes betrothed has her *nedarim* revoked by her husband and her father together (10:1). They may revoke even *nedarim* that she declared prior to the *erusin* (10:3). However, once this marriage is completed, and she enters the husband's domain completely, although her husband can revoke her *nedarim* on his own, he cannot revoke those made before the marriage was completed (ibid. and mishnah 9).

The coming mishnah presupposes knowledge of the above laws, and illustrates the different sequence of events which can make a girl's *nedarim* irrevocable.

וְהִיא ,,יְתוֹמָה''; (ג) נַעֲרָה שֶׁלֹא בָגְרָה,
וְהִיא ,,יְתוֹמָה''; (ד) בּוֹגֶרֶת, וּמֵת אָבִיהָ;

ר' עובדיה מברטנורא

נערה ובגרה והיא יתומה. שֶׁנְּשֵׂאת וּמֵת בַּעְלָהּ, שֶׁנָּדְרָה כְּשֶׁהִיא נַעֲרָה וּבָגְרָה לְאַחַר מִכָּאן, וְהִיא יְתוֹמָה בְּחַיֵּי הָאָב כִּדְפָרִישְׁנָא: **נערה.** בְּשָׁעָה שֶׁנָּדְרָה שֶׁלֹּא בָּגְרָה עֲדַיִן, וְהִיא יְתוֹמָה בְּחַיֵּי הָאָב. וְהָכָךְ תִּלְתָא יְתוֹמָה בְּחַיֵּי אָב קָא חָשִׁיב לְהוּ: **בוגרת ומת אביה.. בְּשָׁעָה** שֶׁנָּדְרָה הָיְתָה בּוֹגֶרֶת, וּמֵת אָבִיהָ, דְּהַיְינוּ יְתוֹמָה מַמָּשׁ:

יד אברהם

"an orphan in her father's lifetime."]

Rambam (*Commentary*) notes that the cases which begin with *bogeres* refer to cases in which, at the time she declared the *neder*, she had already reached that stage. Thus, this case is of a girl who was betrothed as a *naarah* (see commentary above), then completed her marriage, and was then divorced or widowed while not yet a *bogeres*. She then reaches this stage and makes a *neder*. Her father cannot revoke it for two reasons: 1) Having gone through a completed marriage while yet a *naarah*, she is "an orphan in his lifetime" (see preface), and 2) she is a *bogeres* (*Rav* from *Rambam*; cf. *Meiri*).

נַעֲרָה וּבָגְרָה, וְהִיא ,,יְתוֹמָה''; — *[2] A naarah who became a bogeres, and is an "orphan"*;

[Here, too, it means she becomes an "orphan," as it were.]

The cases listed here that begin with *naarah* are those in which she made her *neder* before reaching maturity (*Rambam Commentary*). Accordingly, this second case involves a girl who was betrothed as a *naarah*, made a *neder*, became fully married, then was divorced, and then was betrothed again. After all this, she became a *bogeres* (ibid.; *Meiri*).

Her second betrothed would ordinarily have been able to revoke the *nedarim* she had made before their

erusin, in combination with her father (10:3). However, because she was divorced from a full marriage making her "an orphan in her father's lifetime," and because she is already a *bogeres*, the father's right of revocation ceases. Since the betrothed husband cannot revoke *nedarim* on his own, her *nedarim* must stand (ibid.). He cannot revoke these *nedarim* even if he completes the marriage, since even a fully married husband cannot revoke *nedarim* which were made prior to the marriage (*R' Avraham min HaHar*).

Rav, following *Ran*, construes the case almost identically, but omits the second betrothal. Thus, she is single when she becomes a *bogeres*, and — as in the previous example — the point here is that the father cannot revoke her *nedarim*, since she is like an orphan, and is a *bogeres*. The difference between the first case and the second one is that, in the former, she vowed as a *bogeres*, while in the latter instance she vowed as a *naarah*.

Tos. Rid, following his opinion that a girl becomes a *bogeres* in one of two ways — completing six months as a *naarah*, or displaying physical signs of maturity (see preface) — construes the mishnah as referring to a "*naarah* who is a *bogeres*"; that is, a girl who becomes a *bogeres* by displaying these signs before the standard six months as a *naarah* have passed. This is in contrast to the first case, which deals with a girl who became a *bogeres* following six month as a *naarah*.

YAD AVRAHAM

In the commentary to 10:5, it was mentioned that *Tos. Rid* advances a novel interpretation of that mishnah, according to which a betrothed *bogeres* can have her *nedarim* revoked by her husband alone (see also commentary to 10:2). Similarly, he maintains that "an orphan in her father's lifetime" who is betrothed can have her *nedarim* revoked by her husband alone. Accordingly, the present mishnah is discussing only why these girls are beyond their *father's* jurisdiction. If they would become betrothed, their betrothed husband could indeed revoke their *nedarim* (*Tos. Rid* 10:7, 11:24).

נַעֲרָה שֶׁלֹּא בָגְרָה, וְהִיא ,,יְתוֹמָה'' — *[3] a naarah who has not become a bogeres, and is an "orphan";*

[I.e., "an orphan in her father's lifetime."]

This is identical to the preceding case, except that here she has not yet become a *bogeres* (*Rambam Commentary*). Thus, this third case deals with a girl who is betrothed as a *naarah*, makes her *neder*, and then becomes fully married, divorced, and then betrothed again. Her divorce from full marriage makes her like an orphan, so that her father can no longer revoke her *nedarim*, and consequently, neither can her second betrothed. Unlike the previous examples — in which two factors removed her from her father's authority — being an "orphan" and a *bogeres* — in this instance, only one factor is present — her "orphanhood" (*Meiri*).

The point of this case is that the second betrothed cannot revoke the *nedarim* she had made during her first betrothal, even though she is a *naarah* throughout. The reason for this is that, following this *neder*, she became an "orphan in her father's lifetime"

(by being divorced from a completed marriage). If, however, she became an "orphan," and only then made her *neder*, should she subsequently be betrothed (while a *naarah*), her *nedarim* could be revoked by her betrothed together with her father. Thus, if she were fully married and divorced, and only then, after the divorce, she vowed, and was then betrothed — all as a *naarah* — her new betrothed can revoke that *neder* together with her father. According to this view — which is attributed by some version of the *Gemara* (89b) to R' Meir (see *Meleches Shlomo*) — divorce from a full marriage precludes the father only from revoking those *nedarim* made before the divorce; those made after it, however, can be revoked by him in conjunction with her new betrothed if she becomes betrothed again. As explained below, this position is contested in part by R' Yehudah, and in its entirety by the Sages (*Rambam Commentary*, as explained by R' Avraham min HaHar; cf. *Meiri*).

Rav, following *Ran*, again constructs the case without a second betrothal. Upon being divorced from a full marriage, her father loses his authority over her, so that even though she is still a *naarah*, he cannot revoke her *nedarim*. According to this interpretation, this law is not disputed.

בּוֹגֶרֶת, וּמֵת אָבִיהָ; — *[4] a bogeres, whose father died;*

She was betrothed as a *naarah*, and became a *bogeres*; then, her father died. If she vows after becoming a *bogeres*, her betrothed cannot revoke it, since her father — even while he

(ה) נַעֲרָה בוֹגֶרֶת, וּמֵת אָבִיהָ; (ו) נַעֲרָה שֶׁלֹּא בָגְרָה, וּמֵת אָבִיהָ; (ז) נַעֲרָה שֶׁמֵּת אָבִיהָ, וּמִשֶּׁמֵּת אָבִיהָ בָּגְרָה; (ח) בוֹגֶרֶת, וְאָבִיהָ קַיָּם; (ט) נַעֲרָה בוֹגֶרֶת, וְאָבִיהָ קַיָּם. רַבִּי יְהוּדָה אוֹמֵר: אַף הַמַּשִּׂיא בִּתּוֹ הַקְּטַנָּה, וְנִתְאַלְמְנָה אוֹ נִתְגָּרְשָׁה וְחָזְרָה אֶצְלוֹ — עֲדַיִן הִיא נַעֲרָה.

[נַעֲרָה וּבוֹגֶרֶת. וכו']. והנך תלתא נמי מת אביה כייל להו: **נערה שמת אביה ומשמת אביה בגרה כו'.** הנך תלתא דקתני בוגרת כייללא להו. ובגמרא (פט, ב) אמרינן דחכמים לא שנו אלא שלש נערות, בוגרת, ויתומה, ויתומה בחיי האב: **רבי יהודה אומר כו'.** דכיון שנכנסה לחופה ילדתה מרשות אביה בהנהו נשואים:

יד אברהם

was alive — could not join him in the revocation once she has reached that state (*Rambam Commentary; R' Avraham min HaHar; Meiri*).

Rav follows *Ran*, who constructs the case without a betrothed husband: A single girl becomes a *bogeres*, loses her father, and then vows. Since there is no one to revoke her *nedarim*, they stand. As in the first case, two factors make her independent — her father's death and her being a *bogeres* (*Tos. Yom Tov*).

נַעֲרָה בוֹגֶרֶת, וּמֵת אָבִיהָ; — *[5] a naarah [who became] a bogeres, and her father died;*

This is similar to the previous case, except that here she vowed while still a *naarah*. By the time her betrothed husband learned of her *neder*, she had become a *bogeres*, and her father had died. Consequently, her betrothed husband cannot revoke her *neder* (*Rambam Commentary; R' Avraham min HaHar; Meiri*).

[*Rav* and *Ran* do not comment about this case, but — following their interpretations to the first two cases — we assume that they construe this case as dealing with a *naarah* who vows,

becomes a *bogeres*, and then loses her father. This is different than the fourth case, in which she vowed after becoming a *bogeres* and losing her father.]

נַעֲרָה שֶׁלֹּא בָגְרָה, וּמֵת אָבִיהָ; — *[6] a naarah who has not yet become a bogeres, and her father died;*

She is betrothed as a *naarah* and then makes a *neder* and, before becoming a *bogeres*, her father dies. Her betrothed cannot revoke her *nedarim* on his own. Unlike the fourth and fifth cases, in which two factors — being a *bogeres* and her father's death — account for the betrothed husband's inability to revoke her *nedarim*, here it is only one factor — the father's death (*Rambam Commentary; R' Avraham min HaHar; Meiri*).

[*Rav* and *Ran* presumably interpret this case as involving a single *naarah* who makes a *neder*, and loses her father before becoming a *bogeres*. The fact of her father's death alone leaves her *nedarim* standing.]

— נַעֲרָה שֶׁמֵּת אָבִיהָ, וּמִשֶּׁמֵּת אָבִיהָ בָּגְרָה; *[7] A naarah whose father died, and after her father's death, she became a bogeres;*

[5] a *naarah* [who became] a *bogeres*, and her father died; [6] a *naarah* who has not yet become a *bogeres*, and her father died; [7] a *naarah* whose father died, and after her father's death, she became a *bogeres*; [8] a *bogeres* whose father is living; [9] a *naarah* who became a *bogeres* and whose father is living. R' Yehudah says: Also, if one married off his minor daughter, and she became widowed or divorced, and returned to him, she is still a *naarah*.

YAD AVRAHAM

This is identical to the fifth case, except that here her father died before she became a *bogeres*. Thus, the sequence is that she is betrothed as a *naarah*, makes a *neder*, loses her father, and becomes a *bogeres*. Her betrothed cannot revoke her *neder* without being joined by the father who — even if he were alive — would by now have lost his authority over his daughter (*Rambam Commentary; Meiri; R' Avraham min HaHar*).

[*Rav* and *Rav* presumably understand this case to involve a single *naarah* who vows, loses her father, and becomes a *bogeres*; there is no one who can revoke her *nedarim* as in cases 1 and 4. Two factors make her independent — her being an orphan and a *bogeres* (*Tos. Yom Tov*).]

בּוֹגֶרֶת, וְאָבִיהָ קַיָּם; — [8] *a bogeres whose father is living;*

She is betrothed as a *naarah*, becomes a *bogeres*, and then makes a *neder*. Her betrothed husband cannot revoke it without the father, who lost his authority over her *nedarim* when she became a *bogeres* (*Rambam Commentary; R' Avraham min HaHar; Meiri*).

[*Rav* and *Ran* will explain this case as dealing with a single girl who becomes a *bogeres* in her father's lifetime. Any *nedarim* she makes after reaching that stage are beyond the father's control.]

נַעֲרָה בוֹגֶרֶת, וְאָבִיהָ קַיָּם. — [9] *A naarah who became a bogeres and whose father is living.*

This is similar to the previous case, but here she vows as a *naarah* (*R' Avraham min HaHar*). Thus, she is betrothed and makes a *neder* while she is a *naarah*, and then becomes a *bogeres*. At that point, her husband and father learn of the *neder*. Even though her father is alive, her *neder* cannot be revoked, since her becoming a *bogeres* has eliminated his authority over her *nedarim*, and her betrothed cannot revoke on his own (*Rambam Commentary; Meiri*).

[*Rav* and *Ran* will explain this case to involve a single *naarah* who vows, but whose father learns of the *neder* only after she becomes a *bogeres*. At that point, she is out of his domain, and therefore, the *neder* stands.]

רַבִּי יְהוּדָה אוֹמֵר: אַף הַמַּשִּׂיא בִּתּוֹ הַקְּטַנָּה, וְנִתְאַלְמְנָה אוֹ נִתְגָּרְשָׁה וְחָזְרָה אֶצְלוֹ – עֲדַיִן הִיא נַעֲרָה. — *R' Yehudah says: Also, if one married off his minor daughter, and she became widowed or divorced, and returned to him, she is still a naarah.*

According to some versions of the

[יא] **קוֹנָם** שֶׁאֵינִי נֶהֱנֵית לְאַבָּא וּלְאָבִיךְ אִם
עוֹשָׂה אֲנִי עַל פִּיךְ"; "שֶׁאֵינִי
נֶהֱנֵית לָךְ אִם עוֹשָׂה אֲנִי עַל פִּי אַבָּא וְעַל פִּי

─── ר' עובדיה מברטנורא ───

(יא) קונם שאיני נהנית לאבא ולאביך כו׳ הרי זה יפר. דכיון דנמסרה בהנאת אביה וחביו
על ידי שהיא עושה לבעלה לבעלה, גנאי הוא לבעל, והוי דברים שבינו לבינה:

יד אברהם

Gemara (89b; see *Rambam Commentary*; *R' Avraham min HaHar*, *Meiri*, *and Meleches Shlomo*), the mishnah, until this point, follows the view of R' Meir. As noted in the commentary to the third case, R' Meir distinguishes between *nedarim* made before she is divorced from a full marriage, and those made afterward, in the event that she is later betrothed while still a *naarah*. Her betrothed husband cannot revoke, even together with her father, those *nedarim* made before her divorce, as in the third case of the mishnah. R' Yehudah disagrees, and rules that, even if she was fully married as a minor (i.e., she was less than twelve years old), and the marriage was terminated before she had become a *bogeres*, she retains the general law of a *naarah*, which is that if she becomes betrothed, her father and her husband together revoke her *nedarim*, including even those she made while married to her first husband. Thus, for *nedarim* made under her second betrothal, even though their betrothal followed a divorce from a full marriage, both R' Meir and R' Yehudah agree that these may be revoked by her betrothed together with her father. The dispute is only in regard to *nedarim* she made before her divorce. R' Meir considers them beyond the domain of her new betrothed, but R' Yehudah maintains that the betrothed, together with her father, can revoke even these.

The *Gemara* (89b) goes on to say that the Sages disagree with both R' Yehudah and R' Meir, and maintain that, once she has been divorced from a full marriage, her father can no longer exercise any control over her *nedarim* — not those made prior to her divorce and not those made during her subsequent betrothal (*Rambam Commentary*, as interpreted by *R' Avraham min HaHar.*).

Ran has a different version of the *Gemara*, according to which there is no legal dispute here at all; *Rav* apparently follows his interpretation. The entire mishnah is in accordance with R' Yehudah, who adds at the end that divorce from a full marriage when she is a minor also constitutes a release from the father's authority. The issue of possible revocation during a subsequent betrothal is not dis-cussed at all by the mishnah, whose sole intention is to illustrate how a daughter leaves her father's domain. Thus, the first three cases demonstrate how a girl can become "an orphan in the father's lifetime"; cases 4-6 demonstrate the termination of the father's control due to his death; and the last three cases show how becoming a *bogeres* makes a woman independent.

The *Gemara* (89b) states that the Sages listed three cases rather than nine. To be sure, they agree with the laws of the mishnah, but — rather

11. [**I**f a woman said:] "*Konam,* my benefit regarding Father or your father if I work for your benefit"; [or "*Konam*] my benefit to you if I work for the benefit of Father or

YAD AVRAHAM

than confusing the matter by enumerating all nine possibilities — they list only the three factors above which release a woman from her father's jurisdiction. Accordingly, R' Yehudah's statement — *she is still a naarah* — which is a ruling — must be read: *and she is still a naarah.* He is completing the description of his case, which is just an additional elaboration of an instance in which

the girl leaves her father's control. Thus, the sequence here is: She is married off as a minor, is divorced or widowed from full marriage, but still has not become a *bogeres.* R' Yehudah is telling us that despite the fact that she was married as a minor, her subsequent divorce removes her from her father's domain (*Rav; Ran; see Tos. Chadashim, Shoshannim LeDavid,* and *Tif. Yis.* 52).

11.

קוֹנָם שֶׁאֵינִי נֶהֱנֵית לְאַבָּא וּלְאָבִיךְ,, — *[If a woman said:] "Konam, my benefit regarding Father or your father*

[She directed this *neder* to her husband.]

Rav follows *Rosh,* who interprets this part of her declaration as prohibiting the benefit of her father or father-in-law. *Shalmei Nedarim* explains *Rosh* to mean that she forbids benefits from herself to them (see, however, *Keren Orah*). Thus, essentially, they are forbidden to derive benefit from her, but she is permitted to benefit from them. Since the prohibition does not deprive her from receiving benefits, it is not a *neder* of self-denial. However, if her father or father-in-law became forbidden to benefit from her as a result of her fulfilling the condition of the *neder* (see below), it is embarrassing for her husband. Consequently, this declaration qualifies as a *neder* that affects their mutual relationship (*Tos.* 89b, s.v. תניא; *Shalmei Nedarim*).

Others explain the prohibition to

forbid *her* from deriving benefit from her father or father-in-law which makes the *neder* one of self-denial (*Ran; Nimukei Yosef*).

אם עושָׂה אֲנִי עַל פִּיךְ"; — *if I work for your benefit";*

I.e., if I make any food or do any other work for you (*Nimukei Yosef*). [The expression עַל פִּיךְ, which literally means *on your mouth,* is thus equivalent to *for your benefit.*]

Rambam (*Commentary*) interprets this as meaning: "*if I obey you.*" [Apparently, he construes the literal meaning to be: "if I work on your word."]

The *neder* is thus conditional on her working for her husband. If she does things for her husband, the prohibition involving her father and father-in-law takes effect, which, as noted, is at the least a *neder* that affects their mutual relationship. If she refrains from doing work for her husband, no prohibition ensues, but this in itself is something which obviously affects

אָבִיךְ״ — הֲרֵי זֶה יָפֵר.

[יב] **בָּרִאשׁוֹנָה** הָיוּ אוֹמְרִים: שָׁלֹשׁ נָשִׁים
יוֹצְאוֹת וְנוֹטְלוֹת כְּתֻבָּה:
הָאוֹמֶרֶת: ״טְמֵאָה אֲנִי לָךְ״; ״שָׁמַיִם בֵּינִי
לְבֵינֶךְ״; ״נְטוּלָה אֲנִי מִן הַיְּהוּדִים״. חָזְרוּ לוֹמַר,

---

ר' עובדיה מברטנורא

(יב) האומרת טמאה אני לך. באשת כהן מיירי, דנאסרה לבעלה באונס, ולא הפסידה כתובתה,
והאמינוה חכמים לאסור עצמה על בעלה. וכיון דיוצאה בגט נוטלת כתובתה, דמספר כתובתה
כלמוד, לכשתנשאי לאחר תטלי מה שכתוב ליכי: **השמים ביני ובינך.** מפרש בגמרא (נא, א) דאינו
יורה כחן, כלומר דברים דקמי שמיא גליא ואינה יכולה לברר. ומיירי בבאה מחמת טענה, דאמרה
בעינא חוטרא לידא ומרא לקבורה, דאי לאו הכי, אמרינן לה זילי לא מפקדת אפריה ורביה: **נטולה
אני מן היהודים.** שאסרה תשמיש של כל ישראל עליה. ואף על גב דאמרינן בפרק המדיר (כתובות
עא, א) היכא דנדרה מיהי דיוצאה בלא כתובה, דהיא נתנה אצבע בין שיניה, רש"י פירש ביבמות
(דף קיב, א) כיון שאסרה הנאת תשמיש של כל ישראל עליה ודאי אנוסה היא, כי קשה תשמיש לה.
וסברה משנה ראשונה דאפילו דברים שבינו לבינה לא הוי, דאפשר שיגרשנה: **חזרו לומר כו'.**
נתקלקלו הדורות וחשנו שהיא משקרת להפקיע עצמה מתחת בעלה:

יד אברהם

their mutual relationship. Thus, no
matter how she acts after this *neder*, it
can be revoked (*Ran*).

שֶׁאֵינִי נֶהֱנֵית לָךְ אִם אֲנִי עוֹשָׂה עַל פִּי אַבָּא
— וְעַל פִּי אָבִיךְ״ - הֲרֵי זֶה יָפֵר. *[or
"Konam] my benefit to you if I work
for the benefit of Father or your father"
— this he can revoke.*

This is similar to the previous case,
except that here the prohibition affects the husband, while the condition
concerns her father or father-in-law.
If she is prohibited to either give or
derive benefit to or from her husband,
it certainly affects their mutual relationship. However, she can avoid the

prohibition by refraining from doing
anything for her father and father-in-
law. Nevertheless, for her to avoid
them is also embarrassing for the
husband, so that this, too, would be
something which affects their mutual
relationship (*Tur Yoreh Deah* 234; *Tos.
Yom Tov*). *Ran* explains that it is
inevitable that she will, at some point,
do something for her father or father-
in-law. Thus, since it is all but certain
that the prohibition for her husband
will take effect, he can revoke it as
soon as she makes the *neder* (see *Shach
to Yoreh Deah* 234:45,85).

12.

בָּרִאשׁוֹנָה הָיוּ אוֹמְרִים: — *At first they
used to say:*
[I.e., originally the Rabbis ruled.]

שָׁלֹשׁ נָשִׁים יוֹצְאוֹת וְנוֹטְלוֹת כְּתֻבָּה: —
*There are three women who must be
divorced (lit., go out), yet they take*

their *kesubah:*
[In general, if the infidelity of a wife
necessitates a divorce, she forfeits her
kesubah — the marriage settlement
(*Kesubos* 100b-101a; *Rambam*; *Hil.
Ishus* 24:6f.; *Even HaEzer* 115). In the

your father" — this he can revoke.

12. **A**t first they used to say: There are three women who must be divorced, yet they take their *kesubah:* One who says: "I am unclean to you"; [or] "Heaven is between me and you," [or] "I am removed from all Jews." They later retracted

YAD AVRAHAM

following three cases, however, the Rabbis insisted at first that, although a divorce is necessary, the wife receive her *kesubah* nevertheless.]

הָאוֹמֶרֶת: "טְמֵאָה אֲנִי לָךְ"; — *One who says: "I am unclean to you";*

[She claims to have had relations with another man.] The case involves the wife of a *Kohen* who claims to have been raped (*Rav*). Had she claimed that she willingly engaged in adultery, she would not be entitled to her *kesubah* (*Kesubos* 101a-b). On the other hand, if she was married to a non-*Kohen*, and was raped, she would be permitted to continue her marriage (ibid. 51b). Since here the ruling was that she must be divorced, but nevertheless receives her *kesubah*, the case must be of a woman married to a *Kohen* who claims to have been raped (*Meiri*).

The Rabbis believed her claim, and thus ruled that she must be divorced (*Rav*). They did not deprive her of her *kesubah*, since the divorce is necessary due to her husband's status as a *Kohen*, and not because of any improper action on her part (*Tos. Yom Tov*). Her claim was believed because for a woman to admit to having been raped is embarrassing, and she would not have done so unless she was telling the truth (*Ran*).

"שָׁמַיִם בֵּינִי לְבֵינָךְ", — [*or*] "*Heaven is between me and you,*"

Here, she alleges that her husband is impotent, a fact which would be known only to Heaven. Although a woman is not commanded to have children, she can argue that she wants children in order that she might be cared for in her old age, and attended to upon her death (*Rav*). [Thus, her accusation is sufficient to warrant divorce, and so, the Rabbis — believing her claim — obligated the husband to divorce her. She does not lose her *kesubah*, since she has done no wrong.] Her accusation was believed, since she would have to explain in detail in what way she discovered her husband to be impotent, and this was an embarrassing ordeal. It was initially assumed that she would not subject herself to this unless she was telling the truth (*Gem.* 91a).

"נְטוּלָה אֲנִי מִן הַיְּהוּדִים", — [*or*] "*I am removed from all Jews.*"

This is a *neder* which forbids her to have relations with any Jew (*Rav*). A woman who makes such a declaration must surely experience pain during intimacy, and thus, she is considered to have been driven by this to declare such a prohibition. The Rabbis necessitated divorce in this case, because a marriage could not be allowed to continue without conjugal relations. However, they allowed her to receive her *kesubah*, because they took into consideration the extenuating circum-

שֶׁלֹּא תְהֵא אִשָּׁה נוֹתֶנֶת עֵינֶיהָ בְּאַחֵר
וּמְקַלְקֶלֶת עַל בַּעְלָהּ. אֶלָּא, הָאוֹמֶרֶת: ,,טְמֵאָה
אֲנִי לָךְ" — תָּבִיא רְאָיָה לִדְבָרֶיהָ; ,,שָׁמַיִם בֵּינִי
לְבֵינָךְ" — יַעֲשׂוּ דֶרֶךְ בַּקָּשָׁה; ,,נְטוּלָה אֲנִי מִן
הַיְּהוּדִים" — יָפֵר חֶלְקוֹ, וּתְהֵא מְשַׁמַּשְׁתּוֹ,
וּתְהֵא נְטוּלָה מִן הַיְּהוּדִים.
סליק מסכת נדרים

ר' עובדיה מברטנורא

תביא ראיה לדבריה. ולא מהמנינן לה בלי ראיה: **יעשו דרך בקשה.** יבקשו ממנה שלא
תדבר עוד בו, ובירושלמי (יא, יב) מפרש יעשו סעודה ויפייס: **יפר חלקו ותהא משמשתו.**
דהוי דברים שבינו לבינה ומיפר לטעמו:

יד אברהם

stances which led her to make the
neder (*Rav*, from *Rashi* to *Yevamos*
112a). Although a *neder* such as this
ought to be one that affects their
mutual relationship, the Rabbis initially maintained that, since the husband could divorce her without
revoking the *neder*, he could not
revoke it (*Rav; Rosh*).

Meiri explains that, although he
could revoke the prohibition as it
applied to him, he had no power to
revoke the interdiction directed at the
rest of the Jews, since her being
prohibited from relations with other
Jews while married to him is neither
self-denying, nor something that affects their relationship. Initially, the
Rabbis maintained that, if he could
not revoke some part of the *neder* (i.e.,
what related to others), he could not
revoke it at all.

חָזְרוּ לוֹמַר, שֶׁלֹּא תְהֵא אִשָּׁה נוֹתֶנֶת עֵינֶיהָ
בְּאַחֵר וּמְקַלְקֶלֶת עַל בַּעְלָהּ. — *They later
retracted this, so that a wife should not
set her eyes upon another [man] and
behave immorally toward her husband.*

In all the above cases, the Rabbis
originally established the law on the
assumption that she was telling the
truth. Later on, as the level of morality
deteriorated, there was strong suspi-
cion that a woman who made such
claims may have done so in order to be
free to marry some other man and was
not being truthful (*Rav*). They therefore amended their ruling as follows:

אֶלָּא, הָאוֹמֶרֶת: ,,טְמֵאָה אֲנִי לָךְ" — תָּבִיא
רְאָיָה לִדְבָרֶיהָ; — *Rather, one who says:
"I am unclean to you," must prove it*
(lit., *bring proof to her words*);

In the absence of proof, she would
not be believed and her husband
would not have to divorce her (*Rav*).
Initially, she had been believed because the Rabbis could find no motive
for her to make such a self-humiliating
claim. But, when they saw that women
would do so in order to gain a divorce,
they insisted on more substantial
evidence before obligating her husband to divorce her (*Ran; Tos. Yom
Tov*).

,,שָׁמַיִם בֵּינִי לְבֵינָךְ" — יַעֲשׂוּ דֶרֶךְ בַּקָּשָׁה; —
"Heaven is between me and you" —

11
12
this, so that a wife should not set her eyes upon another [man] and behave immorally toward her husband. Rather, one who says: "I am unclean to you" must prove it; "Heaven is between me and you" — they should plead with her; "I am removed from all Jews" — he should revoke his share, so that she can continue in marital relations with him, but she is removed from [other] Jews.

YAD AVRAHAM

they should plead with her (lit., *they should act by way of pleading*);

[Here again, since an ulterior motive was available to explain her claim, the Rabbis no longer accepted it and did not demand a divorce.]

By *they should plead with her*, the mishnah means that the Rabbis would try to prevail upon her to withdraw her allegations (*Rav*). *Yerushalmi* explains that a feast was made in which the husband attempted to placate his wife and restore their marital harmony. Another explanation is that the Rabbis prayed (i.e., pleaded with God) that she bear a child from this husband, thus silencing her claims (*Rabbeinu Chananel*, quoted in *Tos.* 90b).

‏נְטוּלָה אֲנִי מִן הַיְהוּדִים" – יָפֵר חֶלְקוֹ, וּתְהֵא מְשַׁמַּשְׁתּוֹ,‏ — *"I am removed from all Jews"* — *he should revoke his share, so that she can continue in marital relations with him,*

The Rabbis later decided that, although there was the option to divorce his wife without revoking her *neder*, the *neder* did qualify as one affecting their relationship, and could be revoked (*Rav; Rosh*).

[Alternatively, they came to the conclusion that he could revoke what affected him, even though the prohi-

bition with regard to others still stood. (See *Meiri* cited above, s.v. נְטוּלָה, and preface to mishnah 1.)] Thus, they ruled that he should revoke the part of the *neder* that affected him, and continue the marriage.

וּתְהֵא נְטוּלָה מִן הַיְהוּדִים. — *but she is removed from [other] Jews.*

That is, the husband's revocation of the *neder* releases only him from the prohibition, but all other Jews are still forbidden to have relations with her. Thus, if she is later divorced or widowed, she will be forbidden to marry anyone because of her *neder* (*Tos.* 90b; *Meiri*).

The *neder* was made while she was married, and she was thus forbidden in any case to have relations with anyone other than her husband. In that case, asks *Tosafos* (ibid.), how does the *neder* prohibition take effect on other Jews? There is a general principle that אֵין אִיסּוּר חָל עַל אִיסּוּר, *one prohibition does not take effect on top of another* (*Yevamos* 32a,b). How, then, is the prohibition effective for people who are already forbidden due to her status as a married woman? *Tosafos'* question, however, is somewhat puzzling, since the *Gemara* (ibid.) establishes that, although a second prohibition does not take effect if one already exists, it is only suspended, and not altogether ineffective. Thus, if the first prohibition should end, the second — which had been in suspension all this time

— takes effect. Here, too, although — while she is married — the prohibition on the other people is suspended, it should take effect as soon as her marriage ends. What is *Tosafos'* difficulty?

Shaar HaMelech (*Hil. Issurei Biah* 17:8) suggests, on the basis of *Tosafos'* question, that *nedarim* are different than other prohibitions, in that if a *neder* cannot take effect immediately, it is void, and cannot be reactivated at some later time when the earlier prohibition ends (see *Tos. R' Akiva Eiger* at length and commentary to 11:4, s.v. רַבִּי יוֹחָנָן).

⊷ Glossary

bogeres – בּוֹגֶרֶת: a mature girl. This stage is usually reached at the age of twelve and a half years and a day. See preface to Chapter 10, s.v. *A Girl's Stages of Maturity*.

chalitzah – חֲלִיצָה: the procedure of taking off the shoe — a mechanism provided by the Torah to release the brothers and the widow of a deceased man when they do not wish to perform *yibum*. See General Introduction to ArtScroll *Yevamos*.

chupah – חוּפָּה: (1) the procedure by which *nisuin* is effected (see preface to Chapter 10, s.v. *Eruvin and Nesuin*); (2) the bridal canopy used for this purpose.

dinar – דִּינָר: a type of coin. A silver dinar equals one *zuz*. One golden dinar is equivalent to twenty-five silver dinars.

erusin – אֵרוּסִין: the first stage of marriage, during which the couple is considered legally married in most respects. The term *betrothal*, albeit a poor and misleading translation, has sometimes been used for the sake of convenience. See preface to Chapter 10, s. v. *Erusin and Nisuin*.

Gemara (abbr. Gem.) – גְּמָרָא: the section of the Talmud that explains the Mishnah.

halachah – הֲלָכָה: (1) a religious law; (2) the accepted ruling; (3) [cap.] the body of Jewish law.

kares – כָּרֵת: a form of excision meted out by the Heavenly Tribunal, sometimes as premature death, sometimes by one being predeceased by his children.

kesubah, pl. **kesubos** – כְּתוּבָה (כְּתוּבוֹת): (1) the agreement made between a man

and his wife upon their marriage, whose foremost feature is the dower awarded her in the event of their divorce or his death; (2) the document upon which this agreement is recorded. See General Introduction to ArtScroll *Kesubos*.

Kohen, pl. **Kohanim** – כֹּהֵן (כֹּהֲנִים): a member of the priestly family descended from Aaron.

konam – קוֹנָם: a commonly used substitute for the term *korban* as a reference in a *neder* (see General Introduction, s.v. כִּנּוּיִים, *Kinnuyim*).

korban – קָרְבָּן: an offering. Originally, this had been the standard reference used in *nedarim*. In this context, it referred to an animal designated to be sacrificed in the Temple (see ibid.).

lulav – לוּלָב: branches of the date palm that are taken on the festival of Succos.

mikveh – מִקְוֶה: ritual pool of water for the halachic cleansing of one who is ritually contaminated.

mishnah, pl. **mishnayos** – מִשְׁנָה (מִשְׁנָיוֹת): (1) [cap.] the section of the Talmud consisting of the collection of oral laws edited by R' Yehudah HaNasi (Judah the Prince); (2) an article of this section.

mitzvah – מִצְוָה: a Biblical or Rabbinical precept.

naarah, pl. **naaros** – נַעֲרָה (נְעָרוֹת): a girl over the age of twelve years and one day who has already grown two pubic hairs. This stage ends six months later when she becomes a *bogeres*. See preface to Chapter 10, s. v. *A Girl's Stages of Maturity*.

neder, pl. **nedarim** — נֶדֶר (נְדָרִים): (loosely) a vow. In this tractate, the term always refers to the prohibitory *neder*, in which a person prohibits an item to himself or to others (see General Introduction, s.v. *Types of Nedarim*).

shekel — שֶׁקֶל: a type of coin mentioned in the Torah, known as *sela* in Mishnaic nomenclature. One silver shekel equals four *zuz*. See Appendix I to ArtScroll *Shekalim*.

shevuah, pl. **Shevuos** — שְׁבוּעָה (שְׁבוּעוֹת): an oath (see General Introduction, s.v. *Nedarim and Oaths*).

succah — סוּכָּה: the temporary dwelling used as a domicile during the festival of Succos.

Tanna, pl. **Tannaim** — תַּנָּא (תַּנָּאִים): a Sage quoted in the Mishnah or in works of the same period.

tefillin — תְּפִילִין: phylacteries.

terumah — תְּרוּמָה: a portion of the crop sanctified and given to a *Kohen* who — together with his household — may eat it, but only if both the one who eats the *terumah* and the *terumah* itself are ritually clean.

yavam, pl. **yevamin** — יָבָם (יְבָמִין): the surviving brother upon whom the obligation of *yibum* falls.

yevamah — יְבָמָה: a widow who falls to *yibum*.

yibum — יִבּוּם: levirate marriage, i.e., the marriage prescribed by the Torah between a widow and her late husband's brother when the husband had died childless. See General Introduction to ArtScroll *Yevamos*. Cf. *chalitzah*.